MOSCOW GUIDE

DON'T JUST SEE THE WORLD - EXPERIENCE IT!

OPEN ROAD TRAVEL GUIDES SHOW YOU
HOW TO BE A TRAVELER – NOT A TOURIST!

Whether you're going abroad or planning a trip in the United States, take Open Road along on your journey. Our books have been praised by **Travel & Leisure, The Los Angeles Times, Newsday, Booklist, US News & World Report, Endless Vacation, American Bookseller, Coast to Coast,** *and many other magazines and newspapers!*

Don't just see the world – experience it with Open Road!

GW00722720

ABOUT THE AUTHORS

Yves Gerem is a travel writer who now makes his home in Dallas, Texas. Originally from Slovenia, Yves and his wife Larisa Nikolayevna Gerem (a native Muscovite) spend part of each year in Moscow and traveling around Russia.

BE A TRAVELER, NOT A TOURIST - WITH OPEN ROAD TRAVEL GUIDES!

Open Road Publishing has guide books to exciting, fun destinations on four continents. As veteran travelers, our goal is to bring you the best travel guides available anywhere!

No small task, but here's what we offer:

• All Open Road travel guides are written by authors with a distinct, opinionated point of view – not some sterile committee or team of writers. Our authors are experts in the areas covered and are polished writers.

• Our guides are geared to people who want to make their own travel choices. We'll show you how to discover the real destination – not just see some place from a tour bus window.

• We're strong on the basics, but we also provide terrific choices for those looking to get off the beaten path and *experience* the country or city – not just *see* it or pass through it.

• We give you the best, but we also tell you about the worst and what to avoid. Nobody should waste their time and money on their hard-earned vacation because of bad or inadequate travel advice.

• Our guides assume nothing. We tell you everything you need to know to have the trip of a lifetime – presented in a fun, literate, no-nonsense style.

• And, above all, we welcome your input, ideas, and suggestions to help us put out the best travel guides possible.

MOSCOW GUIDE

DON'T JUST SEE THE WORLD - EXPERIENCE IT!

YVES GEREM

OPEN ROAD PUBLISHING

OPEN ROAD PUBLISHING

We offer travel guides to American and foreign locales. Our books tell it like it is, often with an opinionated edge, and our experienced authors always give you all the information you need to have the trip of a lifetime. Write for your free catalog of all our titles, including our golf and restaurant guides.

Catalog Department, Open Road Publishing
P.O. Box 20226, Columbus Circle Station, New York, NY 10023

Or you can contact us by e-mail at:
Jopenroad@aol.com

1st Edition

Dedicated to my son Michael Yves and my wife Larisa Nikolayevna. Without them this project might never have been begun or completed.

Library of Congress Catalog Card No. 96-72605
ISBN 1-883323-51-7

Front cover photo courtesy of Itar-Tass USA, New York. Back cover photos by Nick Gheissari, ESCOAA Images. Maps by Rob Perry.

The authors have made every effort to be as accurate as possible, but neither they nor the publisher assume responsibility for the services provided by any business listed in this guide; for any errors or omissions; or any loss, damage, or disruptions in your travels for any reason. No fee, service, or discount of any kind was accepted from anyone for their products or services.

The author wishes particularly to thank Larisa Nikolayevna Gerem for her invaluable assistance in the research and preparation of this guide.

TABLE OF CONTENTS

CONTENTS

CONTENTS

CONTENTS

MAPS

Russia & Neighbors   13
Moscow's Ring Roads   71
The Kremlin   261
Central Moscow Sights   296-297

SIDEBARS

Russian Words for Identifying Addresses   13
The Greening of Moscow   16
Russian Names   20
Black Magic Fires of 1547   24
The Many Wives of Ivan the Terrible   27
Moscow's Mayor   40
Weather Chart   42
An Important Word About Hats   46
The Fluctuating Ruble   83
Crime in Moscow   88
Diphtheria, Cholera, Polio, & Measles   98
Soaps Vs. Solzhenitsyn   105
Country & City Telephone Codes   111
Emergency & Useful Telephone Numbers   113
Cellular Phones   114
What Food Is It?   135
Try a Kvas!   140
Coke Vs. Pepsi   143
Hot Water & Heat   146
The Hotel Floor Attendant   150
Stalin's Wedding Cakes   306
Statues of Moscow   333
First Prize Goes to an American   356
Look for the Asterisk   358
Contemporary Theater   365
Ernst Neizvestny   379
Gustav Faberge   437
Women's Clothing & Shoe Sizes   441

1. INTRODUCTION

So you are going to Moscow? Relax. Our guide book is so thorough, complete, and detailed that every conceivable question or concern you might have is answered in the pages that follow. We offer you the Moscow of both ancient and recent history, the Moscow of churches, street markets, museums, unique restaurants and cultural delights.

You've seen those exotic Cyrillic letters and worry about how you will cope with life beyond your hotel entrance? Not to worry, our instructions on how to get anywhere in the city are so detailed you will be able to find them practically blindfolded. You don't need a chauffeured car – just read the section about the Moscow metro and you will get to your destination well before your Western friends who are still stuck in Boulevard Ring Road traffic. And yes, in this guide you will find directions from the Kremlin and the nearest metro station, or two, for nearly every address listed. You will also find every interesting sight in Moscow included.

Which Moscow hotels have the best swimming facilities? You want to buy an English-language book, but where are the English-language bookstores? You have brought your child and want to take her to a children's club for her birthday party – are there any? Do you know where to find a rest room outside your hotel? These are just a handful among the hundreds of questions that are answered in this guide.

There are more hotel and other lodging options here than in any other Moscow guide. You can select from among more than 100 restaurants – again, more choices than in any other English-language Moscow guide – broken into three geographical areas, then listed according to their cost. You'll find the same extensive coverage of bars, nightclubs, and casinos. We review a dazzling array of theaters, art galleries, and shops. Nearby excursions are featured, as well as a separate excursion chapter to St. Petersburg.

We have words of warning when we feel that visitors could be unfairly treated, whether by surly waiters in restaurants or indifferent salesclerks in stores. We put ourselves in your shoes and give you our opinions. And our opinions are completely independent.

Moscow is like no other city in the world. With this book by your side, we know you're going to enjoy it!

2. EXCITING MOSCOW! — OVERVIEW

Based on the cost of food, housing, services, transportation, and entertainment, Moscow is one of the most expensive cities in the world.

Nevertheless, Moscow can still be reasonably priced if you don't expect every Western convenience and comfort, both of which come at a price. You can still eat reasonably well in this city for under $20 a meal, if you know where to go, but you have to stay away from Western restaurants, where a dinner for two quickly adds up to $100, before wine and gratuity. If you stay for a month, you will sleep almost as well in a $500-a-month furnished one-room apartment in the suburbs as you would in a downtown hotel, where you can easily pay more than that for one night's lodging. Although you could, for four weeks, be out of hot water in the middle of the summer. With a few exceptions, like the Kremlin, museum admissions are reasonable by Western standards.

Because of Russia's Communist past, most Western travel guides until recently dealt primarily with her history and culture. A handful of restaurants and tourist sights were thrown in as an afterthought, the assumption being that you would stay at a state-run Intourist hotel, eat prepaid voucher meals and tag along on highly structured tours. You can still do that, but now that the KGB is no longer hovering over you, you need a lot more practical information.

ORIENTATION

You will quickly find out that even with a good map it can be frustrating to find a restaurant, an office, or a gallery. We will help you locate most addresses in this guide with the location of the nearest metro station or stations, although that can sometimes mean an additional 20-minute walk. To save time we sometimes suggest that you continue on a bus, or even take a taxi.

We will always tell you in which direction a certain site is in reference to the Kremlin. We also tell you whether an address is centrally located inside the Boulevard Ring Road, whether it is between the Boulevard and Garden Ring Roads, or outside the Garden Ring Road so you can estimate the approximate distance from where you are. Following that, we might narrow a location still further by other reference points.

Most Russian addresses in this guide are transliterated right down to their Russian capitalization, unless we used an English equivalent, such as Red Square or Pushkin Square.

RUSSIAN WORDS FOR IDENTIFYING ADDRESSES

Ulitsa is street, **prospekt** *is avenue,* **bulvar** *is boulevard,* **ploshchad** *is square,* **pereulok** *is lane,* **naberezhnaya** *is embankment,* **proyezd** *is passage, and* **shosse** *is highway.*

For the sake of clarity, however, a few major tourist attractions have been anglicized to serve as your orientation anchors. They are the Kremlin, Red Square, the Bolshoy Theater and Pushkin Square. We refer to these locations often, assuming that you know their approximate position. Whether you do or not, buy a separate city map if you stay more than just a couple of days because that, too, will save you time and indigestion.

The **Boulevard Ring Road** (Bulvarnoye koltso) is the innermost among the boulevards that circle Moscow, or rather it is a 4.5 mile horseshoe-like semi-circle road formed by ten wide boulevards merging into one another with a narrow park running down the middle of each one. In the south, the Moskva River acts as an imaginary continuation of the Boulevard Ring Road. No matter where you are, practically any address inside the Boulevard Ring is within walking distance, at least by Moscow standards.

More than five hundred years ago the Boulevard Ring was walled off in white stone to defend the city-state of Muscovy. Around 1775, Catherine the Great divided the city into two parts; what was then inside the Boulevard Ring Road was considered part of Moscow, beyond it were the suburbs. In the late 18th century, the ring was planted with trees and gardens as they are seen today.

The **Garden Ring Road** (Sadovoye koltso) is the next, larger ring of 16 merging streets and 16 squares, which form a full circle 9.5 miles in circumference, with the Kremlin almost in the center, and a radius up to a couple of miles from the Kremlin. Shaped like a donut, the Garden Ring Road is sandwiched between the Boulevard Ring Road and the suburbs.

It was indeed a garden-like tree-lined boulevard until the 1930's, when the Bolsheviks nearly destroyed parts of it, and then it was widened into one of the city's busiest ring roads, with large buildings on both sides. This is one of Moscow's widest avenues.

The outermost ring is the **Moscow Circular Road** which marks the city's current boundary. These rings have nothing in common with what is sometimes called the **Golden Ring**, a circle of towns like Sergiyev Posad northeast of Moscow.

Hotels, restaurants, nightclubs, casinos, and bars are divided into one of these three geographical areas: **Inside the Boulevard Ring**, which you can consider tantamount to downtown; **Between the Boulevard & Garden Rings**, a donut-shaped band around the central city and; **Outside the Garden Ring**, which can safely be called the Moscow suburbs

Museums, theaters, art galleries, some stores and other sights and facilities are usually broken into the same three geographical categories, unless otherwise noted. The shopping chapter is broken down according to major shopping streets, with additional clumps of shops noted. Because Western clothing, footwear, toiletries and supermarkets are not as readily available as in the West, we also list a small cluster of the best known shops for such items.

We have added some of the best known excursions around Moscow and a few, such as the Dulyovo Porcelain Works and Zhostovo Trays, that you may not have heard about before. And, finally, there is a short chapter about St. Petersburg, just in case you decide to hop over for a day or two.

3. LAND & PEOPLE

LAND

Measuring six and a half million square miles, Russia is the world's largest country and almost twice as large as either the US or China. Having a population of more than nine million, Moscow is the largest city in Europe and indeed one of the largest in the world; its size puts it somewhere between Rio de Janeiro, Brazil, and Cairo, Egypt. St. Petersburg is its second largest city, with about five million inhabitants, followed by Nizhny Novgorod and Novosibirsk, with about 1.5 million each.

Some would say that Moscow is more imposing than beautiful, especially after 70 years of Communist neglect. It will indeed overwhelm and humble you with its endless dusty boulevards with as many as a dozen lanes, immense apartment complexes and monstrous high rises. Hundreds of thousands of shoppers from the provinces invade the city every day in search of food and other products. Three million visitors in all pass through Moscow daily.

Moscow has developed outwardly from the Kremlin in concentric circles like a spider's web. The **Bulvarnoye koltso** (Boulevard Ring Road) and **Sadovoye koltso** (Garden Ring Road) are the major roads around Moscow.

The Bulvarnoye koltso is the nearest of the four rings to the city center and forms a semi-circle on the northern banks of the Moskva River. The Sadovoye koltso, which measures about four miles in diameter, is a wide boulevard that intercepts all the main streets radiating outward from Moscow's center. It is within this Garden Ring Road that most of the sites of interest to Westerners are located.

The boundaries of Moscow are marked by a 68 mile long circular bypass with a distance of about 25 miles from the north to south and 18 miles from the east to west, and covers an area of about 400 square miles. The city of Moscow has grown roughly four times since the late 1950's.

Located at an altitude of 656 feet, Moscow is about three-quarters the size of Los Angeles and has six percent of Russia's population. Like

Rome and Lisbon, Moscow is built on seven barely perceptible hills, which have reverted to their original pre-Revolutionary name Sparrow Hills. Moscow has about 100 parks and 600 gardens, with more than 100 varieties of trees and shrubs, and there are thousands of elks in the woods around Moscow. The Moscow River has 600 tributaries and is spanned by 16 bridges.

The city is divided into ten administrative districts, with each one headed by a prefect appointed by the mayor. Most heavy industries are located in eastern and southern Moscow; there are more than 1,600 factories within the city limits.

THE GREENING OF MOSCOW

If you are sensitive to trees, you might go through sneezing fits in Moscow in late May and early June when seemingly millions of poplars go through their annual propagation process, shedding billions of tufts of cottony hairs, called **pukh.**

Blame the **pukh** *on 6,000 Moscow gardeners, who in 1948 were under orders from Stalin "to turn Moscow green in 15 days," according to recent testimony of one of the gardeners. The city planted tens of thousands of female poplar trees, starting with Sparrow Hills overlooking Moscow, only to find the down they shed all over the streets each June causes allergies and fires. There are more than 500,000 poplar trees in Moscow today.*

"We didn't think of consequences, we were in a hurry to follow Stalin's orders," says a gardener at the Moscow's greenery department. "We choose the poplar because it is a very oxygenic species, it is tenacious and grows very quickly."

The issue of the poplars and the problems they cause were taboo under the Soviet regime. With the advent of perestroika, Muscovites began complaining to city authorities about the allergies they suffer as a result of the trees depositing a thick white cover of seed everywhere. They were told to wait a couple of weeks and it would all go away.

"We only discovered the error after 25 years, when the trees matured," says the gardener, adding that because the male trees become female after repeated cutting it only aggravates the problem.

PEOPLE

About 75 percent of Russia's nearly 150 million inhabitants are urban residents and the same percentage are also Russian Orthodox. The capital, you will find, is a mosaic of the former Soviet Union. Russians and Ukrainians are the largest ethnic groups in the city, followed by some 200,000 Tartars.

Russia ranks about ninth in its gross national product and has a per-capita income of about $4,800, compared with $27,600 for the US. Crime and unemployment are still relatively low, although the crime rate has been rising for several years. There is one doctor for every 220 Russians, as opposed to one for every 391 Americans. The Russian literacy rate is above 99 percent, compared with 96 percent for the US.

First time visitors to Russia and Moscow will be struck by the lack of small courtesies, but particularly smiles. Except for Muscovites who deal with Westerners on a regular basis, you will sooner convince an adult that Lenin has risen from his Red Square tomb than make him smile. Even when you get to know them a little, Russians seem reserved. Actually, when you contrast them against 70 years of totalitarian rule, it may surprise you that they can smile at all.

Russians are bitterly critical of their country, their government, and their circumstances when speaking with Western friends and acquaintances, sometimes almost competing with each other as to who can be more negative, but they are surprisingly unreceptive to hearing Westerners bashing Russia, even if in much less vehement terms.

Russians are good-natured, hospitable, down-to-earth people who seem to instinctively dislike pretense and smooth talk, even if they are sometimes a bit naive in their judgements and they themselves are not beyond deception. If you should find time and again that they cannot keep their word or turn out to be a little unreliable, just remember that it was the Soviet state that infantilized them. Whether because that is a national trait or perhaps because Russian literature seems to have accentuated these characteristics, they do appear to alternate between gaiety and a morose melancholy. But they also have a wonderful sense of humor and a proclivity for biting satire and it is perhaps traits like these that made it possible for them to suffer the tyrants of centuries past.

So what is a Russian? According to the Greek writer Nikos Kazantzakis, who had spent close to two years in Bolshevik Russia in the 1920's, "The Russian is like the old man Karamazov: He has rich, primitive and overwhelming passions, but he also irresistibly fascinates us, for we sense that his soul is vast and that his heart is full of human warmth."

THE RUSSIAN LANGUAGE

Do not worry about your Russian, whether you know any or not. Russians, like citizens of most of the world's countries will expect you to stumble in your search for a word or two. Americans and the French may be the only global species that expects everyone to speak their language.

It is said that perhaps one hundred times more Russians speak some English than Americans speak any Russian. Many Russians speak some

English, but they may not understand **your** English. Beyond saying that you should speak English very slowly, with lots of illustrative help from your hands, it is impossible to explain to native Americans why Russians do not understand them. Most immigrants to America have no difficulty communicating with Russians in English, although it can be an exhausting process.

Compared with English, there are extra letters in the Russian alphabet - three are actually borrowed from Greek - and pronunciation is a little easier. Russian has separate letters for most sounds so it is easier to read words as they are written. The pronunciation rules are much simpler and easier to remember than in English. Just as there seem to be no rules for pronunciation in English, there are none as to where the **stress** comes in Russian. It may fall on any syllable and even on different syllables of the same word according to its case or number.

The Russian language has no definite or indefinite articles. Nouns and adjectives have different endings according to their grammatical case and number, and there are additional inflections according to the three genders. The **Cyrillic** alphabet, which most Russians and many citizens of the other republics of the former Soviet Union use, was initiated by the brothers **Constantine (St. Cyril)** and **Methodius**, who were born in Greece. Their intention was to ease the spread of Greek liturgical books in Slavonic-speaking countries. Slightly modified, the Cyrillic alphabet is also taught in Bulgaria and half of the former Yugoslavia.

There are quite a few Russian words that are similar to English and other European languages, such as aeroport, kafe, metro, otel, restoran, taksi, teatr, telefon, televizor. Many science and technology words have Latin or Greek roots and are quite recognizable if you can memorize where the stress is.

Russians hardly ever use the verb "to be" in the present tense. Words in plural mostly end with "i" or "y". The absence of definite and indefinite articles and light use of possessives in Russian actually makes you wonder why, in English, you have to say, for example, **I** went to see **my** doctor in **his** office.

Nyet (no) and **nelzya** (it's forbidden) seem to be two very common words; indeed, the Russian language uses negations constantly. But when somebody tells you that something is forbidden, it may just mean that he does not know the answer to your question.

The Russian equivalent to the English-language four-letter words are richly embroidered five-letter words, for which Russian is legendary. This practice goes back for centuries, although as early as in the 17th century the government made an effort to eradicate public use of coarse language. Profanity and obscene language were forbidden on pain of public flogging administered on the spot.

There are several ways of transliterating Russian letters into English. A pre-Revolutionary Russian ruler could be written as **czar** or **tsar**. Some letters in the Russian alphabet have no English equivalents and vice versa. The Russian letter that looks identical to an English-language X, for instance, is not pronounced like an X; the Russian X is pronounced gutturally as if you were clearing your throat. Khrushchev's name, for example, starts with such an X, but is rendered in English through letters "Kh".

The Russian alphabet has no sound similar to the English H; Hamlet in Russian thus becomes Gamlet.

You will want to carry a pocket Russian-English/English-Russian dictionary with you. German Langenscheidt is recommended for its quality and durability. You can buy it at home or in downtown Moscow. A good dictionary is more valuable than a phrase book, which has limited usage. With a dictionary you can always point to a noun or verb or adjective to make yourself understood.

A FEW CULTURAL DIFFERENCES

It is dangerous to generalize about any nation, but here goes! Of course, bear in mind that these are broad, sweeping characterizations and you can (and hopefully will) meet many Russians who defy these stereotypes.

If you are an English-speaking Westerner, you will be viewed differently than the French, Germans, or Italians. Many of these generalizations apply particularly to Americans because of their visibility, but are also attributed to some extent to other English-speaking visitors from Canada, Australia, and Britain.

Many Russians wonder why Westerners smile so much in public, even if there seems to be little to smile about. They are puzzled that a Westerner would ask them, and each other, every day, "How are you?" (when they should already know the answer) and wonder why they have to keep repeating "Fine" over and over again, even when no one is interested in hearing how they really are.

If you are an American, Russians will probably take note of your casual dress and your casual manners. We seem to take everything so easily, as opposed to their grim determination to conquer another day of adversity. If you are friendly, gregarious, and unceremonious, some Russians might mistake these traits for friendship.

They see Americans as being very competitive and brash. They think Americans think that their political system and way of life should be a model copied everywhere. It would not be unusual if some among the well-educated Russians gloat over what they see as America's cultural

RUSSIAN NAMES

Unlike natives of English-speaking countries, Russians always have three, and only three, parts to their full name: the first or given name, the patronymic which is derived from the father's name, and the family name. The patronymic of Ivan would be Ivanovich, and when Ivan is addressed formally he becomes Ivan Ivanovich. If his father had been Grigori, he would be called Ivan Grigorevich.

The same is true for women, except that a feminine ending is added: so an Anna whose father is Dmitry is formally addressed as Anna Dmitriyevna, which means Anna, daughter of Dmitry.

poverty, or appear delighted that the German and Japanese economies outperform the US economy.

America in particular, in their eyes, is a violent society, a reflection, really, of our country's entertainment. Random violence in America's cities, serial murderers, or public health scares from mentally unbalanced individuals are quite incomprehensible to most Russians, even as they themselves begin to experience violent crime on Moscow streets. They like America's seemingly casteless society, but if they lived in America they might feel that service employees are not deferential enough. Frankly, while this is of course a generalization, Russians are a bit wary of anyone who is not a white European, in part because they have had strained relations with the Caucasus and other outlying former Soviet regions for generations.

Russians, like some Europeans, might never fully understand the boundless individual freedom in America and other English-speaking countries, which to them verges on lawlessness. It appears to them that criminals have more rights than their victims and all might be forgiven, as long as you do not get caught in the actual commission of a crime.

They see Westerners, again particularly Americans, as having a disregard for their elderly in a kind of throw-away society that thrives on youth. Russians have very strong bonds with their parents and would be hard pressed to believe that one's elders would enter a nursing home of their own accord. Teachers, even policemen, the Russians might feel, are not respected, but are ridiculed and held up to the standards of public caprice.

Even the peculiarly American "sale" is a great puzzle to Russians: how can you sell something at 75 percent off the original price? It means that you either charged too much in the first place or are using another gimmick to pull a fast one on the customer. They, like their Eastern

European brethren, think that a two-for-the-price-of-one sale encourages senseless consumption and is a waste of global resources. Those Russians who have had an opportunity to walk through a large American supermarket and see 20 kinds of detergents are frustrated by all the choices because, after all, one or two would be perfectly sufficient.

And then there is this business of privacy. In Russian, like in Portuguese, and some other languages, there is not a word to describe what privacy means exactly. Why do English-speaking Westerners want to be shut up alone, and not bothered by neighbors or strangers alike? If they want to be left alone, there must be something wrong with them.

4. A SHORT HISTORY

Moscow, whose Russian name *Moskva* might be of Finnish origin, is one of the younger capitals of Europe. It is believed to have been founded by Prince **Yuri Dolgoruky** (1090-1157), who mentions it in correspondence to a relative in 1147. That year he and his followers made a social call on a noble who had a hunting village built on the hill. Dolgoruky had his host murdered, took his wife, and gave the host's daughter to his son. He constructed a wooden fort and encircled the settlement with a rampart and a moat in 1156 – the original Kremlin. The structure was only about one-twentieth the size of today's.

At the beginning of the 13th century, tens of thousands of ferocious Mongol horsemen, led by **Batu Khan**, the grandson of Genghis Khan, spilled across Russia and kept it under their yoke for more than two centuries. They defeated the Russians in a three day battle near the Kalka River and captured three Russian princes. The treatment of the princes by their captors was described this way in *Russia Under the Czars*, American Heritage Publishing Co., Inc., 1992: "Their custom forbade them to shed the blood of rulers, so they laughingly used the three princes as foundation for a platform on which the Mongols feasted to celebrate their victory. The princes were crushed to death, their blood unshed."

During the winter of 1237-38, about 120,000 Tartars, again led by Batu Khan, invaded the hamlet of Moscow, located in the forest where the Kremlin now stands. They burned it to the ground and Batu demanded the right ear of every citizen as proof that Moscow was destroyed. He extracted heavy annual tributes through the collaborators they cowed into submission. Taxes were imposed on both rich and poor, and the ruling princes were expected to assist the Mongol tax collectors. Those unable to pay were sold into slavery or had their heads chopped off on the spot.

Moscow became the capital of the principality of **Muscovy** as the 13th century drew to an end. **Ivan Kalita** (1304-1341), whose reputation for economic stangleholds over other principalities earned him the nickname Moneybags, was just one such mercenary who extracted taxes on the Mongols' behalf. He was named the first Grand Prince of Moscow by the Khan and moved from Vladimir. The **Metropolitan**, or the head of the Russian Church, also gave legitimacy to Muscovy by moving the seat of the Orthodox Church from Vladimir. The church was exempt from Tartar taxes, in part because the Mongols were superstitious and feared the Christian god. To escape the tribute, thousands of Russians became monks and the church's wealth became enormous.

By the time Catherine the Great ruled Russia, the Orthodox Church owned almost a million serfs. In a custom that lasted for more than two hundred years, free noble women were confined to their chambers, forbidden to go out unaccompanied, and forced to veil their faces to all men except their husbands.

Moscow was becoming the political and religious capital of **Rus**. By the time the first stone buildings were constructed inside the Kremlin walls, about 25,000 people lived in Moscow. Traders and artisans began settling east of the Kremlin in what was later to become Kitay-gorod, or Chinatown. In Sergiyev Posad, northeast of Moscow, **Sergiy Radonezhsky**, who became the patron saint of Russia, founded the **Holy Trinity Monastery**. Around 1367, while the Black Death plague raged in Europe and Asia, the wooden walls of the Kremlin were being replaced by white stone and fortified monasteries were built at strategic points to secure its defenses.

THE END OF MONGOL DOMINATION

The Muscovy principality became more assertive with the rise of the **Grand Prince Dmitry Ivanovich** (1350-1389), who balked over the annual tribute and repelled two sieges by the Tartars. On September 8, 1380, an event took place that Russians still remember to this day. Prince Dmitry, the grandson of Ivan Kalita, brought 100,000 troops to the field of **Kulikovo**, near the upper reaches of the River Don, and in one of the greatest battles in Russian history crushed a much larger Mongol force.

The victor became known as **Dmitry Donskoy** ("of the Don"), was canonized after his death, and the Donskoy Monastery was erected in the area where his army prayed for victory. To avenge their defeat, the Mongols laid siege to Moscow two years later and burned it to the ground. But before the century was out, Moscow recovered and extended its influence. Iconist and monk **Andrey Rublev** (1360/70-1430) was in the midst of creating some of his best work.

Moscow emerged as the most powerful of the Russian city-states in the 15th century, after almost 250 years of Mongol domination. In 1453, after Constantinople, which was the center of the Greek Orthodox Church, was taken over by the Turks, the Metropolitan declared Moscow the Third Rome and the true heir of Christianity. During the reign of **Ivan**

BLACK MAGIC FIRES OF 1547

If floods have been a threat to St. Petersburg throughout its history, fires were even more frequent in Moscow, particularly before Napoleon's invasion of Russia in 1812. Most houses were built of logs. They were heated in winter by stoves and became so dried out that it took but a single accident to char entire neighborhoods. Moscow has suffered hundreds of fires during its 850-year history.

One such fire broke out on April 12, 1547, in Kitay-gorod, then already a well-known merchant quarter. All traders' stalls and warehouses perished in flames. A tower used to store gunpowder exploded, blowing parts of the city wall into the Moskva River. The fire smoldered for several days until, rejuvenated by winds a few days later, it destroyed the district beyond the Yauza River, where the smithies and tanneries were concentrated. Again, the fires died down or remained dormant.

A high wind was blowing on June 21, 1547, when fire broke out in the Arbat district, then a suburb west of the Kremlin. The Vozdvizhenskaya Church burned to the ground. The fire spread rapidly, reducing to ashes the entire western part of the capital, all the way to the banks of the Moskva River. Then the wind changed direction and carried the fire to the Kremlin, which was soon ablaze. "The palace, the treasury, armories, all the state offices, private houses, the Metropolitan's palace, the cathedrals and churches, all were destroyed," notes Ian Grey in his book, Ivan the Terrible. The books and manuscripts, the treasures of the Kremlin, including icons such as the miracle-working icon of the Virgin of Vladimir, perished. The Uspensky Cathedral was partly spared but structurally damaged. The great bell of Moscow fell from its burning belfry to fracture on the ground below. There were enormous explosions of gunpowder in the state arsenal. The Metropolitan Makary had gone to the Uspensky Cathedral to pray for the deliverance of Moscow, but the smoke almost suffocated him.

Driven by the high winds, the fires raged across Moscow. Few buildings escaped damage and most districts were reduced to smoldering ruins. Almost 2,000 people, including many children, perished. Heavy clouds of smoke hung over the city for days. The survivors, with singed hair and blackened faces, searched futilely among the charred ruins for missing relatives and what might have been left of their property.

The Metropolitan and his retinue told the tsar that black magic was responsible for the fires. They said that sorcerers had torn out the hearts of human corpses, soaked them in water, and then sprinkled this water on the streets of Moscow causing the fire. The tsar readily accepted this explanation and gave instructions for the rebuilding of the nobles' palaces in the Kremlin.

the Great (1440-1505), who in 1472 shrewdly married the 350-pound niece of the last Byzantine emperor, Russians overthrew the Tartar yoke. While the Sistine Chapel frescoes were painted in the Vatican and Leonardo da Vinci created his immortal painting *The Last Supper*, Italian architects and artisans from Pskov and Vladimir came to Moscow to supervise the construction of the Kremlin cathedrals and its brick wall.

The city, which now covered an area of more than two square miles, and whose expanded Kremlin grew to its present 70-acre size, was soon to grow to 100,000 people and become one of the most populous in Europe.

IVAN THE TERRIBLE

Ivan IV, known as **Ivan the Terrible** (1530-1584), was born in the Kremlin amid a terrifying storm and deafening claps of thunder, or at least so the legend goes. His father Vasily III, unable to have an heir from his first wife, carted her off to a monastery in Suzdal and married Princess Elena Glinskaya two months later. When she bore him this child, Vasily rejoiced and, following an earlier vow, built a church in Kolomenskoye, where he himself helped lay the foundations. Three years later, while on a pilgrimage to **Sergiyev Posad** (see Chapter 18, *Excursions & Day Trips*), he fell ill of blood poisoning and died. Four months short of his eighth birthday, the boy lost his mother to poisoning.

Ivan the Terrible, who later earned his reputation for brutality, was crowned in Moscow as the first Tsar of All Russia at the age of 17 in the same year much of the city was damaged by fire in 1547 (see sidebar in this chapter). The young Ivan, having lost both his parents at an early age, became a pawn in Kremlin politics. As a child, he was often left "cold and hungry" by the **boyars** (nobles of the court) who hoped to regain their former glory, but did not dare to kill him outright. It is, in part, because of such neglect that Ivan later earned his title "the Terrible," when he indiscriminatley killed many of them.

In 1564, general Andrey Kurbsky became the first defector in Russian history when he sided with the Polish king and was commissioned to fight Ivan. A year later, Ivan organized the **oprichniki**, a band of about 10,000 bandits and criminals, to help him in his pursuit of those he wanted to eliminate. Clad in black, riding black horses, and carrying a dog's head and broom emblems, they killed, maimed and raped with impunity. Ivan defeated the Tartars in Kazan in 1552 and had St. Basil's Cathedral built as his thanks, although a legend persists that he gouged out the eyes of its architects so they could never again create a sight of equal beauty. In 1553, the first printing house opened in Moscow, where dirt and mud abounded and few streets were paved, and those that were, were paved with logs only.

In 1560, his beloved wife Anastasia died, supposedly of poisoning, and Ivan earned his nickname "the Terrible" by exiling thousands of boyars and indiscriminately killing his perceived enemies. He is said to have been "untidy, wild-eyed, with scraggly beard and the look of a madman." In a fit of rage captured so profoundly by painter Ilya Repin on a canvas now exhibited at the Tretyakov Gallery, Ivan murdered his own son. The climax of his brutal rule came perhaps in 1569, when 60,000 citizens of Novgorod were killed for allegedly plotting to betray him to Poland. Cruelty extended to the weak and powerless as well, among them Moscow women who, when caught in marital unfaithfulness, would often be buried up to their necks and left to die.

In the winter of 1584, Ivan felt a portent of his death while gazing at a comet in the sky. He summoned 60 astrologers who agreed that the terrible tyrant was to expire on March 18. And sure enough, his body became swollen and on March 15 he became delirious. Three days later he collapsed dead and was buried in the Cathedral of the Archangel Michael in the Kremlin.

In 1571, when both Shakespeare and Galileo were seven years old, the Crimean Tartars, 200,000 strong, burned Moscow for the last time, although the Kremlin was spared. They kidnapped hundreds of Moscow women and sold them into slavery. In addition to the existing stone wall on the Boulevard Ring Road, a protective barrier was erected on today's Garden Ring Road.

TIME OF TROUBLES

Because of the Livonian War with Poland and Sweden, in which Ivan the Terrible lost his far-flung territories and access to the Baltic, Russia was left in chaos. His feeble-minded son was crowned tsar, but died in 1598. **Boris Godunov** (1551-1605) was elected the next tsar, a shrewd man of Tartar descent, unable to read and write. The time between his assumption of power and 1613 is known as the **Time of Troubles**, a period of suffering and devastation, when boyars struggled against the tsar. One of the worst famines raged in the years 1601-1603, fostering social unrest among peasants and driving some to brigandage and cannibalism. It is believed that the population of Russia was reduced from 14 million people to about nine million during those 15 years.

At the turn of the century, Godunov had another wall built around the Kremlin and Kitay-gorod, which remained until the 19th century, when it was demolished to make way for the Boulevard Ring Road. An additional defense line was established where the Garden Ring Road runs today. There were more than 200 churches by the end of the 16th century, when Shakespeare wrote *Romeo and Juliet*. Novodevichy and Danilovsky

THE MANY WIVES OF IVAN THE TERRIBLE

Ivan was crowned the first tsar of Russia in 1547 and at once dispatched senior officials all over the land ordering boyars to submit their daughters to an inspection of their "comeliness, piety and good character." Almost 2,000 of the most beautiful maidens were assembled in Moscow for the tsar's final selection. He picked Anastasia, a girl of Prussian origin.

Like most Moscow noble wives, Anastasia was closely guarded and displayed her virtue by being shut up at home with nothing to do but to bear children. As a result of the cold and hardships suffered in late 1559, when she and Ivan were returning from Mozhaysk (65 miles southwest of Moscow), Anastasia, who had borne him six children, only two of which survived, died the following year.

Ivan went into deep mourning, but eight days later the church hierarchy suggested that he remarry. The tsar announced such intentions eleven days after his wife's death. In 1561, Ivan heard that a Circasian leader had a daughter of remarkable beauty named Mariya. He at once sent for her and was struck by her sensuality. They were married that same year, but once sated, he lost interest in her. Eight years later she died unexpectedly, but possibly of poisoning. Eighteen months later, messengers again rode the tsardom drumming up new maidens, which were brought to Aleksandrov, near Moscow. Ivan chose 12 finalists, who were then handed to his doctor and to old women of the court "for more intimate examination." But beauty was just one criteria; a maiden who snored in bed was immediately disqualified. Marfa, the daughter of a Novgorod merchant, was chosen as the next bride and immediately her entire family was rewarded with high rank and received big estates. Even before Marfa warmed the bed of Ivan, surely by now also "the Terrible," she fell ill (at the time of her wedding) and "after 16 days of unconsummated marriage, the maiden, chosen from 2,000 for her beauty and character, passed away."

Ivan the Terrible remarried within two months of Marfa's death. His fourth wife was Anna, but he married her without any of the proclamations or the usual searches, for he knew well that to take a fourth wife was forbidden by canon law. Tsaritsa Anna held Ivan's affection for three years and when she failed to conceive, she was sent to a monastery and shorn as a nun, which had the effect of a divorce. That same year the Terrible Ivan took a fifth wife, again named Anna, but without a church ceremony and without her parents being present at court. His sixth wife was a widow called Vasilisa. In 1582, soon after he took his seventh wife, another Maria, and married her without any ceremony or the blessing of the church, he proposed to Lady Mary Hastings, Queen Elizabeth's cousin, but fortunately never married her.

monasteries were already erected as defense outposts outside these ramparts. Red Square became a flourishing market and also the place where executions were carried out. The area just east of the Kremlin also thrived as the center of commerce. The Arbat district, then a suburb of Moscow, became populated by thousands of craftsmen and laborers who were employed in the Kremlin and lived on streets you can still see today, such as Carpenters Lane and Old Stables Lane. Potters lived around Taganka Square and weavers in Khamovniki.

Two pretenders, both named Dmitry, claimed the throne during the Times of Troubles. In 1603, **False Dmitry I** appeared in Poland and claimed to be the son of Ivan the Terrible who was thought to have died under suspicious circumstances in 1591. With the backing of the Polish troops and discontented Russian peasants, he marched on Moscow in 1605, just as Boris Godunov died, and proclaimed himself tsar. His rule lasted less than a year before he was murdered in the Kremlin by his boyar supporters.

The **False Dmitry II** also tried to gain control with the help of the Poles and established a rival government in the village of Tushino, near Moscow, but was also killed. In 1610, the Poles occupied Moscow and held it for three years until driven out after days of starvation by two Russian patriots, a Nizhny Novgorod cattle merchant named **Kuzma Minin** and Suzdal Prince **Dmitry Pozharsky**, and a volunteer army financed by the citizens of the two cities. Two hundred years later a statue was erected in their honor and now stands in Red Square in front of St. Basil's Cathedral. Five claimants to the throne declared themselves to be the youngest son of Ivan the Terrible.

THE ROMANOV DYNASTY

In January 1613, an assembly that represented most upper classes of the day selected the 16 year-old **Mikhail Romanov** (1596-1645), the grandnephew of Ivan the Terrible, as their tsar and the 300-year dynasty of the Romanovs began. After half a century of chaos and terror, Russia lacked doctors, engineers, and other professionals and the Romanov tsars encouraged some 30,000 of them to come to Moscow from European countries. However, the church insisted that these so-called **nemtsy** (stupid foreigners who could not speak Russian) live in the suburban settlement of Nemetskaya Sloboda, east of Moscow and on the Yauza River. Nemets is now a regular word for German.

Because of the cruelty of the Time of Troubles, many thousands of peasants fled to Siberia or to the fertile Volga valley, where colonization had begun toward the end of the 16th century and serfdom was unknown. Others became brigands ambushing traveling merchants and defenseless estates. The landlords, unable to find enough hands to tend to their properties, lobbied the tsar and by 1646 the peasants' right to leave their masters was abolished and inherited occupations became a norm. They lost all their rights to the land and, like **serfs** (slaves), could be sold at any time. In 1649, serfdom was declared hereditary.

Some peasants resisted enserfment by joining Cossack peasant leader **Stepan Razin**, who in 1667 led a band of 1,000 in his first attack on a convoy of trading vessels owned by the tsar. Cossacks originated as runaways from serfdom. Three years later his ragtag army numbered 20,000 men, and were driven by anger and craving for vengeance. By the spring of 1671, the legendary Razin was caught, clapped in irons and brought to Moscow, where Tsar Aleksis interrogated him. Razin was beaten with a knout (a whip for flogging) and his limbs were pulled out of their joints, but the peasant leader endured his torments without a sound. On June 6, 1671, he was taken to the execution block on Red Square, and as a warning to others he was dismembered and some of his body parts were mounted on stakes.

Of all the extraordinary men who have ruled Russia, none is more fascinating than Mikhail Romanov's grandson, Peter I, known as **Peter the Great** (1672-1725), who became tsar, along with his half-brother Ivan, in 1682 under the regency of Ivan's sister Sofiya. Almost seven feet tall, he was also prodigiously strong. Intellectually curious, he often visited Nemetskaya Sloboda, Moscow's European district, to educate himself about the West; he also drank and partied to excess.

Starting in 1697, Peter spent 18 months in Western Europe, learning and recruiting specialists from Germany, Holland, England and Austria for service in Russia. He was only the second Russian ruler ever to travel abroad. Except for diplomats, leaving Russia was considered treasonable. But before Peter's tour was over, the **streltsy**, those pesky soldiers going back to Ivan The Terrible who formed the Kremlin palace guard, rebelled again, so he returned home and had more than a thousand executed.

In 1709, Peter defeated the Swedes at Poltava in southern Russia in one of the most decisive battles in world history, and reigned supreme in northeastern Europe. He adopted the Julian calendar, created the Russian navy, and introduced Western culture and customs to Russia, which included cutting off beards and a European dress code. He deliberately knouted his own son, who hated him as a betrayer of Russian tradition and fled to the court of the emperor of Austria. On land he took from Sweden and on the backs of more than 200,000 laborers and serfs, who perished from exposure, he built St. Petersburg, which became the Russian capital in 1712.

By 1721, the Russian empire replaced Muscovy. Four years later Peter the Great died and was succeeded by his bawdy peasant widow **Catherine**

I (1684-1727). The vain and pleasure-seeking **Elizabeth** (1709-1762) ruled for the next 20 years and on her death left behind 15,000 gowns and 2,500 pairs of shoes. In 1762, she was replaced by Catherine II, commonly known as **Catherine the Great** (1729-1796).

Although Peter moved his court to St. Petersburg, Moscow remained the seat of the Russian Orthodox Church. Many opulent estates that can still be seen today were built here. Tverskaya Street became perhaps the most exclusive street in Moscow and many nobles built their palatial homes along this ancient trade route. Although relegating Moscow to provincial town status, Peter still used Tverskaya for his ceremonial entries to the city. In 1737, Moscow experienced one of the most damaging fires in almost 200 years, and in 1755, scientist **Mikhail Lomonosov** (1711-1765) drew up plans for Moscow University.

During the reign of Peter and Catherine the Great, the lot of serfs only worsened. The gentry could buy and sell farm laborers at will or send them to permanent hard labor at their whim. Between 1740 and 1801, more than 1.3 million peasants were handed over to wealthy landowners. Catherine the Great gave away nearly a million peasants and forbid complaints against their masters on penalty of the knout. As late as 1858, some 1,400 landowners owned an average of 2,200 serfs each.

Conditions grew so unbearable that a civil war broke out again. The rebel this time was another Cossack rebel, **Yemelyan Pugachev** (1726-1775), who proclaimed himself to be Peter III, who had already been murdered. Pugachev's 7,000 rebels captured Kazan in 1774, burning 2,000 of the town's 2,800 houses and killing hundreds. Several thousands more were killed in other towns along the Volga River. Landowners were terrified and Moscow was panic stricken at the prospect that the rebels would head their way. But, like Stepan Razin and others before him, Pugachev was betrayed by his fellow Cossacks, and was seized with his wife and children and put in a small iron cage specially built to take him to Moscow like a wild beast. Catherine conceded in a letter to the French philosopher **Voltaire** (1694-1778) that Pugachev was "an uncommonly brave and resourceful person." She considered George Washington (1732-1799) a rebel, too.

On January 10, 1775, Pugachev was taken to a square on the banks of the Moscow River below the Kremlin walls. Paul Avrich in his book *Russian Rebels 1600-1800* describes Pugachev's execution this way: "There he was beheaded at a blow and then quartered. His head was mounted on a pike and the sections of his body put on wheels and exposed in different parts of Moscow for all to see." Thousands of Muscovites witnessed the execution. By Catherine's edict of March 15, 1775, all matters concerning the rebellion were consigned to "eternal oblivion and profound silence."

Just a year later, a dance company was founded which was later to become known as the **Bolshoy Ballet**. Catherine hated Moscow; she always complained about the Kremlin living quarters and criticized the city's nobility and the church. She said more than once that Moscow was full of thieves.

In the 1782 census of male citizens, Russia numbered 28 million – the gentry and clergy each accounting for one percent – while Moscow' population surpassed 277,000. There were more than 480 separate churches in the city by then.

Lady Londonderry, who visited Moscow in 1836, described it as "the most singular and beautiful town that I ever saw... The immense extent, the gardens, the variety and the hundreds of gold domes and cupolas of every color and shape and shade and pattern and the spires and crosses... and the glorious Kremlin."

NAPOLEON INVADES RUSSIA

On June 24, 1812, when the beloved Russian poet **Aleksandr Pushkin** (1799-1837) was 13 years old and Beethoven completed his Seventh Symphony, **Napoleon** (1769-1821) crossed the Neman River into Russia with his multinational Grande Armee. Moscow was more than 500 miles to the east. On September 12, he surveyed with satisfaction from the hills just outside Moscow the great city below him and awaited its surrender, just like Batu Khan had done 575 years before. But his sentries instead brought him the news that the city of 250,000 seemed entirely deserted.

"Moscow deserted! A most unlikely event!" he exclaimed. Two days later, his troops entered the city through Trinity Gate and Napoleon set up his headquarters inside the Kremlin. Soon fires began breaking out all over deserted Moscow. At first, it was believed that they were set by his own looting troops, but some surmise that the Russians decided to scorch the city rather than turn needed supplies over to Napoleon. Moscow was set on fire on September 14, the fire destroying about three-quarters of the city. The Governor of Moscow posted a notice on his palace, taunting Napoleon: "I set fire to my house so that it may not be polluted by your presence."

"What people! Such tactics have no precedent in the history of the civilization!" exclaimed Bonaparte in disbelief. Surrounded by flames, Napoleon late in the night, by the light from the blazing city, sent a letter to **Tsar Aleksandr I** (1777-1825) demanding his surrender. But as if in reply, the fires soon reached the Kremlin itself and Napoleon was forced to flee through a narrow winding street already afire from one end to the other. The emperor fled to the accompanying roar of the crashing buildings. On September 18, a heavy rain fell and extinguished the fires after four days, making it possible for Napoleon to return. Inside the

Assumption Cathedral, the French built a furnace to melt down treasures for their gold. The Archangel Cathedral served as a wine cellar and St. Basil's as a stable.

Field Marshall **Mikhail Kutuzov** (1745-1813) repulsed their advances and the tsar refused to negotiate a truce. There was nothing left for the occupiers to do, already hungry and fatigued, but to practically retrace their way back to where they came from. As they left Moscow, on October 19, the troops were held down by 700 pounds of gold and five tons of silver. Soon one of the harshest winters on record began, made many times worse by Russian troops and guerillas pursuing the occupiers at every turn. More than 25,000 prisoners were taken by Kutuzov and only about 20,000 of Napoleon's 550,000 troops survived the Russian campaign. Aleksandr I pursued Napoleon's exhausted troops to Paris and occupied it in 1814.

With Napoleon out of the way, Tsar Alexander began rebuilding Moscow. The Kremlin Palace and the Armory were built, as well as many private residences that still stand today. The moat which had run through Red Square was eliminated and the Neglinka River, which bordered the western wall of the Kremlin, was diverted underground in 1821. The **Bolshoy Theater** was about to be rebuilt and **Maly Theater** was planned for. Moscow grew to a city of 350,000 by 1863 and to 750,000 by 1882, when composer **Igor Stravinsky** was born. Most buildings until then were made of wood and were regularly destroyed by fires. Because of this, nearly all the surviving historical sights in Moscow are churches and monasteries built in stone. Many were demolished in the Soviet era, but the Kremlin and some other sights in the center of Moscow survived untouched, most notably St. Basil's Cathedral.

Observed an 1824 guide to Moscow: "No city like Moscow arose with such brilliance and so swiftly from almost complete destruction by fire. Before the great fire, there were 9,158 houses in the city; 6,341 of these burned. Since then, 8,027 houses have been built."

Exposed to the more developed countries as a result of the Napoleonic war, Russian officers could see how good life could be without serfdom and even with a few freedoms of expression. But **Tsar Nicholas I** (1796-1855) and the aristocracy were not about to succumb to reforms, so the opposition festered underground. Later known as **Decembrists**, because of their unsuccessful coup in December 1825, 3,000 of the plotters, who wanted to replace the existing autocratic order, were arrested and hundreds of others were exiled to Siberia. Russia embarked on a systematic campaign of obliterating all dissent, even in literature. With the exception of **Nikolay Gogol** (1809-1852), many writers, including Pushkin, **Mikhail Lermontov** (1814-1841), **Ivan Turgenev** (1818-1883), and **Fyodor Dostoyevsky** (1821-1881) were harassed by the authorities.

On March 3, 1861, one day before Abraham Lincoln's inauguration in America, Nicholas' son **Aleksandr II** (1818-1881) abolished serfdom (several years before Lincoln abolished slavery). More than half of all Russians were serfs then. Thirty years of repression by his father had left the country impoverished, backward, and fearing a serf uprising. The peasants wanted land and other reforms, yet their pleas fell on deaf ears. After an attempt was made to assassinate him, Aleksandr tightened the screws; three more attempts were made against him, until in 1881 he agreed to establish a legislature to win back popular support. He was assassinated that same day.

Many of the landless peasants flooded cities like Moscow, which by 1890 saw its population swell to more than one million. Meanwhile, a railway line between Moscow and St. Petersburg was opened, the **Moscow Conservatory** was inaugurated, electric trams were introduced and in 1837 the stock exchange was founded. But instead of continuing his father's work, **Aleksandr III** (1845-1894) abandoned the constitutional experiment and watered down the emancipation of serfs. The terrorists went to work again. One of them was the brother of Lenin (1870-1924), who was trapped in an 1887 plot against Aleksandr III and hanged.

In 1894, after studying Karl Marx, **Vladimir Lenin** moved to St. Petersburg to organize the Union for the Liberation of the Working Class. That was also the year when Aleksandr III died and **Nicholas II** (1868-1918) became tsar. His domineering wife bore him four daughters and a son, Aleksis, who was born with hemophilia; she came to rely heavily on a Siberian peasant and monk, **Rasputin** (1872-1916), hoping to have the hemophiliac crown prince healed by the time he became tsar of Russia.

Lenin was arrested for his clandestine work and exiled to Siberia for three years. In 1898, the first Marxist party was formed in Russia (in 1903 they split into Mensheviks, less radical communists, and Bolsheviks). In 1900, Lenin left for Switzerland, where he plotted against the tsar as the leader of the Bolsheviks.

Russia fought a war with Japan in 1904-05 to gain control of the Korean peninsula, a war which Russia ultimately lost at the cost of many lives. Corruption was rampant and hunger became widespread and intolerable. The war and Nicholas's refusal to grant freedom of religion and speech ended in 200,000 people marching in the streets of St. Petersburg on January 22, 1905, which became known as **Bloody Sunday**. Led by a priest, the unarmed workers stormed the Winter Palace, demanding an eight-hour workday and a minimum wage of one ruble a day. More than 500 were killed and thousands more wounded. The discontent was so great that by the end of the year more than 1,500 government officials were assassinated. Riots followed throughout the country, with schools, government offices, and railways forced to close.

The revolt was crushed, but the tsar sanctioned the formation of a legislative body, the **State Duma**. The tsar dissolved the Duma in 1906 and 1907, but the third Duma ran for five years (the fourth was cut short by the 1917 Revolution).

On the eve of World War I, Moscow was a prosperous city with bustling business districts, wide boulevards, and large public squares. Following the abolition of serfdom, it became a great industrial center, with railways and roads converging from different parts of Russia. But overpopulation and housing shortages also led to slums, which contributed to the working class unrest of 1905 and the Revolution twelve years later.

THE RUSSIAN REVOLUTION

On June 28, 1914, Archduke Franz Ferdinand of Austria-Hungary was assassinated by a Bosnian Serb terrorist, and World War I broke out in August 1914. Germany and Austria-Hungary declared war on Russia, and Russia declared war on Ottoman Turkey and invaded Hungary. All told, more than 15 million Russians were drafted, and six million were killed.

By 1916, the mad monk Rasputin was poisoned and then shot at the Moika Palace in St. Petersburg. Still not dead, the four noblemen who had hoped with this murder to save the monarchy stuffed the kicking Rasputin into a sack and threw the half-dead monk into the icy Neva Canal.

In February 1917, the Revolution broke out, when thousands of hungry Russians stormed the St. Petersburg bakeries. In March, the tsarist troops fired upon and killed many of the bread seekers, but later themselves joined in the demonstrations. Later that month, lawyer **Aleksandr Kerensky** (1881-1970), who was born in Simbirsk, the same town as Lenin, took over a provisional government. Nicholas II abdicated on March 15, but his brother, **Grand Duke Michael**, refused to take the throne unless through a free election. The Russian monarchy, in power since 1462, came to an end.

Germany, intent on upsetting the pro-allied Russian provisional government, sent Lenin in a sealed train from Switzerland to Russia on April 16. Lenin, **Leon Trotsky** (1879-1940) and **Josef Stalin** (1879-1953) promised their people "peace, bread, and freedom." In October, Lenin was appointed Chief Commissar and inaugurated the "dictatorship of the proletariat." On November 7, 1917 (or October 25 by the old calendar), Bolsheviks took control of key buildings in St. Petersburg with hardly a shot being fired; Moscow, however, took a week of savage fighting. After 206 years in St. Petersburg, Lenin transferred the capital back to Moscow in 1918, when the first attempt was made on his life (by a young woman) which, unfortunately, led to widescale reprisals. The Bolsheviks also dissolved the Constituent Assembly in 1918 and created the secret police, **Cheka**, which arrested, tried, and executed anyone perceived as an "enemy of the people." In 1918 alone, the Cheka shot more than 500 members of the privileged classes in St. Petersburg alone. All debts were canceled and all foreign property nationalized; Kerensky, seeing the writing on the wall, fled abroad.

On the night of July 16-17, 1918, Tsar Nicholas II and his entire household, who were held in detention in Yekaterinburg, Siberia, were suddenly awakened at midnight and brought to the basement of the cold, damp house where they were held prisoners. While the tsar's five children shivered and cried, the Bolshevik guards, on direct orders from Lenin, shot and bayoneted the entire family. Before they were killed, several rescue attempts had been made by the **Whites**, soldiers loyal to the tsar who fought the **Reds** under Lenin in the **Civil War** (1918-1921). While there was some Allied Western intervention to help the Whites take back Russia from the Bolsheviks, the support was token and Lenin ultimately prevailed.

In 1922, the **Union of Soviet Socialist Republics** (USSR) was born, as was Lenin's **New Economic Policy** (NEP) of limited free enterprise – initiated to buy Soviet Russia time before entering an era of state planning. Russian industry was in shambles since workers were placed in control of factories; peasants refused to grow crops. Hunger was so extreme that there were frequent incidents of cannibalism, and five million peasants are believed to have perished.

Incapacitated by several strokes from 1922 on, Lenin died on January 21, 1924. There followed a struggle for power, principally between the articulate and more popular Trotsky, architect of the Civil War victory and Lenin's top advisor, and the crafty and vulgar Stalin, who began building a bureaucratic organization within the Communist Party and currying favor with influential **apparatchiks** (party functionaries). Stalin, whose thick Georgian accent Lenin and others used to make fun of, the man Lenin warned his wife on his sickbed to be wary of, won the power struggle. Trotsky fled to Mexico City in 1929, where Stalin's agents eventually caught up with him in 1940; he was killed most unpleasantly, with an ice pick.

Stalin, who was dismissed for many years as a mediocrity, methodically eliminated one enemy after another, beginning with many of the Old Bolsheviks – the old guard who had been with Lenin from the beginning well before the Revolution. Stalin confiscated private land from the peasants and forced them to join collective farms. They resisted by slaughtering their cattle, burning their crops, and killing many officials. Millions were exiled and a war was declared against the middle peasants (slightly better off than the average peasant), who were known as **kulaks** (the phrase of the day was "Beat the Kulaks"). Many were killed and sent to prison camps, and some three million are estimated to have died of starvation.

More than 60% of private homesteads were collectivized by 1932, when the first Five Year Plan was supposedly completed ahead of time. That same year another famine broke out, claiming five million Ukrainian and Volga peasants, whom Stalin sacrificed by dumping scarce Soviet grain on world markets. He used rapid industrialization as another excuse to gain total control over the Soviet populace; internal passports were introduced for the first time since the tsarist era. And then the purges came.

By the time Stalin had finished with the **purges**, more than 70% of the Central Committee of the Communist Party was eliminated, as was more than 25% of the officer corps of the Red Army. To appreciate the terrors of the Stalin era, take a look at any number of books written about this horrible time in recent Russian history. For the academically minded, one of the classics is Roy Medvedev's *Let History Judge*; for those of you interested in reading a very moving (and short) novel, pick up Lydia Chukovskaya's *The Deserted House*.

A huge reconstruction began in the 1930's under the carnivorous Stalin, including the seven high-rise "wedding cake" buildings, placed at strategic points around Moscow, which transformed it into a city of large block apartment buildings and government offices, while destroying many historical landmarks. In 1935, the first metro line was inaugurated to provide "palaces for the people," whose food was scarce and even the tiniest apartments hard to come by.

In 1939, Hitler and Stalin signed a non-aggression pact and agreed to divide Eastern Europe into two spheres of influence. Russia was to get Poland and the Baltic states. But when Germany invaded Poland that same year, Stalin moved his troops into eastern Poland. The Russians annexed Finland the following year. On June 22, 1941 – almost 129 years to the day after Napoleon made a similar mistake – Germany invaded Russia. More than three million German troops broke into Russia without a declaration of war. A month later, Moscow and the Kremlin suffered the first Nazi bombardment. Hitler instructed his air force "to destroy the monument of Russian barbarism, the Kremlin."

THE BATTLE FOR MOSCOW

The initial German drive toward Moscow had stopped near Smolensk for most of September 1941, while Nazi Field Marshall Bock sent two armies south to close a pincer movement at Kiev. On October 2, the reassembled force of 60 divisions resumed its attack, hoping to overcome the remaining 200 miles toward Moscow before winter. The Russian government, but not Stalin, withdrew to Samara, a city on the Volga River, where in 1892 Lenin practiced law.

The resisting Russians and roads soaked by heavy rains slowed the enemy's advance and, by mid-November, a vicious Russian winter fell upon the Germans, paralyzing men and machinery. In a final effort on December 2, the second panzer division came so close to the capital that the German commanders could see the familiar roofs of the Kremlin, just 38 miles away. But they could not make any more headway. The 258th infantry division of the fourth army fought its way into the suburbs of Moscow, but was repulsed by factory workers who fought the Germans practically bare-handed. By November 29, the temperature fell to 54 degrees Celsius below freezing.

On December 6, 1941, Russian General **Georgy Zhukov** (1896-1974) launched a counter-offensive with 100 fresh divisions. By then, the Germans had already lost some 830,000 men and had to pack newspapers into their thin uniforms to ward off the bitter Russian winter. By Christmas 1941, the temperature was still 45 degrees Celsius below freezing and some German troops had not had a hot meal for over a week. Col. Albert Seaton, in *The Battle for Moscow*, writes: "The plight of many of the isolated German stragglers was almost indescribable. Their lips were cracked and faces frost-bitten, their legs numbed and without feeling; one by one men sat or dropped down to await death because they could go no further; no reasoning could make them continue. Some begged to be shot or shot themselves."

The battle for Moscow lasted from September 1941 to April 1942 and involved more than 1.5 million troops and 1,600 tanks. It was Germany's first major defeat on land in WWII, and the turning point on the central front.

THE WAR'S END & ITS AFTERMATH

By the summer of 1942, German casualties had climbed to nearly two million. Many battles were fought on Soviet territory and in Eastern Europe, as the Soviet military recouped and eventually drove the Nazi forces back into Germany. By the end of WWII, more than 20 million Soviet soldiers were killed.

Unfortunately, even after the war was over, Soviet prisoners of war (who were considered deserters) and hundreds of thousands of other Soviet citizens who came in contact with foreigners, were investigated and many shipped off to slave labor camps. The countries of Eastern Europe, with the exception of the former Yugoslavia, which was never occupied by Soviet troops and which split with Moscow in 1948, became Soviet puppets. They all suffered depravation and depredations that still haunt them.

Reconstruction continued after the war and many of the already wide avenues, such as Mira, Kutuzov, Lenin and Leningrad, were enlarged still more and lined with enormous public buildings or apartment blocks. The new Moscow State University was completed in 1953, the year of Stalin's death, towering 787 feet above Sparrow Hills.

THE COLD WAR & SOVIET POLITICS

After a brief struggle with the barbaric head of state security forces (whose name changed several times until they settled on KGB), **Lavrenty Beria** (1899-1953) was tried and executed like countless thousands of his victims. **Nikita Khruschev** (1894-1971) elbowed his way to the top and, in February 1956, delivered a surprising, secret speech at the Twentieth Party Congress. Word got out, and for the first time, Stalin's shocking crimes were revealed to the Soviet people. But the chubby and flamboyant Nikita was no slouch himself; in 1956, he brutally suppressed the Hungarian rebellion. Although the first earth satellite, Sputnik, was launched during Khruschev's rule, the Soviet leader backed down in his contest of wills with President John F. Kennedy during the 1962 Cuban Missile Crisis. While vacationing on the Black Sea in 1964, he was replaced by the short-lived duo of **Leonid Brezhnev** and **Aleksei Kosygin** for his "hare-brained scheming." Kosygin soon dropped out of the duopoly, and Brezhnev's era began.

The Brezhnev reign was characterized by economic stagnation, fitful periods of détente and pull-back, and ongoing human rights abuses. **Aleksandr Solzhenitsyn** (b. 1918), who had published his *One Day in the Life of Ivan Denisovich* with Khruschev's approval, fell out of favor by the late 1960's when his other books were published abroad. Things worsened for him when he was awarded the Nobel Prize for Literature in 1970. After his *Gulag Archipelago* was published in 1973 in the West, the author was exiled, settling as a recluse in rural Vermont. Physicist Andrei Sakharov (1921-1989) became a leading dissident and countless others followed in his footsteps.

The East-West confrontation, known as the Cold War, lasted from 1946 to 1988 or so, and resulted in throwing away hundreds of billions of dollars in bizarre weaponry on both sides of the Iron Curtain (a phrase, by the way, coined by Winston Churchill in a 1946 speech given in President Harry Truman's home town). Relations between the US and USSR improved after the first major nuclear arms control accord in 1972, and worsened after the Soviets invaded Afghanistan in 1979. Americans did not participate in the 1980 Moscow Olympics, and President Ronald Reagan ushered in the 1980's by calling Soviet rule an "evil empire." But things began to pick up with the elevation of a new Soviet leader in the mid-1980's. **Mikhail Gorbachev** (b. 1931), who was chosen General Secretary of the Communist Party by one vote in April 1985, described capitalism in his speech to the 1986 Communist Party Congress as "the most frightening and dangerous monster" of our time – yet he lost no time by initiating a program of far-reaching reforms, including expanded freedoms and the democratization of the political process through openness (**glasnost**), and restructuring of the economy (**perestroika**).

On April 26, 1986, a great catastrophe befell the Soviet Union – specifically the Ukraine – when a reactor at the Chernobyl nuclear power station exploded during a test in which the emergency cooling system had been switched off. It was 36 hours before the first residents were evacuated. It is estimated that more than 4,000 people died as a result of explosion.

In 1987, national elections were held for the first time since 1917. The voters were able to vote for their favorite candidates or against those they did not want in office. The Russian Congress of People's Deputies was inaugurated in May 1990, after 500,000 demonstrated in Moscow in support of the democratic process. The last Soviet troops left Afghanistan; the Berlin Wall fell; and the Communist regimes in Eastern Europe began collapsing one after another amid Soviet troop withdrawals. The Baltic republics too finally got their independence shortly after the other Soviet satellite states did.

In August 1991, a coup d'état shook Russia and a state of emergency was declared. Boris Yeltsin (b. 1931), already elected President of the Russian Republic since the previous year, joined 50,000 countrymen demonstrating at the Russian Parliament (known as the Russian White House). The coup failed and Gorbachev was restored to power, but it was short-lived. In December 1991, Gorbachev resigned and the USSR was declared over and done with at year's end. The 15 separate republics that made up the Soviet Union became independent nations.

The Parliament approved the country's first law granting Russians the right to travel. Yeltsin was handily reelected in 1996, despite his declining health. Many problems now beset the Russian Republic, not the least of which is rampant official corruption and the growth of a mafia. Still, the Russian people and especially Muscovites struggle on, hoping to build a better and safer future.

MOSCOW'S MAYOR

Yuri Luzhkov, 60, a carpenter's son, is the mayor of Moscow - some consider him the second most powerful politician in Russia. When 19, he was among the students sent by Nikita Khrushchev to the countryside to clear virgin lands. Luzhkov was not elected until his second term in 1996; as a vice mayor he succeeded the previous mayor in 1993. Luzhkov personally makes decisions ranging from multi-million-dollar contracts to deciding which roads will be repaved. An agrochemist by profession, he has the reputation for getting things done, whether it is renovating a dilapidated building or filling potholes on street Prospekt Mira. A populist with an uncanny political sense, Luzhkov in 1995 ordered the city treasury to come up with financing for a $300 million project to rebuild a cathedral near the Pushkin Museum, razed by Stalin, by 1997.

The mayor, who is at times accused of corruption, sometimes sues those making such accusations. He won token damages from Mikhail Gorbachev, who had said in a television interview that Moscow officials diverted public money to build dachas, or country summer homes. Although the mayor earns what equals a few hundred dollars a month in salary, he lives in the same exclusive suburb as President Yeltsin of Russia. He has stood behind Yeltsin in two major crises, during the 1991 coup attempt and during the Yeltsin's assault on the parliament building two years later. After the 1993 crisis, Yeltsin granted him broad new powers to administer Moscow free from most federal controls. In 1996, Luzhkov was reelected by 90 percent of the voters, an unheard of margin in democratic Russia.

5. PLANNING YOUR TRIP

WHEN TO GO

If you travel on business or will attend a conference the question of when to go may be irrelevant. Otherwise, a good time to go is between April and October. Unless you have urgent official or personal business in Moscow, there is little sense in going to the capital during the frigid Russian winter.

June, July, and August are the hottest months and daylight sometimes lasts until 11pm in June. December, January, and February are the coldest, with seemingly countless days of frosty bleakness, when it's dark by the late afternoon. Spring and autumn are both shorter than in Western Europe.

The average January temperature in Moscow is 14 degrees Fahrenheit (-9.9 degrees Celsius), similar to temperatures in Montreal, Canada, or Minneapolis, Minnesota. The average for July is 66 degrees Fahrenheit (19 degrees Celsius) or about the same as in Duluth, Minnesota, but a couple degrees warmer than in London.

Moscow has about 21 inches of precipitation annually; it comes as snow mostly in the winter and as thundery rain in the summer. But take nothing for granted, some summers are chilly and rainy enough that you'll need a sweater, raincoat and an umbrella if staying for more than a few days.

Understandably, you will save money on your airfare and possibly hotel during the off-season, but that should not be your primary consideration when deciding whether to come to Moscow in March instead of June. Also, while in Western Europe you will likely get more efficient and courteous service during off-season, in Russia, we fear, the lack of business will not make your maid or waiter any friendlier or quicker, perhaps even the opposite.

WEATHER CHART

Here is a month by month indication of what to expect during a typical year. From November-March, expect snow; from April-May, expect rain; from June-August, expect sunshine; from September-October, rain.

	F/High	F/Low	C/High	C/Low
Jan.	14	5	-18	-27
Feb.	19	8	-13	-29
Mar.	29	15	-3	-1
Apr.:	43	29	11	-3
May:	60	42	28	10
June:	67	50	35	18
July:	71	54	39	22
Aug.:	68	51	36	19
Sept.:	56	42	24	10
Oct.:	44	33	12	1
Nov.:	28	21	-4	-11
Dec.:	17	10	-15	-22

Practically every larger English-language daily in the world publishes the daily temperature range and precipitation for the previous day in Moscow.

WHAT TO PACK

Most of us carry too much luggage. Travel as light as you can. Before packing your luggage at home, spread out all the clothing you are planning to take with you, then pick those pieces that you can wear in different combinations. Do not take brand-new clothes to Russia, baggage space is too precious to waste on clothing you will lug around but perhaps never wear. If your visit is informal and you plan to stay for just a couple of weeks, less is more. Take only the basics. Women, however, will probably want to carry along a somewhat larger selection, if for no other reason than to inspire their Eastern sisters.

Shoes should be well broken in before you take them overseas. Make sure they are as comfortable as can be because you may end up doing a lot more walking than you anticipated. Low-heeled, thick-soled walking shoes with good arch supports are recommended. Depending on how long you stay, you may need more than one pair.

If you go to Russia on business, you can never dress too conservatively, and two conservative suits should be more than enough. It is better to carry a couple of extra shirts (particularly silk shirts) than to save space and rely on spotty laundry services, unless you stay at one of the three five-star hotels, Baltschug, Metropol or Palace, where they will take good care of you - at a price. Pick accessories that you can wear with every suit.

For women, in spite of what they may have told you at home, Russian businessmen will take you seriously only if appropriately dressed and if you really know the ins and outs of your business. While Russian men are strutting about, it is the women who seem to keep the country humming. Russian women have a lot more power than some Western feminist monologues would have you believe.

You may find this advice useless if all your suitcases are lost, but we nonetheless suggest that you divide everything among all your suitcases so if one disappears you still have something to wear the following day.

Most international airlines will allow you two pieces of luggage and a smaller one that you can carry on, provided you can stow it in the overhead bin or under the seat in front of you. You can also carry a handbag and a camera. A businessperson may get away with a thin suit bag instead, but do not press your luck unless you are prepared to pay for any extra weight. Extra weight usually means anything over 20 kilograms in coach class or 30 kilograms in first class. We are happy to say that most international airlines will go out of their way to accommodate you and unless you carry suitcases of bricks for your dacha outside Moscow they will likely overlook a couple of extra pounds.

Label each piece of luggage outside and inside with your name, address and telephone number. We suggest that you place a copy of your itinerary in all your suitcases. This way, if one is temporarily lost chances are the airline may be able to return your luggage quickly. If you forget to label your suitcases on the outside, or if the tags fall off, the airline will try to open your bags to find out who they belong to.

Never, ever, store valuables in your luggage. Soft and hard luggage can be slashed open or simply crushed and your possessions stolen.

It was never in good taste to advertise your Western affluence in Russia. You do not want to call attention to yourself, whether an American or Canadian, in what you wear or say. The more costly your possessions the more likely someone will try to take them from you, whether by force or guile. Wealth is a relative term in Russia. Twenty dollars may be small change to you, but to a pensioner in Moscow it may mean a month's pay. Most of the time, if you have something worth stealing, you are "rich" in the petty thief's eyes. In Russia, your seemingly expensive clothes still imply affluence. Pickpockets usually look for such signs in their victims, in addition to crowded surroundings, distractions and a clear getaway.

It is not unusual to see jeans-clad students at the Moscow Conservatory classical music concerts, where ties are optional for men. But, man or woman, do not get carried away by wearing shorts to the theater or concerts because you will look foolish and attract unnecessary attention.

If you go out for dinner, to the opera or another formal event, you will be expected to dress up, otherwise jeans and sneakers are always a fashionable form of casual dress. Shorts are seldom acceptable when dining in restaurants.

Western women visiting the historic Russian religious center, Sergiyev Posad, north of Moscow, must be dressed conservatively when visiting its Orthodox churches. They should wear skirts and have their heads covered with scarves, while men must remove their hats.

Ready-made Russian clothing – cheap imports are better – are generally drab, ill-fitting and unfashionable so you are advised to bring your own. There is hope, however, that you can find an urgently needed article of clothing in a Western-style clothing store. How long it might take you is an entirely different question.

Indispensible Items

You would be well advised to bring items you consider indispensable with you, depending on the length of your stay, because it could very well be too difficult or too expensive to replace them. Items that do not take a lot of space, but may be considered indispensable include: color negative and slide film, batteries for your camera, alarm clock and watch, toothpaste, soap, cosmetics, shampoo, pantyhose, a small pocket knife, nail clippers and a sewing kit with extra buttons.

You may not miss the big items because you have resigned yourself to not having them, but realizing that you forgot to bring your shaving kit will likely irritate you. A certain minimal quality of toilet paper is also taken for granted in the West, but may not be readily available in Moscow, except in a few Western stores and at the luxury hotels.

If you bring an electric hair dryer, curling iron or razor bought in the West, you will need a transformer, unless your appliance has one built in. The electric current is 220 volts, AC. You will also need an adapter because Russian plugs have two round pins slightly less than an inch apart.

A comfortable pair of previously worn walking shoes is also essential if you hope to keep up with Muscovites who think nothing of walking for an hour. American-made sneakers are increasingly worn by Russians in their spare time.

Your Coat

When dining in an elegant restaurant, visiting the Tretyakov Gallery or the Pushkin Museum or going to the Bolshoy Theater, you will always be expected to check your coat and any other article larger than your purse. If you refuse there may be a tense moment or two and you will be considered obtuse. Most of the time you will not be allowed to enter until you surrender your coat.

Food

While it seemed worth the bother until about 1993, bringing in any but the most coveted brand-name foods would almost seem foolish.

Western stores, Moscow kiosks and increasingly the better stocked state stores are so well provisioned these days with Western European and North American brands of food that you will readily find everything from cereal to Wrigley chewing gum to Snickers bars. If you stay long enough to be able to test the integrity of local street merchants, you will find that prices are quite uniform and that a Snickers bar will cost you about the same on Novy Arbat as it would at Pushkin Square, even if you cannot utter a word of Russian.

So far, an overwhelming majority of street merchants have been surprisingly honest, whether selling a can of Pepsi or a pack of cigarettes, and they almost never charge a foreign visitor a higher price than a Muscovite. We would also like to add that in spite of everything you might have heard or read, bargaining on small inexpensive items will get you nowhere, except make you look ridiculous in the eyes of Muscovites who, with incomes that are a fraction of yours, pay the very prices you are trying to knock down. Again, use common sense.

Medication

Although there are Western medical facilities and pharmacies all over Moscow, do not take any chances and bring a good supply of any prescription drug you must have. Other medication that do not take a lot of space, but will save you from a headache, literally, are aspirin, cold formulas, anti-diarrheal remedies, indigestion tablets, travel sickness pills and perhaps vitamins. It is not that you cannot find most of these items in Moscow, but rather the time and hassle it could take to find something that you take for granted at home.

If you are susceptible to allergies, bring some over-the-counter remedy because it would not be out of the ordinary to develop an allergy in Moscow. This could happen because environmental allergens are different than what you are accustomed to at home. There is perhaps more dust in Moscow than in most other European capitals and your nose might complain noisily and repeatedly. And if you are affected by ragweed and other weeds, you may feel the consequences between late August and the first frost. Antihistamines will usually take care of your discomfort. If you are sensitive to trees, you might go through fits of sneezing in Moscow in late May and early June when seemingly millions of poplars go through their annual propagation process, shedding billions of tufts of cottony hairs, called **pukh**, that no one can escape.

AN IMPORTANT WORD ABOUT HATS

The winters in Russia can be so frigid that you will be desperate for a hat. Try not to buy it from a fast-talking street vendor, who may sell you dog hair as beaver at a mink price. Styles of fur hats seldom change. Among the most popular are these:

Ushanka (from the Russian word ukho, or ear), is the most common, traditional, square-shaped hat with ear flaps, mostly intended for men but often worn by women as well. It is made in most furs, including rabbit, mink, beaver, raccoon and sable. Ushanki are sold as genuine furs or as fakes, which often have ear flaps that are only cosmetic and do not fold down.

Sharik, or ball hat, is shaped as the name implies and has a soft structure. Sharik is worn mostly by women, is often made out of fox fur, and is particularly welcome in very cold weather.

Eskimoska is similar to sharik, but has pom-poms which can be tied under the chin, and is made of fox fur.

Boyarka, with its little dome, sturdy frame and all-around brim, is usually available in mink and beaver.

Kubanka (a tall rigid hat, often made from Persian lamb), pilotka (almond-shaped, stiff and asymmetrical, meant for older women) and tabletka (pillbox-shaped and smaller, meant for younger women) are other popular styles of women's hats; the last two types are associated with the Anna Karenina look.

To check the quality of the hat, feel it; it should be dense and soft. Blow on the fur; if it parts and springs back at once, it is likely of good quality. A soft hat should immediately regain its shape if scrunched. Check the label, it often contains the date of manufacture. Experts recommend that you purchase a hat of recent manufacture. Always keep your hat away from direct heat, let it dry at room temperature if it gets wet, brush it to keep it free of dust, and wrap it in paper and store it in a box during the summer.

The following three state-owned Mekha stores offer a good selection in various price ranges, starting as low as $25: Mekha, 13/15 Stoleshnikov pereulok, metro Kuznetsky Most, Tel. 928-8862; 28 Ulitsa Stary Arbat, metro Arbatskaya; and 13 Ulitsa Pyatnitskaya, metro Novokuznetskaya, southeast of Kremlin and across the Moskva River.

Summer

Summers are mostly warm and somewhat humid, but quite bearable, unless you come from Alaska. But take an undershirt or a light sweater with you, just in case mother nature shows her distress.

Winter

Please use common sense. You should not endanger your health in the dead of the winter, when Moscow temperatures plummet to those comparable to Fargo, North Dakota. It can snow as early as October and as late as April. Remember that even Napoleon and Hitler capitulated against the Russian winter so there is no point in your trying to rewrite history. About 500 Muscovites die from the cold every winter, mostly men, and three-quarters of them drunk. Boots, a heavy coat and warm gloves are indispensable in the cold and dampness of Moscow winters; a rain coat with a zip-out lining will come handy as well, as will long underwear. For more informal occasions during the winter, you will appreciate a wool sweater and a ski-type jacket. Dress in layers because most interiors are well heated from October through April.

During other times of the year, you might shiver indoors now and then because the entire city gets heat at the same time, an inefficient relic of Soviet-era planning, which has created a tradition of waste. Heat in Moscow is delivered from some 75 steam-generating stations.

CUSTOMS & IMMIGRATION

Whether entering or leaving Russia, you are required to fill out a customs declaration form stating the amount of cash, travelers checks and other negotiable instruments you are bringing in, or taking out, as well as other valuables. Guard your customs declaration form as you would your passport and cash because there will be no end to your headaches if you lose it. You can bring in practically unlimited amounts of foreign currency (cash and travelers checks) as long as you declare them, but you must not bring in or take out Russian currency, bonds or lottery tickets.

Should you bring valuables, such as cameras, watches, binoculars, even a laptop computer, be prepared to prove that they were purchased abroad — declare them on your arrival in Moscow.

It is against the law to take established works of art, such as paintings or sculptures, out of Russia. Most antiques, such as icons, old coins, books in any language published before 1975, and musical instruments, may only be taken out of the country with a permit from the Russian Ministry of Culture. Expect to pay 100 percent duty. Since late 1992, the Ministry also requires buyers to obtain permission before taking art objects dated after 1945 out of the country.

Most contemporary art, for which you paid less than $200, can probably be exported duty-free if you keep the receipt from the seller. Check with the seller before you leave the store. Dealers should provide all paperwork for objects above that amount. See Chapter 12, *Culture* for more details, as well as details about the Art-Tour Agency under the

Moscow Collection Art Gallery. For some artworks you will need an export license and might have to pay an export duty. Even if a work of art is given to you free, it must be valued and a duty may be assessed.

Have your customs declaration ready when leaving Russia. You should have less money than when you entered the country or be prepared to document the discrepancy. If you have invested in large quantities of caviar, they will show up on the X-ray machine at the airport and may be confiscated; actually, you can never be sure what will happen. But legally you cannot take out more than 200 grams of caviar.

Importation and exportation of weapons and ammunition, of course, are strictly forbidden, except for hunting guns with a permit, as are narcotics or any devices for their use. You may not bring in or take out gold coins and precious metals without prior authorization.

Visitors who are at least 21 years old may carry 200 cigarettes or 200 grams of tobacco per person. You are also allowed 1.5 liters of spirits or 2 liters of wine. It is recommended that you bring in a variety of gifts - as opposed to carrying 20 calculators or 15 digital watches - to avoid the suspicion of being something that you obviously are not.

After you have collected your luggage from the conveyor belt, do not let it out of your sight! Proceed to customs and go through the green exit if you have nothing to declare or through the red exit if you have something to declare. A customs official will circle the stated currency amount in red so alterations on your part are not advisable. Guard that customs declaration form as you would your passport because you will have to surrender it on your departure from Russia.

Now, only the stars can predict what will happen. What was once a scary bureaucratic experience has now become completely unpredictable. While passing through customs, about the only thing you can do is smile. Based strictly on our personal experience, chances are you will just be waved through in what may turn out to be one of the most generous customs inspections in the world. All in all, allow at least one hour to pass through passport and customs controls, whether arriving or leaving.

HEALTH INSURANCE

NEAR, *P.O. Box 1339, Calumet City, Illinois 60409. Tel. 800/654-6700 (US), Tel. & Fax 708/868-6700 (outside the US, you can call collect), cable NEAR.*

NEAR is a worldwide membership club, not an insurance company. NEAR's services are available anywhere in the world to citizens of any country. The company offers short-term foreign hospitalization coverage and $100,000 medical coverage, with a $100 deductible and emergency dental coverage. Coverage includes required medical staff, evacuation to your home, medical care during transport, standby ambulance service, and hospital arrangements. NEAR will arrange for supervised repatriation of minor children traveling with a parent who requires hospitalization.

TravMed, *Tel. 800/732-5309 or 410/296-5225, Fax (410) 453-6371.*
TravMed is open from 8am to 4:30pm EST. The insurance they offer is designed exclusively for US citizens (except residents of New York and Minnesota) working, traveling, or living outside the US for up to 70 days. Their Medex worldwide travelers assistance includes "emergency evacuation if medically necessary."

TravMed also provides up to $100,000 coverage for sickness or an accident, which includes physicians' fees and hospital expenses, emergency dental expenses, medical evacuation to your home or hospital, and expenses for bringing a family member to your side. The coverage costs $3.50 a day and the deductible is $25 per accident or sickness.

HealthCare Abroad, *107 West Federal Street, Middleburg, Virginia 20118-0480. Tel. 800/237-6615 or 540/687-3166, Fax 540/687-3172.*

HealthCare Abroad is administered by Wallach & Company. It is a comprehensive $250,000 accident and sickness insurance plan designed to provide coverage of up to 120 days for Americans under age 76 traveling abroad. **HealthCare Global** provides coverage similar to HealthCare Abroad, but only up to $100,000 and the insurance may be purchased for up to six months for travelers up to 84 years of age.

They also sell trip cancellation insurance.

OTHER TRAVEL INSURANCE

Buying **death and accidental travel insurance** seldom makes sense if you carry proper coverage at home. Talk with your insurance agent to find out what exactly is covered under your existing policy. We advise against insurance policies from airport vending machines, which prey on your fears of mortality and are drastically overpriced. However, you may decide that even airport insurance is better than no insurance at all if you have young dependents.

On international flights via the US, most airlines value your life at up to $75,000, or as little as $10,000, depending on where your travel arrangements were made. Survivors may spend half of that in court, litigating for the benefits.

Americans charging their tickets on their American Express cards currently receive $100,000 worth of flight insurance automatically. For an additional fee, charged to your Amexco card, you can buy $250,000 of additional insurance. If you charge your airline ticket on your Amexco card, you can also receive luggage insurance of up to $500 for each trip, again at an additional charge. Check with American Express to confirm their rates on your particular card.

Carte Blanche gives you $150,000 of life insurance automatically if you charge your ticket on their credit card. Diners Club is even more generous, giving you $350,000 of automatic insurance when your ticket is paid for on your Diners card. Again, check with both these companies to confirm their rates for your particular card.

Baggage insurance is a toss-up if you carry the usual items needed during your trip, but when going to Russia it may make a little more sense because luggage is sometimes stolen at Sheremetyevo 2 International Airport. Check with your insurance agent whether your luggage and its contents are already covered or whether you need a supplement. You can insure your luggage throughout your trip; your air ticket protects such belongings during your flight only.

If you carry valuables worth more than what your airline's maximum reimbursement would be, you may want to consider additional coverage from your airline.

Major credit card companies will also sell you coverage for lost and sometimes even delayed luggage in addition to the coverage by your airline. You usually benefit by their basic coverage provided you have charged your ticket to their credit card.

American Express will sell you $500 worth of coverage for checked luggage for a fee and up to $1,250 for bags that you carry on the plane for an additional charge. Carte Blanche and Diners Club give you $1,250 of free insurance for checked or carry-on bags that are lost or damaged as long as you charge your ticket on their credit cards.

Travelers interested in short-term policies that combine some or all of the above types of coverage can also check with: **NEAR Services** in Calumet City, Illinois, *Tel. 800/654-6700* in the US and Canada and *Tel./ Fax 708/868-6700* in Chicago. In addition to complete medical coverage, NEAR also provides trip cancellation and 24-hour lost and found baggage insurance, as well as insurance for valuable items, such as cameras. It also has insurance covering lost or stolen airline tickets. But you can only receive these services at a stiff membership charge of a somewhat dubious value.

Travel Guard International, *Tel. 800/826-1300 or 715/345-0505, Fax 800/826-0838, Internet http://www.travel-guard.com*, is located in Stevens Point, Wisconsin. Their package contains $15,000 trip cancellation or interruption, $10,000 worth of medical coverage, $20,000 worth of emergency medical transportation, and $1,000 in baggage coverage. Children 16 and under are included at no additional cost. If you buy the policy within seven days of booking your trip, pre-existing medical conditions will be waived; a comprehensive package costs just $40.

PASSPORTS & VISAS

If you are a citizen of the US, Australia, Canada, or the United Kingdom, you must have a valid passport and a visa to enter Russia. If you travel with family, every adult member must have a separate passport. If you have an American passport that is not older than 12 years, you can apply for a replacement by mail. Carry 6 to 12 extra passport photos, depending on the length and complexity of your travel because you never know when they will be needed abroad, particularly if your passport is lost or stolen.

Getting an American passport can take up to six weeks, unless you are willing to pay for rush processing services. An emergency passport can actually be issued in hours, depending on your emergency, such as a death in the family or if you already have flight reservations and your ticket. But you will only be issued a Russian visa when you submit copies of the relevant pages from your passport.

Carry your passport with you whenever you need not surrender it because in quite a few places in Moscow, such as your country's embassy, you may be turned away without a passport. The State Department's **Overseas Citizens Services** office in Moscow can generally replace your passport within 24 hours, provided you can prove your identity and have photos available.

Visas

To enter Russia you must have one of several kinds of visas, depending on whether you travel with a group, as an independent tourist or on business.

Ten years after perestroika has begun, Russia is still one of the most inaccessible countries in Europe. Its visa procedures make about as much sense as a fur coat in Burkina Faso. To get one - a visa, that is - you effectively must have someone who will guarantee your well-being while in Russia, not that dissimilar to an American sponsor who guarantees that an immigrant will not become a public charge while in the US.

Unless you've made arrangements with Intourist, the Russian state travel agency for foreigners, you will have to obtain an invitation from an individual or organization before you can apply for a visa. Fortunately, it is not uncommon for mere acquaintances or even complete strangers to provide such invitations as your sponsors, particularly if they can charge you a fee. The **Traveller's Guest House**, *50 Ulitsa Bolshaya Pereyaslavskaya, 10th floor, Moscow, Metro Prospekt Mira, Tel. (011-7-095) 280-4300 or 8562, 971-4059, or 974-1781 or 1798, Fax (095) 280-7686, E-mail tgh@glas.apc.org,* located outside the Garden Ring Road, northeast of the Kremlin, provides such invitations for as little as $40 for a tourist visa up to 25 days.

You can return the required forms by fax or E-mail and charge the fee on your MasterCard or Visa card. While you can thereafter apply for your visa at a Russian consulate yourself, we strongly recommend that you let a travel agent handle this for you at an additional cost because the bureaucratic entanglements can be overwhelming. Have your visa sent to your home by registered mail.

Otherwise, you have to send your hosts an application in duplicate which they must take to the state visa registration office. If you are on business, your employer will obtain an invitation through a counterpart organization or governmental entity.

Some travel agencies in the US sell invitations for about $100 each, which is semi-legal but overlooked in a society where attempts to evade the system are tolerated.

The Russian Foreign Ministry consular service introduced new visa procedures in 1995 in an attempt to stem the growing numbers of what it called "forged" invitations being used by foreigners within Russia. A standardized invitation form was introduced to enable the ministry to control the movement of foreigners inside the country.

In the US, we suggest that you apply for your visa at least three months before you travel, although you can receive it within one week if you are willing to pay for such service. It can cost up to several hundred dollars.

Your visa is valid only for the cities you specify when you submit your application, so apply for all the cities you think you want to visit even if you do not know whether you will have time to get to all of them (although there is only enough space on your visa for a few cities).

Theoretically, you are not allowed to visit areas not on your visa, but with the increasing liberalization in Russia, few officials will bother to check. You may have difficulty, however, when purchasing your airline or train tickets because you will need to show your passport and your visa to do so.

Until recently, the outermost ring road, which forms the city boundary, was also the 40-kilometer (24-mile) limit of your Moscow visa, but now you can travel farther as long as you register at your destination within 48 hours.

RUSSIAN EMBASSY & CONSULAR OFFICES

To apply for your visa for Russia and for some of the republics of the Commonwealth of Independent States, you can go in person to the consular division of the **Russian Embassy**, *1825 Phelps Place, N.W., Washington, D.C., 20008.* For the sake of your sanity, however, we suggest that you pay for this service through your travel agent or a specialized visa provider.

The republics of the Ukraine, Latvia, Lithuania and Estonia require their own visas.

- **Russian Embassy in Washington, DC,** *2650 Wisconsin Ave., Washington, DC, 2003, Tel. 202/298-5700 or 5701–04, Fax 202/298-5735*
- **Russian Consulate in Washington: DC,** *1825 Phelps Place, N.W., Washington, DC, 20008, Tel. 202/939-8912 or 8913 or 8918, Fax 202/986-1207 (general); 483-7579 (visa section)*
- **Russian Consulate in New York,** *9 East 91st Street, New York, New York, 10128, Tel. 212/348-0955 or 0626, Fax 212/831-9162*
- **Russian Consulate in San Francisco,** *2790 Green Street (at Baker), San Francisco, California, 94123, Tel. 415/928-6878 or 9809; Visa Section 415/929-0862, Fax 415/929-0306*
- **Russian Consulate in Seattle,** *2001 6th Avenue, Suite 2323, Seattle, Washington, 98121, Tel. 206/728-1910, Fax 206/728-1871*
- **Russian Embassy in Ottawa,** *285 Charlotte St., Ottawa, Ontario, Canada, Tel. 613/236-0920 or 613/235-6342*
- **Russian Consulate in Montreal,** *3655 Avenue du Musee, Montreal, Quebec H3G 2E1, Canada, Tel. 514/842-5343, Fax 514/842-2012*

Should you need to extend your visa while in Russia, you will have to go to the **Russian Visa and Registration Office** (OVIR), located in every Russian city.

In Moscow, OVIR is located at *42 Ulitsa Pokrovka, metro Kurskaya or Kitay-gorod,* the first room to the left on the first floor. OVIR's number for private visas is *Tel. 207-0113,* and *207-3032* for business visas. English is understood.

OVIR is open from 10am to 1pm and after lunch from 3pm to 6pm on Mondays, Tuesdays and Thursdays. It is open from 10am to 1pm and after lunch from 3pm to 5pm on Fridays. OVIR offices are closed on Wednesdays, Saturdays and Sundays.

The maximum extension of your visa is five days and it starts on the day you apply for extension, even if your visa has not yet expired. You must bring your passport and your current visa with you. Before applying for your visa extension, make sure you pay the required fee at the savings bank across the street. Your extended visa will be ready the following afternoon.

RUSSIAN NATIONAL TOURIST OFFICE

This office might assist you if you only have questions about major tourist attractions in Moscow or St. Petersburg. We contacted them and were asked to submit our questions in writing. We faxed five most basic questions about the town of Dulyovo, near Moscow (see Chapter 17, *Excursions & Day Trips*), where a well-known porcelain factory is located.

Our fax went unanswered, but in a follow-up telephone call we were told the office does not provide information about "a small village with one factory."
· **The Russian National Tourist Office**, *800 Third Avenue, Suite 3101, New York, New York, 10022, Tel. 212/758-1162, Fax 212/758-0933; Internet http://www.russia-travel.com*

TOURS & INTERPRETERS

Russia is so vastly different from the West that, in my opinion, having a guide and interpreter will be make for a more pleasurable trip than if you were left to fend for yourself, particularly if you do not speak Russian. The longer you stay, the more you will appreciate having one, even for just a few hours every other day. While it may not save you any money, it certainly will save you from everyday frustrations; there are advantages to having a private guide that cannot be measured in dollars or pounds.

Whether you have a toothache and are looking for a Western dentist or are trying to close on a business deal, the guide could be an invaluable resource. Perhaps he, but more likely she, will get you the tickets you want to the Bolshoy Theater, will take you to the Pushkin Museum and find out for you where those Rembrandts or Van Goghs or Picassos that you've always wanted to see are displayed. Or she will make reservations for you at an Azeri restaurant that has no sign out front and looks like a private residence to the uninitiated.

If you are in Moscow on a bed & breakfast program, you probably already have your guide and interpreter through someone in the family with which you are staying. Women, again, will probably welcome a guide the most because he or she will be all of the above and a personal bodyguard, too.

There are hundreds of university students who welcome an opportunity to show you around and every time you pass by Aleksandrovsky Gardens or the Kremlin or Red Square you are likely to see more than one student giving a personalized tour to Westerners.

To get an idea about the cost, start with **Intourist**, the Russian state travel agency. Intourist still deals with more visitors than any other travel organization. It provides English-speaking guides for sightseeing and professional translators for business people. You will have to pay in dollars and probably twice as much than if you hire a student, but you will also know exactly what you are getting.

Our preference is to hire one of the **Patriarshy Dom** guides, *Tel. 926-5680*, who are available for private tours, usually at a little over $10 an hour.

Intourist's **Central Bureau of Interpreters**, *23 Leningradsky prospekt, Metro Dinamo, Tel. 250-1723*, is located in northwest Moscow, outside the

Garden Ring Road. It is open daily from 9am to 6pm, Fridays from 9am to 4:30pm, with a lunch break from 1-3pm; closed Saturdays and Sundays.

Other translation and interpreting services include **All-Russia Translation Center**, *14 Ulitsa Krzhizhanovskogo, Bldg 1, Entrance 2, Office #318, Tel. 124-7263 or 7265 or 5231*; **International Association of Translators**, *86 Prospekt Vernadskogo, Tel. 403-0372 or 399-0062*; **International Business Service**, *27 Ulitsa Prechistenka, Tel. 201-3148, Fax 201-5954*; **International Translation Center**, *Tel. 177-8251, Fax 177-8069*; and **Translation & Information Bureau**, *Tel. 374-7603 or 5740.*

Guided Tours

If you want to get to know Moscow, consider a guided tour. You can see the capital with one of the entrepreneurs that advertise their services on bullhorns around Red Square, or pay Patriarchy Dom or Intourist to take you around with expert guides.

To see the city or its individual sights through **Intourist**, *13 Ulitsa Mokhovaya, metro Okhotny Ryad, Tel. 292-1278*, you have to go to their offices near Manezhnaya Square, or one of the branch offices in various hotels. You can arrange for individual guided tours for about $20 an hour within the city limits. A three-hour group sightseeing tour of Moscow with an English-speaking guide is $12 per person. A three-hour Armory Chamber and Kremlin grounds group tour is $20. To see the Pushkin Museum of Fine Arts is $10. A group visit to Sergiyev Posad, formerly Zagorsk, is $40. Be prepared, however, for a specific tour on a certain day to be cancelled, either because the bus broke down or a guide is not available. Intourist's tours are impersonal if adequate, but nothing more.

Patriarchy Dom, *in Moscow at Tel. 926-5680, in Washington, D.C. at Tel. 202 363-9610*, a non-profit Russian-American cultural center established in 1993, is our choice for whatever sightseeing you do. It is located near the American Embassy and the Garden Ring Road, but registration is handled over the phone. Telephones are answered between 9am and 6pm, Monday through Friday and messages left between noon and 6pm on weekends will also be returned. Their selection of tours is at least ten times that of Intourist's, their prices are competitive, and all of their guides speak good English.

In addition to the standard city sightseeing tours and visits to the Kremlin and major museums, Patriarchy guides can also take you on foot down Tverskaya Street or through the Arbat neighborhoods, exploring even the most obscure parts of Moscow, or show you sights hundreds of miles away. Patriarchy offers more tours than all other companies combined. On weekdays you usually have a choice of two excursions, and three on weekends. Most city tours start between 9am and 11am and last for about two hours; excursions outside of Moscow take at least half a day.

The cost is usually $15-40 per person and sometimes includes a sack lunch on daylong excursions. The meeting place for about half of the excursions is at the south gate of the **American Embassy** compound on Bolshoy Devyatinsky pereulok, near the Mir Hotel and the **Russian White House**. Several city tours begin at the Starlite Diner near the Tchaikovsky Concert Hall, across the street from the Pekin Hotel. Only cash payments in dollars or rubles are accepted.

TRAVEL RESTRICTIONS

Your status as a visitor is still somewhat murky under the current laws. Theoretically, you are only allowed to travel to the cities specified in your visa, although some limitations have been abolished or are rarely enforced. You are permitted to travel to locations other than those specified in your visa provided that you notify the Russian Visa & Registration Office (OVIR) once you arrive.

There are still satellite towns around some large cities, Moscow being just one of them, that are off-limits to foreigners because they are military or nuclear sites. Often it is all but impossible to find out beforehand where the restricted areas are. The best advice we can give you is to be alert to where you are and keep that camera away from what could conceivably be a strategic installation of any kind.

You must report to the local authorities within 48 hours of your arrival in any city, which may mean nothing more than handing your passport to your hotel, something that you would do anyway. If you stay with friends, you or they must report your arrival.

Russian authorities can be quite lenient about your overstepping your travel restrictions. But you could run into problems when buying airline tickets and some other services because you have to show your passport and possibly your visa, which always specifies where you are allowed to travel.

Since 1993, passport checks have also been introduced when you purchase your railway tickets. This is being done not to control your travel, but rather to curb speculation in tickets. Before this requirement went into effect, someone could buy a large number of tickets and then resell them at railway stations to foreigners and Russians at a hefty profit.

US & CANADIAN CONSULAR REPRESENTATION

In addition to issuing replacement passports and visas, your consulate can perhaps assist you with limited business advice, depositions and a notary public. If you get seriously ill, the consulate will suggest an English-speaking doctor or a hospital, contact your family or act as conduit for the funds that may have to be sent from your home.

While the consulate can notify your relatives if you should be arrested and assist you in finding a lawyer, it cannot take responsibility for your welfare while you are detained.

You will see a military guard at every embassy and consulate, and not necessarily for your protection. Until Gorbachev came to power these guards, whiling away tedious hours in their tiny huts next to the consular entrances, were there to keep away Russian citizens. Embassies and consulates are typically open from 9am to 1pm and after lunch from 2pm to 5pm.

In 1985, the new American embassy building, just behind the old one, was scheduled to open, but so many bugging devices were discovered that the newly-erected structure was abandoned. The new Russian embassy in Washington, D.C., was held hostage in return and did not open until 1994, when President Yeltsin visited the US.

In the early nineties, the American government often considered reopening the already shabby red-brick building, rather than destroying it and constructing a new embassy. In 1995, a rocket-propelled grenade was fired across Novinsky bulvar and blasted through the embassy wall, damaging an office but causing no injuries. About 950 Americans and Russians work in the embassy compound.

- **United States Embassy**, *19/23 Novinsky bulvar. Tel. 252-2451 to 2459, Fax 956-4261 or 4270, Telex 413160 USGSO SU, Nights & Weekends, Tel. 252-1898 or 255-5123.* Metro Barrikadnaya or Smolenskaya, on the Garden Ring Road, northwest of Kremlin, one block northeast from the Russian White House.
- **Embassy Medical Clinic**, *Tel. 252-2451*
- **Consular Office**, *Tel. 956-4235, Fax 255-9965, Open Monday through Friday, 9am to 6pm*
- **US Foreign Commercial Service**, *15 Novinsky bulvar. Tel. 255-4848 or 4660, Fax 230-2101.* Metro Barrikadnaya or Smolenskaya, and open Monday through Friday, 9am to 1pm and after lunch 2pm to 6pm.
- **Canadian Embassy**, *23 Starokonyushenny pereulok. Tel. 956-2358 or 6666, Fax 241-4400, Night Duty Officer, Tel. 961-7940, Fax 956-1577.* Metro Kropotkinskaya or Smolenskaya, between Boulevard and Garden Ring Roads, southwest of Kremlin. Open Monday through Friday, 9am to 1pm and after lunch from 2pm to 5pm. Visa applications are accepted 9am to noon, except Wednesdays.

WHAT NOT TO EXPECT

It is said that whatever you expect in Russia, your expectations will be frustrated. The question, then, is rather what **not** to expect. For more details or how to handle some of these unexpected situations, see related chapters.

Business: Do not expect that an address or telephone number you had before leaving for Moscow is still valid; the company may have moved last week and the phone number could have changed twice.

Your money: Do not expect to be able to pay with travelers checks for anything; you will even be charged to cash them. Increasingly, when you visit a museum, take a train to St. Petersburg or fly to Vladivostok, be prepared to pay several times more than your Russian counterpart.

Your hotel: Do not expect that your Russian female friends will be readily admitted to most state-owned hotels and their restaurants, which have doormen who assume most women are there to sell their bodies. Once in your room, do not expect to find soap, shampoo or moisturizer, except in the most luxurious hostelries.

Apartment: Do not expect that your apartment, many offices, even concert halls, will be air-conditioned in the summer or heated for parts of the spring and autumn.

Telephone: Do not expect to get the number you dialed right away, although you could get lucky. Do not expect that anyone will pick up the phone before the sixth ring and you should be pleasantly surprised if they do. Do not expect to reach your relatives in New York just before you leave for the Bolshoy Theater; it may take half an hour to get through.

State-owned restaurants or cafes: Do not expect that a waiter will come rushing up to you and smile, with a menu, and greet you in English, even if he speaks a little of it. Do not expect to readily find a place serving breakfast, except in luxury hotels. Muscovites are not in the habit of eating breakfast away from home. Do not expect napkins and ice in inexpensive cafes, unless you ask for them.

On the street: Do not expect that the directions a Muscovite gives you to get to some back street restaurant will actually make it any easier to find it. Following the wholesale street name changes inside the Garden Ring Road, the change is confusing to residents, too.

Metro: Do not expect every Muscovite to know where to make a transfer to get to your station, even if you show them the metro map.

State-owned and some other stores: Do not expect that you will just walk in and buy whatever you need; there are sometimes lines even in bakeries. Do not expect that your purchases will be wrapped unless the saleswoman takes pity on you; always carry an inexpensive shopping bag with you.

Newspapers: Do not expect to find today's American and British newspapers until tomorrow, if then; but the Moscow Times and the Moscow Tribune will do in an emergency. Do not expect to find newspapers from Australia or Canada.

Cinema: Do not expect to find readily a cinema showing a Russian-made film, now that American junk and French erotica have drowned the city.

Sightseeing: Do not expect that you can just walk into the nearest restaurant, if you can find one, when the urge comes to use the rest room. Read the section about Moscow toilets and you could be spared some physical pain. Do not expect that all streets will be referred to with their new names, some old names still linger, even in the press.

So expect the unexpected and you will never be disappointed.

6. ARRIVALS & DEPARTURES

You may have heard terrifying stories about the Soviet Union and read spy novels about the Cold War, so now you're just a bit apprehensive as your plane taxies in. Relax. Things have changed a lot already and will keep changing, hopefully for the better. For example, gone are the days when all foreign airlines landing in Moscow were required to gather and lock up copies of Western magazines and newspapers distributed during the flight.

As you pass through passport control, you will stand in front of an official for a couple of minutes. He or she will look at you and your passport more often than you think reasonable, at least on your first visit, without saying anything. These officials look like they take their job seriously, but you may be surprised at how politely they return your passport, excluding one part of your three-part visa.

On arriving at **Sheremetyevo Airport**, try to get a luggage cart if you have a lot of baggage as soon as you pass through passport control, even if you do not have any rubles. And of course, how could you since it is illegal to enter or leave Russia with rubles and thus impossible to pay for your cart in rubles, which, officially, is the only acceptable currency. Do not despair, there is a way to solve every problem in Russia; sometimes the cashier at the cart desk will accept dollars, otherwise try to get a cart from one of the porters who might be willing to take dollars. The key is to stay calm. You are now in a culture radically different from yours, not better or worse, just very different, so forget how things are done at home. Enjoy the experience if you can.

BY AIR
Aeroflot Russian Airlines
Once the world's largest airline, which employed 600,000 people and carried more than 138 million passengers a year in 5,400 planes, **Aeroflot** has been divided into more than 100 independent aviation companies and 15 airlines in as many republics. The transition has been troublesome

and Aeroflot is not immune to threats of strikes. As fuel prices have risen, the company is suspected of neglecting regular maintenance because it could not afford it.

While flying Aeroflot internationally is comparable to other airlines, Westerners and Russians alike who have survived the ordeal will tell you that flying Aeroflot within the former Soviet Union can be a harrowing experience. In 1994, the International Airline Passenger Association recommended that no one fly over Russia or any part of the former Soviet Union. "Overloaded airplanes, lack of cockpit discipline, pilot error and aging aircraft" are all common, the agency said, in the first such warning it has ever issued. It continued that procedures taken for granted in the US, like safety inspections and regular maintenance, are often absent in the countries of the former Soviet Union.

Instead of meals, movies, and blankets or pillows, you will be lucky if you can get a cup of water on many of these internal routes. Until recently, some Russian travelers on Aeroflot's domestic flights paid bribes to use waiting rooms, to bump other passengers and even to get a drink from a flight attendants while in the air. Carry snack foods and reading materials with you when boarding your domestic Aeroflot flight.

Come to the airport at least one hour before your domestic flight's departure and be alert to what is going on; just because you have a ticket does not mean you will get on board. Some internal flights are overbooked. Foreigners are sometimes checked in as a group, either first or last.

Every year, Russian airport officials confiscate hundreds of guns, thousands of knives and clubs, and tens of thousands of rounds of ammunition, even grenades, from passengers intent on boarding Aeroflot planes and unaware of the regulations. The Russian daily *Pravda* said once that "flying Aeroflot is about as safe as playing Russian roulette."

When you travel within Russia, try to buy your round-trip ticket before you start your trip because you may have difficulties buying the return ticket later on. Aeroflot's toll-free number in the US is *Tel. 800/995-5555*; their offices in the US and Canada are:

• **Chicago**, *255 North Michigan Avenue, Suite 2304, Illinois, 60601, Tel. 312/ 819-2350*
• **Miami**, *80 S.W. 8th Street, Suite 1970, Florida, 33131, Tel. 305/577-8500*
• **New York**, *630 Fifth Avenue, Suite 1710, New York, 10111, Tel. 212/332-1050*
• **San Francisco**, *291 Geary Street, Suite 200, California, 94102, Tel. 415/ 434-2300*
• **Washington, DC**, *1620 I Street, NW, DC, 20006, Tel. 202/429-4922 or 202/466-4080*
• **Montreal**, *615 de Maisonneuve, Quebec H3A 1L8, Tel. 514/288-2125 or 2126, Fax 514/288-5973*

In Moscow, Aeroflot's offices are at *4 Frunzenskaya nab., Metro Park Kultury, Tel. 245-0017 or 2750; 20/1 Ulitsa Petrovka, Metro Teatralnaya;* and *7 Ulitsa Korovy val, Metro Dobryninskaya.*

Call *Tel. 155-0922* for information on domestic flights within the CIS, Georgia, Estonia and Latvia, or *Tel. 155-5045* and *Tel. 926-6278* for information on international flights.

Aeroflot's reservations and ticket offices are also located in these hotels: Kosmos, Mezhdunarodnaya, Rossiya, and Ukraina. Except for Rossiya, which is located inside the Boulevard Ring Road, next to St. Basil's Cathedral, the remaining three are all situated outside the Boulevard Ring.

Other Airlines

Western airline office hours are generally Monday through Friday, from 9am to 6pm, with a lunch break from 1 to 2pm. Most are open Saturdays from 9 or 10am to 5 or 6pm.

In the US, **Delta Airlines** flies to Moscow via New York and Frankfurt. The following addresses and phone numbers will help you contact Delta:
• international reservations in the US, *Tel. 800/241-4141*
• in Canada, *Tel. 800/221-1212*
• Arrival/Departure Information, *Tel. 800/325-1999*
• Moscow Reservations, *World Trade Center (Sovincenter), 12 Krasnopresnenskaya nab., Office 1102-A, Metro Ulitsa 1905 goda. Tel. (095) 258-1288 or 578-2939, Fax 258-1168 or 578-2062.*
• St. Petersburg Reservations, *Tel. (812) 311-5819 or 5820.*
• Delta Airlines at **Sheremetyevo 2 International Airport**, *Tel. 578-2738 or 2939.* Open Tuesdays and Sundays from noon to 2pm, other days from 7am to 8:30am and from noon to 2pm. This is the only place to handle Delta's amended, prepaid, reissued and penalty-charged tickets, as well as excess baggage and luggage insurance.

Other Western airlines in Moscow include:
• **Air France**, *Tel. 237-2325*
• **Alitalia**, *Tel. 923-9840*
• **British Airways**, *Tel. 253-2492*
• **Finnair**, *Tel. 292-8788*
• **Iberia**, *Tel. 923-0488*
• **Japan Air Lines**, *Tel. 921-6448*
• **KLM**, *Tel. 258-3600*
• **Lufthansa**, *Tel. 975-2501*
• **Sabena**, *Tel. 578-3310*
• **SAS**, *Tel. 925-4747*
• **Swissair**, *Tel. 253-8988*

Transaero, *Moscow Reservations, Tel. 241-4800 or 7676*, founded in 1991, the maverick Russian airline with Western planes and Israeli-trained crews, introduced Western standards to the post-Soviet skies. It now flies the much needed Moscow-St. Petersburg route and competes for business with **Pulkovo Airlines**, based in St. Petersburg, one of a hundred of "baby-Aeroflots" that were created after mother Aeroflot collapsed.

The one-hour round-trip air fare between Moscow and St. Petersburg costs from $170 to $350 for foreigners and $64 to $190 for CIS passengers. We do not recommend that you check your baggage on any domestic flight.

Airports

The main airport for international visitors is **Sheremetyevo 2 International Airport**, *Tel. 578-5614 or 5633 or 7518 or 9101*. In case you need them, here are the airport's various phone numbers:
• **Airport Security**, *Tel. 578-0125 or 578-0102*
• **Customs**, *Tel. 578-2208 or 578-2125*
• **VIP Arrivals**, *Tel. 578-7518 or 8224*
• **Departures**, *Tel. 578-7816 or 8286*
• **VIP Lounge**, *Tel. 578-2132 or 8620*
• **Lost & Damaged Baggage**, *Tel. 578-5633*
• **Lost & Found**, *Tel. 578-8248 or 578-5612*
• **Intourist Office**, *Tel. 578-7179*
• **Traveler's Aid**, *Tel. 578-5633*

The international airport is located about 19 miles northwest of downtown Moscow. It was built in 1979 on the design of German architects for the 1980 Moscow Olympic Games. The terminal is an eight-storied decagon with a facade of aluminum and sun-resistant glass. More than 40 foreign airlines fly from Sheremetyevo 2.

The facility is named after the Sheremetyevs, one of the oldest and richest Russian noble families, who once owned the land now occupied by the airport. At their height, the Sheremetyevs owned 200,000 serfs and entertained up to 25,000 guests a day at their estate ten miles east of Red Square; see **Kuskovo** in Chapter 18, *Excursions & Day Trips*.

On the ground floor arrival level, you will find a doctor, currency exchange, drugstore, Intourist office, cafe and toilets.

On the departure level, you can make international telephone calls, and send a fax, regular or express mail. Also on this level are automatic and teller currency exchange facilities, and a MasterCard automatic teller machine. There are clothing and food stores where you can buy everything from Coke to toothpaste.

In addition to several third-rate eating facilities, there is a 24-hour moderately-priced restaurant, **Palette**, *Tel. 578-3135*, on the fifth floor. It boasts a chef who did stints at several Rodeo Drive restaurants in Beverly Hills. But you are in Moscow now so don't be overly optimistic.

The **City Air Terminal**, *37 Leningradsky prospekt, Tel. 155-0922*, is open 24 hours a day, and is located in northwestern Moscow, outside the Garden Ring Road and near the Aerostar Hotel, at Metro Aeroport or Dinamo.

When leaving Moscow, you can go to the airport after you have checked your luggage at the Air Terminal, then take a bus to Sheremetyevo. We do not recommend that you sweat your way to the Air Terminal and Sheremetyevo, even if it means saving $20 or $30, unless you have minimal luggage or are a student traveling with a companion and want to save every penny. Otherwise, hire a taxi, or a rental car with a driver from a well-known company for peace of mind (and because you will need that extra energy at the airport to elbow your way through several security checks on your return home).

The other airport is **Sheremetyevo 1 Airport**, *General Information, Tel. 578-2372 or 3610 or 9101*; *Arrivals & Departures, Tel. 578-2372*; Intourist, *Tel. 578-4110 or 5975*; *Customs, Tel. 578-2137*; *Lost & Found, Tel. 578-2326*. This airport is located about 22 miles northwest of the city, and serves flights primarily to St. Petersburg, the Baltic republics and Russia's northwest.

Arrive at this or any domestic airport at least one hour before the scheduled departure, otherwise there is a possibility that your seat will be taken by someone else. Because of the scarcity of jet fuel there always seem to be more passengers for most destinations than there are seats available.

Domodedovo Airport, *Tel. 323-8652 or 8656*, is located about 30 miles southeast of downtown Moscow and is the largest airport in Russia. It serves most domestic flights to and from places in eastern Russia. At Domodedovo, Vnukovo, *Tel. 436-2674*, and Bykovo, *Tel. 558-4738*, are special Intourist lounges for foreigners, but do not expect anything more than a bench to sit on.

JET LAG

Drink lots of non-alcoholic beverages, preferably water, prior to boarding and while aloft. You can easily become dehydrated during your flight because water evaporates from your skin through respiration, and the humidity is extremely low in the aircraft. Stay away from alcohol, and possibly coffee, because they both aggravate this condition.

Smoking is prohibited on all European flights of six hours or more and all flights within Russia.

And when you finally lay down your weary body for your first night of sound sleep in Moscow, after countless hours of hanging around terminals, sitting cramped in the planes, and taxi rides, you may realize, in disbelief, that you cannot sleep, no matter how tired you are. Jet lag and insomnia have taken over.

We do not recommend that you take sleep-inducing drugs, unless prescribed by your physician. Stay away from coffee or tea if caffeine keeps you awake. A glass of beer or wine may put you to sleep. A warm bath will also relax you. Keep out the noise and light. It is said that the harder you try to go to sleep the less successful you will be. If you cannot sleep, get up and read a book, or this guide.

Unless it is evening already, you may want to try to stay awake until then. Take a walk, go to a museum, even if you haven't had a decent night of sleep for two days. Chances are, when evening comes you will be ready to sleep, not count sheep.

LOST & DAMAGED LUGGAGE

Report the loss of your luggage to your airline immediately. When it comes to Moscow's Sheremetyevo International Airport, take no chances. As soon as the last bags are sent through the conveyor, if yours is not there, file a written claim. Enclose as complete a list of the contents as you can possibly reconstruct. We know from experience how lonely it can be hanging around Sheremetyevo and pleading with indifferent clerks to help you locate your suitcases. Some will pretend they do not understand English or will try to get rid of you by telling you that it will be sent to your hotel as soon as it arrives. No matter how enraged, try to stay calm because your fury will only worsen the problem.

Leave written instructions on how and where the airline can find you when your bags turn up. Call from where you are staying a few hours later, just to see if there is any news.

Should your luggage be permanently lost, or stolen, your airline's liability may be considerably less than the value of your suitcases and their contents. You will be reimbursed at a rate of $9.07 per pound, or $20 for each kilogram, for checked baggage and up to $400 per passenger for unchecked baggage on most international flights. These limits were set in 1929 at the Warsaw Convention and have not been increased since. You can buy insurance for such an eventuality, but it is relatively expensive.

Luggage damage is an everyday occurrence - and not only in Russia. If yours is damaged, check its contents and file a claim at once. You should be reimbursed for damage or loss to the contents as well as damage to the suitcases.

Always carry a survival kit with the very basics you think you can never do without should your baggage get lost or stolen: passport, all your prescription medications, travel documents, prescription eyewear, cash and credit cards, important telephone numbers and addresses, and perhaps a change of underwear, a few basic toiletries, maybe even a few of your favorite snacks so you will be able to tackle the world.

GETTING TO AND FROM THE AIRPORT

Allow at least two hours to get to or from Sheremetyevo 2 International Airport.

By Rental Car

We suggest that you never drive yourself anywhere in Moscow. But if you absolutely must, these telephone numbers are for airport car rentals at Sheremetyevo 2:

- **Auto-Sun**, *Tel. 578-9166*, Russian-Japanese
- **Budget**, *Tel. 578-7344*, American
- **Europcar**, *Tel. 578-3878*, Russian-British
- **Hertz**, *Tel. 578-7532*, American
- **InNis**, *Tel. 230-6162*, Russian-Japanese
- **MosrentService**, *Tel. 578-0919*, Russian-German-Belgian
- **Rasco**, *Tel. 578-7179*, State-owned

By Car & Driver

If you made prior arrangements for a car and driver, he will most likely meet you on your arrival, as you exit near the customs area, perhaps holding up a sign with your name, and whisk you to your destination. Some days, it is quite chaotic in this area as dozens of other people are also waiting for their guests. If you make arrangements through the state Intourist agency, the procedure will be similar; there is a 24-hour Intourist desk in the main terminal.

By Taxi

Taxis at the airport, like in many other parts of the world, have a particularly bad reputation, and horror stories about rip-offs, true or assumed, abound. If you decide to take a taxi, there are about half a dozen taxi services located at Sheremetyevo 2. None should charge you more than $50-60, in rubles or on your credit card, to almost anywhere downtown or back to the airport, but make all arrangements beforehand if you can. If this is not possible, always find out the price of your ride first or do not get inside the car.

Do not succumb to the persuasiveness of men who promise you a cheap ride downtown. The moment you open your mouth, your fare may double from the usual $50 for the one-hour drive into central Moscow. The line between the regular and gypsy cabs has become so blurred that even Russians can barely make sense of it. It is better to pay an extra $20 to a reputable company than be endangered by an individual posing as a cabbie. Women should never enter a taxi with more than one person, the driver, already in it. Even men should think twice.

There are plenty of reliable taxi services, including **Intourtrans taxi** to central Moscow, **Intourist taxi** service to the Hotel Metropol, **Rasco Taxi** to the Hotel Slavyanskaya, **Mosrent Taxi** to the Hotel Aerostar, and **Auto-Sun Taxi** to the Renaissance Moscow Hotel (formerly known as Olympic Penta).

BY TRAIN

Within European Russia, railways are the most common and popular means of passenger transportation. Chances are that you will fly, but for those hardy adventurous souls who are considering a train journey, there are many bumpy rail hours to contemplate. Unlike Russian air service, which is sometimes unreliable, you can depend on Russian trains to leave Moscow on time, even if they arrive late.

If you are a foreigner, even if your spouse is a Russian citizen, you cannot buy your railway tickets at the regular ticket offices inside train stations, like Russians do. Rail and air travel are more expensive for foreigners than for Commonwealth of Independent States citizens. When buying your tickets, you will have to show your passport and, after waiting in long lines, will probably be sent to an address, where the railway cashier assumes foreigners must buy their tickets. Even if you fool the railway cashier, you will be confronted by a stone-faced **provodnik** (conductor) once you get to the railway platform and she will not let you on the train until you pay the difference.

The least painful, but the most expensive way to purchase your rail tickets is through the state Intourist agency or a private travel agent, both foreign and Russian, authorized to sell train tickets to foreigners. However, if you want to maximize your savings, go directly to the **Central Railway Agency**, *1 Ulitsa Krasnoprudnaya, Tel. 266-0004*, which is located near Metro Komsomolskaya, just east of Yaroslavsky and Leningradsky railroads and a bit farther northeast from Kazansky station.

Other Central Railway Agency offices, where you can buy your tickets two to 30 days ahead of your travel, are located at: *4/6 Mozhaisky val, Tel. 240-0505*, Metro Kievskaya; and *1 Leningradsky prospekt, Tel. 945-0807*, Metro Belorusskaya. Working hours are from 8am to 7pm, excluding the lunch break from 1 to 2 pm.

Until 1994, tickets could be bought at train stations by anyone who was willing to pay a higher rate to a scalper, often just a few minutes before the train's departure. Since then, to put an end to heavy speculation in tickets, a passenger's name must be printed on it. You will have to show your passport when you purchase your ticket and, if you are a male, possibly again when you show it to the conductor on the train.

Overnight Trains

You can save one night's hotel lodging by taking an overnight sleeper to and from St. Petersburg. The high-speed 5-hour Aurora Express to St. Petersburg departs from Moscow every morning just after midnight.

While taking a train from Moscow to St. Petersburg may promise to be romantic, you would be better off flying. There are reports that thefts are occurring on this line. If you do take the train, lock the compartment door from inside. If all passengers in your compartment are Westerners, wind some wire around the locks on the inside to prevent anyone else form entering at night.

You can also take the train from Helsinki to Moscow, with an afternoon departure and arrival the following morning; or from Moscow to Helsinki, departing in the early evening.

Overnight trains usually have sleeping compartments for two or four persons to each cabin. They are not segregated so, conceivably, an American female traveler might have a Russian male passenger sleeping in the same compartment. Clean sheets and pillow cases can be had from the conductor for a small fee. Many long-distance trains have dining cars, but regardless of how far you go, you can buy tea or coffee from the conductor at specific times. You can ask the train attendant to knock on your compartment door before your station comes up if you think you may not wake up by yourself. It is only then that your ticket will be returned to you.

If you travel beyond the Russian borders, remember that Belarus, Estonia, Latvia, Lithuania and Ukraine all require their own entry visas. The telephone numbers for their Moscow consular representations are, **Belarus**, *Tel. 924-7031*, **Estonia**, *Tel. 290-5013*, **Latvia**, *Tel. 925-2707*, **Lithuania**, *Tel. 291-2643*, **Ukraine**, *Tel. 229-1079*. You can obtain visas at their Moscow consular offices Monday through Friday, between 10am and noon. Americans can receive complementary visas from the three Baltic states.

For general telephone inquiries about all train departures and arrivals call *Tel. 266-9333*. For ticket reservations, call *Tel. 292-2260 or 2450*.

Railway Stations

Moscow's nine railway stations, which handle almost 400 million passengers annually, are located around the Garden Ring Road:

Belorussky Station, *7 Ploshchad Tverskoy zastavy, Tel. 251-6093*. Located northwest of the Kremlin, at Metro Belorusskaya, with trains to Brest, Bryansk, Kaunas, Minsk, Smolensk and Vilnius. Also departures for Berlin, Paris, Stockholm, Vienna and Warsaw.

Kazansky Station, *2 Komsomolskaya ploshchad, Tel. 266-2843*. Located northeast of the Kremlin, at Metro Komsomolskaya, with trains departing for the east and southeast, the former Soviet central Asian republics, the Altay and Siberia, Bashkiria, Kazan, Krasnodar, Rostov-on-Don, the Urals and Volgograd.

Kazan is the busiest passenger train depot in Moscow. It was being reconstructed into 1997, when it became the largest railway station in Russia and Europe. The station was designed by architect Aleksey Shchusev, who also designed the Lenin's Tomb.

Kievsky Station, *Ploshchad Kievskaya, Tel. 262-6230*. Located west of the Kremlin, Metro Kievskaya, with trains departing for the southern regions, Chop, Kaluga, Kiev, Kishinev, Lvov, Odessa and Yuzhgorod. Also departures for Belgrade, Bucharest, Budapest, Cierny, Karlovy Vary, Prague and Sofia.

Kursky Station, *29 Ulitsa Zemlyanoy val, Tel. 924-5762*. Located east of the Kremlin, Metro Kurskaya, with trains to Armenia, Azerbaijan, the Caucacus, Caucasian mineral spas, Crimea, Georgia, Kharkov, Tver and Tula.

Leningradsky Station, *3 Komsomolskaya ploshchad, Tel. 262-4281*. Located northeast of the Kremlin, Metro Komsomolskaya, with trains to the north and northwest, to St. Petersburg, Novgorod, Pskov, Tallinn, also Helsinki.

Paveletsky Station, *1 Paveletskaya ploshchad, Tel. 233-0040*. Located southeast of the Kremlin, Metro Paveletskaya, with trains to the southeast, the Donbass, Saratov, Volgograd and Astrakhan.

Rizhsky Station, *Rizhskaya ploshchad, Tel. 266-1372*. Located northeast of the Kremlin, Metro Rizhskaya, with trains to the northwest, like the health resorts on the Gulf of Riga, Velikiye Luki and Rzhev.

Savelovsky Station, Savelovskaya ploshchad, Tel. 285-9000. Located northwest of the Kremlin, Metro Savelovskaya, with trains going northwest, to Kalyazin, St. Petersburg and Uglich.

Yaroslavsky Station, *5 Komsomolskaya ploshchad, Tel. 266-0595*. Located northeast of the Kremlin, Metro Komsomolskaya. This station is the starting point of the Trans-Siberian line across Russia to the Pacific Coast, Vladivostok and Petropavlovsk-Kamchatsky. Also going north, to Novgorod, Pskov and Uglich.

It was at Yaroslavsky station that writer Aleksandr Solzhenitsyn, after 20 years of forced exile and a 4,000-mile train journey through Russia, from Vladivostok to Moscow, returned home in 1994.

7. GETTING AROUND MOSCOW

BY BUS, TROLLEYBUS, & TRAM

Buses, trolleybuses, and trams together carry 13.5 million passengers every day. None have conductors and rely solely on the honor system, but you will have to pay a fine if you are caught without a ticket. You punch your own ticket on the bus and retain it until your destination.

Buses operate from 6am to 12:30am and are also reasonably priced, regardless of the distance you go. You can buy your bus or trolley tickets, usually in sets of ten, from the driver and at kiosks or you can travel on a monthly pass. Drivers are allowed to charge you a price higher than elsewhere. You must not enter through the front door: it is only for the exiting passengers.

Etiquette still requires you to offer your seat in the metro or on the bus to an elderly person or a woman of almost any age, even if some try to ignore it.

BY CAR

We suggest that you never drive in Moscow. If you can afford it, you would be well advised to arrange for a private car with driver, even if for just a small part of your stay, or a few hours every other day. You can hire a car with driver by the hour or by the day and it will save you plenty of headaches. If the expense is too big, read the section on the metro, which is actually the fastest and the most efficient way to travel in Moscow.

We do not mean to frighten you, and although there are about ten times fewer cars in Russia than in the US in relation to their populations, you are much more likely to have an accident in Moscow than in the West. Thus, when you are in a car on the streets of Moscow, you need someone who knows how the other drivers think and react behind the wheel.

Even if you know some Russian and have a good map of the city and plenty of time, stay away from driving around the capital by yourself,

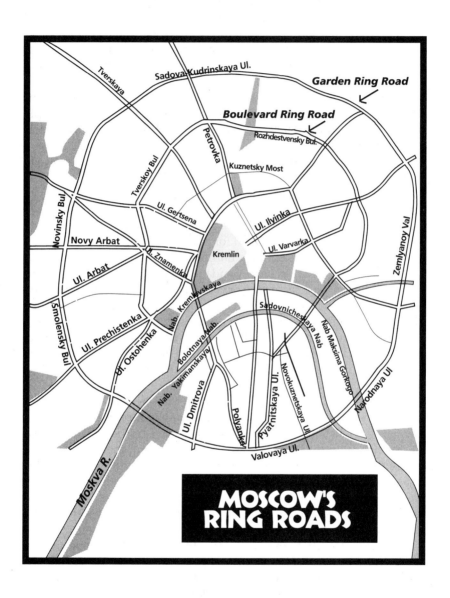

MOSCOW'S RING ROADS

unless you have to. Street signs and house numbers are often difficult to see from the car, but that is only the beginning of your headaches.

The number of private cars in Moscow has tripled since 1993; one estimate has it that there are almost two million cars in the capital today and that nearly 500 additional cars appear every day. Car ownership, says a *New York Times* dispatch from Moscow, "is no longer a vague dream. It is a frightening, traffic-stopping, ear-shattering reality." It adds that the five-mile drive across the city, that once took ten minutes, may now take up to five hours. A bit of an exaggeration, but still scary. There are about 10,000 car accidents in Moscow every year, in which some 1,500 people are killed and almost 10,000 injured, although Moscow does have nearly ten million inhabitants.

Driving speeds are seldom enforced, although they are, officially, 60 kilometers (37 miles) an hour in the city and 90 kilometers (56 miles) an hour in unpopulated areas, and 120 kilometers (75 miles) an hour on highways. Gasoline may sometimes be hard to find when needed, depending on where you are. A Westerner must have an international driver's license issued in Russian. It is valid for one year. Be prepared to operate a stick-shift transmission on most European cars.

Wearing seat belts has been mandatory since 1984, whether you are the driver or front-seat passenger, or you can be fined, the same as in many other countries. Unlike in some Western cities, you may not use the horn within the city limits, except in emergencies.

License plates are color-coded; foreign businessmen, for example, have yellow plates with a black letter M and a number. Each country has a designated license plate number: Canada 003, United Kingdom 001, and the US 004.

Since 1992, your car can be towed away anywhere in Moscow if you are illegally parked. Another hassle that affects foreigners as well as Russians has taken effect in 1994: if you receive a traffic violation, GAI, the Russian state traffic police, will confiscate your driver's license to ensure that you pay your fine at a GAI office and not in the street. This is supposed to alleviate the problem of bribes, but it also means you may wait in lines for hours before you recover your license. Should you accumulate 15 violations, your driver's license could be permanently suspended.

If you are stopped by one of the more than 500 GAI traffic patrolmen that police the streets of Moscow at any given time, there is a chance that you might have to pay a fine for a real or imaginary infraction. Official fines range from a few cents for jaywalking to a few dollars, and much worse for violations committed while drunk. You may not drive under the influence of even the smallest amount of alcohol or you will pay a severe penalty.

Bribery is alleged to be fairly common, but perhaps less likely when a foreigner is involved. Whether you drive yourself or are a passenger in someone else's car, your vehicle may be stopped by a GAI traffic patrolman anywhere and anytime for a quick driver's license check and whether your car meets all regulations. We will not deal here with accidents because they are truly a nightmare in Moscow. No matter how slight the damage, you could have a problem having your car repaired without an accident report from GAI.

Renting a car makes just slightly more sense if you will drive it outside of large cities, but even there you are exposing yourself to risks you may never have anticipated.

But if you must, you can rent a car from the companies below. Direct cost comparisons are practically impossible. Ask as many questions as you can think of **before** renting a vehicle.

Intourist state travel agency, its competitors, and some luxury Western hotels in Moscow can provide you with a car, with or without a driver.

For names of rental agencies operating at Sheremetyevo 2 International Airport and telephone numbers there, please see section **Getting To and From the Airport** in Chapter 6, *Arrivals & Departures*. You can use a chauffeur-driven car as a taxi substitute to and from the airport from most of these companies; the ride will be more comfortable and safer and, of course, more expensive.

Rental Companies

Here are some car rental companies in various parts of the city:

Olga Car Service, *Metropol Hotel, 1/4 Teatralny proyezd, Reservations Tel. 927-6972, Tel. & Fax 927-6973, International Satellite Fax (7-501)927-6976.* Open daily from 8am to 11pm, located near Metro Teatralnaya. Rents Mercedeses, Fords, Opels, Nissans and Russian Zil limousines, as well as Ford minivans, with or without driver, with unlimited mileage.

Air-conditioning is an additional ten percent and travel outside Moscow an additional 30 percent. Between 10pm and 7am, there is an additional charge of 30 percent. Rentals include insurance, third party liability and maintenance, but exclude gasoline and insurance on tires. For cars without the driver the minimum rental time is 24 hours. Delivery and pick up are at an additional charge. Payment by major international credit cards or through a bank.

Rasco State Company, *6/8 Second Paveletsky proyezd, Tel. 235-8190, Fax 235-7297.*

Located in southern Moscow near Metro Tulskaya. Rents Russian Volgas, Mercedeses, and Russian Chaikas. Payment by credit card, cash or bank transfer. Gasoline and insurance not included in prices for cars without driver.

MosrentService, *79 Ulitsa Krasnobogatyrskaya, Tel. 963-9145 or 9173.*
Located in northeast Moscow, Metro Preobrazhenskaya ploshchad.
Rents Fords, Mercedeses, and minibuses, mostly with driver. Payment by
credit card or in rubles. Prices include gas and insurance. Rentals without
drivers also available.

Auto-Sun, *29 Grokholsky pereulok, Tel. 280-3400 or 3600.*
Located in northeast Moscow, Metro Sukharevskaya or Prospekt
Mira. Rents Nissans, with or without drivers. Payment with credit card or
bank transfer. Gasoline not included. Renter's minimum age 20 years.

Avis, *12 Berezhkovskaya nab., Tel. 240-9932 or 9974.*
Located in southwest Moscow, Metro Kievskaya. Rents French
Peugeots, with or without driver. Payment with credit card or bank
transfer. Gasoline, insurance and value added tax are not included in the
quoted price. Driver's minimum age is 20 years.

Budget Rent-a-Car, *16 Verkhnyaya Radishchevskaya ulitsa, Tel. 915-
5237, Fax 915-5940.*
Located in northeast Moscow, Metro Taganskaya. Vehicle rentals
with chauffeurs and long-term leasing of American and European cars.
All major credit cards are accepted.

Hertz, *49 Prospekt Mira, Tel. 284-3741.*
Located in northeast Moscow, Metro Prospekt Mira. Rents Volvos
and Toyotas, with or without driver. Payment with credit card or bank
transfer. Gasoline not included. Price includes value-added tax, and
insurance. Driver's minimum age is 18-21 years.

InNis, *32 Ulitsa Bolshaya Ordynka, Tel. 230-6160, Fax 230-6213.*
Located in southwest Moscow, Metro Dobryninskaya or
Novokuznetskaya. Rents Nissans, Pugeots, Opels and Nissan vans, with or
without driver. Payment with credit card or bank transfer. Rental price for
car without driver does not include gasoline. Driver's minimum age is 21
years.

Europcar, *12 Krasnopresnenskaya nab., Tel. 253-1369/2974.*
Located in west Moscow, Metro Ulitsa 1905 goda. Rents Volvos and
Mercedeses, with or without driver. Rates based on the German mark
exchange rate. Payment with credit card or bank transfer. Minimum
rental is 24 hours. Driver's minimum age is 25 years.

BY FOOT

You cannot hope to get to know any city in the world without strolling
down a few streets. It would be a crime to claim that you have seen Moscow
without spending several days on foot. You will feel adventurous as you
step out from your apartment or hotel on your own and boldly set out in
whichever direction. There is no better way to get to know Moscow, or her

citizens, than by strolling around, studying faces, randomly walking into stores to see what's for sale, even if you buy nothing. Moscow is a city of walkers, not because of some health fad, but often out of necessity – to save every possible ruble. When we say that some establishment is so many excruciatingly long blocks away from something, this should not be taken as a mere figure of speech; some Moscow blocks can be two or three times as long as in New York City.

The Russian Cyrillic alphabet will add suspense to your boldness, perhaps even a tiny bit of fear because, unless you memorize some distinct site, it is possible to get lost in this city, where many streets look alike. Most people are too preoccupied with the problems besetting their daily lives to pay you more than a cursory glance, but if you do need help they will show you the way back and you will be surprised by how many speak at least a few words of English.

In Moscow, cars have the right of way, not pedestrians, which leads us to the observation that many hapless citizens, trying to get across a street, instead might get run over. But if you need to cross a wide boulevard, look for a street sign with a blue walking stick-figure on a white square descending stairs, which means that an underground passageway is nearby.

Russian street numbers can be confusing. A building with several entrances can have one street number for the entire building, with the entrances numbered separately. Often a street address consists of two numbers divided by a slash, like 7/12, which usually implies a corner location. Sometimes these numbers are not posted near an entrance, but instead at either end of the building and quite high. Another peculiarity are buildings behind the one facing the street, which have the same street numbers, but are differentiated as Dom 1, Dom 2, etc.

In the same fashion that every American town has a Main Street, there are street names in Russia that you will come across in every city. Until recently, Lenin, Stalin, and Karl Marx had no competition, but now that Communism has been stripped of its invincibility, these names are rapidly being replaced by the pre-Revolutionary names of the streets. Other standby street names, for the last 70 years, were the dates of Communist victories or other dubious accomplishments.

In 1990, the Moscow City Council voted to rename the first batch of streets, squares, boulevards and metro stations on the very eve of the anniversary of the Russian Revolution. Still more street-name changes followed afterwards and they are continuing, sometimes to the ire of Muscovites. Only the streets and squares inside the Garden Ring Road are being given their pre-Revolutionary names.

In this changeover, not even the national poet Pushkin and playwright Chekhov have been spared. In 1993, for example, the Council decided to rename 76 streets, including Pushkinskaya, which became Ulitsa Bolshaya Dmitrovka, and Chekhova, which reverted to Ulitsa Malaya Dmitrovka.

If you want to combine your walking with shopping or sightseeing on some of Moscow's most famous streets, such as Stary Arbat, Tverskaya, or Kuznetsky Most, please see the individual sections in Chapter 17, *Shopping*.

BY METRO

The decision to build the Moscow metro was taken in 1931 on Stalin's orders and the first line was inaugurated in May 1935. More than 60,000 laborers and 5,000 engineers worked on the venture intended, in part, to distract their citizens from everyday problems. Some 84,000 square yards of marble were used in the first 14 metro stations, which is more marble than was used in all the courts built by the Romanovs during their 300 years of rule. Curiously, the opulent chandeliers at many stations reminded the older generation of pre-Revolutionary ostentation. Several American engineers helped with the construction. By the time of Stalin's death in 1953, four lines were completed. The system is continuously being expanded and even during the World War II new metro stations were completed.

The Moscow metro is the simplest way to get around the city quickly and inexpensively; its ten underground lines stretch for 150 miles. Almost nine million Muscovites use the metro daily (more than any other subway system in the world) so it does get crowded, especially during rush hours, from about 8 to 10am and from 5 to 7pm.

If the metro appears as though it is showing signs of age, remember that it celebrated its 50th anniversary at about the time that Gorbachev came to power. While you will not likely be arrested for eating a banana on the Moscow metro, like in the one celebrated case in the Washington, D.C. metro, eating and drinking is nevertheless not allowed. Smoking is forbidden, too.

If the escalators seem to make you dizzy the first time around, plunging precipitously as deep as 300 feet, it is because they indeed are faster than in the West and many were meant to double as air raid shelters when built.

You will seldom wait more than a couple of minutes for your train. The metro is punctual, something that cannot be said about Moscow's buses, trolleybuses and trams.

The whole system is one gigantic museum, what with stained glass windows, mosaics set with gold, crystal chandeliers, marble columns and bronze statues, but how unfortunate that it should be a Soviet proletarian museum. It is unthinkable what this art could have been were it not for a Communist dictatorship that built the metro. Many older metro stations have a unique, if somewhat austere, look and they will immediately remind you of the Stalinist or Soviet era. The metro stations of interest to Westerners are described in more detail in the section **Unique Metro Stations** in Chapter 13, *Seeing the Sights*.

The 150 metro stations are identified on the street level by a letter M and have separate passages for arriving and departing passengers. Quite a few have two or three entrances and exits, sometimes a block apart, which can be confusing to first-time passengers who cannot read the Cyrillic signs.

When you get out of the train, and if you do read a little Cyrillic, look at the signs inside the station, which will direct you to the exit, a transfer station, and the neighboring streets outside. There are even signs for the bus routes that you will find at each side of the station exit. The three words that you must recognize in Cyrillic to be able to get anywhere underground are **vkhod** (entrance), **vykhod** (exit) and **perekhod**, a passage or crossing over to another line.

Each ride through this entire system will cost you about 50 cents and you can make as many transfers and detours as you want as long as you do not exit through the turnstiles. You insert the plastic **zheton** in the slot on your right upon your entry, similarly as you do on the New York subway. If you plan to ride the metro regularly even for as little as two weeks, consider buying a **proyezdnoy bilet**, a monthly metro pass, the cost of which is less than $20. You will then have to enter not through turnstiles, but through the gates nearest an attendant who will check that your pass is current. This is a valuable convenience to have in lieu of a pocketful of **zhetony** or standing in line to buy them. The monthly passes for the metro and other forms of transportation go on sale a couple of days before the beginning of the month and are only available for about a week.

The metro system is operational from about 5:30am until 1am, depending on the station's location. Electronic clocks at each station tell you the time and how long you have to wait for the next train. The clocks have room for only one digit for minutes because the next train is never more than nine minutes away, and often fewer than that. The Metro has a **Lost & Found**, *Tel. 222-2085*. There is a police station at every metro station.

In addition to the north-south, east-west and other lines crisscrossing whichever way, there is also the Circle Line (Koltsevaya linya), which follows roughly the outline of the Garden Ring Road. It was built in the 1950's and has a total of 12 stations from which you can make transfers in every direction. Remember that transfer stations have more than one name, a different one for each line they serve. Aleksandrovsky sad, Borovitskaya, Arbatskaya and Biblioteka imeni Lenina, for example, are the four interconnected stations several blocks apart, located in eastern central Moscow, that serve the Light Blue, Gray, Dark Blue and Red Line; you never need to exit to catch any of the four trains. Depending on where you want to go, you may be able to go directly or may have to change lines once or twice. An anglicized metro map is a nice convenience to have, but every station has a map displayed on the wall and each car has two or three large maps displayed, showing all transfer stations. They are in Cyrillic, however.

The announcer talking just before the train pulls out is cautioning the passengers about the closing doors and alerting them to the next station, which he announces again just before the train stops. Listen for the announcement, **Ostorozhno, dvery zakryvayutsa** (Caution, doors closing) because the car doors slam shut with considerable force. Next you will hear, **Sleduyushchaya stantsiya**, (Next station), followed by that station's name.

Some Westerners gripe that the metro station signs are difficult to see and figure out from the trains, especially because they are in Cyrillic. We suggest that you **count** the number of stops before you get inside the train so you will know you have to exit at the fourth stop, for example.

We have included, with all addresses in this guide, the nearest metro station, not because you will travel around the capital by metro only - although you could - but to make it easier for you to locate the addresses of various establishments. When we list more than one metro station it simply means that two stations are at a similar distance from the address, sometimes on the opposite sides.

The **Museum of the Metro**, *Tel. 222-7309*, is housed above the Sportivnaya metro station, southwest of the Kremlin and outside the Garden Ring Road. It is open Tuesday through Friday, from 9am to 4pm, and Monday from 11am to 6pm; it is closed weekends.

BY TAXI

There are said to be only about 4,000 licensed taxis left in Moscow, down from 11,000 in 1993, but few Muscovites seem to know who or where they are because so many private citizens, known as **chastniky**, from the word "private," ferry passengers now and again to supplement their income or pay for the scarce gasoline in their cars.

Actual taxis - usually pastel Volgas with checkered patches - are more often than not clustered around the fancy hotels rather than cruising the streets, whether their drivers still work for the city or have become essentially chastniky themselves.

Muscovites, when asked, will tell you that they do abide by three basic rules when flagging down a car on the street: They do not get in the car if they feel uncomfortable about its driver; They never get in the car that has more than one occupant, the driver; and They negotiate the fare **before** getting into the car.

Unless you are with your Russian friends, and particularly if you are a woman, you should never get in a car, any car, alone.

In the past, taxis could be recognized by a green light on the windshield; when the light was on it meant that the taxi was available. But now, most Muscovites just stand on the curb, flagging down cars until one stops, agrees to go their way, and the price is right.

The experience of several long-term Western visitors has been that not many Russians will take advantage of you, even in the current economic malaise, but you should never take chances, especially at night, because every large city in the world has its bad apples.

Perhaps you should think twice before trying to get a taxi anyway, unless it is to an out-of-the-way address. No matter how far you go, if there is a metro line to your destination, you will probably get there twice as fast by subway. Particularly inside the Garden Ring Road and during the day, it will seem as though it takes forever to get from one place to another by car.

In 1995, new regulations went into effect governing Moscow taxis. Accordingly, a taxi driver can serve clients only within the boundaries of the zone indicated on his license, which he must get from the Moscow Transport Inspection. At taxi stands, stations and airports, the driver must not leave his vehicle in search of passengers, even if there is no line.

If you need a taxi, ask your Russian friends or someone at your hotel to assist you. Negotiate the price and currency in which you will pay **before** you get in or your driver will likely insist on being paid in dollars, which could mean you will overpay; set taxi fares are a thing of the past.

You can arrange for a taxi by calling the **state taxi depot**, *Tel. 927-0000 or 927-2108,* around the clock. The charge is 50 percent more for a taxi at night. The line is often busy and when it is not you may be offered a Mercedes at a lofty rate.

Another form of transportation that began reappearing in 1995 is **marshrutnoye taksi**, a Soviet institution that died during perestroika. These powder-blue fixed-route Avto Line vans can be seen zipping all over Moscow. By 1997, there were 1,500 of them serving almost 300 routes. Their prices are about double the regular bus fare.

INTOURIST STATE TRAVEL AGENCY

Intourist, although no longer a monopoly, is still the nation's largest travel agency with many branches all over Russia. Hundreds of guides and interpreters, who speak all major languages of the world, still work for Intourist. Its name is a word composed of **inostranny** (foreign) and **turist**. Until recently Intourist owned scores of hotels, motels and restaurants. The agency works through many foreign travel organizations and offers services in all large cities in Russia and all the former Soviet republics. It also rents cars and buses for individuals and large groups, and has a large position in Moscow's retail foreign currency exchange.

• **Intourist office in the US,** *610 Fifth Avenue, Suite 603, Rockefeller Center, New York City, Tel. 212/757-3884 or 3885, Fax 212/459-0031*
• **Intourist office in Canada,** *1801 McGill College Avenue, Suite 630, Montreal, Quebec, H3A 2N4, Tel. 514/849-6394, Fax 514/849-6743*
• **Main Intourist office in Moscow,** *13 Ulitsa Mokhovaya, Tel. 292-6269*

The main Moscow office is located just across Manezhnaya Square from the northernmost tip of the Kremlin triangle, Metro Okhotny Ryad. The building was originally constructed in 1934 as an apartment block on the site of the 16th century Church of St. George, but soon afterwards housed the American embassy. The renovated luxury hotel Natsional is next to the Intourist. For general inquiries call *Tel. 292-2260.* The Intourist American Department's phone is *Tel. 292-2054 or 2384 or 2386 or 2471 or 5214.*

There are Intourist offices in all major airports, as well as in the Belgrade, Intourist, Izmaylovo, Kosmos, Mezhdunarodnaya, Novotel, Sofitel Iris, Rossiya and Ukraina hotels.

Additional Travel Agencies
Intourservice, *4a Nikitsky pereulok, Tel. 203-3191, Fax 200-1243,* centrally located near Metro Okhotny Ryad, was formerly a branch of Intourist, but is now its competitor. It also provides many services to foreign tourists, from airport limousines to hotel reservations and meals, to excursions to Sergiyev Posad and elsewhere.

Intourtrans, *15/13 Ulitsa Petrovka, Tel. 921-8394 or 8783 or 8741,* another competitor, centrally located at Metro Kuznetsky Most, also books and sells tickets, organizes excursions to all Russian cities, and has special programs for children. Call *Tel. 929-8890* for information about obtaining airline tickets and *Tel. 929-8758* for rail tickets.

CITY MAPS

The first accurate maps of Moscow came out in 1989; Gorbachev's predecessors did not want outsiders to know what was situated where and previous maps were intentionally printed with some glaring errors to confuse Westerners, who, in the minds of the Soviets, were bent on destroying them.

No matter which travel guide you buy, get a separate, independent map of Moscow. One quick, unscientific way to see whether it is fairly up-to-date is to look for the renamed street Ulitsa Bolshaya Dmitrovka, formerly called Pushkinskaya, which runs in a northwesterly direction from Okhotny Ryad metro station to Pushkin Square. Also, find the metro station Ploshchad Ilicha, southeast of the Kremlin and outside the Garden Ring Road, then look for the metro station Rimskaya nearby, which was inaugurated in 1996; if it is not shown, the map may still be useful but it is out-of-date. Maps still showing Ulitsa Gorkogo, instead of what is now Tverskaya Street, are really old and of limited use, although only the streets inside the Garden Ring Road have been renamed since the Communists tumbled from power.

One of the more up-to-date American products is the 1994 English-language map of Moscow by Northern Cartographic; inexplicably, it omits almost all monuments and statues, but redeems itself by showing the location of many hotels, restaurants and theaters.

Also consider the easy-to-read *Traveller's Yellow Pages City Map*, which shows many monuments and statues and can be bought separately or with their Russian or English-language Moscow Yellow Pages. Updated information is also available on the Internet at www.infoservices.com.

A useful Moscow map in Latin transliteration - showing trolleybus and tramway routes - was published as a Euro-City map in 1995 by the American Map Corp., which is part of the German Langenscheidt Publishing company. None of the above maps, by the way, shows the metro station Rimskaya, but all three have the renamed Bolshaya Dmitrovka Street.

Perhaps the most simplistic, and of limited use, map is Kuperard's self-folding *Moscow at a Glance*, published in the UK and the US; you can find better maps for free if you stay in Moscow long enough.

One such complimentary map, in Russian and English, is published by Visitor Guide Publishing in Boston; you can get it at Baltschug Kempinski or the Savoy Hotel. Another free map, 75,000 copies of which are regularly distributed to leading hotels, restaurants and other businesses, is simply called Moscow Map and is updated three or four times a year.

8. BASIC INFORMATION

BANKING & MONEY

As much as Muscovites and their government hated to admit it, the US dollar was a bona fide currency in Russia between 1991 and 1994, when many restaurants, hotels, and retailers would serve only those who could pay in dollars. Most financial transactions among individuals and businesses are still set against the backdrop of the American dollar. Some Russians, who themselves have dollars stashed away as a barrier against inflation, resented this trend, even if only for its symbolism, because they felt that Russians should be able to pay in rubles in their own country.

The Russian government has threatened more than once to outlaw the dollarization of the Russian economy and, perhaps out of fear that such a law would be enacted, many currency stores and restaurants began accepting rubles at that day's dollar exchange rate. Finally, in 1994, the Russian Central Bank banned all cash transactions in foreign currencies. All establishments can only accept rubles for cash sales. Non-ruble credit and debit cards, however, are still permitted. Most hard currency shops have set up currency exchange posts.

To strengthen control over hard currencies and Russian taxpayers, the Central Bank also ordered banks and currency exchanges to issue receipts and to ask for passports when they sell or buy foreign currency, a requirement that is often ignored unless large amounts of dollars are involved.

Banks

Russian banks are not geared to accommodate your financial needs, like in the West. The *Wall Street Journal* quoted a Moscow-based Western banker, who said: "It can still take several months to get money from one part of Russia to the other." An overwhelming majority of Russians get paid in cash.

However, Dialog Bank branches will cash your personal checks against your American Express credit card for a fee of three percent, to a maximum of $1,000 a month.

THE FLUCTUATING RUBLE

One hundred years ago, one Russian ruble was worth 51 cents. After the 1917 Revolution, the **chervonets** *was introduced into Bolshevik Russia as the monetary unit; it equalled ten gold rubles of the former Russian empire. A new gold ruble was introduced in 1936 and its value was set at three French francs to a new ruble. In 1950, the ruble was placed on the gold standard which worked out to four rubles equaling one US dollar. In 1961, it was revalued upward to 0.987412 grams of pure gold and the official rate of exchange until the 1972 devaluation of the US dollar was one ruble for $1.11. In 1965, one Canadian dollar was worth 83 kopecks and a US dollar 90 kopecks. Nineteen years later, the ruble's worth was $1.32.*

In the spring of 1992, a milestone of sorts was reached when the US dollar was valued at 100 rubles for the first time. By the summer of 1993, it broke the 1,000-to-a-dollar barrier and fell as low as 1,500 rubles to the dollar when the government troops stormed the Russian White House to smoke out the renegade Parliament in October 1993. Its value was pegged at 2,000 rubles to the dollar by early 1994. The following spring, the dollar already stood at 5,000 rubles and in 1996 leaped beyond 5,500 rubles.

The inflation of the ruble dropped from 2,000 percent in 1992 to about 20 percent in 1996.

In 1994, 290 years after it was first introduced, the Russian kopeck, the smallest denominated coin and made worthless by galloping inflation, was officially withdrawn from circulation and is now a collector's item.

Cash

Russia is a cash-based society where checkbooks are unknown and credit cards reserved for the very upper crust of society who have regular contact with foreigners. Bring a small amount of US dollars in various denominations, then immediately deposit the excess cash in your hotel safe. Russians are the largest holders of American currency outside the US, but they are obsessed with clean bills. Wrinkled, soiled, or torn cash is not accepted. Avoid bringing old $100 bills because many Russians fear that they will become invalid and you may be charged a fee to exchange them. To answer questions from the jittery public about the new $100 bills, the US Treasury Department opened a public telephone line in Moscow in 1996.

Aside from this, a couple of major credit cards and a personal checkbook are all you will need to keep going indefinitely. Be prepared, however, for a service charge every time you cash a personal check.

Exchange Rates

The ruble keeps losing its value steadily, which puts you at a disadvantage if you exchange too much hard currency at any one time. We do not recommend exchanging more than $100 at a time, unless you have a specific need to do so. Perhaps the biggest nuisance is that you will carry around a fistful of rubles, even though things have improved since the 50,000 and 100,000-ruble notes came into circulation. All banknotes printed before 1993 are invalid. You will recognize them by the portrait of Lenin; most of them are worth more as collectors items.

You are breaking the law by buying rubles on the street, even if nobody seems to care, because Article 88 of the Criminal Code on illicit foreign currency transactions is still in effect. There are now countless exchange bureaus and mobile bank branches, where the buying and selling rates are clearly spelled out, all over central Moscow. It would be foolish to roam the streets for a couple of extra rubles on the dollar.

If you find yourself without rubles after the regular exchange offices close (about 8pm) and you cannot pay with a credit card, go to the underground MontazhSpets Bank branch at the radial Prospekt Mira metro station, north and outside the Garden Ring Road, which works the same hours as the metro, from 6am to 1am.

The exchange rate, at press time in February 1997, is **approximately 5,665 rubles to the dollar**. While no big jumps in the exchange rate are expected in the near future, you should check with the business section of a major newspaper or your bank to get an up-to-date rate.

Credit Cards

Now that foreign currency cash sales have officially been outlawed, we suggest that you use your credit card wherever they are accepted because the exchange rate for credit card purchases is often better than for cash payments. Some stores will even give you a discount on credit card purchases. When using your credit card, be prepared to show your passport or another picture identification, such as your driver's license. In restaurants, do not add your tip to the credit card slip because your waiter will probably not see the money. Leave cash.

You can get cash at a a number of automated teller machines (ATM) throughout Moscow with your credit card(s).

For **American Express** card holders, the monthly withdrawal limit is $1,000 for holders of Green cards, $5,000 for Gold, and $10,000 for Platinum cards. The cost is three percent or $30, whichever is higher.

Although we have never seen kids loitering in this area, American correspondents in Moscow caution their readers at home to be careful with their money on the streets around the American Express office. Some people have been robbed by gangs of Gipsy children after they've withdrawn cash from the ATM there. Incidentally, you can only enter the anteroom where the ATM stands with your credit card when the office is closed.

Regardless of where in Russia you are, if you lose your American Express card, immediately call American Express, *Tel. (095) 956-9000 or 9004 - 9007*, in Moscow.

Amexco 24-hour cash-dispensing machines:

• **American Express ATM**, *Hotel Mezhdunarodnaya's World Trade Center*
• **American Express ATM**, *21a Ulitsa Sadovaya-Kudrinskaya, Tel. 956-9000, 956-9001 or 956-9006*

The machine is in lobby of the American Express office on the Garden Ring, northwest of the Kremlin, halfway between metro stations Mayakovskaya and Barrikadnaya, north of the Pakistani embassy and southwest of Intercar Supermarket. It is open Monday through Friday, 9am to 5pm.

You will be able to get cash on your **Diners Club**, **MasterCard** or **Visa** credit cards from some Western hotels and many banks all over central Moscow, just look for their symbols; the fee is usually two or three percent. There is a Visa ATM outside the Metropol Hotel on Teatralny proyezd, near the entrance to the restaurants Teatro Lobster Grill and Mediterraneo, and another in the middle of Novy Arbat Street promenade. There are some 20 branches of Avtobank all over Moscow, where you can receive cash on your Diners Club, MasterCard and Visa credit cards, including the exchange office at 28/35 Novinsky bulvar, Metro Barrikadnaya, on the corner with Povarskaya Street, just northeast from the American Embassy and next to a Reebok store.

You can also get a cash advance on your Visa card at any of the six Dialog Bank branches, including the American Express office, and inside the Radisson Slavyanskaya Hotel in western Moscow or at the newest luxury hotel Tverskaya on the First Tverskaya-Yamskaya, not far from the Palace Hotel. But do call ahead and ask questions if you are pressed for time because you do not want to spend an hour getting to a bank to find that their office is closed for lunch.

To report the loss of your Diners Club, MasterCard, Visa or any other credit card, call *Tel. (095) 956-3456 or 3556* or go to the nearest Western hotel and ask for assistance.

Travelers Checks

Unless you want to protect yourself against loss, we do not recommend that you buy travelers checks when traveling to Moscow because you may not be able to find a single establishment that will accept them as a form of payment. Aside from the American Express office, Dialog

Bank branches and some other banks, the only establishment that would cash them for us, at a fee of three percent, was Progress Supermarket, *17 Zubovsky bulvar*, on the Garden Ring near the Park Kultury metro station.

Even when you take them to the American Express or Dialog Bank, you will pay a hefty fee of up to five percent and get a lousy exchange rate if you take rubles instead dollars. It is absurd to pay American Express, or another issuer, for the privilege to carry their travelers checks and then end up paying another five percent to cash them. True, they will be replaced if lost or stolen, but you are better off with credit cards.

Wiring Money

You can have funds wired to any of the Dialog Bank branches from anywhere through the Dialog correspondent in New York, but the minimum is $1,000. There is a small service charge.

BUSINESS HOURS

Business and government offices are usually open from 9am to 6pm, with a lunch break somewhere between noon and 2pm.

Banks are open from 8:30 or 9am to 4 or 4:30pm, Monday through Friday, and take a break for lunch for one hour between noon and 2pm.

Stores usually open at 8 or 9am, some even at 10 or 11am, and close at 7 or 8 or 9pm, and some close for up to one hour for lunch.

Most **food stores** are open from 8am to 8pm and close for lunch between 1 and 2pm. Many are open until 6pm on Sundays. **Western-style supermarkets** do not close for lunch.

Department stores normally keep their doors open between 8am and 9pm and take no lunch breaks. **Small department stores** close from 2 to 3pm for lunch. **Other stores** may well be open from 11am to 7pm, with a lunch break from 2 to 3pm. Most non-food stores are closed on Sundays.

In the past, state-owned stores regularly closed for a day or two for "cleaning" or, seemingly for no reason at all, and it still happens to this day.

Hairdressers usually work all day, from 8am to 9pm, without closing for lunch.

Garages and repair shops work from 8am to 8pm, with a break from 2 to 3pm.

COST OF LIVING

Moscow has overtaken the notoriously costly Zurich and Geneva as the world's most expensive city outside Asia, according to one international survey, which covers 136 major cities on all continents. The survery is based on the cost of 155 products and services, including food, clothing, utilities, transportation, leisure and entertainment. Only Tokyo and Osaka in Japan, Beijing and Shanghai in China, and Hong Kong are more expensive than the Russian capital. Oslo and Copenhagen are less costly than Moscow. While New York City might be the most expensive city in the US, according to this survey, it was in 56th place and Washington, DC, about 92nd.

The average wage in Russia was about $150 a month at the end of 1996 and the minimum income needed to keep body and soul together, was about half of that. Some 28 percent of Russians, or 42 million people, received less than this subsistence level income.

The "New Russians," or people earning monthly salaries of $500 to $100,000 or more per family member, make up about five percent of the population, or 7.7 million people.

CRIME

Crime has skyrocketed in Moscow in the last few years, it is true, but remember that violent crime was practically nonexistent for a metropolis of this size until Russia's independence. It is believed that Moscow was free of deathly criminal violence for so long because, in addition to the authoritarian rule, its inhabitants did not have access to firearms, drugs and cars. But even today, it is safer to walk the streets and parks and metro of Moscow than those in Washington, D.C., and many other American cities.

If we had to single out one serious threat to your life in Moscow it would be getting killed crossing streets clogged with cars that never stop for pedestrians. One is tempted to add that more people get killed by everyday acts of rudeness than crime, but that would be trivializing a serious problem.

No matter what the headlines, New York City, for example, had eight times the number of rapes and 13 times the number of assaults of Moscow in a recent year. Even the *New York Times* noted, "Compared with New York, Moscow is not especially crime-ridden."

And when you consider that Moscow has almost ten million inhabitants, and another two million visitors every day, its crime rate is less than half that of Los Angeles or Baltimore. New York, which has 1.7 million fewer inhabitants than Moscow, has more than double the murders of Moscow.

Many crimes are the fruit of bloody clashes among a dozen competing mafia gangs in the suburbs, which do not affect Western visitors, unless you find yourself in the wrong place at the wrong time. But as a rule, vicious murderers are practically unheard of in Russia.

CRIME IN MOSCOW

"Robbery and murder were no less chronic than fires. At night the city would be taken over by holdup men and thieves, and hardly a night would pass without several murders. Every morning the police would pick up the dead lying in the streets, bring all the unidentified bodies to the City Yard, and leave them there for identification by relatives or friends. Unidentified bodies would be taken to the poorhouse, where they were kept, along with the bodies of executed criminals, those who died in prison, and those dead of excessive drinking, until Trinity Week, when they were buried in a common grave. The citizens of Moscow were so terrorized by nightly robberies that nobody dared to respond to cries for help; citizens were even afraid to approach the windows to see what was going on. Burglary was just as frequent as street robbery."

No, this is not description of Moscow today, although some media would have you believe it is. It is actually a paragraph taken from Arthur Voyce's 1964 book **Moscow**, *which describes the capital's daily life in the 17th century, when Moscow had fewer than one-twentieth of the inhabitants it has today.*

However, listening to some people quoting half-baked horror stories from the newly spawned tabloids, you would think murder is rampant in Moscow. It is not. Many women have stopped riding the metro in the early evening, when perhaps the most appalling crime they would witness is some poor slob throwing up. An American correspondent claimed in his dispatch from Moscow that an expensive pair of sneakers could put your life in danger. What nonsense!

Gypsies are not as common a sight on Moscow streets as they were just a couple of years ago, and they can be very persistent. You will notice that panhandlers in large American cities are far more menacing. While there are throngs of elderly and crippled beggars all over the central Moscow, mostly just lying about the metro staircases, with cardboard boxes lying next to them, you will be surprised at how few actually harass you.

But we do *not* wish to lull you into a false sense of security. Moscow, like any city half its size, *can* be dangerous if you are not careful. If you come from a large American city, you must be as vigilant in Moscow as you are at home. If you come from a small town, you must redouble your defenses.

Never display large amounts of cash and do not advertise jewelry that may appear valuable, even if fake. A $25 Japanese watch may pass for a much more valuable timepiece by its appearance.

Americans who want to know more about the unexpected eventualities when they collide with the Russian law, or have other general questions, may call the US State Department's **Overseas Citizens Services** in Washington, DC, *Tel. 202/647-5225, Monday through Friday, from 8am to 5pm EST*. OCS claims to have an office in every American embassy and consulate around the world.

For **emergencies** between 5pm and 10pm, call *Tel. 202/647-5226*. To reach the State Department's switchboard operator at any time call *Tel. 202/647-4000*. The Russian Desk at the State Department, *Room 3316, Tel. 202/647-9806*, can answer your questions about Russia, but remember their role is not to provide travel information and citizen emergencies should be referred to Overseas Citizens Services.

OCS will deliver a truly urgent message from your family or, should something happen to you, contact your family. The service can help you receive urgent funds from your family and relatives if you are robbed or lose all your money and credit cards. This service is available to American citizens only.

The Center also maintains a 24-hour travel advisory that you can access by telephone or by fax. If you have a fax machine with telephone dialing capability, call *Tel. 202/647-3000* to receive faxes about Russia. Recorded messages can be heard at *Tel. 202/647-5225*. On the Internet, Consular Information Sheets about Russia and other countries are available at *http://travel.state.gov*.

DRIVING

We suggest that you never drive in Moscow. Life is difficult enough without having to worry about wrecking a rental car or even getting killed. The Moscow metro is a much more efficient, safe and cheap mode of transportation. If you absolutely must drive, you would be better off hiring a car with driver for a specific situation. To go to an out-of-the-way restaurant, call for a taxi and ask the driver to come back to pick you up in two hours.

And if you wish to visit historic sights outside of Moscow, you can see many of them through Patriarshy Dom or Intourist tours; please see Chapter 18, *Excursions & Day Trips* for more details.

DRUGS

Russians do not take kindly to drugs and consider them a degenerate habit. If they can cope with shortages, inflation and unemployment, one could hardly expect them to tolerate such weaknesses from the citizens of the most prosperous nations in the world.

We have only one piece of advice for you: Stay away from drugs! Russians, like most other Europeans (with a possible exception of the Dutch and some Swiss) do not sympathize with the drug users.

If you carry medication to Moscow that contains controlled substances, make sure you also bring along a current prescription from your doctor as a proof that it is for medical purposes only. Keep all such medicines in their original containers with your name and date when purchased.

And do not, ever, carry in or out of Russia any package for anyone you do not know, even if it is supposedly only a "gift" for a person that will meet you at the airport.

ELECTRICITY

Dual-voltage appliances are your best bet. The electrical current in Moscow is 220 volt AC, 50 Hz, and sockets require an adapter or a Continental type of round two-pin plug. You will also need a transformer.

ETIQUETTE

If the British are said to be excessively polite, you can safely generalize that Muscovites are too rude. Even a New Yorker, accustomed to aggressive behavior and taking nothing for granted, might be appalled at how inconsiderate Muscovites can be, whether in the metro or waiting in a line. Expect to be yelled at by **babushky**, elderly women, if you do not meet their exacting standards and expect to be ignored at counters, where sales personnel assume they are doing you a favor by just coming to work. Russians appear to be willing to bend only to authority, then they will be all milk and honey; better get out of their way when they flex their superiority. One suspects that this rudeness goes hand in hand with 70 years of Bolshevik disregard for human rights and respect toward another person.

You will sooner see a full moon at midday then get a Muscovite to apologize for stepping on your foot, even though it may be completely accidental. It would appear to an outsider that politeness is mistaken by many Russians for a sign of weakness. Holding the door for someone could elicit stares of incredulity. Even beggars will forego the opportunity to thank you after your drop some change in their lap.

GAYS IN MOSCOW

Article 121 of the Criminal Code, whereby "sexual relations between men are punishable by prison terms of up to five years" was abolished in 1993. It was assumed all along that lesbian sexual relations were ignored since the Code did not even mention them. Although the government has sentenced some two dozen men to prison for homosexuality as recently as 1992, most men are more scared of their neighbors' judgement than the law. Russian public opinion polls reveal a highly negative attitude toward homosexuals: in one survey 23 percent of respondents said that homosexuals should be killed and 24 percent said they should be isolated from society.

It was only in 1996 that Russia's first homosexual community center opened in a small two-room basement in the Izmaylovsky region, where you have to enter through a steel door marked only by a small pink triangle.

Research into the spread of AIDS in the former Soviet Union shows a surprisingly low incidence of the virus. Russia's rate of HIV infection is negligible compared with that in the US. The number of AIDS cases in Russia is growing rapidly, nonetheless. Moscow has the largest concentration of AIDS cases. When AIDS appeared in the US and Europe in the 1980's the Soviet Union was a closed country with practically no AIDS cases.

Before Gorbachev's time, the threat of Article 121 was used by the KGB to blackmail artists into cooperating in their schemes. Film director Sergey Paradzhanov, a homosexual, was arrested in 1974 under Article 121 and sentenced to five years in labor camps.

While Moscow homosexuals still congregate at night around the fountain in front of the Bolshoy Theater, they now also have several clubs and meeting places. Most are owned by people who are not homosexual and charge a higher admission than normal clubs would. "In some parts of town," says a *New York Times* dispatch, "private clubs are like American speak-easies of the Prohibition era. You need a password to get in. To get out without being beaten by thugs, many patrons stay all night." For details about **Shans** (Chance), one of Moscow's largest and most liberal homosexual clubs, see Chapter 15, *Nightlife & Entertainment*.

GIFTS

If you are going to give a gift, give an American-made gift if you are an American. No matter how small the gift, make sure it is of good quality. Choose a personalized gift and give it at the end of your visit. Do not perpetuate the worst of Western excesses by giving chewing gum or cheap pens.

Gift-giving in Russia is quite flexible and guided mostly by common sense. You can bring a gift to a business associate, his or her spouse and their children, as well as to people of the same or opposite sex.

Books are among the best gifts you can give to Russians. Their literacy rate is more than 99 percent, considerably higher than in the US, and they know great literature better than most among us. Find out their interests and give books on that subject. Quality picture books for their children are difficult to find and also make for terrific gifts.

Do not expect valuable gifts in return. Russians are going through the most wrenching economic times in well over half a century so their gifts will be given more as a gesture of friendship than for their value. Russians often give gifts that really are beyond their means so consider paying for some of their expenses for other things.

Western women may want to make sure that their gifts will not be misinterpreted by their Russian associates as an invitation to something other than intended.

If you give flowers, remember that they have certain personal connotations and their color may unintentionally say things that you do not want said. Red and pink flowers are always appropriate, but yellow flowers are rarely exhanged between spouses or lovers. Always bring an odd number of flowers, unless you go to a funeral, where even-numbered bunches are expected.

Common sense should be your sole guide on how to give or accept a gift, but it is said that you should not give a present with your left hand and that you should accept it with both hands. We do think that the American custom of urging recipients to open their gifts right away is inappropriate in Russia.

HANDICAPPED TRAVELERS

Handicapped facilities are practically unheard of in most of Moscow. Except for the newest and plushest among the Western hotels, restaurants, stores and business establishments, you will seldom, if ever, find anything that will assist the handicapped. All public means of transportation are completely inaccessible to wheelchairs.

If being in your 60's or 70's could ever be considered a handicap, it would be so in Moscow, where you have to be of nimble foot and in constant readiness for the unexpected.

HEALTH

Medical facilities in Moscow are often inadequate by Western standards. The problem is seldom lack of doctors. Moscow has more of them on a per capita basis than almost any other city its size in the world; one doctor for every 220 Russians, as opposed to one for every 391 Americans. They attend medical school for six years and spend another four years learning their specialty.

But doctors are among the worst paid professionals in Russia; some earn as little as $150 a month, which is about one-half of what an ambulance driver is paid in Moscow. Perhaps because a much larger proportion of Russian doctors are women than in the US, the medical profession has never had the prestige it enjoys in the West. Some doctors work at one or two other jobs just to make ends meet.

There are plenty of hospital beds and in most Moscow neighborhoods there are state-run polyclinics offering residents a variety of health services at no charge. The problem is the appalling shortage of medical equipment and supplies. Something as basic as rubber gloves or disposable syringes are sometimes reused, if they are readily available at all. That there are not enough antibiotics one can understand, but not having enough bandages is inconceivable but sometimes true.

Since 1995, there have been shortages of insulin in Moscow and across Russia. They were created by the Russian Health Ministry, which is trying to force Moscow and other cities to purchase domestically produced insulin, even though it was not available at that time and had not even been approved by the ministry.

If you are in doubt at all as to your health, go to your regular physician before you leave the country. Carry an adequate supply of prescription medications with you at all times because having your prescription filled in Moscow is often difficult if not almost impossible. Have at least one extra pair of glasses with you, even if they are just the $15 drugstore kind to help you with reading. Carry a healthy supply of over-the-counter medications, such as aspirin, depending on the length of your stay.

The **Overseas Citizens Services** office in Moscow can provide lists of doctors and dentists, as well as hospitals and clinics to handle some of your medical emergencies. If you are injured or become ill, the OCS can contact your family or relatives, perhaps even assist you in returning home, at your expense and on a commercial flight. In case of death, the same office can notify your next of kin. If there is a natural disaster or civil unrest in Russia, the office will also assist you if you are registered with the embassy. And finally, if you are arrested, a consular officer can visit you in jail.

Medical Services

For your medical needs in Moscow consider one of the following services:

International SOS Assistance, *8 Neshaminy Interplex, Suite 207, Trevose, Pennsylvania 19053, Tel. 800/523-8930 or Tel. 215/244-1500, Fax 215/244-2227 or 0165 (Emergency Tel. 215/244-0165), or Place Bonaventure, Montreal, Quebec H5A 1C1, Tel. 800/363-0263 or 514/874-7674.*

SOS provides emergency medical, personal and travel assistance worldwide 24 hours a day. Medical assistance includes pre-trip medical referral, medical monitoring while out of the country, dispatch of a doctor if you need one, emergency evacuation, and medically supervised repatriation.

SOS Assistance in Moscow, *Polyclinic No. 1, 31 Grokholsky pereulok. Tel. 280-7133, Fax 280-7329, telex 412257.*

SOS owns the only medically-equipped jet based in Moscow. Those not having medical evacuation insurance might have to pay $10,000 for an evacuation to the West.

Delta Consulting Group, *7/5 Ulitsa Bolshaya Dmitrovka, Bldg. 3, Office 38. Tel. 229-6536 or 229-7892, Fax 229-2138, telex 412257.*

It is centrally located near metro Teatralnaya or Okhotny Ryad, which is north of the Kremlin. Delta's head office is located at *8, rue des Taillandiers, Paris, France. Paris Tel. (331) 48-05-2913, Fax 47-00-7254, telex 212946.*

Athens Medical Center, *6 Michurinsky prospekt, Tel. 143-2387 or 143-2503 or 147-9121.*

Athens Medical Center is located across the Moskva River from the Luzhniki Sports Complex, and north of metro station Universitet. It provides emergency medical assistance and transportation around the clock. Diagnostic and outpatient services are available Monday through Friday, from 9am to 5pm. They can also assist you with hospitalization in Moscow.

Western-Style Outpatient Clinics

American Medical Center, *10 Second Tverskoy-Yamskoy pereulok, Tel. 956-3366, Fax 956-2306, located northeast of metro Mayakovskaya, four blocks southeast of the Palace Hotel, northwest of the Kremlin and outside the Garden Ring Road. It also has an office in St. Petersburg, Tel. (812) 325-6101.*

AMC, which opened its Moscow outpatient clinic in 1991, occupies two floors of a Russian medical diagnostic center and shares the building with **Medicina**, Russia's first for-profit private clinic. It has several examination rooms and access to ultrasound, CAT-scan and X-ray equipment in the same building.

The clinic is open Monday through Friday, from 8am to 8pm, Saturdays from 9am to 5pm, and Sundays for emergencies. The Center is a Western-style facility staffed by American and Canadian physicians, and Western-trained registered nurses. The annual membership is $375 and a general consultation for non-members is $215.

AMC, like all clinics in this category, refers seriously ill or injured patients requiring surgery or hospitalization to Moscow's hospitals, such as the Kremlin Hospital, or, if needed, coordinates medical evacuations by air to Helsinki or London. It also maintains a 24-hour emergency service. For the AMC pharmacy, please see the section on pharmacies in this chapter.

European Medical Center, *10 Second Tverskoy-Yamskoy pereulok, Tel. 250-5523, after hours, Tel. 250-0730 or 1302 or 6099.*

European Medical Center is located at the same place as AMC (above) at metro Mayakovskaya, northwest of the Kremlin and outside the

Garden Ring Road. Its clinic is open Monday through Saturday, from 9am to 7pm.

EMC's doctors are Western-trained, but, like at other medical facilities, they seldom stay in Moscow for more than a couple of years. EMC provides a Western-trained pediatrician, dermatologist, gynecologist and radiologist for procedures such as ultrasound. There is no annual membership at EMC and a general consultation for non-members is $80.

International Medical Clinic, *Polyclinic No. 1, 10th Floor, 31 Grokholsky pereulok. Tel. 280-7138 or 7177 or 8374 or 8388, Fax 280-8677. Pharmacy, Tel. 280-8765.*

This clinic is located near metro Prospekt Mira, northeast of the Kremlin, outside the Garden Ring Road and near the Botanical Gardens.

IMC also houses the offices of **International SOS Assistance.** Twenty minutes by foot from the metro, IMC is not as accessible at the above two clinics if you have to rely on metro for your transportation.

IMC employs Western-trained physicians. The annual membership at IMC is $350 and a general consultation for non-members is $80.

Mediclub, *56 Michurinsky prospekt, Tel. 931-5018, Fax 932-8653, located at Metro Universitet, southwest of the Kremlin and outside the Garden Ring Road.*

A Canadian clinic, Mediclub is one of the most inaccessible clinics if you have to rely on metro for transportation.

Mediclub, which opened in 1994, is a joint venture between Mediclub of Montreal, Canada, and Glavmosstroy, Moscow's largest construction company. Canadian physicians provide outpatient consultations in all specialties. Mediclub is the only clinic where physicians answer all members' telephone calls. Ambulance service and vaccinations are available. It has one of the best private laboratories. There is a pharmacy on the premises. The annual membership is $250 and a general consultation for non-members is $90.

Sana Medical Center, *65 Ulitsa Nizhnaya Pervomayskaya, Tel. 464-1254 or 2563, Fax 464-4563.*

Sana Medical Center is located at the French-Russian Hospital, Metro Pervomayskaya. This is northeast of the Kremlin and outside the Garden Ring Road, just west of the Moscow Circular Road on the city boundary.

Sana is open Monday through Friday, from 10am to 8pm, closed Saturdays and Sundays. It is staffed by Russian and foreign specialists. For its pharmacy, please see the section on pharmacies in this chapter. It also provides eye exams and offers frames and lenses.

If you need soft contact lenses, you can also go to the Russian-American joint venture, **Optic Moscow,** *30 Ulitsa Stary Arbat, Bldg. 2, Tel. 241-1577,* which is open from 11am to 7pm. It is located between Boulevard and Garden Ring Roads, at Metro Smolenskaya.

Dental Emergencies

U.S. Dental Care, *8 Ulitsa Shabolovka, Bldg. 3, Tel. 931-9909*, became in 1995 the first facility in Russia dedicated exclusively to providing state-of-the-art dental care by a full-time American dentist. It is located at Metro Oktyabrskaya, which is south of the Kremlin and just outside the Garden Ring Road.

A Russian-German dental joint venture, **Intermed**, *26 Ulitsa Durova, Block 5, Tel. 288-9679 or 284-7403*, is located north of the Kremlin and beyond the Garden Ring Road, at Metro Prospekt Mira. The treatment of one tooth costs about $100 and a new metal-ceramic tooth is about $275. It is open Monday through Friday, from 9am to 8pm.

The Belgian-Swiss-Italian-Russian joint venture, **Medical Interline**, *5 Ulitsa Tverskaya, Tel. 203-8631 or 956-8964*, is centrally located inside the Boulevard Ring, at the Intourist Hotel, Rooms 2030-2031, at Metro Okhotny Ryad. Open Mondays, Wednesdays and Fridays 10am to 2pm.

A Western-style private **Dental Clinic**, *10 Korovinskoye shosse, Tel. 488-8000*, opened in Sofitel Iris Hotel complex in 1993, near Fyodorov's Eye Clinic, in far northwest Moscow. It is located at Metro Vladykino or Petrovsko-Razumovskaya. Western technology, including an X-ray department, is available for cash or on credit cards.

A well-equipped Russian-owned Western-style dental clinic **Praktik**, *43 Ulitsa Bolshaya Polyanka, Building 2, Tel. 238-1002 or 934-3391*, at Metro Polyanka or Tretyakovskaya, opened in 1994. It is situated south of the Kremlin, across the Moskva River, in the vicinity of the Tretyakov Art Gallery, in a two-story former mansion. Hours are 9am to 8pm, Monday through Friday; closed Saturdays and Sundays.

The clinic occupies both floors; general dentistry is performed on the second floor and new technology on the ground floor. Eight Russian dentists, surgeons, therapists, orthodontists and periodontists work along with hygienists.

Also consider the **Dental Clinic on Kuznetsky Most**, *9/10 Kuznetsky Most, Tel. 923-5322 or 928-6788*, now run by Russians, centrally located inside the Boulevard Ring Road at Metro Kuznetsky Most, and open Monday through Friday, from 8:30am to 8pm, Saturdays 9am to 5pm.

Pharmacies

Not one pharmaceutical factory has been built in Russia in more than 20 years and the equipment at most of the existing ones has gone through 80 to 90 percent of its life cycle. Even in Western pharmacies, medications which were registered by the old Soviet Ministry of Health are mostly sold.

There are only about a dozen Western-style pharmacies scattered through the capital, where you can buy Western medications with your credit card or for rubles at that day's exchange rate. These are among the best supplied pharmacies in Moscow. All except the Stary Arbat Pharmacy accept credit cards.

American Medical Center, *10 Second Tverskoy-Yamskoy pereulok, Tel. 956-3366.*

See Western-Style Outpatient Clinics earlier in this section for more details. Stocks American, Canadian and Western European medications. Located at metro Mayakovskaya. Open Monday through Friday, from 8:30am to 6:30pm; Saturdays, from 10am to 2pm; No lunch break.

Eczacibasi Drugstore, *2/15 Ulitsa Maroseyka, Tel. 928-9189 or 921-4048, Fax 921-2709.*

Stocks American, German and Turkish medications. Located at Metro Kitay-gorod or Lubyanka. Open Monday through Friday from 10am to 7:30pm, Saturdays from 9am to 6pm; No lunch break.

Farmakon, *4 Ulitsa Tverskaya, Tel. 292-0301 or 0843.*

Stocks medications of various European countries. Located at Metro Okhotny Ryad. Open Monday through Friday, from 9am to 8pm; Saturdays 9am to 6pm; Lunch break from 2-3pm.

Interoko Drugstore, *10 Ulitsa Petrovka, 2nd floor, Tel. 292-3451, Fax 938-2033.*

Stocks American, French and German medications. Located at Metro Teatralnaya. Near the Petrovsky Passazh Mall and Bolshoy Theater. Open Monday through Saturday, from 9am to 8pm.

Salute Drugstore, *12 Krasnopresnenskaya nab., Tel. 253-2018.*

Stocks American and medications from Western Europe. Entrance 3, First Floor of Mezhdunarodnaya Hotel, Metro Ulitsa 1905 goda. Open Monday through Sunday from 9am to 9pm; No lunch break.

Sana Drugstore, *65 Ulitsa Nizhnaya Pervomayskaya, Tel. 464-1254, Fax 464-2563.*

Located at the French-Russian Hospital, see Western-Style Outpatient Clinics in this chapter. Stocks mostly medications from France. Located at Metro Pervomayskaya. Open Monday through Friday, from 10am to 8pm; No lunch break.

Stary Arbat Pharmacy, *25 Ulitsa Arbat, Tel. 291-7101 or 7105, Fax 931-5567.*

Stocks American, Belgian, British, French, German and Polish medications. There is also delivery service. Located at Metro Arbatskaya, about five minutes on foot, southwest of metro Arbatskaya. Open Monday through Friday from 9am to 8pm, Saturdays from 10am to 6pm; No lunch break. No credit cards are accepted.

Vita Drugstore, *6 Ulitsa Poklonnaya, Tel. 249-7818, Fax 249-9428.*

Stocks American, French, German and Swiss medications. Located at Metro Kutuzovskaya. Open Monday through Friday, from 10am to 7:30pm, Saturdays from 11am to 6pm; Lunch break from 2-2:30pm.

There are more than 500 state-owned pharmacies in Moscow and at least a dozen of them are open continuously. Some of the above pharmacies display names and addresses of 24-hour state pharmacies.

Health Regulations

American and Canadian citizens do not need a health certificate on their arrival in Moscow, unless they come from a severely compromised location.

These same nationals coming from regions where yellow fever is prevalent, particularly in some areas of Africa and South America, will have to have an international certificate of vaccination. A cholera and tetanus vaccination certificate may also be required.

The Russian president has signed an AIDS law that imposes mandatory testing on nearly all foreigners, including Americans and Canadians, who remain in Russia more than three months. They must provide documentation that they are not infected with the virus that causes AIDS when they apply for a visa. If found that they are HIV positive after they enter Russia, they face deportation. Short-term travelers arriving from AIDS-infected regions may also be required to take an AIDS test.

DIPHTHERIA, CHOLERA, POLIO & MEASLES

Diphtheria, an acutely infectious disease that has been practically eliminated in the West, has been spreading throughout the Commonwealth of Independent States (CIS) since 1990. About 35,700 cases have been reported in Russia during 1995, with 1,746 deaths reported due to diphtheria. In Moscow alone, hundreds of cases have been registered, resulting in several deaths. One case of diphtheria in an American citizen visiting Moscow was reported in 1995. The CIS accounts for more than 90 percent of all diphtheria cases in Europe.

For adults, current immunization usually means getting a booster shot, the tetanus-diphtheria vaccine, unless one has been received in the last ten years. The booster shot is best administered at least two weeks before your trip to allow antibodies to build up.

Cholera, a severe form of bacterial dysentery, has also become a problem since 1994. Flourishing in regions where water is dirty and sanitation poor, it broke out in several Russian provinces and former Soviet republics. Moscow, having old water pipes that are sometimes tainted with bacteria, is not immune from the spread of cholera, in part because of enormous numbers of immigrants from the former Soviet Union republics. At least a couple of people die from cholera each month in Moscow.

One hundred and fifty-two cases of polio and 28,672 cases of measles have also been registered in Russia in 1995.

The Russian requirements for foreigners are more stringent than those of most European countries, but are somewhat similar to requirements in the US. During a parliamentary debate on the new AIDS law, a female legislator claimed that sexual contact with a foreigner "is 100 times more dangerous than with a Russian."

Chances are that your most serious emergency will be a case of diarrhea. Americans who are in doubt as to whether they need to take certain medical precautions should call the **Centers for Disease Control and Prevention**, *Tel. 404/639-3311, Atlanta, Georgia*, and ask for the International Traveler's Health Hotline. You can also have such information faxed free of charge by calling CDC, *Tel. 404/332-4564*, and following the prompts. Canadians can check with the travel information offices of Health and Welfare in all large Canadian cities.

We strongly recommend that you see both your dentist and your physician for a quick checkup before traveling abroad. There is nothing more annoying than a toothache on Red Square. Have all your prescriptions filled before leaving your home.

HOLIDAYS & NOTABLE DAYS

Most businesses, government offices and museums are closed on New Year's Day, International Women's Day, May Day, Victory Day, Russia's Independence Day, National Accord & Reconciliation Day and Constitution Day. Food stores and restaurants seldom close for these holidays.

•**January 1**	New Year's Day
•**January 7**	Russian Orthodox Christmas
•**March 8**	International Women's Day
•**May 1-2**	May Day
•**May 5-13**	Festival of Moscow Stars
•**May 9**	Victory Day (Veterans Parades)
•**June 6**	Poet Aleksandr Pushkin's Birthday
•**June 12**	Russia's Independence Day
•**June** (odd years)	International Film Festival
•**August 22**	Flag Day
•**Every August**	Moscow International Marathon
•**Day in September**	Moscow Day
•**November 7-8**	October 1917 Russian Revolution Day Now National Accord & Reconciliation Day
•**December 12**	Constitution Day
•**December 25-January 5**	Russian Winter Festival of Arts

LAUNDRY & DRY CLEANING

It is difficult to find a Westerner who is satisfied with laundry or dry cleaning services in Moscow, while Muscovites think it is adequate and do not understand what all the fuss is about.

If you stay in a luxury hotel, Western-style laundry and dry cleaning are always available. At a more modest hotel, your floor woman, the **dezhurnaya**, can advise you.

Some luxury hotels provide 24-hour cleaning services for nonresidents, but it will cost you. At the Savoy, the Renaissance Moscow, or the Mezhdunarodnaya Hotel, you can have any article laundered or dry cleaned, man or woman.

If you live in an apartment, these services can clean your garments at prices lower than hotels, and pick up and deliver them at an additional charge:

California Cleaners, *Tel. 497-0005 or 0011, or 493-5271*, from 9am to 10pm. This service has 12 collection points where your laundry or items to be dry cleaned can be picked up. For an additional charge, you can have it picked up and delivered at your residence. Ten pounds of laundry will cost you about $20. This company has been serving Westerners for several years.

Another firm to consider is **Service A.N.**, *Tel. 448-9573 or 9590 or 1098*, which has been providing dry cleaning services within 24 hours for several years. Pickup and delivery are available.

There is also **BFT-Diana**, *Tel. 291-6676*, where laundry and dry cleaning is done in 24 or 72 hours, with a special express service in two hours. Pickup and delivery service are available.

MAIL & COURIERS

Mail delays are a Russian mystery that has no match in the world. Your best bet is to send everything by registered air mail. That is no insurance against your mail being opened, however.

Moscow's **Main Post Office**, *26 Ulitsa Myasnitskaya, Tel. 928-6311 or 924-0250*, is located northeast of the Kremlin, on the Boulevard Ring Road, at Metro Chistiye prudy.

The **Central Telegraph Office**, *7 Ulitsa Tverskaya*, which is part of the Russian Post Office, is across the street from a McDonald's, just north of the Kremlin, near the Intourist Hotel, at Metro Tverskaya.

The **International Post Office**, *37 Varshavskoye shosse, Tel. 114-4645 or 4584*, is located in southern Moscow, outside the Garden Ring Road, at Metro Nagatinskaya. The international post office also has an express mail counter, which is called **Garantpost**, *Tel. 114-4613*. You can reach an English-speaking operator at the international post office by calling *Tel. 117-0040 or 8560*.

Russians write their addresses in reverse order from Westerners, starting with the country on the first line; city and zip code on the second; street, house number and block (if any) on the third, and their names on the bottom line. On the envelope, they write their name and address **below** yours.

When writing abroad, it might help if you write the name of the country of destination in Cyrillic or ask a Russian to do so for you.

There are three privately owned mail companies, all three established after 1991, that can assist you with your mail:

Post International, *1/2 Putinkovsky pereulok, Tel. 200-3373*, behind the Rossiya cinema at Pushkin Square, has a $30 minimum monthly fee, charges $2 to send one 20-gram letter to the US, and ships mail to the US outside the postal channels six times weekly.

P.X. Post, *22b Ulitsa Tverskaya, Tel. 956-2230*, under the arch of the Minsk Hotel, has a $10 monthly minimum fee, charges $1.25 to send one 20-gram letter to the US, and ships mail to the US outside the postal channels five times a week.

Global Post, *55 Leninsky prospekt, Entrance 15, Tel. 135-1172*, has a $30 minimum monthly fee, charges $1.75 to send one 20-gram letter to the US, and ships mail to the US three times weekly.

Courier Services

Courier services are scattered all over Moscow and, amazingly, are able to carry on their business almost as efficiently as in the West, which is not something you can often say in Russia. The usual delivery is three to five workdays.

The **DHL**, *11 Third Samotechny pereulok, Tel. 956-1000, 971-1884 or 281-8671, Fax 974-2106*, head office is located at Metro Novoslobodskaya, north of the Kremlin and outside the Garden Ring Road. US toll-free number is *Tel. 800/225-5345*.

EMS Garantpost, *37 Varshavskoye shosse, Tel. 117-0040 or 8560 or 116-5065, Fax 230-2719*, a private international and domestic express courier, has its main office at the International Post Office, at Metro Nagatinskaya. It accepts letters and packages until 6pm and guarantees delivery abroad within three days. It has two other pick-up locations.

For overnight mail delivery, you can call **Federal Express**, *12 Krasnopresnenskaya nab., Tel. 253-1641 or 262-5034; Tel. 800/238-5355 in the US*. It is located on the first floor of the Mezh Hotel office building, known as the World Trade Center (Sovincenter), Entrance 3, at Metro Ulitsa 1905 goda.

TNT Express Worldwide, *3 Third Baltiysky pereulok, Tel. 156-5682 or 5689 or 5760 or 5771 or 5872, Fax 151-2277; in the US, Tel. 800/558-5555*, is located at Metro Voykovskaya, in northwest Moscow. TNT has worldwide door-to-door delivery. The Moscow office delivers in the metropolitan area only.

United Parcel Service, *12 Krasnopresnenskaya nab., Tel. 253-1937*, is located at Metro Ulitsa 1905 goda, in western Moscow. In addition to Moscow and St. Petersburg, it also serves many other cities in the Commonwealth of Independent States.

United States Postal Service maintains express mail service to most of the larger cities in the Commonwealth of Independent States.

PHOTOGRAPHY

Things have come a long way from the days when a stern voice on the Aeroflot's speaker system would warn apprehensive foreigners: "We have crossed the Soviet border. Taking photos is prohibited." But to be on the safe side, take some basic precautions and never photograph what until recently the Intourist labeled as "military objects and institutions."

Keep your still or movie camera's lens away from the 25-kilometer zone inside border areas, from airports, railway and highway bridges, hydro-electrical installations, dams, pumping stations, railway junctions, tunnels, industrial establishments, scientific research institutions, laboratories, electric power stations, radio and television stations, and telephone and telegraph facilities.

Mostly because of Russia's political and economic disarray, some Westerners are detecting a slight backlash against foreigners in today's Russia and you surely do not want to give anyone a reason to attack you, even verbally, for taking inappropriate photos.

Film

Western-made film is somewhat expensive and sometimes not as fresh as you might wish so carry enough of it with you to see you through your visit. Should you have any left over before you return home, give it to your Russian friends. If you travel with your video camera, remember that video tapes are even more scarce, particularly outside of Moscow.

To guard against X-ray machines, if you are a serious photographer, we recommend you get the lead-lined bags for film before you leave home. For the film already in your camera, have your camera bag hand-checked at all airports. At the very least, carry all your extra film in a plain see-through plastic bag so the airport personnel can tell at a glance what its contents are. Sometimes that will not keep either Russian or American inspectors from making you open every single plastic container with your exposed and unexposed film, even though your connecting flight may be leaving in five minutes. Unless you have exceptional fine-grain film requirements, we recommend film with a sensitivity of at least ISO 400 to guard against the necessity of having to use electronic flash. No photos inside churches, please! If you run out of film, good places to replenish your supply would be your Western hotel; anywhere on Novy or Stary Arbat promenades; **Petrovsky Passazh Shopping Mall**, *10 Ulitsa Petrovka*, Metro Kuznetsky Most; or at **GUM Department Store** and shopping arcades on Red Square, Metro Ploshchad Revolutsiyi. You can get all photographic supplies at **Jupiter** store, *19 Novy Arbat*. For passport photos, head to **Fokus**, *4 Stary Arbat*.

There are many places where you can have your film developed in Moscow today. Try any of the 40-plus Fokus photographic franchises, including these three that are centrally located at *2 Okhotny Ryad Street*, at *4 Tverskaya Street*, and *19 Novy Arbat Street*. You can have your film processed and photos made in one hour or in 24 hours, depending on the price you are willing to pay, although you may want to have all processing done upon returning home. They also sell film and other photographic supplies.

Kodak is now all over Moscow, including in many Western and state hotels, Petrovsky Passazh and GUM malls, where their brightly colored kiosks are easy to identify.

Some of these stores also carry a limited supply of video tapes.

PRESS & BROADCASTING

Newspapers

Although the availability of foreign newspapers is spotty, it is a far cry from yesteryears, when only Communist propaganda from Socialist countries was available.

American or European English-language newspapers published outside of Russia are never available on the day of publication and don't be surprised if you have to pay $2 for yesterday's paper. English, French, German and Italian newspapers and magazines are available in many luxury hotels, such as the Metropol or Slavyanskaya. A few downtown street kiosks sell a limited number of them too, particularly on Tverskaya Street and Pushkin Square.

You can buy the *International Herald Tribune*, published six days a week, in many hotels and shops mentioned in this guide. The European edition of *The Wall Street Journal/Europe* is available in some luxury hotels; some days complimentary copies are stacked on the counter at the Metropol Hotel. *USA Today*, the British *Financial Times*, *London Times*, *The Guardian*, and *The European* are also available at such locations.

The international editions of the American *Time* magazine and *Newsweek* will often be found alongside the British *Economist* and a variety of other Western European periodicals.

Moscow News is published weekly in separate English and Russian editions by its Russian parent, Moskovskiye Novosti. The tabloid-size English-language edition is your best alternative if you cannot read Russian, but want to get a Russian point of view. It carries articles on politics and culture, and news about Moscow.

The tabloid-sized English-language *Moscow Times*, which is controlled by foreigners, is published five days a week and available free of charge in every establishment where Westerners can be found. It has excellent write-ups of events in Moscow that are of interest to Westerners, but spotty coverage of American and Canadian news. Its direct competitor is the bit thinner *Moscow Tribune*, which is also published five times a week.

Hearst brought the Russian-language edition of the American *Cosmopolitan* to Russia in 1994 and hit the jackpot; its racy articles are so successful that the company began publishing a Russian edition of *Good Housekeeping* the following year.

It was, of course, just a question of time, before an American sex magazine appeared in Russian. That dubious distinction goes to *Penthouse*, which already distributes several other international editions. While nothing seems sacred in the American edition, its Russian counterpart is not nearly as raunchy. Not yet.

Perhaps the most widely read Russian-language daily in the capital is *Moskovsky Komsomolets* (Moscow Young Communist), which is now known under its acronym *MK*.

Radio

Radio stations jockeying for status as Moscow's most popular are **Evropa Plus**, at 69.8 FM, and **Radio 101**, which has a bit of English-language programming. Among other radio stations of interest to Westerners is **Radio 7** (104.7 FM frequency and Russian ultra-short wave band 73.4), which also has some English-language programming.

Short-wave Radio

If you have a short-wave radio, tune in to one of these international broadcasters:

British **BBC World Service** broadcasts news every hour on the hour, for up to one hour of in-depth news reports and analysis. There is a variety of 15-minute and 30-minute programs on different subjects, as well as World Business Report, broadcast daily.

American **Christian Science Monitor** World Service broadcasts news every weekday. Americans may find these weekday broadcasts more satisfying than those of the Voice of America. On weekends, most of the Monitor's air time is devoted to religious programming.

Radio Canada International broadcasts can be heard daily.

Voice of America broadcasts some programs in "special English," which has a restricted vocabulary so that it can be easily understood by foreign nationals. While these may not satisfy native Americans for lack of detail, there are VOA's news bulletins every hour. **Radio Moscow** English language service is at 918 kHz on AM, with news on the hour. You can hear the BBC World Service at 1508 MHz.

Television
There are five government television channels and one private channel available in Moscow.

Channels 1 and 2 are the national TV channels. **ORT, Channel 1** is the state-run Ostankino channel, which broadcasts about 23 hours daily and boasts up to 200 million viewers in the former Soviet Union. **RTR, Channel 2**, began broadcasting in 1991, and is also government-owned. It is the second most watched channel and particularly strong in Moscow. It broadcasts about 17 hours daily.

SOAPS VS. SOLZHENITSYN

Upon returning to Russia in 1994, after 20 years of exile, Aleksandr Solzhenitsyn, the great anti-Soviet dissident and winner of the 1970 Nobel Prize in Literature, hosted his own TV talk show on the government-controlled Ostankino Channel 1 for a few months. He was as uncompromising as ever and the show was taped in Solzhenitsyn's Moscow apartment. The 20-minute program followed the evening news and competed against a popular movie channel. A survey disclosed that 12 percent of viewers watched Solzhenitsyn's program. But the show with the highest ratings was **Wild Rose**, *a Mexican soap opera, with 27 percent viewership.*

Commented contemporary intellectual, writer Artyom Troitsky, who had his own post-midnight talk show, to the New York Times: "For the post-perestroika generation, he really means nothing. Why should anyone now care about the Gulag Archipelago? I'm afraid that Solzhenitsyn is totally, totally passe."

Added Viktor Yerofeyev, a novelist and literary critic: "It's better to have him speak than write. He writes such ugly Russian. He is once again what he always was at heart - a provincial schoolteacher."

MTK, Channel 3, founded in 1990, is the Moscow channel owned by several private investors. Until 6pm, it is a privately-owned commercial channel, known as **2 X 2**, and from 6 to 11pm it is a Moscow channel.

NTV, Channel 4, owned by a Russian real estate, banking and media tycoon, is the independent national channel, founded in 1993.

Channel 5, founded in 1938, comes from St. Petersburg and is also state-owned. It broadcasts about 18 hours daily.

Channel TV 6, founded in 1993, is privately owned and originates in Moscow.

The Turner Broadcasting System initiated Russia's first independent cable television channel, CNN International, in 1993, in a joint venture with a Moscow partner. Its programming consists of nightly Russian and American films, interspersed by CNN news in synchronized translation.

You can watch CNN International at most Western and other luxury hotels in Moscow, such as the Baltschug, Marco Polo Presnya, Metropol, Mezhdunarodnaya, Moscow Renaissance, Palace, President, Radisson Slavyanskaya, and Savoy.

Other cable choices available are BBC, MTV, Super Channel and EuroSport.

PROSTITUTION

Prostitution is illegal, but then, you already know why it is called the oldest profession in the world. It is as common in Moscow as anywhere in the world. Night clubs are the favorite prowling grounds for Moscow call girls who will spend the night with you for no less than $100. In ritzy clubs and casinos, where formal attire is required, there are so many of them they sometimes outnumber the customers.

Tverskaya Street is a favorite outdoor haunt of Moscow's female prostitutes, especially around the Intourist Hotel. Western tourists are sometimes awakened by knocking on the door by desperate women who want to earn foreign currency. The ground-floor courtyard Osborne Bar inside that hotel is crawling with women of every description displaying their wares while sipping coffee or nursing a drink. Others spill over the remaining eating and drinking establishments throughout the Intourist and there are still plenty left to linger on various floors, hoping to get lucky.

But one also has a nagging impression that, with some exceptions, many women here engage in prostitution because they are single mothers trying to survive in a harsh economic climate and often are morally obligated to support their aging parents, whose monthly pensions amount to less than the admission price to some clubs. Were it not for all those doormen to pay off, who also prostitute themselves, if in another fashion, these women could perhaps work only a few days each month.

The head of Moscow's criminal investigation department says that the Moscow police can barely cope with the explosion in prostitution. There are 200 sex businesses operating in the city and some even advertising their services in newspapers. He says that women between the ages of 20 and 30 are recruited from the Russian interior to engage in sex and provide massages for which they charge up to $100 an hour.

PUBLIC REST ROOMS

We hope you will not judge Moscow by the availability of her public rest rooms, but must caution you that with some exceptions they are deplorable and sometimes harder to come by than camel's milk.

Our best advice would be that you use a rest room every time one is available, starting with your hotel or apartment. Public toilets in Moscow are few and far between and when you leave the Garden Ring Road you should plot your course as if you would never find another one.

Even when they are open and consist of nothing more than just a hole in the ground over which you must force your unaccustomed body to perform contortions worthy of Houdini, never, ever, expect to find toilet paper in them. When you do it will likely be of a variety you'd only use to sand down your furniture at home. Always carry a small packet of paper napkins or moist towelettes with you.

When sightseeing the city, you will have to be as clever as Field Marshall Kutuzov if you want to return with dry underwear. Establishments catering to Westerners are your best bet when the urge comes. If one of them is not nearby, try a Russian hotel, although many still have guards or doormen that take longer to convince to let you in than your bladder would allow. Russian restaurants are a gamble, but if desperate, you should try them.

As you sightsee the capital, keep these establishments in mind because rest rooms are plentiful:

The **Baltschug Kempinski Hotel**, located south of the Kremlin, across the Moskva River, might have the cleanest bathrooms in Moscow and the kind of toilet paper you would expect in a luxury hotel. Their washing facilities are sparkling. After a particularly trying experience, you will want to linger here in luxurious comfort.

The **Metropol Hotel**, overlooking Teatralnaya Square, has very clean rest rooms with toilet paper always available and washing facilities that compare with those in the West. You can even make a free local phone call on the way in or out. The **Savoy Hotel**, a couple of blocks northeast of here, is comparable.

The **Slavyanskaya Hotel**, next to the Kievsky Railway Station, has bathrooms as clean as you would expect at any American hotel, at home or abroad. The same goes for the **Mezhdunarodnaya Hotel** in the World Trade Center, west of the Kremlin and outside the Garden Ring Road.

Arbat Irish House Supermarket & Bar, *21 Novy Arbat, 2nd floor*, centrally located just outside the Boulevard Ring Road and west of the

Kremlin, is your best bet if shopping on Novy Arbat promenade or walking the Stary Arbat pedestrian mall. But you will have to go through the Shamrock Pub to reach the rest rooms and will need to hold your breath while you wade through the thick clouds of cigarette smoke from the bar patrons. The cleanliness of their rest rooms has gone down since Russians took over the business.

McDonald's Restaurants, on *Pushkin Square*; across the street from the Central Telegraph Office on Tverskaya; at *50/52 Stary Arbat*, near the Ministry of Foreign Affairs; and at two locations on *Prospekt Mira*, might be more desirable for their very clean public rest rooms than for their fast food (to some).

Intourist's main office, *13 Ulitsa Mokhovaya and Manezhnaya Square*, is only a passable choice, especially before or after an Intourist sightseeing tour, but do not expect toilet paper to be available and when it is, it will not be of the gentle variety.

Most Western-style hotels, such as the **Palace, Aerostar, Marco Polo Presnya, Moscow Renaissance** or **Sofitel Iris**, are also reliable if you happen to be in the vicinity of one of them. The same goes for most expensive restaurants, listed elsewhere, some of which are located in these same hotels.

Independent restaurants are a more complex problem because many of them have doormen or guards in front of them and it might be difficult for you to explain yourself. Some will simply refuse to let you enter just to use their toilet.

Recently, the city drew up plans to build a number of portable public toilets in central Moscow. They are to be located at train stations, markets and other public areas.

RELIGIOUS SERVICES

During Soviet times there were fewer than a dozen churches open in Moscow. Today you can practice your faith freely at a number of churches. These are the most often recommended options:

The **Anglican Church**, St. Andrew's Church, *8 Voznesensky pereulok, Tel. 245-3837 or 275-6221*, holds services Sundays at 10am and Wednesdays at 7:30pm, Metro Pushkinskaya, which is northwest of the Kremlin and inside the Boulevard Ring Road.

The **Calvary Church** (Protestant), *29 Ulitsa Presnensky val, Tel. 573-9185 or 195-4605*, holds services in English with Russian translation Wednesdays at 7pm and Sundays at 2:30pm, Metro Belorusskaya, which is northwest of the Kremlin and outside the Garden Ring Road.

The **Catholic Chaplaincy**, *78 Leninsky prospekt, Tel. 243-9621*, holds masses in English on Sundays at 10am, Metro Universitet, which is southeast of the Kremlin and outside the Garden Ring Road.

Christian Science Group, *14 Ulitsa Sushovskaya, Tel. 415-5257 or 417-9028*, holds Russian-English services Sundays at 11am and every first Wednesday of the month at 7pm, Metro Novoslobodskaya, which is northeast of the Kremlin and between the Boulevard and Garden Ring Roads. Their library is open for one hour after Sunday services.

Church of Jesus Christ of Latter-Day Saints, *2 Second Zatchatievsky pereulok, Tel. 247-1136 or 291-3283*, holds English-language services on Sundays from 9am to noon at a red brick school, Metro Park Kultury, which is southwest of the Kremlin and between the Boulevard and Garden Ring Roads.

Congregation Hineini (Reform Judaism), *26 Ulitsa Novoryazanskaya, Tel. 161-1673, 270-9343 or 918-2696*, holds services Fridays at 5pm in the Autoworkers Palace of Culture, Metro Komsomolskaya, which is northeast of the Kremlin and outside the Garden Ring Road.

The **International Baptist Fellowship**, *15 Ulitsa Druzhinnikovskaya, 5th Floor, Hall 5 (through the office entrance), Tel. 971-3558*, offers prayer and Bible study Sundays at 10am, with a service at 11am at the Kinotsentr, Metro Krasnopresnenskaya, which is northwest of the Kremlin and outside the Garden Ring Road.

The **International Christian Assembly**, *10 Krymsky val, Tel. 337-8000 or 8155 or 338-1150*, holds English-language services Sundays at 11am, and Christian Growth classes at 10am, in the Concert Hall of the Central House of Artists, Metro Oktyabrskaya, which is southeast of the Kremlin and inside the Garden Ring Road.

Moscow Charismatic Church, *97 Ulitsa Pervomayskaya, Tel. 461-9874*, holds services Thursdays at 7pm and Sundays at 10:30am in Russian with English translation, metro Pervomayskaya, which is northeast of the Kremlin and outside the Garden Ring Road.

Moscow Christian Center, *24 Ulitsa Novy Arbat, Tel. 344-1344*, holds services on Fridays at 7pm and Sundays at 10am in the Oktyabr Cinema, Metro Arbatskaya, which is east of the Kremlin and between the Boulevard and Garden Ring Roads.

The **Moscow Protestant Chaplaincy**, *36 Prospekt Mira, Tel. 143-3562*, holds services in English on Sundays at 11am on the 2nd floor offices of the Peace Federation, Metro Prospekt Mira, which is northeast of the Kremlin and outside the Garden Ring Road.

The **Moscow Synagogue**, *14 Bolshoy Spasoglinishchevsky pereulok, Tel. 923-9697*, holds services on Fridays at sunset and Saturdays at 9am, Metro Kitay-gorod, which is northeast of the Kremlin and between the Boulevard and Garden Ring Roads.

Mosque, *7 Vypolzov pereulok, Tel. 281-3866*, has services on Fridays at 1pm, Metro Prospekt Mira, which is north of the Kremlin and outside the Garden Ring Road.

Russian Orthodox Church, Church of St. Catherine, *60/2 Ulitsa Bolshaya Ordynka, Tel. 231-8226*, holds services in English on Sundays at 10am, Metro Dobryninskaya, which is south of the Kremlin and inside the Garden Ring Road.

Seventh-Day Adventists, *37 Ulitsa Donskaya, Tel. 126-8767 or 135-3920*, holds bilingual services on Saturdays at 10:30am, Metro Shabolovskaya, which is south of the Kremlin and outside the Garden Ring Road.

ROMANCE

While everything is possible in love, it is highly unlikely that more than a few Western women will ever have an affair with a Russian man. It is men who are still adventurous or foolish enough to go to the ends of the earth for the promise of that one woman that might fulfill whatever their desires might be. In droves, Russian women are trying to get hooked up with Western men.

Today, thousands of English-speaking Westerners meet Russian women without ever leaving their living rooms. Tens of thousands of Russian women are spending their last ruble in hopes of being noticed by some Westerner who will want to bring them to the US or Canada. There are so many matchmakers in the West catering to both sides one would think there could not possibly be enough women available in all of Russia to keep them in business. But there are, and then some. Done properly, meeting through correspondence takes plenty of time and money with no assurance whatsoever that you will be happy forever after. All it takes to get started is a fax machine and a credit card.

After an exchange of several letters, you may decide to call your penpal on the phone. Perhaps you have already decided to go to Moscow and meet her in person. The woman you will likely meet is usually well educated and will likely surprise you with her knowledge of literature, classical music or theater, even if she has difficulty verbalizing it.

A Russian woman can come to the US on a visitor's or fiancée visa, which allows her to stay for a specific time. If she came on a fiancée visa, she must marry within three months or return home. However, a fiancée visa can only be issued after the couple has met. So, if this is something you really want to do, you have to go to Russia to meet her first – which is probably your best insurance that you will not act rashly.

SMOKING

Cigarette smoking is a favorite Russian indulgence. Men and women puff away with such gusto that you almost hate to remind them there are people even in Moscow who find smoking bothersome. Before perestroika,

Russians smoked cigarettes so strong they could send a grown man to the hospital, but have since progressed to Western brands and, as one would expect, now smoke even more to make up for less nicotine. While the current life expectancy for Russian men hovers in the fifties, there are so many smokers in their eighties and nineties that some Muscovites might laugh at you if you tried to make smoking a health issue.

While smoking is prohibited in most public buildings, including museums, the metro, and railway waiting rooms, you can smoke to your heart's content in 99 percent of the restaurants. Only the most exclusive eateries, such as those in the Baltschug Kempinski Hotel, segregate their diners into smoking and non-smoking wings. Even at the Russian Orthodox Church-owned Danilovsky Hotel, guests can smoke wherever there is no portrait of the Patriarch on display, but, fortunately, not in the restaurant.

If cigarette smoke really bothers you, speak to your waiter and ask for another table. After one such relocation, however, you may be left to your own devices as to how to cope with smoke from another neighboring table. If you are in a Georgian, Azeri or Armenian restaurant, where men seem to compete with each other as to how many cigarettes they can smoke, you may look foolish asking for a non-smoking table.

TELEPHONE, TELEGRAM, & FAX

You can make a telephone call, mail a letter, send a telegram, fax or telex from the **Central Telegraph Office**, *7 Ulitsa Tverskaya*, centrally located one block north of the Intourist Hotel. It is open 24 hours a day and you can pay in rubles only.

Telephones

The Russian telephone system is badly in need of modernization; it will eventually cost billions of dollars. Until 1991, the entire Soviet Union could receive fewer calls from abroad than a medium-sized Manhattan apartment building in New York City.

COUNTRY CODES
Russia 7
United States 1

CITY CODES
Moscow 095
St. Petersburg 812

There are some 28,000 telephone booths in Moscow, but none have telephone directories, which are only now beginning to be published regularly. Telephone calls from public pay phones are made by inserting a brown plastic disk, called **zheton**, that you can buy at post officea, some kiosks and metro ticket windows. Their price is usually the same as the metro fare. Lift the receiver and dial the number if you hear a continuous buzzing sound. Make sure you hear the dial tone before you insert your **zheton** or it may mean that the phone is broken. Long rings mean your party's phone is ringing, short rings let you know the line is busy. The zheton will drop into the box as soon as your party answers the phone.

Expect that you may have to dial the same number two or even three times before you reach your party. At other times you might cut right into another party's conversation. Speak fast because Muscovites are in no mood to linger on the phone to find out who is calling. If the other party doesn't speak English, or even if he or she does, you may be unceremoniously cut off without the slightest explanation. One never seems to cease wondering, nevertheless, how many Muscovites answer in English, even if they are not the party you want.

Never, ever, take any telephone number for granted, whether you find it in this guide or any other. In a ritual that no one comprehends, telephone numbers change quickly and often.

If you go to the **GUM Shopping Mall Business Center**, *3 Red Square, Tel. 921-0911 or 7853 or 9447, Fax 921-4609*, you will pay about $1 for each local telephone call. The center has a comfortable lounge on the second level, overlooking Red Square and Lenin Mausoleum. You can have a drink or snack at the bar, while making local or international calls. You can also send and receive faxes, use a computer and have photocopies, printing, binding and laminating done on the premises. There is a DHL express mail counter at the Center.

If you only need to make a phone call, you can also head for the Metropol Hotel, two blocks north, where local calls are free if made from one of the three telephones in the area to your left before entering the lobby. Just dial 9 and your seven-digit number.

The Baltschug Hotel, across the Moskva River from St. Basil's Cathedral, also has nice courtesy telephone booths in their lobby, where complimentary local calls can be made by dialing 11, then the local telephone number.

At the Radisson Slavyanskaya, there are a couple of phones for complimentary calls in the area just before you enter the lobby. Meant for helpless foreigners, these phones are often mobbed by native Muscovites who do not want to pay for their local calls.

EMERGENCY TELEPHONE NUMBERS

Fire (Pozharnaya okhrana) 01
Police (Militsia) 02
Ambulance (Skoraya pomoshch) 03
Gas Leaks (Sluzhba gaza) 04

USEFUL TELEPHONE NUMBERS

Local Information 05
Telegram by Phone 06
Information on Dialing Other CIS Cities 07
Moscow Telephone Numbers Inquiries 09 (or 927-0009 at a charge)
Exact Time 100
International Calls Inquiries 8-190
International Calls Service Hotline 333-0565
Western Union Money Transfers 119-8250.
Accidents Registration Bureau 284-3055
For-Fee Emergency Medical Service 176-7919
Business Inquiries 299-0004
Missing Children 401-9982
Lost Documents 200-9957
Property Lost in Metro 222-2085
Moscow Addresses 943-5001
Finding Your Way Around Moscow 927-0001
Theater Repertoire 975-9122
Moscow Weather 975-9133
Weather in World's Capitals 975-9111

International Telephone Calls

Weekend and nightly telephone calls to North America from the Central Telegraph Office now cost about the same as they would if you called from an apartment, with a 3-minute minimum, but you may have to wait for your connection longer than you want.

Many Western-style Moscow hotels and other establishments catering to foreigners have direct-dial telephone booths where you can call North America on your credit card, but the rates can go as high as $25 per minute in prime time.

At your hotel, find out the cost of your overseas telephone calls before you make them or you may require shock therapy on checking out; your calls could in some circumstances cost even more than your room.

We suggest that you dial all overseas calls yourself directly from a private phone if you can and preferably after 8pm, or on weekends, because it is the least expensive way.

To call the US, for instance, you first dial 8 and wait for the dial tone, then dial 10, then 1, which is the US country code, and finally the area code and the number. Do not get discouraged if the line is busy, eventually you will get through.

To reach an English-speaking international operator from your apartment, dialing **8** and wait for a dial tone, then dial **194** or **196** and wait for the answer. It may take a while because these numbers are often busy.

When you call a Moscow telephone number from the US, dial 011 first to dial overseas directly, then the number 7, which is the country code for Russia. Moscow's telephone code is 095, which you dial next, and finally the 7-digit telephone number. You can now call collect from Russia, but it will take some explaining.

If you call within Russia, do not forget the proper city code before the telephone number. The total must always add to ten digits.

CELLULAR PHONES

If a telephone in your bag and the ability to call worldwide at any time are the only way to make you feel secure in Moscow, consider renting a cellular phone. Two companies you should consider are listed below.

For less than $100 a week both companies will provide you with a cellular phone, extra battery, overnight charger, and a personalized number. Actual calls are additional. Ask as many questions as possible before renting because the extras can add up quickly. You can start using the phone or receiving calls the moment you land at Sheremetyevo International Airport and it will probably cost you less than if you made such calls from your hotel. Your drivers license and credit card are all you need to receive the package in the mail before you leave home. (Your US cellular phone will not work overseas.)

• WorldCell International Service, 4340 East-West Highway, Suite 1020, Bethesda, Maryland, 20814, Tel. 888/967-5323 or 301/652-2075, Fax 301/652-2732

• Worldwide Cellular, Inc., 10777 Northwest Freeway #560, Houston, Texas, 77092, Tel. 800/938-0282 or 713/681-0282, Fax 713/681-0211

Telegrams

Telegrams are a favorite way for Russians to reach each other quickly when they do not know the person's telephone number or the person they want to contact does not have one. You can send a telegram from any post office anywhere in Russia. Faxes and telexes are often the preferred ways of communication among businesses because the mail is unreliable.

To send a telegram abroad, go to the Central Telegraph Office, *7 Ulitsa Tverskaya*, or the International Post Office, *37 Varshavskoye shosse*, Metro Nagatinskaya, which is south of the Kremlin and outside the Garden Ring Road.

Faxing
Faxing services and most other office services are available in many large hotels, as well as specialized service providers, such as **AlphaGraphics**, *53 Leningradsky prospekt, Tel. 258-7500, Fax 258-7501*, Metro Aeroport, northwest of the Kremlin and outside the Garden Ring Road. AlphaGraphics is next door to MicroAge computer store. They are open Monday through Friday, from 9am to 9pm, Saturdays from 9am to 6pm.

TIME
Russia has 11 time zones. Moscow is 8 hours ahead of New York City and Toronto.

Noon in Moscow is 1pm in Tbilisi, Georgia; 2pm in Sverdlovks; 3pm in Tashkent, Uzbekistan; 4pm in Novosibirsk; 5pm in Singapore; 6pm in Tokyo; 7pm in Vladivostok; 8pm in New Caledonia; 9pm in Wellington, New Zealand; 10pm in American Samoa; 11pm in Honolulu; midnight in Anchorage, Alaska; 1am in Los Angeles; 2am in Denver; 3am in Dallas; 4am in New York; 5am in Halifax, Canada; 6am in Rio de Janeiro; 8am in Azores; 9am in London; 10am in Paris; and 11am in Helsinki.

Russian daylight savings time begins at 2am on the last Sunday in March, when clocks are moved up one hour, and it ends at 3am on the last Sunday in September, when they are turned back.

Russians, like most Europeans, operate on the 24-hour clock. The numbers 0001 to 1200 indicate the time from one minute after midnight through noon. From 1201 to 2400 means one minute after noon through midnight. Thus 08:30 is 8:30 in the morning and 13:15 is 1:15 in the afternoon.

TIPPING
Gone are the days when tipping was considered a degrading, as well as an illegal Western relic (although it continued discretely). Tipping then was officially regarded as a "vestige of capitalistic degeneracy."

Only in 1988 did the Trade Ministry begin to allow certain restaurants to take an additional five percent of the bill for quality service. The money would then be divided up throughout the restaurant.

The tipping protocol in Russia is still unclear and, apart from some restaurants which gleefully tack on gratuity charges, there are no clear-cut rules. There are only so many ways to tell your waitress that you appreciated her courtesy and service and tipping her accordingly could be one of them. We say "could be" because not all Russian waiters are driven by greed, even in this economic climate. They, however, increasingly depend on tips and some say that almost a quarter of their income comes from the money left **na chay**, which literally means tea money.

When you like the service, show your appreciation by tipping 10 to 15 percent, depending on the quality and speed of it.

Australians, New Zealanders and to some extent the Irish, where tipping is not customary or confined to taxi drivers and porters, will have no problem recognizing the instances where a Russian does not care for a tip. Americans may sometimes have difficulty understanding this.

If you pay with a credit card, do not write your tip on the credit card slip because your waiter will not receive the money. Leave cash instead.

WATER & AIR

Water

You will hear the most fantastic stories about **Moscow** water and likely be advised to brush your teeth with mineral water.

Moscow water comes from reservoirs outside the city, not from the polluted Moskva River, but you should still exercise caution and drink as little as possible or none of it. When the snow melts in the spring, it could contaminate the water supply. Muscovites themselves will suggest that you boil all drinking water for ten to fifteen minutes if you live in an apartment.

But brushing your teeth with mineral water! Let's be realistic, even if you inadvertently swallowed a gulp or two of tap water, we doubt there would be any consequences. Common sense should be your best guide: drink juices, tea, soft drinks or boiled water, but lose no sleep over brushing your teeth with tap water.

The situation is more serious with the water in **St. Petersburg**, where a parasite called **giardia** infests the water system and can cause upset stomach and diarrhea. To eradicate it, you would need the prescription drug **Flagyl** (metronidazole).

Air

The level of air pollution, as measured by the amounts of nitrogen dioxide in the air, often exceeds the norm between five and 15 times, according to federal environmental monitors. Exposure to high nitrogen dioxide concentration weakens the defense mechanism of the lungs against influenza viruses, causing sore throats, coughs and colds. A large egg-shaped area starting immediately south of the Kremlin contains up to five times officially accepted level of nitrogen dioxide. Far northeast and far northwest Moscow have the cleanest air.

The major polluters of Moscow air are the high auto emissions from almost two million cars, which are responsible for 87 percent of all the city's pollution. The number of cars doubles every three years, according to the Moscow ecological center, and in 1996 the city already had as many cars on its streets as it had expected to have by the year 2000.

Auto emissions and excessive amounts of chloride, to control the snow and ice on city streets, have damaged many trees, even those that survived the Bolshevist regime, since perestroika. Up to ten percent of Moscow trees are presumed dead and another 50 percent are diagnosed as sick.

Dust and grime seem to cover every outdoor surface in Moscow. Wash your hands every time you use a toilet and never use the reusable towels in public rest rooms.

WEIGHTS & MEASURES

Russians use the metric system, so lengths are measured in cenitmeters and meters, distances are measured in kilometers and weight is measured in grams and liters.

Measurement conversion factors: To change from one measurement to another, **multiply** by the factor shown:

acres to hectares: by **.4047**
acres to square feet: by **43,560**
centimeters to inches: by **.3937**
centimeters to feet: by **.03281**
feet to meters: by **.3048**
gallons to liters: by **3.7853**
grams to ounces: by **.0353**
grams to pounds: by **.002205**

hectares to acres: by **2.4710**
inches to centimeters: by **2.5400**
inches to millimeters: by **25.4000**

kilograms to pounds: by **2.2046**

kilometers to miles: by **.6214**

meters to yards: by **1.0936**
miles to kilometers: by **1.6093**
miles to feet: by **5280**
millimeters to inches: by **.0394**
ounces to pounds: by **.0625**
pints to liters: by **.4732**
pounds to kilograms: by **.3782**
pounds avdp to kilograms: by **.4536**
pounds to ounces: by **16**
quarts to liters: by **.9463**
square feet to square meters: by **.0929**
square kilometers to square miles: **.3861**
square meters to square feet: by **10.7639**

liters to U.S. gallons: by **.2642**

liters to pints: by **2.1134**

liters to quarts: by **1.0567**

meters to feet: by **3.2808**

meters to miles: by **.0006214**

square meters to square yards: by **1.1960**

square miles to square kms.: by **2.5900**

square yards to square meters: by **.8361**

yards to meters: by **.9144**

yards to miles: by **.0005682**

WOMEN'S CONCERNS

As you probably already know from visiting other European countries, men are different in each one, from Portugal to Norway. Russian men seem more compliant than most in Europe and it is not very likely that a male stranger will proposition you unless drunk. Russian women say that when one does, you should tell him firmly, or imply so with a decisive gesture, that you are not interested and he will probably go away.

Moscow has a surplus of single and divorced women, so a man would not be surprised by such a reaction. Revealing clothes have similar implications as in most other countries, so if you do not want male attention your clothing can make a difference. Prolonged eye contact means the same thing as at home.

Tens of thousands of Western men are falling in love with and marrying Russian women; see the *Romance* section in this chapter about this phenomenon. Although it seldom happens the other way around, there is always a chance that a Muscovite will find you irresistible and will start a conversation. Do not immediately assume the worst, even if the men approaching you may do so differently than at home.

Going to a restaurant alone, you may be seated at the best or the worst table and you may never know why. It is highly unusual to see a Russian woman in a restaurant alone, even in Moscow, but you will see groups of three or four together and nobody thinks anything of it. Women, Russian women, are sometimes harassed if they go to a restaurant alone because it is assumed that they are looking for company - and more. A Russian woman almost never goes out alone at night, whether to a restaurant or bar, because if she does other people (men and the women they accompany) will be quick in their negative judgement.

Unlike at home, where leaving an establishment makes a statement that you do not appreciate being treated in a certain manner, in Moscow your hasty departure from a restaurant because of bad service will have no effect whatsoever on anyone, except your empty stomach. However, before you judge the whole country as misogynistic, remember that you do not have to be a woman to be treated rudely in Russia.

Except in special circumstances, women are not expected to pay the bill in a restaurant or drinking establishment when men are present. For you to insist would reflect unfavorably on you. In the interest of **safety**, avoid traveling late at night if you can and when you must, avoid being alone in a taxi. If you have to use public transport, we suggest the metro. You would be a statistical aberration if you were bothered on the metro, even in the late evening, except for an occasional drunkard. If things get out of hand, bystanders are much more likely to intervene on your behalf then in the West.

Traveling light will also make you less vulnerable. Other suggestions you might consider to avoid being molested or robbed: Do not wear flashy jewelry that calls attention to your assumed affluence. In Moscow, even an accessory may single you out in generally drab surroundings. If at all possible, keep away from dark or deserted streets, whether during the day or at night. Whether in Moscow or Milan, it is better to turn back halfway down a dark alley that suddenly appears too dangerous than taking your chances. Hold your purse under your arms or inside your coat if you fear an unpleasant encounter. You should take the same precautions in Moscow as you would in Chicago, Liverpool, or Houston.

For fear of sounding ridiculous, we would like to suggest that if you are mugged, try to stay as calm as you can. Do not argue with your assailant and hand over the money if it is clear that's what he wants. Try to commit to memory anything you can about his appearance and clothing. As soon as the ordeal is over, go to the nearest Western hotel or a place where foreigners gather and ask for assistance to report the attack.

Some women supposedly claim to have had success in carrying two wallets. In the event they are robbed, they can hand over the one with a handful of $1 bills and some worthless documents and expired cards, perhaps even a couple of travelers checks because those can be replaced. We think that these ploys are hatched by clever travel writers to appear original and sell their books, but if you think it will work for you, then it's worth trying.

If you take basic precautions, as you should everywhere in the world, your chances of being molested or robbed are quite small. Moscow is a lot safer than you think.

While still in the US, you can call the State Department's **Overseas Citizens Service**, *Tel. 202/647-5225*, for more information about current health conditions and travel safety. See also Crime, Health, and other sections in this chapter. In Canada, call the **Department of External Affairs**, *Tel. 613/992-3705* in Ottawa, for similar information.

9. CHILD'S PLAY

The younger the child you are traveling with, the more planning it will take on your part. Be particularly thoughtful if traveling with a baby; consider feeding times and unexpected changes of diapers. Make sure you have a pacifier or a bottle available on take-off and landing to relieve the pressure that will build up in your baby's ears if he or she does not keep swallowing.

Children two years of age through 12 generally receive at least a 50 percent discount from the regular full fare that you might pay on most international flights. If your child is under two years of age, you may pay as little as ten percent of your air fare.

If the children that will accompany you are of school age, keep them busy even before you set foot on Russian soil. Give them research assignments on Russian culture, food, geography, climate and sports. Have them read Russian literature that is appropriate for their age and read newspaper articles about various facets of Russian life with them. Be sure to bring books and toys to keep them entertained on the long flights to and from Moscow.

Watch video tapes on Moscow that explain Russian culture and history. Buy Russian language cassette tapes and have them teach you how to pronounce words and everyday phrases. The more involved they get, the less surprised, or even disappointed, will they be by the lack of gadgets, mindless cartoons, and video games in Moscow. The city has but a fraction of the entertainment that even preschool Western children take for granted, and it is a tall order to keep them entertained in Moscow.

One of the major problems with Western children in Moscow is their sophistication. A ten year old American child will likely seek out entertainment that in Russia is meant for a much older kid. Consider this when selecting your son's or daughter's diversions.

The venues below are grouped by subject and then listed in ascending distance from central Moscow. Always call ahead to make sure the place is open and what you hoped for.

THE CIRCUS & ANIMAL THEATERS

The circus is an institution that will always enchant your kids with acrobats, clowns, tigers, bicycling bears and trapeze acts, and there are two circus companies in Moscow. They are different, and both are worth visiting. The New Circus, however, has more modern shows and more varied programs, such as a skating show or show in a swimming pool. During the summer, there is often a smaller circus in Gorky Park. You can buy tickets at kiosks throughout the city, at your hotel, or through Intourist.

OLD MOSCOW CIRCUS, *13 Tsvetnoy bulvar, south of the metro station Tsvetnoy bulvar. Tel. 200-6889 or 165-7227. Performances are held daily at 3pm and 7pm, except Tuesdays; also Saturdays at 3pm and 7pm, Sundays at 11:30am, 3pm and 7pm.*

The Old Moscow Circus is located north of the Kremlin, between the Boulevard and Garden Ring Roads. It's the smaller of the two circuses and features animals, acrobats and clowns who entertain by jumping into the audience. The Old Circus was built during the 1880's by a Russian entrepreneur and rebuilt by Finns almost a hundred years later.

NEW MOSCOW CIRCUS, *7 Prospekt Vernadskogo, metro station Universitet. Tel. 930-2815. Performances are held daily at 7pm, except Mondays and Tuesdays; also Saturdays and Sundays at 11:30am, 3pm and 7pm.*

The larger New Moscow Circus is located southwest of the Kremlin, outside the Garden Ring Road, and close to the Children's Musical Theater (see later in this chapter). The Great Moscow Circus features five interchangeable arenas and more than 1,000 artists.

DUROV ANIMAL THEATER, *4 Ulitsa Durova at Ulitsa Delegatskaya, Metro Prospekt Mira. Tel. 971-2785 or 281-2914. Performances are held Wednesday through Friday at 5pm, Saturdays and Sundays at noon, 3pm and 5:30pm. Admission for children up to three years of age is free. Durov is closed from the beginning of June to mid-September.*

The Durov Animal Theater is about four long blocks northeast of the Obraztsov Puppet Theater (see this chapter) and just as far west from Mira Avenue. The shows are mostly for younger children, and were created by the Durov dynasty of trainers. The actors are the animals, and the show combines elements of the circus and the theater. Before and after the show, children can ride the camels, horses and ponies.

The prestigious but impoverished Durov Circus had to let go many of its long-time workers. A well-known animal trainer who had worked for the circus for 30 years now trains laboratory rats to race for the enjoyment of members of the Grand Dinamo private social club, where an annual membership costs upwards of $3,000.

KUKLACHEV CAT THEATER, *25 Kutuzovsky prospekt, Metro Studencheskaya or Kutuzovskaya. Tel. 249-2907. Shows begin Wednesday through Friday at 4pm, Saturdays and Sundays at 11am and 1:30pm. Closed Mondays and Tuesdays.*

This theater is situated west of the Kremlin and outside the Garden Ring Road. The cat trainer Yuri Kuklachev keeps youngsters spellbound with his trained cats and comic routine.

MUSEUMS

ZOOLOGICAL MUSEUM, *Moscow State University, 6 Ulitsa Bolshaya Nikitskaya, Metro Okhotny Ryad. Tel. 203-3569 or 8923. Open daily Tuesday through Sunday, from 10am to 5pm; closed Mondays and last Tuesday of the month.*

This museum is centrally located inside the Boulevard Ring Road, two blocks southeast of the Moscow Conservatory. This is an indoor museum that may be of interest to children of all ages. It exhibits the earth's plant and animal life at different stages of development. In addition to a mammoth skeleton and stuffed bison and bears, it displays more than 10,000 species of animals, birds, fish and insects.

MUSEUM OF SPORT, *located in the eastern wing of the Lenin Stadium in Luzhniki, Metro Sportivnaya. Tel. 201-0747. Open daily from 10am to 6pm, but closed Mondays.*

The Museum of Sport is situated southwest of the Kremlin and outside the Garden Ring Road.

This is the largest sports museum in Russia and documents the development of physical education and sports in the former Soviet Union. On display are medals from Olympic Games and other prizes won by Soviet and Russian athletes at the world and European championships.

DARWIN MUSEUM, *57 Ulitsa Vavilova, Metro Akademicheskaya. Tel. 135-3382. Open daily from 10am to 6pm, but closed Mondays and the last Friday of the month.*

The Darwin Museum is southwest of Kremlin and outside the Garden Ring Road.

The only connection between the Darwin Museum and Charles Darwin are five letters written by the evolutionist and held by the museum. Opened in 1922 by a biology professor, the museum moved to this modern complex (which took 20 year to build) in 1995. It displays sculptures of animals, such as a giant prehistoric sloth in white plaster that dominates the main hall, as well as stuffed originals. To most it will look more like a natural history museum than a museum on evolution. The three-level Darwin Museum does not have much that you have not already seen at some museum back home and all explanatory text is in Russian.

However, there is a rare 19th century edition of *The Birds of North America* by the American ornithologist James Audubon on display and valued at $1 million. It was appropriated by the Bolsheviks from a private collector after the Revolution.

PALEONTOLOGICAL MUSEUM, *123 Ulitsa Profsoyuznaya at Sanatornaya alleya, Metro Teply stan. Tel. 339-1500. Open daily from 10am to 5pm, but closed Mondays and Tuesdays.*

This museum is in far southwest Moscow. It features dinosaurs, cavemen, mummies, skeletons, and stuffed animals.

POLYTECHNICAL MUSEUM, *3/4 Novaya ploshchad, metro Kitay-gorod or Lubyanka. Tel. 923-0756 or 925-0614, Fax 925-1290. Open daily from 10am to 5:30pm, closed Mondays and last Thursday of the month. Small admission fee.*

This centrally-located museum, northeast of the Kremlin, is best for older children interested in old cars, motorcycles, bicycles, typewriters, cameras, watches and other mechanisms. For more details, see the musuem listing in Chapter 13, *Seeing the Sights.*

PARKS & GARDENS

Muscovites love their parks and few things in post-Communist Russia give them more pleasure than relaxing in a park with friends, relatives or their favorite newspaper. The many couples seated on the benches, often oblivious to everyone except their favorite person next to them, will remind you a little of Paris. At a time of severe housing shortages and lack of privacy at home, these parks provide a valuable substitute.

There are two types of parks in and around Moscow: "parks of culture and rest," which usually have sports fields, playgrounds and cafes, and **lesoparks,** which are woodland preserves with trails for walking, horseback riding and cross-country skiing. The most popular among some 100 Moscow parks and gardens are:

ERMITAZH GARDEN, *Karetny Ryad, metro Chekhovskaya or Pushkinskaya. Open from May to September, from 10am to 11pm.*

Located north of the Kremlin, between the Boulevard and Garden Ring Roads. This small park in the center of Moscow has been popular since the 1890's. From the 18th century on, many French settled in this district and, according to playwright Griboyedov, more French was spoken here than Russian. During the summer there are concerts and puppet theater performances. It has several restaurants and cafes.

GORKY PARK, *Krymsky val, Metro Oktyabrskaya. Open from 10am to 5pm weekdays, and 10am to 11pm on weekends.*

Located southwest of the Kremlin, bordering on the Garden Ring Road. This is a large and perhaps the most popular Moscow park, made famous the world over by Martin Cruz Smith's novel of the same name.

It was named after the socialist writer Maksim Gorky, when he died in 1936. The 593-acre facility stretches for four miles along the right bank of Moskva River. Once a showpiece for the Soviet Union's support of athletics and cheap family amusements, the Gorky Central Park of Culture and Recreation began to decay in the 1980's and has acquired reputation as seedy, overpriced and unsafe.

Near the main entrance on Krymsky val, across the street from the **Central House of Artists** (see Art Galleries in Chapter 14, *Culture*), workers tend to green lawns, but deeper into the park, the grass becomes scraggly, waist-high weeds take over flower beds and the park's white swans share the reed-choked Golitsyn Pond with soft drink cans. A few collapsing buildings will further mar your joy.

The park's backwoods of hidden meadows and overgrown stone bridges, known as Neskuchny Sad, boasted classical French parks and a botanical garden in the 17th century, when it belonged to the Trubetskoy, Golitsyn and Demidov estates. The main part of the park was home to mineral spas and a race track before becoming the Park of Culture in 1928. **Lunapark**, a Russian-Italian complex of used Italian children's rides, charges kids exorbitant rates for its floating inner tubes, shabby carousels, miniature steam engine, and Chamber of Horrors. The newest attraction at Gorky Park is an authentic Russian space shuttle, the Buran, on which you can experience a simulated flight in the cosmos.

The park also has the open-air Green Theater, which seats several thousand, a shooting gallery, tennis courts, a chess club, and several cafes. Sometimes rock music is blaringly loud at Gorky. In the summer, you can take boat excursions along the Moskva River, in the winter the ponds of Gorky Park are usually solid enough for you to skate.

SOKOLNIKI PARK, *Metro Sokolniki. Open from 10am to 11pm.*

Located northeast of the Kremlin and outside the Garden Ring Road. This 1,530-acre park, named after the **sokolniki** (falconers) who attended the tsar's hunting parties, is twice as large as Gorky Park. The park, which dates from the 1840's, is laid out with seven pathways radiating from a central circle. It is the site of many fairs. The rock music that you might hear from loudspeakers at the gates of Sokolniki will remind you that this park is for those who prefer noise over solitude. Saturdays and Sundays there is ballroom dancing on an outdoor veranda after 3pm.

Sokolniki gained fame in the summer of 1959 as the site of the American National Exhibition, where Richard Nixon and Nikita Khrushchev had their famous kitchen debate. Since then, large exhibitions have been organized here and they can be noisy.

There is an open-air theater accommodating 5,000, an amusement park with carnival rides, a bicycle-rental facility, cafes and shish kebab stands. In the winter you can skate and cross-country ski.

IZMAYLOVSKY PARK, *Metro Izmaylovskaya. Open from 10am to 11pm.*
Located northeast of the Kremlin and quite a way outside the Garden Ring Road. Once a summer residence and hunting reserve of the Romanov family from the mid-16th century, this park stretches over 2,950 acres and includes large stretches of pine forests. There are plenty of winding pathways for hiking and tables for picnicking. In the summer, children will enjoy the Serebryanka River flowing through the park, in the winter there are sledding hills and cross-country skiing trails.

Tsar Aleksey established a farm here in 1663, complete with a zoo, where the metro station stands today. Izmaylovo is also said to be the birthplace of the Russian navy; in his childhood, Peter the Great found an old boat on the estate and supposedly cultivated his interest in what later became the Russian fleet. An 8-acre section of Izmaylovo, named **Mir Skazok**, has been built for children.

Between the Izmaylovo tourist complex and the Sports stadium, you will find **Vernisazh**, Moscow's largest outdoor market, where on Saturdays and Sundays everything from matryoshka dolls to fake icons can be found, usually overpriced.

BOTANICAL GARDENS, *Metro Botanichesky sad or VDNkH. Open from 9am to 5pm, and in winter from 10am to 4pm.*
Located north of the Kremlin and outside the Garden Ring Road. The Gardens, founded in 1945, are spread over 890 acres and lie just north of the Russian Exhibition Center.

There are more than 1,700 kinds of trees and shrubs planted in the 185-acre dendrarium. There is also a large rose-garden containing some 16,000 roses of more than a thousand varieties. One section displays 3,000 native Russian plants, going all the way to Vladivostok.

Additional Parks

A much smaller botanical garden, belonging to Moscow University, is located northeast of the Kremlin, just north of the Garden Ring Road, at Mira Avenue, Metro Prospekt Mira. It was founded back in 1706.

Other large parks include **Frunze Central Army Park**, north of the Kremlin, where the Armed Forces Museum and Russian Army Theater are located; **Krasnaya Presnya Park**, in far west Moscow, where the World Trade Center and Mezh Hotel are located; and **Tsaritsyno Park** (please see Chapter 18, *Excursions & Day Trips*) in far southern Moscow.

For more about **Aleksandrovsky sad** (Alexander's Park), at the foot of the Kremlin, see Chapter 13, *Seeing the Sights.*

RESTAURANTS & CLUBS

Before getting into the details about diversions of interest to children, here are four restaurants that offer special meals for kids and have a children's menu. For more details please see Chapter 12, *Where to Eat*. Unfortunately all these restaurants are somewhat expensive and far from central Moscow.

The all-day restaurant **Vienna**, *Renaissance Moscow Hotel, 18/1 Olimpiysky prospekt, Metro Prospekt Mira*, serves a breakfast, lunch and dinner buffet, has a children's menu and kids eat at a discount.

Santa Fe, *near the Mezh Hotel, 5/1 Ulitsa Mantulinskaya, Building 6, Metro Ulitsa 1905 goda*, serves Sunday brunch from noon to 5pm and includes free dinners for children under six years of age.

Cafe Taiga, *at the luxurious Hotel Aerostar, 37 Leningradsky prospekt, Bldg. 9, Metro Dinamo or Aeroport*, has a children's menu featuring chicken fingers, burgers and hot dogs, all with fries. One of the few restaurants where high chairs for children are readily available.

The expensive **Le Cafe Francais**, *Sofitel Iris Hotel, 10 Korovinskoye shosse, Metro Petrovsko-Razumovskaya*, also serves children's meals for kids under 12.

Clubs

ARLEKINO CHILDREN'S CLUB, *19/3 Ulitsa Verkhnyaya Radishchevskaya, Bldg. 1, metro Taganskaya. Tel. 915-1106 or 9907. Open daily from 11am to 7pm.*

Located on the Garden Ring Road and southeast of the Kremlin. This club is a special treat for children from three to about ten years of age. They can use Arlekino's playrooms for as long as they wish, be entertained by clowns, magicians and illusionists, watch children's films or use computers. The $10 admission fee includes a buffet, a piece of cake, fruit and a drink. Champagne and other beverages are available for adults.

LIMPOPO CHILDREN'S CLUB, *10b Pervaya Vladimirskaya ulitsa, metro Shosse Entuziastov. Tel. 302-3302. Open daily from 10am to 8pm.*

Located even farther out from central Moscow, at the Prozhektor Dom Kultury (Projector Palace of Culture), east of the Kremlin and outside the Garden Ring Road. This children's club is three very long blocks east of the metro station and one block south of Entuziastov Highway. Limpomo is an American-style entertainment center for children ages one to eight.

ZEBRA CHILDREN'S CLUB, *14 Ulitsa Tallinskaya, metro Krylatskaya or Shchukinskaya, in the district of Strogino. Tel. 499-2990. Open Sundays from noon to 4pm.*

The Zebra Children's Club consists of a theater, clown shows, a variety of toys, and other entertainment.

Unfortunately, it is located much too far from either metro station to walk to, in far northwest Moscow, three very long blocks east of the Circular Road, which forms the boundaries of today's Moscow.

THEATERS

The Russian theatrical tradition is so strong that even now there are more than half a dozen children's theaters in Moscow. All of them have matinee performances. While the theaters listed below specialize in children's fare, most adult theaters, described in Chapter 14, *Culture*, also stage one or two children's plays every season.

CENTRAL CHILDREN'S THEATER, *2/7 Teatralnaya ploshchad, Metro Teatralnaya or Okhotny Ryad. Tel. 292-0069.*

Centrally located north of the Kremlin and directly across the street from the Maly Theater.

This is one of four major children's theaters in Moscow. It was founded in 1921 and is the second oldest children's theater in Russia. Before the Revolution, no such theater existed. According to historians, attempts to create a children's theater continuously failed. At first it staged only fairy tales, but later graduated to Russian classics, as well as Mark Twain, Victor Hugo, Shakespeare and even William Faulkner. Most of its plays are for kids ages 7 to 16 years.

YOUNG SPECTATORS THEATER, *10 Mamonovsky pereulok, Metro Tverskaya or Mayakovskaya. Tel. 299-5360 or 9917.*

Located northwest of the Kremlin, between the Boulevard and Garden Ring Roads, a couple of blocks northwest of Pushkin Square, and behind the Museum of the Revolution on Tverskaya Street.

First known as the Moscow Children's Theater, it has been in existence since 1927. It differs from other children's theaters in that it admits mostly school children ages 7 through 13. This theater is also distinct in its staging; it involves the spectators, who never know when they will become actors, and actors who turn into spectators. The theater's repertoire includes the plays by Jules Verne, Mark Twain, Lillian Hellman, Hans Christian Andersen, Alexander Dumas, and even episodes from Dostoyevsky's *Crime and Punishment.*

OBRAZTSOV PUPPET THEATER, *3 Ulitsa Sadovaya-Samotechnaya, Metro Tsvetnoy bulvar. Tel. 299-3310 or 6313. Afternoon performances at various times for children only; evening performances are held at 7pm.*

Located north of the Kremlin, on the Garden Ring Road, and northeast of the Hermitage Gardens.

Russian puppetry dates back to the Middle Ages, when performers belonged to the manors of the feudal nobility. By 1700, puppetry in Moscow was a tradition fortified by many foreign puppeteers.

This theater dates from 1931 and it is named after its founder Sergey Obraztsov, who became its director in 1945. Puppetry is a popular form of artistic expression in Russia and the Obraztsov is a troupe known worldwide. Even though Obraztsov died in 1993, a staff of more than one hundred continues drawing on a repertory of some 40 plays. This is a favorite theater of Russian children. Take your kids whether they understand Russian or not, they will have fun.

Although it is primarily a children's theater, some of its plays, such as *Don Juan*, are staged for adults. During these performances only, children under 18 will not be admitted. It also has a mechanical cuckoo clock, in front of the building, which is a popular tourist attraction.

In the foyer, you will see a showcase displaying hundreds of puppets and masks collected by the company in some 50 countries where they performed.

The puppet plays shown here include Pushkin's *A Tale about Tsar Saltan*, Gernet's *The Magic Lamp of Aladdin*, as well as *Hercules* and *Pinocchio*. It also shows Obraztsov's own, *An Unusual Concert* and *Noah's Ark*, a puppet version of the biblical story.

Since 1994, NTV, Moscow's Channel 4, uses actors and puppeteers from the Obraztsov Theater in Russia's first televised weekly political satire, *Kukly* (Puppets), to poke fun at Russian government officials with life-size puppets.

BALAGAN THEATER, *Russian Exhibition Center, Prospekt Mira at metro VDNkH. Tel. 426-6562.*

The Balagan Theater has puppet shows Saturdays and Sundays, starting at noon and then every 30 minutes. Three popular shows are *Morning on the Planet of Monsters*, *King Herod*, and *Macbeth*.

CHILDREN'S MUSICAL THEATER, *5 Prospekt Vernadskogo, Metro Universitet. Tel. 930-7021 or 6364.*

Located southwest of the Kremlin, outside the Garden Ring Road, and close to the New Circus, near Sparrow Hills.

One of Moscow's four children's theaters, Children's Musical Theater was originally located in the former Nezlobin Theater, near the Bolshoy Theater. It reopened at this location in 1979 to educate children between 10 and 16 years of age about the theater. Before each play the actors come to the foyer to talk to the children about the play they are about to see. Bring yours and let them examine the bird atrium on the second floor.

Composer Sergey Prokofiev collaborated on his symphonic fairy tale for children, *Peter and the Wolf* (Opus 67) here. He was fascinated by children's theaters and knew the Children's Musical Theater because he brought his three children to the theater a year earlier. "We must start with something full of contrasts, something that makes a strong impression," he told the theater director. "The most important thing is to find a common language with the kids." They created a story involving animals and at least one human character; each animal is personified by a different instrument of the orchestra, and the human character by the more complex string ensemble. The orchestration was finished one day after Prokofiev's 45th birthday.

At its first impromptu performance for a group of children at the theater, with Prokofiev at the piano, *Peter and the Wolf* was an immediate success, and became one of the most popular children's classics in many languages.

The theater's repertoire also includes *Winnie the Pooh*, an innovative interpretation of the Shakespearian tragedy *King Lear* and Mozart's opera *The Magic Flute*.

TOYS, CLOTHING, & ACCESSORIES

Looking for children's toys, clothing or accessories? Except for Children's World downtown, they are hard to find and prices are uniformly high. Try one of these stores, which, again, are listed in order of ascending distance from central Moscow:

DETSKY MIR (Children's World), *5 Teatralny proyezd, Metro Lubyanka, Tel. 927-2007.*

Centrally located inside the Boulevard Ring Road and across Lubyanka Square from the former KGB headquarters. This former Soviet toy and clothing store dinosaur is changing and trying to make it in the competitive free market. There are five well-stocked departments on the second floor, including Barbie and Lego salons.

GOETZ, *1 Ulitsa Solyanka, Bldg. 2, Metro Kitay-gorod, Tel. 921-6820.*

Centrally located east of the Kremlin and inside the Boulevard Ring Road. A high-quality store tucked into a quiet side street, it has a good selection of dolls, Fisher-Price products, Playmobile figures, and Lego blocks. On the upper level, you will find a good selection of infant and children's clothing.

MOTHERCARE, *Valdai Center on Novy Arbat, Metro Arbatskaya, Tel. 291-7185.*

Located just a few steps from the Arbat Irish House, west of the Kremlin, between the Boulevard and Garden Ring Roads. This is a branch of a British franchise offering the latest in baby technology and it is very expensive. Their second location is at *83 Leninsky prospekt, Metro Universitet,* southwest of the Kremlin and outside the Garden Ring Road.

DOM IGRUSHKY (House of Toys), *26 Ulitsa Bolshaya Yakimanka, Metro Polyanka, Tel. 238-0096.*

Situated south of the Kremlin and inside the Garden Ring Road. One of the best toy stores in Moscow, Dom Igrushky is located on the second floor of a large brick building near the President Hotel. It has separate departments for infant accessories, dolls and stuffed animals, battery-operated toys, as well as cars and trucks.

BARBIE, *97/1 Prospekt Mira, Metro Alekseyevskaya, Tel. 216-6775.*

Located northeast of the Kremlin and outside the Garden Ring Road. This store has a good selection of Barbie dolls and accessories from Mattel, but is not a Mattel store.

WINTER ACTIVITIES

If you find yourself in Moscow during the winter, take your kids sledding in **Kolomenskoye Park**, Metro Kolomenskaya, outside the Garden Ring Road and southeast of the Kremlin. You and your children can do the same on **Sparrow Hills**, on the other side of Luzhniki Stadium, Metro Sportivnaya, southwest of the Kremlin and outside the Garden Ring Road.

Skating or hockey for children older than seven years is available at **Luzhniki Northern Lights**, *24 Luzhnetskaya nab., Metro Sportivnaya, Tel. 201-0218.* You can rent skates, and there is a cloakroom, first aid station and a cafe. It is open from 5pm to 9pm daily, except Mondays.

Sokolniki Park, *16 Sokolnichesky val, Metro Sokolniki,* has natural and artificial ice skating, available from 10am to 7pm, at hourly rates that are reasonable.

You can also take your children skating in **Gorky Park**, *9 Krymsky val, Metro Park Kultury or Oktyabrskaya, Tel. 237-1266,* southwest of the Kremlin and just outside the Garden Ring Road. There are cloakrooms available, a first aid station and a cafe. The hours of operation are from 10am to 10pm daily, except Mondays, 5 to 10pm, and you can rent skates.

There are several other outdoor skating rinks as well, where children can also play hockey. **Dinamo Rink**, *36 Leningradsky prospekt, Metro Dinamo,* northwest of Kremlin and outside the Garden Ring Road, is just one, but we recommend that you come during the day because in the evening adults play hockey here.

Finally, there is the **AZLK Ice Palace**, *46/15 Volgogradsky prospekt, Metro Tekstilshchiki,* southeast of the Kremlin and outside the Garden Ring Road. It is open from 7am to 8pm.

You and your kids can even go skiing in Moscow during the winter. Among several parks where skiing is enjoyable are **Sokolniki Park**, **Izmaylovsky Park**, and **Gorky Park**, all three outside Garden Ring Road.

ZOO

MOSCOW ZOO, *1 Ulitsa Bolshaya Gruzinskaya, Metro Krasnopres-nenskaya or Barrikadnaya. Tel. 255-5375 or 252-3580. Open daily, except Mondays, from 10am to 6pm, between May and September.*

The Moscow Zoo is located northwest of the Kremlin and outside the Garden Ring Road, and is about three blocks northwest of the American Embassy.

The pond inside is all that is visible of the Presnya River since it was forced underground in 1908.

Founded in 1864, the oldest Russian zoo began extensive reconstruction in 1992, and it will continue until the end of the century. The is the first reconstruction effort since 1919, when it was nationalized. You can already see a difference for the better, although some of the animals appear undernourished.

Fewer than one-third of the zoo's 5,000 animals are on view because of cramped conditions inherited from the Soviet era. One reason for this is that despite a 1932 expansion plan, the 50-acre zoo remained confined when neighboring houses, which were slated for destruction, were appropriated by such powerful organizations as the KGB and the Ministry of Internal Affairs. One of the playwright Anton Chekhov's targets for his sardonic derision included the "scandalously neglected Moscow Zoo," a topic which was to rankle him for a decade.

In 1996, a 60-foot-high bronze statue called the Fairy Tale Tree by renowned artist Zurab Tsereteli was erected next to the wolf lair. Atop it sits an eagle whose wingspan measures 20 feet.

OTHER ENTERTAINMENT

AQUARIUM WORLD, *22 Novinsky bulvar, Metro Barrikadnaya or Smolenskaya. Open daily from 11am to 6pm, closed Mondays.*

This aquarium is located on the Garden Ring Road, across from the American Embassy. There are more than 150 kinds of fish and turtles on display.

PLANETARIUM, *5 Ulitsa Sadovaya-Kudrinskaya, Metro Barrikadnaya or Krasnopresnenskaya. Tel. 254-0153 or 1838. Open daily from 1pm to 6pm; closed on Tuesdays.*

Moscow's planetarium is located northwest of the Kremlin and three blocks north of the American Embassy, on the Garden Ring Road. The Chekhov Museum is on the other side of Garden Ring Road.

The Planetarium was built in 1928. It highlights Soviet space missions in particular and the cosmos in general. Sophisticated devices reproduce the movements of the sun and other planets and stars, as well as solar and lunar eclipses, polar lights and comets on the planetarium's spherical ceiling.

DOLPHINARIUM (Sea Circus), *27 Ulitsa Mironovskaya, Metro Semyonovskaya, then take trolleybus #22. Tel. 369-7966. Open Wednesdays and Thursdays at 4pm and 6pm; Fridays at noon, 4pm and 6pm; Saturdays and*

Sundays at noon, 2pm, 4pm and 6pm. Children under six years of age are admitted free.

Dolphinarium opened at the Izmaylovo Dvorets Vodnogo Sporta (Palace of Water Sports) in 1994. It is situated northeast of the Kremlin and outside the Garden Ring Road.

North Sea lions, walruses, a white beluga whale, and Black Sea dolphins entertain children of all ages. This was originally an animal show performing in Argentina, Chile, Israel and the former Yugoslavia, but decided to move inland and settle in Moscow permanently.

LITTLE BEE CHILDREN'S RAILROAD, *24 miles southeast of Moscow. Open Thursdays, Fridays and Saturdays from 10am to 2pm, and Sundays from 10am to 5pm, but from June 1 to August 25 only.*

To get to the Children's Railroad by car, drive to the town of Zhukovsky through Lyubertsy and turn at the railway station in Otdikh. The Little Bee children's railroad is next to it. You can also get there in about an hour's time by train from the Kazansky Railway Station.

This miniature railroad is good for kids up to age 9. It has about 2.3 miles of track and is run by kids 11-16 years of age who work as conductors and ticket collectors. A round-trip tour takes about 40 minutes.

Miscellaneous Options

If you cannot find a baby-sitter for your preschoolers, there is always **Sesame Street**, which is shown late in the afternoon three times a week on Moscow's NTV independent television network. Big Bird in **Ulitsa Sezam** has been replaced by a doglike creature named Zeliboba, while other characters come from Russian fairy tales.

As a last resort, take your kids atop the **Ostankino Television Tower**, where they can have dessert while all of Moscow unfolds before them. They are bound to be impressed by the elevator ride. For details, see **Sedmoye Nebo** in Chapter 12, *Where to Eat.*

For older boys who never tire of weapons and seem to have an infinite curiosity about destruction, there is the **KGB Museum**, the **Museum of the Revolution**, the **Armed Forces Museum**, the **Battle of Borodino Panorama**, the **Museum of Cosmonautics**, the **Frunze Aviation & Space Museum**, and **Victory Park**. Please turn to Chapter 13, *Seeing the Sights* for more details about these museums.

Boys or girls, young or old, will enjoy a **boat cruise** on the Moskva River, which is 312 miles long and flows through the capital for 50 miles. Small ships make regularly scheduled trips on the river daily, from 9am to 9pm, between May and August. The trips last about an hour and a half, with ten stops, and are reasonably priced; children's fare is one-half the adult's. On warm days you can admire the scenery on the open deck and on cooler days you can sit in a downstairs lobby with wide windows. A convenient way to start your trip would be at the Kiev Pier, which is located on Berezhkovskaya Embankment, near the Kievsky Railway Station and Kievskaya metro. For more information call the **City Ticket Office,** *Tel. 257-7119 or 118-7811.*

If you and your kids want to swim outdoors (for indoor swimming facilities see Chapter 16, *Sports & Recreation*), probably the only safe beach in Moscow is at **Serebryany Bor Park**, northwest of the Kremlin and east of the Circular Road. The official beach area, not the surrounding islands, is clean, the water is monitored for pollution and the sand is regularly disinfected. There are lifeguards on duty and the banks are shallow enough even for young children to wade in.

To get there, follow Khoroshevskoye Highway, starting at Begovaya metro station, and continue into Prospekt Zhukova to the end.

10. FOOD & DRINK

FOOD

While Americans will do everything they can to stay away from meat and other fatty foods, most Russians want as many calories as they can get and consider meat a luxury.

In some ways, the Russian diet today is similar to that of Western Europe forty years ago. Unless you cook your meals yourself or stay with a family that will cater to your whimsy, forget the calories and your cholesterol count because it is practically impossible to follow a dietary regimen short of starving yourself. Meals in Russia mean nourishment for your body, not something to trick your body into believing it has processed more calories than it really has. If you are on a diet make prior arrangements because it is a concept alien to most Russian citizens. There are only a handful of restaurants that carry salad bars, the most popular among them being **Patio Pizza**.

Food in Russia is expensive and a pensioner can easily spend his entire month's income on a few pounds of meat. An average Russian may spend as much as one half of his or her income on food, as compared with Americans, Britons or Canadians who average less than a quarter.

More food is purchased raw in Russia than in the West and all the preparation and cooking is done in the kitchen. A meal like that obviously takes much longer to prepare than a ready-to-eat packaged meal.

A continental European breakfast, and to some extent a Russian breakfast, is typically a roll, jam, cold meats and cheese, and pastries, not ham or sausage with eggs, hash browns, toast and coffee, like in the US and other English-speaking countries. Russians also eat boiled or fried eggs and **kasha** (hot cereal), and drink tea more often than coffee.

For many central and northern Europeans and European Russians, the main meal of the day is served at midday, not in the evening, like in Italy or Spain. It often begins with an array of **zakuski** (appetizers), which include a variety of smoked fish, meat cuts, fish, and salads, followed by beet soup or chicken broth.

WHAT IS IT?

Bliny - thin, leavened pancakes; *borsch* - beetroot soup; **chay** - tea; **dolma** - meat stuffed in grape leaves; **golubtsy** - cabbage leaves stuffed with ground meat; **govyadina** - beef; **griby** - mushrooms; **ikra** - black or red caviar; **kartoshka** - potatoes; **kasha** - boiled buckwheat porridge; **khachapuri** - doughy bread with melted cheese; **khlyeb** - bread; **khinkaly** - spicy Georgian meat dumplings; **kofe** - coffee; **kotlety** - fried meat patties; **kuritsa** - chicken; **kvas** - popular Russian soft drink made from black bread and yeast; **lavash** - freshly baked thin Caucasian bread; **lobio** - spicy red or green marinated bean salad; **maslo** - butter; **morozhenoye** - ice cream; **napitok** - flavored drink; **okroshka** - cold kvas soup with chopped vegetables and meat or fish; **pelmeny** - Siberian meat-filled dumplings; **pirozhki** - stuffed doughy turnovers; **pirozhnoye** - pastry; **plov** - pilaf; **ryba** - fish; **satsivi** - chicken or turkey in walnut sauce; **sevruga** - sturgeon; **shashlik** - shish kebab; **shchy** - cabbage or sauerkraut soup; **skoblyanka** - meat with mushrooms and fried potatoes; **smetana** - sour cream, **sok** - juice; **solyanka** - spicy meat or fish soup; **sosiski** - sausages; **chicken tabaka** - Georgian-style fried chicken with garlic sauce; **telyatina** - veal; **tost** - toast; **zakuski** - hors d'oeuvres; **zharkoye** - beef stew.

Beef, fish, or chicken, all of which are beyond the means of many Russians these days, are served with potatoes, rice or noodles. Other main courses include beef Stroganoff, which is fried, then sauteed beef with mushrooms and onions, **satsivi** (chicken with walnut sauce), as well as chicken Kiev, **shashlik** (shish kebab), and **kotlety** (fried meat patties).

Salads are served and eaten with, not before, the main course, like in the US, unless they include meat, when they could be a main dish. Muscovites love ice cream; they eat about 170 tons of it a day, whether in the summer or winter. Hot dogs are called **sosiski** in Russia and hamburgers are known in Moscow mostly thanks to the mushrooming McDonald's franchises.

If you are a committed vegetarian at home, you may be disappointed by the size and quality of vegetables you will find in your average Moscow restaurant plate. Vegetables, cooked or raw, are expensive. You might think that the cucumber is Russia's national vegetable, and maybe it is, it is very popular; you will see young and old eating them, often with bread.

There are many varieties of Russian bread and unless you are addicted to the gummy supermarket mass that Americans call bread, you will appreciate the taste and texture of Russian breads. Like French baguettes, you can eat fresh Russian breads alone, without butter or anything else. Bread has a special place in Russia, treat it with respect.

Keep your hands on the table, not in your lap if you want to appear well-mannered. Most Europeans eat with the fork in their left hand, while holding the knife in their right. Many restaurants, except for the expensive restaurants, expect you to use the same knife and fork for your entire meal. Americans place their knife and fork side by side on the plate when they are finished eating, while Europeans might cross them.

There are few non-smoking sections in Moscow restaurants. If smoke from a nearby table really bothers you, ask for another table. Also, do not be surprised to see Russians smoking during their meals; you will also encounter this habit among other Europeans.

WHAT TO EAT & WHAT NOT TO EAT

Food poisoning can disable you for days. It often rears its ugly head as nausea, a severe headache, and possibly vomiting and diarrhea. Diarrhea is a serious problem for any traveler and more so if you go to Moscow than in most European capitals. Be aware that you can get it anywhere in the world, from St. Petersburg to St. Tropez. Diarrhea, in short, is the result of your ingesting bacteria or a virus that your system does not recognize. Even if you eat in all the safe places, you can come down with diarrhea.

Over-the-counter medications, such as Pepto-Bismol or Kaopectate, might alleviate most of your diarrheal problems; if it persists for more than three days, it may indicates symptoms of a more serious illness and you should seek out a doctor. Be aware that some diarrheal medications have side effects which may make your discomfort even worse. When nothing else is at hand, take a couple of aspirin, it just might do the trick. Eat bland foods with as low a fat content as you can find. Some travelers swear on bottled water with a spoonful of honey and a pinch of salt.

If you are taking them now or have done so recently, antibiotics may actually bring on an onset of diarrhea because they sometimes destroy your intestinal bacteria. When that is the cause, try yogurt, which contains acidophilus bacteria that cooperates with your digestive tract. Coffee causes diarrhea in some people so you already know whether you should avoid it at certain times.

A major problem caused by diarrhea is dehydration so irrigate your system with additional beverages, which will replenish the sodium and potassium your body needs to function properly. In Moscow, the best remedy to prevent dehydration, in addition to drinking bottled water, is to drink a lot of fruit juices or bottled carbonated water.

While Moscow's water supply is generally satisfactory, you should limit the amount of tap water you drink or, preferably, drink none at all. To be on the safe side, drink bottled water, soft drinks, tea, beer or wine.

Ice seldom comes automatically with a glass of water, or a soft drink, as it does in American restaurants, and remember that ice is usually made from the tap water you do not want to drink. Iceless drinks are the safest alternative. If bottled water is not available, but you live in an apartment, you can purify your water by boiling it for at least ten minutes, then store it in the refrigerator.

In spite of all the silly stories you might have read, you should have no problem bathing or brushing your teeth with tap water.

Milk and milk products should be somewhat suspect because you do not know whether they have been properly pasteurized, or pasteurized at all. Avoid all meats and fish that are not thoroughly cooked. When eating in a restaurant, a medium-done steak is much safer than a medium-done hamburger because the hamburger is ground processed meat that had plenty of opportunities to attract harmful bacteria inside and out, while the steak is usually one solid slab of meat.

Salads can be a gamble because you do not know whether its ingredients were properly washed. Fruits and vegetables that can be peeled are a safe alternative.

Do not buy foods from the kiosks or street vendors! The food fare sold by street vendors is rough even on native stomachs; it is bought mostly by people who come to Moscow from the interior and cannot afford to buy better quality food. The Moscow Sanitary Control Authority says that up to 98 percent of these salespeople do not have health permits to sell food. The Moscow press reports that some sellers have infectious forms of tuberculosis and other contagious diseases.

TYPES OF RESTAURANTS

No one knows how many restaurants, cafes, snack bars and cafeterias there are in Moscow, but one estimate has it at more than 8,500. Unless you are adventurous and your stomach can take it, we suggest that you stick mostly with those mentioned here.

The first foreign-owned restaurants in Moscow opened in the fall of 1987. In the following three years, nearly all served hard-currency patrons only, although most of them were well-to-do Russians. The 1987 change in the law, which allowed cooperatives to get into the restaurant business, had a major impact on Moscow restaurants and most agree that the change made vast improvements in how well you can eat today.

The reason, of course, is competition. While a restaurant you visit today may not have everything listed on the menu, be thankful; as recently as 1986, it was the other way around — there were only a couple of dishes available from the entire menu.

Restaurants in Moscow almost never display their menus and prices outside as their Parisian counterparts so proudly do. Often, state-owned restaurants are a better value, if the food is edible, because their prices are much lower than what you will pay in a Western-style eatery.

Most state restaurants have a **kniga zhalob**, or a book where you can register your complaints. Just do not be under the illusion that your griping will quickly affect the service and quality of food like it could in the West.

There are four kinds of restaurants in Moscow:

The **state-owned**, where efficiency and service have improved somewhat, although it is still only a question of time before many will turn private or go out of business. Some of them have twice as many workers as they need.

State-run eateries usually list hearty and heavy food, as well as rather bland dishes. You will find pretty much the same type and quality of food in most state restaurants, although a rare few are as good as private cooperatives. Many state-run restaurants have live music and gaudy floor shows at night.

Next are **cooperatives**, often called cafes, but in fact they are restaurants that compete for their patrons with the quality of their food and service, although their prices are out of reach for many Russians. Most cooperatives offer at least acceptable service and have friendlier staff than their state counterparts. The quality of their fare is better, more dishes are available, and their choices are more varied.

Most cooperative restaurants serve specific cuisine or have other peculiar features that distinguish them from their competitors. Usually they serve from 25 to 75 guests in two or three dining rooms. Their musicians may still play too loudly for Western taste, but when it comes to food, you often get what you pay for.

Then there are the **joint-venture** type of restaurants, which almost always meet Western standards. Until 1994, when hard currency cash was outlawed as a form of payment, they served food mostly for US dollars. They are expensive even for middle-class Westerners. These last two types are the two most changeable eating establishments. Do not be surprised if a few listed below have changed their telephone numbers or location, and a couple may even have gone out of business by the time you read this.

There is also a fourth type of restaurant, a true state-owned **cafe** type of eating place, where the quality of food and service are much lower and so are the prices. We have not listed any such cafes here.

Some restaurants may try to get you started with a tableful of **zakuski** (appetizers), sometimes automatically served when you sit down at your table. You do not have to take them, either because you think they are too expensive or too stale or just amount to altogether too much food. But speak up as soon as you come in, do not just nibble selectively or you may be charged a lot more than you anticipated. When making reservations, ask for **chisty stol** (clean table), which will free you from fretting about appetizers when you arrive.

While reservations are seldom required for lunch, we suggest that you call several hours ahead for your dinner, sometimes several days, if your time is valuable and you want to secure a table for a specific time.

It is quite common for Muscovites to eat at hotel restaurants, even if they are not staying there. We have listed many such hotel restaurants below. Others, which are average enough to mention only along with hotel descriptions, like the four at the Kosmos Hotel, are listed briefly under their hotels.

There are also some restaurants, mostly Georgian, Azeri or Uzbek, that will allow you to bring your own alcoholic beverages, a perfectly acceptable practice in Russia, as in several other European countries.

In restaurants, particularly where prices are listed in US dollars, check the cost of extras like wine, bottled water, coffee or tea because prices for these can be numbing.

No matter how confusing or unreadable your check, and particularly if you are in the company of a Russian that can help you, always verify the prices before paying. When a service charge is included, you do not owe the waiter anything more, unless you want to show your appreciation for superb food and service. Our experience, however, has been that only rarely will waiters try to cheat you, even if you do not speak a word of Russian. How long that will hold is, of course, anyone's guess.

It is more likely that you will have overlooked paying for extras, such as bread and butter with your meal, which can run as high as $3 with a meal for two. So when the waitress asks you whether you want bread, ask how much they charge for it.

DRINK

An ordinary Russian will likely out-drink many if not most Westerners. Sometimes it is best to pretend that you do not drink at all because of health reasons. If you slow down when drinking, Russians will try to speed it up by shouting "*Do dna!*" or Bottoms up!

Should you accept the challenge and drink like the Russians do, drink your shot-glass of vodka straight in one gulp and follow it quickly by eating a piece of bread to shorten the burning sensation in your throat.

Vodka

Mixed drinks are not well-known in Russia, a country where straight liquor, like vodka, reigns. Russians have been drinking their beloved

vodka - diminutive of voda (water) - since 1174. Scotch whiskey became popular in 1490. Five hundred years ago, Tsar Ivan the Terrible started a government monopoly on the production of vodka, which is basically made from rye and water. The monopoly has since been abolished and reestablished several times.

In the 1920s, the Kristall factory began to produce vodka that has since won more than 40 international awards. While you can buy Kristall vodka everywhere, the largest selection will be found at the factory store, *40 Ulitsa Volochayevskaya*, near Stroganovsky proyezd (east of the Kremlin, outside the Garden Ring Road, about four blocks northwest of the metro station Ploshchad Ilyicha, and a couple of blocks northeast of the Spaso-Andronikov monastery and Rublev's museum).

It may seem unthinkable, but it is true, Russia cannot keep up with the demand for vodka so her citizens are drinking more imports from Poland, Germany and the Czech Republic than ever before. Moscow kiosks and shops are full of inexpensive European vodkas with names such as Gorbatchov and Rasputin, even Jeltsin, which sell for $3-6 a bottle. These brands are more expensive than some Russian-made brands. The price of Russian vodka is still set by the state because it is considered a basic necessity and politicians fear the wrath of drinkers.

In recent years, almost one-half of some 30 million decaliters of vodka produced in Russia annually have been bathtub brews gussied up with

---

TRY A KVAS!

*For centuries **kvas** was second only to vodka in Russia. These days, however, it is easier to find a gold watch on the Arbat promenade than a bottle of kvas in the summer.*

Kvas, which tastes like liquid toast, is brewed the same way as beer, but uses rye instead of barley and contains little alcohol. Russians enjoy its natural flavor, spiced in more than 50 varieties with everything from horseradish to berries.

Despite a loyal following by some, kvas has become a major casualty in Moscow's cola wars. Many kiosks which once sold kvas are either closed or pushing Western soft drinks. Meanwhile the cola business is booming and Pepsi and Coca-Cola billboards are everywhere. Some hope the taste for Western sodas is just a temporary fad, but others think the future of kvas is uncertain.

When there were four kvas breweries in Moscow, the Ostankino Soft Drink Factory produced nearly a gallon (or three liters) a year per capita for Moscow's eight million residents and visitors. Now only three plants are left and the total output is down by 97 percent. Ostankino Factory, for one, makes extra money by bottling Pepsi Cola.

counterfeit labels to look like respectable brands. Chances are if you paid less than $3 for a bottle of vodka it is either a harmless fake or a danger to your health. The high-quality Russian vodkas, such as Stolichnaya, seldom appear in the state stores. Other popular Russian brands are Russkaya and Starka. About one million decaliters of vodka is consumed in the US every year.

In the early 1990s, Smirnoff vodka appeared in Moscow stores for the first time since the Smirnoff factories were nationalized after the 1917 Revolution. Descendants of Pyotr Smirnoff, who supplied vodka to Russian czars, brought out a Genuine Smirnoff Vodka, although the arguments as to who makes the best vodka and who has the right to sell the name still rage inside and outside the courts.

Vodka comes plain or in several flavored varieties: **Okhotnichaya** (or hunter's) is strong and flavored with bitter herbs, which gives it a distinctive sharp taste; it is 56 percent alcohol; **Gorilka s pertsem** (Ukrainian with peppers); **Krepkaya** (strong) is 56 percent alcohol; **Lemonnaya**, with a bitter lemon taste, is popular with fish dishes and is 40 percent alcohol, but some Russian men shy from it believing it is a woman's drink; **Moskovskaya osobaya** (Moscow special) is a classically produced vodka that is 40 percent alcohol, 80 proof; **Osobaya** (special) is excellent and approximates Moskovskaya osobaya and is 40 percent alcohol; **Pertsovka**, with a peppery taste, is believed to be effective against colds, when it should be drunk before bedtime and is 40 percent alcohol; **Posolskaya** (ambassadorial) is of high quality and purity at 40 percent alcohol; **Russkaya** (Russian) is made in part with potatoes and distilled water and is of inferior quality (40 percent alcohol); **Sibirskaya** (Siberian) is good tasting and 45 percent alcohol; **Starka** (old) is a dark color with an herb flavor, and is 40 percent alcohol; **Stolichnaya** (Capital) is the most popular with Muscovites, who consider it the purest (40 percent alcohol); **Tminaya** is made with caraway seeds; **Zubrovka** is made with bison grass and is 40 percent alcohol; and **Zveroboy** (animal killer).

Vodka is served before, during and after meals, often with **zakuski**, or appetizers. It is ordered by the bottle or in grams and served in an open carafe. One hundred grams is about one drink each for four persons. It should be drunk cold.

Alcoholic drinks are served from 2pm to 10pm; later in bars, nightclubs, casinos, and some restaurants. You must be at least 18 years of age to purchase and consume alcohol in Russia.

Toasting

Refusing a drink or a toast is a serious breach of etiquette and once the bottle is uncorked it must be finished. The first toast, akin to a blessing, is quickly followed by the second. In the dictatorial Soviet times, the first toast was most often to Stalin, even at events as unrelated to politics as a child's birthday. Among friends, the first toast is often a brief *Budem zdorovy!* (or Let's be healthy!) At birthdays, the first toast is to the health of the celebrator and next to his or her parents.

At weddings, the first toast is to the newlyweds and the second to their parents. While the guests drink champagne, someone will invariably shout, "It is bitter, make it sweeter!" and before long there is a rhythmic chorus chant from the rest: "Gorko! Gorko! Gorko!" (or Bitter, bitter, bitter). The newlyweds can only stop the chanting by a long kiss, during which relatives and friends count in unison: "One, two, three." The longer the kiss, the greater the applause.

Wine

If you opt for a domestic wine, your best choices will probably come from the now-independent republic of Georgia. The most common choices are:

White Wine: The light yellow, fruity **tsinandali** (10 to 12 percent alcohol); the astringent **gurdzhaani** (ten to 12 percent alcohol); or the smooth-tasting **vazisubani** are among the dry wines. **Tvishi** or **tetra** are popular among the medium dry white wines.

Red Wine: Both **mukuzani** and **saperavi** (10.5 to 12.5 percent alcohol), made from the same grape and named after a Georgian village, are among the dry red wines. Try Stalin's favorite, **odzhaleshi** (ten to 12 percent alcohol) or **kinsmarauli** for medium dry red wines. Raspberry-flavored **khvanchkara** and **akhasheni** (both 10.5 to 12 percent alcohol) are also widely available.

Dry champagne is called **sukhoye**, medium dry **palusukhoye**, sweet is **sladkoye**, and red medium dry champagne is called **tsimlyanskoye**.

The Russian equivalent for Port is **portvein**, Madeira is called **madera**, vermouth is **vermoot**. The best brandy comes from Armenia and is known as **armyansky kanyak**.

Water

And then there is the blessed water in one-and-a-half liter bottles, the heavenly **Saint Springs** water, advertised in the Moscow English-language press as quite simply "the best water in the world, and it's Russian."

Bottled since 1994 from underground springs of exceptional purity, located about 15 miles outside of Kostroma and owned by the Russian Orthodox Church, Saint Springs water claims to be certified to meet or exceed international standards for purity. Patriarch Aleksey II blessed the spring and signed the joint venture contract that was initiated by a California businessman.

The Archbishop of the Church in the Kostroma region says it was the first commercial enterprise of the church and the first such plant in Russia. All revenues from Saint Springs water are supposed to go toward restoration of churches and for charitable works. A Golden Ring city of about 300,000, Kostroma was founded in the 1150s.

In the pre-Revolutionary Russia, the Church ran many prosperous agricultural businesses. The Church was once the richest landlord whose wealth was envied even by the tsars.

Tea

No discussion about the Russian kitchen would be complete without mention of the samovar, or self-boiler, which in the West was once called a Russian tea machine. Writer Fyodor Dostoyevsky thought that the samovar was the most essential Russian thing.

It was first introduced in the early 18th century in the Urals. The uniqueness of the Russian samovar is that all its separate parts - the vessel, the furnace, the wind-box, the pipe and the tap - are combined into a contraption that resembles a boilerhouse, with a teapot atop it. Water is kept boiling by a tube filled with charcoal that passes through the center. A porcelain teapot usually sits on the chimney, containing tea concentrate that is diluted with boiling water.

COKE VS. PEPSI

In 1974, Pepsi Cola was the first and only Western product available in the Soviet Union. The first seed for Pepsi's entry to Russia was planted in 1959, when the company's chairman met Nikita Khrushchev during Richard Nixon's visit to the Soviet Union. Khrushchev was said to have downed five bottles of Pepsi in a row.

It was Brezhnev, however, who authorized the actual deal in which Pepsi marketed Russian vodka in the US and Russia used the hard currency earnings to purchase Pepsi concentrate. The company now has 20 franchised bottling plants in Russia, but it can barely ward off Coca-Cola, which entered the market in 1991. By the time you read this, Coca-Cola may already have surpassed Pepsi in sales. The problem with Pepsi is that it has been around for such a long time few Russians consider it a Western drink anymore.

The samovar played an important role in the daily life of Russians; it was a mark of hospitality and a symbol of a family's prosperity. It was usually made out of brass or copper and, for the wealthy, even out of silver.

There were more than a hundred samovar manufacturers in the early 19th century. In the second half of the century, when the town of Tula became a center of samovar manufacturing, more than half a million of them were made every year. Today, only electric or purely ornamental samovars are made in Russian factories.

If you want to buy a an old-fashioned samovar, whether for tea or just as decoration in your home, the sole options seem to be an antique store on Stary Arbat Street or the Izmaylovo outdoor market. For suggestions on where to buy one, please see Souvenirs & Antiques on Old Arbat Street in Chapter 17, *Shopping*. Some samovars are considered antiques and cannot be taken out Russia without permission from the Ministry of Culture.

11. WHERE TO STAY

APARTMENTS

Whether you stay for a couple of weeks or three months, living in a private apartment in Moscow makes more sense than perhaps anywhere else in Europe because hotels are either exorbitantly expensive or are sorely lacking by Western standards.

A private apartment is nearly always an actual residence, most likely temporarily vacated by Russians who want to earn some hard currency. While you occupy their apartment, they are likely staying with relatives. Often, these are well educated and relatively prosperous professionals or elderly and their apartments reflect that.

A reasonably well appointed Moscow hotel downtown start at about $250 a night and can go up two or three times that amount, depending on the conveniences included. If you travel as an individual through Intourist, the minimum rate in one of the Intourist hotels is about $100 per person at a depressing dump like the Hotel Belgrad 2, near the Arbat McDonald's restaurant. One night for a single can go as high as $1,000 per person at the Metropol, a top Moscow hotel. With rates like these, you can get a decent apartment for much less.

But brace yourself for shabby exteriors, fetid halls, trash and broken glass, even in the more exclusive areas of central Moscow, like the Arbat and around the Ministry of Foreign Affairs, unless you are willing to pay a hotel-size rent. Most apartments are considerably cleaner than their filthy exteriors would imply. Until recently, these buildings were the property of the state, which was also responsible for their upkeep, so tenants had little incentive to keep them clean. Since Moscow's privatization program began in 1992, about a million apartments have been privatized, or well over one-quarter of all municipal housing.

Do not expect an American style condominium with Calvin Klein bedding, but you can lease a satisfactory apartment with a small living room, a tiny bedroom and kitchen at a reasonable rate. The toilet and bathroom are sometimes separate. You will be able to cook if you so desire

HOT WATER & HEAT

Josef Stalin decided in the 1930's that the state should control Moscow's hot water, which is used for steam heat, as well as in baths and kitchens. Today, 15 huge plants produce most of the capital's hot water, which heats perhaps 95 percent of the apartments and offices.

*However, a city bureaucrat decides when to turn the heat on and off. Sometimes it is so hot in the middle of the frigid winter that you might have to open the **fortochka**, a small ventilation window. In the spring, the director of the Government Energy Department decides which day to turn the heat off. During the summer, every Moscow district has its hot water turned off for a month of ritual "cleaning and repairs," although no one can explain this. These shut-offs are rotated from one district to another - affecting tens of thousands of residents at a time - and you may never know precisely when your hot water will be back. If you love hot water, you will have to boil it on the stove and improvise with a washbowl, which might be the ultimate inconvenience for some Westerners. Even for Muscovites it is a hated legacy of the Stalinist system.*

"When we turn off the hot water in the summer, people are ready to kill us," says the man responsible for this unpopular task. Fortunately his neighbors, even his own wife, do not know who makes that decision.

The Kremlin, of course, has its own water heaters.

or be bothered by nothing more strenuous than making a cup of coffee. Both television and telephone will be at your disposal and you can arrange for other conveniences.

Very few Moscow apartments have air-conditioning and most hardly ever need it. The city government decides when to turn on the heat in the fall and when to turn it off in the spring, a leftover from the Stalinist era that still affects most Muscovites. The same with hot water.

What the British call the ground floor is the first floor to the Russians as it is to Americans.

Private apartments are regularly listed in the classified sections of Moscow English-language newspapers. Among the real estate companies advertising in newspapers, there are:

Barin's Realty, *Tel. 124-7211 or 7526*, Fridays and Saturdays, *Tel. 967-5472*; **Best**, *Tel. 151-5950, Fax 151-5920*; **Blackwood Real Estate Co.**, *Tel. 915-4000, E-mail black@blackw.msk.ru.*; **Continental Holding**, *Tel. 151-5950, Fax 151-5920*; **Delight Real Estate**, *Tel. 246-8179 or 248-4408, Fax 209-6342*; **Evans Property Services**, *Tel. 973-3805 or 3886 or 3892*; **Home Sweet Home**, *Tel. 237-2269 or 3068 or 4659*; **Ivanishka**, *Tel. and Fax 564-8013 or 244-2662 or 2714*; **JAT Rental Service**, *Tel. 915-0014 or 912-4103*;

Moscow Realty, *Tel. 928-5093 or 944-2489*; **Novy Gorod**, *Tel. 975-3136, Fax 975-1466*; **Notra**, *Tel. 291-4554 or 4783 or 290-0017*; **Penny Lane Realty**, *Tel. 931-9653 or 235-6539*; **Slavyansky Dvor**, *Tel. 155-7702 or 7901.* Moscow area code is (095).

When dealing with apartment services, be prepared to pay about double the rent you would pay if you rented directly from an individual. But, in either case, beware of scams because the housing shortages that have ailed Moscow through most of its 70 years of Communism have grown even more desperate in the new age of capitalism. There are more than half a million persons on various waiting lists for apartments in Moscow, although the city builds fewer than half that number in a year.

Since 1994, there have been almost no restrictions on foreigners renting apartments, according to the Russian Security Service (successor to the KGB). The government no longer seems not to be interested in where you live and how much rent you pay. But the Service adds that if you stay for three days or longer, you must register at the local police station within 48 hours of your arrival and pay a small fee. Call *Tel. 200-8427 or 924-0045* for more information. Your landlord, apartment agency or your guide-interpreter can also register you. If you travel to more than one city specified in your visa, you must register on the first leg of your trip.

Luxury Western Apartments

Moscow apartments that meet the criteria of Western executives rent for $1,000-4,000 a month, depending on size and location. Most of the above realty companies can assist you in finding one.

Perhaps the most expensive and expansive of these Western dwellings is the $88 million, 478-townhouse development, **Rosinka**, constructed around a 40-acre lake, 15 miles from downtown Moscow.

Houston developer Hines manages a 48,000-square-foot, 333-unit residential and office complex, **Park Place**, the brainchild of a member of the Russian Academy of Architecture. It is situated about nine miles southwest of Moscow, on the way to the Vnukovo airport.

Another complex is the Russian-American joint venture, **Perestroika**. Perestroika leases 2, 3 and 4-bedroom townhouses on a 23-acre park and 5-acre pond near the River Syetun, an hour's drive from the Kremlin. Amenities include a health club, heated garages, satellite TV, international telephone line, and day care facilities.

BED & BREAKFASTS

A Bed and Breakfast is another option to consider, particularly for those who enjoy family surroundings and the protection of a Russian family that will take pride in having you as their guest. You may have to forgo some privacy, but the family with which you stay will probably go out of its way to keep you as busy as you want to be.

Cost varies depending on single or double occupancy, meals and other amenities. Should you arrange for your room through a B&B service, the cost will likely be about double what it would cost you to contract for it directly with an owner. You will, however, be spared the headache of searching for an appropriate dwelling because most B&B facilities have been screened by the B&B service. B&Bs also gives you the luxury of having all the answers even before you set out for the airport.

Ideally, you should start making arrangements for your B&B at least three months ahead of your arrival, but absolutely no later than one month before you go. Proceed carefully as you could lose the required deposit or part of your payment if you cannot travel at the agreed upon time. Among the B&B organizations in the US to consider are the following:

American-International Homestays, *17360 Highway 119, Rollinsville, Colorado 80403, P.O. Box 7178, Boulder, CO., 80306. Tel. 800/876-2048 or 303/642-3088, Fax 303/642-3365, E-mail ash@igc.apc.org.*

AIH was founded in 1988 by a former computer consultant who speaks Russian, a former tax consultant and a former educator. Each Homestay city has a local manager and staff. AIH is a private company - not a travel agency - and is a member of the Better Business Bureau. A homestay usually includes round-trip air fare from New York and all meals and lodging with your English-speaking hosts in their homes for two one-week stays in two cities. Usually two travelers are placed in each home, but single or family placements are also possible.

Host Families Association (HOFA), *16 Mevan Avenue, Englewood, New Jersey, 07631. Tel. 201/569-4967, Fax 201/569-1782, e-mail lemee@carroll.com.* In **St. Peterburg**, *5-25 Ulitsa Tavrisheskaya.*

HOFA, founded in St. Petersburg in 1991, is a group of English-speaking families, most of whom are members of faculties or research staff at local universities and research institutes. They arrange for home visits in Moscow, St. Petersburg and a dozen other locations in Russia and the former Soviet Union. HOFA's deluxe service plan includes a private bedroom, meals and beverages, host-guided walks, and an English speaker to accompany you. The standard plan consists of a private bedroom and breakfast. There are several other plans, including plans for students who wish to visit St. Petersburg and Moscow. HOFA will assist you in obtaining your visa at an additional cost.

International Bed & Breakfast, *Post Office Box 823, Huntingdon Valley, Pennsylvania, 19006. Tel. 800/422-5283 or 215/663-1438, Fax 215/379-3363, Internet: http//www.libertynet.org. ~ ibb.*

IBB was founded in 1990 to enable Americans and other visitors to Russia to enjoy the amenities of private homes rather than staying in hotels. It has its own office and staff in Moscow and contacts with Russian families who welcome having Americans in their homes. IBB accommodations are available in Moscow, St. Petersburg and other CIS cities. They will assist you with your visa. Moscow tours, excursions, translations and interpretation services are also available.

IBV Bed & Breakfast Systems, *13113 Ideal Drive, Silver Spring, Maryland, 20906. Tel. 301/942-3770, Fax 301/933-0024.*

IBV provides a B&B program throughout Russia and the former Soviet Union. There is a small non-refundable booking fee. IBV's cancellation policy is flexible, we were told. While, theoretically, you would lose 50 percent of your total cost if you had to cancel 7 to 14 days prior to your scheduled arrival, IBV will work with you if you reschedule your trip within a reasonable time frame. However, there would be some incidental costs, such as securing a new visa for you.

HOTELS

Moscow has never been a tourist mecca and has always had a shortage of luxury hotels. Nevertheless, by 1915, the capital had 250 hotels in every conceivable price range, all privately owned. Today, Moscow has about 170 hotels, but fewer than half of these have facilities and amenities that would satisfy Western visitors at any price. Many state-owned hotels are a depressing combination of overpriced, nonfunctional rooms with cheap or nonexistent furniture, where a television set implies luxury, and indifferent service, where complaints often fall on deaf ears. It will take years of competition before the state-run hotels understand the meaning of service.

When you check into a Russian hotel, your passport will be held for 24 hours, while you are registered with the authorities, not unlike in some other European countries. In return, you will receive a card with the hotel's name and your room number. This will be your identification until you get your passport back.

All Western-run and several better state-owned hotels listed below have service bureaus that will assist you in calling for a taxi, reserving tickets to the Bolshoy Theater or a restaurant and will facilitate your telephone calls abroad, if they cannot be placed directly from your room.

Except at a handful of the top Moscow hotels, do not ever assume that one will provide complimentary shampoo, soap, moisturizer or sewing kit, like most of them do in the US.

If cost is an important consideration for you, remember that the more English-speaking guests there are the more likely the rates will be higher.

THE HOTEL FLOOR ATTENDANT

*Most state-owned hotels have a female attendant, a **dezhurnaya**, on each floor. A mother and a policewoman in one, she knows everything that is going on on your floor and probably in your room as well. She will take your room key when you go out and give it back when you come in. Men, before you try to entice that young Russian thing to your room, watch out; you smuggled her past the doorman by speaking to her in English (which she hardly understands), but do not try the same trick on your dezhurnaya, you probably will not outwit her.*

Only luxury hotels have room service so these attendants can also help you with other needs, such as obtaining extra towels, blankets, or coffee if none is provided in your room. If you need to call someone outside Moscow, the dezhurnaya will make arrangements for you and afterwards tell you how much you owe - a throwback from the olden days, when she could have reported you to the KGB. If you need soap, stamps for your postcards, or have to have a button sewed on your pants, well, by now you know who to ask. At some state-owned hotels, she is even responsible for your hotel bill so please pay it on time or she will remind you about it at 5:30 in the morning.

But the dezhurnaya is even more, if you can believe it, much more. This is how the New York Times describes, in part, a fairly typical one:

"Long seen as a particularly unpleasant sentry of Soviet authority, the floor lady is always stationed near the elevators at the entrance to every corridor. She - and it is always she - controls all room keys, adjudicates all disputes and dispenses justice as she sees fit. When they are nice they can take the edge off the bleakest hotel experience, but there is nothing scarier than a dezhurnaya with a bad attitude.

There are some cost-conscious hotels that have discarded the floor-lady system. Nor will they be found at those fancy Western hotels with minibars and CNN. It's got to be a Russian hotel: a big, ugly, concrete fortress with hundreds of rooms and one roll of toilet paper."

Large hotels in the center of Moscow will generally cost much more than the smaller ones on the periphery, but, of course, you may not be willing to tolerate the primitive conditions in some of the smaller hotels.

Before you call your family in New York or that client in Toronto, check the price of your international telephone calls. Sometimes they can cost more than your room. Please see also the section Telephone, Telegram & Fax in Chapter 8 *Basic Information*.

If you are a male, your Russian female partners, friends or companions might find it difficult to get into your state-run hotel, sometimes even the hotel restaurant with you accompanying them, supposedly to protect foreigners from pesky individuals or prostitutes. Not infrequently, speaking English to such a woman, even if she does not understand a word, while passing those righteous doormen looking for bribes, will do the trick.

In the former Soviet Union, there was a rule that no citizen could stay in a hotel in his home city. It was impossible to evade this because you had to show your internal passport when checking in, and your place of residence was clearly shown. Although that rule was finally abolished in 1994, an average Russian may still have a hard time understanding why another Russian would stay in a hotel in his home city - unless, of course, he is up to something fishy. It is only since 1994 that the state-owned hotels are officially required to change sheets and bathroom supplies twice weekly, deliver guest's mail, provide hot water, accept wake-up calls and charge no more than 25 percent of their nightly fee to reserve a room.

Do not to leave any **valuables** in your room; everything from your airline tickets to your excess cash should be stored in the hotel's safety deposit box. Do not try to outsmart a hotel thief by hiding your jewelry or cash in what may seem to you an unlikely place. Other guests before you have probably tried and failed because thieves earn their living by knowing where you stash those $100 notes.

During the summer, be prepared to be without hot water for up to four weeks in many secondary hotels, supposedly for **remont**, or renovation and cleaning.

To women, we repeat our often-stated suggestion that if you stay at a hotel, check into the most expensive one you can afford, then get the least expensive room, because it is usually safer and there will be less harassment.

A Moscow hotel day is considered roughly from noon to noon.

All the hotels we reviewed are divided into one of the following geographical areas: **Inside the Boulevard Ring Road**, or what Westerners would call the downtown area; **Within the Boulevard & Garden Ring Roads**, a bagel-shaped band around central Moscow; and **Outside the Garden Ring Road**, an area that encompasses the Moscow suburbs.

Within each of these three geographical areas, the hotels are divided into three categories, based on their prices, starting with the most expensive and ending with the least expensive:
• **Expensive** – More than $200 a night per person
• **Moderate** – Between $100 and $200 a night per person
• **Inexpensive** – Up to $100 a night per person

Beyond generalizations based on the price, these categories do not imply a recommendation, unless so stated specifically in the text. Only Western-style hotels readily accept credit cards, and when they do we note it after the address and telephone number. Do not be surprised if a state-owned hotel charges you more for an identical room than it does to a Russian-born guest.

When considering an inexpensive hotel, use our price quotes as a starting point only in your selection process because sometimes there is more than one rate.

INSIDE THE BOULEVARD RING ROAD

Quick Overview: The **Baltschug Kempinski** and **Metropol** hotels are two of the three five-star hotels in Moscow. Also inside the Boulevard Ring Road are two four-star luxury hotels, **Savoy** and **Natsional**, which cater mostly to Western businessmen. They all meet Western standards of amenities and service since they were mostly built or rebuilt with the help of Western partners. Women, if they can afford to stay at these four-star hotels, should feel entirely safe if traveling alone.

What follows are hotels, such as **Intourist**, **Moskva**, and **Rossiya**, which some Westerners would consider barely adequate in amenities and service. Women will find most of them safe enough to stay in by themselves, but they should be cautious.

Following those are top Class B hotels, such as **Budapesht**, where amenities are often even more modest. Women may want to inspect their rooms before staying alone in hotels of this category.

Expensive

BALTSCHUG KEMPINSKI HOTEL, *1 Ulitsa Baltschug, Metro Novokuznetskaya or Tretyakovskaya. Tel. (095) 230-6500, Fax (095) 230-6502 or 6504, Telex 414873 HBKMO RU; Satellite Tel. 7 (501) 230-9500, Satellite Fax 7 (501) 230-9502 or 9503 or 9511. Toll-free reservations in the US, Tel. 800/426-3135, Internet edp@kempimos.msk.ru. Major credit cards accepted.*

Located across the Moskva River, just south of the Kremlin and Red Square, and northeast of Tretyakov Gallery. Baltschug is centrally located, but not accessible by public transportation, and most attractions are across the river to the north or across the canal to the south.

If status is your nourishment and you expect formally-attired doormen and bellhops to snap at attention and jump to open the doors for you, this is the place to impress somebody, although you better be dressed up yourself or you might get one of those haughty Teutonic looks in return. This is not a place to wear jeans.

Reconstructed in 1992 at a cost of $80 million and brought up to Western standards, this facility is owned by Lufthansa German airlines.

The site of Baltschug once housed the Bukaresht Hotel and before that the Novomoskovskaya Hotel, but all that is left of the original hotel built in 1898 is its facade. It has a wonderful view of Red Square and the Kremlin. There are 202 air-conditioned rooms and 32 soundproofed luxury suites, many done in red and cream. Singles, some of which face a factory on the eastern side, start at about $400 a night, doubles at $550, plus 20 percent value added tax. Children under 12 years of age stay free. Suites are priced from $800 to $2,500 a night, and, yes, you guessed it, 20 percent VAT. All rooms have direct-dial satellite-telephone, Fax and computer facilities.

For more details about its **Le Romanoff** and **Baltschug** restaurants, please turn to Chapter 12, *Where to Eat*. The breakfast buffet is about $30. **Cafe Kranzler** on the ground floor is convenient for afternoon tea and pastries. A nightclub in the basement is open until 3am. There is a VIP lounge, **Bibliothek**, on the 8th floor with some 2,500 books in German, English and Russian - and a good view of Moscow.

If true that a house can be judged by the cleanliness of its rest rooms, then Baltschug is the best hotel in Moscow because they are absolutely spotless. Secretarial and translation services are available on the premises, as is the laundry and dry cleaning. Other amenities include a Lufthansa airline counter, a hairdresser, a tailor shop, a food store and a post office. A swimming pool and fitness center with sauna are also on the premises.

METROPOL HOTEL, *1/4 Teatralny proyezd, Metro Teatralnaya. Tel. (095) 927-6000 to 927-6009 or (095) 927-6453, Fax (095) 927-6010; Satellite Tel. 7 (501) 927-1000, Fax 7 (501) 927-6010. Toll-free reservations in the US, Tel. 800/327-0200. Major credit cards accepted.*

Centrally located north of the Kremlin and overlooking Theater Square, and roughly between the Bolshoy Theater and Red Square.

There are 400 rooms and suites that can accommodate 700 guests. The top suites go for $1,650 a night, while the singles start at $330. You will also be charged a 20 percent value added tax on top of the room rate. All rooms have mini-bars and computer connections, many feature hardwood floors and oriental rugs, and all suites are decorated with antiques.

An old brick wall behind the hotel is a remnant of the wall that once surrounded the oldest part of the city, known as Kitay-gorod (Chinatown). This section of Moscow was a bustling commercial center for hundreds of years after the 1300's.

In 1917, the new Soviet government was headquartered in this turn-of-the-century gem in the heart of Moscow and Lenin often spoke inside it. The Communist Party's favorite son, Nikolay Bukharin, who fell in love with this art nouveau building and his beautiful 20-year-old future wife,

Anna Larina, who grew up in Room 305, had many dinners here with Lenin and Stalin. After she bumped into Stalin in the corridors, he actually delivered her first love note to Bukharin because she was too bashful to bring it herself. This did not keep Stalin from having Bukharin arrested in 1937 and executed, following a show trial at which he was accused of leading "a gang of spies, terrorists and thieves." Anna Larina died in 1996.

The Metropol was designed by William Walcott, the Russian-born English architect. Note the hotel's mosaic facade on Teatralny pereulok, *Princess Dream,* created by the mad genius Mikhail Vrubel, who died in a mental hospital. The five-story building was completely restored in 1990, when it became the first Moscow hotel ever to earn five stars. Before that, Lee Harvey Oswald stayed here, at the KGB's expense.

The Metropol is now managed by Inter-Continental Hotels. An oasis of peace in turbulent Moscow, it has a laid-back elegance and comfortable overstuffed leather chairs in the lobby. Even if you cannot afford Metropol's prices, use its free local-calls-only phones next to the lobby; you will appreciate the management's understanding of how helpless a Westerner can feel in Moscow. A simple telephone call can be a major undertaking.

You may want to stop at the **Artist's Bar** or **Cafe Confectionery** for a cup of coffee to repay their generosity. True, at $3.50 a cup, it is an expensive cup, but no tastier cup will you find in all of Moscow. There are few confectionery delights that your Russian acquaintance will appreciate more than the scrumptiously rich desserts, served on exquisite china and with civilized service. Both shops are open Monday through Saturday, 10am to 8pm.

Metropol's Service Bureau, open from 8am to 10pm weekdays, and until 8pm on weekends, will arrange for guides and interpreters and help you reserve tickets for most events. You can rent a computer or a laser printer and make international direct-dial telephone calls from your room. A heated swimming pool, fitness room and saunas are also available.

For details about **Boyarsky, Evropeysky, Metropol, Teatro Lobster Grill**, and **Teatro Mediterraneo** restaurants, please see Chapter 12, *Where to Eat.* Metropol is one of only a handful places in the city where you can find a hearty breakfast, without having to be a hotel guest, even if it does set you back well over $20.

Every Sunday, from 11:30am to 4pm, you can enjoy a brunch to the sounds of the Moscow Conservatory Orchestra in the Metropol restaurant. **Chalyapin Bar** is on the ground floor. Adjacent to the hotel is a women's clothing shop, **Modus Vivendi**, *Tel. 927-6060*, which is open from 11am to 8pm. Behind the hotel is **Olga Car Rental**; please see Car

Rental in Chapter 7, *Getting Around Moscow* for more details. **EPS**, *Tel. 927-6982 or 83*, just off the lobby, sells tickets for a variety of events, including the Bolshoy Theater and is open Monday through Friday, from 10am to 6pm, Saturdays 10am to 3pm. The barber and hair dressing salon, *Tel. 927-6670*, is open from 8am to 8pm Monday through Saturday, and until 4pm on Sundays.

SAVOY HOTEL, *3 Ulitsa Rozhdestvenka, Metro Lubyanka. Tel. (095) 929-8500 or 8557 or 8590, Fax (095) 230-2186, Telex 411620; Satellite Fax 7 (501) 929-7571. Major credit cards accepted.*

Located inside the Boulevard Ring, northeast of the Kremlin and west of Lubyanka Square, near the Bolshoy Theater and Red Square.

Another turn-of-the-century hotel, the Savoy was constructed in 1912, when Russia celebrated the 300th anniversary of the Romanov rule, for a well-known insurance company and rebuilt in 1989. After the Revolution housing was in such short supply that the Savoy became a hostel for members of the Commissariat for Foreign Affairs. This Russian-Finnish joint venture, formerly named the Berlin Hotel to emphasize good relations with East Germany, has 86 somewhat small rooms and suites and can accommodate about 155 guests. Singles start at about $325 a night, suites go up to $900. One of the suites contains the piano purchased for the Italian tenor Luciano Pavarotti when he stayed here during his Moscow performance. The lobby, however, is surprisingly cramped for such an illustrious hostelry.

Curiously, but probably by chance, Khrushchev ordered it to drop the name Savoy and become the Berlin shortly after he issued his famous Thanksgiving Day 1958 ultimatum on Berlin, which led to negotiations with Western powers.

The Savoy has the comfort and service that is lacking at many other Moscow hotels. Only hard currencies were accepted until the law mandated otherwise and credit cards are preferred. The staff is trained in Helsinki, Finland, and the hotel is managed by Finnair. You can watch CNN news in your room.

Savoy Restaurant, about which you can read in the restaurant section, receives its food supplies from abroad and is one of the plushest eateries in the city. Savoy also boasts the first gambling casino in Moscow. The hotel also has the **Hermitage Bar**, where you can argue politics over $3-a-cup coffee. Several shops are located on the premises, as is an art salon. You will have an English-speaking concierge and 24-hour room service. Other amenities include a business center with the Reuters financial news wire, computers and photocopiers.

NATSIONAL HOTEL, *14/1 Okhotny Ryad, Metro Okhotny Ryad. Tel. (095) 258-7000, Fax (095) 258-7100; Satellite Tel. 7 (501) 258-7000. Toll-free reservations in the US, Tel. 800/225-5843. Major credit cards accepted.*

Centrally located and overlooking Red Square and the Kremlin across Manezhnaya Square. Bolshoy and Maly Theaters are but two blocks away, Intourist's main office is next door and the fashionable Tverskaya Street begins on the other corner.

Natsional was built in the then-popular art nouveau style in 1901, the same year that Leon Trotsky escaped from Siberian exile and settled in London. It reopened in mid-1995, after four years of reconstruction at a cost of $78 million. A Victorian-style hotel that before its renovation exuded a certain genteel poverty, it is now once again a top Moscow hotel, with neo-Baroque ceiling paintings and murals that were covered up by the Soviets.

Eleanor Roosevelt was a guest in the old ambassadorial Suite 115, followed by actress Elizabeth Taylor and Sir Winston Churchill's son. Today, you are just as likely to find a Russian millionaire here, like the 33-year-old Oleg Boyko (the owner of Moscow's OLBI-Diplomat electronic stores), who has a $500-a-night suite at the Natsional. And who could blame them, the view alone is unforgettable.

Moscow architect Lev Lavrenov has redesigned or enlarged the 213 rooms, of which 170 are standard singles and doubles, that altogether accommodate more than 300 guests. Most rooms feature polished oak furniture upholstered in silk. Singles with air-conditioning, satellite television and mini-bar start at $300 a night, doubles at $400 and suites go from $450 to $1,200. Rooms overlooking the busy Manezhnaya Square are soundproofed. Non-smoking rooms, a rarity in Moscow, are also available.

The Natsional dining room, where satirical writer Mikhail Bulgakov and poet Vladimir Mayakovsky often ate, has reopened as a branch of **Maxim's** restaurant in Paris; please see Chapter 12, *Where to Eat* for more details.

Other restaurants include **Moskovsky**, where a traditional Russian dinner is served from 6pm to 11pm and accompanied by balalayka music. The opulent **St. Petersburg** restaurant, located on the second floor and claiming a terrific view of the Kremlin and Red Square, serves European dishes to the sound of Russian folk music, from noon to 11pm; it also hosts a Sunday brunch. **Slavyansky Buffet** serves breakfast, lunch and dinner from 7am to 10pm.

Natsional is a sort of national monument and for several years prided itself with having Lenin and his wife Nadezhda Krupskaya as occupants of Room 107, after the Bolshevik government moved its headquarters from St. Petersburg to Moscow in 1918. The large balcony on the corner of the hotel was his platform for exhorting the proletarian masses.

Natsional has a flat roof constructed as an observation platform with an excellent view of central Moscow. Many of its rooms overlook the

Kremlin and St. Basil's Cathedral. Equally appealing are the rooftop fitness center and the pool with sauna.

A $1-billion underground 161,000-square-yard complex of restaurants and shops, a theater, bank and casino, as well as large parking lot, is being built on Manezhnaya Square, in front of the hotel. Until the lot is completed, the Natsional is severely handicapped by the lack of parking space.

Moderate

INTOURIST HOTEL, *3/5 Ulitsa Tverskaya, Metro Okhotny Ryad. Tel. (095) 956-8304 or 8400 or 8426, Fax (095) 956-8450. Major credit cards accepted, except American Express.*

Centrally located and within easy walking distance of the Bolshoy and Maly Theaters, and almost as close to the Kremlin and Red Square if you take the metro passageway under Manezhnaya Square.

Built in 1970, the year of Kerensky's death, Intourist has 466 plain rooms in an ugly 22-story high-rise that stands out from the surrounding buildings like a sore thumb. Some rooms on the top floors have excellent views of the Kremlin, though. Like so many state-owned hotels, Intourist is depressingly drab and shabby, the furniture is worn out and carpets stained. Singles start at about $150 a night, not counting the 20 percent value added tax. The rooms have not been renovated in a quarter of century and it shows.

This hotel, although sometimes rated as one of the better state-run hostelries in Moscow, is also the cause of complaints among Westerners for its poor service. Saleswomen in the boutiques on the ground floor are sometimes so engrossed in their recreational reading that a casual browser would hate to wake them up with a possible purchase. Arcade action games in the back of the lobby make the Intourist look like an 1890's Wild West saloon. While rude doormen crassly stop everyone not meeting their expectations, supposedly to weed out the guests from the pretenders, judging by the number of prostitutes always loitering inside, they can probably be persuaded to show a bit more understanding with a little bribe.

Persistent Gypsy beggars, currency dealers, kids pushing Soviet stamps, women hoping to make a quick $50, and an assorted collection of other characters prey on the guests from the sidewalk throughout the day and into the night. Unmarked taxis, whose owners dream for that elusive American who might drop $100 for a ride to the airport, also litter the street. And a little farther up Tverskaya Street are Soviet immigrants attracted to the Central Telegraph Office like moths to a light bulb, all adding to one's impression of this being a Russian-style New York City Times Square.

Intourist's restaurants and bars seat well more than a thousand diners at a time. For more information about three of them, **Azteca**, **Lili Wong** and **Skazka**, please see Chapter 12, *Where to Eat*; the same about the **Patio Pizza**, located in front of the hotel and overlooking Tverskaya Street.

There is also the second floor European-cuisine **Golden Hall**, open from noon until midnight; and **Swedish Buffet**, serving breakfast from 7:30am to 10:30am, and lunch from noon to 3pm. The **Traveler Bar**, some nights sporting more tight-skirted floozies than patrons, is on the third floor and open from noon to 4am; another bar on the tenth floor is open from 10am to 10pm. The **Tea Bar** on the 16th floor is open from 11am to 11pm. The drab-looking **Osborne Bar** on the ground floor patio, next to the reception area, always adorned with clumps of berouged females, is for males looking for a one night stand.

Intourist **Taxi Service**, *Tel. 203-0247*, has a counter in the lobby. On the 20th floor you will find **Medical Interline**, *Tel. 203-8631 or 9496*, a joint venture dentist with some Western equipment. **Jindo Rus**, *Tel. 230-9742*, a men's and women's fur and clothes store, is also on the premises.

In 1995, two armed men burst into the Intourist's lobby, shot a policeman in the leg, forced some 50 people to the floor and cleaned out a foreign exchange office and a jewelry store before making a clean get-away in broad daylight. As they left, the men set off a smoke bomb to cover their escape. To assure their getaway they also took cover behind a woman from the hotel. The Intourist is renowned for its surly security guards who loiter around the entrance, a holdover from the Soviet times when no one was allowed inside without a visitor's pass.

BUDAPESHT HOTEL, *2/18 Ulitsa Petrovskiye liniyi, Metro Kuznetsky Most. Tel. (095) 921-1060 or (095) 924-8800 or 8820, Fax (095) 921-1266 or 5290, Telex 411662 HBR SU.*

Centrally located north of the Kremlin, north of the Bolshoy Theater, and just around the corner from Petrovsky Passazh, a Western-style shopping mall.

Originally built in 1876, Budapesht was renovated in 1958, the year the Russian poet Boris Pasternak received the Nobel Prize for Literature. The hotel was renovated again in 1994, but it appears that the reconstruction chiefly affected the bathrooms. The lobby is clean and the staff was quite helpful when we asked to see several rooms and complied with a smile.

Budapesht has 200 rooms, from singles to double bedrooms. Singles on the second or third floor start at more than $100, those located higher are cheaper. Like in so many other state-owned hotels, some beds are so narrow they will remind you of your youth camp bunk. The mattresses are mushy and murder on your back, but not more so than in most other hotels in this category. The one disturbing sight, although not that unusual, was openly displayed passports just barely out of reach from the counter. A criminally inclined passerby could have carried away a fistful of them with just a little extra effort.

The hotel's restaurant, also called **Budapesht**, next door, has five dining rooms decorated with Hungarian scenes. Although state-owned, it serves decent European and Hungarian food at reasonable prices, often with a smile, not a small feat in Russia; for more details, please see Chapter 12, *Where to Eat.*

On the corner with Petrovka Street, there is the **News Pub**, whose stock has fallen since its Russian partners took over. Walk south to Kuznetsky Most Street and browse among its many bookstores and outdoor stalls. The service at the nearby English-language **Zwemmer's** book store, 18 Kuznetsky Most, has gone downhill as well; please see Chapter 17, *Shopping.*

MOSKVA HOTEL, *2 Ulitsa Okhotny Ryad, Metro Okhotny Ryad. Tel. (095) 292-1000 or 1100 or 2008 or 4621 or 4615, Fax (095) 928-5938. Cash only.*

Located a block from the Bolshoy Theater and across Manezhnaya Square from the northern tip of the Kremlin, practically next to Red Square. Where the hotel stands today was once a flourishing outdoor marketplace in the 15th and 16th centuries.

It is said that during the Stalin years many Soviet citizens would make a wide detour around the Moskva Hotel because it provided lodgings mostly for foreigners and no Muscovite would risk even the suspicion of being seen near a Westerner. The career of its architect Aleksey Shchusev (1873-1949), who also designed the Lenin Mausoleum, came precariously close to being cut short, while he designed Moskva. This being the first new Soviet-built hotel in Moscow, Shchusev had to have the approval of Stalin before construction could begin. To be on the safe side, the architect submitted two versions of the design for the wings, with no explanation. Stalin signed the plan without indicating which version he preferred. Shchusev knew better than to ask questions and so built the hotel as you can see it today: the wings on either side of the central colonnade are very different from each other.

Upon its completion in 1937, American architect Frank Lloyd Wright was given a tour of the hotel by Shchusev. When asked through an interpreter what he thought of it, Wright is said to have replied, "It is the ugliest thing I have ever seen!" which was graciously translated as "I'm very impressed." Wright stayed at the Hotel Natsional across the street.

This is another example of a hotel with a location comparable to Place de la Concorde in Paris, Copacabana in Rio de Janeiro, or Via Veneto in Rome, that seems to have done everything it could to discourage tourists. The doormen checking guests' identification behave as though the Soviet regime is still in power. Its enormous somewhat murky lobby, where battered and mismatched furniture is an eyesore and a bathroom is harder to find than a 5-ruble gold piece, will remind you of an empty railway station in the Balkans. There is hardly a place to sit down in the lobby, where a few rickety chairs are puffed up from overuse. The receptionists are utterly indifferent to the presence of their guests. Most of the kiosks and shops in the lobby are closed in the mid-afternoon.

Moskva consists of three buildings with more than a 1,000 generally small spartan and bare rooms that can accommodate up to 1,600 guests. The first building was completed in 1935, the same year that the Moscow metro opened, the second in 1977. Singles, mostly overlooking a court-yard, start at about $100 a night, but do not expect much beyond a bathtub and a TV set. The best rooms are said to be on the 15-17th floors. There is a **dezhurnaya**, a female attendant, on each floor, just to make sure you do not sneak someone or something you are not supposed to into your room, even if you already dealt with that at the hotel entrance.

Please see Chapter 12, *Where to Eat* for more details about **El Rincon Espanol** and **Paradise** restaurants on the ground floor. **Paradise Bar** is one of the few Moscow restaurants where you can have a breakfast until 11am.

Moskva restaurant, *Tel. 292-1245*, open from noon to 10pm, serves European-Russian cuisine; there is a variety show and dancing in the evening.

An underground $1-billion shopping and restaurant complex, six stories deep, is being built under Manezhnaya Square next to the hotel.

ROSSIYA HOTEL, *6 Ulitsa Varvarka, Metro Kitay-gorod. Tel. (095) 298-5400 or 5401 or 5402 or 5403 or 5404, Fax (095) 298-5541, telex 411641 HOTEL SU.*

Located opposite St. Basil's Cathedral and the Kremlin, just off Red Square, on what is perhaps the oldest Moscow street.

The foundations on the 33-acre plot of Rossiya were originally excavated in 1950 to house the Soviet Council of Ministers, but the work was abandoned for fear that the planned 32-story building would over-shadow the Kremlin and Red Square. Construction of Rossiya finally began in 1961 and was followed, floor by floor, by the Moscow press almost daily.

"Forward to Victory!" and "Complete the Project Ahead of Time" were among the many red banners on display at the construction site, exhorting the workers not to loaf. By 1966, when the first guest checked into what is still regarded as the largest hotel in Europe, Rossiya's cost soared to 90 million rubles, a staggering sum of money at the time.

The 12-floor Rossiya, which has a separate 10-story building to house its service operations, has three separate lobbies, more than 3,000 rooms and can accommodate more than 5,500 guests. Singles start at about $100 for a livable room. If you changed your accommodations at Rossiya every night, it would take you more than eight years to sleep in every room. It has 90 elevators in four separate wings, the last one finally completed in 1968. Each wing has its own entrance and countless miles of corridors and halls that make you feel as though you are walking the terminals at a deserted airport.

During the summer, Rossiya is filled mostly with Western tourists, who over a year's time account for about one-third of the more than 250,000 guests. The hotel boasts some 3,000 employees and countless directors, too many of whom do not want to or cannot speak satisfactory English, and whose presence often slows service to a crawl. Rossiya's telephone system equals that of a town of 35,000 people and consumes as much electricity. The hotel has nine restaurants and 20 cafes, some with a superb view of St. Basil's Cathedral and the Kremlin. There is an international telephone booth in the lobby, as well as a pharmacy kiosk.

Many celebrities stayed here, as did Russia's official guests, although its fame has been overblown. It is a Soviet labyrinth that will more likely depress rather than cheer you up, and is not exactly the place to recommend to Westerners. If you disregard our advice, take a compass with you or you might get lost walking its corridors. Avoid rooms facing the square, which has noisy tourists coming and going.

The south wing has a 2,500-seat concert hall, which was finally completed in 1971, and two 800-seat cinemas. The American blues singer Ray Charles sang here, but he lodged on the other side of Red Square, at the Metropol Hotel.

By 1994, Rossiya had fallen so low that city sanitation officials were forced to close it down for infestation of cockroaches and mice. The city plans to turn it into a Western-standard hotel. Rossiya will be divided into a 3-star, 4-star and 5-star hotel, with only 1,800 rooms. Even the hotel's director acknowledged that "reconstruction is urgently needed. All our rooms look the same, like barracks."

Manhattan Express, *Tel. 298-5354 or 5355 or 5359*, is a $2-million New York-style dance and supper club, which opened in 1993 on the northwest corner of Rossiya, facing Red Square. See Chapter 15, *Nightlife & Entertainment* for more details.

BETWEEN THE BOULEVARD & GARDEN RING ROADS

Quick Overview: There are no five-star hotels between the two ring roads, although the **Baltschug Kempinski** is actually located across the Moskva River, but is so centrally situated that we included it with lodgings inside the Boulevard Ring Road.

The **Marco Polo Presnya** and the **President** are luxury Western-style hotels that cater mostly to Western businessmen and are safe choices for women; the President is perhaps the most heavily guarded hotel in Moscow and thus as safe as you will find.

Arbat and **Agmos** are in the next lower category of hotels located between the two ring roads. They are generally safe and satisfactory for the Westerners.

Pekin and **Minsk** (Na Tverskoy) are two examples of Class B dumps that have even fewer amenities and women should stay there alone only if with a group or if unable to afford anything else. It may actually be better to stay in a Bed & Breakfast than in the Minsk. The Pekin is not much better.

Expensive

MARCO POLO PRESNYA, *9 Spiridonyevsky pereulok, Metro Pushkinskaya or Barrikadnaya. Tel. (095) 202-0381, (095) 956-3010 or (095) 244-3631, Fax (095) 926-5402/5404, Telex 414748 VIZIT; Satellite telephone 7 (502) 222-0000, Satellite Fax 7 (502) 222-0131 or 0132. Major credit cards accepted.*

Located northwest of the Kremlin, three blocks west of Pushkin Theater on Tverskoy bulvar, a block south of Patriarch's Ponds, and a few minutes walking distance from Pushkin Square, which is northeast of the hotel.

Formerly a Russian Communist Party hotel, it reopened as a Russian-Austrian joint venture in 1991. It has 68 rooms and suites on five floors that do not live up to a luxury hotel designation. Presnya is a small, unobtrusive, and civilized hostelry, although its frumpy lobby does give you a hint that it could still be a Communist-era lodging.

Singles, including value added tax and service charges, start at about $230 a night, or $160 on weekends, in both instances including breakfast. Doubles are $275 on weekdays or $180 on weekends. Suites begin at $350 per person, or $225 on weekends, and go all the way to $500 a night.

Presnya is managed by Marco Polo Hotels of Vienna, Austria, the same as the more expensive five-star Palace Hotel in northwest Moscow. Like many hotels in this category, it is popular with Western businessmen. Marco Polo Presnya has a business center, health club with fitness equipment and sauna, a lobby bar and a terrace cafe. You can also rent a BMW car with driver.

The hotel has a good reputation with its European-cuisine restaurant whose dining room does not match the decor of luxury hotels downtown, but the food is well prepared and the service attentive. The Moscow News food critic says it is "expensive, but worth it."

A couple of houses away, at 5 Spiridonyevsky Lane, is the subdued club **Ekipazh**.

PRESIDENT HOTEL, *24 Ulitsa Bolshaya Yakimanka, Metro Polyanka. Tel. (095) 238-6558 or 7303 or (095) 239-3800, Fax (095) 230-2216 or 2318, Telex 412438 HOTEL SU. Major credit cards accepted.*

Located south of the Kremlin and southwest of Tretyakov Gallery in a historic area known as Zamoskvorechye. The back of the hotel is adjacent to the sculpture park of the Central House of Artists, where you will find, among a hundred artworks, dozens of despised Soviet sculptures relegated here to escape destruction.

Hotel President is a Russian-Italian joint venture that can accommodate 330 guests. If safety is your major concern, this is probably one of the safest hotels in Moscow. Not only is it surrounded by a 6-foot iron fence so thick it can withstand a tank, but there is one controlled entrance only at Third Golutvinsky pereulok. In 1996, there was a presidential election office here and you could only have entered the manicured courtyard upon submission of your passport and telephone verification that you were a guest.

(For a similarly guarded, but less expensive hotel between the American embassy and the Russian White House, please see the description of Hotel Mir, which is situated outside the Garden Ring Road.)

Opened in 1983, the President gives the appearance that it has four times the actual 210 rooms. It was built by the Communist Party of the Soviet Union for its own needs and the service personnel sometimes still act as if the party bosses are staying here, instead of businessmen. Foreign heads of state and other VIP's regularly meet at the President to hold conferences. Former British prime minister Margaret Thatcher lodged here when she visited Moscow.

The President has one of the most imposing staircases to the second-floor lobby that you will ever see in a Russian nongovernmental building. Both the staircase and the lobby are so huge you might need a taxi just to get to the check-in counter. Rooms, at $200 a night per person, are just as large, but tastefully appointed. The place is spotlessly clean inside and out. Because many official delegations, government ministers, and foreign dignitaries stay here, we suggest that you make reservations at least a month ahead. The President's security is very tight, and you will only be able to enter by showing your passport and after telephone verification that you are a guest.

Amenities include a Russian-cuisine ground-floor restaurant, which is open from 7:45 to 10:30am for breakfast, 1 to 4pm for lunch, and 6 to 10:30pm for dinner. There is also an express buffet bar, newsstand, beauty parlor and exchange office, as well as a business center. You can also enjoy a full-size swimming pool, sauna and massage.

ARBAT HOTEL, *12 Plotnikov pereulok at Sivtsev Vrazhek pereulok, Metro Smolenskaya. Tel. (095) 244-0819 or 7635, Fax (095) 244-0093, Telex 414732. Major credit cards accepted.*

Located on a quiet street southwest of the Kremlin, roughly between the Ministry of Foreign Affairs and the Canadian embassy, and just two blocks south from the Old Arbat Street pedestrian promenade. Pushkin's only Moscow apartment is so close you may not be able to resist seeing it, no matter how much you dislike museums.

The Arbat Hotel, once the property of the Communist Party's Central Committee, now continues under state ownership and has 107 rooms and suites. Singles start at $150 a night, doubles $175, plus the 20 percent value added tax. Deluxe suites go as high as $650 a night, before the VAT. It very much looks like a Soviet apartment building. The hotel is bit faded now, but a good choice if you wish to stay in the Arbat area, an ancient district full of surprises. The dilapidated house in the nearby Krivoarbatsky pereulok of Konstantin Melnikov (1890-1974), a leading modernist architect, who, in 1936, was accused of 'formalism' and barred from his profession until his death, is one such site.

The hotel's sales pitch is that the Arbat will remind you of a "small, comfortable and quiet hotel like those you might find in Switzerland or on the side streets of Paris." The Arbat's manager claims that his staff is well trained and speaks several languages, if haltingly. He says that, to please foreign visitors, comfort, a quiet environment and freedom from ill-mannered guests off the street are his goals. He goes on that safety is the hallmark of Arbat Hotel and that you will not encounter rowdy nouveau-riche types, nor "frivolous girls" in his establishment. The hotel is "secure from suspicious and criminal characters," and "gentlemen of fortune" (he means burglars) have no chance of getting in.

A restaurant specializing in Russian cuisine is on the premises, serving Russian cabbage **pirozhki**, among others specialties. Westerners can enjoy an English breakfast or an American steak. The hotel also houses an expensive French wine club.

Old Arbat Street's American **McDonald's** fast food restaurant, which opened in 1993, is so close (within the walking distance to the northwest) that we fear Americans will not be resolute enough to stay away from it.

Moderate

AGMOS HOTEL, *18/73 Krymskaya nab., Metro Park Kultury. Tel. (095) 956-6501 through 6505, Fax 956-6523. Major credit cards accepted.* Docked on the Moskva River, southwest of the Kremlin, inside the Garden Ring Road, and near the Central House of Artists.

Aboard the floating steamship M.S. Valery Bryusov, the Agmos Hotel was named after the Russian poet, born in Moscow in 1873, and a leader in the Russian Symbolist movement. He was an enthusiastic Bolshevist and worked for the cause until his death in 1924.

Inaugurated in 1993, the single daily rate of about $100 includes breakfast.

For more information about **Silla**, its Korean and Asian restaurant, please turn to Chapter 12, *Where to Eat*. It also has a casino, bar and sauna.

PEKIN HOTEL (Beijing Hotel), *5 Ulitsa Sadovaya Bolshaya, Metro Mayakovskaya. Tel. (095) 209-0935 or 2135 or 2442, Fax (095) 200-1420, Telex 411661. Major credit cards accepted.*

Pekin is located northwest of the Kremlin, on the Garden Ring - in this case on Ulitsa Bolshaya Sadovaya - and across the street from the Satira and Mossoviet theaters and Tchaikovsky Concert Hall. A larger-than-life statue of the poet Vladimir Mayakovsky stands on Triumfalnaya Square in front of the hotel, with its back toward the Pekin.

The hotel was completed in 1955, the year when Russian-born writer Vladimir Nabokov published his English-language novel, **Lolita**. This outwardly quite handsome structure of 15 floors faces what until 1996 was the tired, shabby **Sofiya** restaurant.

There are 140 rooms, with singles starting at $95, accommodating 240 guests. Refrigerators and TV sets in some rooms are available on request only, but laundry and dry cleaning are done on the premises. In 1996, Pekin, following in the footsteps of many other Moscow hotels, opened a casino.

But what a letdown after you enter! The cramped lobby looks like some undefined Middle Eastern bazaar and even its marble mosaic floor or walls tiled with marble slabs might not reverse your disappointment.

From the lobby is the entrance to **Pekin** restaurant, until now serving good Chinese, European and Russian dishes.

Texas pianist Van Cliburn, who in 1958 won the first Tchaikovsky International Piano Competition against all expectations, stayed in this hotel during his surprising performance.

Inexpensive

NA TVERSKOY HOTEL (Minsk Hotel), *22 Ulitsa Tverskaya, Metro Pushkinskaya, Tverskaya or Mayakovskaya. Tel. (095) 299-1300 or 1215, Fax (095) 299-1208, Telex 411640 MINSK SU.*

The now privatized Na Tverskoy Hotel, which was known as Minsk while state-owned, is located northwest of the Kremlin and southeast of Tchaikovsky Concert Hall on Triumfalnaya Square.

This depressingly average Soviet-style hotel, which can accommodate 500 guests, was built in 1964, the year when Nikita Khrushchev was sacked as the Soviet Prime Minister. A TV set and refrigerator are available on request only and the rates reflect that; singles start at $50 a night, doubles at $80. The cluttered and worn-out lobby is complemented by halls shrouded in darkness and displaying worn-out carpets. The spartan singles overlook an even more depressing courtyard, while the doubles are subjected to 24-hour-a-day noise from traffic on the busy Tverskaya Street. The beds seem so narrow you might want to hold on to the boards all night, fearful that you will tumble on the floor. Shower areas are often so tiny you couldn't hope to bathe your toes. But an English-speaking receptionist was quite courteous when guiding us through a couple of floors.

Na Tverskoy has its own European-Russian cuisine restaurant, named, what else but **Minsk**, *Tel. 299-1248*, open from 11am to 11pm, and prides itself on its **Minskaya** cutlets.

An American **McDonald's** fast food restaurant is located just south of here, on Pushkin Square. **Pizza Hut**, where prices are as high as in New York, is farther southeast on Tverskaya, near the Prince Dolgoruky statue.

The **Museum of Revolution** is almost across the street, but only worthy of your consideration if you like to read old Soviet newspapers; see Chapter 13, *Seeing the Sights* for more information.

OUTSIDE THE GARDEN RING ROAD

Quick Overview: The selection of hotels outside the Garden Ring Road is perhaps the best, although often it translates into more than an hour's drive by car or thirty minutes by metro to a downtown site like the Bolshoy Theater or Red Square.

Palas is the five-star choice for those who want impeccable lodgings and food and have the means to afford them.

The **Renaissance Moscow**, the American-managed **Radisson Slavyanskaya, Aerostar, Sofitel Iris, Tverskaya, Novotel, Park Otel Laguna**, and perhaps the **Mezhdunarodnaya** are the luxury choices for those accustomed to Western comforts and those concerned about safety.

Danilovsky is owned by the Russian Orthodox Church and one of the safest Moscow hotels. **Kosmos** is a toss-up between a hotel with a few luxuries and a tourist mill of gigantic proportions. **Zolotoye Koltso**, once a concentration-camp-like habitat, has been reconstructed and reopened as a luxury hotel in 1997.

Art, Mir, Sovyetskaya, Tsaritsino and **Ukraina** are in the next class of hotels that are generally satisfactory to Americans, even if single women should exercise caution. Hotel Mir, however, because of its proximity to the Russian White House, is heavily guarded and also one of the safest Moscow hotels. **Inflotel**, like Agmos in the previous section, is a floating boat hotel on the Moskva River.

The following hotels, still another notch down in amenities and service from a Western point of view, just might exhaust the limits of your patience. They include such unwelcome choices as **Belgrad, Veshnyaky, Soyuz, Leningradskaya, Globus** and **Tsentralny Dom Turista**. Women traveling alone might feel safer staying at a pre-screened Bed & Breakfast home instead.

And, finally, there are hotels, such as **Varshava, Izmaylovo, Sheremetyevo, Yunost, Sevastopol, Arena, Orlyonok, Sport,** and **Molodyozhnaya**, where amenities are even more spartan and whose lodgings might well be considered inadequate. Student groups might be the only acceptable lodgers for some of the last two groups of hotels. **Kievskaya**, fortunately, does not even accept foreigners.

On behalf of those pinching pennies, we visited the **Traveller's Guest House**, asked questions, observed and listened to what went on. Frankly, you could do much worse in a hotel at twice the Guest House's rate.

In this section, when you consider an inexpensive hotel, use our price quotes as a starting point only in your selection process because the quotes are not always uniform. When one of us visited Hotel Arena, we were told the single rooms start at $50, but when we called on the phone we were told that singles start at $30. We thus decided to use the single rate of $40 a night.

Expensive

PALAS HOTEL (Palace Hotel), *19 First Ulitsa Tverskaya-Yamskaya, Metro Mayakovskaya or Belorusskaya. Tel. (095) 956-3152, Fax (095) 956-3151, Telex 412794 PALAC SU; Satellite telephone 7 (503) 956-3152, Satellite Fax 7 (503) 956-3151. Major credit cards accepted.*

Located northwest of the Kremlin, four long blocks beyond the Garden Ring Road, and two long blocks southeast of the Belorussky Railway Station.

Inaugurated in 1993, this is a Russian-Austrian joint venture whose hostelry is run by Marco Polo Hotels & Resorts, which also manages the Marco Polo Presnya Hotel. Its Russian partner is the Russian Academy of Sciences, which once owned this building. For a five-star hotel, the Palace has a rather small lobby.

There are 221 rooms and suites - 51 for non-smokers - where prices for singles start at $300 and for doubles at $325 a night. Executive singles are about $350 and almost $400 for doubles. The junior among its 23 suites go from $450 and all the way to $850 for a two-bedroom duplex suite, regardless of the number of guests. The most expensive is the $1,100 two-story two-bedroom Presidential Suite, excluding the 20 percent value added tax; there are two rooms downstairs and bedrooms up the curved staircase, the furniture is luxurious and the bath taps are gold-plated. Most suites have large plate-glass windows offering a panoramic view of Moscow below you. All are air-conditioned, with direct-dial satellite telephones, minibars, satellite TV and VCR.

There are three restaurants at the Palace; for more information about **Vienna**, which serves gourmet international dishes to the accompaniment of live music; **Yakor**, serving seafood; and **Lomonosov** serving breakfast, lunch and dinner buffet, and Sunday brunch, please see Chapter 12, *Where to Eat*. The typically Austrian **Cafe Mozart**, clean and pleasant, serves Austrian pastries and coffee to the music of, who else but, Mozart. You can have a drink in the lobby bar or Hermitage Bar.

A hairdresser, as well as laundry and dry cleaning services are available. The underground garage entrance is on First Brestskaya Street, a sidestreet. The Palace Hotel health club, which is open from 7am to 10pm, offers jacuzzi, saunas, work-outs, aerobics, massages and a solarium; there is a small charge for these facilities. The hotel also rents cars at a discount.

RENAISSANCE MOSCOW HOTEL, *18/1 Olimpiysky prospekt, Metro Prospekt Mira. Tel. (095) 931-9000/9833, Fax (095) 931-9020/9076, Telex 411061 OLIMP RU; Satellite Tel. 7 (502) 223-9000, Satellite Fax 7 (502) 223-9076, Satellite reservations Fax 7 (502) 223-9020. Major credit cards accepted.*

Located north of the Kremlin, east of the Frunze Central Army Park and the Russian Army Theater, and north of the Olympic Sports complex. The quickest way to walk over to the hotel from Prospekt Mira metro station is to go straight west on Kapelsky pereulok and Ulitsa Samarskaya, but it will take ten minutes or more.

The Renaissance Moscow, previously known as Olympic Penta, is a modern 12-story facility that opened in 1991 as a joint venture between Intourist and Lufthansa Airlines. It has 488 rooms, including 12 suites, that can accommodate almost 1,000 guests. Singles start at $300 a night, suites at $500. The 12th floor is for Renaissance Club members, who receive additional luxuries and higher security. Non-smoking rooms are available. Amenities for all guests include an English-speaking concierge, 24-hour room service, individually air-conditioned rooms, minibars, and satellite telephones.

The all-day restaurant **Vienna**, which seats 150, serves breakfast, lunch and dinner buffet and has a salad bar. There is also a Sunday brunch and children eat at a discount. The **Mediterranean Village**, with seating for 130, serves Italian and Mediterranean cuisine to the sounds of live piano and guitar music. **Bierstube**, a traditional German beer restaurant which seats 80, serves German cuisine until after midnight.**The Bakery**, on the lower level, is open daily from 8am to 8pm; it sells croissants, Danish pastries and French baguettes.

The Olympic Health Club includes a 22-meter indoor swimming pool, fitness center, solarium, saunas and massage services. Business amenities include the hotel's business center, meeting rooms, and computer and secretarial services. The hotel has an underground garage.

RADISSON SLAVYANSKAYA HOTEL, *2 Berezhkovskaya nab., Metro Kievskaya. Tel. (095) 941-8020 or 8021 or 8044, Fax (095) 240-6915 or (095) 941-8000; Satellite Fax 7 (502) 224-1225. Major credit cards accepted.*

The 50-million dollar Radisson hotel and business complex is located southwest of the Kremlin, and, inexplicably, next to the congested Kievsky Railway Station, whose unwashed masses spill right to its doorway.

A joint venture between Intourist and Radisson Hotels, built in 1991, this is Russia's first American-managed hotel and you can tell so right away by the comfortable chairs and sofas strewn inside its sprawling two-level lobby, where you have a sense of freedom typically found in large American hotels. Americans will also be pleased to know that a certain informality they are accustomed to at home also reigns here.

Slavyanskaya has 430 rooms and 165 suites that accommodate 1,200 guests. Some Westerners find the rooms a bit cheerless and small, although some have been redone since 1994. Singles start at about $250 a night, doubles at $300, suites go from $500 to $900, plus the inevitable 20 percent value-added tax. When President Clinton visited Russia, he stayed in a $2,000-a-night suite.

For more about **Amadeus Cafe**, **The Exchange**, and **Skandia** restaurants, please see Chapter 12, *Where to Eat*. The **Lobby Bar** is a great place to unwind, while watching for any of your business associates who may be passing through Moscow.

Its business facilities include a 165-suite office building next door, with numerous meeting rooms, as well as a conference hall with the means to translate into five foreign languages.

Slavyanskaya's fee-charging health club is open daily from 7am to

10pm. It features a junior Olympic indoor swimming pool, men's and women's saunas, solarium, a weight and exercise room, aerobics classes and massage services.

There are numerous shops and stores on the ground floor, where you can buy everything from staples to designer clothes, have your film processed, or pick up an expensive, but well-crafted souvenir. **Reuters** news agency bureau is located on your right as you enter the hotel. The **American House of Cinema** shows films in its second-floor cinema.

There is a **Dialog Bank**, *Tel. (095) 956-9877, Fax (095) 941-8424,* currency exchange branch on the ground floor for anyone who lugs around American Express travelers checks, only to find that no establishment in the city will take them; one alternative is to cash them here at a hefty service fee, whether you get dollars or rubles in return. You can also write emergency personal checks against your American Express card for a slightly more bearable charge. Dialog Bank is open seven days a week, from 8am to 8pm.

Upstairs is the **Americom Business Center**, *Satellite Tel. 7 (095) 941-8427 or 243-7518, Fax 7 (095) 240-6915 or 941-8978, E-mail americom@co.ru,* which is open 24 hours a day. Computers, photocopiers, fax machines and direct-dial international telephone service are available. You can rent a computer or have oral and written translations made, from 9am to 9pm every day.

In the fall of 1996, an Oklahoma businessman, one of the hotel's partners with Radisson Hotels and the Moscow city government, was gunned down in broad daylight at the bottom of the Kievskaya metro station staircase, just steps from the hotel and business center he founded in 1991.

Note: While this hotel is more than adequate in every way, we suggest that you avoid walking around the nearby Kievsky railway station at night. The area is a magnet for pickpockets, thieves and an occasional band of street children that can be a nuisance.

AEROSTAR HOTEL, *37 Leningradsky prospekt, Bldg. 9, Metro Dinamo or Aeroport. Tel. (095) 213-9000, Fax (095) 213-9001, Telex 414831 ARSTR SU; Satellite phone 7 (502) 213-9000, Satellite Fax 7 (502) 213-9101. Major credit cards accepted.*

Located on the road to Sheremetyevo 2 international airport, northwest of the Kremlin, southeast of the 60,000-seat Dinamo Stadium, named after a local soccer club, and northwest of the Hippodrome horse racing track. Across the Leningradsky Avenue is the red-brick Petrovsky Palace, where the tsars and their retinues rested when traveling between Moscow and St. Petersburg.

This area is known as **Khodynskoye pole** (Khodynskoye Field), whose history goes back to the 1389 ecclesiastical charter of Grand Duke Dmitry

Donskoy. By 1600's, there was a country court for the reception of arriving foreign ambassadors on the banks of the Khodynka River. In 1896, the coronation of Nicholas II, the last Romanov emperor, took place here, an event that ended in hundreds of Muscovites dying from the crowds pressing forward, fearful that there was not enough of the promised free food and drink for all.

Formerly an Aeroflot hotel, this is a renovated (1992) Canadian joint venture with Intourist state travel agency. It has 417 rooms with European furnishings, with singles running from $250 to $375 and suites from $350 to $450. Non-smoking rooms are available, a rarity in Moscow.

For more information about the restaurants **Borodino**, which was inaugurated in 1993 and features live lobster from Nova Scotia, or about the more casual **Cafe Taiga**, please see Chapter 12, *Where to Eat*. Children eat at a discount at Cafe Taiga. The Terrace Bar, open from 11am to 2am, overlooks the lobby and has live music every evening.

Aerostar provides free shuttle bus service for guests to Izmaylovsky Park on weekends. You will also be served a complimentary breakfast in the lobby, from 5 to 8am. Other amenities include a fully equipped fitness center. You will also have at your disposal an English-speaking concierge, photocopiers, computers and translation services.

If you like to watch horse races, go to the nearby **Hippodrome**, *22 Ulitsa Begovaya, Tel. 945-0437 or 4516*, a few very long, but typical Moscow city blocks southeast of here.

SOFITEL IRIS HOTEL, *10 Korovinskoye shosse, Metro Vladykino. Tel. (095) 488-8000 or 8228 or 8229, Fax (095) 488-8229 or 8230, Telex 413656 BOYG SU; Satellite tel. 7 (502) 220-8000, Satellite Fax 7 (502) 220-8888. Major credit cards accepted.*

Located in the Degunino district in far northwestern Moscow, near the renown Svyatoslav Fyodorov Eye Clinic. There is a free hourly shuttle to and from the city center, from 7:30am to 11pm, with stops at Pushkin Square and the Central Telegraph Office on Tverskaya Street. During exhibitions only, a free shuttle is also available to and from the Ekspotsentr and the Russian Exhibition Center (VDNkH). Limousine service to and from the airports is available 24 hours a day.

Sofitel Iris is a Russian-French joint venture facility built in 1991 in the oval shape of an eye. The hotel has 195 soundproofed and individually air-conditioned rooms, including 39 suites, built around a central atrium, and can accommodate 400 guests. Singles start at $250, doubles at $350, suites at $450, and the Presidential Suite is $750, all excluding the 20 percent value added tax, an additional "special tax" of one percent, and a one-time visa registration fee of $3 per person.

There is a Sofitel sales representative on the lower level at Sheremetyevo 2 international airport; if you come here in person or call *Tel. (095) 578-*

7532, Monday through Saturday, between 11am and 10pm, you can receive a substantial discount. A single will then start at $190, double at $205, and suite at $295.

There is a direct-dial satellite telephone in each room, as well as 30-channel satellite television. Sofitel has 24-hour room service. Safe deposit boxes are complimentary.

The hotel has an excellent French restaurant, **Les Champs-Elysees**, and brasserie **Le Cafe Francais**, about which you can read in Chapter 12, *Where to Eat*. There is a delicatessen boutique, selling homemade pastries and wines, and a lobby bar featuring jazz music. A 24-hour exchange office, a gift shop and a beauty salon are also on the premises. Guests can utilize the hotel's business center, which provides telephone, fax, telex, copier, computer, secretarial and translation services.

Other amenities include a health club with a gym, swimming pool, sauna, solarium and massage services. Laundry and dry cleaning are also done on the premises.

There is a Western-style private **Dental Clinic** at Sofitel Iris; for more details please see Chapter 8, *Basic Information*. You will also find an optician and a pharmacy.

TVERSKAYA HOTEL, *34 Ulitsa First Tverskaya-Yamskaya, Metro Belorusskaya or Mayakovskaya. Satellite Tel. 7 (501) 258-3000 or 7 (502) 290-9900; Satellite Fax 7 (501) 258-3099 or 7 (502) 290-9999. Toll-free in the US: 800/777-1700. Cash only.*

Located northwest of the Kremlin, just a few steps southeast of the Belorussky Railway Station, and a block northwest of the five-star Palace Hotel.

Tverskaya, named after one of the first Moscow streets which ran to the ancient town of Tver, is one of the newest luxury hotels in Moscow. Open for business since late 1995, the hotel caters mostly to businessmen. Moscow mayor Yuri Luzhkov himself came to cut the ribbon at the American-managed hotel, where you can reserve your room or suite on your credit card, but must pay in cash. Colony Hotels & Resorts of Pittsburgh has been hired to manage the 122-room hotel, which has satellite telephones in the rooms and a fitness center on the premises.

Single rooms in this eight-story hotel start at $250 and go to $500 a night for a suite, excluding a 20 percent value added tax. Doubles start at $275 and can climb as high as $600 a night for two. The Presidential suite is about $900, again before the VAT. All are individually air-conditioned and heated.

We unsuccessfully searched for a speck of dirt in the glistening lobby, where two glass-walled elevators allow you a complete view of the interior. Toilets were spotless, too. A business center, safe deposit boxes, laundry and dry cleaning, and underground parking are all available.

There seems to be considerable demand for accommodations in this four-star hotel category. In the US and Europe, cities of Moscow's size have three to four times the number of hotels in this price range. Tverskaya, although admittedly a small hotel, seems to be close to occupied most of the time; we suggest that you reserve weeks ahead. The hotel's cafe and bar are adjacent to the lobby. Its **Seasons** restaurant on the second floor, seating 150, has a prix fixe New Orleans brunch on Sundays, when you can sample such Cajun favorites as chicken and smoked sausage gumbo, etouffe of shrimp and crayfish, all for about $30. Champagne is complimentary. There is jazz music and a ten-ounce prime rib steak special on Friday and Saturday nights.

NOVOTEL SHEREMETYEVO 2, *located at Sheremetyevo 2 International Airport. Tel. (095) 578-9110 and 578-9401 through 9408, Fax (095) 926-5903 or 5904, Telex 911620 NOVSH SU; Satellite Tel. 7 (502) 220 6611 or 6612, Satellite Fax 220 6604. Toll-free reservations in the US and Canada, Tel. 800/221-4542. Major credit cards accepted.*

Located next to the Sheremetyevo 2 International Airport, about 19 miles north of the Kremlin. Allow at least one hour to get to or from downtown. You can be picked up at any airport at any time free of charge. Free shuttle service to downtown Moscow is available hourly between 8am and 10pm. With 24-hour notice, Novotel will assist you in obtaining a 72-hour transit visa.

A Russian-South Korean joint venture, Novotel has 22 suites and 426 well-maintained and comfortable rooms, five of them for "disabled guests," a rare gesture to the handicapped in today's Moscow. All rooms have individual climate controls and are equipped with satellite telephones and minibars. Singles start at $230 a night, doubles at $275, and suites at $400; they include the value added tax. Novotel promises high level, but discreet security.

There is the restaurant **Efimoff**, featuring Russian and international cuisine, a coffee shop, a lobby bar and a nightclub with live music in the evening.

A fitness center with a swimming pool, jogging trail, sauna and massage services are at your disposal. A medical doctor is also on site.

A business center, an independent 24-hour bank and currency exchange, car rental agency, Federal Express office, travel agency, boutique, and in-house laundry and dry cleaning are all available.

PARK OTEL LAGUNA, *95/15 Akademika Pilyugina at Leninsky prospekt, Metro Noviye Cheremushky or Prospekt Vernadskogo. Tel. (095) 133-4393, Fax (095) 938-2100. Major credit cards accepted.*

Laguna is located southwest of the Kremlin, on the northern edge of Vorontsovsky Park, near the former East German embassy, and across Leninsky prospekt from Hotel Sport.

This establishment is a Russian-Swiss joint venture. It can accommodate only about 40 guests; this probably makes it one of the smallest hotels in the capital, where size is often equated with quality. Singles start at $230 a night.

The peaceful and high-ceilinged **Taverna** restaurant, serving international, Russian and Italian cuisine can accommodate up to 100. The piano bar, which shares the dining room premises, has live music.

MEZHDUNARODNAYA (International), *12 Krasnopresnenskaya nab., Metro Ulitsa 1905 goda. Tel. (095) 253-1391 through 1394 and 2840, Fax (095) 253-2400, Telex 411339 INTER SU or 411486 SOV SU. Major credit cards accepted.*

Located west of the Kremlin and the Russian White House and east of Krasnaya Presnya Park, the Mezh, as it is called locally, overlooks the Moskva River. The nearest metro station is a good 15 minutes away and only one city bus stops near the hotel.

Where the Mezh stands today was once the estate of Yekaterina Ushakova, who most of her adult life was desperately in love with Russia's greatest poet, Aleksandr Pushkin. She married only after the poet died in a duel, when she was already 44 years old.

This 23-story Intercontinental Hotel, with a nine-story atrium and glass elevators, was built in 1980 by the late oil tycoon Armand Hammer, who rubbed shoulders with everyone, from Lenin to Gorbachev. Israeli Prime Minister Menachem Begin nominated the fame-starved Hammer for the Nobel Peace Prize in 1989, but Hammer lost out to the Dalai Lama. The Moscow Chamber of Commerce is a major shareholder in the Mezh.

"For years, the Mezh has stood as a monument to the disappointment of perestroika," is how the *Moscow Times* daily once described the hotel. Potentially a top-class hotel, it instead gained infamy for its high prices, surly security guards and for the men and women of dubious purpose who lurked about the lobbies. In 1996, the new management committed itself to refurbishing the interior, retraining its 3,000 employees and replacing the dreaded security men. The Mezh, once one of the most popular Moscow business hotels, has been deserted in droves.

The Mezh is part of Hammer's SovinCenter, an international trade center, which also includes conference facilities and an office building. The upper 15 floors have more than 200 offices, many occupied by international corporations and banks.

Comparable to a Hilton or Sheraton, it has 540 rooms that can accommodate 1,000 guests, but most rooms are said to have narrow single beds. Singles start at $225, doubles at $300, and suites at $400 a night, excluding the 20 percent value added tax.

Used by foreign businessmen and delegations, the hotel has half a dozen restaurants, a coffee shop on the ground floor, and several bars.

For more information about one of them, **Kontinental**, please see Chapter 12, *Where to Eat*. On the ground floor there is a casino and nightclub.

Other amenities include a bowling alley and car rental counter, foreign currency exchange counter, translation services and audiovisual equipment for business meetings. There are swimming pools, saunas, solariums and a gym.

An American Express cash dispensing automatic teller machine is located in the lobby, near the registration desk.

DANILOVSKY HOTEL, *5b Bolshoy Starodanilovsky pereulok, Metro Tulskaya. Tel. (095) 954-0306 or 0503, Fax (095) 954-0750. Major credit cards accepted. Limited smoking is allowed.*

Located south of the Kremlin, a couple of long city blocks northeast or southeast of Tulskaya metro station, depending on where you exit.

The hotel is situated inside the reconstructed Danilovsky Monastery, which was founded in 1272 by the first Prince of Moscow and rebuilt in stone by Ivan the Terrible in the 16th century. It served as a factory from early Soviet times until 1983. Now the Patriarch of the Russian Orthodox Church has his headquarters here.

If the President Hotel on Bolshaya Yakimanka Street in Zamoskvorechye is a majestic bunker beyond penetration, if the Mir Hotel is a nest of gun-toting soldiers and KGB operatives keeping their weary eyes on the Russian White House across Konyushkovskaya Street, then the Danilovsky Hotel perhaps holds the distinction of being the third most closely guarded hotel in Moscow. While no armed soldiers are present, you will not be admitted to the hotel courtyard until your identity has been established - or you calculatingly speak English only to cut through the red tape. Once on the hotel grounds, you will marvel at the manicured gardens and the spotless lobby, where nothing is left to chance and someone is always sweeping, cleaning, dusting. One cannot shake the feeling, however, that the Danilovsky flaunts its newly-found affluence a bit .

There are 120 rooms. Singles start at $200 a night, doubles at $230, and suites at $300, all including one or two breakfasts. Smoking is not allowed in any public area, where the Patriarch's portrait is displayed, although you can puff to your heart's content in your room or in the basement nightclub. You can buy church souvenirs and icon reproductions in the gift shop. Danilov is often filled up so fax in your reservations weeks ahead if you wish to stay here.

There are **dezhurniye** (floor ladies) on each of its four floors, but their demeanor is rather sweet when compared with the stern women guarding the floors (and, they think) the reputation of such Soviet institutions as Hotel Moskva, to name but one. The rooms at the Danilovsky are clean, comfortable and attractive, but no ashtrays could be seen. Many have a lovely view of the gardens and other church properties. Bathrooms are practical and have shampoo available.

The hotel has a good restaurant, serving traditional Russian cuisine; one among the very few non-smoking restaurants in Moscow. For more details, please see the Chapter 12, *Where to Eat.*

ZOLOTOYE KOLTSO (Golden Ring), *5 Ulitsa Smolenskaya, Metro Smolenskaya.*

Located west of the Kremlin, just outside the Garden Ring, and practically across the street from the Ministry of Foreign Affairs. From the beginning of the 17th century, Smolenskaya Street was the road to the historic town of Smolensk.

Like its twin across Smolenskaya, named the Belgrad, the old Zolotoye Koltso hotel could accommodate about 800 guests. It was dreary, unfriendly, austere, and overpriced, the kind of place a hapless tourist often ends up at.

Zolotoye Koltso was completely rebuilt and, according to the Intourist office inside the Belgrad Hotel, across the street, will reopen as a luxury hotel in 1997.

Moderate

MIR HOTEL (Peace Hotel), *9 Bolshoy Devyatinsky pereulok at Ulitsa Konyushkovskaya, Metro Smolenskaya or Krasnopresnenskaya. Tel. (095) 290-9150 or 9518 or 9504, Fax (095) 252-0140.*

Mir is located west of the Kremlin, two blocks west of the Garden Ring Road - in this instance Novinsky bulvar - and practically in the shadow of the Russian White House facing the Moskva River. Sovincenter World Trade Center business offices at the Mezhdunarodnaya Hotel are three characteristically long Moscow blocks farther west, the American Embassy one block northeast of here. The Moscow mayor's office is farther south on the same block.

Mir's lobby has a strong military presence. Some men actually sport weapons and KGB operatives abound. But because of this it is probably one of the safest hotels in Moscow. If you wish to stay close to the American embassy, as well as Novy and Stary Arbat for sightseeing and entertainment, Mir is as good a buy for your money as you can hope to find. It has 220 rooms on eleven floors and can accommodate 300 guests. The daily rate is $100 per person.

Most rooms overlook either the east side of the White House or the American embassy on the other side. The somewhat plain lobby, halls and attractive rooms are clean if a bit spartan. But you better reserve well in advance if you hope to stay here.

Two more expensive alternatives to Mir, both with very strict identification checks, but both as safe as Mir, include the palatial **President Hotel** in Zamoskvorechye and a more private **Danilovsky Hotel**, which is operated by the Patriarch of the Orthodox Church of Russia.

During the bloody struggles for the White House in October 1993, Mir guests were thrown out of the hotel to make room for government forces, who battled the Parliament renegades seeking to overthrow the government. The following year, more than 100 hotel employees protested against plans to transfer its ownership to the KGB to house counterintelligence service staff coming to Moscow from the provinces.

Mir has its own restaurant and bar, but if you do not like theirs, there are many other dining options in this area. Perhaps the only restaurant we wish to caution you against is **Arbat**, situated on the western end of Novy Arbat, close to the corner with Novinsky bulvar. Read about it in Chapter 12, *Where to Eat* and decide for yourself.

KOSMOS (Space), *150 Prospekt Mira, Metro VDNKh. Tel. (095) 217-0692 or 0693 or 0785 or 0786, Fax (095) 215-8880 or 7991, Telex 411488 ZENIT SU. Major credit cards accepted.*

Located northeast of the Kremlin, and facing Prospekt Mira and the enormous Russian Exhibition Center, metro station VDNkH, and the Museum of Cosmonautics behind it. Two blocks northeast of here stands the gigantic sculpture of the Worker & Collective Farm Woman, designed by Vera Mukhina.

Built by the French in 1979 to house their athletes at the Moscow Olympic Games, the 26-story colossus, as big as the universe itself, Kosmos has 1,777 simple rooms and can accommodate more than 3,500 guests. Only in the former Soviet Union would one expect to find a behemoth like this to intimidate tourists.

Singles start at about $100, doubles at $200, and suites at $300 a night.

The two-story lobby has slot machines and is always full of tourists; about half of the rooms are occupied by package tours during the May-to-September high season. According to some disgruntled Western guests that's what Kosmos is, a typical tourist dive. It is also believed that groups get better service than individual lodgers. The prostitutes abound.

It has several airport-sized cafeterias and the following four restaurants of industrial proportions:

The ground-floor **Dubrava**, open from noon to 11pm, serves as a coarse strip-tease stage after 9pm to amuse arthritic Westerners; **Galaktika**, open from 11am to midnight, is located upstairs, across the mezzanine from a casino, where tourists gamble in shorts and sandals; another hangar-like **Kalinka**, open from noon to 11pm; and the still more enormous second-floor **Lunny**, open from noon to 11pm, with bathrooms that sometimes lack toilet paper. Altogether, they can accommodate several thousand diners, but we feel none is distinguished enough to single it out, even if the expensive cherry-tree and fumed oak wood paneling and Austrian crystal chandeliers did add up to $2 million in the renovation of Dubrava. There are several bars scattered about and the **Solyaris** nightclub is in the basement and open from 11pm to 7am.

Other amenities include a swimming pool, saunas and underground parking. Kosmos has four standard American underground-based bowling lanes, which operate from 2pm to midnight. Secretarial services in English, translations, and currency exchange are also available. There is a car rental counter in the lobby.

TSARITSINO HOTEL, *47/1 Shipilovsky proyezd at Orehovy bulvar, Metro Orekhovo or Domodedovskaya. Tel. (095) 343-4317 or 4343 or 4344, Fax (095) 343-4351 or 4363. Major credit cards accepted from Westerners only.*

Located southeast of the Kremlin and southeast of the Tsaritsino palatial ruins, in the Orekhovo district, near the southern city limit.

This Scandinavian type of apartment-hotel, mostly for long-term residents, is situated on the edge of Tsaritsino Park, a few minutes south of Orekhovo metro station. The 17-floor hotel, which opened in 1991, and its parking area are fenced in and have a 24-hour guard. The top floor has a restaurant, bar and sauna.

Daily rentals for Westerners start at about $100. Monthly Western-style one-room and two-room monthly rentals are also available and include breakfast, as well as telephone, satellite TV, kitchen utilities, linens, refrigerator, electric stove, microwave oven, toaster and dishwasher. Also on the premises is a washing machine and drier.

Standard one-room "Russian apartments" are available for a minimum of six months. They do not include the use of the telephone, TV or refrigerator, for which there is a separate monthly charge. Office space rentals are also available on an annual basis.

SOVYETSKAYA HOTEL, *32/2 Leningradsky prospekt, Metro Dinamo. Tel. (095) 250-7253 or 7255, Fax (095) 250-8003, Telex 411671 LOTA.*

Located northwest of the Kremlin, southeast of Dinamo Stadium, northeast of the Hippodrome racecourse, and next to the Romen Gypsy Theater.

All rooms come with color TV sets and refrigerators. The Sovyetskaya is a remodeled hotel with 100 rooms than can accommodate 160 guests. Singles start at $100. At one time, government leaders and other VIP's stayed here. American politician Adlai Stevenson slept under its roof, too.

The original 1911 building, the site of the once famous restaurant **Yar**, was made into a hotel in 1952. Mad monk Rasputin, who really was not a monk at all, but had great influence over the wife of Tsar Nicholas II, caused such a ruckus here in 1915 that even the mild-mannered tsar became enraged.

There is a post and telegraph office on the premises. Sovyetskaya, meaning Soviet, has a restaurant and three banquet halls.

In the Romen Theater, there is the **Golden Horseshoe Club**, open daily from 10:30pm to 6am, where you will enjoy authentic Gypsy singing and dancing.

ART HOTEL, *41 Prospekt Vernadskogo, Metro Prospekt Vernadskogo. Tel. (095) 432-7827 or 431-0822, Fax (095) 432-2757. Major credit cards accepted.*

Located southwest of the Kremlin, between Ulitsa Udaltsova and Ulitsa Lobachevskogo, one block southeast of metro station Prospekt Vernadskogo, and behind the Druzhba Hotel.

This small German-managed hotel, which describes itself as "the first middle-class hotel in Moscow," opened in 1994. It has 53 rooms in art-deco style, with baths or showers, all equipped with satellite telephones and TV's. Singles start at about $100 a night.

There is a restaurant on the premises, open from 7am to midnight, and an open-air beer garden between May and October. A German breakfast buffet is available.

Small pool, sauna, solarium and massage services are also at your disposal.

UKRAINA HOTEL, *2/1 Kutuzovsky prospekt, Metro Kievskaya. Tel. (095) 243-3030 or 2596 or 3246, Fax (095) 956-2078, Telex 411654 LOTOS. Major credit cards accepted.*

Ukraina is located west of the Kremlin, north of Kievsky Railway Station, and across the Moskva River from the Russian White House. The avenue running past the hotel is named after field marshal Mikhail Kutuzov, hero of bloody battles against Napoleon in 1812. The nearest metro station is at least ten minutes away.

This large city-owned hotel, built in 1957 on the bank of the Moskva River, can accommodate 1,600 guests in its 1,000 faded and worn rooms and suites, which are priced, in part, according to how high they are located. Singles start at $100 a night, suites go up to $350. Most rooms have TV sets and refrigerators.

Ukraina was inaugurated by the fanatically dedicated Communist, Yekaterina Furtseva, the first woman in Soviet history to be a member of the Presidium of the Supreme Soviet. Until the completion of the Rossiya Hotel, just east of the Kremlin, Ukraina was the largest hotel in Russia. This, like the Ministry of Foreign Affairs or the Moscow State University building, is one of the seven showpiece anchor buildings Stalin erected simultaneously all over Moscow to display the Soviet Union's might. Guests seem equally divided between Russians and foreigners.

American comedian Bob Hope stayed here and on seeing Ukraina's massive entrance, he is said to have exclaimed: "Now I believe that the

Russians **are** eight feet tall!" But even Bob Hope would not have held much clout in October 1993, when just across the river the Parliament and the Russian President fought for control of the White House building and guests were literally thrown out of this hotel by the government troops because of its strategic location.

The highest among its 30 floors has a nice panoramic view of Moscow. You can make international phone calls directly from your room. Saunas are also available and the hotel has many other amenities, including laundry and dry cleaning services, and foreign currency exchange.

For details about its 3rd floor **In Vino** eatery, please see Chapter 12, *Where to Eat*. Another is **Ukraina**, as well as several bars, among them the **German Wine Bar**.

The 20-foot-tall bronze statue on a pedestal of Ukrainian granite in front of the hotel is that of Taras Shevchenko (1814-1861), a Ukrainian poet who was born a serf in Kiev.

INFLOTEL, *aboard the M.S. Aleksandr Blok, docked opposite the Mezhdunarodnaya Hotel, 12 Krasnopresnenskaya nab., Metro Ulitsa 1905 goda. Tel. (095) 255-9278 or 9284, Fax (095) 253-9578. Major credit cards accepted.*

Situated on Moskva River west of the Kremlin, west of the Russian White House, and northeast of Ekspotsentr, an exhibition center.

This specially equipped river boat is named after the Russian poet Aleksandr Blok (1880-1921), whose verse is characterized by violent Romanticism, and who at first welcomed both the 1905 and 1917 Revolutions, but later became disillusioned.

In 1996, Inflotel unveiled plans for a variety of tourist facilities that would make it a Las Vegas-style entertainment complex with a sandy beach on the Moscow River, an artificial marina and swimming pool, a helicopter to transport club members to the airport, and a gondola to take guests for cruises along the river. Meanwhile, singles start at about $80 a night, suites at $200.

This floating hotel has the well-known **Greek Restaurant**, please see Chapter 12, *Where to Eat* for more information. You can also enjoy its popular **Casino Aleksandr Blok**, described in Chapter 15, *Nightlife & Entertainment*. There is an open air cafe, with an interesting view of the Moscow skyline from the top deck, and a bar.

Inexpensive

BELGRAD HOTEL, *8 Ulitsa Smolenskaya, Metro Smolenskaya. Tel. (095) 248-1676 or 2841, Fax (095) 230-2129, Telex 113259 TOYOTA. Major credit cards accepted.*

Located southwest of the Kremlin, just beyond the Garden Ring Road, at the intersection of the Garden Ring Road and Ulitsa Smolenskaya, across the square from the Ministry of Foreign Affairs. Its newly rebuilt former twin brother, Zolotoye Koltso Hotel, is across the street. It will take you but a couple of minutes on foot to enjoy the Old Arbat promenade or visit Pushkin's only Moscow apartment, which is located two blocks northeast of here.

Belgrad was built in 1973, the year when the Communist Party General Secretary Leonid Brezhnev and Richard Nixon signed a treaty to limit nuclear war. The hotel accommodates about 800 guests and you may be able to see the Russian White House from a few top-floor rooms, but do not expect much beyond cheap plywood furniture. Singles start at $85, more than you should pay for such decrepit lodgings.

There is bedlam in the lobby and, indeed, in every office throughout the building all day, a veritable study of inefficiency. Belgrad, always drab, developed a bad reputation with Westerners for lack of comfort and service. Amenities are minimal; there is no air conditioning in most of the rooms, which is really needed only for a couple of summer months, and many rooms are noisy because of its congested location. Most beds are singles and the mattresses unacceptable, according to some travelers. You will be given accommodations with a telephone and refrigerator on request.

There is a state **Intourist** travel office in the lobby, but the only tour we could book was to the Kremlin.

For more information about the **Dionyssos** restaurant, please see Chapter 12, *Where to Eat*. You can also read more about the Caucasian-cuisine restaurant **Shirak**, on the third floor, which has its second location here. **Belgrad**, on the second floor, offers Russian, Yugoslav and European dishes; there is music and dancing after 7pm. A **McDonald's** fast food restaurant is located less than two blocks northeast of here, on Old Arbat Street, almost across the street from Pushkin's apartment.

Next door is **Union Gallery**, *6 Ulitsa Smolenskaya*, selling everything from Soviet posters to icons.

VESHNYAKY HOTEL, *3 Krasny Kazanyets, Bldg. 3, Metro Ryazansky prospekt. Tel. (095) 171-2500 or 2527, Fax (095) 174-2599. Major credit cards accepted.*

The Veshnyaky is located southeast of the Kremlin and Kuskovo Park, and northeast of Ryazansky prospekt metro station.

A relatively new, but modest hotel that can accommodate 40 guests and has a restaurant and bar. Its rooms and suites, some with kitchenettes, have satellite TV, featuring CNN among other channels. Singles start at $80 per person and include a continental breakfast. You also have access to satellite telephone, fax and international telex.

Guests receive free transportation to and from the airport.

SOYUZ HOTEL (Union Hotel), *12 Ulitsa Levoberezhnaya, near Pribrezhny proyezd, Metro Rechnoy vokzal. Tel. (095) 457-9004 or 2088, Fax (095) 457-2096. Major credit cards accepted.*

The Soyuz is located in far northeast Moscow, on the bank of the Moscow Canal, east of the crossing of the Moscow Circular Road and Leningradskoye shosse. You can get to the hotel from the metro station Rechnoy vokzal, which is south of the hotel, or by bus, but both are inconvenient and a taxi is preferable. The surroundings are depressing. It is situated about 15 minutes from the Sheremetyevo 2 International Airport.

Built by the Yugoslavs in 1980, this 13-story hotel has 157 rooms, with surprisingly attractive furnishings for a hotel in this category. Soyuz can accommodate 280 guests. Singles start at $80 nightly. It has a post and telegraph office.

There is a restaurant on the premises, as well as a bar and cafe.

A short drive south of here is a super hip and super huge nightclub **Water Club/Ptyuch**, where your admission fee depends in part on how hip a dresser you are. It is located at the northern Rechnoy vokzal boat station, where on weekends you can buy tickets for riverboat excursions. Located at 51 Leningradskoye Highway, it is open Fridays and Saturday from 11pm until dawn, and boasting mostly students, artists and musicians. No telephone.

LENINGRADSKAYA HOTEL, *21/40 Ulitsa Kalanchevskaya, Metro Komsomolskaya. Tel. (095) 975-3008 or 3032, Telex 411659 GLORU SU. American Express credit card accepted only.*

Located northeast of the Kremlin, just east of the Kazansky and southeast from Leningradsky and Yaroslavsky railway stations, with enormous masses of the poor, unemployed and unkempt, and southeast of the International Post Office.

Built as Stalin's grandiosely impractical Gothic sky-rise hotel, Leningradskaya has 346 rooms, trademark red carpets, can accommodate 500 guests, and opened in 1957, the year when the Soviet Union launched Sputnik I and II, its first earth satellites. The rate for its Soviet-style rooms starts at $70 a night for singles and runs as high as $250. For a bit of quiet and a better view, ask for the highest-placed room you can get.

Although 26 stories high, several floors are unoccupied and wasted on an ornate tower. This is one of the seven Gothic buildings, constructed simultaneously, known jokingly as Stalin's wedding cakes. These massive granite monsters do provide one useful service to visitors, however: they serve as beacons in Moscow's often unnavigable maze of streets. Some Western lodgers say that staying at Leningradskaya feels like living inside a mausoleum, what with high ceilings, the murals and ornate bronze fixtures. A foreign currency exchange office and men's and women's hairstylists are on the premises.

The hotel, which was named after the city of Leningrad, now renamed St. Petersburg, has a restaurant with average food. Leningradskaya also has one of Moscow's better casinos, **Moscow**. For more information see Chapter 15, *Nightlife and Entertainment*. **Jacko's** bar next door, which until 1996 was run by a popular expatriate Scot, drew disproportionately large crowds of foreigners.

In 1993, a homemade device exploded on the 5th floor, in Room 531, and blew out two adjoining rooms, which belonged to a Russian-Austrian joint venture. No injuries were reported and the motive was never disclosed.

GLOBUS HOTEL, *17 Ulitsa Yaroslavskaya, metro VDNkH. Tel. (095) 286-4189 or 956-2940. Cash only.*

Located northeast of the Kremlin, east of the huge Russian Exhibition Center, northeast of VDNkH metro station and the Kosmos Hotel.

Globus can accommodate 300 guests. There are no single rooms available; doubles start at $70 a night, and no credit cards are accepted.

Globus has a 50-seat restaurant, serving Russian, European and Oriental cuisine, as well as a casino. Tennis court and sauna are available. Also on the premises is a foreign currency exchange office.

The **Museum of Cosmonautics** is on the other side of Prospekt Mira, behind the VDNkH metro station, and **Space Obelisk** with a monument to Konstantin Tsiolkovsky (1857-1935), a rocket and space research pioneer, is a short distance southwest of the hotel. The infamous Soviet propaganda statue, **Worker & Collective Farm Woman**, by Vera Mukhina, is about four blocks east of the museum and obelisk.

TSENTRALNY DOM TURISTA, *146 Leninsky prospekt, Metro Yugo-Zapadnaya. Tel. (095) 434-2782 or 9467 or 438-5510, Fax (095) 434-3197 or 438-7756. Cash only.*

Located southwest of the Kremlin and southwest of Luzhniki sports complex, and north of the former Lumumba University, named after a former Zairian Communist. Metro station Yugo-Zapadnaya is three excruciatingly long Moscow blocks northwest of here.

The 35-story Class A hotel, whose name translates to Central House of Tourist, was built in 1980, has 612 rooms and can accommodate 1,200 guests; a few rooms include a sauna. Singles start at $70 a night, but no credit cards are accepted. Inside there is a post office, a beauty salon and a foreign exchange office. It has its own cinema and a concert hall.

Its restaurants can accommodate several hundred guests in three dining rooms; it also has three bars and a cafeteria. For more about **1001 Nights**, a Middle Eastern cuisine eatery on its premises, please see Chapter 12, *Where to Eat*.

VARSHAVA HOTEL, *1/2 Leninsky prospekt, Metro Oktyabrskaya. Tel. (095) 238-1970 or 4101, Fax (095) 238-9636 or 9639.*

Varshava is located south of the Kremlin, on the Garden Ring Road, southeast of the Central House of Artists and the New Tretyakov galleries, and east of Gorky Park. If you stand in front of the Central House of Artists, you will see the hotel and Lenin's statue near Oktyabrskaya metro clearly.

It opened in 1960, the year when the American U-2 spy aircraft was shot down over the Soviet Union. It has 122 rooms; those with one bed cost $55 a night, plus a 25 percent reservation fee for the first night only; rooms with two beds are $65 a night, plus a 25 percent reservation fee for the first night; two-room accommodations with two beds are $90 a night, plus 25 percent reservation fee for the first night. Some of the rooms overlook Gorky Park and the New Tretyakov Gallery, featuring artwork created after 1917.

There are two lobbies; the first to screen out the riffraff, and the second, a relatively large hallway with sofas, to register or to get your room keys. The lobbies are all right, but the hallways are barely lit and rooms are shabby. Varshava is not as dangerous as it is scary because you never know quite what to expect. The hotel personnel is rather friendly.

Varshava has a Russian-European restaurant good enough to attract patrons who do not care for its lodging. The food and service in a richly decorated dining room are noteworthy. There is dancing in the evening.

IZMAYLOVO HOTEL, *71 Izmaylovskoye shosse, Metro Izmaylovsky park. Tel. (095) 166-0109 or 2572 or 2763 or 3627 or 5272, Fax (095) 166-2180 or 2184, Telex 412226 TUR SU. Only American Express and Visa credit cards are accepted. No reservations are required.*

Located in northeastern Moscow, southeast of Sokolniki Park, southwest of the former Izmaylovo tsarist estate, and across the street from the Izmaylovsky park metro station.

Built on the site of the ancient village of Izmaylovo, which from the middle of the 17th century was the country estate of Russian tsars and where Peter the Great spent his childhood and began the Russian navy, this hotel is part of the largest tourist complex in Europe. It was constructed in four years for the 1980 Summer Olympic Games in Moscow and is now owned by several Russian trade unions.

The neglected five-block structure boasts 5,000 rooms and can accommodate 7,500 guests. Singles start at $50 a night, doubles at $70. It has 24-hour room service and an English-speaking concierge, even if we could not find him. The lobbies will remind you of barracks and, in fact, there are rude surly men in army fatigues guarding the entrances. It is your sensibility, not your person that is under assault here.

Although hotel's monotony and drabness are likely to depress you, at least you can shop at the Izmaylovo outdoor market, the largest in Moscow. Izmaylovo has five restaurants, one in each building, that can accommodate guests in halls for 100-150 diners each. In the evenings there is a variety show and dancing.

The hotel bowling center offers **kegelban** (duckpins), from 1pm until closing. The bowling center is located on the third floor of the Beta building, opposite the nightclub and bingo parlor.

SHEREMETYEVO HOTEL, *Sheremetyevo 2 International Airport. Tel. (095) 578-5753 or 5754, Fax (095) 578-5750.*

The Sheremetyevo Hotel is located about 19 miles north of the Kremlin. You should allow at least one hour to reach it from downtown.

It has rooms to accommodate 550 guests, a restaurant and a bar. Single rooms start at $50 a night, payable in cash only.

YUNOST HOTEL (Youth Hotel), *34 Ulitsa Khamovnichesky val at Ulitsa Dovatora, Metro Sportivnaya. Tel. (095) 242-0353 or 4860 or 4861, Fax (095) 242-0284. Cash only.*

Yunost is located southwest of the Kremlin, and two characteristically long Moscow blocks southeast of the Novodevichy (New Virgin) Convent, where Boris Godunov was proclaimed tsar. The Luzhniki sports complex is two blocks south of here and the nearest metro station, Sportivnaya, is on the same block. A spartan hotel built in 1961, the year when the Russian cosmonaut Yuri Gagarin orbited the earth, Yunost has 203 austere rooms, starting at about $50 per person, as well as a restaurant and bar. It is mostly meant for budget-minded groups or students.

U Pirosmani, *4 Novodevichy proyezd*, a well known tourist restaurant, is situated about six long blocks north of the hotel.

SEVASTOPOL HOTEL, *1a Ulitsa Bolshaya Yushunskaya at Sevastopolskaya ploshchad, Metro Sevastopolskaya. Tel. (095) 318-3881 or 2827 or 0918, Fax (095) 310-7059. Cash only.*

Sevastopol is located in southeastern Moscow, northeast of Bitsa Park and equestrian sports complex.

This austere hotel complex comprises four 16-story high-rises with 2,300 rooms that can accommodate 2,800 guests; only parts of these buildings are air-conditioned. Singles start at about $50. Cheap plywood furniture is the standard issue. Sevastopol has nine restaurants and several snack bars; there is dancing and a floor show in the evening.

ARENA HOTEL, *11 Ulitsa 10-letya Oktyabrya at Ulitsa Usacheva, Metro Sportivnaya. Tel. (095) 245-0662 or 2802 or 3065.*

Located southwest of the Kremlin, five blocks north of Luzhniki sports complex and two blocks east of Novodevichy (New Virgin) Convent, where Peter the Great dumped his first wife when he tired of her. The Arena can accommodate 320 guests in a 12-story apartment tower-like corner building that from the outside promises more than it actually delivers. Singles run about $40 nightly, payable in cash, but the place looks so disorganized from the lobby onward that you may feel cheated even at that low rate. It has a Georgian-cuisine restaurant on the premises.

Another Georgian restaurant, the well-known **U Pirosmani**, that brags having President Clinton as one of its guest, is two blocks west of the hotel.

ORLYONOK HOTEL (Eaglet Hotel), *15 Ulitsa Kosygina, Metro Leninsky prospekt. Tel. (095) 939-8844 or 8845 or 8853 or 8884, Fax (095) 938-1956. Cash only.*

Located southwest of the Kremlin, south of Luzhniki sport complex and west of Gagarin Square, with a 98-feet-tall monument to the Soviet cosmonaut. The metro station is almost 20 minutes southwest of the hotel.

The 17-floor Orlyonok was inaugurated in 1976. It has 395 rooms, with singles starting at $35, and can accommodate more than 700 guests. It is suitable mostly for students, although many rooms have TV and refrigerators. Laundry and dry cleaning services are available on the premises. It has a 650-seat auditorium and a concert hall seating 180.

Orlyonok has three restaurants, bars and a cinema. In 1993, **Russkaya Troyka**, a topless cabaret and strip-tease club opened here; please see Chapter 15, *Nightlife & Entertainment* for details.

SPORT HOTEL, *90/2 Leninsky prospekt at Ulitsa Kravchenko, Metro Prospekt Vernadskogo. Tel. (095) 131-1191 or 1194 or 3515, Fax (095) 131-4141.*

The Sport Hotel is located southwest of the Kremlin, southwest of Sparrow Hills, and one unbelievably long city block southeast of Prospekt Vernadskogo metro station.

It was built in 1979 and has 400 rooms to accommodate 700 guests, including 140 singles starting at $30 a night. Each room has a telephone, color TV set, and refrigerator. There is a post and telegraph office on the premises, as well as safe deposit boxes. Sport has a restaurant seating 600, and a couple of bars.

One block northeast of here is none too friendly **Krapiva Club**, *87/1 Leninsky prospekt*, open from 5pm to 5am.

MOLODYOZHNAYA (Youthful), *27 Dmitrovskoye shosse at Krasnostudenchesky proyezd, Metro Timiryazevskaya. Tel. (095) 210-4429 or 4565 or 4574, Fax (095) 210-4311 or 4565. Cash only.*

The Molodyozhnaya is located northwest of the Kremlin, east of Timiryazeva Academy Park, about five typically long Moscow blocks northeast of the Timiryazevskaya metro station.

It was built for the 1980 Olympic Games and has 600 quite spartan rooms, starting at about $25 nightly, that can accommodate up to 1,400 guests. This hotel is meant primarily for student groups traveling under the auspices of the Sputnik tourist agency. If you are traveling with friends, ask for a three- or five-person room.

There is a European-Russian restaurant on the premises, as well as a cafe and bar.

Every Friday and Saturday, from 11pm to 5am, you can enjoy yourself at **La Bamba** discotheque, a large second-floor dance hall (there is an admission charge). The club is popular for its Latin dancing music, such as salsa and merengue.

KIEVSKAYA HOTEL, *2 Ulitsa Kievskaya, Metro Kievskaya.*

The Kievskaya Hotel is located southwest of the Kremlin and behind the Kievsky Railway Station. The Radisson Slavyanskaya Hotel is on the other side, facing the Moskva River.

Kievskaya, managed by Ukraina Hotel, has 200 utterly shabby rooms, but, fortunately, this miserable hotel does not accept foreigners. If you're a Russian visiting Moscow, well . . .

TRAVELER'S GUEST HOUSE, *50 Ulitsa Bolshaya Pereyaslavskaya at Glinisty pereulok, Metro Prospekt Mira or Rizhskaya. Tel. (095) 971-4059, 974-1781 or 1798 or 280-8562 or 4300, Fax (095) 280-7686, E-mail tgh@glas.apc.org. Major credit cards accepted.*

Located northeast of the Kremlin, northeast of the Olympic sport complex, northeast of Prospekt Mira metro station, and one block west of Leningradsky and Yaroslavsky railroad tracks. Bolshaya Pereyaslavskaya Street runs north to south, roughly parallel with Prospekt Mira, which lies about three blocks east of this street. If coming from the south, look for the four high metal industrial chimneys.

The Guest House, which occupies the entire tenth floor, is owned by the Moscow Institute of Civil Engineering. A cafe on the third floor serves sandwiches and beer. There are no signs directing you to the Guest House outside or in the lobby that looks like a typical Soviet apartment house, where you never know whether the elevators will work in the next five minutes. As you enter the tenth floor, the confusion is of the Soviet type again, although employees in various offices are helpful. Walk the entire corridor on the north side and you will soon have an idea what the dormitories and rooms look like. Although the college set predominates, we also encountered middle-aged couples who told us the amenities are satisfactory for the money spent and that you will probably be too tired to stay awake due to the noise from the street. Dorm beds go for about $20 a night, single rooms are close to $40, and double rooms $50.

The Guest House can also provide you with every conceivable transportation ticket anywhere inside the former Soviet Union, and will arrange for a taxi to Sheremetyevo 2 International Airport when you leave.

12. WHERE TO EAT

Several Muscovites and Westerners have contributed their impressions and opinions for a composite picture of these restaurants so it is possible that your level of satisfaction may differ from ours. All it takes is one surly waiter to ruin your impression of a restaurant. It is perfectly acceptable to look at the menu before you sit down and to leave without any additional explanation.

If you do not make prior reservations, always try to call ahead of your arrival to make sure the restaurant is open. Depending on where you go, it can take as much as an hour to get there, and you'll be awfully steamed if you cannot get in. The restaurant might have changed its hours, may be temporary closed for summer renovation, or could even have gone out of business.

All restaurants are divided into one of the following geographical areas: **Inside the Boulevard Ring Road**, or what Westerners might call downtown area; **Between the Boulevard & Garden Ring Roads**, a bagel-shaped band around central city; and **Outside the Garden Ring**, which encompasses the Moscow suburbs.

Within each of these geographical areas, restaurants are divided into four categories, based on the price of a typical dinner, starting with the most expensive and ending with the least expensive:
- **Very Expensive** – More than $100 per person
- **Expensive** – Roughly between $50 and $100 per person
- **Moderate** – Roughly between $20 and $50 per person
- **Inexpensive** – Less than $20 per person

We tried to use common sense and did not base these ratings on the costliest dishes on the menu, nor the cheapest. An appetizer, a soup or salad, a meat or fish dish, dessert and a non-alcoholic drink, and coffee or tea, are considered in the price categories for all restaurants, except those we labeled inexpensive. Alcohol, tip, and all other extras are not included.

Beyond generalizations based on the price, these categories do not imply a recommendation, unless so stated specifically in the text. None of the establishments knew of the reason for our visits.

INSIDE THE BOULEVARD RING ROAD

Quick Overview: There are more than 40 restaurants listed in central Moscow. If the cost of your meal is of secondary importance, the first eight restaurants in this section, designated as very expensive, are always a safe choice and you will enjoy good quality food. With the exception of two, the Russian-cuisine **Serebryanny Vek** and Spanish **Don Kikhot**, all are located in one of the luxury hotels. With the exception of Don Kikhot, which is located on eastern Boulevard Ring Road, all are within walking distance of each other.

The next twelve are still expensive, meaning you can spend more than $50 for a meal without alcohol and gratuity. While **Azteca** and **El Rincon Espanol** are the friendliest in this lot, we believe they are overpriced. And so are **Gambrinus** and the Chinese-cuisine **Panda**.

We labeled the next 19 restaurants as moderately priced, which means you should be able to eat for under $50, which may not always be the case if you pick one of the most expensive entrees. The renowned **Slavyansky Bazar**, is temporarily closed due to a fire. Overall, we like **Artistico**, perhaps the best in this bunch, followed by **Patio Pizza** for its excellent salad bar and efficient service, Georgian **Iberia** for low prices, and **Bombay Express** for friendliness. We consider the Georgian **Aragvi** and the Russian **Praga** typical tourist dives; be particularly leery of Praga, where every tourist ends up sooner or later. Both are state-owned, as are **Budapesht** and **Tsentralny**, and it shows in service that leaves something to be desired. We recommend the American **Pizza Hut** only if you get homesick and are looking for compatriots; you will find mostly Russians though. **Paradise** is no garden of Eden and **La Cantina** will be of interest if you want a Tex-Mex dish and want to hear live rock or country music. Although **Stanislavskogo** is included, you may not be able to get in, except if you know another patron or try your luck for lunch.

Finally, there are five inexpensive eateries, where you could eat for under $20. Consider **Belfiori** as a stop on your Western-style Petrovsky Passazh shopping trip. The six **Kombi's** sandwich locations will come handy if you need a quick bite or want to take something with you. Do we need to talk about **McDonald's**? That leaves you with **Russkoye Bistro**, a Russian fast food chain with absolutely the lowest prices in Moscow. *Bon appetit!*

Very Expensive

EVROPEYSKY (European) (European-Russian cuisine), *1/4 Teatralny proyezd, Metro Teatralnaya or Okhotny Ryad. Tel. 927-6062, Fax 927-6010. Open daily from 11:30am to midnight for lunch and dinner. Major credit cards accepted. Reservations are always recommended in the evening. Parking is available. Jacket and tie suggested for men.*

Entrance on the Theater Square side of the Metropol Hotel. Centrally located north of the Kremlin and overlooking the Theater Square, between the Bolshoy Theater and Red Square.

Once inside this exclusive culinary mecca, you will feel as though you are in one of the best Western European restaurants, even the prices are comparably stratospheric.

Cold appetizers start with black Astrakhan caviar on ice with *bliny* (pancakes). Next could be Georgian *suluguni* cheese salad with tuna. Salads are followed by traditional Russian *okroshka*, cold soup with ham, egg, cucumbers and *kvas*, served with sour cream; or traditional *botvinya* soup with poached beluga-sturgeon, sorrel, cucumbers and *kvas* with sour cream. Hot soups include the Russian borscht Suzdal-style, with smoked turkey and beef; *solyanka*, Russian fish soup, with sturgeon and crab *pirozhky* (pastries); and pirate shark soup with noodles, soy sprout and paprika.

The chef's pasta creations include the Russian *pelmeny* (Siberian dumplings) stuffed with pork and beef in a bouillon. Poached sturgeon dressed with red caviar is just one of the fish dishes. Among exotic dishes is poached Canadian lobster with vegetables and red caviar, and shark and frog legs *shashlik* (shish kebab) with pineapple sauce. Then it's on to the regular meat dishes, such as fillet of beef with red pepper and mushroom sauce, or baked rack of lamb with vegetable rice. Among the poultry and game dishes, the Evropeysky's chef will surprise you with stewed Ural mountain hare with sour cream; roasted quails stuffed with nuts; and elk *shashlik* with Russian pickles.

LE ROMANOFF (Russian cuisine), *1 Ulitsa Baltschug, Metro Novokuznetskaya or Tretyakovskaya. Tel. 230-6500 to 6507, Fax 230-6502. Open daily from 6pm to 11pm. Major credit cards accepted. Reservations are advisable always. Parking is available. Jacket and tie are recommended for men.*

Located on the 2nd floor of Hotel Baltschug Kempinski. Centrally located just across the Greater Moskvoretsky Bridge, south of the Kremlin and Red Square, and northeast of Tretyakov Gallery, in an area known as Zamoskvorechye. Technically, Le Romanoff is outside the Boulevard Ring Road, but we purposely included it with its rich cousins across the river.

If you want a romantic candle-lit dinner for two this would be a good choice, as long as your ardor matches Le Romanoff's prices. You will appreciate the blend of traditional Russian ingredients in a cleverly conceived nouvelle cuisine menu, which extends from prawns in caviar to duck with pomegranate.

Zakuski (appetizers) start with Beluga caviar. Soups include *Russische Borschtsch a la Romanoff*, named after the distinguished old Russian family. Amid the elegant surroundings of this small custom-furnished, wood-paneled and intimate restaurant, you will savor *pelmeni a la Romanoff* in meat broth with creme fraiche and garlic butter. You will enjoy home-baked breads and elegant desserts, including, what else but, strawberries a la Romanoff. The restaurant's wine selection dates all the way back to 1906.

Baltschug is one of only three five-star hotels in Moscow and its prices are a constant reminder of its luxurious surroundings. You should anticipate spending well over a $100 per person with wine and gratuity.

MAXIM'S DE PARIS (French-European cuisine), *14/1 Okhotny Ryad at Ulitsa Tverskaya, Metro Okhotny Ryad. Tel. 258-7000. Open daily from noon to 3pm for lunch and from 6:30 to 11:30pm for dinner. Major credit cards accepted. Reservations are always recommended. Parking is available. Jacket and tie are suggested for men.*

Inside the Natsional Hotel. Centrally located across Manezhnaya ploshchad north of the Kremlin, on the corner with Tverskaya Street, and next door to Intourist, the state travel agency.

Maxim's, one of the most expensive restaurants in Moscow, is a branch of the renowned Paris restaurant. Pierre Cardin himself came to Moscow for its opening in the refurbished Victorian-style hotel.

The cold starters include caviar at $75 a portion, and duck liver terrine with Port jelly, which is about $20 less. *Consome a la Bouchere*, or fish soup, both run about $20 each, but there is also Saint Germain with croutons, or vegetable soup.

The most expensive meat entrees are lamb noisettes Edouard VII, at $75; duck liver escalope with apple and ginger, at about $65; and pan-grilled beef fillet Gabrielle, at over $60. Other main dishes include butterfly of scampi with champagne and caviar sauce; *sole meuniere a la Grenobloise*; roast rack of lamb with vegetables; veal stew with white Morels sauce; and sweet breads kebab villeroy. There are several fish dishes, such as the $65 Charlotte of scampi with eggplant; and a $60 lobster stew.

With prices like these, you may just as well add dessert, unless that means you will have to take the metro to get home. Try the hot apple pancake flamed with Grand-Marnier, or, if you came here just to show off, three chocolate frozen tears, for an additional $15.

Maxim's serves a business lunch Monday through Friday, from noon to 3pm.

BOYARSKY (Russian-European cuisine), *1/4 Teatralny proyezd, Metro Teatralnaya or Okhotny Ryad. Tel. 927-6063, Fax 975-2355. Open Monday through Saturday, from 7pm to midnight. Major credit cards accepted. Reservations are always recommended. Parking is available. Jacket and tie are suggested for men.*

On the 4th Floor of the Metropol Hotel. Centrally located north of the Kremlin and overlooking the Theater Square, between the Bolshoy Theater and Red Square. Live entertainment.

The name of this restaurant originates from pre-Revolutionary Russia, when the rich landowners (*boyare*) met the tsar at a round table as they enjoyed fine food. The Boyarsky dining room includes a large stuffed bear. A Russian folk orchestra will soothe your frayed nerves, just in case you had to confront another day of bureaucratic runaround. Waiters dressed in 16th century garb used by servants to the boyarsky nobility will restore your sense of civility.

The least expensive starter dish, if you should lower yourself to such banalities as money, costs about what you would pay for a complete meal that we label as inexpensive in this guide. From there you can progress to a spicy Russian salad with walnuts, and turkey-breast and crab-meat salad *Aleksandr*. After that no price is sacred, whether you order black Russian caviar served with *bliny* (pancakes), or *zakuski Boyarsky*. There are soups, of course. *Pirozhki* (pork, beef and lamb meat pastry) with brandy sauce are a tempting hot starter.

Among the hearty entrees, the choices are: pork cutlet, chicken a la Kiev, marinated lamb *shashlik* (shish kebab), and partridge Boyarsky-style with roasted apple. The selection among the fish dishes includes sturgeon with pomegranate sauce, stuffed fillets of river trout, a salmon and scallops combination, and roast baked trout with white cabbage and black caviar.

This is one of the most expensive dining spots in town. You will easily spend upward of $100 before you even have the first bottle uncorked.

SAVOY (European-Russian cuisine), *3 Ulitsa Rozhdestvenka at Teatralny proyezd, Metro Kuznetsky Most or Lubyanka. Tel. 929-8600 or 8574, Fax 230-2186. Open daily from noon to 11pm for lunch and dinner. Major credit cards accepted. Reservations are strongly recommended for dinner. Parking is available. Jacket and tie are suggested for men.*

At the Hotel Savoy. Centrally located northeast of the Kremlin, west of Lubyanka Square (of KGB fame), and one block east of the Maly Theater. Live entertainment.

Unquestionably one of the most glamorous restaurants in Moscow, where you will enjoy an elegant Russian, Scandinavian or international meal, but it is also one of the most expensive. The attentive waiters border on chaperons. Savoy, which first opened in 1914 and seats about 100, has one of the most opulent interiors you will find in Moscow. Enjoy the gilded wall coverings and ceiling paintings that would not at all be out of place in the tsar's palace in St. Petersburg. The Savoy was the first Soviet member restaurant of the world gastronomic association Chaine de Rotisseurs.

In the way of an appetizer, the chef recommends his vegetable salad, Baltic herring a la Russe, or black caviar with *bliny* (pancakes) or toast. Among the entrees, the suggested dishes are snow grouse a la Suvoroff, or pike perch tempura. Other menu highlights include salmon *kulebyaka* with melted butter.

Wild duck with cognac cream sauce will gladden the hearts of those who love fowl. Sample also the borscht, cold salads or marinated pork. Savoy has a superb selection of wines to go with any meal. Prix-fixe lunches are available.

METROPOL (European-Russian cuisine), *1/4 Teatralny proyezd, Metro Teatralnaya or Okhotny Ryad. Tel. 927-6061. Open 7am to 10:30am for breakfast, noon to 4pm for lunch, and 6:30pm to 11:30pm for dinner; Brunch on Sundays. Major credit cards accepted. Reservations are recommended for dinner. Parking is available. Jacket and tie are suggested for men.*

On the ground floor of the Metropol Hotel. Centrally located north of the Kremlin and overlooking Theater Square, between the Bolshoy Theater and Red Square. Live music.

Lenin ranted about his Communist Utopia more than once in this art nouveau dining room, with a remarkable stained glass ceiling and windows, and marble pillars, all of which also served as a backdrop for a few scenes in the film *Dr. Zhivago*. It seats up to 180.

The Metropol has one of better breakfast tables in town - if you are willing to pay $30 for fare as varied as sushi and *bliny* (the Russian pancakes). Try also *syrniki*, the denser, cheesier equivalent of the Slavic pancake that along with *pelmeny* (meat-filled Siberian dumplings) is a major contribution to the Russian culinary art.

Vice president Al Gore lunched here when visiting Moscow. There is a wide selection of fresh salads, soups and desserts. Specialties include beef Stroganoff, chicken Kiev, borscht, chicken *tabaka* (Georgian-style fried chicken with garlic sauce), and fish.

While the full buffet could be had for about $50 per person, the a la carte menu can reduce you to penury. Sunday brunch, with the sounds of your favorite classical selections, is well over $50, the most expensive in Moscow.

Overall, one of the most elegant eateries in town and at prices like these you shouldn't expect anything less.

SEREBRYANNY VEK (Silver Age) (Russian-European cuisine), *3 Teatralny proyezd, Metro Lubyanka or Okhotny Ryad. Tel. 926-1352, Fax 928-*

7929. Open daily from 1pm to 5am for lunch and dinner. Major credit cards accepted. Banquets are regularly held here so make sure you call for reservations. Jacket and tie are suggested for men.

Centrally located northeast of the Kremlin, less than two blocks southeast of the Bolshoy Theater, and almost hidden in an alley across the street from the Tretyakovsky proyezd arch and the Metropol Hotel, in an extravagant complex built more than a century ago. Live music and elaborate entertainment nightly.

The Arkadia Tavern and jazz club were here before the Serebryanny vek. Now, like then, the new Russian *biznismeny* like to show off their money here and it is also a showplace to take visitors to Moscow. Serebryanny vek has one of the most elegant interiors you will see in any Moscow restaurant. A majestic staircase worthy of Versailles leads to the second floor dining room, which has an ornate ceiling and fresco-like wall paintings.

The mind-numbing menu is loaded with 200 dishes, including *Ryumersky* pie, a favorite with Tsar Nicholas II. Among cold *zakuski* (appetizers), you can sample a pickled meat assortment with horseradish or boiled pork with garlic *po-domashnemy* (home-style). Among the poultry dishes, you might enjoy the chicken fillet Serebryanny Vek or chicken *po-moravsky* (Moravian-style). Sturgeon *po-tsarsky* (royal-style) comes with black caviar and $50 price tag, the whole fish stuffed *po-Evropeysky* is even more expensive.

TEATRO/LOBSTER GRILL (Seafood), *1/4 Teatralny proyezd, Metro Teatralnaya. Tel. 927-6068 or 6069, Fax 927-6678. Open daily from 11am to 2am. Major credit cards accepted. Reservations are recommended in the evening. Secured parking is available.*

Shares its side entrance at Metropol Hotel with Teatro Mediterraneo. Centrally located north of the Kremlin and across the Theater Square from the Bolshoy Theater. Live entertainment.

Teatro restaurants have been open since 1992 and are considered among the best in the city. Both are owned by a Swiss national and have a no-nonsense staff which is there to serve you. There are many kinds of salads and soups, including cream of tomato, which is "perfumed with vodka." Two memorable starters are *creuse de Bretagne* (fresh oysters) at $45 for six, and *tagliatelle al caviale* (noodles with cream sauce and black caviar) at $38. Other starters include smoked Norvegian salmon, and *prosciutto di Parma e melone* (Parma ham with melon).

If you desire a lobster, you can start with stuffed lobster Thermidor baked with mozzarella cheese, or steamed lobster with lemon, both of which are $70 per person. There is also *tagliatelle all'aragosta* (noodles with lobster in cream sauce), broiled lobster tail, and steak and lobster. The selection of seafood entrees is even larger, starting with the Alaska king crab legs, at $80. Other seafood specialties include grilled salmon steak, Dover sole, grilled swordfish, and California-style shrimp.

Also on the menu are the *cote de veau* (grilled veal chop with zucchini and potato gratin) at $65, the New Zealand lamb rack, lamb fillet, grilled beef fillet with duck liver and red wine sauce, and *pulcino arrosto* (the whole roasted cockerel with French fries), the preparation of which takes 30 minutes. Beef, imported from the US, includes T-bone steak with herb butter at $51, rib eye steak, and strip steak.

Expensive

TOKYO (Japanese cuisine), *6 Ulitsa Varvarka, Metro Kitay-gorod. Tel. 298-5374 or 5707. Open daily from noon to 11pm for lunch and dinner. Major credit cards accepted. Parking is available.*

On the ground floor of Rossiya Hotel, entrance from Red Square. Centrally located next to St. Basil's Cathedral and the Kremlin, just off Red Square. Live entertainment.

This modernistic pastel-colored restaurant, which seats about 60, may be the only Japanese eatery in Moscow, where dishes are prepared in front of the guest, on a special grill called teppan-yaki. Ingredients for many meals are imported. The food and service are good, but expensive.

Among the appetizers, Tokyo's chef recommends braised crab at $24, as well as fried oyster, shellfish, or crab salad. Among the recommended entrees is sirloin steak, at $60, scallop, tenderloin steak, and matsuzaka beef from Japan.

There is a bar and tea salon.

TEATRO/MEDITERRANEO (Seafood), *1/4 Teatralny proyezd, Metro Teatralnaya. Tel. 927-6068 or 6069. Open daily from 11am to 2am. Major credit cards accepted. Reservations may be in order for dinner. Secured parking is available.*

Shares its side entrance at the Metropol Hotel with the Lobster Grill. Centrally located north of the Kremlin and across the Theater Square from the Bolshoy Theater. Live entertainment and dancing nightly.

Mediterraneo has the same owner, quality of food and service as the Lobster Grill, above. It's a good location for business meetings. Modern Russian art is on display inside. Some dishes are identical in both Teatro restaurants, although there are specials in each one.

In addition to the usual array of salads - Caesar's, for example, is $3 cheaper than at the Lobster Grill - soups and starters, Mediterraneo always has a couple of vegetarian dishes.

Pastas include *spaghetti al funghi* (with mushrooms), and *spaghetti aglio, olio e peperoncino* (with garlic, green and red hot peppers and olive oil). Main courses include *parillada de carne* (fillets of beef, pork, lamb and rabbit) at $45, as well as *chuleta de cerde sol* (grilled pork chop with tomato and olives), *filetes de conejo* (rabbit fillets with cream sauce), chicken curry with exotic fruits and vegetables, and duck breast.

BALTSCHUG (European cuisine), *1 Ulitsa Baltschug, Metro Novokuznetskaya or Tretyakovskaya. Tel. 230-6500. Open daily from 6am to 11am, noon to 3pm, and 6pm to 11pm. Major credit cards accepted.*

Inside the Hotel Baltschug Kempinski. Centrally located just across the Greater Moskvoretsky Bridge, south of the Kremlin and Red Square, and northeast of the Tretyakov Gallery, in an area known as Zamoskvorechye. Technically, it is outside the Boulevard Ring Road, but we purposely included it with its rich cousins across the river.

Baltschug, as compared to its pricey cousin, Le Romanoff, offers a more bearable set-price buffet. Breakfast, lunch and dinner are served in a dining room separated into smoking and non-smoking wings, a rarity in today's Moscow.

You can opt for one of the hot or cold buffets, or order a la carte. In the latter category, try ravioli of rock lobster with wild mushrooms, or roasted loin of lamb. Whether your select grilled salmon steak, or a more traditional *bliny* (pancakes) with red or black caviar, you will not regret your choice. And if you aspire to vegetarianism, try Baltschug's beetroot roulade stuffed with mushrooms.

On Sundays there is a brunch from noon to 4pm. A *Moscow News* food critic describes Baltschug as "expensive, but a good value."

DON KIKHOT (Don Quixote) (Spanish-European cuisine), *4/17 Pokrovsky bulvar, Metro Chistiye prudy or Kitay-gorod. Tel. 917-4757. Open daily from noon until midnight for lunch and dinner. Major credit cards accepted. Reservations are recommended in the evening.*

Located east of the Kremlin, on the Boulevard Ring Road, in the basement of an office building, not far from the Iranian Embassy. Live entertainment includes Flamenco music.

Don Quixote opened for business in 1993. The main restaurant, executed in rustic country style decor, accommodates about 60 diners. All of Quixote's seafood and many other ingredients are imported from Spain. Among the appetizers you might want to try *jamon Serrano* or *queso Manchego*, both starting at about $20. Among entrees the Spanish chef recommends dishes such as *paella de campo, tortilla Espanola, besugo al horno*, and *solomillo a la plancha*. Spanish omelettes and pork in tomato sauce are also noteworthy. *Flan* is popular among the desserts.

GAMBRINUS (Mexican-European cuisine), *3/5 Tverskoy bulvar, Metro Pushkinskaya or Arbatskaya. Tel. 203-0149 or 291-9403, Reservations 291-9474. Open daily from noon to midnight for lunch and dinner. Major credit cards accepted.*

Located northwest of the Kremlin on the Boulevard Ring Road, or Tverskoy bulvar, the oldest Moscow boulevard, where French troops hanged suspected arsonists on the lanterns when fires broke out all over the city during Napoleon's occupation of Moscow in 1812. Just around the corner from Gambrinus, on Bolshaya Nikitskaya Street, is the Church of Great Ascension, where the famous Russian poet Aleksandr Pushkin wed his stunningly beautiful bride Nataliya Goncharova.

Gambrinus was a legendary Belgian king who is said to have invented beer, but the restaurant of the same name is better known for its high prices, even if it looks more like a regular pub. A business-like atmosphere prevails and no-nonsense service makes up a bit for the cost of food prepared by a Mexican chef.

Beef dishes start at about $26 per person, but there is also pork, lamb and chicken. Appetizers include mussels capriccio. There are more than two dozen brands of beer for sale here, from $3 to $15 a bottle. About 40 brands of wine and 20 Mexican drinks are also available.

The owners of Gambrinus also manage **Panda**, a Chinese cuisine restaurant around the corner, with entrance on Malaya Bronnaya Street.

U DYADY GUILYAYA (At Uncle Guilly's) (American cuisine), *6 Stoleshnikov pereulok, Bldg. 1, at Tverskaya ploshchad, Metro Teatralnaya or Chekhovskaya. Tel. 229-2050 or 4750, Fax 229-4295. Open daily from noon to midnight for lunch and dinner. Major credit cards accepted. Reservations are suggested in the evening.*

Centrally located north of the Kremlin, east from Prince Yuri Dolgoruky's statue on Tverskaya Square and west of Petrovsky Passazh department store, in a vaulted cellar that dates back to 1700. During the 1812 invasion, Napoleon's emissary to Moscow stayed here. This was also a Chinese sauna and a bordello before it became Uncle Guilly's. Live entertainment.

Named after a turn-of-the century Moscow writer and actor, Vladimir Guilyarovsky, who was considered a connoisseur of good food. A popular, but expensive steak restaurant and a more economical bar with good food that in the opinion of many is overpriced.

In the way of an appetizer, you can start with buffalo wings or Caesar salad. You can continue with onion or black bean soups. There is fried chicken steak with mashed potatoes or fries. The chef's recommendations include a 22-ounce T-bone steak at a whopping $46, filet mignon at $42, 16-ounce New York sirloin, or lamb chops, which come to about $40.

LE STELLE DEL PESCATORE (Italian cuisine), *7/5 Ulitsa Pushechnaya at Ulitsa Rozhdestvenka, Metro Kuznetsky Most. Tel. 924-2058, Fax 923-1419. Open daily from 10am to 2am for lunch and dinner. Major credit cards accepted.*

Centrally located north of the Kremlin, one block west of the former KGB headquarters, across the street from Savoy Hotel and next to Alitalia airline office. Live entertainment after 8pm.

A rather pleasant four-year-old franchise eatery, owned by a Russian woman, with two connecting dining halls and about two dozen tables. There are contemporary artworks displayed on the walls. But this does nothing for the food served at Stella, which is rather average. We ordered minestrone soup, which cost $10, but what we got was some thin liquid that nobody could mistake for the thick, zesty Italian minestrone.

Zakuski (appetizers), pastas and fillets, they all run close to $30 each, with some fish dishes surpassing $45. Recommended appetizers are *carpaccio di carne* and *bruschette cognac*. The chef also recommends *spigola al forno con patata*, at a whopping $42, *scaloppine limone*, and *bistecca ferri*.

Stella has an interesting, almost a gourmet-like, salad bar, but at $20 a shot we felt it was no bargain. You may be tempted to try Stella's business lunch, but it's so skimpy you'll end spending more on extras and it will be less expensive if you order a regular meal.

AZTECA (Tex-Mex, California & Southwestern cuisine), *8/5 Ulitsa Tverskaya, Metro Okhotny Ryad. Tel. 956-8489 or 8490. Open from noon to 5am. Major credit cards accepted. Reservations are recommended in the evening.*

Located on the 20th Floor of the Intourist Hotel. Centrally located at the foot of Tverskaya Street, near Manezhnaya Square and just a block southeast of the Central Telegraph Office. Live Latin entertainment and dancing from 8pm.

This is a curious spot with about half a dozen tables covered by ponchos and waited on by Cuban and Central American students and a small bar in one of the former hotel rooms. It's one of the friendliest and most popular spots in town, but expensive even by American standards. This is a place where the expatriates go looking for dates with other Westerners and to taste some of the best Tex-Mex food in Moscow. Unless you have reservations, it is not easy to get a table in the evening. The view is spectacular, too.

Azteca serves breakfast from 4am and the menu includes Spanish omelette and chilaquiles with chorizo and eggs. Sunday brunch is served from 10am to 3pm.

You can taste the real southern hemisphere fare: enchiladas, nachos, chili, burritos, tacos and refried beans. Every entree comes with beans and rice. The most popular dish is chicken and sour cream enchiladas with green chili sauce. Pico de gallo, quesadillas, shrimp salad, chips and green chili con queso are also available. Do not forget the tequila-marinated beef tacos. You can wash your food down with Mexican Corona beer, ice-cold tequila or margaritas.

The second **Azteca**, *11 Ulitsa Novoslobodskaya, Tel. 972-0511*, is located across from metro station Novoslobodskaya, northwest of the Kremlin and outside the Garden Ring Road.

PANDA (Chinese cuisine), *3/5 Tverskoy bulvar at Ulitsa Malaya Bronnaya, Metro Pushkinskaya. Tel. 298-6565 or 202-8313. Open daily from noon to 11pm for lunch and dinner. Major credit cards accepted.*

Located northwest of the Kremlin, on the Boulevard Ring Road - in this instance Tverskoy Boulevard - a few steps from Nikitskih vorot Square and the statue to Russian naturalist Kliment Timiryazev.

Panda restaurant is a partnership between a Chinese-American restaurateur Charlie Tsung from West Orange, New Jersey, where he operates two restaurants, and Russian businessmen. Tsung was born in China and moved to Taiwan when he was three years old, after the Communist takeover of the mainland. He once owned restaurants all over the eastern US, but sold all of them except the two in New Jersey.

Panda specializes in the spicy dishes typical of China's Szechwan and Hunan provinces. It is considered by Muscovites as one of the better Chinese restaurants in the city. Most ingredients are flown in from abroad. Although Panda has hardly changed its prices between 1994 and 1996, it is still a place where a meal will easily scale the $50 barrier.

Some among the suggested dishes are chicken and meat for two, prepared in sweet and sour sauce, steamed dumplings and, of course, rice. The most expensive item on the menu is called Dragon & Phoenix, basically Hunan chicken and shrimp, at $60 for two. Other house specialties run from $20 to $40 per person, and include Hunan-style crispy fish, Szechuan-style Snow White Chicken, lamb in two styles from the Hunan province, and sweet and sour fish. The lunch menu provides roughly the same meals as dinner at a lesser cost.

The owners of Panda also manage **Gambrinus**, a Mexican-European cuisine restaurant just around the corner on Tverskoy Boulevard.

EL RINCON ESPANOL (Spanish cuisine), *2 Okhotny Ryad, Metro Okhotny Ryad or Teatralnaya. Tel. 292-6267 or 2893, Fax 292-0294. Open daily from noon to 11:30pm for lunch and dinner. Major credit cards accepted. Reservations are advisable in the evening.*

Inside Hotel Moskva. Centrally located north of the Kremlin across from Manezhnaya Square, south of the Bolshoy Theater, and across the street from Natsional Hotel, with entrance at the southwest side of the hotel, on Manezhnaya Square. Enter through two sets of doors, then turn right. Live entertainment.

A small, noisy, crowded, smoke-filled, but appealing Spanish restaurant and bar in the Moskva Hotel. Seemingly never short of customers in the evening, El Rincon seats up to 70. The service is good and waitresses speak passable English.

Good for a quick lunch or evening snack, although the menu is limited, but it is overpriced; a meal with a couple of glasses of wine or bottles of beer, will run over $50. The chef recommends Galician pie with chicken, or Serano ham as appetizers; and octopus in vinaigrette or roasted meat El Rincon-style as entrees. Consider also *paella*, *fabada* (thick beans stew), and fried *chorizo* (spicy sausage). Spanish wines by the glass and Danish beer by the bottle could be had. This is the kind of spot that hits you with the $4 bill for a small dish of peanuts, or $3 for a cup of coffee without refills.

Moscow's alternative weekly, *Living Here*, presents pros and cons for El Rincon thusly: "Waitresses that look like Frida Kahlo serve sangria fresher than sunshine, braised scallops and refreshing gazpacho. Avoid the Soviet-style bathroom upstairs which smells worse than Communist agitators."

The second location of El Rincon Espanol, called **The Spanish Bar**, *13/8 Ulitsa Bolshaya Dmitrovka, Tel. 229-7023 or 0497 or 0881* is located three blocks northeast of this El Rincon, on the corner with Stoleshnikov pereulok; same metro stations.

SKAZKA (Fairy Tale) (European-Russian cuisine), *3/5 Ulitsa Tverskaya, Metro Okhotny Ryad. Tel. 956-8403. Open daily from noon to midnight for lunch and dinner. Major credit cards accepted. Reservations may be in order in the evening.*

Inside the Intourist Hotel. Centrally located north of the Kremlin, one block southeast of the Central Telegraph Office, next to Natsional Hotel and near Manezhnaya Square. Live Gypsy entertainment in the evening.

The large wood-paneled dining room, which seats about 90, gives the impression of Old Russia. There is a large selection of *zakuski* (appetizers) that include caviar, sturgeon, herring and mushrooms and can quickly add up to the price of a meal. Try the 24-hour-old *shchy* (cabbage soup), *borscht* (beetroot and cabbage) soup, broth with *pelmeni* (Siberian dumplings) and *okroshka* (cold kvas soup).

Skazka's chef recommends *sudak Skazka* (pike perch Skazka), *ryba po-russky* (fish Russian-style), roast meat *Lukomorye*, veal with caviar sauce, *zhar-ptitsa* roasted chicken, *ryba po-asturiysky* (fish Asturian-style), *osetrina tverskaya* (Tver sturgeon), and *osetrina po-tsarsky* (sturgeon a la Tsar), which goes for about $40.

NOLSTAGIE ART CAFE (Continental cuisine), *12a Chistoprudny bulvar, Metro Turgenevskaya or Chistiye prudy. Tel. 916-9478 or 9462 or 9090. Open daily from 11am to 11:30pm for lunch and dinner. Major credit cards accepted. Reservations are suggested in the evening.*

In the Roland Bykov Center. Located northeast of the Kremlin, on the Garden Ring Road, where it occupies a corner site of a distinguished building, across the boulevard from Chistiye prudy (Clean ponds). The Miss Russia organizers and their modeling agency are also housed in this building so do not be surprised at the number of good-looking women coming and going. Live entertainment from 8-10pm, when there is a cover charge.

The history of this cafe goes back to 1927, but the menu today consists of experimental Russian cuisine. Once you step inside, you will find potted palms, colonnades and carved wooden arches. At dusk the candles are lit and soft background music gives way to a live jazz ensemble. Happy hour is from 5:30pm until 7pm.

You can have the suckling pig cassoulet, basically a casserole of white beans baked with herbs and meat, for less than $30. Fresh trout with almonds costs even less. Another option is the veal with exotic fruit and bacon. Nostalgie is known for its coffee and pastries.

Moderate

ANGLETERRE (England) (European cuisine), *5/21 Ulitsa Bolshaya Lubyanka, Metro Kuznetsky Most or Lubyanka. Tel. 926-0781, Fax 926-0062. Open daily from 11am to midnight for lunch and dinner. Major credit cards accepted.*

Centrally located northeast of the Kremlin, across the street from the KGB Museum, in a five-story building completed in 1906. It overlooks Vorovskogo Square, with a statue of Vaclav Vorovsky. Entrance is from the corner of the building. Live entertainment from 8pm to 11pm.

Opened in 1995, this restaurant has about 20 tables and a sunken bar adjacent to it. There is a separate room with four billiard tables. Angleterre has an extensive menu with cold and hot appetizers, which range from $3 to $30, salads from $4 to $23, soups up to $10, meat and fish dishes $10 to $35, and desserts up to $13.

There is live popular music in the evening and just in case you forget how close you are to the various KGB buildings, a bas-relief of Lenin hangs on the wall behind the orchestra stand. The staff, however, is friendly.

PIZZA HUT, *12 Ulitsa Tverskaya at Kozitsky pereulok, Metro Tverskaya or Pushkinskaya. Tel. 229-2013 or 7840, Fax 229-7840. Open daily from 11am to 10pm. Major credit cards accepted.*

Centrally located north of the Kremlin, two long blocks southeast from Pushkin Square, but much closer to Prince Yuri Dolgoruky statue on Tverskaya Square.

You can sample a variety of pizzas, salads, wines and other beverages. The food is overpriced, but you will seldom pass by, whether at noon or night, without seeing a line on the sidewalk to get in.

Another Pizza Hut location is at *17 Kutuzovsky prospekt at Ulitsa Bolshaya Dorogomilovskaya, Metro Kievskaya. Tel. 243-1727 or 9964, Fax 243-1994. Open the same hours.* It is located near Sadko food and department store, four long blocks northwest of Kievskaya metro station, and two just as long blocks southwest of Ukraina Hotel.

KENTUCKY FRIED CHICKEN, *17 Kutuzov Avenue.*

In 1995, this, the first KFC opened, sharing frontage with its PepsiCo sibling. Everything from spicy Hot Wings to corn on the cob to the Colonel's classic chicken sandwiches can be had. Another KFC outlet was slated to open on Nikitsky Boulevard in 1997.

BASKIN ROBBINS, *12 Kutuzovsky prospekt.*

Located across the street from the KFC, this ice cream outlet is one of eleven that are scattered across the city.

ARTISTIKO (Italian-European cuisine), *6 Kamergersky pereulok, Metro Okhotny Ryad, Teatralnaya or Kuznetsky Most. Tel. 292-0673 or 4042, Fax 261-7062. Open daily from noon to midnight for lunch and dinner. Major credit cards accepted.*

Centrally located north of the Kremlin, and practically across the street from Chekhov's Moscow Arts Theater, half a block east from the Central Telegraph Office on Tverskaya and about as far east from Kuznetsky Most and Bolshaya Dmitrovka Streets on the other end of the block.

Ristorante Artistico's face is so plain you may walk by twice and still miss it, but once you step inside you will be pleasantly surprised by its elegant dining room that seats about 60 at 12 tables. Restored walls and painted ceiling suggest a stately pre-Revolutionary interior that has escaped Bolshevist destruction. There is a small bar at the far end of the restaurant. Carved dark wood gives Artistiko a cozy atmosphere that makes you want to linger. On hot days you will appreciate its functional air-conditioning, a rarity in smaller Moscow eateries.

We tried **penne** with roast duck, as well as **fettucine primavera** with shrimps, mussels and salmon and did not regret it. One specialty of the house is veal in Marsala wine. Other dishes include roasted loin of lamb and pan-broiled marinated sirloin steak. Shrimp and seafood kebab are just two among the fish dishes.

Moscow alternative weekly, *Living Here*, describes Artistiko thus: "Small, cozy, chic atmosphere without being pretentious; excellent carpaccio, salads; decent main courses" and adds that in the evening "waits can be long."

The food is well prepared, although you could hit the $50-per-person limit for this price category without great effort or alcohol.

LILI WONG (Chinese cuisine), *3/5 Ulitsa Tverskaya, Metro Okhotny Ryad, Teatralnaya or Kuznetsky Most. Tel. 956-8301, Fax 956-8356. Open daily from noon to midnight for lunch and dinner. Major credit cards accepted.*

Centrally located just north of the Kremlin, at the foot of Tverskaya Street, on the south side of the Intourist Hotel building; you can enter through the hotel or a separate entrance.

Although Lili Wong's English-language advertisements promise "The only real authentic Chinese restaurants and bar in Moscow," the food is rather average.

There are set dinners for two persons for $85, whereby you can pick from a main course consisting of duck, chicken or beef, and also get fried rice, dessert, and tea or coffee. A set-price dinner for three is $125 and for four $165. Among the more expensive a la carte dishes is a combination, with scallops, king prawns, fish, squid and vegetables, at $25.

ARAGVI (Georgian cuisine, with some Russian dishes), *6 Ulitsa Tverskaya at Stoleshnikov pereulok, Metro Chekhovskaya or Pushkinskaya. Tel. 229-1308 or 3762. Open daily from noon to 11pm for lunch and dinner. Major credit cards accepted. Reservations are recommended in the evening.*

Centrally located northwest of the Kremlin, in the theater district, overlooking Tverskaya Square, with the statue of Moscow founder, Prince Dolgoruky, and another of Lenin behind it. Live entertainment nightly.

Aragvi, named after a Georgian river, has a cavern-like cellar rooms with high ceilings and murals depicting Georgian legends. A tourist trap for years, this was once part of the Dresden Hotel, where writers Chekhov and Turgenev stayed from time to time. It was taken over by the Bolshevist propaganda machine in 1917 and it is still state-owned.

Still popular with tourists, as it was with Winston Churchill, for an evening of decent food and merriment, Aragvi, now pushing the sixth decade of its existence, bills itself as the oldest Georgian restaurant in Moscow. Even Stalin liked it, particularly the private rooms on the second floor. But you may want to dress up for dinner because a Westerner in blue jeans elicits befuddled looks from the formally-clad waiters.

Start with appetizers, which include caviar, salmon and cucumbers. The **satsivi** (chicken in walnut sauce) might turn to be one of your favorites. Men, take note: regulars claim that Aragvi serves a Georgian bean dish which will improve your fertility might. Other dishes include chicken **tabaka** (Georgian-style fried chicken), broiled sturgeon, **shashlik** or **suluguni** (cheese) with **lavash** (freshly baked Caucasian bread). Also try **kharcho** (spicy soup).

SLAVYANSKY BAZAR (Russian cuisine), *17 Ulitsa Nikolskaya, Metro Ploshchad Revolutsiyi or Lubyanka. Closed, but expected to reopen in 1997-98.*

Centrally located north of the Kremlin, roughly between GUM department store and Lubyanka Square, in an old Moscow district called Kitay-gorod (Chinatown). Nikolskaya Street was known in the past for its many icon markets.

Slavyansky Bazar was destroyed by fire and closed for renovation. Originally a hotel, it opened in 1873 and re-opened in 1966. This colorful state-run restaurant, which seated about 250, was always jam-packed, particularly with Western tourists. Closed now because of fire, it is expected to re-open once again sometime in late 1997 or 1998.

It had been famous since before the Revolution, when playwright Anton Chekhov, novelist Lev Tolstoy, and director Konstantin Stanislavsky were regulars here; Tchaikovsky and Rimsky-Korsakov also dined at Slavyansky Bazar. The restaurant was originally the dining room of the Hotel Slavyansky Bazar and singled out as one of Moscow's best by the Baedeker guide in 1914. After the Revolution, the hotel was closed and the restaurant became a soldiers' cafe. In a private room of this, perhaps the oldest Moscow restaurant, stage directors Stanislavsky and Vladimir Nemirovich-Danchenko conceived the Moscow Arts Theater (Chekhov) over an 18-hour lunch on June 21-22, 1897; see Theaters in Chapter 14, *Culture* for more details.

PARADISE (Continental cuisine), *Moskva Hotel, 2 Ulitsa Okhotny Ryad, Metro Okhotny Ryad or Teatralnaya. Tel. 292-2030 or 924-8083, Fax 292-1892. Open daily from 8:30am to 1am for breakfast, lunch and dinner. Major credit cards accepted.*

Centrally located two blocks southwest from the Bolshoy Theater and across Manezhnaya Square from the northern tip of the Kremlin, also two blocks northwest of Red Square.

Relegated to the northwest corner of the gray Moskva Hotel, this restaurant, which opened in 1991 and seats about 75, could hardly be called a garden of Eden, but it is pleasant nonetheless. This is one of the few centrally-located Moscow restaurants offering breakfast, from 8:30am until 11am, in the bar, which precedes the restaurant. There is also a special business lunch, served from noon to 3pm, but be skeptical because we have yet to find a restaurant serving a business lunch that won't bleed your wallet dry while you try to get enough food to satisfy your hunger.

Entrees suggested by the chef are Chateaubriand, steak a la Dizo, and veal Marengo. Other main dishes include sturgeon in champagne, salmon steak, Paradise trout, shrimp with garlic sauce, New York steak, lamb chops, beef with mushrooms and cheese, fillet of chicken with peaches, or baked lobster stuffed with crab meat, which runs about $50.

LA CANTINA (Tex-Mex cuisine), *5 Ulitsa Tverskaya, Metro Okhotny Ryad. Tel. 292-5388, Fax 200-3210. Open daily from 8am to midnight for breakfast, lunch and dinner. Major credit cards accepted. Reservations are suggested for weekend nights.*

Centrally located in the building housing the Yermolova Theater, next to the Intourist hotel, and close to Manezhnaya Square. Live rock & roll and country music every night.

This is a small American eatery modeled on those in the southwestern US. You will find everything, from Mexican dishes, like guacamole and nachos, to a flag of Texas here. La Cantina makes its own tortillas. Dishes to consider include the beef or chicken fajitas, chili con carne, and Mexican style marinated ribs. For a little over $20, you can also get any of these four meals: grilled fillet of beef; Cajun-style sturgeon with green salsa; fried breaded Chicken Maryland with pineapple; escalope of pork, all four with mixed vegetables.

Enjoy a hearty American breakfast between 7am and noon, or 7am and 3pm Saturdays and Sundays, not a small feat in a city of almost ten million where no more than a dozen non-hotel restaurants downtown serve breakfast. You can dive into a steak, two eggs, sausage, bacon, tomato, hash browns, toast, and tea or coffee for about $12.

PRAGA (European-Russian cuisine), *2 Ulitsa Novy Arbat, Metro Arbatskaya. Tel. 290-6296 or 6171 or 6152, Fax 290-5693. Open daily from 11am to midnight. Major credit cards accepted.*

Centrally located west of the Kremlin, on the Boulevard Ring Road, facing Arbat Square, where loud jazz bands compete for rubles and attention. Both Novy and Stary Arbat Streets start here. Live entertainment.

Praga has an enormous reputation to uphold and it is barely hanging on in its attempt. More than 35 years ago, when Nikita Khrushchev was in the former Yugoslavia, he invited a group of Western journalists to Moscow, saying that restaurants there were better than in Paris. When a reporter asked him for a specific name, he blurted out the name Praga. This huge pre-Revolutionary restaurant is divided into several dining rooms that seat hundreds. What's left of Praga's grandiose decor will remind you of the Old World cafes in Central Europe. The most desirable are the balcony tables overlooking the Arbat or open-air terrace on the roof with a view of the Kremlin.

Until its 1996 renovation, clusters of waiters preyed on potential guests at the entrance and mercy to the weary travelers who did not know how some state-run restaurants made money, when the lunch or dinner for foreigners was always $25. Nobody knows how many old habits are being carried into the new Praga. Be cautious because this restaurant has a perfect location and it will always find it difficult to resist the temptation of gouging Westerners.

A few Czech and Russian dishes, however, are all right. Among its specialties Praga's menu lists Praga salads and filet with mushrooms. With a little luck you could get a better steak here than at most state-run restaurants; cutlets are good, too.

REPORTER (French-International cuisine), *8 Gogolevsky bulvar, Bldg. 2, Metro Kropotkinskaya or Arbatskaya. Tel. 956-9997. Open daily from noon to midnight for lunch and dinner. Major credit cards accepted.*

Centrally located southwest of the Kremlin, on the Boulevard Ring Road - in this instance Gogolevsky bulvar - in the basement of a building it shares with Fototsentr photographic art gallery (see Art Galleries in Chapter 14, *Culture*), just a short distance north of the metro station. The

Cathedral of Christ the Savior is one block east of here and the Pushkin Museum of Fine Arts three blocks northeast, on Ulitsa Volkhonka. Live entertainment.

Tucked away on the tree-lined Gogolevsky bulvar, this restaurant has undergone a metamorphosis. Until 1996, it was just another state-run Russian-cuisine dinery with rude, indifferent waitresses, then - abraca-dabra - and it is now a French-cuisine restaurant. But old habits die hard; the waiters are still indifferent, but the food is edible. The restaurant bills itself as journalist's club, where you can have "free talks with the most prominent newsmen." There is live jazz in the evening. Lunch is about 30 percent cheaper than dinner.

PATIO PIZZA (Italian cuisine), *5 Ulitsa Tverskaya at Manezhnaya ploshchad, Metro Okhotny Ryad or Teatralnaya. Tel. 956-8362. Open daily 24 hours a day for lunch and dinner. Major credit cards accepted.*

Centrally located north of the Kremlin, one block southeast from the Central Telegraph Office, and in front of the Intourist Hotel. Patio Pizza revolutionized eating habits of many foreigners and Muscovites alike by introducing the first real salad bar. Not only it is an answer to the prayers of those who try to shed a few pounds, but Patio Pizza also started offering unlimited food at a set price, a concept previously unheard of in Moscow. The restaurant is hugely successful. Although there are two Patio Pizza locations (see last paragraph below), you may have difficulty finding a seat in the evening.

The salad bar consists of about two dozen vegetables and greens, attractively displayed, and reasonably priced, at $10 per meal. Pizzas taste all right, too. Meat entrees are puny and the quality of meat average; a grown man can easily eat two of their steaks, meat, vegetables and all. You can order white or red wine by the glass or buy a bottle. The desserts are scrumptious and can easily run up to $10 for some delectable piece of torte. You will appreciate the efficient and polite service, although things can get bogged down as the evening progresses.

The original Patio Pizza, *13a Ulitsa Volkhonka, Tel & Fax 201-4809*, is located across the street from the Pushkin Museum of Fine Arts, three long blocks southwest of the Kremlin and on the northern edge of the new Cathedral of Christ the Savior.

MOSCOW BOMBAY EXPRESS (Indian cuisine), *3 Glinishchevsky pereulok, Metro Pushkinskaya or Chekhovskaya. Tel. 292-9731. Open daily for lunch from noon to 3pm and for dinner until 11:30pm. Major credit cards accepted.*

Centrally located in the theater district north of the Kremlin, north of Prince Dolgoruky statue on Tverskaya Square, and roughly three doors east of Hotel Tsentralny on the corner with Tverskaya Street. Live entertainment nightly.

Opened in the summer of 1993. The owners ran a similar restaurant in Paris, visited by such luminaries as the former French president Francois Mitterand, and it shows in detail to quality and service in Moscow. Come here to experience the marinated and skewered meats grilled in an Indian **tandoor**, the traditional clay-baked oven, which stands behind glass in the corner of Bombay Express. Moscow alternative weekly, *Living Here*, opines that Bombay has "the best **tandori** (salmon or chicken) in Moscow hands-down," and also singles out "casual atmosphere, good prices."

Taste the **shashlik** (shish kebab) appetizer, or **mashli tika** (marinated spiced fish fillets). You will enjoy marinated meats grilled in this clay-baked oven, accompanied by rice. Additional good choices include grilled chicken legs, lamb **biryani**, or **murghi tikka** (diced, marinated chicken cooked over charcoal).

BUDAPESHT (Hungarian-Russian cuisine), *2/18 Ulitsa Petrovskiye liniyi, Metro Kuznetsky Most. Tel. 924-4283. Open daily from noon to midnight for lunch and dinner. Cash only. Reservations are suggested in the evening.*

Part of Hotel Budapesht, but with a separate entrance. Centrally located north of the Kremlin and the Bolshoy Theater, and just around the corner from Petrovsky Passazh shopping mall on Petrovka Street. Music and dancing after 7pm, floor show after 9pm.

Built before the Revolution, Budapesht is an aged matron that still has a little class left with her marble statues, chandeliers and white linen tablecloths in her big dining hall, even if she does look a little pompous with too much rouge and frayed at the edges. This is not the place for a fancy 200-dollar meal and be thankful for it. You will find some good Hungarian specialties and traditional dishes, but you might also get your money's worth. Considering that it is state-run, you may find it friendlier than most in this category. However, should you wish to talk business, better go in the mid-afternoon, when you can be heard.

TSENTRALNY (Russian-European cuisine), *10 Ulitsa Tverskaya at Glinishchevsky pereulok, Metro Tverskaya, Chekhovskaya or Pushkinskaya. Tel. 229-0241. Open daily from noon to midnight. Cash only.*

Centrally located northwest of the Kremlin, amid the theater district, half a block from the Nemirovich-Danchenko theatrical museum on the same lane as the entrance to this restaurant. Live entertainment.

A grande dame of Moscow hotel restaurants, a large baroque dining room of this pre-Revolutionary establishment first opened in 1865 under another name. In 1905, a fashionable cafe was opened by the wealthy baker Filipov and next to it the Hotel Luxe (now known as Tsentralny) in 1911. In the 1920's, the hotel became a hostel for foreign Communists. The service is sloppy, rude and slow, but complements the Old-World atmosphere.

The menu though typical for a state-run eatery is varied and has a dish or two not available at other state restaurants. **Zakuski** (appetizers), alone can be a meal in itself. Meat and fish salads are edible, as are **pirozhki** (stuffed turnovers).

OLD SQUARE PIANO BAR (European-American cuisine), *8/6 Bolshoy Cherkassky pereulok, Bldg. 1, Metro Kitay-gorod, Ploshchad Revolutsiyi or Lubyanka. Tel. 298-4688 or 4738, Fax 298-4738. Open daily from 11am to 5am for lunch, dinner or drinks. Cash only.*

Centrally located northeast of the Kremlin, southwest of Kitay-gorod metro stations, and one block southwest of the Museum of Moscow History.

Opened in mid-1994, this is a classy, cozy place to go for a low-key lunch or dinner, or late coffee and a chat. The ground-level room has a nice bar and several booths overlooking the street. Downstairs, there are four small dining rooms. Italian mozzarella salad and Irish beef stew are the kinds of meals you will find at Old Square, in addition to sandwiches. New York pasta Alfredo, Mexican avocado salad, and a barbecue chicken sandwich are other choices available.

STANISLAVSKOGO (Russian cuisine), *2 Leontiyevsky pereulok at Nikitsky bulvar, Metro Arbatskaya or Pushkinskaya. Tel. 291-8689. Open daily from 6pm to 2am. Cash only. Reservations are mandatory.*

Centrally located in the theater district, northwest of the Kremlin, one block east of the Boulevard Ring Road, and northeast of Mayakovsky Theater. Live entertainment.

Named after the dramatist Konstantin Stanislavsky (1863-1938), this is more of a club than a restaurant, and unless you come with a recommendation from another member you may not be admitted. Strangers are sometimes unceremoniously turned away. Try your luck at lunch. This tiny restaurant offers some of the best Russian food. Mushroom-barley soup, veal and **bliny** (pancakes) are a good bet. To dine here, you might need to reserve the day before.

UZBEKISTAN (Central-Asian cuisine), *29 Ulitsa Neglinnaya, Metro Tsvetnoy bulvar or Kuznetsky Most. Tel. 924-6053. Open daily from noon to 11pm for lunch and dinner. Cash only.*

Centrally located on the edge of the theater district, north of the Kremlin, one block northeast of the Petrovsky Passazh shopping mall and on the southern edge of Trubnaya Square. Live entertainment nightly.

Loud tourists and Central-Asian men stand out in this Uzbeki restaurant, opened in 1949 to celebrate the "friendship" of another ethnic group in the Stalinist Soviet Union. There are paintings of Uzbeki scenes and the ceiling is decorated in a mosaic pattern.

Try **tkhumdulma** (boiled egg with a fried meat patty), or **shashlik** (shish kebab) Uzbeki-style. **Plov** (Asian pilaf), which is rice mixed with fried onions and lamb meat, is always a safe choice; flavor and color are added with prunes and carrots. You might want also to taste Uzbeki native bread, called **non**, which is baked on the premises. You should eat it by simply breaking off pieces with your hands, do not use a knife.

U NIKITSKIH VOROT (At Nikitin's Gates) (Georgian cuisine), *23/ 9 Ulitsa Bolshaya Nikitskaya at Nikitsky bulvar, Metro Okhotny Ryad. Tel. 290-4883. Open daily from noon to 11pm for lunch and dinner. Cash only.* Centrally located northwest of the Kremlin, on the Boulevard Ring, between the Mayakovsky Theater on Bolshaya Nikitskaya Street and U Nikitskih Vorot Theater on Nikitsky Boulevard. Itar-TASS news agency is across the street from the restaurant entrance.

The menu consists of basic Georgian dishes, whether you pick **zakuski** (appetizers) or grilled meats. Among the zakuski, you pick between the boiled beef tongue or **satsivi** (chicken in walnut sauce). Hot entrees include at least four kinds of **shashlik** (kebab) of sturgeon, veal, pork or mutton, as well as pork chops and roasted chicken.

IBERIA (Georgian cuisine), *5/7 Ulitsa Rozhdestvenka, Bldg. 2, Metro Kuznetsky Most. Tel. 924-8694 or 928-2672, Fax 924-7146. Open daily from noon until 5pm for lunch, and from 7pm to midnight for dinner; kitchen closes at 11:30pm. Accepts American Express credit cards only or cash. Reservations may be advisable in the evening.*

Centrally located northeast of the Kremlin and one block north from the Savoy Hotel and restaurant. Live folkloric and classical music after 8pm.

Open since 1992, Iberia is a cozy candle-lit restaurant that seats about 70, has a small bar and a private dining room. You can also eat at one of the tables on the sidewalk. The menu is basic and somewhat limited. Among the dishes to sample are **khachapuri**, a cheesy Georgian bread which is supposed to be served at least warm, but came to our table cold and stale; bean-based **lobio**; and a variety of grilled Georgian meats. Fried sturgeon entree goes for about $15.

We tried roast pork, with good taste if somewhat tough meat, and fried trout which also tasted respectably, and had a glass of Georgian house wine that makes all the difference in how much you will enjoy your Georgian meal.

Inexpensive
BELFIORI (Beautifu Flowers) (Italian cuisine), *10 Ulitsa Petrovka at Ulitsa Kuznetsky Most, Metro Kuznetsky Most. Tel. 925-5423 or 6469. Open daily from 11am to 6pm for lunch and dinner. Major credit cards accepted.*

On the 3rd floor of the Petrovsky Passazh shopping mall. Centrally located north of the Kremlin and the Bolshoy Theater, three blocks east of the Prince Dolgoruky statue on Tverskaya Square overlooking Tverskaya

Street. Live entertainment. Convenient if you are shopping at the Petrovsky Passazh mall and need a quick meal.

Appetizers include carpaccio, stuffed aubergines, and an Italian meat appetizer. Among the hot entrees, you can choose such standard Italian dishes as **spaghetti alla carbonara**, lasagna, and stuffed lobster.

KHRAM LUNI (Temple of the Moon) (Chinese cuisine), *1/12 Bolshoy Kislovsky pereulok, Metro Arbatskaya. Tel. 291-0401, Fax 291-1300. Open daily from 1pm to 11pm for lunch and dinner. Major credit cards accepted.*

Centrally located just four blocks west of the Kremlin, off Vozdvizhenka Street, and one block northeast from the Arbat metro station. Live music.

This small, cozy and comfortable Chinese cuisine restaurant, decorated in yellow and red, seats only 25. If you are hungry, try the fish. The chicken is another good choice, as are the salads.

KOMBI'S (Sandwich shop), *4 Ulitsa Tverskaya, Metro Okhotny Ryad. Tel. 292-3911. Open daily from 10am to 10pm. Cash only.*

Centrally located north of the Kremlin, at the foot of Tverskaya Street, across the street from the Intourist Hotel, on the second floor, above the Fokus photographic store.

An attractive, clean and quick self-service sandwich shop chain that has stores all over Moscow. At one time you could eat at Kombi's for under $5, but those days are gone and the major reason for eating here would be the still-competitive prices and lack of time. You can eat on the premises or take your food with you. All of Kombi's restaurants are clean and their rest rooms are spotless - not an insignificant detail when you look for a place to wash you hands. Kombi's may be the only Moscow fast food restaurant where employees wear disposable plastic gloves while preparing your food. The workers are generally friendly.

There are almost two dozen kinds of sandwiches on the menu, served on rolls or make-believe croissants. When the bread is fresh, they taste terrific, but just as often, the bread is stale by noon. Kombi's has an interesting fruit cake.

Other Kombi's are located at:

• *40 Ulitsa Stary Arbat, Metro Smolenskaya. Tel. 241-2202.* Centrally located west of the Kremlin, on the Old Arbat promenade, two blocks east of the Garden Ring Road, near the Pushkin Museum and the Georgian Cultural Center.

• *32/1 First Ulitsa Tverskaya-Yamskaya. Tel. 251-2578.* Located on the Garden Ring Road, diagonally across the street from the Tchaikovsky Concert Hall, just a door or two from the American Bar & Grill, with which it shares the same owners and address, and literally a few steps from the metro station Mayakovskaya.

• *46/48 Prospekt Mira at Protopopovsky pereulok, Metro Prospekt Mira. Tel. 280-6402.* Located three long blocks north of the Garden Ring Road,

northeast of the Kremlin, east of the Olympic Sports Complex, and near McDonald's.
• *180 Prospekt Mira at Ulitsa Borisa Galushkina, Metro VDNkH. Tel. 283-0651.* Located outside the Garden Ring Road, northeast of Kremlin, across the street from the Russian Exhibition Center, and one block north of the Kosmos Hotel.
• *4 Michurinsky prospekt at Ulitsa Kosygina, Metro Leninskiye gory. Tel. 437-5443.* Located outside the Garden Ring Road, southwest of the Kremlin, and at the foot of Sparrow Hills.

McDONALD'S (American fast food), *29 Ulitsa Bolshaya Bronnaya at Pushkin Square & Tverskaya Street, Metro Pushkinskaya or Tverskaya. Tel. 200-0590. Open daily from 10am to 10pm for lunch and dinner. Cash only.*

Centrally located northwest of the Kremlin, just off the Boulevard Ring Road, on the northwestern edge of the Pushkin Square, and two blocks southeast from its Russian fast-food competitor Russkoye Bistro (see below).

McDonald's, a joint venture with the Moscow municipal government, was the capital's first fast-food altar when it opened in 1990. It has 27 registers, seats more than 700 at a time, and employs 1,000 workers who serve up to 40,000 patrons daily. Sad to say but true: McDonald's on Pushkin Square is a tourist sight more popular than the Kremlin, Lenin's Tomb, and the Pushkin Museum put together. Other locations include:
• Another, smaller McDonald's, opened in 1993 on the ground floor of an 11-story McDonald's office building farther southeast, just off Tverskaya Street, across from the Central Telegraph Office, *17/9 Gazetny pereulok, Tel. 956-9816.* At the other end of this lane is Abacus Club, at 3 Gazetny pereulok, Bldg. 1.
• West of Kremlin, just inside the Garden Ring Road and next to the Ministry of Foreign Affairs and Pushkin Museum on the Old Arbat pedestrian walkway, is another McDonald's housed in a restored two-story 200-year-old house, *50/52 Stary Arbat, Tel. 241-3681.*
• Outside the Garden Ring Road, northwest of Kremlin, west of the Moscow Zoo and four very long blocks northeast of the World Trade Center and the Mezh Hotel, a McDonald's is located on the west side of the square in front of the metro station Ulitsa 1905 goda.
• Also outside the Garden Ring Road, northeast of Kremlin, east of the Olympic Sports Complex, *39 Prospekt Mira and Protopopovsky pereulok, Tel. 288-2177,* you will find a two-story McDonald's next to the stadium.
• Still outside the Garden Ring Road, northeast of Kremlin, south of Sokolniki Park, and across the street from the Sokolniki metro station, there is a McDonald's, *26 Ulitsa Rusakovskaya and Ulitsa Bardolina, Tel. 269-1493.*

• In 1996 McDonald's introduced a drive-thru McAvto, where Muscovites can yell their orders into the static-filled speakers without getting out of their cars. It is located at 63 Leningradskoye Highway on the way to Sheremetyevo 2 International Airport. The restaurant can serve up to 60 cars each hour.

• Another McAvto location opened at the end of 1996 on Yaroslavskoye Highway near Krasnaya Sosna Street, in the far northeast Moscow.

RUSSKOYE BISTRO (Russian-Fast Food), *10 Bolshoy Gnezdnikovsky pereulok at Ulitsa Tverskaya, Metro Pushkinskaya. Located northwest of Kremlin and a few steps from its chief competitor, McDonald's; 14 Ulitsa Varvarka at Ploshchad Varvarskiye Vorota, Metro Kitay-gorod. Located east of Kremlin, north of Rossiya Hotel, on one of the oldest Moscow streets; there are also several other locations throughout Moscow, Ulitsa Tverskaya, across the street from the Minsk/ Na Tverskoy Hotel. Open daily from 11am to 10pm.*

The first Russkoye Bistro, located in the narrow Gnezdnikovsky Lane that is parallel with Tverskoy Boulevard, was inaugurated by Moscow mayor in August 1995.

Like all other Bistros, it is decorated with the imitation Kremlin paintings, bright mirrors and symbols of Moscow. The employees wear Cossack blouses, black slacks and hats similar to those worn by Russian troops when they drove Napoleon from Moscow. It was those Russian soldiers, who pursued Napoleon's troops back to Paris between 1812 and 1814, that coined the word "bistro," which in Russian means "fast." It was adopted by the French after the hurried Cossacks who shouted impatiently for their food: "Bistro! Bistro!"

Perhaps taking a clue from their American competitor, one of the largest McDonald's restaurants in the world, which is located just two blocks northwest of here, across Tverskoy Boulevard, the Bistro employees are surprisingly cheerful and polite.

Russkoye Bistro concentrates on inexpensive food that all Russians know. Most dishes, such as **pirogi** (small pastries stuffed with meat, vegetables or fruit), thin pancakes called **bliny**, and mushroom soup, cost under $2 apiece. The Bistro is the last inexpensive restaurant left in Moscow. You can have a meal here for under $5. Bistro also offers **kvas**, a Russian drink made from fermented bread.

"This food is very, very tasty," said the mayor during the Gnezdnikov Lane Bistro opening ceremonies, adding, "I don't like McDonald's. I only go to one for the opening ceremonies." The city, incidentally, owns 51 percent of Moscow's McDonald's and you won't hear the mayor complaining about sharing those fat profits from McDonald's.

The Varvarka Street Bistro received another booster of even higher caliber; in January 1996, the mayor and President Yeltsin both stopped by to grab a bite to eat.

BETWEEN THE BOULEVARD & GARDEN RING ROADS

Quick Overview: You will find listed below some three dozen restaurants inside this donut-shaped area between the two major ring roads. The first two, **Imperial** and **Glazur/Rusalochka**, have impeccable food and service and are comparable to the top downtown restaurants inside the Boulevard Ring Road.

The 13 that follow them have been estimated to be expensive, where a complete meal will probably cost you more than $50. Some, like the **Ambassador** and **Kropotkinskaya 36**, have been around for a long time, others, like **Ampir** and **Dorian Gray**, are of a more recent vintage. We also like **Amsterdam** for its no-nonsense food, service and cleanliness, and **Danilovsky**, which is part of the hotel at the Danilovsky Monastery. We are still wary of the former tourist dive, the state-owned **Arbat**, because of its past practices, although the restaurant has had a profound face-lift and it shrank considerably.

The next 16 restaurants have been placed in the moderately-priced category, where you can eat for under $50 a meal. We do not recommend any restaurant located on the Stary Arbat promenade on food merits, including **Pizza Italia**, **Arbatskiye Vorota**, or **Russky Traktir** that are listed below, unless you enjoy the atmosphere on the street and do not mind paying a little extra. We like the friendliness, food and atmosphere at the American **Starlite Diner**, but not at its neighbor **American Bar & Grill**, whose reputation at this central location is sliding. **Tandoor** and **Palms Cafe** are owned by the same company and both merit your consideration. Westerners swear that eating at **U Babushki** is just like going to your grandmother's, which is the translated name of this Russian-cuisine restaurant. **Sports Bar** is suggested for only the young and restless. The old, tired, state-owned **Sofiya** and the Azeri-Arabian-Lebanese **Baku/Livan-Nassr** were under reconstruction at the end of 1996.

Among the inexpensive eateries, **Cafe Margarita** and **Moskovskiye Zori** are especially good choices for the college set. **U Mamy Zoyi** is one of the most popular Georgian cafes in Moscow at any price. That leaves us with **Dunkin' Donuts**, which shares its space with **Baskin-Robbins**, as the least expensive alternative, if you can call it a restaurant at all.

Very Expensive

    GRAND IMPERIAL (Russian cuisine), *9/5 Gagarinsky pereulok at Chertolsky pereulok, Metro Kropotkinskaya or Smolenskaya. Tel. 291-6063, Fax*

290-0249. Open daily from noon to 11pm for lunch and dinner. Cash only. Reservations are mandatory in the evening. Jacket and tie are suggested for men.
Located southwest of the Kremlin, east of the Ministry of Foreign Affairs and half that distance southeast of the Canadian Embassy, and north of the Tolstoy museum on Prechistenka. Live piano music.

The entrance is dominated by an old Russian wooden double-headed imperial eagle that the owners chanced upon in the loft of an old house. The proprietors are a husband and wife team. In 1994, Imperial became the first Russian restaurant to be awarded the International Certificate of Quality; it was also one of the first private restaurants in the capital in 1987. Imperial, which can seat up to 50, has the class and the atmosphere of a time long gone, but now revived for you to appreciate. There are Russian mafia and diplomatic corps limousines parked in front of it most evenings. A doorman will greet you in formal attire. There are two dinning rooms, the larger having seven tables with blue velvet chairs that seat perhaps 40. A fountain in the middle is complemented by antiques displayed elsewhere. White linen tablecloths bring out the beauty and age of antique handmade platters, crystal and old silverware. There are fruit bowls and freshly cut flowers on each table. Original canvases by Russian and European artists grace the walls.

The food is well prepared and tastefully arranged. **Zakuski** (appetizers) include Chef's Salad Grand Imperial and frog's legs. The signature soup is named after Catherine the Great. Among entrees, try the roasted **sevruga** (sturgeon) named Griboyedov, or the smoked fish, or the meat **pirozhki**, or stuffed turnovers. There are also veal Romanoff, roast flambe a la tsar, and pancakes with caviar. You may be able to have a lunch here for under $100, without alcohol and gratuity, of course. The dinner is more expensive, but you will not feel cheated. You will experience imperial Russian grandeur in a city ravaged by the Communists.

GLAZUR/RUSALOCHKA (Danish-Russian cuisine), *12/19 Smolensky bulvar, Metro Smolenskaya or Park Kultury. Tel. 248-4438, 230-2319. Open daily from noon to midnight for lunch and dinner. Major credit cards accepted. Reservations will be needed in the evening.*
Located in a renovated 19th century mansion southwest of the Kremlin, on the Garden Ring Road, three blocks south of the Ministry of Foreign Affairs, and about the same distance southwest of the Danish embassy. Live classical, jazz and folk music in the evening.

Rusalochka, or Little Mermaid, meaning the well-known Copenhagen mermaid, is the only Danish cuisine seafood restaurant in Moscow and one of the oldest such eateries in town. This elegant cooperative, which seats about 50, serves good food and a varied selection of international wines. Rusalochka is a separate dining hall serving Russian food. Glazur's chef recommends boiled pork with eggplant, or stuffed tomatoes as appetizers. For an entree, he would have you pick among baked salmon a la Russe or steak with Madeira sauce. Several other main courses, such as chicken cutlets, are also worthy of note. They, as well as the fish, flown from Copenhagen, lobsters and shrimp can be washed down with the best international wines or Danish draft beer.

The service is professional, just what you would expect in an establishment with Copenhagen-like prices. You will have no problem shelling out $100 per person by the time the dessert cart rolls out.

Expensive

AMPIR (Russian cuisine), *4/10 Ulitsa Sadovaya-Triumfalnaya, Metro Mayakovskaya. Tel. 299-7974, Fax 299-7514. Open daily from noon to 1 am for lunch and dinner. Major credit cards accepted. Reservations are recommended for dinner.*

Located northwest of the Kremlin, on the Garden Ring Road, one block northeast of the Tchaikovsky Concert Hall, and on the same block as one of the Mayakovskaya metro exits.

An elegant dining room, where prices match the ambiance. Among the chef's recommendations are frog's legs, escargo Bernard, and the $77 lobster with lemon sauce, as well as **pelmeny** (meat-filled Siberian dumplings), and cassoulet, which is a French-style casserole of white beans baked with herbs.

Zakuski (appetizers) range from salmon with fritters to soft caviar. Soups include pike perch chowder and **okroshka** (cold kvas soup with meat or fish). Among the hot fish entrees, there is a $40 steak of salmon from Norway, sturgeon with barbecue sauce, or roasted trout with sour cream. Selections from the grill are just as ample: $25 pheasant with wine; roast pork with pineapple, or roasted fillet of beef. From the pan, there is the $50 suckling pig with buckwheat porridge; $45 duck fillet with honey sauce; fried boar fillet, and roasted quail. Desserts include the Hopless Drunkard pear, which is boiled in red wine. A bar and billiard room are also at your disposal.

AMBASSADOR (Old Russian & European cuisine), *29/14 Ulitsa Prechistenka, Metro Park Kultury or Kropotkinskaya. Tel. 201-4014, Fax 291-4196. Open daily from noon to 11pm for lunch and dinner. Major credit cards accepted. Reservations are recommended for dinner.*

Located southwest of the Kremlin, in one of the most beautiful historic districts of Moscow. The palace across the street from Ambassador, at 32/1 Prechistenka, for example, belonged to the a royal guard officer until 1879, when it became the renowned Polivanov Gymnasium, where writer Lev Tolstoy educated two of his sons. Live entertainment.

This stylish restaurant bills itself as "an ambassador from the old Russian aristocratic culture to the world of the new Russian service."

Clean and elegantly decorated. Offers recipes from old and forgotten Russian cuisine, such as rolled port, chicken liver with mushrooms, or tsar and celery pancakes. Among the appetizers, you can enjoy lobster with raspberry sauce, among entrees sturgeon marinated in champagne or salmon in white wine.

The owner of Ambassador was a deputy to the founder of the renowned **Kropotkinskaya 36** restaurant, located diagonally across Prechistenka Street, and another choice for elegant dining.

DOM LITERATORA (Writer's Union Restaurant) (Russian cuisine), *50 Ulitsa Povarskaya, Metro Barrikadnaya. Tel. 291-1515. Open daily from noon to midnight for lunch and dinner. Major credit cards accepted. Reservations may be in order evenings. Jacket and tie are suggested for men.*

Located northwest of the Kremlin, just inside the Garden Ring Road, and northeast of the American embassy, on one of the oldest and most fashionable Moscow streets.

This house was built in 1887. The light-brown wood-paneled dining room, a former Masonic salon became a nursery school in 1917, and in 1932 a privileged hiding place for the most trusted Party literary hacks and their sycophants. Dissenters, like Pasternak and Solzhenitsyn, were expelled. President Reagan gave his televised address on the freedom of the press here during his 1988 visit.

Still a state-owned eatery, it is now run by the considerably more impoverished Writer's Union and is no longer just for the authors who can still afford to eat here. Its menu can now be inspected at the door so you can catch your breath over its high prices before entering. While appearing without a tie would be considered blasphemous just a few years ago, the doorman took it all in stride when an informally-clad Westerner showed up to test the waters. **Zakuski** (appetizers), such as crab, carp, potato pancakes and **pirozhki** (stuffed turnovers) are some of the available choices. Try also the chicken Kiev or sturgeon, two more among the dishes whose quality just barely keeps up with the lofty prices.

KROPOTKINSKAYA 36 (Russian cuisine), *36 Ulitsa Prechistenka, Metro Park Kultury, Kropotkinskaya or Smolenskaya. Tel. 201-7500 or 203-8259, Fax 200-3217. Open daily from noon to 5pm for lunch and from 6pm to 11pm for dinner. All major credit cards accepted. Reservations are suggested.*

Located southwest of the Kremlin, on one of Moscow's grandest streets, where nobles built their opulent homes to the blueprints of architect Osip Bove, and two blocks southeast of Ambassador, a continental restaurant of similar class. Entrance is actually on Kropotkinsky pereulok, which also shelters the Australian and Finnish embassies. Live entertainment nightly.

This venture was in 1986 the first private cooperative restaurant in Moscow. Since then the name of the street has reverted to the pre-

Revolutionary Prechistenka, but the restaurant has kept the previous name of the street, named by the Soviets after the anarchist Pyotr Kropotkin. The staff is friendly, once you pass the stern doorman. Although today Kropotkinskaya 36 seems just another expensive restaurant, it is still a good place to taste a **bliny** (pancakes) with caviar. It has a somewhat formal 1920's style upstairs room on the street level, with a pianist, and a cozy room downstairs in the basement tavern. Both of them seat about 80. Note the copy of an old, now just decorative, tiled ceramic stove in the anteroom. **Shchy** (cabbage soup), classic Russian mushroom julienne, or crab Kamchatka soup would all be a good start. Siberian meat dumplings, or **pelmeny**, are another worthwhile choice. Among the entrees, the chef recommends Kropotkinsky-style pork and beef in beer with lemon. Try also broiled shrimp and sturgeon prepared in Russian style, roasted **sevruga** (sturgeon) on a spit, or Russian-style lamb.

DORIAN GRAY (Italian cuisine), *6/1 Kadashevskaya nab. at Staromonetny pereulok, Metro Tretyakovskaya or Novokuznetskaya. Tel. 237-6342 or 6313, Fax 237-6313. Open from noon to midnight for lunch and dinner. Major credit cards accepted. Reservations are suggested for dinner.*

Located south of the Kremlin, across the Moskva River in Zamoskvorechye, an old Moscow district, and two blocks northwest of Tretyakov Gallery.

One of the best and most expensive Italian restaurants in Moscow. It has a pleasant interior with a bar along the dining room and classical music to entertain you. Among the hot entrees, its well-known chef recommends **spaghetti con frutti di mare**, **salmone al Carry**, or **costolette d'agnello**, which runs over $30. There are more than 20 kinds of spaghetti to choose from and an extensive seafood menu. For dessert, treat yourself to tiramisu.

The Moscow alternative English-language weekly, *Living Here*, praises "Good location, atmosphere, fresh pasta dishes," then adds: "Overpriced; cellular phones blaring through your meal. Shootings have occurred."

AMSTERDAM (European cuisine), *30/4 Ulitsa Pyatnitskaya, Metro Novokuznetskaya. Tel. 231-4244. Open daily from noon to 10pm for lunch and dinner. Major credit cards accepted. Reservations are suggested in the evening.*

Located southeast of the Kremlin, in the historic Zamoskvorechye neighborhood, just south of Klimentovsky pereulok and one block south of Novokuznetskaya metro station, almost across the street from the Tanzanian embassy.

This is a pleasant, simple, clean, efficient Dutch-controlled eatery with about a dozen tables and a tiny bar. White tablecloths add to the feeling of luxury and attentive service. Not a well known restaurant, but just right for an intimate, quiet conversation or to close a business deal.

Whether you have a steak or one of the seafood dishes, you will feel that you got your money's worth even if prices are relatively high. A fenced terrace has been added for those who want to enjoy their food and drinks outdoors and are willing to tolerate the noise of Pyatnitskaya Street.

LAZANYA (Lasagna) (Italian cuisine), *40 Ulitsa Pyatnitskaya at Golikovsky pereulok, Metro Tretyakovskaya or Novokuznetskaya. Tel. 231-1085. Open Monday through Friday, from noon to 11pm, Saturdays and Sundays from 3pm to 11pm. Major credit cards accepted.*

Located southeast of the Kremlin, in an old Moscow neighborhood across the Moskva River, known as Zamoskvorechye, and southeast from Tretyakov Gallery. The house, now a museum, where playwright Aleksandr Ostrovsky was born is just northwest from here.

An Italian cooperative with two dining rooms that seat a total of about 40. During the years when you could pay in dollars in Moscow restaurants, it was so popular you had to make reservations days ahead to get into the dining hall where rubles were accepted. Modernistic painters display their work on the walls.

Their lasagna is sometimes just average. Pasta, chicken and veal are only three among the almost 50 dishes that are worthy of your consideration.

LE CHALET (Swiss-French cuisine), *1/2 Korobeynikov pereulok, Metro Park Kultury. Tel. 202-0106 or 2611, Fax 202-7166. Open daily from noon to midnight for lunch and dinner. All major credit cards accepted. Reservations are recommended in the evening.*

Located southwest of the Kremlin, around the corner from the Moskva River's Prechistenskaya embankment, across the river from the Central House of Artists, in the Chaika sports complex.

This is one of the few Moscow restaurants serving Swiss food, as well as French. It seats about 50 and is promoted as a place for businessmen with quiet and unobtrusive service. The menu features beef and cheese fondues, carpaccio, steak tartare. The chef recommends the **fondue bourgignone**, **darne d'esturgeon en piperade**, and **blanguettes de veau**.

ARBAT (Russian-European cuisine), *21 Ulitsa Novy Arbat, Metro Arbatskaya or Smolenskaya. Tel. 291-1445. Open daily from 10am to midnight for lunch and dinner. Major credit cards accepted. Reservations may be in order in the evening.*

Centrally located west of the Kremlin and just inside the Garden Ring, on one of the most popular sidewalks in Moscow, and within a short walking distance south of the American Embassy.

Beware of this restaurant! Before its 1995 reconstruction, their unappetizing food was served in the Arbat's cavernous dining hall that seated over a thousand people. Waiters preyed on unsuspecting tourists looking for a respite, exhausted from sightseeing with no place to sit. No matter what you ate the tab was always $25, without alcohol. But even in a city of ten million, where there are plenty of people to make money from, Arbat's business was wilting.

While the new, substantially smaller Arbat restaurant has made great cosmetic changes, along with new menus and more appetizing food, we cannot shake off a conviction that you cannot teach an old dog new tricks. We recommend this eatery only to those who have the courage to complain if they did not get their money's worth. You can always have hamburgers at McDonald's on the nearby Stary Arbat.

Inside the old restaurant premises there is also the **Tropicana** club on the second floor, serving Polynesian cuisine from 7pm to 4am. It is expensive and as warm as a slab of marble. **Casino Arbat** (same phone), on the ground floor, is open from 2pm to 6am.

SILLA (Korean-Chinese cuisine), *Aboard M.S. Valery Bryusov, Krymskaya naberezhnaya, Metro Park Kultury or Oktyabrskaya. Tel. 956-6527. Open daily from noon to 3pm for lunch and from 6pm to 11:30pm for dinner. Major credit cards accepted.*

Docked on the Moskva River, southwest of the Kremlin, and inside the Garden Ring Road.

The ship is named after the Moscow-born poet, Valery Bryusov, who was greatly influenced by the French. He wholeheartedly embraced the Bolsheviks in 1917 and served their cause tirelessly until his death in 1924. Silla was the name of an ancient dynasty in Eastern Asia; today the name belongs to many cafes and restaurants in Seoul.

If you wish to start with an appetizer, the Silla's chef recommends fried prawns or stewed dumplings. There are several hot entrees to pick from, among them the roasted duck, or spicy raw beef. Also on the ship is a bar and casino.

DANILOVSKY (Russian cuisine), *Danilovsky Hotel, 5b Bolshoy Starodanilovsky pereulok, Metro Tulskaya. Tel. 954-0306 or 0503, Fax 954-0750. Major credit cards accepted. Reservations are suggested in the evening.*

Located in the reconstructed Danilovsky Monastery, south of the Kremlin, a couple of long city blocks northeast of Tulskaya metro station, depending on where you exit.

Danilovsky has a reputation for good food and the prices are not too bad either if you come from the West. **Zakuski** (appetizers) go up to $32 for black caviar. Fish appetizers are just as expensive. Soups go up to about $12. Fish entrees range from $15 to $35, for the baked sturgeon **po-monastyrski** (Danilovsky-style). Steam-boiled salmon is also on the menu. Meat dishes will cost you anywhere from $13 to $23 for roast calf meat, Russian-style.

You can choose from a good selection of wines and a variety of desserts. There is no smoking in the restaurant or in public areas which display the portrait of the Patriarch of the Russian Orthodox Church, which owns Danilovsky hotel and restaurant. Believe it or not, in the basement of this church-controlled building there is a nightclub.

PEKIN IN MOSCOW (Chinese cuisine), *1/5 Ulitsa Bolshaya Sadovaya, Metro Mayakovskaya. Tel. 209-1865 or 1815, Fax 209-1863. Open daily from 2pm to 2am for lunch and dinner. Major credit cards accepted.*

Situated northwest of the Kremlin, on the Garden Ring Road - in this instance Ulitsa Bolshaya Sadovaya - across the square from the Tchaikovsky Concert Hall and across the street from Satira and Mossoviet theaters. Located inside the Pekin Hotel, behind the larger-than-life statue of Russian revolutionary poet Vladimir Mayakovsky (see Chapter 13, *Seeing the Sights* for his museum). The hotel is striking from the outside, but a dreary sight inside. Entertainment nightly.

Pekin restaurant opened during a time when China and Soviet Union were of the same mind about Communism. You might still bump into a Chinese diplomat or a journalist here and there, but the restaurant is a favorite with Moscow's younger set now. This large eatery serves fine food, particularly house specialties, such as Pekin duck. More than 50 dishes are available, among them the chicken strips, and barbecued bean curd, all prepared by Chinese chefs.

DYNASTY (Chinese cuisine), *29 Zubovsky bulvar, Metro Park Kultury. Tel. 246-4936 or 5017 or 5821 or 7071, Fax 246-5502. Open daily from 11:30am to 10:30pm for lunch and dinner. Major credit cards accepted.*

Located southwest of the Kremlin, on the Garden Ring Road, a block northwest from Park Kultury metro station and near the Progress French department store.

Probably the first thing you will notice about this restaurant is that it has a metal detector, a practice that is slowly gaining currency in various Moscow establishments to prevent some of the more unsavory patrons from bringing in guns. The softly lit dining room has rose and mauve velvety walls. There are more than 100 dishes on the menu, from the $65 whole roasted Peking Duck served with pancakes, for which you must give a 24-hour advance notice, to $50 baked lobster prepared in one of the three distinct flavors.

Among the appetizers, you can pick from the Mongolian lamb to Chinese dumplings steamed in a bamboo basket. Shark's fin crab meat soup or shark's fin chicken soup both run about $26. The menu is laden with seafood dishes, such as Peking-style grilled fish, Cantonese-style fried king prawns, and fried squid with pepper and garlic salt. Chicken entrees include fried and grilled dishes in Cantonese and Szechuan styles. There are several pork dishes, including the sweet and sour variety, with six kinds of rice. The menu prices do not include a ten-percent service charge.

Fast Food Fans, a division of Dynasty, serves those on the go and provides delivery at a $5 charge. Its fast food outlets are open from 10am to 10pm and are located at Komsomolskaya, Taganskaya, Mendeleyevskaya, Paveletskaya, Medvedkovo, Akademicheskaya, Kuzminky, Kurskaya, Park Kultury, and Ulitsa 1905 goda metro stations. Its fare includes beef and chicken dishes priced at up to about $5.

Moderate

PIZZA ITALIA (Italian cuisine), *45 Ulitsa Stary Arbat at Plotnikov pereulok, Metro Smolenskaya or Arbatskaya. Tel. 291-8262. Open daily from noon to midnight for lunch and dinner. Cash only.*
Located west of the Kremlin and two blocks east of the Garden Ring Road, across the street from Cafe Mishanka.

We are leery of all eating and drinking establishments on Stary and Novy Arbat, although some are undoubtedly better than others. The temptation to sit down on this handsome and very old promenade is as great for you as the temptation to charge a little extra is for the owners of the increasingly more exclusive eateries lining the street. Our advice is that if you come here for food alone, you may be disappointed. But if you come to shop in the many antique stores, walk up and down, like thousands of Muscovites and foreigners alike, and then sit down at an outdoor cafe for a meal or drink to relax and let the world pass by, go with the understanding that you are paying extra for the show.

Pizza Italia and its sister establishment **Italia Bar**, *49 Arbat*, are typical examples of what to expect on Arbat. Aside from a variety of pizzas, which run from $10 to $30, you will find a fair selection of appetizers and pastas. Seafood starts at $26 and goes all the way to $39 for mixed fish soup. You can buy the house wine by the glass or by the bottle.

There is a 15 percent service charge on top of your bill. Pizza Italia, like most Arbat restaurants, usually does not take credit cards, but when we inquired with the service supervisor, she agreed to take the American Express only.

STRASTNOY 7 (Russian-European cuisine), *7 Strastnoy bulvar, Metro Chekhovskaya or Pushkinskaya. Tel. 299-0498 or 200-1243. Open daily from noon to 11pm for lunch and dinner. Major credit cards accepted.*
Centrally located northwest of the Kremlin, just north of the Boulevard Ring Road, northeast from Pushkin Square, southeast from Lenkom Theater, and north of Rossiya Cinema. Live entertainment in the evening.

One of the more elegant and expensive cooperative restaurants, this one is favored by business people during the day and is the right place for a quiet meal. Neoclassical decor in beige and brown and friendly service are the hallmark of this eatery which opened in 1988 and seats about 45. It is named after its street address.

There are several daily specials, such as Old Moscow roulade or meat-and-ham-filled crepes. The chef recommends the trout in white wine and a fish named sterlet in champagne among the hot entrees.

AMERICAN BAR & GRILL (American cuisine), *32/1 First Ulitsa Tverskaya-Yamskaya, Metro Mayakovskaya. Tel. 251-2847 or 7999 or 250-9525. Open 24 hours a day; breakfast served from 4am to 11am. Major credit cards accepted.*

Located northwest of the Kremlin, on the Garden Ring Road, just east of Tchaikovsky Concert Hall and Mayakovsky statue on Triumfalnaya ploshchad, and a few doors east of Kombi sandwich shop.

Known as "ABAG" to those in the know, this a popular dating spot for the Moscow expatriates. You are bound to run into hordes of Americans, no matter what the time of day, or night. The food is typical fare for an amerikansky bar and grill. If you have a yen for good American steak, like New York strip, this is the place to go, as well as for hamburgers with American cheese. You can sample tangy and spicy Buffalo wings, potato skins with bacon and cheese topping or a chicken Caesar salad. Also available are grilled salmon and succulent BBQ baby back ribs.

For breakfast - and remember there are only a handful of Moscow eateries where you can find it - try pancakes with bacon, ham or sausage, or scrambled eggs with potatoes. The Jesse James breakfast consists of a grilled strip steak served with eggs and toast.

The *Moscow News* food critic, however, believes that "the only redeeming features of the ABAG, the once appealing refuge from the stress of Moscow life, are that it is open 24 hours a day, and is literally across the street from the metro. The service is terrible." This same reviewer suggests that you instead "head across town to its newer, spacier and much more relaxed sister establishment near metro station Taganskaya."

That ABAG, *59 Zemlyanoy val and Nikoloyamskaya nab., Tel. 912-3615,* is also located on the Garden Ring Road at the Yauza River embankment. It is open from noon to 1am, but on Fridays and Saturdays from noon to 2am in the morning.

U BABUSHKI (At Grandmother's) (Russian cuisine), *42 Ulitsa Bolshaya Ordynka, Metro Tretyakovskaya or Novokuznetskaya. Tel. 230-2797 or 233-2110. Open daily from noon to 4am for lunch and dinner. Only MasterCard and Visa are accepted. Reservations are suggested for dinner.*

Located in a low-slung 19th century red house in Zamoskvorechye, south of the Kremlin, on a typically long Moscow block bounded by Pyzhevsky pereulok on the north end and First Kazachy pereulok on the south. Tretyakov Gallery is two blocks north and one block west of here. This street is more than 700 years old.

This restaurant is run by the film actress Alla Budnitskaya and theater actress Svetlana Shvaiko, who know how to make you feel at home. The dining room is cozy, with old photos on the walls and knickknacks on the dresser... well, just like at grandmother's, even if the bill will bring you back to reality. Among the recommended entrees are aromatic **borshch** (beetroot soup), sturgeon soup, **pelmeny** (Siberian meat-filled dumplings) with sour cream, and **bliny** (thin pancakes). **Pirozhki** (stuffed turnovers), Moscow-style sturgeon, fried mushrooms, and suckling pig are also good choices served in an intimate, parlor-like setting.

The English-language weekly, *Living Here*, praises its "home-style atmosphere, good Russian dishes; authentic Russian dining experience," but adds that "prices are too high."

STARLITE DINER (American cuisine), *16 Ulitsa Bolshaya Sadovaya near Ulitsa Tverskaya, Metro Mayakovskaya. Tel. 290-9638, Fax 299-0600. Open 24 hours a day. Major credit cards accepted.*

Located northwest of the Kremlin, just off the Garden Ring Road, in Aquarium Gardens next to Mossoviet and Satira Theaters. Pekin Hotel is across the Garden Ring Road.

Few Western restaurants arrive in Moscow with publicity comparable to the Starlite, a typical 1950's American diner, which appeared here just before Christmas, 1995. After the building was manufactured in southern Florida, complete with Formica countertops, stainless steel stools, and assembled in a tiny park behind the Tchaikovsky Concert Hall, it made the news worldwide. The *New York Times* gave it a quarter page and declared that "There are almost 100,000 Americans and Europeans in Moscow now and many are already overjoyed at the chance to get hold of a good chicken pie and some chocolate milk."

The menu is extensive and it includes all the goodies you loved in the 1950's, if you are old enough, that is, including nine types of salads. Bacon grilled cheese sandwich comes with Hellmann's Real Mayonnaise and hamburgers are just as greasy as at home. You can treat yourself to a 25-dollar 12-ounce boneless New York strip steak. We tried homemade meat loaf and must admit that it immediately brought back memories of a 1960's New York diner. Pastas are worthwhile also.

The English-language weekly, *Living Here*, says, in part: "Your Eurosnob friends who whine about the Americanization of world culture quickly succumb to the Mushroom Onion Swiss Burger with fries; they hate themselves afterwards, but always come back for more."

Perhaps the worst that one can say about the Starlite is that it competes with the Burger Queen on Nikitsky Boulevard for the honors of making the worst coffee in Europe. Starlite is also one among the few places that serve breakfast. For about $15, you will get a 6-ounce steak with three eggs, hash browns, toast and all the bad coffee you can drink.

ZOLOTOY DRAKON (Golden Dragon) (Chinese cuisine), *59 Bolshaya Ordynka, Metro Dobryninskaya or Tretyakovskaya. Tel. 231-9251. Open daily from noon to 5am for lunch and dinner. Cash only.*

Located southeast of the Kremlin, Tretyakov Gallery, and Tropinin Museum, all in descending distance, one block north of the Garden Ring Road, near Pogorelsky pereulok, and across the street from the Kirgiz Republic embassy. On the street behind the Golden Dragon is a branch of Maly Theater.

This is one of the three restaurants by the same owners. There are several basement rooms, that seat about 50 diners, and a bar, decorated with lanterns, mirrors and Chinese landscapes. Some 40 dishes are offered, among them carrot salad and silver mushrooms appetizers. Afterwards you can enjoy hot chicken stew with nuts, meat with mushrooms **siangu**, or carp with soy sauce. You can also try pickled and spiced vegetables with shrimp and chicken, sweetened pickled cabbage, brown eggs, shrimp baked in pastry, **mora** (pieces of meat with uncut black mushrooms), and several varieties of rice.

Two other locations of Zolotoy Drakon are also open from noon to 5am:
• *64 Ulitsa Plyushchikha, Metro Smolenskaya or Park Kultury. Tel. 248-3602.* Located southwest of the Kremlin, outside the Garden Ring Road, and near the stadium of the Medical University;
• *15a Ulitsa Kalanchevskaya at Orlikov pereulok, Metro Krasniye vorota. Tel. 975-5566.* Located northeast of the Kremlin, two blocks outside the Garden Ring Road, and south of Leningradskaya Hotel.

TANDOOR (Indian cuisine), *30/2 Ulitsa Tverskaya, Metro Mayakovskaya. Tel. 299-4593 or 209-5565, Fax 299-5925. Open daily from noon to 11pm for lunch and dinner. Major credit cards accepted.*

Located northwest of the Kremlin, just inside the Garden Ring Road, a block from the poet Mayakovsky's statue on Triumfalnaya Square, and almost across the street from the Tchaikovsky Concert Hall.

This is a pleasant restaurant with white tablecloths and friendly Indian staff. The menu is extensive and includes **boti kebab** (boneless lamb marinated overnight and cooked in a tandoor, the traditional clay-baked oven), **murg malai tikka** (chicken), and **kalmi kebab** (chicken drumsticks marinated with spices). At $23, **jheenga masala** (fresh prawns) is about the most expensive dish on the menu. Other choices are **murg aftab** (boneless chicken), and **gosht awadh korma** (boneless lamb).

SPORTS BAR (American cuisine), *10 Ulitsa Novy Arbat, Metro Arbatskaya. Tel. 290-4311, Fax 290-4498. Open daily from noon to 6am; happy hour from 6pm to 8pm. Major credit cards accepted.*

Located west of the Kremlin, immediately west of **Dom Knigi** book store and across the street from the Arbat Irish House supermarket. The house where poet **Mikhail Lermontov** lived and his statue are behind the Sports Bar, on Malaya Molchanovka Street. Live entertainment nightly, starting at 10pm.

This is a huge two-level American-style bar with greasy food and plenty to wash it down with. Seems a terrific place if you are a male in your twenties and on the prowl. There are more TV sets at Sports Bar then there are customers at noon, showing either sports or MTV. As the sun goes down, the noise level and the smoke go up. There is a bar, billiard table and dance floor downstairs, together with a dozen small tables. The more menacing upstairs has another bar, table tennis, darts, basketball, and more billiard tables.

With all the goings on, who has the time to eat. We tried the beef goulash soup with mushrooms and potatoes and it tasted OK. A Tonya Harding cheeseburger was squeeshy with dripping grease. You can also order O.J. Simpson and Pete Rose Burgers. The barbecue pork ribs and chicken are for those who really want to gain some weight. You will also find several Mexican dishes. Sports Bar also serves breakfast.

ARBATSKIYE VOROTA (Arbat Gate) (Russian cuisine), *11 Ulitsa Stary Arbat, Metro Arbatskaya or Smolenskaya. Tel. 290-1035. Open daily from 11am to 11pm; lunch break from 3 to 4pm. Cash only. Reservations are required.*

Centrally located west of the Kremlin, at the beginning of Stary Arbat promenade, near Praga Cafe.

With just four tables and a tiny bar inside, and a couple more on the street, this may well be one of the smallest restaurants in Moscow. Stary Arbat, as you will soon find out, is one of the oldest and most popular promenades in Moscow. Sooner or later every tourist, and every Russian, walks down this street, where the poet Pushkin once held his stunningly beautiful wife Nataliya Goncharova on his arm . (By the way, his museum is on the other end of Arbat, across the street from McDonald's fast food restaurant.)

And the popularity of Arbat is where, we believe, the problem starts. The food on both Arbat streets is quite average and priced higher than elsewhere. However, if you do not mind spending a few extra dollars, indulge yourself and you will be able to tell your neighbors that you ate on Arbat Street.

PALMAS CAFE (Palms Cafe) (Continental-Thai-Indian-Chinese cuisine), *Valdai Center, 11 Novy Arbat at Arbatsky pereulok, Metro Arbatskaya. Tel. 291-2221 or 2216. Open daily from 11am to 11pm for lunch and dinner. Major credit cards accepted.*

Centrally located on the second floor of the Valdai shopping center, above Most-Bank, just a few doors east of the Novoarbatsky Gastronom supermarket and the rest of Arbat Irish House. Live music in the afternoon and evening.

An interesting place to consider whether you need a quick lunch or dinner or just want to linger and rest after sightseeing and shopping on Novy or Stary Arbat, or in the Valdai Center, which opened in 1994 and boasts several expensive stores. The large wall-sized windows make for an interesting view of Novy Arbat, which is always jammed by throngs of passers-by, and of **Dom Knigi**, the largest Moscow bookstore, on the other side of the street.

The menu includes shrimp cocktail, beef satay, chicken curry with rice, fish and chips, fried prawns, Wiener schnitzel, grilled sandwiches, and Dutch East Indies crepe. Palms Cafe is one of the few of non-hotel restaurants that offer a salad bar. Moscow desperately needs more such eateries, where you can reduce your caloric intake by munching on some harmless vegetables and salads. But the Palms salad bar plates are so tiny you could, with only a bit of exaggeration, confuse them with the tea saucers. You are not allowed seconds, unless you pay for another meal. If salad is what you want, we recommend that you head to one of the two locations of Patio Pizza (see listing), where for the same money you can eat all the salad you wish.

Another thing that sent our temperature soaring is that Palms, like many other restaurants in Moscow, charges for the bread and butter; this can add up to $2. So if you come here and they ask you whether you want bread, you will know what to expect.

SOFIYA (Bulgarian-European cuisine), *2 First Tverskaya-Yamskaya, Metro Mayakovskaya.*

Located northwest of the Kremlin, on the Garden Ring Road, and directly opposite poet Vladimir Mayakovsky's statue on Triumfalnaya ploshchad, where the Tchaikovsky Concert Hall is also located.

This venerable, inefficient, tired, old state-run restaurant looked and smelled musty, although it had some of that Old World atmosphere, even if the food was average. The building housing Sofiya was in reconstruction in 1996.

BAKU (Azeri-Arabian cuisine), *24 Ulitsa Tverskaya, Metro Tverskaya, Pushkinskaya or Mayakovskaya. Tel. 299-8506. Open daily from 11am to 11pm. Major credit cards are accepted. Reservations are suggested in the evening.*

Located northwest of the Kremlin, in the theater district of Moscow, two blocks northwest of Pushkin Square and a block southeast of Tchaikovsky Concert Hall. Variety show in the evening.

Named after the Azeri capital, Baku has several intimate rooms that seat about 200. You should try mutton **shashlik** (shish kebab) with one of the 20 varieties of **plov** (pilaf). Other good choices are beef Stroganoff, **dolma** (meat stuffed in grape leaves) or **golubtsy** (meat stuffed in vine or cabbage leaves). And do not forget **lavash**, the flat Caucasian bread.

LIVAN-NASSR (Lebanese cuisine, with a few Russian dishes), *24 Ulitsa Tverskaya, Metro Tverskaya, Pushkinskaya or Mayakovskaya (the same address as Baku; they share dining facilities).*

Try Livan-Nassr's eggs mixed with greenery and traditional Arab **plov.** Or platters of delicious **falafel, kiobeh** and grilled meats.

DUBROVNIK (Yugoslav-Russian cuisine), *8 Ulitsa Sadovaya-Chernogryazskaya, Metro Krasniye vorota. Tel. 207-5037. Open Monday through Saturday from noon to 11pm for lunch and dinner. Cash only.*

Located northeast of the Kremlin, on the Garden Ring Road, and one block northwest of the Eye Hospital. Live evening entertainment.

This formerly state-owned restaurant that seats about 100 is named after the historic Croatian port on the Adriatic Sea. Dubrovnik serves a variety of dishes of former Yugoslavia, as well as seafood, such as crabs.

ARBATSKY DVORIK (Arbat Courtyard) (Russian Cuisine), *9 Ulitsa Arbat, Bldg. 2, Metro Arbatskaya. Tel. 291-4060. Open daily from noon to midnight for lunch and dinner. Cash only.*

Centrally located west of the Kremlin and south of Praga restaurant. The entrance to this restaurant is from 8a Maly Afanasevsky pereulok, not from Arbat Street: walk south from Praga until you are across the street from **Nikolay Gogol** statue, located in front of you and at the top of Gogolevsky bulvar, also known as the Garden Ring Road. The tiny street on your right is Maly Afanasevsky Lane. Live music nightly after 8pm.

The building on the next block on your right, in a shaded courtyard, is Arbatsky Dvorik. Go up the stairs to the lounge, or through another door to the restaurant that seats about 40 and has a bar near the entrance. Now if that seems like a lot of trouble to get to a perfectly average restaurant, remember that we are suggesting it as a respite from the bustle of the Arbat streets, not for its culinary excellence, although you could do worse. And if you come here during the day, walk down a couple of streets to get the sense of old Moscow, with its narrow, winding streets.

RUSSKY TRAKTIR (Russian Tavern) (Russian cuisine), *44 Ulitsa Stary Arbat, Bldg 1, Metro Smolenskaya or Arbatskaya. Tel. 241-9853. Open daily from 7pm to 5am for dinner. Cash only.*

Located west of the Kremlin, northeast of the Ministry of Foreign Affairs, and close to the poet Aleksandr Pushkin's only Moscow residence, which is now a museum. Live entertainment.

As on the main promenade of any large city in the world, you will probably get less for your money than could elsewhere. Unless you have money to burn be a bit skeptical of all eating and drinking establishments on Arbat. Traktir is situated in a small, dark cellar and the doorman is usually not too friendly.

Some of the standard choices, dating back to the former Soviet Union, are mushrooms in cream, salted mushrooms and fried mushrooms. Also fried fish, like **sudak** (pike perch) and **osetrina** (sturgeon). Then there are borscht and **solyanka**, meat or fish soups. And several meat dishes, all mediocre as well.

CAFE MARGARITA (European-Russian cuisine), *28 Ulitsa Malaya Bronnaya, Metro Pushkinskaya. Tel. 299-6534. Open daily from 1pm to midnight, with a break from 4 to 6pm. Cash only. Reservations are practically a must.*

Located in the Margarita section of Moscow, northwest of the Kremlin, three blocks southeast of the American Express office on Sadovaya-Kudrinskaya Street, or the Garden Ring Road, and diagonally across the street from the Patriarch's Ponds. Live music nightly.

Cafe Margarita is situated in a well-known area of Moscow, which was the setting for Mikhail Bulgakov's most admired novel, *The Master and Margarita.* Patriarch's Ponds - actually, only one remains - are just across the street and have a statue of **Ivan Krylov** (1768-1844), the great Russian fabulist, born in Moscow, on the north end of the Ponds. You can enjoy the shade of lush trees surrounding the pond at the height of summer. The peaceful atmosphere might be disrupted for the next couple of years if plans to build a 500-car garage directly under the pond are carried out.

This cafe is popular with Moscow intelligentsia and Western students of Russian literature alike, with most of the diners college age. Perhaps it's even a bit too popular for its own good and becoming a bit worn as a tourist site. This small eatery has ten tables, lanterns on the walls and lattice-shuttered windows. There are surrealistic paintings on the wall that will remind you of the grotesqueness of Bulgakov's characters. This place has personality. Good, light and inexpensive meals and salads can be had. Mushrooms are all over the short menu, which also has a hand-written English translations tucked in, either in a soup or in casserole.

CAFE YAKIMANKA (Oriental-Mediterranean cuisine), *2/10 Ulitsa Bolshaya Polyanka at Yakimanskaya nab., Metro Polyanka. Tel. 238-8888. Open daily from 1pm to 11pm. Cash only.*

Located south of the Kremlin, just south of Vodootvodny Canal and Maly Kameny Bridge, and northwest of the Tretyakov Gallery. Live entertainment at night.

A mostly Tartar cuisine restaurant that seats about 70, the foreigners stand out against the Central Asians at this candle-lit Uzbeki restaurant. The food is influenced by the Mediterranean and Oriental dishes. Try the **dolma** (meat in grape leaves) and **plov** (pilaf) with beef and vegetables. You can bring your own alcohol.

Inexpensive

KOLKHIDA (Georgian cuisine), *6 Sadovaya-Samotechnaya, Building 2, Metro Tsvetnoy bulvar or Sukharevskaya. Tel. 299-6757. Open daily from* *noon to 11pm for lunch and dinner. Often crowded so make reservations if you want to eat dinner here. Cash only.*

Located north of the Kremlin, on the Garden Ring Road, which in this instance is Ulitsa Sadovaya-Samotechnaya, and across the street from the famous Obraztsov Puppet Theater. Live entertainment. Kolkhida serves authentic Georgian specialties. The atmosphere is friendly, but the piano and violin players sometimes are too loud. Red beans **lobio** (carrot and cabbage salads with spices), **phali** (noodle cake with cheese), all their other appetizers are tasty. For your main course, **dolma** (meat stuffed in grape leaves) would be your best choice, also calf **shashlik** (shish kebab) or **khinkali** (large, juicy dumplings). **Golubtsy** (meat in cabbage leaves) or stuffed tomatoes and peppers are tasty too.

MOSKOVSKIYE ZORI (Moscow Dawn) (Russian cuisine), *11 Maly Kozikhinsky pereulok, Metro Pushkinskaya. Tel. 299-5725. Open daily from noon to 11pm for lunch and dinner. Cash only.*

Located northwest of the Kremlin, east of Patriarch's Ponds of Bulgakov fame and just a block east from Margarita Cafe.

This log cabin was one of the first coop restaurants in Moscow. Although dark inside and quite small, it is cozy and suitable for a quick lunch or if you wish to linger over your meal in the summer, when a few tables are set outside.

The menu is somewhat rich in calories. Those who are regulars here suggest that you start with Stolichny Salad, rice-crab salad, or slices of **sevruga** (sturgeon) fish, or calamari. The breaded chicken cutlet, sauteed chicken legs, and the pork fillet are somewhat greasy main dishes. There is a good selection of Georgian wines, from Kinsmarauli to Mukuzani, to wash down your entree.

U MAMY ZOYI (Mama Zoya's Cafe) (Georgian cuisine), *8 Sechenovsky pereulok, off Prechistenka Street, Metro Kropotkinskaya or Park Kultury. Tel. 201-7743. Open daily from 11am to 11pm. Cash only. Reservations would be a smart move in the evening.*

Located southwest of the Kremlin, two blocks southwest of the Lev Tolstoy Museum, and four from the metro station Kropotkinskaya, on a side street between Prechistenka and Ostozhenka Streets. The entrance to the cafe is from the courtyard behind the building; you might smell the food before you get there. This friendly, unpretentious and casual cafe, somewhat at odds with its noble surroundings, is run by the wife of the owner of **Guriya Cafe**, also one of the better Caucasian restaurants in Moscow; see the listing below. Live entertainment some evenings.

Mama Zoya will overwhelm you with her appetizers, which include red and green bean salad, called **lobio**. **Satsivi**, a cold dish of chicken pieces in walnut sauce, and delicious **pkhali**, fried eggplant slices topped with walnut sauce and garlic.

Among the main courses, you can select **shashlik** (grilled chunks of pork or lamb served with raw onion), **khinkali** (spicy meat dumplings with onions), or tasty **khachapuri**, a cheesy bread that you can dip in sauces in front of you. The menu also includes spicy mutton and rice stew, called **kharcho**, and a thick yogurt known as **matsoni**.

DUNKIN' DONUTS (Donuts), *24 Ulitsa Myasnitskaya at Bankovsky pereulok, Metro Chistiye prudy or Turgenevskaya. Open daily from 10am to 8pm. Cash only.*

Located northeast of the Kremlin and Lubyanka Square, southwest of either of the two metro stations.

The first Moscow Dunkin' Donuts, which shares its retail space with **Baskin-Robbins** ice cream parlor, opened in the summer of 1996 and sells about 50 varieties of **donats**. Espresso, cappuccino, Arabica, and the American-style coffees are available, as well as hot chocolate and tea. There is a lot of coffee in Moscow that can pass for dish-washing water; Dunkin' Donuts coffee, we are happy to say, is good.

At least a dozen more Dunkin' Donuts shops are planned for. They and the **John Bull** pubs, which also has a couple of locations in Moscow, are owned by the same company.

OUTSIDE GARDEN RING ROAD

Quick Overview: There are some 50 restaurants listed in the endless suburbs outside the Garden Ring Road. This vast area, however, also includes parts of Moscow where many Westerners conduct business and lodge: the World Trade Center west of the Kremlin, and the area between Ukraina and Radisson Slavyanskaya hotels — the nearest suburban parts of western Moscow.

The first ten restaurants in this section are for those on a corporate expense account or living on an inheritance. **Borodino**, **Les Champs-Elysees**, **Yakor**, **Vienna**, **The Exchange**, **Lomonosov**, and **Taiga** are all luxury hotel restaurants with excellent reputations. The only non-hotel eateries in this bunch are the Japanese **Sapporo**, the tsarist Russian **Aleksandrovsky**, and the Italian **Arlekino** restaurants.

The next eleven are still expensive, but the quality of their food, service and decor lags behind the first group, particularly in the case of **Planet Hollywood**. A more typical example in this group would be the Italian **Kaprichio**, which serves good food, but expensive if you stay in Moscow more than a couple of weeks. Filipino-cuisine **Manila** also has decent food and service, but it so far away and for some so difficult to find, you might consider it if you stay in far southwest Moscow. **Karusel** and

Zolotoy Ostap are, we fear, overpriced. There are a dozen restaurants and bars at the Ekspotsentr, southwest of the World Trade Center, convenient only if you have independent transportation or if you want a respite from the Mezhdunarodnaya Hotel food. The next seven restaurants will generally give you your money's worth, even if they are a bit expensive. **U Pirosmani**, always somewhat of a tourist dive because of its location near the **Novodevichy Convent**, has deteriorated since President Clinton ate there in 1996. **Chopsticks** will probably be of interest mostly to golfers since it is located at the Tumba golf course club.

The next group of 14 eateries is more reasonably priced and some like **Brasserie du Soleil** and **Gian Carlo** are also attractive. Radisson's **Skandia** and **Amadeus Cafe** will be welcomed by those seeking a bit of Americana in Moscow. **U Yuzefa** is the only Jewish restaurant featured in this guide. **Sedmoye Nebo**, atop the Ostankino television tower, is recommended for its view only and it is a spectacular one. **Razgulyay**, unlike U Pirosmani, has been able to handle the hordes of foreign tourists without compromising the quality of its food. If you want solid Middle-Eastern fare, complete with belly dancers, you might consider **1001 Nights**, located all the way in the extreme southwest.

Hanoy is a surly dive that we do not recommend. Deciding between the Caucasian cuisines of **Mush Cafe** and **Shirak**, whose Oktyabrskaya Street locations almost face each other, is not easy, but we liked Shirak.

Finally, our choice among the inexpensive restaurants outside the Garden Ring Road, particularly if you like the Georgian food, is **Guriya**, followed by the friendly Cuban **Las Palmas**, near the Spasso-Andronikov Monastery.

Very Expensive

BORODINO (French-European cuisine), *located on the 5th floor of the Aerostar Hotel, 37 Leningradsky prospekt, Bldg. 9, Metro Dinamo or Aeroport. Tel. 213-9000. Open daily from 6pm to 11:30pm. Major credit cards accepted. Jacket and tie are suggested for men.*

Located northwest of the Kremlin, west of the Dinamo soccer stadium and southeast of the Airline Terminal. Live entertainment.

Borodino steak and seafood restaurant, named after a historic battlefield village southwest of Moscow, will more likely win your praise for its culinary artistry than Napoleon did in his frustrating pursuit of Russians in 1812, when more than 80,000 troops were killed during the 15-hour battle. Fortunately, nobody has to die while enjoying Borodino's superb cuisine, except possibly from overeating the Canadian chef's gourmet spread.

You could start with snails or sliced raw venison served with garlic sauce. Perhaps even lamb **pelmeni** (meat-filled Siberian dumplings). How about medallions of veal that are served with shrimp and Georgian white wine sauce? The main courses can be complemented by a large selection of French and American wines. The service is faultless, the 19th century Russian period style decor includes a portrait of the plump Kutuzov, suggesting that he seldom went hungry, and the music is unobtrusive. You can spend $100 here even before your date reaches for his or her dessert; and by then the value-added tax will almost lose its meaning on an already Utopian bill.

LES CHAMPS-ELYSEES (French cuisine), *located inside Sofitel Iris Hotel, 10 Korovinskoye shosse, Metro Petrovsko-Razumovskaya. Tel. 488-8000 or 8131. Open daily from 7pm to 10:30pm. Major credit cards accepted. Jacket and tie are suggested for men.*

Located in far northwestern Moscow, north of St. Boris and Gleb Church and close to the renown Fyodorov Eye Clinic. Sofitel Iris is located close to the northern limits of Moscow and too far to walk to. If you can eat here you surely must be able to afford a taxi; if you are just trying to impress someone, take the bus #56 from Petrovsko-Razumovskaya metro station. Live entertainment.

Authentic French cuisine, superb service and atmosphere to match all showcase an elegant dining room. Many ingredients are imported from France. Among the entrees, you can choose from Normandy-style hot oysters, snails casserole, smoked fish platter, or caviar with buckwheat bliny. Other choices include lobster in cream sauce, sea scallops with Ural caviar, thin veal fillet or roasted rack of lamb for two. Fish dishes menu will surprise you with salmon paupiette with lobster mousse, scallops with chicory shred, and eel cassoulet with white wine sauce. Among the desserts, you can choose crispy raspberry biscuit, lime pancake souffle and glazed apple tart, which takes 20 minutes.

Menu Gourmand at a fixed cost changes weekly. Plat du jour changes daily. For four or more diners, who reserve 48 hours in advance, there is free limousine service.

YAKOR (Anchor) (Seafood), *at Palas Hotel with separate street entrance, 19 First Ulitsa Tverskaya-Yamskaya at Ulitsa Bolshaya Gruzinskaya, Metro Belorusskaya or Mayakovskaya. Tel. 956-3152, Ext. 121, Fax 956-3151. Open daily from noon to midnight for lunch and dinner. Major credit cards accepted. Reservations are recommended for dinner. Underground parking is available.*

Located northwest of the Kremlin, four long blocks beyond the Garden Ring Road, and two long blocks southeast from the Belorussky Railway Station. Live entertainment.

Inaugurated in 1993, Yakor is located in almost the same spot as the original Yakor restaurant, which was then run by the USSR's Academy of

Sciences. The restaurant's dining hall is constructed in the form of a frigate deck. Appetizers and soups are abundant, with prices just as robust. You can tickle your palate with everything from carpaccio of salmon to fresh oysters on a half shell, at $55 for a dozen. You can sample Yakor's new Russian cuisine with poached breast of chicken stuffed with crab meat, or pan-fried sturgeon fillet with mushroom sauce. And if you are willing to spend upwards of $35 for an entree, then you can also enjoy sauteed fillet of beef with foie gras, pan-fried lamb with mustard, or sauteed fillet of Dover sole with almond at about $50. The restaurant's shellfish is imported from Maine, other items are from Scandinavia and France, and the prices reflect that. Any one of the five lobster dishes, grilled or roasted, costs more than $60 each. Yakor also serves Cajun foods, such as jambalaya, which is Cajun shrimp and chicken steamed in rice.

SAPPORO (authentic Japanese cuisine), *14 Prospekt Mira, Metro Sukharevskaya or Prospekt Mira. Tel. 207-8253 or 0198 or 7093, Fax 207-7869. Open daily from noon to 4pm for lunch and 6pm to 11pm for dinner, Monday through Saturday; 6pm to 10pm Sundays. Major credit cards accepted. Secured parking. Reservations are suggested for dinner.*

Located northeast of the Kremlin, one block north of the Garden Ring Road, north of Baskin-Robbins ice cream parlor and next door to Japro, a Japanese supermarket. Live entertainment and dancing.

A exclusive Japanese restaurant, where you can spend as much for dinner as you would at one of the three downtown five-star hotel restaurants. Sapporo is located on four floors each with different decor, and an elevator that whisks you to your location.

One of the less expensive lunches includes **tempura mori** (shrimp, squid and vegetables), **unaju** (fried eel), and **wafu**, which is roast beef steak. Salad **kaisen mori** (raw fish and vegetables) is a 25-dollar appetizer. Now you are ready for the dinner menu: **matsuzaka** (roast beef steak in sauce with hot vegetables and salad) is $100, as is **matsuzaka** filet. Sushi of assorted raw sea food is about $50, followed by **botanebi** (raw shrimp), **maguro** (raw tuna), **sashimi mori** (assorted raw sea food), and **kaki furai** (fried oyster).

The bill will probably make you break out in a rash anyway so go ahead and have that 5-dollar ice cream and coffee dessert.

VIENNA (Continental cuisine), *inside Palas Hotel, 19 First Ulitsa Tverskaya-Yamskaya at Ulitsa Bolshaya Gruzinskaya, Metro Belorusskaya or Mayakovskaya. Tel. 956-3151, Fax 956-3152. Open daily from 7pm to 11pm for dinner only. Major credit cards accepted. Reservations are recommended. Parking is available. Jacket and tie suggested for men.*

Located northwest of the Kremlin, four long blocks beyond the Garden Ring Road, and two long blocks southeast of the Belorussky

Railway Station. Tverskaya Hotel is diagonally across the street from Palace Hotel. Live entertainment.

Appetizers include warm smoked salmon, crawfish tails and lobster mousse with spinach dumplings. Among the seafood entrees, the dish recommended by the chef is a whole poached lobster at about $56. There is fillet of sea bass, or **turbot** with langoustine tails. Treat yourself to duck breast with Merlot sauce or roast rack of lamb. There is also tenderloin of veal with wild mushrooms, and fillet of beef in onion sauce.

You can stop here and calculate the value-added tax instead of dessert or go for broke and splurge on a bottle of wine that could cost as much as your entire meal. You probably think you deserve it so go ahead and have that $22 crepes Suzette, flamed at your table, while you enjoy the soothing Viennese classics played by a harpist from the Bolshoy Ensemble.

Expensive

THE EXCHANGE (American cuisine), *on the Ground Floor of Hotel Radisson Slavyanskaya, 2 Berezhkovskaya nab., Metro Kievskaya. Tel. 941-8020 or 8333. Open Monday through Friday, from noon to 3pm, for lunch and daily from 6pm to 10:30pm for candlelight dinner. Major credit cards accepted. Reservations are advisable in the evening.*

Located southwest of the Kremlin, southwest of the Borodinsky Bridge and the river boat stop, and next to the Kievsky Railway Station.

Arguably the best American steak house in Moscow, with real American cuts of sirloin and porterhouse, flown in from the US. The dark wood-clad, dimly lit Exchange seats up to 100 guests and is a good place for business meetings with solid food and attentive service. The prices go up as the sun goes down.

Appetizers include shrimp cocktail, escargot burgundy, and cured ham with asparagus, as well as black caviar with **bliny** (pancakes), marinated salmon in olive oil, and shrimp cocktail with avocado. This is a veritable Taj Mahal for the serious steak aficionado stranded in a country where a scraggly piece of wiry meat often passes for steak: real fillet mignon, New York sirloin, rib eye and pepper sirloin steak, you will find them all, but at the soaring prices you would expect to pay at Morton's in New York, most of them costing between $30 and $40. The real American apple pie is supposedly so good you will forget its lofty price tag.

If you are an American who has just come in after several months of deprivation in the Kazakhstani oil fields, you will want to spend the rest of your life here. And you could. Delta Air Lines' *Sky Magazine* notes this is "The only place to go when you are serious about beef. Close your eyes and you could be in New York, Chicago or Houston."

ALEKSANDROVSKY (traditional Russian cuisine), *17 First Ulitsa Tverskaya-Yamskaya at Ulitsa Bolshaya Gruzinskaya, Metro Belorusskaya or Mayakovskaya. Tel. 251-7987 or 289-9939, Fax 250-8448. Open daily from noon to 11pm for lunch and dinner. Major credit cards accepted. Reservations are suggested in the evening. Parking is available.* Located northwest of the Kremlin, four long blocks beyond the Garden Ring Road, and two long blocks southeast of the Belorussky Railway Station. The Palas Hotel is around the corner and the Tverskaya Hotel is one block north and across the street. Live entertainment.

Named after Tsar Aleksandr II, whose portrait hangs in this spectacular 19th century regal dining room, the prices are just a bit steep for the quality of the food. Aleksandrovsky aims to emulate the olden days when merchants would sit around tables laden with food, enjoying the feast, while the Gypsies would provide entertainment.

Sterlet a la Merchant is the most expensive entree at $56, followed by Lobster **Ekzotik** at about $50. Other second courses include steak Aleksandrovsky; sturgeon Potemkin; **ryba po-tsarsky** (sturgeon or salmon tsar-style); **osetrina po-monastirsky** (grilled sturgeon); trout fried in wine sauce; spicy shrimps; fried veal; liver Boyarsky; mutton with olives and walnuts; and Russian ravioli with cheese.

LOMONOSOV (European-Russian cuisine), *inside Palas Hotel, 19 First Ulitsa Tverskaya-Yamskaya, Metro Belorusskaya or Mayakovskaya. Tel. 956-3152, Fax 956-3151. Open daily from 7am to 10:30am for breakfast, from noon to 3pm for lunch, and from 7pm to 11pm for dinner. Major credit cards accepted. Reservations are recommended for dinner. Underground parking is available.* Located northwest of the Kremlin, four long blocks beyond the Garden Ring Road, and two long blocks southeast of the Belorussky Railway Station. Live entertainment.

A quality restaurant with a high reputation and almost as high prices. Deep-red decor and richness of the wood stand out against the white tablecloths, candles and freshly-cut flowers on your table. Whether a hotel resident or an outsider, you can enjoy breakfast, lunch and dinner, Monday through Saturday. On Sundays, an equally expensive brunch, with live music and magic show, replaces breakfast and lunch. Champagne is free for adults as is the food for kids under 12 years of age.

Lomonosov has an outstanding array of dishes; fish, meat, pork and fowl. Goose and duck are also on the menu. The chef recommends pork with onions and chilli peppers, or chicken and veal zucchini and red peppers, at about $40 each.

ARLEKINO (Arlecchino) (Italian cuisine), *15 Ulitsa Druzhinnikovskaya, Metro Krasnopresnenskaya or Barrikadnaya. Tel. 255-7088 or 9056, Fax 973-2029. Open daily from 12:30pm to 3:30pm and from 6 to 11pm. Major credit* *cards accepted. Reservations are recommended for dinner. Jacket and tie suggested for men.*

Located northwest of the Kremlin and south of the Moscow Zoo, in the Cinema Center northwest of the American Embassy.

Arlekino, which seats 200, is rated among the 20 best Italian restaurants outside of Italy, according to one survey. Popular with businessmen on expense accounts; the majority of the guests are Westerners and the so-called "new Russians" with money to burn. The restaurant takes pride in reminding its guests that most ingredients are imported from Italy. The chefs are mostly native Italians and Arlekino claims to be the first Italian restaurant in Moscow.

The **risotti** are tasty, and the pastas include **farfalle with gorgonzola**. The chef likes to highlight his **prosciutto di Parma** appetizer and **ossobuco a la Milanese** entree. A few Russian dishes are also available. Do not pass up the scrumptious desserts if your midriff can take it.

Arlekino Night Club is at the same address and open Friday through Sunday, from 11pm to 5am. A variety show is featured evenings. You can dance away the night. The cover charge in the past was as high as $50, which included one drink.

CAFE TAIGA (Russian-Continental cuisine), *inside Hotel Aerostar, 37 Leningradsky prospekt, Bldg. 9, Metro Dinamo or Aeroport. Tel. 213-9000, Fax 213-9001. Open daily from 7am to 11:30am for breakfast, noon to 6pm for lunch, and 6pm to 11pm for dinner. Sunday brunch is served from noon to 4pm. Major credit cards accepted.*

Located northwest of the Kremlin, west of **Dinamo** soccer stadium and southeast of the **Airline Terminal**. Live entertainment.

Its big elegant dining room seats about 400, olive and pink colors predominate, and the food, like its lodgings, is meant to please the Western businessman. The business lunch buffet is under $25. Taiga's chef recommends sauteed tiger shrimp at $33, grilled New York sirloin steak, and grilled swordfish with maple glaze at prices a bit below that. Several pastas are on the menu as well. Other main dishes, aside from the chef's recommendations, include roasted chicken, broiled red snapper, roasted duckling, beef Stroganoff, and Georgian **shashlik** (shish kebab). You can choose among several vegetarian main courses.

Taiga is perhaps best known for its Sunday brunch, at $35 per person. Even the irreverent English-language Moscow alternative weekly, *Living Here*, acknowledges that this "huge buffet spread offers one of the best values in town," and also mentions its "pasta bar, omelettes made to order, juices and desserts."

PLANET HOLLYWOOD (American), *23b Ulitsa Krasnaya Presnya, Metro Krasnopresnenskaya or Ulitsa 1905 goda. Tel. 255-0539 or 0569. Open daily from 11am to 1am for lunch and dinner. Major credit cards accepted.*

Located northwest of the Kremlin, three blocks west of the Moscow Zoo, and three blocks southeast of the metro station Ulitsa 1905 goda.

The Moscow version of Planet Hollywood opened in the fall of 1996, but just weeks after its gala opening, the waitresses often outnumbered the customers. The fact that Arnold Schwarzenegger and Patrick Swayze flew in to breath some life into the joint seems to have made no difference. And how could it, for Planet Hollywood is expensive, even in one of the most expensive capitals in the world. The cheapest food item on the menu is the $10 nacho appetizer. The $15 cheeseburger is possibly the most expensive burger in town. The Cajun chicken sandwich is $17 and pizzas are just as high. The portions are ridiculously small.

AROMAT (Aroma) (Russian cuisine), *12 Ulitsa Rogova, Bldg. 2, Metro Oktyabrskoye pole or Shchukinskaya. Tel. 947-2645, Fax 947-0024. Open daily from 6pm to 4am. Major credit cards accepted. Reservations are recommended for dinner.*

Located northwest of the Kremlin, southwest of Kurchatov Atomic Energy Institute, northeast of the October Stadium and west of Oktyabrskoye pole metro station. While there is bus service to Rogova Street from either metro station, you will save some shoe leather if you come by car or take a taxi from either metro station. Live music and variety show after 7pm.

This dark-wood-accented restaurant with white tablecloths, which opened in 1988, has chefs who once cooked their elaborate meals for the Communist bigwigs in the Kremlin. It tries to attract the Moscow elite, Western businessmen and foreign tourists with deep pockets.

Among the **zakuski** (appetizers), the chef recommends pike perch roll with shrimps, among the entrees **volovany** (dumplings) of potatoes with sturgeon, brisket with apples, or chicken fillet. If in the mood, try the **pelmeny** or a sturgeon dish.

SIRENA (Siren) (European Seafood), *15 Ulitsa Bolshaya Spasskaya at Skornyazhny pereulok, Metro Sukharevskaya or Krasniye vorota. Tel. 208-1412 or 0200. Open daily from 2pm to midnight, Saturdays & Sundays from 1pm to midnight, for lunch and dinner. Major credit cards accepted. Reservations are advisable for dinner.*

Located northeast of the Kremlin, one characteristically long Moscow block from the Garden Ring Road, and across the street from Volga Hotel. Live entertainment.

A wood-paneled, little-known and expensive restaurant serving a broad variety of fresh Mediterranean fish and live lobsters. Quiet music, several aquaria and model ships of yore atop them, create an atmosphere of ocean calm and respectable coziness. Taste the sliced smoked veal, salmon with black caviar, or smoked sliced chicken. There is also Florida sea turtle soup. Sirena is one among the handful of Moscow restaurants where you will find frog's legs and escargot. Also impressive is its stuffed grilled shrimp from Kamchatka, lobster and stuffed trout with almonds.

ATRIUM (Russian-European cuisine), *44 Leninsky prospekt, Metro Leninsky prospekt. Tel. 137-3008. Open daily from noon to 4pm and from 6 until 11pm. Major credit cards accepted. Reservations are suggested for dinner. Take-out is available.*

Located southwest of the Kremlin, a 15-minute walk from Gagarin Square, and one block southwest of Sputnik Hotel, on the ground floor of an apartment building.

The dining room has marble columns, statues, bas-reliefs and elegant decor, seats about 40, and may remind you of 16th century Rome.

The fixed menu features typical Russian cuisine. **Zakuski** (appetizers) include baked pork and garnished veal or sturgeon. Among the entrees, choose from the baked sturgeon Atrium, pork brisket stuffed with mushrooms, **pelmeny** Atrium (Siberian meat dumplings), stewed veal with mushrooms, and roast veal with mushrooms.

KAPRICHIO (Capriccio) (Italian cuisine), *8/40 Goncharny proyezd, 2nd Floor, Metro Taganskaya. Tel. 915-6492. Open daily from noon to midnight for lunch and dinner. All major credit cards are accepted. Reservations may be in order in the evening.*

Located southeast of the Kremlin, on the Garden Ring Road, just off Taganka Square in a Brezhnev-era building, two minutes from the metro station on foot. Secured parking. Live music nightly.

Opened in 1994, this pleasant but not exactly intimate restaurant, seating more than 150, is located on the southwest corner of Taganka Square, where Moscow coin, medal, pin and stamp collectors meet daily in the open air to trade their wares. The worn-out but renowned Taganka Theater is also located in this historic part of the city.

Capriccio is owned and operated by a friendly Italian from Palermo. Its Italian chef dishes out authentic Italian fare. The menu is practically the size of a telephone book, everything from **antipasti** (appetizers) to **primi** and **secondi piatti** (entrees) and **pesce** (fish). You might start with **antipasta di mare**, an assortment of seafood, or marinated red, green and yellow peppers. There is a large assortment of spaghetti, fettuccini, cannelloni, tortellini and risotti.

For dessert, try **tiramisu**, the Italian-style cheese cake, or **torta di frutta**, a light white cake.

LA CIPOLLA D'ORO (Zolotaya Lukovitsa) (Italian cuisine), *39 Ulitsa Gilyarovskogo at Kapelsky pereulok, Metro Prospekt Mira. Tel. 281-1339, Fax 281-9498. Open daily from noon to 11:30pm for lunch and dinner. Major credit cards accepted.*

Located northeast of the Kremlin, north of the Irish Embassy, a block west of Prospekt Mira, on the ground floor of a 12-story residential building, two blocks east of Renaissance Moscow Hotel. Live music Friday and Saturday nights.

La Cipollo D'Oro has an attractive and brightly-lit large dining room and bar with big windows and sparkling kitchen. The food, under the new management from Rome, matches the surroundings and attentive service. A terrace with about 15 tables is located in front of the dining room and walled off from the street. A la carte menu offers an abundance of choices. The antipasti are worthwhile, as are Tuscan soups and pasta dishes that change daily. All meats are grilled over open flame in the style of **girarrosto fiorentino**. You may enjoy lamb chops or suckling pig, spicy sausage or stuffed chicken. A large selection of Italian wines, some of which exceed the price of meals, is displayed in a glass refrigerated case.

Moscow's alternative weekly, *Living Here*, which is never shy with its opinions, declares: "The best Italian restaurant in Moscow."

MANILA (Filipino, Portuguese, & Spanish cuisine), *81 Ulitsa Vavilova, near Ulitsa Panferova, Metro Profsoyuznaya or Universitet. Tel. 132-0055, Fax 938-2285. Open daily from noon to 4pm for lunch, and from 5pm to midnight for dinner. Major credit cards accepted. Reservations are suggested for dinner.*

Located southwest of the Kremlin, northwest of Profsoyuznaya metro station, southeast of the Anglo-American School and Fairn & Swanson department store on Leninsky prospekt, on the ground floor of an apartment complex. One cannot help but be intrigued by how a luxury non-Russian cuisine restaurant in the middle of nowhere can survive in this economic climate. We set on foot from the metro station Noviye Cheremushky - something we do not recommend unless you are as fanatical about Moscow as we are - and it took more than an hour to get to the restaurant. A bit spartan but elegant, the Manila, with about a dozen tables, good air-conditioning and attentive service is quite a contrast to the grime and sorrow outside. Live piano and violin music at dinnertime.

Start out with the devil fish salad at $40, or seafood and vegetable salad at half the price. Manila's specialties include the whole lobster sauteed with spices, but it comes to almost $100. A bit easier on your wallet is **surgo terminador**, or king prawns with milk sauce and baked with cheese. If this is still too much, go for **camaron rebosado**, pickled prawns baked with sweet and sour sauce, at about $50. We stuck with the conservative chicken Mandarin, as well as chicken fillet in vegetable sauce, with nuts and pineapple and felt we received our money's worth.

KONTINENTAL (Russian-European cuisine), *inside Hotel Mezhdunarodnaya, 12 Krasnopresnenskaya nab., Metro Ulitsa 1905 goda. Tel. 253-1934, Fax 253-7998. Open daily from noon to 11pm for lunch and dinner. Major credit cards accepted. Reservations may be advisable in the evening.*

Located west of the Kremlin, east of Krasnaya Presnya Park, and next to the World Trade Center. Live music and dancing in the evening.

The well decorated dining hall seats up to 250, is a little on the dark side, but has a pleasant atmosphere; there are no windows overlooking the city, however.

Appetizers and cold dishes include caviar, cold-smoked salmon and sturgeon, as well as cold boiled pork. Also traditional Russian **sudak**, **sevruga** and **osetrina**, all of them expensive fish, both fried and as cold dishes. There are almost a dozen kinds of salads. Meat and fish **solyanka** soups are also on the menu. Main courses include languette with Madeira sauce, fillet, and steak.

LE CAFE FRANCAIS (French cuisine), *inside Sofitel Iris Hotel, 10 Korovinskoye shosse, Metro Petrovsko-Razumovskaya. Tel. 488-8000 or 8131. Open daily from 7am to 10:30pm for breakfast, lunch and dinner. Major credit cards accepted.*

Located in far northwestern Moscow, north of St. Boris and Gleb Church and close to the renown Fyodorov Eye Clinic. Sofitel Iris is located close to the northern limits of Moscow and is too far to walk to. We suggest you take a taxi from Petrovsko-Razumovskaya metro station, or bus #56 to get to the restaurant.

Le Cafe Francais has an upgraded coffee-shop-like atmosphere, but think twice before coming if you hope to dine in style at coffee-shop prices; the dinner buffet alone runs close to $50. Be prepared — your expectations about the food may not be met; such was the case with a **Moscow News** food critic who labeled a four-course gourmet dinner at Sofitel "a dinner more redolent of the rubber-chicken circuit than gourmet French cuisine."

Entrees include French onion soup, hot or cold Vichyssoise, and **solyanka** Russian soup. You can select from among the following meat and fish dishes: grilled steak Bearnaise, lamb steak, veal escalope with melted cheese, pork tenderloin in paprika, duck steak, Dover sole with mushrooms and shrimp. Snacks for paupers with deep pockets include King Burger, Italian lasagna, ham or cheese omelet and Club sandwiches.

KARUSEL (Carousel) (Italian-European cuisine), *7 Ulitsa First Tverskaya-Yamskaya, Metro Mayakovskaya. Tel. 200-5763 or 251-6444, Fax 250-9598. Open daily from noon to 6am for lunch and dinner. Business lunch from noon to 5pm. Major credit cards accepted. Reservations are suggested in the evening.*

Located northwest of the Kremlin, roughly halfway between Triumfalnaya Square with a statue of poet Vladimir Mayakovsky and Belorussky Railway Station on the other end with a statue of writer Maksim Gorky. Live entertainment.

Karusel has a restaurant at this address, including a casino upstairs and a bar next door; Karusel Klub, a disco that is open from 10pm to 6am, is located on the north side of the next block. Of the four Karusel establishments, we recommend the restaurant only. For more about Karusel Klub, please see Chapter 15, *Nightlife & Entertainment.*

The menu is groaning under the weight of the appetizers, pastas and fish pastas, soups, various meats, and special dishes that you can order in advance, and desserts. Among the Russian specialties, you might enjoy stuffed roasted pork, **okroshka** soup made of kvas and served cold, grilled fresh river trout, or skewers of sturgeon.

The half a dozen blocks of First Tverskaya-Yamskaya Street have one of the largest concentrations of restaurants on a Moscow street if Karusel doesn't appeal to you.

ZOLOTOY OSTAP (Golden Ostap) (Georgian-Russian cuisine), *3 Shmitovsky proyezd at Second Zvenigorodskaya ulitsa, Metro Ulitsa 1905 goda. Tel. 259-4795 or 256-0939. Open daily from 1pm to 4am for lunch and dinner. Major credit cards accepted. Reservations are suggested in the evening.*

Located west of the Kremlin, north of the World Trade Center and the Mezh Hotel, and four very long blocks southwest of the metro station. You may find this restaurant too far to walk to from the metro; take a taxi from the Ulitsa 1905 goda metro or a bus on Presnensky val Street nearby, across the street from Sixteen Tons restaurant and pub. Live entertainment.

Zolotoy Ostap restaurant and piano bar is owned by Archil Gomiashvili, a well-known Georgian film actor. There is a small casino next door, about which you can read more in Chapter 15, *Nightlife & Entertainment.* You will be greeted by a liveried doorman, a surprise for the proletarian Krasnaya Presnya district. Waiters wear white gloves. Muscovites in the know say that the Golden Ostap is generally overrated for what you get for your money.

Cold appetizers, which run up to $30, include **satsivi** (chicken in walnut sauce). Among the hot entrees, the chef recommends Ostap aromatic fillet with fried apples and almonds, as well as pork cutlet. Georgian entrees include a $30 sturgeon barbecue, as well as **kuchmachi** (fried chicken liver), and **chakapuli** (lamb), which may consist mostly of gristle and fat. A harp player will entertain you during the lunch; after that you can listen to a trio named Zolotoy Ostap, singing Georgian and Russian songs, then see a live show.

SADKO ARCADE (various cuisines), *Ekspotsentr, 1 Krasnogvardeysky Pervy proyezd, Metro Ulitsa 1905 goda. Tel. 259-5656, Fax 973-2185. Open as shown under individual entries. Most accept major credit cards.*

Located west of the Kremlin, southwest of Krasnaya Presnya Park, as well as the World Trade Center and Mezhdunarodnaya Hotel, inside the Ekspotsentr exhibition park, near Sadko supermarket.

Sadko Arcade has a number of eating establishments serving cuisine from all over the world. Caution: We do not recommend that you walk to any of the Ekspotsentr establishments below, either from the metro station or the Mezh Hotel; it is too far and not entirely safe. If you must go, take a taxi or bus #12 at the metro station square, across the street from the pub Sixteen Tons.

These restaurants might only be of interest if you have business at the exhibition park. Except for the side facing Moskva River, the area surrounding the Ekspotsentr borders on the somewhat neglected **Krasnaya Presnya Park**.

These establishments are located at Sadko Arcade and all accept major credit cards:

- **Beer House**, *Tel.* 940-4072, German food; see individual listing below
- **Chico's Cafe**, *Tel.* 940-4068, Italian cafe, selling pastries and ice cream
- **Club 21 House**, *Tel.* 255-2742, Bar and nightclub with DJ music and more
- **Golden Lotus**, *Tel.* 255-2500, A Chinese restaurant
- **Mistral**, *Tel.* 940-4071, Mediterranean restaurant; see listing below
- **Remy's Piano Bar**, *Tel.* 940-4065, Cocktails and array of other beverages
- **Steak House**, *Tel.* 256-2206, American steak house; see listing below
- **Swiss House**, *Tel.* 940-4069, Swiss food; see listing below
- **Swiss Pastry Shop**, *Tel.* 253-9592, Swiss and European pastry and candies
- **Trattoria**, *Tel.* 940-4066, Italian restaurant; see listing below

BEER HOUSE (German-European cuisine), *Sadko Arcade. Tel. 940-4072. Open daily from 11:30am to 11:30pm for lunch and dinner.*

The Beer House, a casual and unassuming German-style eatery, seats 75. Start with the cabbage-and-bacon salad, then have an old-fashioned wurst or schnitzel. There are various kinds of sausage and other meals you would expect to find in a central European restaurant, along with the obligatory draft beer. Live entertainment.

MISTRAL (Seafood-Mediterranean cuisine), *Sadko Arcade. Tel. 940-4071. Open daily from 4pm to 11:30pm, Saturdays and Sundays from 11am to 11pm, closed Mondays.*

This restaurant, close to Beer House (above), opened in 1995 with simple Greek decor, if you can call it that. You can watch your meal being cooked in an area between the two large dining rooms.

Appetizers include at least half a dozen seafood tapas, from prawns to smoked fish fillet. The seafood entrees range from fresh mussels prepared in a creamy fish stock to **sole Estoril**, an oven-baked dish with garlic and bacon. Chicken **souvlaki** and grilled lobster with lemon butter are both tasty. Scampi Mistral has excellent sauce seasoning. The grilled red snapper fillet with peppers and garlic is also on the menu. The lamb soup with barley and fresh vegetables is worth trying. The meat dishes include the Yugoslav **satarash** with sliced pork fillet and egg, and grilled lamb fillet, which costs $25.

SWISS HOUSE (Swiss-International cuisine), *Sadko Arcade. Tel. 940-4069. Open daily from 5pm to 11:30pm, Saturdays and Sundays from 11:30am to 11:30pm.* This restaurant has a pleasant light wood-paneled dining room, bright and airy, with lots of colorful flowers. The owners call it "a Swiss cottage of the Engandin Valley - in the heart of Moscow."

Swiss House's soups are priced up to about $10, hot appetizers and salads up to about $15, cold appetizers $20, meat dishes $35, and fish dishes up to about $40.

Among the appetizers, the chef recommends the original Swiss dried beef or snails with garlic butter. For a hot entree, you may consider his recommendation of halibut Lucern-style or a rack of lamb Provencale.

STEAK HOUSE (American cuisine), *Sadko Arcade. Tel. 256-2206. Open daily from 11:30am to 11:30pm for lunch and dinner.*

The Steak House has a pleasant dark wood-clad interior, accented by fresh flowers and beige tablecloths. A patio overlooking the Moskva River is open in the summer. The Steak House promises sirloin, rib eye and T-bone cuts of beef, "all flown directly from the U.S. For seafood lovers, we offer shrimp along with a full salad bar of fresh greens and vegetables. So if you've been to the Palm in New York, Blacky's in Washington, and now you are looking for the true steak lover's restaurant in Moscow, come to the Steak House."

Veal loin steak with fried mushrooms, French fries and vegetables is about $33. You can also try their mushroom burger. Appetizers include the original Hungarian goulash soup.

There is live music in the evening, from Wednesday through Saturday.

TRATTORIA (Italian cuisine), *Sadko Arcade. Tel. 940-4066. Open daily from 11:30am to 11:30pm. Note: this is the last of the Sadko Arcade restaurants.*

A brightly lit pastel-colored restaurant, the Trattoria seats 110. There is a variety of northern and southern Italian dishes, including veal, fish and seafood. Start with a tomato-mozarella salad, then enjoy one of the many pastas, like **marinara** and Alfredo.

Appetizers include **avocado ripieno con insalata di calamari**, as well as **zuppa di pesce**. Among the entrees listed on the menu are **romba alla griglia**, and **piccata di vitello alla parmigiana**, but there is also a large selection of other northern and southern Italian specialties. For an Italian dessert try **tiramisu** or **pasticceria della casa**.

TRIUMF-KOENIG STUBE (German-Russian cuisine), *36 Kutuzovsky prospekt at Kutuzovsky proyezd, Metro Kutuzovskaya. Tel. 249-6965 or 6529. Open daily from noon to midnight. Major credit cards accepted.*

Located southeast of the Kremlin, south of Fili Park, northeast of Victory Park and Triumphal Arch, and one blocks east from the Kutuzov's Hut, Borodino Diorama and Kutuzov's statue. Music entertainment nightly.

This is a good place for lunch and dinner, if you like German food, particularly after you have walked yourself unconscious at the behemotic Victory Park on a hot summer day. Upon ascending one more set of winding stairs, you will reach a restaurant in the style of a German hunter's lodge. Triumf seats about 150 in a dining room on the second floor overlooking Kutuzov Avenue, and has a small banquet room set aside for private parties.

Soups and appetizers go as high as $25. Try the Berlin liver with fried onion as an entree. The German chef recommends lobster, or smoked eel with tartar sauce. You should also consider the flounder, grilled shrimp, grilled steak, baked lamb, or schnitzel.

U PIROSMANI (At Pirosmani's) (Georgian cuisine), *4 Novodevichy proyezd at Ulitsa Pogodinskaya, Metro Sportivnaya. Tel. 247-1926 or 246-1638, Fax 246-1638. Open daily from 1pm to 10:30pm for lunch and dinner. Major credit cards accepted. Reservations are suggested for dinner.*

Located southwest of the Kremlin, south of Ukraina and Radisson Slavyanskaya Hotels, on the northeast side of the 16th century Novodevichy Monastery, near the Moskva River. Boris Godunov was proclaimed tsar in Novodevichy. The convent was established in 1524 to shelter the ladies of royal birth and widowed or unwanted wives. Live entertainment.

This large cooperative restaurant is named after the Georgian primitive painter Niko Pirosmanashvili (1860-1918). The son of a gardener, he was a self-taught painter of tavern signs and was discovered in 1912. The crude directness of his work can be observed at the Tretyakov Gallery.

U Pirosmani has always been somewhat of a tourist dive, probably because of its proximity to the Novodevichy Convent, although not to the extent of the Aragvi restaurant on Tverskaya Street downtown. On April 20, 1996, President Clinton ate here, while visiting Moscow, and complaints are already mounting that prices have gone up and the quality of service down as a result. The menu abounds in appetizers and Georgian dishes, such as **khinkaly** (meat-filled dumplings Georgian-style) and **lobio** (spicy red or green marinated bean salad). You have not tried Georgian cuisine until you taste the **lavash** (freshly baked Caucasian bread) or **khachapuri** (bread with melted cheese). Sample the cabbage, beet and carrot salads, as well as a variety of cold meats. The main dishes are usually listed on a chalkboard at the entrance and may include **karcho** soup and **shashlik a la Mirasaan** (kebab).

GREEK RESTAURANT (Greek-European cuisine), *aboard the M.S. Aleksandr Blok, docked opposite Mezhdunarodnaya Hotel, 12 Krasnopresnenskaya* *nab., Metro Ulitsa 1905 goda. Tel. 255-9284 or 9278, Fax 253-9578. Open daily from noon to 3pm for lunch and from 7 to 11pm for dinner. Major credit cards accepted.* Located west of the Kremlin, near the World Trade Center and the Mezh Hotel. Live Greek music on piano and guitar.

This British-managed restaurant that can seat up to 50, is next door to a casino at the Inflotel floating hotel.

Among the seven main courses, 12 kinds of salads, cold appetizers and desserts, there is also a seafood menu. It features lobster, shrimp, swordfish, and filet of sole. Buffet luncheon is available weekdays; buffet dinner, with live bouzouki music, weeknights except Thursdays. On Thursday nights, there is a fresh fish buffet dinner at $50 per person. A buffet luncheon is also held on Saturdays and Sundays.

IN VINO (European-German cuisine), *on the 3rd Floor of Ukraina Hotel, 2/1 Kutuzovsky prospekt, Metro Kievskaya. Tel. 243-2316 or 2444. Open daily from 7:30am to 11am for breakfast, from noon to 4:30pm for lunch, and from 6pm to midnight for dinner. Major credit cards accepted. Reservations may be in order in the evening.*

Located west of the Kremlin, north of Kievsky Railway and metro stations, and across the Moskva River from the Russian White House.

The dining room, with a large bay window overlooking the river, can seat up to 50. The service is attentive and the small menu changes frequently.

For starters, you can try one of the vegetable salads. **Bliny** (pancakes) with caviar, shrimp, crabmeat and tomato soup are other choices. Among the main dishes is one with shrimp and vegetables. Fillet of beef and fillet of pork, both with vegetables, are priced at about $25, while the fillet of chicken in wine sauce is a bit extra.

There are other eating facilities inside the hotel, such as **Ukraina**.

IL PESCATORE 90 (Italian cuisine), *36 Prospekt Mira, Metro Prospekt Mira. Tel. 280-2406 or 3582, Fax 280-3582. Open daily from 7pm to midnight for lunch and dinner. Major credit cards accepted.*

Located northeast of the Kremlin, southeast of the Olympic Sport Complex, on the same block as the southern metro station exit, and next to the University Botanical Garden.

This rather popular Italian restaurant, which seats 120, whips up dozens of dishes with ingredients flown in from Italy. Even Italians like to eat and relax here. Pescatore features a wide variety of pastas, veal and rabbit. As the name implies, it also excels in seafood. The **Milanese** and salmon are good follow-ups to the small pasta dishes.

The owners also manage **La Cipolla d'Oro** (see listing) on nearby Gilyarovskogo Street, which runs almost parallel to Prospekt Mira, northeast of the metro station.

SANTA FE (American southwest cuisine), *5/1 Ulitsa Mantulinskaya, Bldg. 6, at Ulitsa Anny Severyanovoy, Metro Ulitsa 1905 goda. Tel. 256-1487 or 2126, Fax 256-2451. Open daily from noon to 2am, Fridays and Saturdays until 3am.*

Situated west of the Kremlin, three very long winding blocks east of the Ekspotsentr exhibition park and Sadko Arcade, one block west of Mezhdunarodnaya Hotel, and near the entrance to the Krasnaya Presnya Park. Unless you stay at the Mezh Hotel, we do not recommend that you wander around here at night. Arrange for a taxi or at least take the bus. Live entertainment and dancing.

Located inside what looks like a beautiful former mansion, this large restaurant has two dining rooms and just as large a bar and two patios. Opened in mid-1994, this is a popular spot for Moscow expatriates seeking dates with other Westerners; and no wonder, it is comfortable, pleasant, relaxing and bright, something you would find in New Mexico.

The menu is large and offers infinite choices, starting with appetizers, such as Caesar's salad with grilled peppers, or jumbo shrimp taco salad. From there, you can progress to grilled king prawns and broiled sirloin steak, each of which will set you back $35. Southwest swordfish, fajitas, salmon fillet and grilled beef tenderloin fillet, however, are all under $30. Other entrees include a rack of pit-smoked ribs New Mexican-style, a couple of kinds of chicken, marinated snapper and scallops.

For more about the **Hippopotam** club, below Santa Fe, see Chapter 15, *Nightlife & Entertainment.*

CHOPSTICKS (Chinese-European cuisine), *1 Ulitsa Dovzhenko at Ulitsa Ulofa Palme, Metro Universitet. Tel. 147-7368, Fax 143-7832. Open daily from noon to 11pm. Major credit cards accepted.*

Located southwest of the Kremlin, south of the Setun River, at the Tumba golf course club, northwest of Sparrow Hills, formerly named after Lenin, in the embassy section of southwestern Moscow. Mosfilm studios are located a few long blocks southeast of here. Difficult to reach unless you have a car.

Open to both members and non-members. If you love golf, this is a good place to discuss and lock in that business deal that brought you to Moscow in the first place. Formerly called the Savoy Club, Chopsticks seats about 60. They offer a broad selection of Chinese dishes, including seafood. Try the shrimp soup, and among the entrees, try the beef fillet with garlic or asparagus sauce. A wide variety of wine is also available. European cuisine is served on the first floor.

Moscow's English-language alternative weekly, *Living Here*, comments: "Tasty fried prawns, Sezchuan dishes; friendly service; interesting view of the 10th hole of the Tumba golf course." A disco and a bar are also on the premises.

Moderate

BRASSERIE DU SOLEIL (European cuisine), *21 Ulitsa Taganskaya at Marksistsky pereulok, Metro Marksistskaya. Tel. 258-5900. Open daily from 11:30am to 11:30pm for lunch and dinner. Major credit cards accepted.*
Located southeast of the Kremlin, and southeast of Taganka Square, in the Mosenka Park Towers.

This hardwood-floor restaurant is divided into eight sections with about two dozen seats each, which gives it an intimate cafe-like setting. Mostly red couches, topped with wrought iron and frosted glass, divide each section. Brasserie flung its doors open for the first time in 1996. The bar and lounge sport aged leather armchairs purchased at the auction of a bankrupt French club.

The menu is not large, but has enough options to display the virtuosity of its Belgian chef. Most of the ingredients are brought in from Belgium. For starters, you can try scampi shrimp cooked with garlic butter. Brasserie has already gained a reputation for its hot Touraine goat cheese salad; it comes on a bed of salad greens decorated with slices of grapes, kiwi, plum and strawberries. As an entree you can select from pork tenderloin, or veal medallions with fried potatoes. The beef and pork are sometimes tough and the salmon in white wine cream sauce is not always fresh. Sole Meuniere is at $30 one of the most expensive entrees, but a good choice.

GIAN CARLO (Italian cuisine), *2/1 Ploshchad Pobedy at Kutuzovsky prospekt, Metro Kutuzovskaya. Tel. 148-7556, Fax 148-6208. Open daily from noon to midnight for lunch and dinner. Major credit cards accepted.*
Located southwest of the Kremlin, southeast of Fili Park, northeast of Victory Park, and roughly between the Triumphal Arch and Borodino Diorama on the opposite end of the restaurant.

After an exhausting tour of the huge Victory Park and taking in all the monuments honoring the World War II victims and memorializing Napoleon's invasion in 1812, this is the nearest decent restaurant where you can collapse in abandon knowing they will nourish you before your next tour starts. It is clean and comfortable, airy and pleasing to the eye. There is also a bar in the back of the restaurant.

After the usual array of appetizers, you can settle for one of the pastas, which run up to $15, or a pizza that goes a little over that. Perhaps the most expensive entree is veal fillet at about $35. Other main dishes include grilled fish; prawns in cognac; swordfish with fresh tomatoes; salmon; lamb in red wine; lamb chops; and veal scallops in wine.

SKANDIA (European cuisine), *ground floor of Radisson Slavyanskaya Hotel, 2 Berezhkovskaya nab., Metro Kievskaya. Tel. 941-8020, Ext. 3268, Fax 271-0998. Open daily from 7am to 11am for breakfast; noon to 2:30pm for lunch;*

5:30 to 10:30pm for dinner; and noon to 4pm for Sunday brunch. Pipe and cigar smoking is discouraged. Major credit cards accepted.

Located southwest of the Kremlin, south of the Russian White House, and next to the Kievsky Railway Station.

This plain but comfortable restaurant features hearty buffet-style meals that will remind you of the good ole' USA at a time when you may genuinely miss her. Like the **Amadeus Cafe** or **The Exchange** steak house, both on the ground floor of the Slavyanskaya, Skandia offers good food, pleasant environment and (a bit) high prices.

Breakfast buffet is $15, but includes fresh fruit, **bliny** (thin pancakes), meats and cheeses, cereals, ham, bacon and sausage, juices, scrambled eggs, pastries, as well as coffee and tea. Lunch buffet runs about $25 and is just as generous in selection as in calories. Dinner buffet goes for $30 and, again, the tables are groaning under the mountains of food. The Sunday Champagne Brunch costs $33.

A la carte items are priced relatively high, whether you have spinach fettucini alla carbonara, pan-fried salmon with mashed potatoes, a salad buffet, spaghetti Bolognese, a cheeseburger, hamburger, or grilled cheese sandwich.

U YUZEFA (Jewish-European cuisine), *11/17 Ulitsa Dubininskaya, Metro Paveletskaya. Tel. 238-4646. Open daily from noon to 11pm for lunch and dinner. Major credit cards accepted.*

Located southeast of the Kremlin, a couple of blocks south of the Garden Ring Road, and one block south of the Paveletsky Railway Station. "Look for the church and you'll find us," says its owner, referring to the Church of Saints Flor and Paul in Zatsepa, north of the restaurant. Live entertainment.

This is one of only a handful Jewish restaurants in Moscow. It opened in 1988 and already boasts diners such as Princess Ann and poet Yevgeny Yevtushenko, not to mention countless former dissidents. Its owner, Yuzef Maksovich, who likes to sit with the guests, moving from one table to another, wrote ten cookbooks. He says, "our dishes are kosher, we don't use pork and use only natural oils - cotton, olive and vegetable oil."

The menu is large, but not all the dishes advertised are available. Among more than a dozen kinds of hors d'oeuvres, you might enjoy the cooked eggplant salad with carrots. Try the mutton stew in an earthenware pot. Also worthwhile is herring under boiled beets and gefilte fish. You might also enjoy fried carp.

There is a good selection of kosher wines. Various folkloric ensembles accompany singers who perform Jewish songs in Hebrew and Yiddish in the evening.

SEDMOYE NEBO (Seventh Heaven) (Russian cuisine), *atop the Ostankino Television Tower, 15 Ulitsa Akademika Korolyeva at Ulitsa*

Novomoskovskaya, Metro VDNkH. Tel. 282-2293 or 2038. Open daily from 11am to 11pm. Cash only. Entry by passport only. Admission to the tower $4. Located north of the Kremlin, south of the Botanical Gardens, and east of the International Television Center. Sedmoye Nebo is almost straight west of the Kosmos Hotel, about half a dozen blocks, but they are so infinitely long, you may want to take a bus on Akademika Korolyeva Street.

The **Ostankino Television Tower**, the second tallest free-standing structure in the world, was completed in 1967 and has three observation platforms with a bar and a two-platform restaurant, which seats more than 200. This is the only restaurant of its kind in Moscow. The tower is 1,200 feet high and the platforms make one complete circle every 45 minutes, enabling you to view the entire city. The view is absolutely spectacular, the food is average, and the service is exactly what you should expect in a typical state-run establishment, where waiters seem to think they are doing you a favor just by being there.

In the top-level restaurant you can order your food a la carte, which will also free you from the silly rule of being seated and having your meal at specific times. The next level down is a set-menu restaurant, which has several fixed lunch-time and dinner periods, 11am, 1pm, 3:45pm, 5:45pm, and 7pm. Below the restaurant is another platform with a bar.

For security reasons, you must bring your passport and you have to secure reservations in an office next to the tower, where you can also buy Ostankino Tower trinkets. To a Westerner it is a baffling experience with no comparison, and you will also have to fill out a questionnaire about your current residence. Only after these 15-20-minute distractions will you be allowed to enter one of the high-speed elevators. Leave your bags and briefcases in your hotel or you will encounter additional complications.

Instead of the fixed menu, which contains **zakuski** (appetizers), a main course and dessert, we suggest that you select something just a bit more edible. **Osetrina po-petrovsky** (sturgeon Peter's-style) is about the most expensive hot entree at $25. Pork roast meat **po-ostankinsky** (Ostankino-style), **ptitsa v gorshochke po-rossiysky** (Chicken pot Russian-style), and **baranina po-tiflisky** (mutton Tiflis-style) are other hot-dish choices.

If the weather is good, you will see all seven of the Stalin's "wedding cakes," those awful Gothic buildings simultaneously erected all around Moscow during his dictatorship.

RAZGULYAY (Authentic Russian cuisine), *11 Ulitsa Spartakovskaya at Yelokhovskaya ploshchad, Metro Baumanskaya. Tel. 267-7613, Fax 265-0079. Open daily from noon to 11pm for lunch and dinner. Cash only. Reservations are suggested for dinner.*

Located northeast of the Kremlin, three blocks west of the Baumanskaya metro station and one block from the Cathedral of the Epiphany, built in 1750's and the largest in Moscow until the Cathedral of Christ the Savior was erected. The restaurant faces a small park with the Bolshevik revolutionary Bauman's statue. Live gypsy entertainment nightly.

Named after nearby Razgulyay Square, one of the oldest in Moscow, where merchants of old came for a jug of honey drink or to have a beer. There were many restaurants, casinos and other places of entertainment here in the 18th century. A restored basement of the former nunnery provides the three cellar dining rooms, each with about six tables, each one painted in an old Russian style, Gzhel, Khokhloma and Beresta.

The menu has plenty of typical Russian dishes and most of them are worth trying. Try the beef baked in a pot village-style or the roast meat with prunes and mushrooms. Both entrees are hearty and tasty and only about $12 each, and just what you'd expect. The one sour note is a $1.25 charge for bread and butter, not unusual in Moscow.

Also tasty are **skoblyanka** (meat with mushrooms and fried potatoes), house-specialty **pelmeni** (Siberian meat dumplings), and meat in jelly. Other main dishes on the menu include stuffed chicken Razgulyay-style, chicken cutlet Slavic-style, Moscow-style sturgeon, and beef steak with mushrooms.

Razgulyay, which seats 65, is clean and has satisfactory service, particularly for a state-run restaurant. Gypsy vocalists will try to "cheer you up," which is the translation of the name of this restaurant.

DIANA (Russian-European cuisine), *22 Ulitsa Timura Frunze at Zubovsky proyezd, Metro Park Kultury. Tel. 246-5448. Open from 11am to 11pm for lunch and dinner. Major credit cards accepted. Reservations are suggested for dinner.*

Located southwest of the Kremlin, one block beyond the Garden Ring Road, and another from Lev Tolstoy's Museum in Khamovniki, although you will have to make a long U-shape detour northwest or southeast from the restaurant to get to it because Timura Frunze is a three-block-long uninterrupted street.

Open since 1994, it consists of three intimate tiny dining rooms. The one thing that surprised us at Diana, however, were tables laden with **zakuski** (appetizers), waiting for someone to claim them. This was once a standard practice in Soviet restaurants that is quickly disappearing. We are a little concerned about the health aspects — meat displayed unrefrigerated for an hour or two at room temperature. The easiest way to dispense with this relic is to ask for **chisty stol** (clean table) when making reservations or to refuse the zakuski outright upon your arrival.

Among the many hot entrees on the menu is French-style sturgeon, trout stuffed with walnuts, and Russian-style salmon. You can also try steak **po-derevensky** (village-style), almond cutlet with brandy, and

Argentinean style pork. There are also home-style **pelmeny** (meat-filled Siberian dumplings), and beef with prunes. Most entrees are under $20.

AMADEUS CAFE (American-European cuisine), *located on the ground floor of Slavyanskaya Hotel, 2 Berezhkovskaya nab., Metro Kievskaya. Tel. 941-8020. Open daily from 6:30am to 11pm. Major credit cards accepted.*
Located southwest of the Kremlin, and across the Moskva River, next to the Kievsky Railway Station.

If you have been in Russia for a month and long for pancakes with maple syrup or a bagel with cream cheese for breakfast, this is the place to go. While there, you can pick up the English, French, German or Italian newspapers in the nearby hotel kiosk. Amadeus is believed to be one of the best informal Western-run lunch spots in Moscow, particularly when in a hurry.

The menu also includes club sandwiches, lasagna, wurst, green salad, and daily soups. It's known for having good coffee and great burgers. Try the salmon burger with melted Swiss cheese, or the baby shrimp, mushroom and bean sprout salad. Quick, friendly service, but the prices are a bit high.

MEI-HUA (Plum Blossom) (Chinese cuisine), *2/1 Ulitsa Rusakovskaya, Bldg. 1, Metro Krasnoselskaya or Sokolniki. Tel. 264-9574. Open daily from noon to midnight for lunch and dinner. Major credit cards accepted. Reservations may be advisable in the evening. Monitored parking.*
Located northeast of the Kremlin and Kazansky Railway Station, south of the Sokolniki Park, and three blocks northeast of Krasnoselskaya metro station. Live music.

The appetizers are delectable, whether beef in orange sauce, sweet-and-sour cucumbers or spicy carrots. The chef actually recommends his vegetable salad, meat in soy sauce, or shark-fin soup. Among the entrees you might enjoy deep-fried chicken, barbecued pork or spicy pork with peanuts. The chef's suggestion for the main dish is beans with meat, or seafood in the Chinese tradition.

U BANKIRA (At Banker's) (Russian-Caucasian cuisine), *24/1 Ulitsa Chasovaya at Third Baltiysky pereulok, Metro Sokol or Aeroport. Tel. 155-4554. Open daily from noon to 11pm for lunch and dinner. Cash only.*
Located northwest of the Kremlin, four long blocks northeast from the Sokol metro station, and three blocks northwest from the Leningradsky farmer's market. Live entertainment.

Seating about 100, this restaurant opened in 1992. The chef here is a former personal cook to Andrey Gromyko (1909-1989), the longest-serving Soviet foreign minister.

The menu includes cold hors d'oeuvres, such as Baltic cheese salad, assorted fish, sturgeon and salmon caviar, followed by meats like beef tongue with horseradish, and Georgian **satsivi** (chicken in walnut sauce), concluding with vegetables, such as marinated mushrooms, **lobio** (bean salad with nuts), fresh cucumber salad, beet salad with nuts, and tomato salad. Hot fish dishes include sturgeon brochette, roasted sturgeon, Polish boiled pike, and fried trout. Other hot meat dishes to consider are baked suckling pig and Armenian **dolma** (meat stuffed in grape leaves). Among the chef's specials are merchant's sturgeon and chicken casserole with mushrooms.

1001 NIGHTS (Tysyacha I Odna Noch) (Middle-Eastern cuisine), *inside Hotel Tsentralny Dom Turista/Central House of Tourist, 146 Leninsky prospekt near Ulitsa 26 Bakinskih Komissarov, Metro Yugo-zapadnaya. Tel. 438-9554 or 9556. Open daily from 10am to midnight for lunch and dinner. Cash only.*

Located southwest of the Kremlin, near the Moscow city limit, one very long block northeast of Hotel Salyut; its entrance is off an alley in the back of the Central House of Tourist. Live entertainment.

A spacious, exotic Jordanian restaurant, cafe and bar, with stained glass windows, far from the central Moscow, but worthwhile if you are in this part of the southwestern suburbs. The name suggests a nightclub, but once you are inside, you will find a clean, efficient Arab restaurant, whose service and attention to detail explains why you will find Arab diplomats and businessmen working in Moscow dining here.

For starters, try the asparagus salad. There are many grilled meats and barbecued kebabs to get you going on the main course. You can also try mixed grill comprised of beef, chicken and pork, or perhaps the Jordanian chicken flavored with lemon, or ground lamb mixed with mint. The floor show is unobtrusive; the belly dancers and Arab music are sedate compared to what is performed in some other Moscow restaurants.

RAVI (Pakistani cuisine), *7 Stoliarny pereulok at Ulitsa Presnensky val, Metro Ulitsa 1905 goda. Tel. 253-9485. Open daily from 11am to 11pm for lunch and dinner. Cash only.*

Located northwest of the Kremlin, east of the southern metro station exit, and next to Krasnopresnenskaya banya (baths). Live entertainment.

While Moscow is full of Indian restaurants, Ravi is perhaps the only Pakistani-cuisine restaurant in the Russian capital. One of the basic differences between Pakistani and Indian foods is the bread; the northern wheat-eating Pakistani Muslims contrast with their southern neighbors who eat mostly rice. Ravi offers half a dozen kinds of such **nans** (breads) and similar stuffed **parathas**, in addition to a potato-stuffed **paratha**, fried **tandoori roti** (thick corn bread), and meat-filled **paratha**.

Chicken **karai**, which is chunks of boneless chicken simmered in walnut and chutney sauce, is a popular Ravi dish available with fresh Indian vegetables, such as okra and squash, which are difficult to find in Moscow. For lunch or dinner, you may want to try chicken **tandori**, **seikh** kebab, fish **tikka, bhuna gosht**, and a vegetable **bhujia**. A lunch buffet is available at $20 per person. In the evening, a Russian belly dancer clad in an Indian hula skirt will entertain you.

BUSINESS CLUB NEVKA (Russian-European cuisine), *16 Ulitsa Novopeshchanaya, Metro Sokol. Tel. 943-4152 or 4197, Fax 943-4197. Open daily from noon to midnight. Major credit cards accepted.* Located northwest of the Kremlin and southeast of the Sokol metro station. Nevka is perhaps too far from the metro station to walk to so you might consider it only if you have other means of transportation. Live entertainment.

This is probably the only Moscow restaurant and club that also has a gym, sauna and solarium. It is a cozy restaurant, accented with dark-wood furniture, dark tablecloths with white napkins, and black-and-gold-colored wallpaper. It is a comfortable place to sit down and talk leisurely over a meal.

After you have had an appetizer, such as Salad Gurman or a plate of prunes stuffed with nuts, Nevka's chef recommends entrees such as salmon with garnish, or the 50-dollar dish of chicken breast stuffed with big shrimps. Several kinds of salads, homemade pizza, mushrooms in cream and salty mushrooms are also on the menu.

DIONYSSOS (Greek-Cypriot-International cuisine), *located on the ground floor of Belgrad Hotel, 8 Ulitsa Smolenskaya, Metro Smolenskaya. Tel. 248-2312 or 2416. Open daily from 1pm to midnight. Cash only.*

Situated southwest of the Kremlin and just off the congested Garden Ring Road and Smolenskaya Street, across the square from the Ministry of Foreign Affairs.

The Dionyssos, a small dining room of polished wood and glass on the ground floor, is a restaurant, cafe, bar and pizzeria all in one.

The menu is extensive and includes several Cypriot specialties. Among the Greek dishes, you can try the classic lemon-egg soup. Taste one of the Greek appetizers, perhaps the yogurt and garlic dip or shrimp and crab cocktail. The salad menu includes shrimp, crab, tuna, ham and chicken salad. The Greek salad, consisting of fresh cucumbers and tomatoes on a bed of sliced cabbage, is also served. Among the hot courses there are Cypriot specialties, like **moussaka, stifado, afelia, cleftiko** and **souvlaki** (shish kebab). You can also choose from a grill menu that includes four kinds of steaks, lamb, chicken and pork. The fish menu offers you the choice of salmon, prawns and calamari.

There are supposedly 12 varieties of pizza available at about the same prices as the main courses. The service is friendly.

DELHI (Indian cuisine), *23b Ulitsa Krasnaya Presnya, Metro Ulitsa 1905 goda. Tel. 255-0492. Open daily from noon to 11pm for lunch and dinner. Major credit cards accepted.*

Located northwest of the Kremlin, southeast of the metro station, and west of the Moscow Zoo. Live entertainment in the evening.

Delhi was born in 1987 as the first Indian restaurant in Moscow when a festival of India was held. There were once separate ruble and hard currency rooms here. Indian chefs and waiters, clad in Nehru jackets, as well as Indian-style paintings on the walls, add to the unique atmosphere of this establishment which seats more than 200.

Try various curries, as well as lamb or chicken **tandoori**, with crisp Indian bread baked in a traditional tandoor oven. There are also several vegetarian alternatives. During dinner traditionally-clad Indian women perform native dances.

HANOY (Vietnamese-Russian cuisine), *20/21 Prospekt 60-letya Oktyabrya, Metro Akademicheskaya. Tel. 125-1438 or 6001. Open daily from 1pm to midnight for lunch and dinner. Cash only.*

Located southwest of Kremlin, in the Cheremushky area, southwest from Gagarin Square, at Dmitriya Ulyanova and Profsoyuznaya Streets, directly across the street from the Ho Chi Minh monument. Live music and variety show in the evening and its own casino.

A dumpy and disappointing Vietnamese restaurant that seats 90, often in exaggerated darkness. The bottled water is not always available and soft drinks may arrive warm.

The food is average and may start with a nondescript Vietnamese soup with pork and vegetables. The standard **zakuski** (appetizers) include salads, various combinations of fish, and caviar. **Osetrina po-moskovski** (Moscow-style fish), fillet with Madeira sauce, two kinds of shish kebab, escalope, and home-style **pelmeny po-domashnemu** (home-style) pretty much exhaust the menu choices. You will likely end up paying more than you planned to, no matter what you eat.

MUSH CAFE (Armenian cuisine), *2/4 Ulitsa Oktyabrskaya at Institutsky pereulok, Metro Novoslobodskaya or Mendeleyevskaya. Tel. 284-3670, Fax 284-5509. Open daily from 10am to 11pm for lunch and dinner. Cash only.*

Located north of the Kremlin, west of the Renaissance Moscow Hotel, northwest of the Frunze Central Army Park, north of the Russian Army Theater, and almost across the street from Shirak, a Georgian-cuisine restaurant. There is a substantial walk from any metro station so consider taking a taxi (there is no bus). Live entertainment.

A modest Caucasian cuisine restaurant that seats 60, with well-prepared food. The cross that adorns the door lintel outside will remind you that Armenia was the first nation to adopt Christianity as its national religion. Giant portraits of Armenian national freedom fighters are on display inside. Check out the old Armenian rifles on the walls.

Appetizers include dried and smoked slices of beef resembling jerky in texture and mild yellow cheese. The main dishes includes **dolmas** (which are prepared with cabbage leaves) and mutton, green beans, trout, and **shashliki** (shish kebabs). The trout is served whole with its head and tail. Also on the menu is a spinach dish, as well as a stew of meat and vegetables. **Lavash**, the thin Caucasian bread, is delicious.

ORIENT (European-Russian-Asian cuisine), *1/9 Pervy Nikoloshchepovsky pereulok, Metro Smolenskaya. Tel. 241-1078, Fax 244-7387. Open daily from 10am to 11pm. Cash only.*

Located west of the Kremlin, just outside the Garden Ring, north of Belgrad Hotel, and west of the Smolenskaya metro station. Live entertainment.

Formerly named Smolensky Traktir, or Smolensk Tavern. Fried pork, fried tomatoes and fried sturgeon, along with **satsivi** (cold chicken in walnut sauce), and salads are suggested choices. Among the Mediterranean dishes, you can order frog's legs, clams and shrimp.

ROBIN HOOD (Russian-European cuisine), *42 Ulitsa Bolshaya Gruzinskaya at Bolshoy Tishinsky pereulok, Metro Belorusskaya or Mayakovskaya. Tel. 254-0738 or 8930 or 4457, Fax 254-0738 or 4457. Open daily from noon to midnight. Major credit cards accepted.*

Located northwest of the Kremlin, four typically long blocks north of the Moscow Zoo, and three almost as long blocks northwest of the American Express office on the Garden Ring Road. Live entertainment.

The walls of this restaurant, recreating the feeling of a wilderness area, whose owner is fascinated by the famous British brigand Robin Hood, are clad with bark, the ceiling with wickerwork, and the floor with green felt. Unremarkable non-meat **zakuski** (appetizers) consist of beetroot salad and cold fish. The better main dishes include spicy Georgian stew and Robin Hood Steak. Many of the dishes are prepared according to old recipes.

VSTRECHA (Georgian-Armenian-Italian cuisine), *3 Ulitsa Gilyarovskogo at Sukharevskaya ploshchad, Bldg. 1, Metro Sukharevskaya. Tel. 208-4597. Open daily from noon to midnight for lunch and dinner. Cash only.*

Located northeast of the Kremlin, southeast of the Olympic sports complex and Durov Animal Theater, one block west of Prospekt Mira. Live entertainment.

This is a popular cooperative restaurant and bar where you will be served a Georgian or Italian meal. It seats 36. **Shashlik** (shish kebab) and stewed chicken with potatoes and tomatoes are quite popular. Other Caucasian dishes are also available, in addition to a few Italian specialties.

SHIRAK (Georgian cuisine), *5 Ulitsa Oktyabrskaya at Institutsky pereulok, Metro Novoslobodskaya or Mendeleyevskaya. Tel. 281-8991 or 288-7533. Open daily from noon to 11pm for lunch and dinner. Cash only.*

Located north of the Kremlin, west of the Renaissance Moscow Hotel, northwest of the Frunze Central Army Park, north of the Russian

Army Theater, and almost across the street from Mush Cafe, another Caucasian-cuisine option for you to consider. Live entertainment.

If you should walk to Shirak from Prospekt Mira metro station or from the Renaissance Moscow Hotel, which is even closer to this restaurant, be prepared for a 15-minute walk on the streets that are difficult to identify. Unless you possess a drop of fanatical curiosity about Moscow, we suggest you cut your exploration short by taking a taxi.

The tile-ceilinged restaurant has a tiny bar. Shirak's food is standard Caucasian cuisine that will not disappoint you. Cold and hot fish and meat appetizers, soups and salads go up to about $22. The **shashlik** (shish kebab) and **dolma** (meat stuffed in grape leaves), each one costing under $20, are worth their price. Some other dishes on the menu include the beef tongue with mushrooms, Shirak stuffed pork, **khinkali** (spicy meat dumplings), and beef with mushrooms **po staro-russky** (the old-fashioned Russian style), and none go for over $20.

But you do not have to go all this way to sample Shirak's food; there are three other Shirak restaurants located at these addresses:

• **Shirak**, *on the 2nd floor of Belgrade Hotel, 8 Ulitsa Smolenskaya, Metro Smolenskaya. Tel. 248-2652/2380.* It is located southwest of the Kremlin, on the Garden Ring Road, and west of the Ministry of Foreign Affairs.

• **Shirak**, *126 Volgogradsky prospekt, Metro Kuzminky or Ryazansky prospekt. Tel. 175-6422.* It is located southeast of the Kremlin, outside the Garden Ring Road, and two very long blocks southeast of the Kuzminky metro station.

• **Shirak**, *29 Ulitsa Botanicheskaya, Bldg. 3, Metro Petrovsko-Razumovskaya. Tel. 219-4007, Fax 219-6564.* It is located northwest of the Kremlin, outside the Garden Ring Road, and one block west from the Botanical Gardens.

SKAZKA (Fairy Tale) (European-Russian cuisine), *1 Tovarishchevsky pereulok at Ulitsa Taganskaya, Metro Taganskaya or Marksistskaya. Tel. 911-0998. Open daily from noon to 6pm for lunch and from 7 to 11pm for dinner. Major credit cards accepted.*

Located southeast of the Kremlin, one block east of the Garden Ring Road and Taganka Square. Live entertainment.

A dark-wood interior, the paintings and carved furniture illuminated by candles, almost makes good the restaurant's name, which translates as "Fairy Tale." It seats about 50. Try the **bliny** (pancakes) with caviar, **pelmeny** (tender dumplings floating in sour cream), one of several veal dishes or the pork in mushroom sauce. Also on the menu is boar cooked in wine; Veal Perestroika, which is marinated before being cooked; and slices of veal and chicken stuffed with butter, named cutlet **Pozharsky**.

The floor show includes acrobats, Cossacks, and Gypsies performing to a variety of music.

VIALE (Italian cuisine), *12 Leningradsky prospekt, Metro Belorusskaya or Dinamo. Tel. 214-2158, Fax 214-2158. Open daily from noon to midnight for lunch and dinner. Major credit cards accepted.* Located northwest of the Kremlin, east of the Hippodrome racetrack, and north of the Belorussky Railway Station.

This restaurant opened its doors in 1994. The interior is dark and cozy, with a candle on every table, but the food is average. Standard Italian fare, with cold and hot appetizers, soups, pizza, and several meat and pasta dishes. Carpaccio, lightly marinated thin slices of raw beef, is one dish on the menu. Pasta with spicy tomato and garlic sauce, is also available. **Scalloppine al vino blanco**, with two large slices of veal, lightly breaded and served in a creamy white wine sauce, is worth trying.

LAS PALMAS (Cuban cuisine), *5/2 Ulitsa Sergiya Radonezhskogo at Khlebnikov pereulok, Metro Ploshchad Ilyicha or Rimskaya. Tel. 278-8403. Open daily from noon to midnight. Cash only.*

Located east of the Kremlin, southeast of Spasso-Andronikov Monastery, on the corner with Khlebnikov Lane. When you come out of the Ploshchad Ilyicha metro station, walk away from the Lenin statue on the square until you get to Ulitsa Sergiya Radonezhskogo, on the way to the monastery. As you approach the Church of Sergey of Radonezh, directly in front of you, the second street on your right will be Khlebnikov Lane.

The cute tiny Las Palmas, which opened in 1996, has barely enough space for five tables in the main dining room and a slim waitress to walk in-between. Next to it is just as tiny a bar that would barely accommodate four grown men with their elbows on the bar. The background music is hot and the proprietor as friendly as you will ever find in Moscow.

A dozen appetizers stretch from **tortilla a la Cubana** to the $17 **pulpo a la vinegreta** (octopus in vinegrette). The most expensive dishes are **enchilado de langosta** (Cuban-style lobster) and **langostinos a la plancha** (grilled prawns), each one costing about $33. The rest of the seafood dishes are much more reasonably priced and include **camarones rebozados** (breaded shrimps) and **trucha al ajillo** (trout in garlic sauce). Choices among the meat dishes are even more varied and range from **parrilla a Las Palmas** (Las Palmas-style grilled meat), **chilindron de chivo** (Cuban-style lamb), **chuleta de cerdo** (pork chop), to **lomito en salsa de champinones** (fillet in champignon sauce) and all under $15 for each.

Inexpensive

CAFE AGDAM (Azeri-European cuisine), *4 Khlebnikov pereulok, Bldg. 1, Metro Ploshchad Ilyicha or Rimskaya; Tel. 278-6057 or 7149. Open daily from noon to midnight for lunch and dinner. Cash only.*

Located east of the Kremlin, halfway through a run-down side street, southeast of Spaso-Andronikov Monastery. When you come out of the Ploshchad Ilyicha metro station, walk away from the Lenin's statue on the square, until you get to Ulitsa Sergiya Radonezhskogo, on your way to the monastery. As you approach the Church of Sergey of Radonezh, directly in front of you, the second street on your right will be Khlebnikov pereulok. Live music and variety show daily from 7pm on

Caution: Do not confuse Khlebnikov pereulok with Khlebny pereulok, which is located a few blocks east of the American Embassy, or you will wander around hungry, hopelessly searching for a restaurant on the street that has none.

Agdam, which seats about 60, is not aseptic, like a McDonald's, but you can have a lively meal, after you have seen the staid Spaso-Andronikov Monastery. Among the dishes from Azerbaijan are a large variety of mutton, turkey, chicken and sturgeon **shashliki** (shish kebabs) or **dolmas** (meat stuffed in grape leaves) entrees.

GURIYA (Georgian cuisine), *7/3 Komsomolsky prospekt, Metro Park Kultury or Frunzenskaya. Tel. 246-0378. Open daily from 11am to 11:30pm for lunch and dinner. Cash only.*

Located southwest of the Kremlin, southwest of the Aeroflot office, four blocks southeast from the Lev Tolstoy's house in Khamovniki and two block from the Church of St. Nicholas of the Weavers. The entrance is from the courtyard behind building No. 7. Live entertainment - a Gypsy band.

This restaurant consists of two small dining halls that seat 32. It's a disorganized Georgian eatery, but the service is personable. This is one of the most popular Moscow cafes serving Caucasian dishes. The dishes are tasty and somewhat spicy.

Baklazhany (eggplants stuffed with nuts), cold green beans and hot red beans, vegetable salad, **kuchma** (liver), kidneys and other bowls cooked in a sauce, are served as **zakuski** (appetizers). Also available are chicken in tomato, **adzhab-sandal**, pepper, **lobio** (spicy beans), tomatoes and potatoes prepared in hot sauce, and **satsivi** (cold chicken in walnut sauce). And try the flat bread or the famous **khachapuri** bread with cheese. You can bring your own wine.

13. SEEING THE SIGHTS

This chapter will introduce you to the major sights, some of which no visitor to Moscow will want to miss; to see them all you would need weeks, not days. The most important museums, churches, art galleries, monuments, and parks, the zoo, and other diversions are included. With out-of the-way sights we also include the name of a restaurant or two so you can recharge yourself before or after your visit.

Russians are justifiably proud of their cultural sights and have preserved them down to the smallest detail. Most are guarded by **babushki**, Russia's elderly women, who working for practically nothing, will run after you to make sure you follow the exhibits in the order they were meant to be appreciated.

Except for the Kremlin Museums, Tretyakov Gallery, and the Pushkin Museum of Fine Arts, admission to most museums is often quite low for Russians, but foreigners may have to pay an admission double or triple or ten times that of Russians. Many secondary museums are in dire financial straights because the government allocation toward their upkeep has been shriveling since the country's independence in 1991.

Whether you are interested or not, you cannot skip the Kremlin and its surroundings, for to do so is the equivalent of going to Paris and not seeing the Louvre, visiting Rome and skipping the Vatican, or traveling to London and ignoring the British Museum. We also suggest that you visit at least one of the major galleries: Tretyakov for its Russian treasures or the Pushkin for its international collection.

Russia is a land of museums; there are about 150 in Moscow alone to keep you busy for a year, although, some deal in questionable former Communist propaganda not worthy of your time.

There is not a single national museum of modern art in Russia today, thanks to 70 years of Communist folly, when anything outside of socialist realism was frowned upon. The Russian aristocracy invested great fortunes in the acquisition of Russian and international art, even if many of these collections were stolen from their heirs by the Communists and are now on display in museums and galleries all over the country.

If at all possible, call ahead to make sure the museum or sight you want to visit is open. In spite of all the posted times, the hours of operation are constantly modified.

In some museums and palaces described below, you will be asked to put on **tapochky**, special slippers available at the entrance that must be worn over your shoes to protect the wooden or marble floors.

Other Russian words, aside from **tapochky**, that you are likely to read or hear are: **gardyerob** - cloakroom, **ekskursavod** - guide, **kassa** - ticket office, **muzey** - museum, **Na remont** - Closed for Repairs, **Nye trogat!** - Don't Touch!, **otkryto** - open, **vystavka** - exhibition, **zakryto** - closed, **zal** - hall

SIGHTS INSIDE THE BOULEVARD RING ROAD

THE KREMLIN MUSEUMS

The Kremlin, Metro Aleksandrovsky sad or Ploshchad Revolutsiyi. Tel. 202-4256 or 1420 or 921-4720. Open daily from 10am to 5pm, closed Thursdays. Admission to all museums for foreigners is about $20.

Tickets can be purchaged at the kiosks next to the Trinity Gates, in front of the Kremlin, at the foot of Vozdvizhenka Street and behind the Manezh Exhibition Hall, from 10am to 4:30pm. There are no public eating facilities on the Kremlin grounds. Anything larger than a standard woman's purse must be checked in at the storage area under the Trinity Gates, where there are also rest rooms. Other rest rooms are available on Cathedral Square, behind Assumption Cathedral.

We regret to tell you that the throngs of tourists during the summer, almost exclusively foreign, are so large they may take away some of the enjoyment in seeing these magnificent structures. While waiting in line to enter the Armory, you will be treated indifferently: do not expect any help from the Kremlin administrators who seem to care most about how many dollars they can squeeze out of Westerners.

The Kremlin complex consists of the **Assumption Cathedral**, **Annunciation Cathedral**, **Archangel Cathedral**, **Church of the Deposition of the Robe**, the **Armory Palace**, the **Belfry** and **Bell Tower** of Ivan the Great, the **Patriarch's Palace**, the **Arsenal Building**, the **Senate**, and the **Palace of Congresses**.

The Kremlin is the heart of Russia and synonymous with her history, her government and her power. The Kremlin is Buckingham Palace, the White House, the Elysee Palace; at once the Vatican, Versailles and the Parthenon.

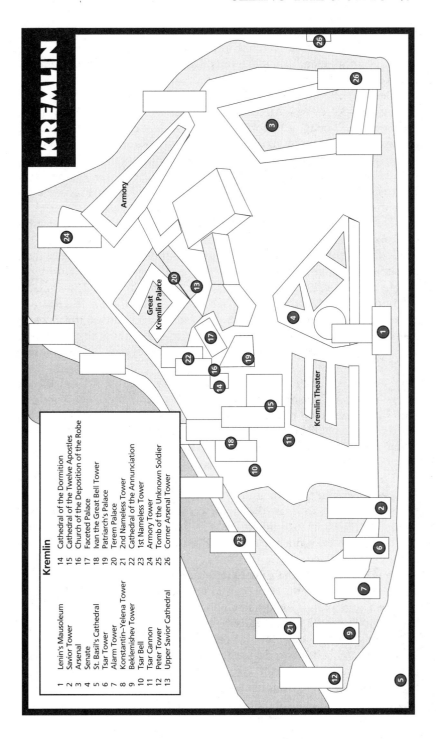

KREMLIN

Armory

Great Kremlin Palace

Kremlin Theater

Kremlin

1	Lenin's Mausoleum
2	Savior Tower
3	Arsenal
4	Senate
5	St. Basil's Cathedral
6	Tsar Tower
7	Alarm Tower
8	Konstantin–Yelena Tower
9	Beklemishev Tower
10	Tsar Bell
11	Tsar Cannon
12	Peter Tower
13	Upper Savior Cathedral
14	Cathedral of the Dormition
15	Cathedral of the Twelve Apostles
16	Church of the Deposition of the Robe
17	Faceted Palace
18	Ivan the Great Bell Tower
19	Patriarch's Palace
20	Terem Palace
21	2nd Nameless Tower
22	Cathedral of the Annunciation
23	1st Nameless Tower
24	Armory Tower
25	Tomb of the Unknown Soldier
26	Corner Arsenal Tower

The **Russian Church** has been headquartered here since the 13th century and all the tsars were crowned and married inside the irregular, walled-in, triangular shaped grounds. Its 70 acres covers the the almost imperceptible Borovitsky Hill and overlooks the Moskva River.

Centuries ago, from this 130-foot hill, a bell would sound when the enemy was spotted to warn Muscovites it was time to seek shelter inside the Kremlin. Today, a 65-foot-high wall, in some parts 13 feet thick, surrounds the Kremlin. The walls, with a circumference of about one mile, were reinforced with 20 towers, five of which were also gates to the fortress Kremlin. In front of Trinity Tower, where you will enter, is Kutafiya Tower, a watch tower built near the Troitsky Bridge over the now-unseen Neglinnaya River.

The **Spassky** (Savior) **Gate and Tower**, now facing St. Basil's Cathedral, are the best known among the Kremlin gates and towers. Until the 1917 Revolution, all men, including the tsars, had to dismount their horses and remove their hats when entering this gate. It was considered holy by the masses, and ambassadors were also met here. The Savior Gate was built in 1491 and the tower above it was added in 1625. The Kremlin chiming clock is incorporated in the tent-like section of the Spassky Tower. It was first installed in the 15th century; the current chiming clock, which weighs 25 tons, was assembled in 1852. Red Square lies just outside the Kremlin's east wall.

The history of the Kremlin is the history of Moscow, indeed the history of Russia. The red fortress rampart was originally of oak wood and built sometime in the 1150's, when Eric of Sweden conquered Finland. It was replaced by white limestone in the 1360's, after Muscovites grew tired of one disastrous fire after another, and by the end of the 15th century it was again replaced by the brick that you can still see today.

The Kremlin was then completely surrounded by the waters of the Moskva River and the now underground Neglinnaya River, as well as a deep moat. In 1475, **Ivan the Great** hired craftsmen from Pskov and architects from Italy to build the three great cathedrals and the new walls, parts of which also remain to this day. The walls were modeled after those of the Sforza Palace in Milan.

It is perhaps fortunate that **Catherine the Great** lost interest after receiving the blueprints for a new complex in the 1770's which was to replace a large part of today's Kremlin. She never got beyond the Senate building behind the Lenin Mausoleum.

After stationing his troops inside the Kremlin for more than a month, **Napoleon** almost destroyed it to the ground in 1812, when his troops had to retreat. Many a ruler, from Ivan the Terrible to Josef Stalin, terrorized their subjects from the safety of this citadel.

During the years before the 1917 Revolution, the Kremlin was mostly deserted except for coronations and occasional visits by tsars who had then lived in St. Petersburg. The masses were allowed in after the Communists took over, but not for long. The Kremlin was closed to all but the most privileged until well after Stalin's death. When it finally re-opened in mid-1955, more than five million Soviets thronged the grounds in its first twelve months.

Stalin, Brezhnev, writer Maksim Gorky, cosmonaut Yuri Gagarin and two Americans, John Reed, who witnessed the Revolution and wrote about it in *Ten Days That Shook the World*, and Bill Haywood, founder of the American Communist Party, are buried on the Kremlin grounds.

The most recent addition to the Kremlin was the large **Congress building**, inaugurated for the 22nd Congress of the Communist Party. The Church of Twelve Saints was destroyed to make place for it. The Kremlin has been the residence of the Russian president since 1992.

The best view of the Kremlin is believed to be from the upper floors of the dinosaur-sized Hotel Rossiya.

It would take a separate volume to describe the palaces and cathedrals inside the Kremlin and if you are interested there are several fine books available in English all over Moscow, describing in detail Kremlin's treasures. Here is a brief outline:

Cathedral Square is the Kremlin's main square where the major churches face each other. It took shape alongside the Kremlin in the late 15th and early 16th centuries. Coronations, receptions for foreign ambassadors, and church processions took place here.

Assumption Cathedral, the oldest and the most elaborate of all the churches on Cathedral Square, was completed in 1479, the year Copenhagen University was founded. The following year, Tatar-Mongol bondage came to an end, after more than 200 years. For centuries, Assumption Cathedral was the main cathedral of Russia; the most important laws and decrees were promulgated here, royal weddings were held, and grand princes, tsars and later emperors were crowned inside this holy edifice. The heads of the Russian Orthodox Church took orders and patriarchs were buried here. This white-stone cathedral on Kremlin Hill dominated the town as a symbol of Russian power at a time when most other buildings were made of wood.

Although built by an Italian architect, Ridolfo Fioravanti, its architectural style is thoroughly Russian because the architect was dispatched to Vladimir, Pskov and Novgorod to absorb the essence of Russian architecture and the outcome was the style of the Assumption Cathedral of Vladimir. The Cathedral has a priceless collection of Russian religious art, including icons dating from the 14th to 17th centuries and frescoes by artists of the Dionysus school of the 14th and 15th centuries.

After Fioravanti finished his masterpiece, he asked the tsar to be allowed to return to Italy in 1485. Instead he was thrown into prison and died in Moscow a year later.

The **Bells of Ivan the Great**, next to the Assumption Cathedral, and their 16th century tower are regarded as a sacred relic related to important events in Russia's history. In the past, they resounded on days of triumph, celebrations of military victories and the coronation of tsars. The belfry was originally the Kremlin's watch tower and the bells served as an alarm, calling on ancient Muscovites to assemble their forces against approaching enemies. The chimes of Ivan the Great were an inseparable part of the rituals of the Russian Orthodox Church. In the old days, when the city was much smaller, they could be heard throughout Moscow. After 1917, the bells fell silent, but now, as part of the restoration of ancient national values, they are chiming again.

Next is the nine-domed **Annunciation Cathedral**, located in the southern part of Cathedral Square, nearest to the Moskva River. It was begun in 1484, when Botticelli painted his **Birth of Venus**, and completed by the masters from Pskov in 1489.

The Annunciation Cathedral was adjacent to the tsar's palace and served as the place of worship for him and his family. The grand dukes and later the tsars attended daily services and all members of the ruling family were baptized and received the nuptial benediction here.

Priceless icons painted by Andrey Rublev and Theophanes the Greek, from the 14th and 15th centuries, are on display. You will notice that none is signed because it was not customary for their creators to sign them until the end of the 16th century. Note also the floor which was constructed from agate-colored jasper.

The **Archangel Cathedral**, whose construction began in 1505, a year before Christopher Columbus died, and completed three years later, was the necropolis of the grand princes and tsars from the early 14th century to the late 18th century. It was named after Archangel Michael, the patron of Russian warriors and contains no fewer than 46 tombs. The grand dukes were buried under the cathedral's floor in wooden coffins which were placed inside stone sarcophagi and covered with tombstones. (Starting with Peter the Great, all Russian emperors were buried in St. Petersburg, which became Russia's capital in 1712 and remained so until 1918.) Traditionally, Russian tsars attended services at the Archangel Cathedral before going off to war.

In the 1960's, the tombs of Ivan the Terrible (1530-1584) and his sons, all near the altar, were opened so the likeness of the tsar could be established because no portraits of Ivan the Terrible were made during his lifetime.

The **Church of the Deposition of the Robe,** another Kremlin museum, was the church of the Patriarch of Moscow and is connected to his palace.

This small single-domed church was started in 1484 by masons from Pskov, the same year as the Cathedral of the Annunciation, and was completed two years later. This is one of the Kremlin's few architectural monuments whose original interior design has been preserved and includes frescoes painted in 1644.

In the church's gallery, you will find an exhibition of wooden sculptures that were quite popular in Old Russia.

The **Patriarch's Palace,** with the Cathedral of the Twelve Apostles adjoining it, stands on the north side of Cathedral Square. It was constructed in 1656 for the ambitious and vainglorious Patriarch Nikon. Today it houses the Museum of Applied Art and Lifestyle of 17th century Russia.

Try not to miss the **Armory Palace,** the oldest museum in Russia, where you will marvel at a unique collection of old arms, decorated weapons and suits of armor, coronation paraphernalia, church utensils, jewelry, rare textiles, costumes and other valuables. Covering two floors, there are more than 4,000 items presented in 55 showcases in nine halls. Objects of applied art from Russia, Western Europe and Asia, dating from the 4th to the early 20th centuries, are displayed in the building which was erected in 1851.

The Armory was initially set up in 1511 by the Grand Prince Vasily III as a court workshop for the production and repair of armaments and as a storehouse of ceremonial armor and firearms. In 1806, it was designated as a private court museum, but the decision did not take effect until 1812, when the treasures were evacuated to protect them from Napoleon's approaching troops.

Many artifacts in the Armory collection are ambassadorial gifts to Russian tsars from England, Holland, Austria and Sweden, presented at special ceremonies that were held in the Palace of Facets in the Kremlin.

Also included are jewel-encrusted crowns, Boris Godunov's throne, and rooms full of tsarist coaches preserved for history along with life-sized model horses. Although New Yorkers can actually see more hand-made Faberge jeweled Imperial eggs in Forbes' collection at the magazine's museum on lower Fifth Avenue than in the Kremlin, you can still enjoy several superb specimens, which were given as gifts to the tsar's family. Faberge, founded in St. Petersburg in 1842, was the largest jewelry firm in Russia and it employed 500 workers.

A crown with 5,000 diamonds, made in 1762 by the court jeweler for Catherine the Great for her coronation, is on display in the Armory annex. You can also admire the Orlov diamond, weighing almost 190 carats, named after Catherine the Great's lover, Prince Grigory Orlov. Found in India in the 17th century, the diamond was brought to Russia in 1773. Orlov presented it to Catherine II at a cost of 100,000 rubles, a staggering sum of money at that time.

The **Tsar's Cannon** stands in the Kremlin's Ivanovsky Square. It was cast in bronze in 1586 at the Moscow Cannon Yard, not far from the Kremlin, and is the world's biggest cannon in caliber size, measuring 890 millimeters. No country in the world had anything like it in the 16th century. The bronze cannon weighs 40 tons. It was positioned near Spassky Gate to defend the Kremlin, but it never fired a single shot. Legend has it, however, that it scared a few of Russia's detractors. The cannon balls next to it weigh one ton each.

The nearby **Tsar's Bell** is the biggest bell in the world. The bell was cast in the Kremlin in 1735 and weighs 200 tons. Two years later a fire broke out in Moscow and spread to the Kremlin buildings. While the fire on the bell's scaffolding was being extinguished, water poured on the bell and the difference in temperature caused it to crack. An 11.5-ton piece broke off, so the bell never rang. After this misadventure, the damaged bell lay buried in its foundry pit for 99 years, until it was extricated in 1836.

One thing that is gone from the south side of Ivanovsky Square is the two-ton **statue of Lenin** that was unveiled in 1967 on the occasion of the 50th anniversary of the October Revolution. It stood there for 18 years, before it was moved to Leninskiye Gorky, where he died in 1924, along with the contents of his former Kremlin apartment.

The **Arsenal Building**, which stands in the western part of the Kremlin, was begun in 1702. Four years later, the construction was interrupted by the war with Sweden. It was finally completed in 1736. A year later the Arsenal was destroyed by fire. Restored, it again suffered from an explosion in 1812, when Napoleon retreated from Moscow. Originally, arms and ammunition were kept in the Arsenal, until it became a museum of the 1812 War.

The **Senate Building** was constructed in 1790, first to hold the assemblies of Moscow nobility, and then was given to the judicial departments of the Moscow Senate in 1856. After the Bolshevik Revolution, when in the spring of 1918 the capital was moved to Moscow again, Lenin, his wife and his sister moved to an apartment on the third floor of this building. Later Stalin had his study in the Senate Building.

In 1961, the **Kremlin Palace of Congresses** was built near Trinity Tower, its main entrance facing the Arsenal building. It is the largest public building in Moscow, with about 800 rooms, some of them five floors under ground. The main conference room, one of the largest in Europe, has some 6,000 seats. It is now used for concerts and stage performances.

RED SQUARE
Krasnaya ploshchad

If Times Square is the crossroads of the world, as New Yorkers would have you believe, then Red Square is the epicenter of Russia. Some claim that only the Place de la Concorde in Paris surpasses it in its beauty. On its south side, **St. Basil's Cathedral** has stood since 1561, on the north is the **Historical Museum**, right where Moscow University was founded in 1755. East and west it is bounded by the Kremlin wall and the **GUM** department store.

For centuries and right into Russia's Communist collapse, this 2,280 feet long and 426 feet wide rectangle has always had a peculiar fascination for Russians and foreigners alike. Although **krasnaya** in Russian translates as both "red" and "beautiful," it must have been the "red" in Red Square that struck Westerners with terror every Revolution Day in November, when tanks and nuclear rockets rolled by, while the stuffy, wily Communist tyrants stood atop the Lenin Mausoleum.

By the Middle Ages, Red Square was already etched into the Russian psyche. It was originally the only dry side of the Kremlin and had a water channel until Napoleon's occupation of Moscow. Battles against the invading Tartars who tried to overtake the Kremlin raged here. From the 1500's on, it was the market place of Moscow, named **veliky torg** (Great Marketplace), as well as the site of festivals and religious processions. "The beggars, the rouged wenches offering their charms, the peddlers, the public executions, the religious services and processions-all greatly contributed to the local color" on Red Square. Author Arthur Voyce also writes that "Public torture of felons was a common sight on the streets of Moscow. Often one could see an executioner leading a half-naked, blood-covered man through the streets and squares, flogging him with a knout and loudly announcing his crime.

Red Square frequently witnessed such spectacles until the end of the 17th century. During the reign of **Ivan the Terrible** a mass slaughter of the **boyare** (medieval Russian noblemen) and their retainers took place in Red Square. Stepan Razin, a peasant leader, was executed in 1671, and 28 years later **Peter I** had many of his **streltsy** (musketeers) publicly put to death in wholesale executions on the square. Employed by the tsars to serve as their military - there were 22,450 musketeers in 1681 - they fell out of favor when opposing Peter's liberal program. Peter himself cut off more than a hundred of their heads in 1668 and 1669.

During the 1917 Revolution, bloody battles were fought over its cobbled 83,720 square yards.

Today, you can casually stroll from one end to the other and admire its vastness and beauty. The only time this is not possible is when Lenin's

Tomb is open to visitors and Red Square is cordoned off. The square is surprisingly clean and free of beggars, although the police keep a weary eye on all who enter it.

On the southeastern end of Red Square, in front of St. Basil's Cathedral, stands the monument to **Minin and Pozharsky**. The statue of the merchant Kuzma Minin and Prince Dmitry Pozharsky was the first statue ever erected in Moscow. Minin rallied his fellow Russians in 1611 to drive out Polish invaders and Prince Pozharsky led this militia, which marched to Moscow and fought a decisive battle on August 24, 1612. Two bas-relief ornaments on the pedestal of the monument depict the citizens of Nizhny Novgorod collecting funds for their struggle on one side and the expulsion of the Poles on the other.

The statue was executed by the Ukrainian-born neo-classical sculptor **Ivan Martos** (1754-1835), who came from an impoverished Cossack family, studied at the Academie in St. Petersburg at the age of ten and was sent to Rome on a scholarship. Originally unveiled in the middle of Red Square in 1818, it was made possible by public donations.

More than 100,000 people packed Red Square in 1993, when cellist and conductor Mstislav Rostropovich led the National Symphony Orchestra of Washington, D.C., in an outdoor performance of Prokofiev and Tchaikovsky, complete with cannon fire and the Kremlin bells ringing. On the 100th anniversary of Tchaikovsky's death (to the day), it was so cold that orchestra members wore gloves, parkas and fur hats. Rostropovich was exiled in 1974 because he sheltered writer Aleksandr Solzhenitsyn.

The following year, an all-star American team played an exhibition basketball game on a hardwood court next to the Lenin Mausoleum with the team of the former Soviet Union that won the gold medal at the 1988 Olympic Games.

On the northern corner of Red Square and Nikolskaya Street stands the rebuilt **Kazan Cathedral**, a monument to Russia's victory over the Poles in 1612. The original cathedral was dedicated in 1636, but destroyed 300 years later and turned into a public restroom. The icon of the Kazan Virgin accompanied Prince Pozharsky on his campaigns, but was moved to St. Peterburg in 1710. It's likely that the cathedral would never have see the light again were it not for blueprints secretly made by architect Pyotr Baranovsky, the same architect who saved St. Basil's cathedral.

Also near Kazan Cathedral are the reconstructed **Iversky Chapel** and **Voskrisenskiye Gates**, one of the original seven gates of Kitay-gorod. The chapel and gates were destroyed along with Kazan Cathedral in the same year as the Cathedral of Christ the Savior to make room for tanks entering Red Square for parades. A copy of an Iberian icon was brought from Mount Athos in Greece and placed in this Holy Virgin of Iberia chapel in 1995.

ST. BASIL'S CATHEDRAL
Pokrovsky sobor

Red Square, Metro Ploshchad Revolutsiyi. Tel. 298-3304. Open daily from 10am to 6pm. Small admission fee.
Located on the southern end of Red Square, between the Kremlin and the Hotel Rossiya.

St. Basil's was erected by Ivan the Terrible in 1561, the same year that London's St. Paul's Cathedral was badly damaged by fire, to celebrate the liberation of the Russian state from the Tartars. Legend has it that when the cathedral was completed, the two architects were blinded so they could never create an equally beautiful sight.

Whatever the veracity of this tale, Ivan originally planned to build eight churches on the square, each one to be dedicated to the saint on whose day he won his battles. But after seven wooden structures were built, he ordered them torn down and stuck with the present brick cathedral in traditional Russian style with onion domes situated over the nine chapels. It was looted by the Poles in 1611 and the cathedral was given its present colorful appearance sixty years later.

Many a traveler has visions of his own in front of St. Basil's and the Greek poet Nikos Kazantzakis expressed his thusly: "In front of the Parthenon my heart does not leap with emotion; only my mind, after long contemplation and intellectual play, understands and is then possessed by a serene, cold admiration that befits that structure. But here in front of this barbaric church, my heart soars and screeches like a hawk. The cathedral appears to me like an immense haughty cactus, its tentacled branches blooming in green, red and yellow. With its Oriental domes that twist like turbans, it resembles a gathering of emirs. This Oriental richness and gentleness and, at the same time, heroic surge to controvert logic are indescribable."

Perhaps Kazantzakis got carried away a bit by its outside appearance. Had he gone inside, he would have seen exhibits telling him about the epoch of Ivan the Terrible and of the history of the cathedral, but he would look in vain for frescoes that really matter.

The cathedral was close to being torn down by Stalin, who wanted better access to Red Square. It was saved by architect Pyotr Baranovsky who threatened to kill himself if Stalin did not spare St. Basil's. Stalin did, but the architect ended up in prison.

Today, the cathedral is threatened with complete collapse because of its age and the negligence of city authorities. In 1991, ultrasonic tests were performed, which disclosed cracks in the cathedral's foundation, threatening the building with collapse. In 1996, the head of the Moscow Historical Museum affiliate said that in two or three years the cathedral will certainly go to pieces.

In front of the cathedral is a statue of a butcher and a prince who raised and led an army that sent the Poles flying from the Kremlin in 1612.

Try this approach to St. Basil's and Red Square when you visit them for the first time and see what it does for your heart beat: Start from the southwest side of the Moskva Hotel, roughly where the entrance to El Rincon Espanol restaurant is, and walk in a southwesterly direction across Manezhnaya Square. As you approach the Voskrisenskiye Gates (Proyezd Voskrisenskih vorot), between the former Lenin Museum and Historical Museum, keep walking while keeping your eyes on St. Basil's Cathedral on the other side of Red Square. The closer to the passageway you come, the higher the Cathedral will rise before you, like a primordial apparition from the sea that will send shivers through your body by the time you pass the gates and approach Red Square. It is an experience.

LENIN MAUSOLEUM
Movzoley Lenina

Red Square, Metro Ploshchad Revolutsiyi. Open Tuesdays, Wednesdays & Thursdays, from 10am to 1pm. No cameras or bags are allowed. No admission fee.

When you consider all the pain, humiliation, and worse, that the Communists have inflicted on millions of their own people, it may surprise you that this red marble bunker, erected in 1930, has not yet become the symbol of their 70-year oppression. One can only surmise that Communist Party members have so thoroughly indoctrinated the masses that children and adults alike could not help but line up for hours on end to steal a glance of the waxen, shriveled, mummified and refrigerated remnants of the man responsible for so much evil.

Lenin's body lies on a pedestal in the bullet-proof sarcophagus designed by Russia's leading modernist architect **Konstantin Melnikov** (1890-1974). Forty years later, when he was destroyed professionally because of his alleged 'formalistic tendencies,' Melnikov recalled in a letter to Nikita Khrushchev that a GPU official, "Comrade Belenko, threatened my life if I failed to complete the sarcophagus on time."

Melnikov's sarcophagus is surrounded by an artificial mystical darkness and hushed tourists who cannot take their eyes off the shiny waxen face. Visitors are not allowed to stop in front of the remains, nor photograph or videotape them.

In the early years, when the mausoleum was still made of wood, mass hysteria engulfed visitors, as described by a sympathetic chronicler, Greek writer Nikos Kazantzakis: "The Russian throngs watch ecstatically. A few years earlier, before this new savior arrived, they had marveled at the rosy, fair face of Jesus in front of the holy altars of churches with the exact same mystical glance."

This "new savior," according to the Russian historian Dmitry Volkogonov, a retired colonel general and senior military adviser to the Russian president who wrote biographies of Trotsky, Stalin and Lenin, despised Russians and often referred to them as "fools" and "idiots."

"Lenin had been embalmed at Stalin's insistence," writes British art critic Matthew Cullerne Bown. When Lenin died in January 1924, his widow Nadezhda Krupskaya called for him to be buried in St. Petersburg next to his mother, but her plea was ignored. His body was given three mausoleums, each more remarkable than the last. The first, erected in two days in January 1924, was a grey-painted wooden hut put up in Red Square to shelter the body while mourners trooped past it. This was soon replaced by a second, more elaborate wooden structure.

In 1925, a competition was announced for a permanent mausoleum to be built in stone. The winning design belonged to **Aleksey Shchusev** (1873-1949), originator of the earlier wooden structures. Before the Revolution, he had helped to restore churches and built Moscow's Kazan station.

"Shchusev's building combined modernist simplicity with veiled glance back at the classical heritage. It even seems possible," writes Bown, "that the design of the mausoleum, like the decision to embalm Lenin's body, was in part a response to the discovery in 1922 of Tutankhamen's tomb in Luxor - an event which made news around the world. Shchusev's return, in 1924, to such an ancient source was in stark contrast to the mainstream of Soviet architecture; and yet it was a gesture that was to prove prophetic."

No other country, except perhaps for North Korea, is attempting to preserve the body of a national figure. The mausoleum's behind-the-scenes control room resembles a nuclear power plant. A monitor displays data and mechanisms that record and control temperature automatically and restabilizes the area when the lights in the viewing room are used for an extended period. It costs the state millions of rubles to keep the Bolshevist's body presentable. The operation is supervised by an officer in a white doctor's gown. Only about ten staff members who work directly with the corpse are permitted inside the lab.

How the corpse is kept in repair is a closely guarded secret. On Mondays and Fridays, when the mausoleum is closed, scientists move the body into the lab for maintenance, working for up to one and a half hours.

How long Lenin's remains will survive in his sarcophagus with the accompanying ceremony is hard to say. Stalin was removed from this same tomb, some three dozen dark steps below Red Square, in 1961, eight years after his death.

In October 1993, after government forces won an armed battle against the Communist-infested Parliament in a struggle for the Russian

White House building, it was suggested that Lenin be removed from Red Square and buried next to his mother in St. Petersburg.

On October 6, 1993, at four o'clock in the afternoon, instead of the usual goose-stepping changing of the guard in front of the tomb, two policemen quietly walked into the mausoleum, and another Communist relic that made no sense, except for attracting hordes of camera-toting tourists, became victim to a presidential decree.

For 69 years, the changing of the guard took place every hour during the day, when new guards stepped out of the Kremlin through the main gate at two minutes before the hour and replaced the old guards at the tomb as the clock in the Spassky Tower chimed the hour. At night, the guards were simply rotated. This hourly changing of the guard in a ceremonious display of military precision was initiated by an order of the Moscow garrison commander on January 26, 1924, five days after Lenin's death.

While the practice of requiring visitors to line up in pairs, take off their hats and remove their hands from their pockets has passed, speaking inside the mausoleum is still discouraged and you can be arrested for trying to take photos. The mausoleum is now sporadically closed to the public, fueling speculation that the embalmed corpse is decaying.

THE RUSSIAN WHITE HOUSE
Bely dom

2 Krasnopresnenskaya nab., Metro Barrikadnaya or Smolenskaya. Closed to tourists.

Facing the Ukraina Hotel across the Moskva River, the White House is located west of the Kremlin, outside the Garden Ring Road and a block southwest of the American Embassy; also across Konyushkovskaya Street from the offices of the Moscow Mayor.

The building, originally intended for the Council of Ministers of the Russian Federation, was built in 1980. It consists of two parts: a seven-story base and a 20-story office tower. The White House, where the Russian Parliament meets, was one of the first Moscow buildings to be fully air-conditioned and to have underground parking.

The White House is so named in part for its bright white marble exterior, as opposed to many other Moscow buildings which are of red brick. During the attempted coup d'etat in August 1991, tens of thousands of Muscovites blocked tank approaches to the building. An armed power struggle between Russian President Boris Yelstin and the Parliament in October 1993 ended in a figurative and actual stain on its face.

It all assumed deadly proportions on September 21, 1993, when the President suspended Parliament and called parliamentary elections for

December, but rejected simultaneous presidential elections. The defiant lawmakers, whose constitution dated from the Communist era, voted to impeach him. Four days later, the Congress of People's Deputies, which convened in the building, had the electricity cut off, but refused to vacate the premises. By September 29, after clashes with the riot police, the building was surrounded by barricades and mounted police.

On October 2, hundreds of stone-throwing Communists and other hard-liners battled the police at several locations and set up burning barricades in sympathy with about 1,500 people remaining inside the White House. The hard-liners attempted to take over the government-run Ostankino television complex, but failed and in the process caused 62 deaths, when they used rocket-propelled grenades to blast their way through the barricaded door. On Bloody Sunday, October 3, the President declared a state of emergency in Moscow after a mob of ten thousand overwhelmed the riot police and seized several government installations, including the Mayor's office which is across a side street.

On the morning of October 4, government troops stormed the White House, while T-72 tanks shelled the building. Fires broke out and clouds of black smoke poured from the upper floors. By the late afternoon, most parliamentarians and their sympathizers surrendered. More than 190 dead and 500 wounded people were left behind. The building, which has since been renamed the **House of Government**, was quickly repaired and reopened in 1994.

Behind the White House you can see the tiny Hunchback Bridge, whose history originated in the 1905 Revolution, when it was part of the barricades erected by the proletarians from the nearby Presnya district to prevent the tsarist forces from crossing over it.

TRETYAKOV GALLERY
Tretyakovskaya galereya
  12 Lavrushinsky pereulok, Metro Tretyakovskaya. Tel. 233-5233. Open daily from 10am to 7pm, closed Mondays. Admission for foreigners is about $4.
  Located south of the Kremlin and inside the Garden Ring Road, across the Moskva River. Pavel Tretyakov's statue, by sculptor **Sergey Konyonkov** is in front of the gallery.
  In April 1995, the renovation of the Tretyakov Gallery was finally completed. The museum was shut down in November 1985, just seven months after Mikhail Gorbachev came to power. All Soviet era art has been removed from the Tretyakov, which now only displays works created before 1917, the year the Bolsheviks clawed their way to power.
  Like many Russian galleries and state art exhibits, Tretyakov could exhaust you with hundreds of paintings, sculptures, drawings, icons and

Byzantine mosaics that are displayed in 60 rooms covering 8,600 square yards and enhanced with skylights.

What was once a musty basement has been turned into a ground-floor entrance that boasts marble floors, chandeliers and an elegant cafe. The renovation cost $50 million and transformed the Tretyakov into the most exhilarating museum in Moscow.

Tretyakov Gallery is one of the great art museums of the world, as well as one of the largest, and it welcomes more than 1.5 million visitors a year. The museum's collections include only Russian art, just as it was conceived by its founder, **Pavel Tretyakov** (1832-1898), a Russian merchant and art patron who founded it in 1850. When in 1892, Pavel, one of the two Tretyakov brothers, presented 1,287 of his paintings and sketches and 518 drawings to the city of Moscow, his collection included the works of almost every 19th century Russian artist of note. For this, Pavel Tretyakov and his brother were named Honorable Moscow Citizens.

Tretyakov's entire collection was initially exhibited at his mansion on Lavrushinsky Lane, but it became so large that he had to construct several exhibition halls in a separate building to accommodate his treasures. In 1904, the museum was incorporated into its present facade.

The gallery was nationalized by the Bolsheviks in 1918. In 1949, its director proclaimed: "Cezanne must be condemned, Matisse cannot draw, Picasso is putrefying; any artist who doesn't follow the example of Soviet art is an enemy of Socialism."

The Tretyakov now has more than 80,000 paintings, icons and other works of art, but it can only display about a third of them at any one time.

Many of the world's most valuable icons, more than 4,500 in all and mostly from the 11th-17th centuries, are displayed. All four great schools of church art are amply represented: Pskov, Kiev, Novgorod and Moscow.

Featured among the countless works are *Our Lady of Vladimir*, brought by Kievan princes from Byzantium in the early 12th century, and Andrey Rublev's *The Old Testament Trinity*, a spectacular work of art executed in 1422-27. You can also appreciate the 14th century's *The Annunciation*, and the 15th century's *St. George and the Dragon*, which is Moscow's symbol.

The exhibition of paintings at the Tretyakov opens with early 18th century portraits by **Ivan Nikitin** (1690-1742), a major artist from the period of Peter the Great, and **Aleksey Antropov** (1716-1795), a portraitist to the Imperial Court. Another court portraitist on display, **Ivan Argunov** (1722-1802) and his two sons were serf artists of the wealthy Count Sheremetyev.

Fyodor Rokotov (1735-1808) created many portraits of women, full of charm and noble grace, although he was the son of a serf and himself owned by Prince Repin. A contemporary of Rokotov, **Dmitry Levitsky**

(1735-1822), influenced by French artists, was considered a polished master of the gallant age with its cult of femininity and grace. The neo-classical sculptor **Fyodor Shubin** (1740-1805) excelled in marble. After the works of **Vladimir Borovikovsky** (1757-1825), you will come upon the outstanding romantic 19th century portraitist, **Orest Kiprensky** (1782-1836). An illegitimate son of a nobleman, he was brought up as a serf and attended the Academie in St. Petersburg at age six. His portrait of Pushkin, painted in 1827, when the great Russian poet returned from exile to St. Petersburg, expresses a melancholy contemplation.

Simplicity is the trademark of **Vasily Tropinin** (1776-1857), who was born a serf during the time of the American declaration of independence and died in the same year as composer Mikhail Glinka. He also studied at the Academie, but was recalled by his owner to work on his estate as a gardener and valet. **Silvestr Shchedrin** (1791-1830), son of the sculptor Shchedrin, spent most of his life in Italy so it is not surprising that many of his canvases are lyrical Italian landscapes. Moscow-born painter of Greek origin, **Aleksey Venetsiyanov** (1780-1847) is considered the father of Russian genre painting.

Karl Briullov (1799-1852), a major Romantic mythological painter, born in Italy, was still another Russian artist that excelled in the portraiture, such as his pale self-portrait, done in 1848. Poet Pushkin and writer Gogol both admired his work. **Aleksandr Ivanov** (1806-1858), the son of a professor of painting, spent almost half his life on one huge painting, **The Appearance of Christ to the People**, which took 20 years to finish. It is perhaps the most celebrated single religious painting of the mid-19th century in Russia.

Watch for the pretended fright of the would-be bride and the staged unexpectedness of the bridegroom in the doorway in the 1848 canvas **The Major's Marriage Proposal** to appreciate the work of the Moscow-born **Pavel Fedotov** (1815-1852), who is the founder of Russian critical realism. **Vasily Perov** (1833-1882) was the first major artist to depict the poverty and sorrow of the peasants and his work on display here will explain why. His portrait of the writer Fyodor Dostoyevsky is a study in pain, too.

Look for **Ivan Kramskoy's** portrait of the writer Leo Tolstoy, painted in 1873; Kramskoy became the leader of the Wanderers movement in 1863. Next are the lyrical landscapes by **Ivan Shishkin** (1832-1898), who specialized in forests and studies of trees. **Viktor Vasnetsov** (1848-1926) is perhaps the most dramatic painter of Old Russia, as could be seen in **The Russian Legendary Heroes**. You might also enjoy the work of **Nikolay Gay** (1831-1894) who, in the opinion of some, employs light source reminiscent of Caravaggio or Rembrandt.

Ilya Repin (1844-1930), is a major Russian painter, who had already painted portraits and icons while still a child. His art represents the summit of Russian critical realism. One of his canvases on exhibit is **The Religious Procession in Kursk Province**, another the melodramatically effective painting of Ivan the Terrible and his son Ivan, whom the tsar killed in a moment of madness. There is also the portrait of Mussorgsky, which was finished just four days before the composer's death. (If continuing north on Lavrushinsky pereulok, you will cross the canal on a bridge to Bolotnaya Square, where a statue of Repin's is prominently displayed. This is also the place where the Cossack rebel leader **Yemelyan Pugachev** (1726-1775) was beheaded; please see Chapter 4, *A Short History* for details.)

Vasily Surikov (1848-1916) is a great Russian historical painter. Perhaps the most important landscape painter in the late 19th century Russia was **Isaak Levitan** (1860-1900); there are several of his canvases on display. Moscow-born **Konstantin Korovin** (1861-1939), you will notice, seems to have been inspired by the Impressionists.

Son of a composer, **Valentin Serov** (1865-1911), is a great Russian master of the late 19th and early 20th centuries. Look at his 1887 portrait of the daughter of the patron of the arts Savva Mamontov, or the 1910 portrait of the famous Russian theater actress Yermolova. Visit next with the Russian Symbolist painter **Mikhail Vrubel** (1856-1910) and see his powerful 1890 canvas **Demon Seated**, which was influenced by Lermontov's poem **Demon**. In and out of hospitals because he suffered from insanity, Vrubel suffered the ultimate tragedy that can befall a painter, he went blind four years before his death. Shown here for the first time is his giant 53-by-23-foot **Princess Gryoza**, which was created in 1896. Believed lost, **Princess** was uncovered in a badly damaged state from a Bolshoy theater warehouse in 1960 and restored just in time for the reopening of the museum.

Anna Golubkina (1864-1927) was a sculptor who may remind you a bit of Rodin, under whom she worked in Paris from 1897 to 1900; see her bronze of Leo Tolstoy. Painter **Kuzma Petrov-Vodkin** (1878-1939) possessed a great originality and admired the tradition of icon painting, which is reflected in some of his work.

The works of Chagall, Kandinsky and Malevich have only been on display since 1991.

Tretyakov has several eating facilities. You can interrupt your visit with lunch or a snack, then return to the exhibition halls, as long as you keep your tickets.

TRETYAKOV GALLERY AFFILIATE

The Central House of Artists, 10 Krimsky val, Metro Oktyabrskaya or Park Kultury. Tel. 230-1116 or 7788. Open daily from 10am to 7pm, closed Mondays. Admission for foreigners $2.

Located southeast of the Kremlin on the Garden Ring Road, across the street from Gorky Park and next to the Moskva River. This gallery exhibits mostly Soviet and post-Soviet art. Be sure to see the outdoor sculpture garden called the Mouseion. More than a hundred statues of disgraced Communist art, brought from all over Moscow after the failed 1991 coup, as well as other works are displayed in this garden. For more details, please see the Central House of Artists in the Galleries & Exhibition Halls section of Chapter 14, *Culture*.

PUSHKIN MUSEUM OF FINE ARTS

12 Ulitsa Volkhonka, Metro Kropotkinskaya. Tel. 203-7998 or 9578. Open daily from 10am to 7pm, closed Mondays. Admission for foreigners $4.

Located southwest of the Kremlin, southwest of the Russian State Library, almost across the street from the Cathedral of Christ the Savior, and a few minutes on foot from practically anywhere in central Moscow.

The former National Museum of Arts has been known as the Pushkin Museum since 1937. The foundation stone of the great marble building was laid in 1898. It was inaugurated by Tsar Nicholas II and his daughters in June 1912, one hundred years after the Napoleon's invasion of Russia.

The Pushkin Museum is modeled on Dresden's Albert Museum and its interiors are decorated to reflect Greek, Renaissance and Egyptian art and architecture. The marble columns of the portico are based on the architecture of the Acropolis and were copied from the ancient temple of Erechtheum (dating from 421-406 B.C.). It contains a trove of half a million works of ancient, Oriental, classical and Western European art on two floors, with 15 exhibition halls each. Cezanne and Gauguin, for example, are displayed in hall 18, the French Impressionists in hall 21, both on the second floor.

Built mostly with public donations, it was originally conceived as a Moscow University educational center on the initiative of professor Ivan Tsvetayev, the father of poet **Marina Tsvetayeva** (1892-1941); please see this chapter for more about her museum. Two-thirds of the construction cost was paid for by the glass manufacturer Yuri Nechayev-Maltsev. The Pushkin still houses an extensive collection of copies of well-known sculptures from ancient times and the Renaissance. They were acquired from museums in Berlin, Munich, Paris, London, Rome and Naples.

The present collection has been assembled from sculptures in the old Pashkov House, which is one of two buildings of the current Russian State Library (formerly Lenin Library) nearby. The paintings, first exhibited at the Pushkin in 1924, come from the Hermitage Museum in St. Petersburg, as well as from a variety of other collections donated to the museum or confiscated from wealthy individuals after the Communists elbowed their way to power. Among the largest plunders were the priceless private collections of Sergey Shchukin and Ivan Morozov, rich Moscow merchants with an uncanny eye for new French art, particularly the Impressionists. In 1925, Western European paintings from Tretyakov Gallery were also transferred to the Museum of Fine Arts.

The Pushkin's ancient art collection includes a rare series of 23 Fayum portraits, which were discovered in the 1880's in the burial places in Fayum, an oasis near Cairo, by the Russian Egyptologist Vladimir Golenishchev. They are the earliest painted portraits discovered to date and were painted in the 2nd century B.C. on cypress panels. Only 600 are known to exist.

The museum holds Italian icons from the 13th-15th centuries, as well as 1,150 ancient Greek vases, one of the largest collections in the world. No Russian icons are on display at the Pushkin. The plaster casts take up several rooms, but there is also an extraordinary collection of authentic Egyptian sculptures and other ancient exhibits. Thousands of items document the early art of Egypt, Assyria, Babylon, Greece and Rome.

There are more than 3,000 paintings and engravings on exhibit from the 13th to 20th centuries, so you will not be able to see them all in one day, but who says you cannot come back for a second or third time. Among the notable painters of the Italian school represented here are Botticelli, Perugino, Boltraffio, Borgognome, and Canaletto. Spaniards are represented by El Greco, Vasquez, Ribera, Murillo, and Zurbaran. Flemish masters include at least three paintings by Rubens and Van Dyke. Somber portraits attest to the great art of Rembrandt. Cranach represents the Germans on exhibit here.

You can spend a day with the French and they are a lot friendlier than those that Napoleon brought over in 1812. There is so much to see you will forget that the gallery closes at 7pm, although you will not be admitted after 6:30 pm. The rooms full of Impressionists paintings will make you wonder how many private collections the Communists plundered to assemble this fine collection.

Eleven canvases on exhibit at the Pushkin represent the art of Claude Monet, one of the leading Impressionists. There is a series of his mills, poplars, haystacks, and the Rouen cathedral painted at different times of day, and the Thames and the water lilies that were painted between 1890 and 1926. Following Monet, you will find several landscapes by Camille Pissarro, and Alfred Sisley's 1873 oils.

Among the five masterpieces by Auguste Renoir, you will find a study for the portrait of the actress Jeanne Samary from the late 1870's and one of Renoir's most productive periods. Three of the Pushkin's four Degas are devoted to ballet, including the *Blue Dancers*. The museum's collection of Paul Cezanne consists of 14 paintings, one of the finest anywhere. You will not soon find a still life as fine as his *Peaches and Pears*, painted in 1889.

Thirteen of the 14 Impressionistic canvases by Gauguin belong to his Tahiti and Dominique periods; only one was painted in France. You can see five works by Vincent van Gogh here, all five painted after 1886 in France: *The Red Vineyard at Arles* and *Fishing Boats at Sea*, both from 1888, the 1889 *Portrait of Dr. Rey*, and *Wheat Fields at Auvers After the Rain*, and *The Prisoners' Round*, both from 1890.

Henri Matisse's 17 canvases at the museum span over a long period of artist's life, from the late 19th century works all the way to 1940.

Some of these canvases had not been seen in the West until the 1960's, when the *Ladies' Homes Journal* was allowed to reproduce several of them.

Older Frenchmen on exhibit at the Pushkin include Poussin, Lebrun, five Claude Lorrains, Wateau, Chardin, three by Fragonard, Delacroix, Ingres's *Virgin*, Courbet and Corot. You can see Francois Boucher 's (1703-1770) *Hercules and Omphale*, which immortalizes "the most passionate kiss in the history of art," according to one Russian guide. There are Toulouse-Lautrec, Utrillo, Bonnard, Signac and Vlaminck works also on display.

Eleven Picassos are in the Pushkin's collection, all from the Blue and Rose Periods done before 1914, among them: *Family of Acrobats, Old Beggar and Child, Little Girl with Balloon, Lady with a Fan, Young Girl on a Ball, Portrait of the Poet Sabartes* and *Spanish Woman from Mallorca.*

The museum possesses three Rembrandts, *Christ Driving Moneylenders from the Temple*, which was painted between 1625 and 1631; *The Incredulity of St. Thomas*, dated 1634; *Ahasuerus, Haman and Esther,* from 1660; and three portraits from the Dresden Collection acquired during the reign of Catherine the Great: *Portrait of an Old Woman, Portrait of Adriaen van Rijn*, and *Portrait of the Wife of Rembrandt's Brother*, all of which were painted in the mid-1650's and "display the painter's profound penetration into the complexities of human life," according to author Boris Brodsky.

French sculptors on display span a period from the 18th century on, including several works by Auguste Rodin, Emile Bourdelle and Aristide Maillol.

The Pushkin also possesses some 300 pieces of antique furniture, but not all are being shown. More than 20,000 graphic works, until 1861 on display at the Hermitage, are also available for exhibit. Marc Chagall is said to have presented more than 70 of his lithographs to the museum.

Among the thousands of drawings and watercolors at Pushkin, you could see Durer's, Rembrandt's, Renoir's, Modigliani's, Toulouse-Lautrec's, Picasso's, Malevich's, and Kandinsky's.

Unfortunately, lighting at the Pushkin sometimes leaves something to be desired and you will find yourself straining from one angle to another to dodge reflections so you can appreciate the works before you.

MUSEUM OF PRIVATE COLLECTIONS

14 Ulitsa Volkhonka, Metro Kropotkinskaya. Tel. 203-9578. Open daily from 10am to 4pm, Saturdays and Sundays noon to 6pm. Closed Mondays and Tuesdays.

Located next to the Pushkin Museum of Fine Arts.

The Museum of Private Collections building is one of the oldest in this area and has undergone several reconstructions. In 1774, it was converted into a palace for Empress Catherine II, who came to Moscow to celebrate Russia's victory over Turkey. This victory made it possible for her to incorporate the Crimean peninsula into her empire.

This building was later divided into offices and private apartments, which the owners rented out. The well-known Russian playwright Aleksandr Ostrovsky lived in one of them. After the 1917 Bolshevik Revolution, the building was taken over by the Communist Academy and in 1928 two floors were added.

The left wing of Golitsyn's manor estate, which now houses the Museum of Private Collections, was a hotel in the 19th century, before it was purchased by the Moscow Art Society. Many prominent artists had workshops and apartments here. Painter Leonid Pasternak and his son Boris, a poet and Nobel Prize winning novelist, moved in in 1911. The younger Pasternak lived in the house until 1937.

The museum was inaugurated in 1995. Its backbone are 12 private collections of 16th-20th century Russian and Western art, displayed in an arresting interior. The exhibit halls flow from one roomful of notable Russian art pieces to another.

Among the artists represented is **Ilya Repin** (1844-1930) with his large and unforgettable 1913 canvas titled *Duel*, which shows the contrition of a surviving duelist. Others include **Vasily Polenov** (1844-1927), **Ivan Shishkin** (1832-1898), **Aleksandr Rodchenko** (1891-1956), **David Shterenberg** (1881-1948), Boris Pasternak's father **Leonid Pasternak** (1861-1945), who is represented with ten oils and graphics, and the French Impressionist **Henri Matisse**.

There is a snack bar on the ground floor and a bookshop. Rest rooms in the back of the ground floor are clean.

ALEXANDER'S GARDENS

Aleksandrovsky sad

Located between the Kremlin and Ulitsa Manezhnaya, Metro Aleksandrovsky sad, Biblioteka imeni Lenina or Borovitskaya.

You can walk to the Gardens from the site of the Historical Museum at the Kremlin's wrought-iron Arsenal Gate or through Biblioteka imeni Lenina metro station, which has an exit directly onto Aleksandrovsky sad.

Leaving the Kremlin itself, you will find yourself in the Gardens by way of Troitskiye Gate.

The Gardens were laid out by Osip Bove between 1819 and 1822 and named after Tsar Aleksandr I, the eldest son of Paul I and grandson of Catherine the Great. The Neglinka River, a Moscow tributary that once snaked its way along the western wall of the Kremlin and formed one of the three water barriers protecting the Kremlin, was diverted into an aqueduct beneath the Gardens after the catastrophic fires of 1812. Gardeners from all over Russia were invited to plant trees, shrubs and flowers. The river, or rather a small portion of it, is being resurrected in 1997 as part of the billion-dollar reconstruction of Manezhnaya Square. It will again flow at the edge of Aleksandrovky sad, but only for a few hundred feet, and will begin and end in fountains. The bridge, which once spanned the Neglinka, has been preserved and is now utilized as a passageway to the Kremlin.

Although the northern end of Alexander's Gardens has been invaded by noise from the $1 billion construction effort going on in Manezhnaya Square, where a multi-level underground shopping center and a parking lot is being built, the rest of the Gardens are an oasis of peace in today's congested Moscow. There are plenty of benches to sit on and relax. It is an acceptable practice to strike a conversation with your neighbor here.

Aleksandr I (1777-1825) reached the summit of his rule with a victory over Napoleon in 1812 and he triumphantly entered Paris on a white horse at the head of Russian troops two years later. He attempted a similar achievement in his domestic policy with liberal reforms, but failing to carry them out, he returned to the traditional despotism of other Russian rulers. Aleksandr supposedly died in the Decembrist uprising of 1825, although his death remains a mystery. Officially he died in southern Russia, but rumor had it that he had secretly renounced the crown and wandered around Russia preaching penitence and humility.

Back in 1801, Aleksandr gave his consent to the overthrow of his father, Paul I, who was half-mad. The coup ended in the emperor's assassination, which probably was not planned by his sensitive son. Later, Aleksandr may have feared that a future coup would lead him to share his father's fate, thus he possibly feigned his death. The closed-coffin funeral of the emperor took place in St. Petersburg in March 1826, four months after his supposed death.

The Eternal Flame of memory burns in Aleksandrovsky sad at the **Tomb of the Unknown Soldier**, at the foot of the Kremlin wall and Kremlevsky Passage. The Tomb has this inscription: "Your name is unknown, your feat immortal." This red granite memorial to the heroes of World War II was unveiled on May 8, 1966, on the eve of Victory Day to commemorate the anniversary of the defeat of German forces in battles near Moscow. The remains of the Unknown Soldier were taken from a mass grave at the village of Kryukovo, at the 41st kilometer of the Leningrad Highway, where enemy troops attacking Moscow had been halted. To the right of the Tomb are six urns holding soil from the six cities that resisted the German occupation: Odessa, Sevastopol, Volgograd, Kiev, Brest and St. Petersburg.

Every May 9, when the victory over Nazi Germany is celebrated in Russia, war veterans and other citizens come to the tomb to pay their respects. The granite slabs lining the tomb are often covered with flowers. Flowers are also laid daily at the Tomb of the Unknown Soldier by many newlyweds who traditionally come here on their wedding day to honor the war's dead and pose for photographs. It is not uncommon to see brides ascend the steps of the tomb in their lightweight dresses when the temperature may be well below freezing.

Not far from the Tomb of the Unknown Soldier, there is a gray obelisk, the **Monument to Revolutionary Thinkers**, that now bears the names of Socialists and Bolshevik revolutionaries. The obelisk was erected in 1913 to mark 300 years of the dynasty's rule. Originally, it listed the names of the Romanov tsars and was crowned with a double-headed eagle. Five years later, the Bolsheviks removed the Romanov eagle, erased the names of the tsars and transformed it into a revolutionary monument by replacing them with the names of Communist theoreticians. It was the first monument of Bolshevik revolutionary Russia.

You may be surprised to find the names of Karl Marx and Friedrich Engels, but not that of Vladimir Lenin. Well, the list of hastily-assembled names was prepared by Lenin himself and, for once, it even included his opponent Mikhailovsky. No one dared to correct Lenin's list and it was reproduced exactly as he had written it.

CATHEDRAL OF CHRIST THE SAVIOR

37 Kropotkinskaya nab., Metro Kropotkinskaya.

Located southwest of the Kremlin, adjacent to the Boulevard Ring Road and the Moskva River, and a block south of the Pushkin Museum of Fine Arts.

In 1883, following 46 years of construction by nearly 100,000 workers and expenditures of 15,125,163 rubles and 89 kopeks, the gigantic Cathedral of Christ Our Savior, commissioned by Tsar Aleksandr I, was erected at this site to honor those killed in the Napoleonic War of 1812. This 338 feet tall, 72,120 square foot cathedral could accommodate 10,000 worshippers. To make room for the original cathedral, the tsar had a convent torn down and legend has it that in retaliation the nuns cursed the site.

Fifty years later, the Communists wanted to build the Palace of the Soviets here, which was to be the tallest building in the world at that time, crowned with a gargantuan 301-foot-tall statue of Lenin. It was to be so gargantuan in fact that Lenin's index finger alone was to be almost 20 feet long. The nearby Kropotkinskaya metro station was built and named Palace of the Soviets in anticipation of the future complex. The Savior's Cathedral was thus one of the first buildings that fell victim to Stalin's reconstruction. After six days of preparations, the tyrant had the cathedral reduced to a heap of rubbish in 1931. But as the huge soft-soiled foundations of the new palace kept shifting, the plans were abandoned and the nuns' curse seemed to have come true when Stalin ordered it blown up. The Bolshevik engineers finally understood why it took architect Konstantin Ton 46 years to build it.

Meanwhile, the cathedral's main altar with its gilded iconostasis (a screen that separates the sanctuary from the nave) was rumored to have been sold to Eleanor Roosevelt. Some believe that she donated it to the Vatican where it supposedly remains today, except that no one will acknowledge its existence. Its marble was used to decorate several Moscow metro stations, and its jasper columns now grace Moscow State University. A few other remnants of the original cathedral, such as the four surviving reliefs that have been kept at the Donskoy Monastery, will be displayed at the cathedral's museum.

In its place, Basin Moskva, a year-round heated open-air swimming pool, was built on orders from Nikita Khrushchev in 1960. In typically Soviet fashion, it was so large that 2,000 people could swim in it at any one time. But the pool had many detractors, including those who claimed that the pool's steam was damaging the artwork in the nearby Pushkin Museum and eroding the foundations of other buildings. By the 1990s, it had a seedy look about it, but it cost just a few cents to use.

In 1994, Moscow's mayor resurrected the idea of rebuilding the cathedral in time for the 850th anniversary of Moscow in 1997. While the upper church is a replica of Ton's original cathedral, the complex also includes a gate church, socle housing, two council halls, a museum, refectory, kitchen and a garage. The new $300 million edifice, which is the principal cathedral of Russia, rises 295 feet high, almost as high as St. Paul's in London. It serves as a reminder that 200,000 clergymen were eliminated in the former Soviet Union. Only **Victory Park**, and perhaps the **Tretyakov Gallery**, come close to the Cathedral in its symbolism in the new Russia. It is one of the most visible structures in Moscow, no matter what part of central Moscow you find yourself.

The main cross mounted on the summit of the cupola is 30 feet tall and gilded with one kilogram of gold. While the cathedral was basically finished for the 850th anniversary, painting it will take several more years.

The pace of the round-the-clock construction was so hectic in 1996 that workers who were just five minutes late were fined $10, not an insignificant amount at the time. Some 40,000 businesses contributed toward its completion; a bank donated 110 pounds of gold and more than a million bricks were received as gifts.

PRINCE YURI DOLGORUKY STATUE

Tverskaya ploshchad at Ulitsa Tverskaya & Stoleshnikov pereulok, Metro Pushkinskaya or Chekhovskaya.

Located northwest of the Kremlin, southeast of Pushkin Square, and across the street from the Moscow city government offices on Tverskaya Street. Aragvi, a Georgian restaurant, is on the southern side of the square and the Moskva bookstore is just north.

Prince Yuri Dolgoruky (Prince of Long Arms), who is believed to have lived from 1090 to 1157, is said to have founded Moscow around 1147, about the same time that the Lisbon Cathedral was built. Commissioned in 1947 to mark the 800th anniversary of the founding of Moscow, this majestic equestrian statue on a high granite pedestal was not completed until 1954. It was sculpted by **Sergey Orlov** (1911-1971). Dolgoruky is so tall in the saddle that he can see inside City Hall across Tverskaya Street.

Additional Sites Near Prince Yuri Dolgoruky Statue

What may surprise a Westerner about this square is a much smaller and quite inconspicuous statue of Lenin sitting in the tiny park behind Prince Dolgoruky. Why the Communists let Dolgoruky overshadow their favorite paternal figure is a mystery. This statue by **Sergey Merkurov** (1881-1952) was exhibited at the New York World's Fair in 1939 before it was unveiled on what was then called Sovyetskaya Square the following year.

The **Marxist-Leninist Institute** archives are held in the building behind Lenin's statue and contain some 40,000 documents, mostly about, who else but, Lenin.

In 1912, a statue of the Central Asian conqueror, general and former governor of Minks, **Mikhail Skobelev** (1843-1882) was unveiled on Tverskaya Square. Five years later it became an irritant to the Bolsheviks so they replaced it with an obelisk in 1919. This was also carted away in the late 1930's.

The **Moscow City Council**, across Tverskaya Street, was designed by the architect Matvey Kazakov in 1782 for Count Chernyshevsky, the first military governor-general who was appointed by Catherine the Great for his valor in the Russo-Prussian war of 1760. It served as the official residence of Moscow governors until the Bolshevik Revolution. One of the governors was Prince Dmitry Golitsyn, who between 1820 and 1844 paved the city streets and commissioned the water system that still serves Moscow. In 1939, when Stalin had Tverskaya Street widened, this building was moved back some 42 feet and two more stories, as well as a new entrance, were added. A balcony still stands over the entrance from which Lenin spoke to the masses.

UNIQUE METRO STATIONS

The 12 stations of the Circle Line, which follows roughly an outline of the Garden Ring Road, were built in the 1950's and connect seven of the nine Moscow railway stations. Most of Moscow's population was concentrated inside the Garden Ring Road at that time. Here is an alphabetical listing of the most interesting metro stations, mostly located on or inside the Circle Line. For more practical information about the metro, please see the Metro and Bus sections in Chapter 7, *Getting Around Moscow*.

Arbatskaya (on the Arbatsko-Pokrovskaya & Filyovskaya lines) is located on the Boulevard Ring Road, west of the Kremlin, and at the foot of Stary and Novy Arbat. Opened in 1953, Arbatskaya is heavy on marble and decorated with ceramic flowers and hanging bronze lamps. The metro was built on the site of Tikhon the Wonderworker Church, which was demolished in the early 1930's.

Belorusskaya (on the Circular & Zamoskvoretskaya lines) is located northwest of the Kremlin and near Belorussky Railway Station. Opened in 1952, it was built with white and beige-colored marble and onyx brought from Siberia. It was designed and decorated by Belorussian architects and artists with scenes from everyday Belorussian life. Its heavy columns are typical for a Circular line station. The tessellated floor is in a traditional Belorussian carpet pattern. The mosaics here are not as compelling as those inside the Chekhovskaya station.

Chekhovskaya (on the Serpukhovsko-Timiryazevskaya, Tagansko-Krasnopresnenskaya & Zamoskvoretskaya lines) is located on the Boulevard Ring Road, northwest of the Kremlin and under Pushkin Square. Opened in 1988, it is dedicated to the Russian classicist **Anton Chekhov** (1860-1904). On nearby Malaya Dmitrovka Street, once named after him, Chekhov lived at three different address between 1890 and 1899. Scenes at both ends of the station depict the playwright and his Moscow museum. The side walls of the station are decorated with marble mosaic scenes from Chekhov's works, such as *Lady with a Dog* and *The Cherry Orchard*. These mosaics were created by Ludmila and Pyotr Shorchev.

Chistiye Prudy (on the Kaluzhskaya-Rizhskaya & Sokolnicheskaya lines) is located on the Boulevard Ring Road, northeast of the Kremlin.

While many metro stations served as air raid shelters during World War II, Chistiye prudy was the headquarters of the General Staff, where Stalin and General Georgy Zhukov (whose equestrian statue is displayed in front of the Historical Museum) plotted their tactics against the Germans.

Kievskaya (on the Circular, Filyovskaya & Arbatsko-Pokrovskaya lines) is located southwest of the Kremlin, outside the Garden Ring Road, and next to Kievsky Railway Station. Opened around the time of Stalin's death, it glorifies, in a typically Stalinist fashion, the achievements of the Ukraine with mosaic scenes, such as Pushkin in the Ukraine, and chandeliers. Kievsky Railway Station was built in 1920.

Komsomolskaya (on the Circular & Sokolnicheskaya lines) is located northeast of the Kremlin, outside the Garden Ring Road, and on the way to Kazansky, Leningradsky and Yaroslavsky Railway Stations. One of the busiest, this station, constructed in 1952, is named after the Communist League of Youth (Komsomol). Built on the design of the well-known architect Aleksey Shchusev (1873-1949), who also drafted the Lenin Mausoleum, it is believed by some to be the most handsome metro station in Moscow. Its design won the Grand Prix in Brussels, as well as the first prize at the New York International Exposition, both in 1958. This is the most baroque of Moscow's stations and late at night, when it's completely empty, it might remind you of a cathedral. The main concourse is 623 feet long and 30 feet wide, and has 72 octagonal marble piers supporting round arches. Amid large chandeliers, there are eight ceiling mosaics, each more than eight feet in diameter. They depict scenes from Russian history, including the 1612 liberation of Polish-occupied Moscow and the 1812 Napoleonic invasion of Russia, as well as Lenin in Red Square in 1917 and Russians at Berlin's Reichstag in 1945. They were created by painter and monumental artist Pavel Korin (1892-1967), whose religious beliefs are clearly detectable. The Red Square parade mosaic has been altered several times because of changing political winds and Stalin, Beria and Khrushchev were all erased.

Kropotkinskaya (on the Sokolnicheskaya line) is located southwest of the Kremlin and inside the Boulevard Ring Road. It is one of seven stations that opened in 1935 between Sokolniki and Park Kultury stations on the oldest metro line. You will be able to tell its age by its classic simplicity interrupted only by a row of marble columns. Kropotkinskaya, which was named after the anarchist Prince Kropotkin, was designed by the same architect who designed Mayakovskaya.

Mayakovskaya (on the Zamoskvoretskaya line) is located on the Garden Ring Road, northwest of the Kremlin, and below the Tchaikovsky Conservatory. Opened in 1938, Mayakovskaya lies on the second oldest metro line and is named after the brash revolutionary poet Vladimir Mayakovsky who killed himself in central Moscow in 1930. Simple, spacious and elegant, accented by rows of stainless steel pillars, it is bejeweled with the same Urals stone used by Faberge in his Easter egg creations. Architect Aleksey Dushkin, who also designed Detsky Mir children's department store on Lubyanka Square, won first prize at the 1938 World's Fair in New York for this metro design. The 36 oval cupolas provide the lighting. On the ceiling are 33 fluorescent mosaics designed by painter Aleksandr Deineka (1899-1969), displaying Moscow sports and aviation themes during a 24-hour period.

On November 6, 1941, Stalin spoke to the Supreme Soviet inside this station, while the Germans advanced within a few miles of Moscow. Aside from being the headquarters for the anti-aircraft defense forces, Mayakovskaya also served as a refuge for women and children during the war.

Novokuznetskaya (on the Zamoskvoretskaya line) is located across the Moskva River south of the Kremlin, inside the Garden Ring Road, and east of Tretyakov Gallery. There once was a church where the Novokuznetskaya metro now stands. It was destroyed in the 1930's and its stones were used in the construction of this station. Built and inaugurated during the World War II, it is decorated with a military bas-relief and athletic theme mosaic on the ceiling; its artist died during the siege of Leningrad. In 1996-97, this station was closed for reconstruction.

Novoslobodskaya (on the Circular & Serpukhovsko-Timiryazevskaya line) is located northwest of the Kremlin and outside the Garden Ring Road. Open in 1952, it is worth seeing for its 36 pleasing stained glass panels made in Riga, Latvia. These panels were created by the icon painter **Pavel Korin**, who also designed the ceiling mosaics in the Komsomolskaya station. The panels are based on the traditional motifs of old Russian embroidery and tapestry, giving it a church-like effect.

Park Kultury (on the Circular & Sokolnicheskaya line) is located on the Garden Ring Road southwest of the Kremlin. This was once the end station of the original Sokolniki line and it opened in 1935. Clad in gray-colored marble, it displays bas-relief medallions with sport and recreation motives, such as chess-players, dancers and musicians. Park Kultury is a bit misleading; it implies that the station is located near what was originally called Gorky Park of Culture and Rest, but it's not. For more about Gorky Park, please see Parks & Gardens in Chapter 9, *Child's Play*.

Ploshchad Revolutsiyi (on the Arbatsko-Pokrovskaya line) is centrally located just north of Red Square and next to what was once the Lenin Museum. Inaugurated in 1936, its architect, Aleksey Dushkin, designed it on the theme of the October Revolution. The red-colored Urals marble-clad concourse is guarded by 36 life-size bronze sculptures of Bolshevik partisans who, at the station's opposite end, transform into peaceful citizens. Among the representations are the crew of the cruiser

Aurora and a mother and child, all from the workshop of the monumental sculptor **Matvey Manizer** (1891-1966). This is the same Manizer who in 1940 erected a colossal 53-foot-high statue of Lenin in his hometown of Ulyanovsk.

Rimskaya (on the Kalininskaya & Lyublinskaya lines) is located southeast of the Kremlin and outside the Garden Ring Road. Inaugurated in the summer of 1996, it is one of the newest stations. The theme is classical Rome: sculptures of Romulus, the founder of Rome, and his brother Remus fed by a she-wolf, four horses pulling an ancient Roman chariot and fallen Corinthian columns with children playing. All the sculptures are made of fire clay and are a modern interpretation of 14th and 15th century Italian sculptures created by the well-known Russian sculptor **Leonid Berlin**. Son of the General Secretary of the Iranian Communist Party who was executed in 1938, Berlin had hard time surviving during the socialist realism period, which, he says, he always detested. The artwork in this station is what Berlin always wanted to create.

Taganskaya (on the Circular & Tagansko-Krasnopresnenskaya lines) is located on the Garden Ring Road, southeast of the Kremlin. This station was inaugurated in 1950 and the marble-clad Taganskaya station uses the Great Patriotic War, or World War II, as its main theme and displays partisans, tank drivers and pilots.

Teatralnaya (on the Arbatsko-Pokrovskaya, Sokolnicheskaya & Zamoskvoretskaya lines) is centrally located north of the Kremlin and near the Metropol Hotel. It was opened in 1940 and dedicated to the arts of the republics of the former Soviet Union. Glazed porcelain figurines come from a porcelain factory near Moscow and the marble was brought in from the Crimea.

Tsvetnoy Bulvar (on the Lyublinskaya & Serpuhovsko-Timiryazevskaya lines) is located north of the Kremlin, inside the Garden Ring Road, and near the Old Moscow Circus. Tsvetnoy bulvar has compelling stain glass panels and excellent ventilation.

FOLK ART MUSEUM

7 Leontiyevsky pereulok, Metro Arbatskaya or Pushkinskaya. Tel. 290-2114 or 5222. Open daily from 11am to 6pm, Tuesdays & Thursdays noon to 7pm; closed Mondays. Small admission fee.

Centrally located northwest of the Kremlin, a few blocks southwest of Pushkin Square, and almost across the street from the Stanislavsky Museum.

Folk arts and crafts of the 18th and 19th centuries, such as carved and painted wood, folk costumes, ceramics, ivory, pottery, chests, toys, lace and embroidery of the peoples of the Russian Federation are on display in this one-room museum. The museum also includes crafts from Fedoskino, Khokhloma, Mstyora, Palekh and Zhostovo, some of the villages around Moscow that produce the crafts.

GOGOL MEMORIAL ROOMS

7a Nikitsky bulvar, Metro Arbatskaya. Tel. 290-5881. Open Mondays, Wednesdays and Thursdays from noon to 7pm, Saturdays and Sundays from noon to 5pm; closed Tuesdays and Fridays. No admission fee.

Located west of the Kremlin, south of U Nikitskih Vorot Theater and the Oriental Arts Museum, both on Nikitsky Boulevard, and northwest of the Arbatskaya metro stations.

This two-room museum is located in the tree-shaded courtyard of city library No. 2 in the house which belonged to Aleksandr Petrovich Tolstoy, the governor of two provinces before he met Gogol in early 1840's.

The father of realism in Russian literature, the great **Nikolay Gogol** (1809-1852) was born in the Ukraine, became disenchanted with being a university lecturer and lived abroad, mostly in Rome, for ten years. By his own admission he never had any relations with women. At first a romantic, Gogol turned prickly with his 1836 drama, *The Inspector-General*, which satirizes the corruption and vanity of provincial officials. Six years later he wrote *Dead Souls*, which some consider the finest comic work in Russian literature. In it small landowners attempt to swindle the government by purchasing the names of dead serfs who were erroneously left on the register. His fantastic imagination is also brilliantly displayed in his short stories that are full of irrational fears and obsessions.

In this house, which became a museum in 1974, Gogol began working on the second volume of *Dead Souls*, but burned the manuscript just ten days before his death. Less than a month before he died, he subsisted on a few spoonfuls of watery oatmeal soup and spent most of his nights in prayer, allowing himself but a couple of hours of sleep. During the last few days he let out intermittent piercing screams that could be heard up and down Nikitsky Boulevard. Gogol died half-starved in a religious fervor in a room now occupied by the library. There are plans to expand the museum in the future.

There are two statues of Gogol in downtown Moscow, only three blocks apart, with interesting histories. A somewhat forlorn-looking one is located in the courtyard of the two-story house, *7a Nikitsky Boulevard*, where Gogol lived from 1848 until his death. It was sculpted by Muscovite **Nikolay Andreyev** (1873-1932) in 1906 and was prominently displayed until it was hidden inside this postage-stamp-sized courtyard north of Arbat. It was paid for by public subscription and originally unveiled in the place of the second statue in 1909.

The second, more upbeat statue is also located on the Garden Ring Road, just south of Arbatskaya Square, at Gogolevsky bulvar and Maly Afanasevsky pereulok. This one was created by **Nikolay Tomsky** (1900-1956) in 1951, and is clearly visible at the northern end of Gogolevsky Boulevard park. It was first unveiled on the centenary of Gogol's death in 1952.

The glum statue by Andreyev, which is now in the courtyard next to his house, was taken from Gogolevsky Boulevard and replaced by the Soviets with Tomsky's more upright and happy creation in the early 1950's. Andreyev's statue, which is still displayed in the courtyard, was removed on Stalin's orders, and sent to **Donskoy Monastery**. It was stored there from 1951 until 1959, when it was safe to bring it to Gogol's last home after Stalin's death in 1953. Muscovites are said to prefer the gloomy statue next to his house because it is more characteristic of the great writer.

HALL OF COLUMNS

Kolonny zal

1 Ulitsa Bolshaya Dmitrovka on the corner of Ulitsa Okhotny Ryad, Metro Teatralnaya or Okhotny Ryad. Tel. 292-4864. Open only when concerts and other events are held.

Centrally located north of the Kremlin, a couple of blocks southwest of the Bolshoy Theater, and across the street from the northern end of the Moskva Hotel.

At the beginning of what was called Pushkin Street in Soviet times, but is today again known as Ulitsa Bolshaya Dmitrovka, there is an old classical building that was once the largest and the most imposing in the district.

The house is known as the Hall of Columns (Kolonny zal), after the four large columns on the face of the building and inside it. The house was designed in 1775 by the Russian architect **Matvey Kazakov** for Prince Vassily Dolgorukov, a governor of Moscow. In 1784, when the prince died, it was sold to the Assembly of the Nobles, and Kazakov built a large hall in place of an inner courtyard to adapt it for public gatherings. It became the Noblemen's Club. The hall, bordered by 28 Corinthian columns, became Kazakov's masterpiece. Only the hall from the original building survived extensive alterations in 1908.

The poets Aleksandr Pushkin and Mikhail Lermontov and the writers Ivan Turgenev and young Lev Tolstoy, all among the most prominent Russian writers, came here to get inspiration for their descriptions of upper crust Moscow society. It was here that novelist Fyodor Dostoyevsky made an impassioned speech about Pushkin when the poet's statue (see Pushkin Statue, below) was unveiled in 1880. Tsars attended balls and concerts here when they were in Moscow, the old capital. Its perfect acoustics made it an excellent place for musical recitals by Tchaikovsky, Liszt and Rachmaninov. In 1856, the same year that he terminated the Crimean War, Tsar Alexander II (1818-1881) came here to speak to the Russian nobles about the abolition of serfdom. When the empire, shaken by internal problems and a disastrous war, collapsed in 1917, the building was taken over by trade unions and is still known to some as the **House of Trade Unions** (Dom Soyuzov).

In 1924, when Lenin died, he lay in state here for public grieving. More than a million hysterical mourners passed through the black-shrouded hall for three days and nights in 30 degrees below zero weather (Celsius) to pay tribute to the man who only now, inside Russia, is widely acknowledged to have been a colossal villain. During the 1930's, the Hall of Columns witnessed hundreds of show trials at which thousands of innocent people were denounced as traitors and enemies of the state. Often it was the starting point of their tragic road to death. One of them, who was not nearly so innocent was Lenin's and Stalin's associate Nikolay Bukharin (1888-1938), who himself sent many people to death.

When Josef Stalin, the clever puppeteer of these atrocities, died in 1953, he was brought here for funeral ceremonies. All passages to the Hall of Columns were barricaded by troops and vehicles to contain the multitudes of misguided citizens who, amid general hysteria, fought each other to pay their respects. The queue is said to have stretched from the Hall of Columns all the way to the Boulevard Ring Road at Trubnaya Square and Tsvetnoy Boulevard. According to one often-quoted estimate, 12,000 people were crushed to death and thousands badly injured in the bedlam.

Starting in the 1940's, winter festivals for children have been held here and still are occasionally to this very day. Soviet dictators Leonid Brezhnev (1906-1982) and Yuri Andropov (1914-1984) also lay in state in the Hall of Columns.

Today, the Hall is also recognized as one of the best concert halls in Moscow. The violin and cello contests of the International Tchaikovsky Competitions have been held here, with soprano Maria Callas and cellist Mstislav Rostropovich acting as jury members.

KGB MUSEUM

12 Ulitsa Bolshaya Lubyanka at Ploshchad Vorovskogo, Metro Kuznetsky Most or Lubyanka. Tel. 224-1982. Open Monday through Friday from 9am to 5pm, for group tours only. Small admission fee.

Centrally located northeast of the Kremlin, north of Lubyanka Square and north of the former KGB headquarters, with the entrance across the street from the restaurant Angleterre.

This museum originally opened for KGB officers in 1984. After a few exhibits were removed, it was opened to Russians in 1991 and two years later to foreigners. Only guided group tours are admitted so if you are interested inquire with a tour operator, such as Patriarshy Dom. Although this is one of the most biased tours you will find in Moscow, it arouses more interest among Westerners than almost any other tour offered by Patriarshy Dom. KGB stands for Komitet Gosudarstvennoi Bezopasnosti which translates to State Security Committee.

As you enter the large murky lobby of the Federal Security Service's (FSB) Cultural Center, you will have just enough time to spy a bust of the rapacious Feliks Dzerzhinsky before you are steered upstairs, where the tour begins in the FSB's ceremonial hall. You will see various uniforms on display here and learn that the Cheka secret police began wearing leather jackets because the service expropriated a warehouse of them from Arkhangelskoye in 1917. From there it's all downhill as far as objectivity is concerned for the tour soon turns into a eulogy for the KGB. I doubt that the tour's content will change by the time you visit.

You will be told that **Feliks Dzerzhinsky** (1877-1926), the founder of Cheka, was of noble birth and joined the Revolution at age 16. The indignant guide might deplore the act of "bandits and terrorists" who tore down the ruthless Feliks' larger-than-life statue on the grassy knoll of Lubyanka Square in 1991. One entire exhibition hall is dedicated to Iron Feliks who, after his death, had the square renamed after him.

It becomes increasingly embarrassing to listen to the guide, obviously a KGB man, who might have been picked for this job because he can be relied upon to defend the honor of his order. He refers to Stalin's repressions mostly because some 20,000 Cheka agents were also executed among the countless millions. The guide claims that only three million people perished under Stalin and adds, following doubts expressed by his audience, that he has access to documents as to the numbers that were executed. He dismisses the figures of 10, 15 or 20 million dead as a figment of an inflated Western imagination.

There are four halls in all and you might quickly tire of this one-sided account concerning the KGB and its predecessor. Except for a few photos, like the huge enlargement of the famous photo showing the soldiers casting down German flags in front of the Lenin Mausoleum in the third hall, you will see mostly copies of various documents, fake identity cards, and weapons allegedly taken from Western spies and Russian criminals. On display are a few personal belongings from Kim Philby, the KGB mole who managed to get inside British intelligence. You can also see the pistol and silencer supposedly taken from the American spy Gary Powers after his U-2 reconnaissance airplane was shot down over the USSR in 1960.

Additional Sites Near the KGB Museum

The 16th century building behind the KGB museum is the **Mansion of Count Rostopchin**, the governor of Moscow who ordered that the city be burned in 1812. According to Tolstoy's *War and Peace*, Muscovites mobbed his mansion to get the arms to fight Napoleon. The count escaped the mobs by throwing an alleged traitor over the balcony and thus saved his own skin. Once also a residence of the Dolgorukys, this same building was the KGB's first headquarters, and was in 1997 renovated for the offices of Inkombank.

Across the street from the KGB museum and behind the restaurant Angleterre, there is a statue of **Vaclav Vorovsky** on a square that bears his name, near Kuznetsky Most Street. Vorovsky was a professional revolutionary and political writer. He was assassinated in Lausanne, Switzerland, in 1923 and buried at the Kremlin Wall. A statue of him stands in the courtyard of the former Soviet Foreign Commissariat.

The only thing worth remembering about Vorovsky today is that he was the reason an old church was torn down. The **Church of the Presentation of the Blessed Virgin in the Temple** was the parish church of Prince Dmitry Pozharsky, an early 17th century hero who saved Russia from a Polish invasion. The prince placed the famous icon of the Kazan Virgin Mary (see the description of Red Square for more details) here, which he carried to Moscow after his victory over the Poles. This is the same icon that he later brought to Kazan Cathedral on Red Square.

After the Revolution, the Church of the Presentation was selected as the sight for the statue of Vorovsky because it was close to the Soviet Foreign Commissariat. This was the first church in Moscow destroyed by the Bolsheviks.

The former KGB building, **Lubyanka Prison**, which overlooks Lubyanka Square, was originally built for the Rossiya Insurance Company in 1906 and taken over by the Cheka in 1918. Among the many hapless victims interrogated here was Aleksandr Solzhenitsyn, who has well documented the excesses of the Cheka and the KGB.

Countless thousands of others have suffered in the recesses of this gray stone and marble trim fortress. The front of the building housed the Ministry of Internal Security. The prison building, with an iron gate, was in the rear. Since Lubyanka is on a hill the first floor becomes the basement in the rear and it is here that many of the cells were located. Walter Laqueur in his book *Stalin: The Glasnost Revelations* describes questioning during the Stalinist years as follows: "...The defendants were interrogated without interruption; they had to stand up and were not permitted to sleep. If this did not produce quick results, they were beaten, and bones were broken. They were not permitted to drink or were given very salty water or compelled to eat and drink excrement. They were kept in very hot or freezing rooms and knifed or burned on various parts of the body. There was an extensive instrumentarium of torture, and the interrogators learned from experience. A favorite gambit was to beat them on the mouth right at the start of the interrogation so that they lost a few teeth. If this did not work, more elaborate and painful methods were used."

According to the film director Andrey Konchalovsky, "In the late 1930's, as many as 1,000 people a day were shot in the Lubyanka." A former Gulag prisoner who has investigated Stalinist crimes for many years said that "on some nights as many as 150 trucks were brought to Lubyanka to cart the corpses away."

Today the building houses the Federal Counter-Intelligence Service, one of several splinter organizations of the old KGB. Cheka grew from an organization with 18 employees in 1918 Leningrad to more than 265,000 by 1922. In 1919, Lenin authorized the creation of the GULAG, a network of 80 forced labor camps that later held millions of often completely innocent people.

Russia has a long history of policing its people, starting with the delusional Ivan the Terrible (1533-1584), who in 1565 founded the **oprichnina**, a dreadful force of 6,000 licensed gangsters who sniffed for anything they suspected as treason. He was followed by Peter the Great (1672-1725), who had secret agents so deadly no one dared to utter a word against the tsar. After the assassination of Tsar Aleksandr II (1818-1881), spying took a new turn with the dreaded **okhrana** which had 10,000 agents that could arrest and imprison virtually anybody.

Detsky mir, a children's department store across the square from the KGB building, was once the site of a foundry where the huge bronze Tsar's Cannon, now inside the Kremlin, was cast.

MUSEUM OF LITERATURE

28 Ulitsa Petrovka at Petrovsky bulvar, Metro Pushkinskaya, then trolleybus #15 or #31. Tel. 925-1226, Fax 923-4175. Open daily from 11am to 6pm, closed Mondays. Small admission fee.

Centrally located north of the Kremlin, three blocks northeast of Pushkin Square and one block south of the Boulevard Ring Road.

If you really enjoy Russian literature, you will find this a gold mine of information, if not, you might get awfully bored. On display are exhibits related to the history of Russian and Soviet literature from the 18th century to the present.

We recommend this museum, founded in 1934, to those interested in Soviet-era writers, such as Maksim Gorky, Mikhail Sholokhov, Aleksey Tolstoy, Ilya Ehrenburg or Vladimir Mayakovsky, many of whom have been tainted by Communist ideology.

There are also rare books, original manuscripts, personal belongings of prominent writers, and plenty of photographs and paintings of poets and playwrights.

Take the dramatist Mayakovsky: after visiting the US in the early 1920's, he published *My Discovery of America* (in 1926) in which he claimed that America was seven years behind the Soviet Union. He was impressed by American technology but regretted what he believed to be a lack of human values in the US.

MAYAKOVSKY MUSEUM

3/6 Lubyansky proyezd at Lubyanka Square, Metro Lubyanka. Tel. 921-9560 or 9387. Open Tuesdays, Fridays and Saturdays, from 10am to 6pm; Mondays from noon to 6pm; Thursdays from 1pm to 9pm; closed Wednesdays, last Friday of the month. Small admission fee.

Centrally located northeast of the Kremlin, just east of Lubyanka Square, in a granite and marble building across the street from the former KGB prison.

Vladimir Mayakovsky (1894-1930) was regarded as the leader of the Russian avant-garde for some twenty years. He had been educated as a painter and was a contemporary of artists like painter Kazimir Malevich. Supposedly, he became a member of the Bolshevik party when only 15 years old.

During the 1917 Revolution, he emerged as the propaganda mouthpiece of the Bolsheviks, decrying bourgeois customs and advocating the overthrow of its aesthetic preferences. In his autobiography, he said about the 1917 uprising: "It was my Revolution." Mayakovsky, a revolutionary from the depths of his soul, died by shooting himself in the heart; some are of the opinion that he became disillusioned when Stalin came to power.

The room in which this futurist poet lived from 1919 to 1930, and the additional extraordinarily large spaces around it for such a secondary artist, opened as a museum in 1989; before that it was a youth hostel. It is recreated here as a futuristic multi-level panorama in true Mayakovsky spirit: revolutionary, unconventional, disdainful of classical art and religion. Documents, newspaper articles and objects of every description are attached to the surfaces, and are next to photographs of Mayakovsky and other revolutionary symbols. Also on display are the poet's manuscripts, paintings, posters, drawings, books and personal belongings.

On the fourth floor, you will find Mayakovsky's tiny original room, with a simple table, writing bureau, and a sofa where the driven poet took his life.

There is a monumental statue of Mayakovsky on Triumfalnaya ploshchad (1935-1991 the square was named after him), in front of

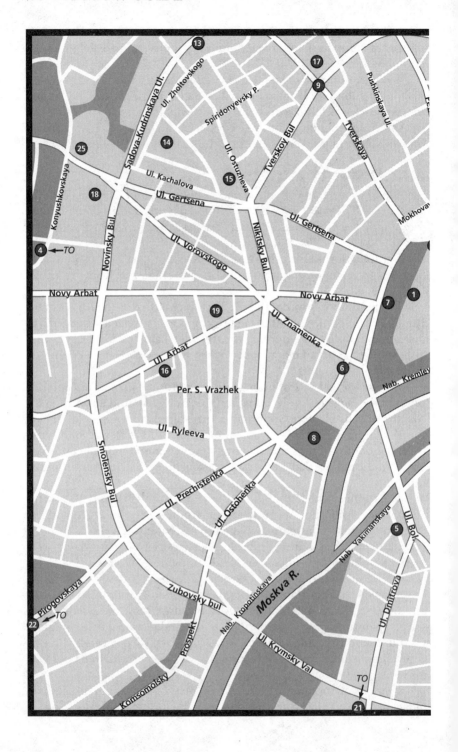

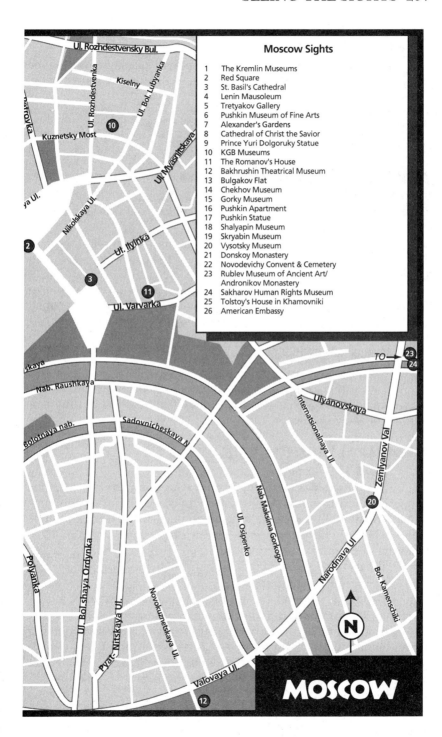

Moscow Sights

1 The Kremlin Museums
2 Red Square
3 St. Basil's Cathedral
4 Lenin Mausoleum
5 Tretyakov Gallery
6 Pushkin Museum of Fine Arts
7 Alexander's Gardens
8 Cathedral of Christ the Savior
9 Prince Yuri Dolgoruky Statue
10 KGB Museums
11 The Romanov's House
12 Bakhrushin Theatrical Museum
13 Bulgakov Flat
14 Chekhov Museum
15 Gorky Museum
16 Pushkin Apartment
17 Pushkin Statue
18 Shalyapin Museum
19 Skryabin Museum
20 Vysotsky Museum
21 Donskoy Monastery
22 Novodevichy Convent & Cemetery
23 Rublev Museum of Ancient Art/
    Andronikov Monastery
24 Sakharov Human Rights Museum
25 Tolstoy's House in Khamovniki
26 American Embassy

MOSCOW

Tchaikovsky Concert Hall, which was created by Aleksandr Kibalnikov and unveiled in 1954, 28 years after his death.

The square is still used for outdoor poetry readings, such as the echoes of this impatient Mayakovsky shout to the Red Guard:

You pinned the Whites to the walls and killed them,
But why forget Raphael?–
Fire, fire, in the museums!
Why don't you pounce upon Pushkin?

MUSEUM OF MOSCOW HISTORY

12 Novaya ploshchad, Metro Lubyanka or Kitay-gorod. Tel. 924-8490. Open daily from noon to 6pm, Wednesdays and Fridays from noon to 7pm, closed Mondays. Small admission fee.

Centrally located northeast of the Kremlin, south of Lubyanka Square, and across the street from the Polytechnical Museum. Entrance is from the courtyard.

This museum was founded in 1896 and transferred to its present location in 1954 when it took over the premises of the **Church of St. John the Divine**, which was closed by the Bolsheviks in 1925. One of the two large halls downstairs features a permanent exhibit about the history of Moscow since medieval times. The second holds interesting temporary exhibitions, often displaying photographs of Moscow that will startle you.

The museum is supposed to vacate the former church, which was originally built in stone in 1658 and rebuilt in 1825-37, but the new location is not yet known.

MUNICIPAL COUNCIL BUILDING

3/2 Ploshchad Revolutsiyi, Metro Ploshchad Revolutsiyi.

Centrally located between the Historical Museum, the Moskva Hotel and GUM Department Stores, just off Red Square.

Erected in 1882, the Lenin Museum occupied this red-brick building from 1936 until the attempted overthrow of the government in 1991, when the museum lost its funding. The building originally housed the pre-Revolutionary city **duma**, or municipal council. In the 15th century there was a tsar's private zoo in this area.

The museum featured Lenin's propaganda in 34 exhibition halls, displaying his manuscripts and other documents, personal belongings and gifts, including his decidedly capitalistic toy, the Rolls-Royce Silver Ghost limousine, which the People's Commissar Krasin bought in England in the early 1920's. The Rolls was later moved to the second floor of the Historical Museum next door through a window with a specially constructed lift.

There were other temporary exhibitions here in the past, from paintings dedicated to the poet Aleksandr Pushkin to landscapes exhibited by the Portuguese Embassy.

In October 1993, two days after government forces won control of the **Russian White House** in bloody battles with the hard-line Parliament that took some 190 lives, the Moscow mayor announced that the Lenin Museum building was being returned to its old function as the headquarters of the Moscow City Council, but nothing came of it.

To this very day, you can still see scores of Communists and nationalists, along with their sympathizers and detractors, arguing their points of view under the portico of the building and at its corner, near the metro station. They also sell their publications, pins and other paraphernalia.

ORIENTAL ARTS MUSEUM

12a Nikitsky bulvar, Metro Arbatskaya. Tel. 291-9614. Open daily from 11am to 8pm, closed Mondays. Small admission fee.

Located northwest of the Kremlin, on the east side of the Boulevard Ring Road, one very long block north of Novy Arbat. The U Nikitskih Vorot Theater is just a few doors farther north.

This museum is also known as the Museum of the Arts of Eastern People. There is a permanent exposition of the arts of Central and Southeast Asia, China, Japan and India and an extensive collection of clothes, arms, jewelry, rugs, utensils, wood and ivory carvings, dolls, pottery and decorative plates.

There is an art shop next door to the museum, but the pickings are average.

Designed by the Italian architect Domenico Gilardi, this is an imposing mansion on Nikitsky bulvar. It belonged to the Lunins, a rich noble family. One of them, Mikhail Lunin, participated in the Decembrist uprising of 1825, an attempt to overthrow a repressive autocracy, and was exiled to Siberia.

Additional Sights Near the Oriental Arts Museum

A bit farther northeast and on the other side of the street, behind the Burger Queen fast food restaurant, is the **Church of St. Theodore Studitus**, where field marshal Aleksandr Suvorov (1729-1800) was baptized. He lead the Russian army across the snow-covered Alps during the Italian campaign in 1799. In the Soviet period, Nikitsky Boulevard was named Suvorovsky and a 30-foot statue was unveiled in his honor in 1982 on the square near Frunze Park, north of the Kremlin. Born in Moscow, the same year as Catherine the Great, Suvorov gained fame over a span of 50 years when he led forces in two dozen military expeditions and won every one of the more than 60 battles under his command.

In 1773, aged 44, Suvorov married on orders from his father (whom he never disobeyed): his one and only defeat. The bride was 20 years younger, tall and stately, and his father's choice. The groom was a short, sickly man who forgot all his tactics when it came to women. When he discovered his wife's adulterous affair, he drove her out of the house and even the empress could not reconcile them.

OSTROVSKY MUSEUM

14 Ulitsa Tverskaya at Kozitsky pereulok, Metro Tverskaya, Pushkinskaya or Chekhovskaya. Tel. 229-8552 or 209-3790. Open Wednesdays and Fridays, from noon to 8pm; Saturdays from noon to 7pm; Sundays from 10am to 5:30pm; closed Mondays and last Friday of each month. Small admission fee.

Centrally located on the south side of the Boulevard Ring Road, south of Pushkin Square and north of the Konyonkov Studio-Museum, on the other side of Tverskaya Street.

This museum is dedicated to the dramatist **Nikolay Ostrovsky** (1904-1936) who was born in Moscow. (Not to be confused with the classical dramatist of world renown Aleksandr Nikolayevich Ostrovsky.) Nikolay Ostrovsky became a Young Communist at 14 and a member of the Communist Party at 20.

After the Revolution, he suffered from polio and by 1929 was completely blind and partially paralyzed. He dictated several novels in this condition and one, *How the Steel was Tempered*, sold more than 20 million copies in 18 languages. It was published in English as *The Making of a Hero* in 1937.

A cartoon on dispaly will remind American visitors that in 1957 the House Un-American Activities Committee of the US Congress suggested that *How the Steel was Tempered* was just unworthy Communist propaganda. This book was already banned in France.

POLYTECHNICAL MUSEUM

3/4 Novaya ploshchad, metro Kitay-gorod or Lubyanka. Tel. 923-0756 or 925-0614, Fax 925-1290. Open daily from 10am to 5:30pm, closed Mondays and last Thursday of the month. Small admission fee.

Located northeast of the Kremlin, southeast of Lubyanka Square, and across the street from the Museum of Moscow History.

This is the largest Russian museum devoted to the history of science and engineering; it receives more than a million visitors every year. It originally opened in 1872 on Prechistenka Street and the construction of its current site began two years later. Its eleven major departments are devoted to physics, chemistry, machine building, power engineering, computer technology and other sciences and branches of engineering.

The 80 halls of the Polytechnical Museum contain more than 140,000 exhibits, including Russia's largest collection of microscopes and one of the largest collections in the world of cameras, sewing machines, typewriters, watches, motorcycles and bicycles. You can see Russia's first motor vehicle, made in Riga, as well as the bullet-proof ZIS-110 limousine taken from Stalin's garage.

The father of Russian science Mikhail Lomonosov, serf artisan Cherepanov who constructed the steam engine, and chemist Lebedev who worked out a formula for the first synthetic rubber, are all recognized here. There is a hall at the museum where lectures are delivered by scientists and designers. In the past, vast audiences gathered here to hear the naturalist Kliment Timiryazev lecture on plant life, Zhukovsky speak about aeronautics and Stoletov talk of physics. Yablochkov showed the first electric lamp here, known as the Russian Candle.

RERIKH MUSEUM

3/5 Maly Znamensky pereulok, Metro Borovitskaya or Kropotkinskaya. Tel. 203-6419. Open daily from 10am to 5pm, closed Mondays. Small admission fee.

Centrally located southwest of the Kremlin and north of the Cathedral of Christ the Savior. Walk between the Pushkin Museum and the Museum of Private Collections to the last yellow building on the left, to reach the museum.

On display are exhibits from India by Nikolay and Yelena Rerikh, also known under the surname of Roerich. Paintings, archive materials, documents and photographs illustrate Rerikh's life.

Nikolay Rerikh (1874-1947) was a painter, graphic artist, theater designer, scholar, archeologist and mystic. His early preoccupation with the themes of a mythical ancient Russia led to his interest in folk art. Born in St. Petersburg, he studied law, then painting at the Academie.

In 1919, Rerikh met Bengali poet Rabindranath Tagore in London, who sparked his interest in India and the Himalayas. He toured America from 1920 to 1923 on the invitation of the Chicago Art Institute, and founded the **Nicholas Roerich Museum** in New York (more below). The following two years, he undertook a journey to India and began devoting ever more time to his interest in anthropology, archeology and esoteric religions. Rerikh returned to Moscow in 1926, then left for Mongolia and Tibet, and from 1928 on directed a research station in the Himalayas. He participated at an exhibition of contemporary Russian art in Philadelphia in 1932. The Communists tried to recruit him to do a little spying overseas on their behalf, but the evidence so far is inconclusive as to whether he compromised himself.

Rerikh created more than 7,000 paintings, some of which you can see at the **Museum of Oriental Art** and at **Tretyakov Gallery**. The Victoria and Albert Museum in London, the Louvre, and Stockholm's National Museum also have Rerikh's works on exhibit. Rerikh wrote nearly thirty books. As an explorer and scientist, he carried out extensive archeological research and excavations in Russia and the Orient. His theater designs can be seen at the **Bakhrushin Theatrical Museum** (see below). Between 1907 and 1922, he created designs for the works of Wagner, Rimsky-Korsakov, Borodin, Ibsen, and Mussorgsky.

On May 28 1913, Stravinsky's *Rite of Spring* (Sacre du Printemps) was inaugurated at the Theatre des Champs-Elysees by Diaghilev and his Russian Ballet on a libretto by Stravinsky and Rerikh. Among the listeners insults flew, some whistled or shouted. When the lights came on, the audience was in uproar that has not been forgotten to this day.

In the US, there's a Roerich Museum in a former townhouse off Riverside Drive, *319 West 107th Street, New York, New York, 10025, Tel. 212/864-7752*. On display are about 100 of his paintings, among them Himalayan, Tibetan, and Indian mountain scenes.

THE ROMANOV'S HOUSE
Palaty V Zaryadye
10 Ulitsa Varvarka, Metro Kitay-gorod. Tel. 298-3706. Open daily from 10am to 6pm; Wednesdays 11am to 5pm; closed Tuesdays and first Monday of the month. Admission fee.

Centrally located just east of the Kremlin and Red Square and north of Hotel Rossiya on what is probably the oldest street in Moscow and the old trade route to Vladimir.

For many years before the 1917 Revolution, Varvarka was a street filled with restaurants, stores and candle-lit churches. In 1671, rebel leader Stepan Razin was led to his execution along street, then named St. Barbara Street. The street was named after him in Soviet times.

This museum displays furniture, clothing and utensils, and shows the daily life of nobles in Zaryadye (an area of the Kitay-gorod behind the shopping stalls of what is now Red Square) during the 17th and 18th centuries. Late 15th century pottery and archaeological finds related to the history of Zaryadye are also on display.

This was once the residence of the first Romanov tsar's parents and home of a Moscow **boyar** (medieval Russian nobleman in the service of the tsar) which includes the study of the master, the dining room, the girls' room, and furnishings dating from 1642. The chambers are among the oldest stone buildings in Moscow. Erected in the 16th century, they formed part of an urban estate of the Romanov boyars. The only part that has survived in its original form, despite alterations, fires and destruction, is the 16th century basement. The building has been a museum since 1859.

Additional Sights Near the Romanov's House

If you walk from Red Square or St. Basil's Cathedral to Varvarka Street, you will pass the **Church of St. Barbara** on your right, which was rebuilt from 1796 to 1801. Behind it, closer to the Rossiya Hotel, is the **English House**, a building dating back to 1556 with a steep wooden roof that Ivan the Terrible gave to English merchants and diplomatic envoys. Queen Elizabeth II visited the house in 1994. Across the street is the **Gostiny Dvor**, or Merchant Arcade, built in the late 1700's and now under reconstruction.

Farther on is the **Church of Maximus the Blessed**, *4 Varvarka Street*, built by merchants from Novgorod in 1698-99. Behind it, at number 8a, stands the **Monastery of the Sign**, erected on the estate of the Romanovs in 1634; its cathedral was converted into a concert hall during the Soviet times. After the above-mentioned House stands the **Church of St. George**, *12 Varvarka*, built in 1657 by merchants from Pskov.

Should you walk across the street from here and continue one block north on Ipatyevsky pereulok and turn right, before you stands the asymmetrical red brick and white stone **Church of the Holy Trinity in Nikitniki** on the lane of the same name. (The church is also just a couple of blocks northwest of Kitay-gorod's southern metro station.) If you want to look inside, it is open daily from 10am to 5:30pm, but closed on Tuesdays, *Tel. 298-3451.* The exhibits shown in this museum, which was built in 1634 by the second wealthiest merchant in Moscow, Grigory Nikitnikov, include icons painted by the well-known 17th century artist Simon Ushakov and his contemporaries.

SHCHUSEV ARCHITECTURAL MUSEUM

5 Ulitsa Vozdvizhenka at Starovagankovsky pereulok, Metro Aleksandrovsky sad, Borovitskaya or Arbatskaya. Tel. 291-2109. Open daily from 10am to 6pm, closed Mondays. Small admission fee.

Centrally located just three blocks west of the Kremlin, across the street from the Russian State Library, and one block south of Timiryazev House, home of a well-known agricultural biologist.

This museum is named after the Russian architect **Aleksey Shchusev** (1873-1949), who designed more than 150 projects, including all three versions of the **Lenin Mausoleum** on Red Square and **Moskva**, the first Soviet-built hotel in Moscow after the Revolution. He was well established before the Bolsheviks took over and easily moved from the neo-classicism of the 1910's to the Socialist Realism of Stalin's 1930's. He incorporated these styles from 1912 to 1940, when designing the vast **Kazan Railway Station** in northeast Moscow.

A painter by training and archaeologist by avocation, Shchusev had carved out a brilliant career for himself before 1917, restoring ancient

Russian cathedrals and designing lordly residences. He set out single-mindedly to adapt to political changes and the new regime received him with open arms. Eminently flexible, he lived until he reached old age at 76. "Shchusev's early work scarcely commands attention today except that it seems to foreshadow the worst features of the Stalinist rococo," wrote S. Frederick Starr, a noted critic. Shchusev was director of the Tretyakov Gallery from 1926 to 1929 and received four Stalin Prizes.

The exhibits feature the history of Russian and Soviet architecture from the 17th to 19th centuries, including photographs, models, original plans and sketches illustrating the old Russian architecture of Novgorod and Vladimir. Additional sketches include the churches and palaces of the Kremlin and other neighborhoods of Moscow.

This mansion was built in 1787 for the courtier and officer Aleksandr Talyzin, who gave Empress Catherine his uniform to wear when she rode out secretly to take the throne from her husband, Peter III. One part of it became the architectural museum in 1945 and was under reconstruction in 1996.

STATE HISTORICAL MUSEUM

1/2 Red Square, Metro Ploshchad Revolutsiyi. Tel. 928-8452. Open daily from 10am to 6pm, Wednesdays and Fridays 11am to 7pm; closed Tuesdays and last Monday of each month. Small admission fee.

Centrally located between the former Lenin Museum and Aleksandrovsky Gardens, just off Red Square.

The dark red State Historical Museum is the largest depository of documents and cultural monuments related to the history of the Russian people. Opened in 1883 on the spot where the original Moscow University was founded in 1755 by the Russian scientist Mikhail Lomonosov, it is one of Moscow's oldest museums. Its inauguration coincided with the coronation of its patron, Tsar Aleksandr III. The museum traces the origins of Russia back to the stone age, although the terms B.C. and A.D. were not used until the Communist collapse.

More than 30,000 works of pictorial and applied arts, jewelry and national costumes are held here. The museum's collection of old Russian icons is one of the largest in the country; it also holds more than 300,000 paintings, drawings and posters. There are 20,000 ancient weapons. Thousands of Old Russian and Western coins, medals and maps going back to the 16th century can also be found. More than 36,000 ceramic items and countless thousands of antique books are stored at the museum. Its furniture exhibits go back to 16th century. A robe worn by Ivan the Terrible, a map of Russia drawn by the son of Boris Godunov, Napoleon's sabre, a clay vase used for storing rain in the second century

B.C., and the cage in which Yemelyan Pugachev, the peasant leader who rebelled against Catherine the Great, was brought to Moscow to be executed, are the kind of exhibits you will find here when the museum is open. Painted from white to red by the Bolsheviks and in disrepair for almost a hundred years, the museum is undergoing an agonizingly slow reconstruction. Hundreds of thousands of objects are shut in crates and some Western Europeans have a better chance of seeing its treasures than Muscovites because foreign museums are paying for the privilege in hard currency.

YERMOLOVA THEATER SALON

11 Tverskoy bulvar, Metro Pushkinskaya or Arbatskaya. Tel. 290-0215 or 5580. Open daily from noon to 6pm, closed Tuesdays and last Monday of each month. Small admission fee.

Located northwest of the Kremlin, on the Boulevard Ring Road - Tverskoy bulvar - the oldest Moscow boulevard; also on the western edge of the theater district, one block southwest from the Pushkin Drama Theater and on the same block as Na Maloy Bronnoy Theater. The newly-unveiled statue of the dissolute poet Sergey Yesenin, briefly husband to dancer Isadora Duncan, is across the boulevard.

Mariya Yermolova (1853-1928), perhaps the greatest Russian theater actress, excelled equally in Friedrich Johann Christoph von Schiller's *Maid of Orleans* as Joan of Arc as in Aleksandr Ostrovsky's Russian plays. All her performances took place in her favorite Maly Theater, where she performed for more than 50 years. She started her career at age 16, when she stood in for another actress who was ill. Yermolova was as popular in Russia as Sarah Bernhardt was in the West.

Her house is one of the very few 18th century buildings that survived the great fires of 1812, during the Napoleonic invasion of Moscow. Yermolova lived here with her husband, a lawyer who later fled into exile, and their daughter. Fyodor Shalyapin, the renowned operatic basso, often visited and sang here. As in several other Moscow salons, you will find paintings and sketches by Boris Pasternak's father, Leonid. After the 1917 Revolution, the actress gave up the first two floors of her house and kept for herself only a couple of rooms on the third floor, where she died in the bed that you can still see. Most of the furniture on this floor is authentic. In all, she spent 39 years of her life in this building, which was converted into a three-floor museum in 1986. After Yermolova's death in 1928, her daughter continued to live on the upper floor.

Yermolova Drama Theater, named after her, is located at 5 Tverskaya Street, between the Intourist Hotel and Central Telegraph Office. After

STALIN'S WEDDING CAKES

In 1947, Stalin decided to decorate Moscow with eight skyrises positioned around one of the buildings, the megalomaniac Palace of the Soviets (the site of today's Christ the Church cathedral). Stalin ordered them built to showcase the Soviet Union's architectural abilities. Fortunately for posterity, the Palace was never realized because of a sinking foundation, but the other seven buildings did materialize. These seven Gothic buildings are jokingly referred to as Stalin's wedding cakes, and are mostly located around the Garden Ring Road. They are also sometimes called the Seven Sisters.

Although considered downright ugly by many, these massive stone monsters do provide one useful service to visitors: they are beacons in Moscow's often unnavigable maze of streets. Except for the two hotels, it is unlikely that you will be able to see these eyesores from the inside. Fret not; there are plenty of more interesting sites.

Hotel Leningradskaya, 21/40 Ulitsa Kalanchevskaya, Metro Komsomolskaya. Located north of the Kremlin, just east of the Kazansky and southeast of Leningradsky and Yaroslavsky railway stations.

Hotel Ukraina, 2/1 Kutuzovsky Avenue, Metro Kievskaya. Located west of the Kremlin, north of Kievsky railway station, and across the Moskva River from the Russian White House.

Moscow State University, Sparrow Hills, Metro Universitet. Located southwest of the Kremlin and southwest of the Luzhniki Sports Complex. Entry is restricted to students.

Ministry of Foreign Affairs, 32/34 Smolenskaya-Sennaya Square, Metro Smolenskaya. Located southwest of the Kremlin and across the street from the Pushkin Museum. Entrance is restricted to those on official business.

Ministry of Transportation, 2 Ulitsa Novaya Basmannaya, Metro Krasniye vorota. Located south of Leningradsky and southwest of Kazansky railway stations, near the Hotel Leningradskaya. Restricted entrance.

Kudrinskaya Square Apartments, Novinsky Boulevard, Metro Barrikadnaya. Located one block north of the American Embassy and next to the Moscow Zoo and the Planetarium. There is a Western-style supermarket on the ground floor, but visitors are not welcomed to explore the rest of the building.

1/15 Kotelnicheskaya Embankment Apartments. Located near the Library of Foreign Literature, northwest of the metro station Taganskaya. There is a movie theater in this building, the Cinema Illyuzion, but it's not likely that you will be able to see the inside of this building for privileged.

the Soviets established themselves, Yermolova became the first person in 1920 to be awarded the title of People's Artist by Lenin.

After you visit the Yermolova Salon, you can get a bite to eat at the moderately-priced Junk Boat, the Chinese restaurant in the basement of the Moscow Art Theater (Gorky), also known by its Russian acronym MKhAT, one long block northeast of here, at 22 Tverskoy Boulevard. The menu is ten pages long and the most expensive item is Peking Duck at $40.

SIGHTS BETWEEN THE BOULEVARD & GARDEN RING ROADS

Revolutionary museums, more than other kinds of museums, should be considered with some skepticism, particularly if you are pressed for time. While many Muscovites consider them part of their history, to Westerners they are but former tombs of Communist propaganda that many Russians have yet to put in proper perspective. The simplest way to say it would be: if in doubt leave it out.

BAKHRUSHIN THEATRICAL MUSEUM

31/12 Ulitsa Bakhrushina, Metro Paveletskaya. Tel. 233-4470 or 5390. Open Monday, Thursday, Saturday and Sunday, from noon to 7pm; Wednesday & Friday, from 1pm to 8pm; closed Tuesdays and last Monday of the month. Small admission fee.

Located southeast of the Kremlin, in Zamoskvorechye, on the corner of Bakhrushina Street and the Garden Ring Road, opposite the Paveletsky Railway Station, one block east of the northern Paveletskaya metro station, and one block west from Stockmann's Finnish supermarket.

Named after the theater lover **Aleksey Bakhrushin** (1865-1929), the museum was founded in 1895 in the house where Bakhrushin lived from 1898 until his death. Bakhrushin was a hereditary honorary citizen of Moscow who was born into a merchant family of art patrons. In 1913, Bakhrushin donated the museum and the estate on which it stood to the city of Moscow. Aleksey and Vasily Bakhrushin were more then just two rich Muscovites, they gave the city a hospital for the chronically ill, an asylum for the incurably ill, an orphanage, two buildings of free apartments, and two trade schools.

This is one of the best museums of its kind in Russia and will acquaint you with the history of Russian and Soviet drama, opera and ballet from the 18th century to the present. Among the 1.5 million articles in the collection only a small part can be displayed since the authorities took away a large part of the estate in the 1930's. On exhibit are sets and costume designs, photographs and other documents such as **Vaslav Nijinsky**'s ballet shoes and the costumes worn by classical bass singer **Fyodor Shalyapin**, who has his own museum next door to the American embassy.

The Jewish restaurant U Yuzefa is nearby if you're looking for a place to eat (see Chapter 12, *Where to Eat* for more information).

BULGAKOV FLAT

10 Ulitsa Bolshaya Sadovaya at Triumfalnaya ploshchad, Metro Mayakovskaya. Open randomly and irregularly.

Located northwest of the Kremlin, on the Garden Ring Road, next to the Aquarium Gardens.

If you proceed in a southeasterly direction on the Garden Ring Road, starting from the Tchaikovsky Concert Hall, you will pass the Satira Theater, the Gardens, and a row of kiosks on your left before you reach the house, whose entrance leads into a courtyard. The bas-relief plaque on the front of the building, facing the Garden Ring, was ripped out by Communist sympathizers during the attempted coup d'etat in 1993, but you can still see where it was attached to honor one of the most popular Russian writers ever.

The courtyard is just as dirty as the fictional one described in **Mikhail Bulgakov's** satirical masterpiece *The Master and Margarita*, written in secrecy between 1928 and 1940, and published in a censored edition only in 1966 by his third wife. The novel is a masterpiece of politcal satire, featuring a visit to Moscow by the Devil himself and involving all sorts of extremely clever digs at Stalinism, power, authority, and human nature.

Built in 1910, this was once a fashionable house that belonged to three Moscow artists. There was at one time a bohemian cafe, **Stables of Pegasus**, in the basement, where the dissolute Russian poet Sergey Yesenin (1895-1925) met his future wife, dancer Isadora Duncan (1878-1927). Ms. Duncan, on the invitation of the Soviets, opened a dance school at an unheated house at 20 Prechistenka Street in 1922.

Bulgakov's flat, #50, is the one on the left on the top floor. From the outside, it is the second window to the left of the drain pipe. Enter through the second stairway on your left and you will immediately recognize the interior, which is painted over from floor to the ceiling with graffiti messages and drawings that deal with Bulgakov's fictional characters. Perhaps the only similar sight you will encounter in Moscow is the outdoor **Tsoy Memorial Wall** (see Old Arbat Street in Chapter 17, *Shopping*) on Stary Arbat at Krivoarbatsky Lane, honoring the rock musician Viktor Tsoy.

Almost any time of the day or night, you might encounter a few rebellious youths who will want to practice their high school English on you by asking you where you are from. The residents of the house have been putting up with this inconvenience since the early 1960's when the house acquired such mythological proportions and its interiors were regularly whitewashed by the authorities. They are outright hostile to all outsiders and aren't likely to look at or speak to you. Unfortunately, the house, which during the Soviet years housed several offices, is also a place of worship for Moscow satanists. Just to be on the safe side, we do not recommend that you visit after sundown.

Mikhail Bulgakov (1891-1940) was born in Kiev and, after completing his medical studies, came to Moscow in 1921. While working in the literary department of the Ministry of Culture he wrote, in this apartment, the novel, *The White Guard*, arguably the best Russian account of the Civil War. Adapted for the stage in 1926 as *The Days of the Turbines*, it must have struck a chord with Stalin, for the carnivorous tyrant saw its performance no fewer than 16 times.

Unhappy with the amount of living space he had been allocated, the satirist petitioned Lenin's wife Nadezhda Krupskaya and, in typically absurd Soviet fashion, received one more room, #34, in a separate building opposite his original room. The writer lived here for almost five years. He died of hereditary nephritis in a large apartment house overlooking the courtyard at 6 Gagarinsky pereulok, diagonally across that lane from what is today the Imperial restaurant. As soon as he was dead, his wife was thrown out of the apartment and moved to a room on Nikitsky Boulevard.

While there was an ad hoc Bulgakov museum here for a couple of years, a fire in 1994 consumed several of Bulgakov's few remaining possessions, and the flat is open only intermittently.

Nearby restaurants include the Starlite Diner, American Bar & Grill, Tandoor and Kombi's (see Chapter 12, *Where to Eat* for more information).

CHEKHOV MUSEUM

6 Ulitsa Sadovaya-Kudrinskaya, Metro Barrikadnaya or Krasnopresnenskaya. Tel. 291-6154, Fax 975-2196. Open daily from 11am to 6pm; Wednesdays and Fridays, 2pm to 6pm; closed Mondays and last day of the month. Small admission fee.

Located northwest of the Kremlin, on the smoggy and congested Garden Ring Road, three typically long Moscow blocks northeast from the American Embassy, and two just as long blocks south of the American Express office. The Planetarium is on the other side of the Garden Ring Road.

Anton Chekhov, the author of such theatrical successes as *The Cherry Orchard*, *The Seagull*, *The Three Sisters*, and *Uncle Vanya* lived in this house from August 1886 to 1890. During this time he abandoned medicine and became a writer. In two months, he wrote his play *Ivanov* here. The museum opened in 1954, the 50th anniversary of the writer's death.

When Chekhov stayed here with his family, the house was known as the Korneyev House, after the doctor who had rented it to his young colleague. At 650 rubles a year it was expensive, but conveniently central. This modest two-story house, built in 1874, was painted red and stood out from the other houses in the neighborhood. Dr. Chekhov had two large rooms and a study on the ground floor where he received his patients (from noon until 3pm). Upstairs is the sitting room where he entertained his friends, such as the composer Tchaikovsky, the painter Isaak Levitan, and the architect Fyodor Shekhtel. In addition to this room upstairs, were the rooms of his parents and his sister, who was in love with the painter Levitan.

You'll find Chekhov's 1908 bust by sculptor **Konyonkov** in the lobby. His writing desk can still be seen, along with many original items displayed on it. You will also find photographs of scenes from his plays.

After spending his first 19 years in the southern Russian port town of Taganrog, where he was born, Chekhov arrived in Moscow, where, between 1877 and 1904, he changed his residence no fewer than 14 times. At first he was enchanted with the city. "I'm terribly in love with Moscow," he wrote after only a few months. He also said "I'm a Muscovite once and for all." Later he insisted on moving to the country, only to return at the end of his life to his beloved Moscow.

GERTSEN MUSEUM

27 Sivtsev Vrazhek pereulok at Maly Vasilyevsky pereulok, Metro Smolenskaya or Kropotkinskaya. Tel. 241-5859. Open daily from 11am to 6pm; Wednesdays and Fridays, from 2-7 pm; closed Mondays. Small admission fee.

Located west of the Kremlin, on a quiet street two blocks south of Stary Arbat and three blocks east of the Ministry of Foreign Affairs.

This museum is named after the Russian political thinker, agitator and writer **Aleksandr Gertsen** (also spelled as Herzen), who was born in Moscow in 1812, the year Napoleon invaded Russia. The illegitimate son of a Russian nobleman and his German governess, he was exiled to the provinces for his socialist ideas from 1834 to 1842. Gertsen left Russia for good in 1847, first for Paris, then in 1851 he settled in London. But after the 1848 revolutions, he became disillusioned with the West and became a hardened Socialist revolutionary and a powerful propagandist. He died in Paris in 1870, the year Lenin was born.

In this house, Gertsen courted his cousin Nataliya, who after their marriage fell in love with a German poet. Their marriage was further strained by the birth of a deaf-mute son, who drowned with his grandmother in a shipwreck near Nice, France. Gertsen's wife took this as god's punishment for her sinful desires and died of a nervous breakdown. Surprised at finding out, after his wife's death, that the wife of his friend Nikolay Ogarev had been passionately in love with him for years, Gertsen eventually married her.

The museum, which opened in 1976, is located in the house where the Gertsens lived from 1843 to 1846, after his second exile to Novgorod. Sparsely furnished, it displays portraits, documents, prints and publications documenting his work. Also on display is a little glove, all that was left behind by their son after he drowned.

A bust of Gertsen can be seen in the courtyard of the **Yakovlev Mansion**, where he was born; see the Pushkin Theater in Chapter 14, *Culture* for more details.

Additional Sights Near the Gertsen Museum

The Nobel Prize winner, novelist Boris Pasternak, set Gromeko House from *Dr. Zhivago* on Sivtsev Vrazhek Lane. Nearby, at 34 Sivtsev Vrazhek, the 22-year-old **Lev Tolstoy** took an apartment in 1850 and began to write in earnest. Poet **Marina Tsvetayeva** lived at number 19 after her marriage in 1911. Writer **Sergey Aksakov** lived at number 30.

GORKY MUSEUM

6/2 Ulitsa Malaya Nikitskaya at Ulitsa Spiridonovka, Metro Arbatskaya. Actual entrance is from Spiridonovka Street. Tel. 290-0535 or 3262. Open Wednesdays and Fridays, from noon to 7pm; Thursdays, Saturdays and Sundays, from 10am to 5:30pm; closed Mondays and Tuesdays. Small admission fee.

Located in the embassy section of western central Moscow, about two blocks northwest of U Nikitskih Vorot Theater and next door to the Aleksey Tolstoy Museum.

It seems ironic that the Gorky Museum is housed in a splendid art-nouveau style mansion that the Bolsheviks stole from Stepan Ryabushinsky, chairman of the Stock Exchange. Ryabushinsky was a discriminating collector of icons, and a patron of the arts, who fled Russia after the Revolution. **Maxim Gorky**, after all, was supposed to be the proletarian hack of the common man and, one presumes, lived like one. But the father of Social Realism seems to have enjoyed creature comforts more than once; in 1921, after conflicts with the Bolsheviks, he left the country and lived in exile on the island of Capri, the Italian playground of the rich. Before and after his Italian escapade, Gorky was a mouthpiece for the carnivorous Stalinist regime whose darkest tales are yet to be told.

The house is one of about 50 buildings designed by the Saratov-born architect **Fyodor Shekhtel** (1859-1926), who came to Moscow as a teenager. His mother served as a housekeeper to the family of art collector Pavel Tretyakov. His friendship with the playwright Chekhov stirred his fascination with theater design and interrupted the completion of his studies at Moscow Architectural School after his first year. In 1902, Shekhtel designed Moscow's **Yaroslavsky Railway Station**. The architect always said that he loved Moscow as a man loves woman. After the 1917 Revolution, his architectural style was rejected as bourgeois, in part because he was a member of the Old Believers sect, and the architect whose work parallels that of Frank Lloyd Wright died sick and destitute at age 67.

The two-story mansion, which was commissioned not only as a home, but also as the setting for his icon collection, represents Shekhtel's best residential work. A startling limestone staircase in the shape of a wave leads to the second floor, splendid oak wood doorways and large windows, all different, can be admired throughout the house, and its ornamental ceiling and stained glass add to its timeless beauty. This work of art became Gorky's residence in 1931, upon his return to Russia, and remained his refuge, complete with 12,000 books, until his death in 1936. Some suspect that he was poisoned on Stalin's orders.

The mansion became a museum in 1965, although members of the Gorky family lived here until 1971. Ryabushinsky, also an Old Believer, had a secret mosaic-lined chapel built up under the eaves of the house, but you are not likely to see it because it is still off limits to the visitors. The Malaya Nikitskaya Street entrance has been closed off since Gorky became too ill to receive all the visitors who came banging on the front door and remains shut to this day. In his study, Gorky kept a copy of Leonardo da Vinci's *Madonna*.

Immediately after 1917, this building served as the Ministry of Foreign Affairs' visa department. Stalin's son Vassily also worked here after Gorky's death.

Additional Sights Near the Gorky Museum

Next to his mansion, Ryabushinsky built other buildings for his servants, including stables and a carriage house. From 1941 until his death, Count **Aleksey Tolstoy** (1882-1945) lived in this adjacent building; he was a minor writer and a distant relative of Lev Tolstoy. A White Emigre, he returned to Russia in 1923, and became such a popular scribe he was awarded the Stalin Prize. His flat, a museum since 1987, is decorated in the bourgeois style, complete with a salon and a tapestry of Peter the Great crowning Catherine I. Next door is a statue of poet **Aleksandr Blok** (1880-1921), who also lived around here for a time.

The **Aleksey Tolstoy Museum**, *Tel. 290-0956*, is open Thursdays, Saturdays and Sundays, from 11am to 6pm; Wednesdays and Fridays, from 1pm to 6pm; and is closed Mondays and Tuesdays.

Across the street from the Gorky Museum stands Osip Bove's **Church of Big Ascension**. It's a bit decrepit, but is gradually being renovated. The original construction dragged on for several decades, until 1840, because of Napoleon's invasion of Russia. It is well-known today because the poet Aleksandr Pushkin married, in 1831, his stunningly beautiful wife, Nataliya Goncharova, here. The Goncharovs, an impoverished noble family, had their mansion nearby, contributed to the church's construction, and insisted that the marriage take place here. Six years later the poet of Russia was killed in a duel due to a fit of jealousy.

The most feared Soviet, **Lavrenty Beria**, once lived at 28 Malaya Nikitskaya Street, where the Tunisian embassy is housed today. In 1993, a mass grave was uncovered in the basement of the mansion, where Beria lived from the mid-1930's until his death in 1953. Workers unearthed piles of human bones, covered by lime and chlorine; these bones are now thought to be the grisly remains of Beria's victims. He was rumored to have maintained a private prison in the basement. Mild-mannered but so vicious that he was nicknamed the "Himmler of Russia," Beria was suspected for years of kidnapping young women off the streets, raping and sometimes murdering them. This was confirmed by a few survivors who have come forth. After Stalin's death, the Georgian was denounced as "a thrice-accursed Judas," and was shot after a brief "treason" trial.

For information about nearby restaurants, Gambrinus, Panda or U Nikitskih Vorot, please see Chapter 12, *Where to Eat*.

GORKY MUSEUM OF LITERATURE

25a Ulitsa Povarskaya, near Borisoglebsky pereulok, Metro Barrikadnaya or Krasnopresnenskaya. Tel. 290-5130. Open Wednesdays and Fridays, from noon to 8pm; Thursdays, Saturdays and Sundays, from 10am to 6pm; closed Mondays and Tuesdays, and last Friday of each month. Small admission fee.

Located west of the Kremlin, two blocks east of the American Embassy, on one of the oldest streets in Moscow which leads from Stary Arbat to the Garden Ring Road and amid the cluster of other embassies in central northwest Moscow.

Maxim Gorky is the pen name of **Aleksey Maksimovich Peshkov** (1868-1936). The Soviet novelist was born in Nizhny Novgorod, a city that assumed Gorky's name until 1991 when it reverted back to its original name.

Brought up in dire poverty and with hardly any education, his deplorable circumstances made an indelible impression on the young Gorky. He began writing for provincial newspapers while holding menial jobs. He rose rapidly from a provincial proletarian background to national prominence and by 1900 became one of the most popular writers in Russia. After he was arrested for his involvement in strikes, Gorky threw his support behind Lenin and the Bolsheviks. He wholeheartedly embraced the Soviet Communist regime and sponsored "social realism" as the official school in Soviet literature and art. He was the first president of the Soviet Writers' Union and for several years a friend of Stalin.

On display are Gorky's manuscripts, documents, letters, photographs and personal belongings, which tell about his life and literary activity, as well as his role in the development of Soviet literature. A statue of Gorky is in the courtyard.

Additional Sights Near the Gorky Museum of Literature

Gorky and his museum are but a footnote in the history of this street. At 52 Povarskaya Street is the 18th century country estate of Baron Bode-Kolychev - a wooden house, really, covered by plaster - believed to be the prototype for the Rostov family home in Lev Tolstoy's epic *War and Peace*. A statue of the author is in front of the estate. Now housing the Union of Writers, the legendary poet Marina Tsvetayeva worked here in the early 1920's and met the just as well-know poet, Aleksandr Blok. The **Tsvetayeva Museum** is just around the corner on Borisoglebsky Lane (a separate entry). The **Russian Academy of Music** is at 30 Povarskaya Street.

Next door, at 50 Povarskaya, is the exclusive Writers Union Restaurant (see Chapter 12, *Where to Eat*).

KONYONKOV STUDIO MUSEUM

17 Ulitsa Tverskaya at Tverskoy bulvar, Metro Pushkinskaya or Tverskaya. Actual entrance is at 28 Tverskoy bulvar. Tel. 229-4472. Open daily from 11am to 6pm, closed Mondays and Tuesdays. Small admission fee.

Located northwest of the Kremlin, two blocks southeast of McDonald's fast food restaurant, and on the southern edge of Pushkin Square.

This museum has a permanent display of sculptures by **Sergey Konyonkov** (1874-1971), a dramatic Michelangelesque sculptor, who was born in the Smolensk region and studied at Moscow College. At the turn of the century, he was awarded the Tretyakov Prize and traveled throughout Western Europe and Egypt. After the Bolshevik Revolution, Konyonkov began a long and distinguished career as a Socialist Realist sculptor and also served as president of the Moscow Union of Sculptors.

During 1919-20, he founded Monolit, a group of sculptors that included such well-known artists as Vera Mukhina, who designed the monumental *Hymn to the New World*, commonly known as the 75-ton sculpture titled *Worker and Collective Farm Woman*, which stands in front of the **Russian Exhibition Center**. In 1923, Konyonkov emigrated to the

US and only returned to Moscow in 1945. His work is featured in Tretyakov Gallery.

In the 1920's, poet Sergey Yesenin and his American wife, Isadora Duncan, often visited Konyonkov. While in his wife's studio, Yesenin would recite his poems while Konyonkov worked.

For information about the nearby fast food restaurants McDonald's or Russkoye Bistro, see Chapter 12, *Where to Eat.*

LERMONTOV HOME-MUSEUM
2 Ulitsa Malaya Molchanovka, near Ulitsa Novy Arbat, Metro Arbatskaya or Smolenskaya. Tel. 291-5298 or 1719 or 1860. Open Wednesdays and Fridays, from 2pm to 8pm; Thursdays, Saturdays and Sundays, from 11am to 6pm; closed Mondays and Tuesdays.

Located west of the Kremlin, two blocks east of Marina Tsvetayeva Museum, and one block north of Novy Arbat Street, almost behind Dom Knigi, Moscow's largest bookstore.

This museum is dedicated to the memory of **Mikhail Lermontov** (1814-1841), a Russian poet of Scottish extraction who was born in Moscow. He lived in this wooden house with his grandmother from 1830 to 1832, while attending Moscow University. The furnishings are sparse and not Lermontov's. In one of the drawing rooms, you can see Lermontov's watercolors, and a copy of a handwritten poem to his first love.

In 1831, when his idol poet **Aleksandr Pushkin** resided on old Arbat, the 16-year-old Lermontov was already writing touching lyrics. Upon leaving Moscow, he attended the military cavalry school in St. Petersburg. He was arrested in 1837 for the poem *The Death of a Poet*, which he wrote on the death of Pushkin. Although published in a **samizdat**-form, it gained enormous popularity. He was exiled to the Caucasus. Reinstated, Lermontov was again banished following a duel with the son of the French ambassador. As a member of Tsar Nicholas's army, he was recklessly courageous. Another duel with an old schoolmate was the cause of his own death at age 26.

A noted musician, painter and mathematician, Lermontov did not publish most of his work until the last years of his life and his fame is posthumous. Along with Pushkin, Lermontov is considered one of the greatest Russian poets.

When Novy Arbat Street was being constructed by the Soviets, they wanted to tear down this house, but a Moscow writer fought them tooth and nail and saved the building.

About one-hour's drive north of central Moscow is the Lermontov estate at **Serednikovo**, where the poet spent several summers during his teenage years. Although much needed restoration work began on the main house in 1994, the rest of the estate is in deplorable shape. Upon reconstruction, one of the buildings to the side of the main house will contain a museum dedicated to Lermontov and his descendant, the assassinated prime minister Pyotr Stolypin (1862-1911). If you drive to Serednikovo, take Leningradskoye shosse, turn left to Firsanovka just before Zelenograd and drive straight for about eight kilometers.

For information about nearby restaurants, Sports Bar, Palmas, Praga and Arbat, see Chapter 12, *Where to Eat*.

ALEKSANDR OSTROVSKY MUSEUM

9 Ulitsa Malaya Ordynka, Metro Tretyakovskaya. Tel. 233-8684. Open daily from 1pm to 7pm, closed Tuesdays and last Monday of each month. Small admission fee.

Located south of the Kremlin, in a historically old part of Moscow called Zamoskvorechye, one block south of the Tretyakovskaya metro station, and one block east from St. Nicholas Church on Bolshaya Ordynka Street which was built in 1670-72 by streltsy (musketeers).

Aleksandr Ostrovsky (1823-1886) is the father of contemporary Russian theater who wrote no fewer than 48 plays during his 40-year career. The son of a government clerk, he was born in this two-story wooden house and grew up among the merchants of Zamoskvorechye, which became the preferred subject of his works. Although the house is full of period furnishings only a few articles are original, and there are many photos and documents to acquaint you with the theater of that time. The playwright's bust is next to the house. The grounds were under reconstruction in 1997 and an adjacent building, the Bakhrushin Center, which will feature artistic events, became part of the complex.

Ostrovsky worked for eight years at the Moscow Commercial Court, which gave him intimate knowledge of the merchant classes. *The Bankrupt*, his first play, was banned by the censors because it exposed the fraudulent practices of merchants. The playwright was forced to resign from government service and was kept under police surveillance. His first work to be staged, *The Poor Bride*, was produced in 1852, followed by a string of other popular works, many of which can still be seen today. He wrote a new play every year until his death, although the first two are still considered among the best.

Among his latter plays, critics single out *Poverty is No Crime*, perhaps the most loved of Ostrovsky's comedies. *The Ward*, in contrast, is one of his gloomiest works. *The Storm*, written in 1860, is believed to be his ultimate masterpiece and his best-known work in the West. Ostrovsky has done in the theater what Gogol accomplished in fiction; instead of the melodramas staged at the time, he introduced realistic plays.

You can see a larger-than-life Ostrovsky statue in front of the **Maly Theater** (see theater section in Chapter 14, *Culture*) on Teatralnaya

Square downtown, across the street from the Bolshoy Theater. It was created by the Muscovite Nikolay Andreyev (1873-1932), who also sculpted Gogol and Chekhov, and unveiled it in 1929. Ostrovsky is considered the adopted son of the Maly Theater, where freshly cut flowers can be found at the base of this statue. The Maly Theater staged 47 of his 48 plays, mostly comedies about the Russian merchant class, and has been nicknamed the Ostrovsky House. During the last ten years of his life, the playwright was the artistic director of Moscow Imperial Theaters.

For information about the nearby restaurant Amsterdam, see Chapter 12, *Where to Eat.*

PUSHKIN APARTMENT

53 Ulitsa Arbat at Denezhny pereulok, Metro Smolenskaya or Arbatskaya. Tel. 241-9295. Open Wednesday through Friday, 11am to 6pm; Saturdays and Sundays, from 11am to 5pm; closed Mondays and Tuesdays, last Friday of each month. Small admission fee.

Located west of the Kremlin, three blocks southwest from the Vakhtangov Theater, two blocks east of the Garden Ring Road, in the shadow of the Ministry of Foreign Affairs and almost across the street from McDonald's fast-food restaurant.

This two-story building with a balcony is typical of what was built in this area after the fire of 1812. It became a museum in 1986. During the immortal poet's time, this was a cobblestone street and part of it still is. Praga restaurant, at the northeastern end, connects the Old Arbat with the New Arbat.

Aleksandr Pushkin rented the second-floor, his only Moscow residence since age 11, in 1831 and personally supervised its completion. On February 18 of that year he married and brought his stunningly beautiful but none too bright 17-year-old bride, Nataliya Goncharova, here following their wedding ceremony in the nearby **Church of the Ascension**. The couple danced away the night in this five-room apartment, which then was located across the street from the **Church of St. Nicholas**. The house was owned by the second daughter of field marshal Kutuzov of Napoleonic fame.

The Goncharovs refused to give Pushkin their daughter's hand several times, but the poet persisted and when his financial prospects improved with his rising fame, they reluctantly agreed. Her beauty was supposedly so magnetic that the tsar himself cast an eye her way.

While the Pushkins lived only in the large parquet-floor living quarters on the second floor of the apartment, the first floor - which in those days always housed servants - is now also part of the museum. The sparse furniture inside did not belong to him, but the desk at which the poet supposedly wrote is there, along with portraits, manuscripts and other documents. There are surprisingly few books on display.

Five days after his wedding, Pushkin wrote to a friend, "I'm married now - and I'm happy; my only wish is that nothing will ever change. I couldn't hope for anything better." Three months later the poet and his bride left for Tsarskoye Selo, near St. Petersburg.

In 1988, Pushkin's three great-great-great-granddaughters (descendants of the poet's youngest daughter), who live in the U.K., were welcomed at this museum by Pushkin's great-grandson Grigory, who lives in Moscow. Grigory Pushkin, who was born in 1913, is the only member of the continuous male line of the Pushkin family.

A small part of this building is occupied by a minuscule museum of the Symbolist poet **Andrey Bely**, who was born here in 1880 and lived in this flat during his first 26 years.

PUSHKIN STATUE

Pushkin Square at Ulitsa Tverskaya, Metro Pushkinskaya or Tverskaya.

Located northwest of the Kremlin, on the Boulevard Ring Road, and in front of the Rossiya Cinema.

There is little that has not already been said about Pushkin, the greatest Russian poet, who was born in 1799 and foolishly perished in a duel in 1837.

"**Eto bog**" (He is god) is how Pushkin has been described for more than a century. If you ever do get to see this monument, reflect for a moment on the founder of modern literary Russian, who had died so tragically at age 37, almost like one of his characters in *Yevgeny Onegin*, his great novel in verse.

Pushkin worked for the Ministry of Foreign Affairs, but was exiled to southern Russia after he wrote his *Ode to Liberty* in 1820; and these lines show why:

> *O tyrants of the world, beware!*
> *And you, good men, take heart and dare-*
> *Arise, O fallen slaves!*

When his statue was unveiled in 1880, Dostoyevsky himself came from St. Petersburg to pay homage to the poet and was joined by Ivan Turgenev, another literary giant. Later Dostoyevsky gave an impassioned speech at the Kolonny zal, on Okhotny Ryad, about the genius of Pushkin. The statue was created by sculptor **Aleksandr Opekushin** (1841-1923).

Stalin, who would not let anyone be, could not resist the impulse and moved the statue from amid the trees of nearby Tverskoy bulvar, Moscow's oldest boulevard, to its present location in 1950.

It is quite common to see bouquets of fresh flowers at the poet's feet; Russians love poetry and they adore Pushkin, even in this age of Mexican television soap operas. Pushkin's statue is one of the most popular meeting places for Moscow lovers. Nearby, at 6 Strastnoy Boulevard, lived the classical composer **Sergey Rachmaninov** from 1905 to 1917. McDonald's fast food restaurant is southwest of here, across Tverskaya Street.

PUSHKIN MUSEUM

12/2 Ulitsa Prechistenka, Metro Kropotkinskaya. Tel. 202-8531 or 201-3256. Open Wednesdays, from 10am to 7pm; Thursday through Sunday, from 10am to 6pm; closed Mondays and Tuesdays, last Friday of the month. Small admission fee.

Located southwest of the Kremlin, two blocks southwest of the southern Kropotkinskaya metro station exit, and a block northeast of the Tolstoy Museum in what is one of the most interesting areas of Moscow.

To make things complicated in a typically Russian fashion, the entrance to the museum is actually at 2 Khrushchevsky Lane, a side street named after the retired captain Khrushchev who built the Empire mansion with columned facades facing the main street and the lane. Again called Ulitsa Prechistenka (the Street of the Immaculate Virgin), this street was named Kropotkinskaya from 1924 to 1991, after the anarchist revolutionary prince, who was born nearby in 1842.

In 1961, the ten-room Pushkin Museum was opened; thousands of individuals and organizations contributed some 100,000 exhibits, including 66,000 books.

Pushkin's first success was his romantic poem, *Ruslan and Ludmila*, followed by the masterly *Yevgeny Onegin*, an 1828 novel in verse, somewhat in the style of Byron. *Boris Godunov* is considered his finest tragedy. Pushkin often had to rely on his poetic gift to keep his income flowing because his family estate was in shambles.

The poet never lived in this house, but had many friends in the neighborhood, including some Decembrists who were exiled to Siberia after their unsuccessful attempt at democracy in December 1825. On display are editions of Pushkin's works from all over the world. While the originals are mostly in St. Petersburg, where the writer spent many years, copies of his manuscripts, letters and documents on the paper manufactured in Pushkin's time are also on display. A couple of portraits of his beautiful wife Nataliya Goncharova can be seen here.

The museum closed for a complete restoration in 1996. If you are pressed for time and prefer best-sellers over Russian literature, you can safely skip this museum.

Nearby restaurants include the Imperial and Reporter, see Chapter 12, *Where to Eat.*

THE MUSEUM OF THE REVOLUTION

21 Ulitsa Tverskaya at Mamonovsky pereulok, Metro Tverskaya or Pushkinskaya. Tel. 299-5217 or 6742, Fax 299-8515. Open daily from 10am to 6pm, Sundays 10am to 5pm, closed Mondays. Small admission fee.

Located northwest of the Kremlin, a block northwest of Pushkin Square, and on the same block as the Stanislavsky Drama Theater.

The red building dates from 1780, when it was built for Count Razumovsky. It was first used for Masonic meetings and in 1831 became the **English Club**, so named because almost no Englishmen belonged to it; women were not admitted. It soon became a club of idlers and gamblers. Tolstoy once lost a thousand rubles at cards here. The two funny-looking lions at the entrance were immortalized by Aleksandr Pushkin in his poem *Yevgeny Onegin.* The building was badly damaged during Napoleon's occupation in 1812. The last great event at the club was a costume ball set for Tsar Nicholas II in 1913 to celebrate the 300th anniversary of Romanov rule. It was turned into the Museum of the Revolution in 1923.

We only recommend this museum if you have plenty of time on your hands or a burning desire to understand how the Bolsheviks strong-armed their way into the government in 1917. Why else would you want to look at home-made bombs that were retrieved from the hiding places of revolutionaries? While there is a small section that deals with the 1991 and 1993 attempted coups d'etat, you will have to look hard to find a mention of either Trotsky or Gorbachev.

The museum has a million exhibits related to the struggle of the working class and the peasantry in the 1917 Revolution. There are hundreds of articles about and portraits of Lenin and Stalin. Chances are you will be exhausted and remain indifferent long before you have seen half of it. In the courtyard, you will pass an armored car used in the battles for Moscow in 1917 and a burned out trolley bus that was used as a barricade at the **Russian White House** in 1991.

Although the admission is negligible, you might resent paying twenty times more than Russians do to see this clutter.

The fast food restaurants McDonald's and Russkoye Bistro are nearby; see Chapter 12, *Where to Eat* for more information.

SHALYAPIN MUSEUM

25 Novinsky bulvar, Metro Barrikadnaya. Tel. 252-2530 or 205-6236. Open Tuesdays and Saturdays, from 10am to 5pm; Wednesdays and Thursdays, from 11:30am to 6pm; Sundays from 10am to 4pm; closed Mondays and Fridays. Small admission fee. Located west of the Kremlin, two blocks north of Novy Arbat, and next to the American Embassy building on Garden Ring Road.

The great Russian bass singer **Fyodor Shalyapin** moved into this house in 1910 and had it completely reconstructed. He was born in 1873 (the same year as the Italian singer Enrico Caruso) in Kazan, on the Volga. The son of a clerk, there was much poverty, misfortune and hard work in Shalyapin's youth. "I was beaten mercilessly," he wrote about his apprenticeship in a cobbler's workshop.

Shalyapin began his operatic career in 1884 as an extra. In 1893, he was appointed a soloist at the Tiflis opera house and the following year set off for Moscow. He became member of the Bolshoy Opera in 1899 and sang there for 15 years. He had his La Scala debut in 1901 and sang for the first time at the Metropolitan Opera in New York in 1907. Shalyapin established himself with roles like Boris in Mussorgsky's *Boris Godunov*, Mephistopheles in Gounod's *Faust* and Don Basilio in Rossini's *The Barber of Seville*, but he had a lifelong phobic fear of losing his voice. His success enabled him to acquire this Moscow mansion on which he spared no expense.

He lived here until 1920 with his Italian wife, a ballerina, and five children. Shalyapin and composer Sergey Rachmaninov rehearsed in the house every day. The dining room table, where Shalyapin enjoyed the company of intimate guests, can still be seen, as can most of the other original furnishings. Some of the best known Russian artists displayed their works in his drawing room, where at other times he enjoyed singing in the nude to the astonishment of passersby on Novinsky Boulevard.

Shalyapin's Bechstein piano still stands in the White Hall. His study was Shalyapin's favorite room and it is still decorated with portraits of his friends, including Tolstoy, Chekhov and Boris Pasternak's father Leonid.

When the Bolsheviks came to power, Rachmaninov left the country, but Shalyapin stayed, hoping the Communists would let him keep his house. Instead, it was converted into communal apartments for 65 people and left rotting away until it was renovated for the 1980 Moscow Olympic Games. Shalyapin and his entire family of seven stayed in one room from 1918 to 1922. His daughter Irina continued to live here until her death in 1978.

In 1922, Shalyapin left Russia and settled in Paris. "For the rest of his life Shalyapin would be tormented by uneasy, gnawing feeling about the country he had left behind," writes one of his biographers. In 1927, he was stripped of his title of the People's Artist and was threatened with being deprived of his citizenship because he helped starving Russian children in Paris by contributing 5,000 francs.

The year before Shalyapin died, the American impresario Sol Hurok was introduced to Stalin, who asked him "Why doesn't Shalyapin come to Moscow? We'll give him money, if it is money he needs. We'll give him a house in Moscow. Just tell him to come home." When Stalin's words were repeated to him, Shalyapin muttered: "You'll give me a house? And what about my soul? Can you give me back my soul?"

Suffering from terminal leukemia, he died in 1938 and was buried in Paris until the former Soviet government allowed his ashes to be buryed at Novodevichy Cemetery in Moscow in 1984.

Shalyapin's daughter, Tatyana, came from Paris for her father's 120th anniversary celebrations in 1993, but died of lung failure at the age of 88 in her room at the Minsk, now the Na Tverskoy Hotel, near Pushkin Square.

The Arbat and Sports Bar restaurants are nearby, please see Chapter 12, *Where to Eat*.

SKRYABIN MUSEUM

11 Bolshoy Nikolopeskovsky pereulok, near Stary Arbat, metro Smolenskaya or Arbatskaya. Tel. 241-1901 or 0302 or 5156. Open Wednesday through Sunday, from 10am to 6pm; closed Monday and Tuesday, last Friday of each month. Small admission fee.

Centrally located west of the Kremlin, one block northwest of the Vakhtangov Theater, and on the same block as Spasso House, the American ambassador's residence on Spasopeskovsky Square.

This museum honors native Moscow virtuoso pianist and composer **Aleksandr Skryabin** (1872-1915), who studied at the Moscow Conservatory with Rachmaninov and was a professor there from 1898 to 1904.

At about that time, the extremely self-centered Skryabin became increasingly preoccupied with philosophical and mystical ideas that influenced his life and music. He left Russia for many years, abandoning his wife and four children for a young female admirer, and toured many European countries. He also appeared in a series of recitals in the US. Skryabin wrote three symphonies, ten piano sonatas, 80 preludes, 21 mazurkas, and many other piano works. The composer dreamed of having his work performed in the Himalayas with an orchestra of 3,000 musicians.

The museum is located in the second-floor flat that Skryabin rented from 1912 until his sudden death from blood poisoning in the bed you can still see today. It is somber and dark because the composer disliked direct light (Skryabin's armchair always stood with its back to the window) and mystical because it reflects Skryabin's deeply-held ideas. Each room reflects the composer's idiosyncrasies. The floor where his study is located is covered with a red-brown carpet which dulled the sounds because Skryabin was annoyed even by the slightest interference with his creative process. There is also a Bechstein grand piano in the study, where Skryabin often worked at night. In this room, you will also see books in French in the glass-door bookcase (Plato, Spinoza, Schopenhauer) and a photographic memorial of ten photos that Skryabin made of himself. You will find Leonid Pasternak's sketches of Skryabin in the dining room, and Leonardo da Vinci's *The Last Supper* in his bedroom.

Soviet statesman Vyacheslav Molotov, originally surnamed Skryabin, played cello in the composer Skryabin's orchestra and was instrumental in this becoming one of the first Soviet museums.

Additional Sights Near the Skryabin Museum

Next door to Skryabin's house, *13 Nikolopeskovsky Lane,* was an acting school founded by Fyodor Shalyapin and Igor Stravinsky. The Skryabin and Glinka Museums function as museums during the day and hold concerts on some evenings.

TSVETAYEVA MUSEUM

6 Borisoglebsky pereulok at Ulitsa Bolshaya Molchanovka, Metro Arbatskaya or Smolenskaya. Tel. 202-3543. Open Wednesdays and Thursdays from noon to 5pm. Small admission fee.

Centrally located west of the Kremlin, three blocks east of the Garden Ring Road, and two blocks north of Ulitsa Novy Arbat.

A close friend of Marina Tsvetayeva's sister camped out in this house for seven years, enduring life without water, gas and electricity to save it from destruction by Moscow authorities and in 1992 succeeded in opening it as a museum.

In the poverty of her self-imposed Parisian exile, the great Russian poet **Marina Tsvetayeva** expressed her predicament as a poet: "Here I am not needed; there I am not possible."

In 1937, Tsvetayeva attempted the impossible; she returned to the Soviet Union in the midst of Stalin's Great Terror and to Moscow, where she was born in 1892 and grew up on Trekhprudny Lane, near the Patriarch's Ponds. Her father, the Moscow University professor Ivan Tsvetayev, founded what is today the **Pushkin Museum of Fine Arts**, and her mother was a pianist.

Not long after her return, both her husband and their daughter, who had preceded her home, were arrested; he was shot and she spent 19 years in labor camps. Her other daughter Irina died of hunger in an orphanage. On August 31, 1941, after having been evacuated with her son to Tartarstan, when the bombing of Moscow began, and from there to the bleak village of Yelabuga on the Kama River, Tsvetayeva, unable to bear her despair and loneliness, hanged herself.

An extremely poor and hungry Tsvetayeva lived in this 19th century house with her husband from 1914 to 1922, renting one or two of the communal rooms on the second floor. The snippets of poetry you can see written on the walls of her room imitate what Tsvetayeva did when she lived here and ran out of paper, which was often. A mirror, a table, and a dress are the only items on display that the poet owned. Forced to burn almost all of her furniture to keep warm and barter many of her possessions in exchange for food, Tsvetayeva left Moscow with practically nothing when she followed her husband into exile.

The museum organizes readings of her poetry. Tsvetayeva loved Moscow and dedicated several cycles of her verse to the city, mostly written in 1916. *After Russia*, published in Paris in 1928, is arguably the best book of verses by any modern Russian poet. Her poetry is a torrent of passion, pain, metaphor and music.

Another Tsvetayeva museum opened in 1995 in the village of Novo-Talitsy in the Vladimir region.

"The poet in Russia is more than a poet," the bard of Russian poets, Yevgeny Yevtushenko, once said, referring to the exceptional importance poetry played in the Soviet Union. Poetry has long stood in for other, more censored forms of public discourse. Since the fall of communism, however, the role of the poet has changed somewhat. "The poet in Russia has ceased to be more than a poet. He has become neither more nor less than himself," says poet Yevgeny Bunimovich.

APOLLINARY VASNETSOV MUSEUM

6 Furmanny pereulok at Ulitsa Chaplygina, Apt. 21/22, Metro Chistiye prudy or Turgenevskaya. Metro 208-9045. Open Wednesdays and Fridays, from 2pm to 8pm; Thursdays, Saturdays and Sundays, from 11am to 5pm, closed Mondays and Tuesdays. Small admission fee.

Located three blocks northeast of the Garden Ring Road - in this case Chistoprudny bulvar - two blocks northeast of the Sovremenik Theater, and about four very long blocks northwest of the Gogol Drama Theater.

A brilliant collection of oils and water colors of Moscow and country landscapes by **Apollinary Vasnetsov** (1856-1933) are on exhibit in this museum.

Vasnetsov was born in a remote village in the province of Viatka, in the Kirov region. His father was a village priest, and he received his artistic training from his brother **Viktor Vasnetsov** (see Viktor Vasnetsov Museum in this chapter). Vasnetsov lived in St. Petersburg from 1872 to 1875 and learned from the great Russian painter Ilya Repin. From 1883 on, he participated in traveling art exhibitions and in 1891 published his illustrations for poet Lermontov. He exhibited in Paris in 1900, in Munich in 1913, and in New York, Boston and Baltimore in 1924. From 1901 to 1919, Vasnetsov taught painting at the Moscow School of Painting, Sculpture and Architecture. He was also known as a book illustrator and stage designer. His work is exhibited at the **Tretyakov Art Gallery** and **Bakhrushin Theatrical Museum.** Also shown at this apartment-museum is 19th century furniture made to Vasnetsov's design.

VYSOTSKY MUSEUM

3 Nizhny Tagansky tupik at Ulitsa Verkhnyaya Radishchevskaya, Metro Taganskaya. Tel. 915-7578. Open weekdays from noon to 5pm.

Located southeast of the Kremlin, just inside the Garden Ring Road, in a dead-end alley, around the corner from the Taganka Theater's new stage.

This museum is a bit confusing to find the first time: enter Verkhnyi Tagansky tupik from Verkhnyaya Radishchevskaya Street, roughly between the children's **Klub na Taganke** on the southeast corner and **Taganka Blues** night club, across the street, then continue straight northwest until the last building on your right. Do not wander in this blind alley at night by yourself, it might not be safe.

Moscow-born poet, actor, singer and composer **Vladimir Vysotsky** (1938-1980) was already a legend before his unexpected death in 1980. He achieved enormous fame as an actor at the **Taganka Theater** (see Chapter 14, *Culture*), and in 26 films, but particularly as a bard of his people. Unfortunately, he was unable to record his songs and was barred from publishing his poetry.

"Moscow gave birth to two outstanding minstrels: the singer-poets Okudzhava and Vysotsky," says poet Yevgeny Yevtushenko. "Bulat Okudzhava, who sings the praise of the old Moscow streets, is a subtle lyric master, the father of Russian bards. Despite the fact that his songs were not played on the radio or television or recorded, they spread like wildfire and were heard in every Moscow house.

"Vladimir Vysotsky, an actor at the Taganka Theater who played Hamlet and Brecht's *Galileo,* came later. His songs were the complete opposite of Okudzhava's: they were not as melodic but much harsher, much more exposed. Vysotsky's voice was hoarse and growling. The words of his songs are written in Moscow's rude slang and sometimes resemble satire set to guitar. Vysotsky died young and his funeral turned into an all-city procession: about three hundred thousand people followed his coffin."

When Vysotsky died, his admirers took part in a three-day mourning, although the Soviet press ignored him completely. Even now, every July 25 hundreds of people from all over Russia gather at his grave in Moscow's Vagankovskoye cemetery to commemorate his death at the age of 42.

During the years since his death, the Vysotsky Center was created and houses a museum, archives and a publishing department. The center is located in one of those decrepit Moscow buildings where no one lives and where people still work.

A **statue** of Vysotsky was unveiled in central Moscow, at Ulitsa Petrovka and Strastnoy bulvar in the summer of 1995.

NOTABLE SIGHTS OUTSIDE THE GARDEN RING ROAD

ARMED FORCES MUSEUM

2 Ulitsa Sovyetskoy Armiyi, Metro Mendeleyevskaya, Novoslobodskaya or Prospekt Mira. Tel. 281-4877. Open daily from 10am to 5pm, closed Mondays and Tuesdays. Small admission fee.

Located north of the Kremlin, in the northeasternmost part of Frunze Central Army Park, northwest of the Dostoyevsky Museum and the Russian Army Theater.

This museum is devoted to the history of the Russian armed forces since the time of Peter the Great. It has a collection of 600,000 items, including weapons, military equipment, uniforms, toy soldiers and photos. On exhibit are the captured German standards that were cast down in front of the Lenin Mausoleum on Red Square in 1945, as well as the wreckage of the American U-2 reconnaissance aircraft brought down over the Urals in 1960, together with Gary Powers (shown in hall 20). The Soviet invasions of Hungary and Czechoslovakia are barely dealt with and the war with Afghanistan is confined to photos.

In 1965, the museum moved to its present location, where the exhibits are arranged in 25 halls, some of which were closed in 1996 until the more gruesome Stalinist era could be reassessed. On the grounds outside the museum is a large collection of Soviet tanks, artillery, aircraft and an armored train of the type that carried Trotsky into battle during the Civil War.

For information about the Caucasian-cuisine restaurants Shirak and Mush Cafe nearby, please see Chapter 12, *Where to Eat*.

BATTLE OF BORODINO PANORAMA MUSEUM

38 Kutuzovsky prospekt at Ulitsa 1812 goda, Metro Kutuzovskaya. Tel. 148-1927. Open daily from 11am to 4pm, closed Fridays and last Thursday of each month. Small admission fee.

Located southwest of the Kremlin, west of the Kievsky Railway Station, and northeast of Victory Park.

The panorama, painted in 1912 by Russian artist **Franz Roubaud**, depicts the battle between field marshall Mikhail Kutuzov (1745-1813) and Napoleon's Grand Army of 130,000 men on the vast field near the village of Borodino, 75 miles southwest of Moscow, on August 26, 1812. Kutuzov, who according to one estimate engaged 120,000 men, was defeated at Borodino but won victory over Davout and Ney at Smolensk during the French retreat in November 1812. During the 15-hour Borodino battle, 80,000 men perished. Kutuzov later pursued the enemy into Poland and Prussia, where he died the following year.

The picture's dimensions are 377 feet by 49 feet (115 meters by 15 meters).

Kutuzov holds a special place in the history of Russia. Born in 1745, the year when the French defeated the English at Fontenoy, the field marshal had an illustrious career. He served in Poland and fought against the Turks. He was an ambassador at Constantinople, governor of Finland, and governor of St. Petersburg.

Additional Sights Near the Battle of Borodino Panorama Museum

Behind the panorama building is **Kutuzovskaya izba**, the wooden hut where Kutuzov met with his staff and made the decision to retreat from Moscow.

In the summer of 1995, while the museum was being restored for the 250th anniversary of Kutuzov's birth, 180 items were stolen from Kutuzov's Hut. Among the artifacts taken were four valuable icons, Kutuzov's uniforms and weapons, as well as an ancient porcelain collection and paintings.

Next to the panorama building is a larger-than-life equestrian bronze **statue of Kutuzov**, sculpted by **Nikolay Tomsky** (1900-1956) and unveiled in 1973. Near Kutuzov's Hut, built in 1868, a grey marble **obelisk** marks the grave of 300 of Kutuzov's officers and other men killed in the battle against Napoleon.

And while at Kutuzovskaya metro station, you might continue on to Fili, the next station, and go on foot in a northwesterly direction, to 6 Ulitsa Novozavodskaya. The old village of Fili was once the center of the Kuntsevo estate, which Peter the Great granted his uncle, Lev Naryshkin, in 1689, upon his ascending the throne. Naryshkin built a new mansion there and laid out a large garden with ponds.

He also built the **Church of the Intercession at Fili**, a splendid example of the Russian baroque style, also known as Naryshkin Baroque. It is open daily from 11am to 5:30pm, closed Tuesdays and last Friday of each month. The building actually consists of two churches: the winter Church of the Intercession on the ground floor, which is heated by stoves and open year-round, and the Church of the Savior Nerukotvorny on the upper level.

For information about Triumf-Koenig Stube and Gian Carlo, two nearby restaurants, see Chapter 12, *Where to Eat*.

MUSEUM OF COSMONAUTICS

111 Prospekt Mira and Alleya Kosmonautov, Metro VDNkH. Tel. 283-7914 or 1837. Open daily from 10am to 7pm, closed Mondays and last Friday of each month. Small admission fee.

Located northeast of the Kremlin, southeast of the Russian Exhibition Center and west across the street from the Kosmos Hotel and next to VDNkH metro station.

The museum is located in the plinth of the **Space Obelisk**, designed as an arrow in the form of a shooting titanium-plated rocket, which was designed by sculptor **Andrey Faidysh-Krandiyevsky** and unveiled in 1964. It was built to commemorate the conquest of outer space and achievements in space exploration. Items on display include articles used by astronauts during space flights and their personal belongings.

In front of the 330-feet-high obelisk is a monument to scientist **Konstantin Tsiolkovsky** (1857-1935), the father of Russian cosmonautics, gazing over the **Alley of Cosmonauts** (Alleya Geroyev Kosmosa), a walkway flanked by the bronze busts of cosmonauts **Yuri Gagarin** (1934-1968), the first Soviet cosmonaut to travel in space; **Valentina Tereshkova** (born 1937), once an amateur parachutist and in 1963 the world's first female astronaut; and **Aleksey Leonov**, **Pavel Belyayev** and **Vladimir Komarov**.

At the end of the alley are two busts. One is dedicated to **Sergey Korolev** (1906-1966), the designer of the Soviet space system; his **house-museum**, *Tel. 283-7914*, is not far from here. Korolev received this house from the Soviet government as a gift for his successful launching of the first Sputnik in 1957. Korolev was accused of subversive activities during the Stalinist regime and was exiled to Siberia in 1938. The other bust is of the academician **Mstislav Keldysh** (1911-1978), mathematician and mechanical engineer who headed many Soviet space programs.

Konstantin Tsiolkovsky was a scientist who not only predicted interplanetary flight within the solar system, but also created the theory of modern rocketry and astronautics. Albert Einstein was keenly aware of his work. Tsiolkovsky died deaf, neglected and isolated by poverty. His mother died when he was 13 and at 16 the youth went to Moscow with his father's allowance of fifteen rubles a month, most of which he spent on books not available in the libraries. "I had nothing to eat but dark bread and water, he recalled later. "I would go to a bakery once in three days and buy nine kopecks' worth of bread." Only in 1900 did he obtain a small grant from the Academy of Sciences to do research in rocketry. In 1935, dying of cancer and hoping to secure a posthumous pension for his family, he bequeathed all his work to the Bolsheviks. Two days before his death Stalin sent him a thank-you telegram.

After spending billions of dollars in a cold-war space rivalry with the Russians, in 1993 the National Aeronautic and Space Administration (NASA) began working with the Russians to design a smaller and cheaper space station. The Russians had previously suggested several cooperative ventures. By 1995, eight Russian and American astronauts, who took part in the first American-Russian space linkup in 20 years, returned to Earth after nearly four months in orbit.

If you are interested in Russia's space program, see the **Russian Exhibition Center** in a separate entry later in this chapter.

If you get hungry, the restaurant Oskar, *3 Ulitsa Akademika Koroleva*, is just one long block southwest of here.

DECORATIVE & FOLK ARTS MUSEUM

3 Ulitsa Delegatskaya at Ulitsa Sadovaya-Samotechnaya, Metro Tsvetnoy bulvar or Mayakovskaya. Tel. 923-1741 or 7725. Open Mondays, Wednesdays and Saturdays, from 10am to 6pm; Tuesdays and Thursdays, from 12:30 to 8 pm; closed Fridays. Small admission fee.

Located just outside the Garden Ring Road, two blocks east of the Glinka Museum and one block west of the Obraztsov Puppet Theater.

This museum is housed in what was originally a 16th century estate. In 1812, the complex was greatly damaged by Napoleon's invasion. It was reconstructed in 1834-44 for the theological seminary of the Russian Orthodox Church, which occupied it until 1917. When government personnel stationed here moved to the Russian White House in 1980-81, this building was ceded to the Decorative Arts Museum.

More than 40,000 objects of wood, metal, glass and clay, from the 14th century to the present are on display, all folk and applied art of the peoples of the Russian Federation.

Included are crafts from the villages of Fedoskino, Gzhel, Mstyora, Palekh, and Zhostovo. They include crafts made of wood and metal, as well as lacquered miniatures. Lacquer arts originated in China before the birth of Christ. In the 18th century, workshops opened in France. A

Russian merchant brought this craft from Germany to Fedoskino, near Moscow.

There is a collection of samovars and cast iron pieces, religious utensils, Faberge jewelry, china, glass, pottery and toys. In the section on Bolshevik propaganda porcelain, you can see a decorative plate with this inscription: "If you are not with us, you are against us." In another section, an old-fashioned stylized typewriter is displayed, with keyboard containing portraits of well-known Russian writers, such as Pushkin, Akhmatova, Tsvetayeva, and Solzhenitsyn.

You will see arts and crafts from **Sergiyev Posad** and the Kuznetsov porcelain factory in the village of **Dulyovo**, both near Moscow and both described in Chapter 18, *Excursions & Day Trips*. One of the largest furniture collections in Russia is on display here, including works by Yelena Polenova from the **Abramtsevo** group (also in Chapter 18, *Excursions & Day Trips*). Textiles are represented by national dresses, embroidery, weaving and lace.

For information about the nearby Georgian restaurant, Kolkhida, see Chapter 12, *Where to Eat*.

DONSKOY MONASTERY

1 Ploshchad Donskaya at Ulitsa Donskaya, Metro Shabolovskaya or Leninsky prospekt. Tel. 952-1646. Open Tuesday to Friday and Sunday, from 11am to 6pm. A notice near the entrance informs visitors that women are not allowed to enter in trousers or go into the churches with their heads uncovered. Shorts are strictly prohibited for both sexes.

Located southwest of the Kremlin, roughly between Gorky Park and Danilovskoye Cemetery.

Like many other ancient Russian monasteries, Donskoy, with its seven churches and twelve towers, was built as a defensive fortress outside the city walls to shield Moscow from the Tartars. It was founded by **Boris Godunov** in 1591 on the site of Russia's 1571 victory over the Crimean Tartars, which was attributed to a miraculous icon of the Virgin of the Don. Earlier, the icon also accompanied Dmitry Donskoy (Dmitry of the Don) in his war against the Mongols and brought him victory during the Battle of Kulikovo near the River Don in 1380, the first decisive Russian conquest over the Tartars since the 13th century.

A cathedral was constructed here in 1593, but the icon, which was originally displayed inside, is now shown in the Tretyakov Gallery. The **Old Cathedral** was the monastery's only building until the **New Cathedral**, with its defensive walls, was founded in 1684 by Peter the Great's half-sister Sofiya and built between 1686 and 1711. North of the New Cathedral is the **Church of the Deposition of the Robe**, which was constructed in 1701.

By the late 18th century, the monastery's cemetery became a fashion-able burial ground. Pushkin's grandparents, Tolstoy's grandmother and Turgenev's mother are buried here, as is the well-known Moscow archi-tect Osip Bove. There is a temple of the Patriarch Tikhon, who lived here under house arrest in the 1920's and was buried in an unmarked grave in 1925. He challenged Lenin and denounced Bolshevik terror. After his reburial in the Old Cathedral in 1992, a fire destroyed most of the icons in the cathedral, except for the copy of the Virgin of the Don. For many Russians this monastery symbolizes the triumph of the Russian spirit over evil.

During most of the Bolshevik reign, Donskoy was closed, although its monks survived until 1928, when the entire complex became part of the **Shchusev Museum of Architecture** (see separate entry), displaying art-works from the destroyed Moscow churches.

The museum in the New Cathedral contains drawings, plans and sketches about Russian architecture from the time of Peter the Great to the present. You can also see sketches and photographs of Moscow buildings that have been demolished.

Additional Sights Near Donskoy Monastery

South of the monastery, on Ordzhonikidze Street, you can see the former **Patrice Lumumba University**, named after the former Belgian Congo Communist agitator and the first prime minister of Zaire who was killed in 1961. The ugly Stalinist complex opened in 1960 to export the Bolshevik revolution to the Third World. Among its many notable visitors during its heyday were PLO Chairman Yasir Arafat and Cuba's Fidel Castro. The university, now renamed the **Russian People's Friendship University**, is still the institution of choice for those who want a degree on $2,000-a-year tuition.

DOSTOYEVSKY MUSEUM

2 Ulitsa Dostoyevskogo at Pereulok Dostoyevskogo, Metro Mendeleyevskaya or Novoslobodskaya. Tel. 281-1085 or 284-8642. Open Thursdays, Saturdays and Sundays, from 11am to 6pm; Wednesdays and Fridays, from 2pm to 8pm; closed Mondays and Tuesdays. Small admission fee.

Located in northwest Moscow, west of Frunze Central Army Park, and behind the star-shaped Russian Army Theater. There is a long walk from either metro station so walking may be an unacceptable option.

Fyodor Dostoyevsky was born in 1821 at St. Mary's Hospital for the poor, where his father began working as a surgeon eight months before. The ground-floor flat, a museum since 1928, is located in the building where the great Russian novelist lived from 1823 to 1837.

When the three-room museum opened, the former Ulitsa Novaya Bozhedomka was renamed in the writer's honor. Not far from the hospital lay a cemetery for vagrants, suicides, criminals and their victims. It was called the House of the Wretched (Ubogy dom); thus the original street name. As a schoolboy, Dostoyevsky was educated at the Academy in Ulitsa Novaya Basmannaya, in northeast Moscow; his father also taught him Latin. Dostoyevsky left for St. Petersburg in 1837 at the urging of his father who wanted him to attend the Military Engineering School.

Joining revolutionary circles in St. Petersburg, he was condemned to death in 1849, reprieved at the very last moment and sent to hard labor in Siberia, where he met atheists, nihilists, sensualists and criminals that litter his novels. If you want to know more, read *House of the Dead*. Dostoyevsky suffered from poverty, hunger and illness all of his life. On display at the museum are a few pieces of original furniture, photographs, photocopies of manuscripts, documents and the writer's personal belongings that were brought from St. Petersburg and elsewhere. Just enough to get you started rereading *The Brothers Karamazov* or *Crime and Punishment,* where "the dark heart, the mystical turmoil and chaos rule."

There is a Dostoyevsky statue in the courtyard of the hospital, where he was born and lived the first 16 years of his life. This is the only Moscow outdoor monument to the novelist. It was designed by **Sergey Merkurov** (1881-1952), who also created Kliment Timiryazev's on Tverskoy Boulevard, unveiled in 1918.

For information about on two nearby Georgian-cuisine restaurants, Shirak and Mush Cafe, see Chapter 12, *Where to Eat.*

FRUNZE AVIATION & SPACE MUSEUM

4 Ulitsa Krasnoarmeyskaya at Ulitsa Seregina, Metro Aeroport or Dinamo. Tel. 212-5461. Open daily from 10am to 6pm. Small admission fee.

Located northwest of the Kremlin and the Dinamo Sports Complex, and north of Aerostar Hotel. Petrovsky Palace, where the tsars rested when traveling between Moscow and St. Petersburg, is also nearby.

Mikhail Frunze (1885-1925) was a Soviet army commander who took part in the Bolshevik uprising in Moscow in 1905. He was arrested for it and sentenced to death. He also took an active part in the 1917 Bolshevik Revolution and is considered the father of the Red Army. In 1924, Frunze became Trotsky's deputy, but the following summer he fell ill and was dead by the end of October. Rumor had it that he was the victim of a "medical murder," when forced to undergo an operation urged on him by Stalin, who had him replaced with Voroshilov.

Exhibits include models and photographs of aircraft, telling the history of Russian aviation from its origins to the present.

STATUES OF MOSCOW

Statues of Lenin, Stalin, Marx and Engels were on practically every corner of every town in the former Soviet Union and in some towns, they abound to this day.

Many are still scattered all over Moscow. One of them, of Karl Marx, seems to taunt Westerners on Teatralnaya Square in the middle of the city. It's kind of ironic that it is in front of what is today the pillar of capitalist luxury hotels, the Metropol, even if the graffiti messages scribbled on the statue are not of the kindest sort. Lenin himself spoke at the ceremony when its foundation was laid in 1920, concluding: "I am certain that this monument to our great teacher will serve as a motivation for you to devote all your attention to the necessity of working hard to create a society free of exploitation." The 160-ton granite block has this inscription: His name will endure through the ages and so also will his work! Engels.

In Moscow, the one remaining truly monumental statue of Lenin stands on Oktyabrskaya Square, south of the Kremlin and overlooking the Garden Ring Road.

Since 1976, Friedrich Engels has stood six feet tall in bronze on Prechistenskaya Square, seemingly aghast at the newly rebuilt Cathedral of Christ the Savior across the square.

In 1992, a brash Dallas fast food restaurant owner visited Russia and bought a Lenin statue that for 40 years stood in front of the Odessa Crane Factory in the Ukraine. The 8-foot-high, 700-pound statue cost $500. It arrived in Texas ten months later in several pieces and the rabid anti-Communist owner had it reassembled. It still stands in front of Goff's Hamburgers on Lovers Lane, at the edge of ritzy University Park. Goff's restaurant once wanted to add a Leninburger to its menu, which would consist of a hamburger on red cabbage, but abandoned the idea for lack of interest.

GAGARIN MONUMENT

Ploshchad Gagarina at Leninsky prospekt, Metro Leninsky prospekt.

Located southwest of the Kremlin, southeast of the Luzhniki Sports Complex, and southwest of Donskoy Monastery. The square, previously known as Kaluga Gate, was renamed after a hundred thousand Muscovites welcomed Gagarin home following his 1961 flight.

There is little else to see around the square, except for a multiplicity of kiosks where private enterprise thrives. Leninsky prospekt, which stretches for nine miles in a southwesterly direction from the Oktyabrskaya metro station on the Garden Ring Road, is Moscow's longest avenue.

On April 12, 1961, Gagarin became the first human to make a manned orbital flight around the earth. His 43-feet-tall titanium monument stands on a vertigo-causing 98-feet-high fluted column. Gagarin seems to soar so high as to be practically able to observe events at the Cape Canaveral space station in Florida. At the foot of the pedestal is a model of his spaceship Vostok, erected here in 1980. It was along Leninsky Avenue that Gagarin made his triumphant entry into Moscow; in 1812, when Napoleon was retreating from Moscow, he took it in the opposite direction toward Kaluga.

Yuri Gagarin (1934-1968) was born in a village in the Smolensk region and joined the Air Force in 1955. After studying at the Chkalov military aviation school, he served as a fighter pilot, and in 1960 joined the group of pioneer Soviet cosmonauts. He was killed in a flying accident in 1968. The cosmonaut is buried behind the Lenin Mausoleum on Red Square with the likes of Stalin and other henchmen of Lenin's.

Gagarin was attractive in a down-to-earth way, with a round face and broadly set, light-blue eyes, says Leonid Brezhnev's niece in her memoirs (she's been living in California since 1990). She remembers that he danced oddly, pulling in one leg for some reason. Fame never spoiled him, she recalls; he retained his winning simplicity and positive outlook and, except for some envious souls, was loved by everyone.

Another statue of Gagarin is displayed in the **Alley of Cosmonauts** in the **Museum of Cosmonautics**, a walkway flanked by bronze busts of several space exploration pioneers, near Prospekt Mira and metro VDNkH.

GLINKA MUSEUM OF MUSICAL CULTURE

4 Ulitsa Fadeyeva at Pykhov-Tserkovny pereulok, metro Mayakovskaya. Tel. 972-3237 or 251-1066, Fax 972-3255. Open daily from 11am to 7pm; Tuesdays and Thursdays, from 2pm to 8:30pm; closed Mondays. Small admission fee.

Located just north of the Garden Ring Road, northwest of the Kremlin, northeast of Tchaikovsky Concert Hall and Satira Theater on Triumfalnaya ploshchad, and three blocks west of The Decorative & Folk Arts Museum.

This museum will acquaint you with the life and work of classical composer **Mikhail Glinka** (1803-1857), a civil servant who, upon returning from Italy, decided to study music in Berlin. There are more than 800,000 exhibits about the music of most nations throughout history. A book of musical sketches by Beethoven is on display here, dated 1803.

In this museum you will also get to know the Russian classical composer **Modest Mussorgsky** (1835-1881), who was educated for the army, but in 1858, after the onset of a nervous disorder, began the serious study of music. You will also learn about **Nikolay Rimsky-Korsakov** (1844-1908), who started out as a naval cadet before devoting himself to classical music, and about other Russian composers of the 19th century. Also on display is a unique collection of 1,500 musical instruments from throughout the world. The $650,000 Stradivarius violin presented by Queen Elisabeth of Belgium to the Russian violinist **David Oistrakh** (1908-1974) as a token of her appreciation was stolen from this museum in the summer of 1996, along with a Jacob Steiner violin appraised at $300,000.

Another instrument on display is the **balalaika**, the Russian national musical instrument. The classic balalaika consists of three strings on a triangular body, although there are also many oval instruments with two or four strings. The balalaika was mentioned first around 1715, when Peter the Great initiated the creation of an orchestra made up of players and instruments from all regions of the Russian Empire. The balalaika has always been popular among the peasants who have spun many folk songs on it. It was often made from an inexpensive fir tree, which did not exactly help the quality of its sound. In the 19th century, the balalaika was overshadowed by the guitar and accordion.

KRASNAYA PRESNYA REVOLUTIONARY MUSEUM

4 Bolshoy Predtechensky pereulok at Maly Predtechensky pereulok, Metro Krasnopresnenskaya or Barrikadnaya. Tel. 252-3035 or 2900. Open daily from 10am to 6pm, closed Mondays and Tuesdays. Small admission fee.

Located northwest of the Kremlin, roughly between the Moscow Zoo and World Trade Center's Mezhdunarodnaya Hotel.

Krasnaya Presnya is a working-class district that even today retains a high percentage of Communist sympathizers. The American embassy annex, the Russian White House and the World Trade Center with the Mezh Hotel are all located in Krasnaya Presnya. Originally named just Presnya, after a tributary of the Moskva River, which is now visible only inside the Zoo, it earned the adjective **krasnaya** (red) during the December 1905 uprising, when district workers attempted to overthrow the tsarist government, but failed to reach central Moscow.

This neglected museum, which opened in 1924, tells you what the Communists did before the Revolution. The leadership of the Communist Party convened in this building to plot its strategy. Most notable among the thousands of exhibits is a diorama, reproducing the December 1905 battles at Presnya in which more than a thousand lives were lost. It tells of the courage of the workers during the uprising and the development of the Krasnopresnensky district today.

For information about the nearby Italian restaurant Arlekino (Arlecchino), see Chapter 12, *Where to Eat.*

THE LENIN FUNERAL TRAIN PAVILION

1 Paveletskaya ploshchad, Metro Paveletskaya. Tel. 235-2898. Open daily from 10am to 6pm, closed Saturdays and Sundays.

Located southeast of the Kremlin, a block south of the Garden Ring Road, in a small park east of Paveletsky Railway Station.

In a pavilion of marble, glass and concrete you can see the 1910 U-127 steam engine and wagon of the funeral train that brought Lenin's body from Gorky to Moscow for his January 23, 1924 funeral on Red Square.

Built in St. Petersburg, this locomotive served the railroads of the Russian Empire and broke down soon after the Revolution. The railway workers of the Paveletsky depot fixed it up and presented it to Communist Party members, who in turn presented it to their leader, already dying in Gorky. The memorial has been displayed in its present form since 1980 and more than eleven million people have visited it since it went on display.

However, for one to appreciate the scope of Lenin's death, you should know that more than a million people waited night and day, for an average of five hours in the arctic cold (30 degrees Celsius below zero), to pass through the **Kolonny Zal**, where his body lay in state.

Today, a car dealership shares space with the hearse. You can buy irons and washing machines here, as well. On the ground floor, right under the train, there is a bar, open until 10pm, where you can have such capitalist delicacies as champagne, coffee, whiskey and caviar.

For information about the Jewish restaurant **U Yuzefa**, see Chapter 12, *Where to Eat*.

MUSEUM OF THE MINISTRY OF INTERNAL AFFAIRS
MVD

11 Ulitsa Seleznevskaya at Sushchevsky tupik, Metro Novoslobodskaya. Tel. 258-0659. Open daily, except Mondays, from 10am to 5pm, but with guided group tours only. Small admission fee.

Located north of the Kremlin, east of Frunze Central Army Park, and one block northeast of Novoslobodskaya metro station.

In one exhibition room of this museum, there is a case devoted to the memory of one man and to the fire-fighting branch of the MVD. Inside its protective glass walls hang the uniform, hat and coat of **Vladimir Maksimchuk**. This restrained exhibit commemorates the actions of a man who, in the words of one MVD chief, "saved half of Europe." There is a special helmet awarded to him by the Germans.

Maksimchuk was the chief fire fighter at Chernobyl in April 1986, when the reactor headed toward a meltdown. He led his men in the successful battle to extinguish the fire before the entire plant exploded, but could not prevent radioactive fallout from spewing over much of Eastern Europe. Maksimchuk died of his Chernobyl injuries in mid-1994. Except for his family and fellow officers who reconstructed the case in the museum, practically no one remembers the fireman. This is a sobering way to begin a tour of one of Moscow's most controversial bastions of historical record.

The museum covers the history of MVD from the days of the tsarist police to Chernobyl. MVD claims not to be political, but merely a federal police force. Until 1991, it was responsible, together with KGB, for internal security. The museum has several exhibition halls that note similarly momentous historical events, along with bizarre crimes. You can see the white flag of surrender from the October 1993 siege at the Russian White House, as well as the photos of Anatoly Chikatilo, the schoolteacher from Rostov-on-Don, who killed 53 people before being caught.

NOVODEVICHY CONVENT

1 Novodevichy proyezd, Metro Sportivnaya. Tel. 246-8526 or 2201. Open daily from 10am to 5pm, closed Tuesdays and first Monday of each month. Small admission fee.

Located southwest of the Kremlin, west of Gorky Park, north of the Luzhniki Sports Complex, and at the bend of the Moskva River.

After the Kremlin museums, this is one of the most gratifying historical sights, as well as a tourist circus. If you come in the morning, you will have to rub shoulders with the hordes of mostly-Western tourists, who come here for a cursory look at the 15 buildings and 16 gilded domes before boarding their buses for Sheremetyevo airport. Expect some rude treatment from the guardians of the convent who have yet to realize that it is these same tourists who make their jobs possible.

The Novodevichy (New Maiden) Convent, is an outstanding example of early 16th century architecture. It is called "new" because there was an older monastery here in the 14th century. The convent's brick walls measure 3,000 feet in length and up to 35 feet in height. Novodevichy was a powerful fortress at the southwest approaches to Moscow. It was founded in 1524 under the reign of Vassily III in honor of his 1514 recapture of Smolensk from the Lithuanians who controlled it for more than a hundred years. In 1571, this fortress withstood a Tartar attack.

Novodevichy was long associated with the royal family and witnessed historical events, such as election of Boris Godunov as tsar in 1598. It acquired its present appearance in the 1680's during the regency of Peter the Great's half-sister Sofiya, who was banished here in 1679. By then the convent had lost its military and defensive importance. Chroniclers of the late 17th century recount that 195 of the tsar's **streltsy** (musketeers) were hanged from 35 gallows erected under Sofiya's window, in front of the convent. Sofiya was allegedly involved in the soldiers' mutiny against Peter's reforms. Peter did not believe in monasteries and at one time turned Novodevichy into a children's shelter.

The convent's entrance is through a passageway beneath the **Church of the Transfiguration**. West of it are the **Lopukhina Chambers**, where Peter the Great's pious first wife, Yevdokia Lopukhina, lived from 1727 until her death four years later. This was the only way for a tsar to get rid of an unwanted wife; divorce as we know it did not exist. The Lopuhina Chambers are now utilized by the Metropolitan of Moscow.

The **Cathedral of the Virgin of Smolensk**, a six-column church with five large domes is reminiscent of the Kremlin's Assumption Cathedral. When completed in 1525, it was the first stone building in the convent; its basement served as a burial place for women of noble families, such as the daughter of Ivan the Terrible. Peter's wife and his half-sister are also buried underneath the cathedral. Icons painted by Simon Ushakov in the 1680's can be seen here.

East of the cathedral is the 240-feet-tall **Bell Tower**, and on the west is the **Refectory** (the monastery's dining room). On the south wall of the convent is the **Intercession Church**. Next to it is the **Church of St. Ambrose** and the **Old Refectory**, also known as Irina Godunova's Chambers, which were named after Boris Godunov's sister and widow of Tsar Fyodor, who stayed here from 1598. Between the refectory and the Lopukhina Chambers is one of the four nun's buildings.

Over the centuries Novodevichy received presents of land and other valuables, together with exiled noble women. It accumulated paintings, as well as gold and silverware, old books and other art objects of the 16th and 17th centuries. It boasted more than 15,000 serfs (slaves, in effect) at the height of its prosperity. At the end of the 18th century Novodevichy became a regular convent, where mostly women were admitted, but in 19th century even criminals were incarcerated here.

Napoleon used the monastery briefly as a provisions depot in 1812 and ordered it blown up when he had to beat his retreat. However, a nun extinguished the fuses at the last moment and saved this fine piece of architecture for posterity.

Next to the cathedral you can see the tomb of the poet Denis Davydov, a Hussar who fell under the French. The convent became a museum in 1922, although the Smolensk Cathedral was returned to its spiritual owners after World War II. In Soviet times and until 1991, there was a museum of ceramics here.

NOVODEVICHY CEMETERY

50 Khamovnichesky val, with entrance on Luzhnetsky proyezd. Open daily from Wednesday through Sunday, from 11am to 4pm; closed Mondays and Tuesdays. Small admission fee.
Located next to Novodevichy Convent.

The Novodevichy Cemetery, probably the most prestigious necropolis of Moscow, occupies an area of almost 16 acres and holds the remains of many Russian writers, artists and politicians, among them the playwright Anton Chekhov, composers Aleksandr Skryabin, Sergey Prokofiev and Dmitry Shostakovich, writers Nikolay Gogol and Mikhail Bulgakov, painters Levitan, Serov and Nesterov, film directors Pudovkin and Eisenstein, theatrical director Konstantin Stanislavsky, poet Vladimir Mayakovsky, Stalin's second wife Nadezhda Alliluyeva, and Soviet premier Nikita Khrushchev, whose monument, at the request of Khrushchev's family, was created by his longtime adversary, the modernistic sculptor **Ernest Neizvestny**, now an American citizen. For more about this, please see the sidebar in Chapter 14, *Culture.*

For information about the nearby Georgian restaurant U Pirosmani, see Chapter 12, *Where to Eat.*

OSTANKINO PALACE

5 First Ulitsa Ostankinskaya at Ulitsa Novomoskovskaya, Metro VDNkH. Tel. 286-6288 or 283-4645, Fax 286-0288. The Italian Pavilion is open between May 1 and October 1, from 10am to 5pm; closed Mondays and Tuesdays. When raining or when there is 80 percent humidity, the Pavilion is closed. Admission fee.

Located north of the Kremlin, south of the Academy of Sciences Botanical Gardens, southeast of the Russian Exhibition Center, west of Kosmos Hotel and VDNkH metro station, and two typically long Moscow blocks northeast of the Ostankino Television Tower. It is a long walk west from the VDNkH metro station to Ostankino so consider taking a bus anywhere on Akademika Koroleva Street.

In the late 1980s the estate, which had been converted to a state museum during the Soviet period, was closed completely because of the dismal condition of many of the buildings. It has been under construction for several years and continues to be renovated, however, the Italian Pavilion has reopened.

The village of Ostankino had been known for centuries. The estate once belonged to Ivan the Terrible. From 1620 on, it was the property of Prince Mikhail Cherkassky whose last daughter married a Sheremetyev in 1743 and brought the land into his family. By that time, it was just a few miles from Moscow.

Ostankino is an outstanding example of 18th century architecture and interior design, which were provided by serfs. While construction began in the late 1500's, the palace and park grounds were bought by the Sheremetyevs in the 1750's and the present palace was completed in 1795, when it was inherited by Nikolay Sheremetyev, a well known patron of the arts. He originally planned to erect an arts palace on one of his properties in Moscow, but instead built this classical masterpiece of deception. It looks like masonry but is really a wood frame covered with stucco.

The Sheremetyevs's holdings at the height of their influence included more than two million acres spread over 17 provinces and more than 200,000 serfs. To have 200 servants was believed normal for an affluent household. It was not unusual for a landowner like that to have a man whose sole responsibility was his master's pipe. Key employees were the housekeeper, steward, butler, cellar keeper and chamberlain, who sometimes supervised a staff numbering into the dozens.

A wealthy landowner might have up to a hundred entertainers, such as actors and musicians, singers and dancers, fools and dwarfs. The lowliest among them all were house serfs, who cared for the furnishings, did the laundry and staffed the kitchens. Sometimes the staff would include individuals responsible for polishing the silver, washing the windows or polishing the furniture their entire lives. Above them were chefs, stable keepers and gardeners, and still higher nannies, which were considered almost family members. These positions were often passed down from generation to generation.

Nikolay Sheremetyev, one of the richest and most educated aristocrats of his time, began the construction of a theater on the estate in 1790, with the help of peasant architects, and it was completed about seven years later. Five ground-floor central doors lead into the **Blue Room**, which is the most opulent of all interiors, and gets its name from the color of the drapes, wall coverings and upholstery. Speculation has it that it was designed as a bedroom for Catherine the Great, but she died just as the palace was being finished.

The **Picture Gallery** is also the main foyer of the theater, which is 120 feet long and 58 feet wide. The **Egyptian Pavilion**, another major interior which resembles a Roman atrium, was a concert hall. The **Italian Pavilion** lies on the western side of the palace and is almost as lavish as the Blue Room. A parquet floor of rosewood, ebony and walnut reflects the Italian Pavilion's ceiling pattern. The Italian Pavilion serves as a gallery for more than two dozen sculptures; it and the Egyptian Pavilion are connected to the theater by closed galleries.

The **theater** is the heart of the palace. Ostankino's was the best equipped Russian theater of that time, with a stage that allowed for quick set changes and complicated scenic effects, and it could be converted into a ballroom in about 30 minutes. The stage, the auditorium, makeup rooms and some of the stage machinery have been preserved to this day. Although the serf theater was formed in the 1760's, it truly blossomed 30 years later under Count Sheremetyev's supervision. Talented serf children were taught by professional actors and musicians, then enlisted into the company to perform. Their level of acting was so high they successfully competed with the professional theaters of Moscow and St. Petersburg. The Ostankino theater had a collection of 5,000 costumes.

We can only speculate how the Ostankino estate would look today were it not for the fact that sometime in 1790 the middle-aged Count Sheremetyev fell in love with a serf girl, named **Praskovia Kovalyova-Zhemchugova**, who had worked on his **Kuskovo Estate** (see Chapter 17, *Excursions & Day Trips*). The Ostankino palace was built to enable her to escape Kuskovo. Praskovia Zhemchugova was a gifted and popular actress and singer at Sheremetyev's theater. Debuting at the age of 11, she went on to perform with success in more than 50 Italian and Russian operas. She was granted her freedom and Count Sheremetyev married her in 1805 against all customs of the times, infuriating Moscow high society.

Misfortune seemed to wait in the wings, however, for less than three years after their marriage, Praskovia died of tuberculosis after the birth of her son Dmitry. As an adult, Dmity, in an experiment before the royal decree of 1861, gave his serfs their freedom. While devoting himself to the poor by supporting what is today the Sklifosovsky Hospital (formerly the Count Sheremetyev Hospital for the Poor and Ill), on Sukharevskaya ploshchad at Prospekt Mira, which he dedicated to Praskovia after her death, the count died of grief.

The Ostankino palace was seriously damaged during the French occupation of 1812, when pillagers looted its stage equipment, stripped the silk upholstery from the palace walls and curtains from the windows. Original oils by Rubens, Rembrandt and Titian were stolen from the gallery nearby. The last theater performance took place in 1817 and 101 years later the Ostankino palace was turned into a museum.

Additional Sights Near Ostankino Palace

The **Church of Trinity**, west of the palace entrance, was built more than a hundred years before the palace by Prince Cherkassky, who had the distinction of being the only courtier of Peter the Great that did not have to shave his beard.

North of the palace stretch the 860 acres of the **Botanical Gardens**, which were founded in 1945 as an extension of the original **Russian Exhibition Center**, and contain one of the best collections of Russian flora. The gardens are open Wednesday through Sunday, from 10am to 4pm, or until 8pm in the summer.

For information about the restaurant **Sedmoye nebo**, atop the Ostankino Television Tower, see Chapter 12, *Where to Eat*.

RUBLEV MUSEUM OF ANCIENT ART
Andronikov Monastery

   10 *Androniyevskaya ploshchad, Metro Ploshchad Ilicha or Rimskaya, one of the most recently completed stations. Tel. 278-1489. Open daily from noon to 5pm, closed Wednesdays and last Friday of the month. Admission fee.*

   Located east of the Kremlin, northeast of Taganka Square, and inside the Spaso-Andronikov Monastery. When you exit Ploshchad Ilicha metro station, walk east on Sergiya Radonezhskogo Street; the fourth street on your right will open on Androniyevskaya Square.

   The monastery, where the great Russian iconist in Byzantine style, **Andrey Rublev**, worked, was founded by **Metropolitan Aleksey** in 1360, in fulfillment of a promise he made after getting lost in a storm in the Black Sea upon his return from Constantinople. It was named after its first abbot Andronik, who was the disciple of St. Sergiy of Radonezh. St. Sergiy stayed here during his travels to Moscow. Originally built as a wooden fortress with churches to defend Moscow, it was gradually rebuilt in stone as you see it today and is based on Vladimir and Suzdal architecture.

   This museum, which opened in 1960, displays masterpieces of 13th to 18th century Russian art, collected from all over Russia. It includes icons, or holy images, of the Moscow, Tver and Northern schools, fragments of monumental painting, early Russian wooden sculptures and facsimile copies of frescoes. Oddly, it does not display a single work by the man after whom it is named, Rublev, whose best artwork, including some painted while he lived at this monastery, can be seen in the Tretyakov Gallery. Rublev's monument is amid the trees on the plaza in front of the monastery.

   Andrey Rublev (circa 1360/70-1427/30) is the most celebrated of Russian icon painters. He is thought to have been an assistant to the iconist Theophanes the Greek (circa 1350-1410) and became a monk as an adult. Little is known about his life. He is believed to have painted the celebrated 1410-20 icon, *The Old Testament Trinity*, depicting three archangels who appeared to Abraham and his wife as travel-weary angels asking for shelter; it is exhibited at the Tretyakov Gallery. The icon has been called "a painting of great refinement, elegance and even tenderness" by one historian, while another says "Rublev depicted the three angels as an embodiment of the concept of spiritual perfection."

   Rublev is presumed to have painted icons or murals at the **Cathedral of the Annunciation** in the Kremlin in 1405 and is also believed to be the author of the panels of saints that were painted at the Uspensky Cathedral in Vladimir in 1408. He also worked at the Trinity Monastery in Sergiyev Posad.

Rublev was buried by the ancient walls of the **Cathedral of the Savior**, the oldest stone building in Moscow, erected in 1420-27, which stands in the center of the monastery, but his grave was lost after the 1917 Revolution. Left of the cathedral as you enter it, stands the **Church of the Archangel Michael**, whose construction was completed in 1739. The red-brick refectory building next to it was finished in 1504.

Rublev was one of only seven artists listed as worthy of monuments in Lenin's plan issued in 1918.

Additional Sights Near the Rublev Museum of Ancient Art

West of this square stands the **Sergiy of Radonezh Church**, *59 Nikoloyamskaya Street*, which was completed in 1838. St. Sergius, now the patron saint of Russia, was born in 1314 in a family of a pious Rostov medieval nobleman and became a hermit in the forest in the 1340's. At the age of 26, he founded the now-exalted monastery, **The Holy Trinity St. Sergius Lavra**, in Sergiyev Posad, Russia's spiritual capital northeast of Moscow (see Chapter 18, *Excursions & Day Trips*). In 1380, when Muscovy was confronted by an army of 400,000 Mongols, St. Sergius encouraged Prince Dmitry Donskoy and his 100,000-strong army to fight the Tartars. This ended in the famous battle of Kulikovo, where the infidels were beaten decisively for the first time in 140 years.

For information about the Cuban-cuisine restaurant **Las Palmas** or the Georgian **Cafe Agdam** nearby, see Chapter 12, *Where to Eat*.

THE RUSSIAN EXHIBITION CENTER

Prospekt Mira at metro VDNkH. Tel. 181-9504 or 9758. Open daily from 10am to 8pm, Saturdays and Sundays from 10am to 9pm; the pavilions close at 7pm. No admission fee, except for a few pavilions.

Located north of the Kremlin, northwest of **Sokolniki Park**, and southeast of the **Botanical Gardens**. Within walking distance of the VDNkH metro station, and the Kosmos Hotel across the street.

This gigantic sight has no peer. The grounds of the Communist-inspired Exhibition Center, along with the Botanical Gardens and park, were once part of the enormous Ostankino estate of more than 2,500 acres. The estate belonged to Count Nikolay Sheremetyev, where he had tens of thousands of serfs.

The exhibition originated in Gorky Park in 1923 with some 50 pavilions illustrating agricultural products, but closed after three months. A permanent complex at the present site was started in 1937 and an agricultural fair opened in 1954, displaying the country's achievements in agriculture to inspire Soviet farmers. As other exhibits were being added, it came to be called, in 1959, the **Exhibition of Economic Achievements**.

The exhibition covers 570 acres of gardens, walkways and fountains, as well as some 80 pavilions. All major industries of the former Soviet Union are highlighted, from tractors to electronic equipment. Each of the 15 former republics has its own building in that region's style. The obligatory larger-than-life statue of Lenin stands just inside the VDNkH entrance in front of the central pavilion.

A huge monument of a peasant couple striding forth in unison, holding aloft the hammer and sickle, titled *Worker & Collective Farm Woman*, has towered over the entrance since 1939. It is by its sheer size a Communist monstrosity that you might not be able to ignore, and to some, it will be as startling as the 70-year-old history of the communist Soviet Union. Sculpted by the Riga-born **Vera Mukhina** (1889-1953), who also created the statue of Tchaikovsky in front of the **Moscow Conservatory**, this stainless steel behemoth represented the Soviets at the 1937 World Exhibition in Paris. For many years the statue was also the symbol of Mosfilm, the state film company.

It is almost 83 feet high and weighs 75 tons. To the former Soviet Union tyrants, it expressed the strength and confidence of their people; today many a Muscovite merely sneers in derision on seeing it, while you may not know how to react. It was the Soviet Union's answer to the exhibitions of Paris and New York.

After World War II, Mukhina was asked by Stalin to do his portrait, but she cleverly avoided the assignment by wanting Stalin to pose for her, which the vain tyrant, insecure about his appearance, would not allow.

Once inside, you might enjoy sitting in front of the **Fountain of Friendship**, with its gilded statues of maidens, representing the former Soviet republics, encircling a giant sheaf of wheat. Jets of water shoot high into the air and are illuminated at night by 500 spotlights.

After the Soviet Union's collapse, the exhibition center was neglected and almost abandoned until new Russian capitalists took over. Today, you can buy a Swedish sewing machine, a pair of German shoes, or a Japanese vacuum cleaner. At the pavilion which once honored space exploration, you can now purchase a Cadillac automobile. Cameras and skis are sold at what was once the Pavilion of Agronomy.

In the winter there is ice skating and troyka rides.

If you get hungry, there are several cafes and kiosks selling a variety of food, but you might confine yourself to bottled water and soft drinks unless you have some assurance that the food will not ruin the rest of your trip. But if you would like to conclude your VDNkH marathon with something more memorable, try **Bali**, the first Indonesian restaurant in Moscow which opened in 1996. It is located southeast of the Kosmos

Hotel, *15 Ulitsa Kosmonavtov at Ulitsa Yaroslavskaya*, and is open from 4pm to midnight.

SAKHAROV HUMAN RIGHTS MUSEUM

57 Ulitsa Zemlyanoy val, Bldg. 6, at Poluyaroslavskaya nab., Metro Kurskaya. Tel. 916-2653. Open daily from 10am to 5pm, closed Mondays. Small admission fee.
Located east of the Kremlin, about five blocks south of Kursky Railway Station, and north of the bank of the Yauza River, on the second floor of a restored police station, opposite the house in which Sakharov lived before dying.

This **Peace, Progress and Human Rights Museum** was inaugurated on May 20, 1996 on the eve of the 75th anniversary of the birth of the creator of the hydrogen bomb and a dissident. The museum consists of three sections: Russia's totalitarian past, Russia's contemporary problems, and the life of Sakharov. It was named the Peace, Progress and Human Rights Museum after the lecture Sakharov delivered when he received the Nobel Peace Prize in 1975.

The museum is designed to foster intellectual freedom, tolerance and civil responsibility, values which are still not widely shared in Russia, according to **Yelena Bonner**, Sakharov's widow who attended the opening ceremony. "We have yet to say farewell to our totalitarian psyche, even though we now live in a different state," she said.

Since the center was to provide access to documents on the history of totalitarian rule in Russia, the architect Ilya Voznesensky divided it with two high file cabinets, thus creating three separate sections, which also include a library and a computer center. The first section contrasts the Communist myth with the totalitarian reality by displaying samples of official propaganda. The second section contains biographies of persons executed under Stalin and the dossiers of those who resisted the regime. On a computer monitor in this section, you can see a map of the Gulag, the Soviet forced-labor camps. The third section presents the human rights situation in Russia today and tells about Sakharov's life. Childhood photos, covers of his early books and his letters to political leaders are displayed.

Andrey Sakharov (1921-1989) studied physics at Moscow State University. Upon graduation in 1942, he worked as engineer in an arms plant on the Volga River. Three years later he began graduate work in theoretical physics in Moscow. In 1948, Sakharov played a crucial role in the development of the first Soviet hydrogen bomb, which was tested in 1953. Later in that decade he became concerned about the harmful effects of radioactive fallout and campaigned for an end to nuclear weapons testing. He was eventually barred from secret work and deprived of many privileges.

In 1980, Sakharov was banished to Gorky (now Nizhny Novgorod) for his decade-long campaign against human rights abuses in the Soviet Union. Mikhail Gorbachev released him in 1986 after phoning him personally and telling him he was free to return to Moscow. Sakharov became a deputy to parliament three years later.

The museum is sponsored by the Sakharov Foundation, the Moscow city government, the Berlin Wall Museum, United States Agency for International Development, and other organizations.

TOLSTOY MUSEUM

11 Ulitsa Prechistenka at Lopukhinsky pereulok, Metro Kropotkinskaya. Tel. 202-2190, Fax 202-9338. Open daily from 11am to 4:30pm, closed Mondays and last Friday of each month. Small admission fee.

Located southwest of the Kremlin, four typically long Moscow blocks southwest of the metro station Kropotkinskaya, and one block southeast of the Pushkin Museum on the other side of the street.

This museum is installed in the one-story Empire-style Lopukhin mansion, whose stucco finish conceals a wooden villa. As with the house, the six Ionic columns supporting the portico are not made of stone. It was designed by serf architect Afanasy Grigoriyev, who earlier built Khrushchev's house, which is now the Pushkin Museum.

Lev Tolstoy never actually lived here, although his children attended a school on Prechistenka Street. The Museum's nine halls contain a large number of manuscripts, some 70,000 pages in all, documents and pictures, as well as books and letters, related to the great Russian novelist. Compared to his house in Khamovniki district (see below), the rooms here are bright, airy and high-ceilinged. Room 4 is devoted to *War and Peace* and Room 5 deals with *Anna Karenina*. You might not enjoy this museum unless you are interested in Tolstoy or his time in Russia. If you can only visit one, go to Khamovniki.

Ilya Repin's painting of Tolstoy, finished less than a year before the writer's death, will greet you on the first room's wall facing the entrance. There are illustrations by Boris Pasternak's father, Leonid, scattered throughout the house.

In the courtyard stands a granite statue of a gloomy Tolstoy, with his head bent and his hands behind his belt. It was created by sculptor **Sergey Merkurov** on the 100th anniversary of the novelist's birth. Merkurov's inspiration came after taking the writer's death mask at the Astapovo railway station where Tolstoy died in 1910. This monument was originally placed in a triangular public garden, Maidens' Field, near Zubovsky

Square in 1928. Forty-four years later, in 1972, a new one was sculpted by Portyenko and this sculpture was exiled to Prechistenka Street.

Additional Sights Near the Tolstoy Museum

A few houses away is the House of **Denis Davidov**, *17 Ulitsa Prechistenka*, a hero of the Napoleonic war of 1812, after whom Tolstoy named his character Denisov in *War and Peace,* his monumental work that required six years at Yasnaya Polyana estate to complete. That estate, near Tula, lies 200 miles south of Moscow and requires a full day to visit. Please see Chapter 18, *Excursions & Day Trips* for more information.

For information about the nearby Georgian restaurant **U Mamy Zoyi**, see Chapter 12, *Where to Eat.*

TOLSTOY'S HOUSE IN KHAMOVNIKI

21 Ulitsa Lva Tolstogo at Obolensky pereulok, Metro Park Kultury or Frunzenskaya. Tel. 246-9444 or 6112. Open Tuesday through Sunday, from 10am to 5pm; in winter 10am to 3:30pm; closed Mondays. Small admission fee.

Located southwest of the Kremlin, northwest of Gorky Park across the Moskva River, and two long blocks west of Park Kultury metro station. A beer brewery next door is still operational after more than 100 years.

Lev Tolstoy Street approximately parallels the Garden Ring Road and his former 16-room cottage faces what must surely be one of the longest city blocks in central Moscow. If you approach the street from Zubovsky proyezd, you will have to make a long detour to the northwest or southeast before reaching Tolstoy Street.

An old pink-and-green wooden country-style house with a garden, both hidden behind a wooden fence, is the residence where the writer, philosopher, moralist and mystic lived every winter from 1882 to 1901 to enable his many children to attend proper schools in the city. Built in 1820's and characteristic of the homes on the outskirts of Moscow, it is located in an area known as Khamovniki. After 1901, Tolstoy lived in Yasnaya Polyana and began devoting himself to the welfare of the peasants on his estate, denounced his earlier masterpieces, and repudiated his wealth. After his death, the 18-room building was nationalized and in 1921 was made into a museum. Tolstoy had neither electricity nor running water and the house remains without electricity to this day. He bought the cottage mostly to placate his wife who wanted to enjoy the conveniences of Moscow and a cultural life.

In this house, which belonged to the Tolstoys for almost 30 years, recitals and literary soirees were organized in the upstairs drawing room, even if the head of the family shunned many of them later in his life. Sergey Rachmaninov played the piano and Fyodor Shalyapin sang here. The family also entertained the painter Ilya Repin until his affair with their daughter Tatyana; several of his portraits of family members are on display. In Tolstoy's writing room, you will see his desk with a low chair because he was shortsighted.

Outside his work room is the bicycle that Tolstoy learned to ride when he was 70 years old. By the time he moved to this spacious home, he had already written *War and Peace* and his other great work, *Anna Karenina*. His manuscript draft for *The Resurrection*, part of which was written in this house in 1900, is still in Tolstoy's study; it strayed so far from orthodoxy that the Holy Synod excommunicated him the following year. *The Kreutzer Sonata* was also written here.

The kitchen, where Tolstoy's meals were prepared, still stands. The room of his first son, Sergey, a lazy Oblomov-type cynic, is also located upstairs, next to the dining room. Under the Communists, Sergey was the director of the Tolstoy museum in Yasnaya Polyana for 40 years. And near the stables there is the cabin where his wife Sofiya Andreyevna worked on her husband's manuscripts; legend has it that she copied *War and Peace* 16 times and *Anna Karenina* nine times. In the end, Tolstoy ran from home in a fit of argument and died at a small railway station in Astapovo in 1910, the same year as the great artist Mikhail Vrubel.

This house, preserved just as it was in his lifetime, is a better choice for a hurried visitor than Tolstoy Museum on Prechistenka Street, described above. The curator of both Tolstoy museums until her death in 1957 was Sofiya Aleksandrovna, one of the writer's granddaughters, who was also the first wife to poet Sergey Yesenin.

For information about two nearby restaurants **Diana** and **Dynasty**, should you get hungry, see Chapter 12, *Where to Eat*.

Additional Sights Near Tolstoy's House in Khamovniki

Either before or after you visit the Khamovniki house, stop at Tolstoy's statue at **Maidens' Field**, at the far end of Lva Tolstogo and Bolshaya Pirogovskaya Streets. Inside this small triangular park young maidens were once left as a tribute to the Tartars. The novelist's statue was created by Aleksey Portyanko and unveiled in 1972.

Going in southwesterly direction on Bolshaya Pirogovskaya, toward the Novodevichy Monastery, there are five other statues of notables within a few minutes' walking distance: botanist Mikhail Filatov, oncologist A.I. Pirogov, physiologist Ivan Sechenov, Semashko and neurosurgeon V.S. Snigirev.

MOSCOW STATE UNIVERSITY

Vorobyovskiye (Sparrow) Hills, Metro Universitet. Restricted entry.

Located southwest of the Kremlin and southwest of Luzhniki Sports Complex. It is within walking distance from the metro station.

Moscow University's 32-story 787-foot high-rise towers over the 220-acre campus and overlooks the capital from what were in Soviet times Lenin Hills and are now again called Sparrow Hills. It was the tallest structure in Europe when built, except for the Eiffel Tower. Built by thousands of slave workers from 1949 on and inaugurated in 1953, it had a teaching staff of 1,800, some 20,000 students and 1,900 laboratories. This is one of the so-called "Seven Sisters," buildings of repelling Gothic appeal, with which Stalin implied to the West that Russians can match the West in anything, including dubious architecture. It is located in a favorite recreation area with good skiing.

Moscow University is the largest in the country. About 10,000 students take entrance tests at the university's 20 faculties every year, but only about 3,500 are admitted. The enrollment has now ballooned to about 30,000, but the university, like all educational institutions, has fallen on hard times and is falling apart for lack of sufficient funding. Mikhail Gorbachev graduated here in law in 1955. There are up to 15 applicants for every vacancy at the foreign languages faculty. The students, many of whom subsist on grants as low as $10 a month, live in rooms measuring about four feet by nine feet and every two rooms share a common entrance and other facilities.

Dr. Michael DeBakey, the world's imminent heart surgeon and a pioneer in heart transplants, is just one of the many Westerners cooperating with Moscow University. The famed Texas surgeon, who received an honorary degree from Moscow University in 1993, three years later witnessed the heart bypass operation on President Boris Yeltsin.

VIKTOR VASNETSOV MUSEUM

13 Pereulok Vasnetsova at Ulitsa Meshchanskaya, Metro Sukharevskaya, Tsvetnoy bulvar or Prospekt Mira. Tel. 281-1329. Open daily from 10am to 5pm, closed Mondays and last Thursday of each month. Small admission fee.

Located north of the Kremlin, three blocks north of Garden Ring Road and four blocks west of Prospekt Mira, on a tiny patch of land set against the apartment blocks nearby.

This little log house was home to **Viktor Vasnetsov** (1848-1926) for more than 30 years. A painter and theater designer, he was **Apollinary Vasnetsov's** brother (see Apollinary Vasnetsov Museum in this chapter).

Born into the large family of a priest, Viktor Vasnetsov began drawing at an early age, but because of his father's calling he was sent to the theological seminary. He did not become a priest as his father wished; instead he entered St. Petersburg Academie of Arts, where he made friends with one of the most respected Russian painters, Ilya Repin. From 1874 on, he exhibited, like his brother, at traveling art exhibitions. In

1878, Vasnetsov moved to Moscow and later to Kiev where he created murals for the Cathedral of St. Vladimir. He joined his brother Apollinary at the **Abramtsevo** (see entry in Chapter 18, *Excursions & Day Trips*) art colony in 1879.

Influenced by folk legends and epic tales he heard in his childhood, Viktor Vasnetsov is one of the most dramatic painters of themes of Old Russia and his canvases are displayed in museums all over Russia, including the **Tretyakov Gallery**. He also refaced the Old Tretyakov Gallery in a striking medieval Russian style.

The interior of his house has been preserved to the last detail, with icons hung in a corner and the heavy dining table at which the artist spent many an evening with his friends. Black and white family photos and the artist's sketches are hung on the walls. Upstairs is Vasnetsov's large studio.

VICTORY PARK
Park Pobedy

Kutuzovsky prospekt at Ulitsa Generala Yermolova, Metro Kutuzovskaya.

Located southwest of the Kremlin, northwest of Sparrow Hills, and southeast of Filyovsky Park.

It was at the edge of Victory Park on Poklonnaya gora (The Bowing Hill) that Napoleon stood in 1812, looking at the Kremlin and awaiting the keys to the city of Moscow, which would symbolize the city's surrender to the invader. But Moscow was quickly abandoned and Napoleon waited in vain. Soon fires broke out, Napoleon withdrew and the rest is history. Poklonnaya Hill has since been leveled to a hillock that even Napoleon would not recognize and today, you cannot see very far from it. It was leveled to make room for the enormous Victory Park, a park to honor the millions who died and those who survived World War II.

The huge complex was 15 years in the making and was finally completed in 1995. It consists of an obelisk, a large museum, a church, and several monuments.

A narrow **obelisk** with Nike, the Greek goddess of victory, flanked by two angels with golden trumpets at her side, soars more than 410 feet skyward in the center of the square. It displays battle scenes and the names of Soviet cities that were designated as hero-cities because of their contribution during the war. At its base, St. George, the symbol of the city of Moscow, pitches a final, mortal lance from his rearing horse into the dying, dissected dragon of fascism.

The multi-level **Museum of the Great Patriotic War** behind the obelisk is the largest such memorial to veterans of World War II in Moscow. It is open Wednesday through Sunday from 10am to 6pm and there is no admission fee. Toilets are downstairs, on your left as you reach the bottom of the moving stairs.

Downstairs, in the **Hall of Memory**, you will see thousands of tiny lights suspended in the darkened hall as "tears" of memory for the fallen, while funereal music is heard. Russians have plenty to remember. Their war loses are estimated at 32 million dead, but even if the numbers are smaller, they are still well beyond what any other nation suffered during the World War II. There are six dioramas on the same level, among them those featuring the battles of Stalingrad, Moscow, Leningrad and Berlin, where the Russians are shown raising their flag over the Reichstag.

Upstairs, in the **Hall of Honor**, you can read the names of the 11,700 men and women who received the title of Hero of the Soviet Union, and 13 cities that were similarly honored for the war effort. The museum has one of the largest displays of documents, photos, uniforms, weapons and mementos anywhere. There are continuous showings of wartime documentaries. The mood is somber and the multiplicity of displays may wear you out.

A handsome stylized ancient-style **church**, the first one built since the 1917 Revolution, was completed in 1995 in record time. Instead of paintings, it is decorated with relief panels in bronze. The icon of St. George on the wall to your left as you enter was donated by the Moscow mayor. Other churches are planned nearby.

Another impressive monument outside is the huge sculptural ensemble, titled **Tragedy of the Peoples**, which was sculpted by the noted Georgian artist **Zurab Tsereteli**, who also created the obelisk and St. George with the dragon at the foot of the obelisk. Muscovites found the clothesless figures of male and female prisoners and their children, all of whom are falling back into each other, obviously doomed to death, so oppressive they convinced the mayor to move the enormous metallic composition away from the central square of Poklonnaya Hill.

Between the figures and a massive metal wall stand several more blocks dedicated to those who died during the war with inscriptions in several languages of the former Soviet Union. Behind the wall and the figures, metal reproductions of shoes, toys, books and suitcases are strewn on the monument's platform. Tsereteli also sculpted the monument of a dragon destroying missiles, which was inaugurated in front of the United Nations in New York in 1991.

If you want to see how strongly Russians feel about their losses in World War II, come here on May 9th, commemorated as the Victory Day.

On the eastern edge of the Victory Park, in the middle of Kutuzov Avenue, stands the **Triumphal Arch**, designed by **Osip Bove** and erected at the Belorussky Railway station in 1834, to commemorate Russia's victory over Napoleon. Razed in the 1930's and lying forgotten, like so many other treasures, at the **Donskoy Monastery** (see separate entry), it was resurrected and moved here in the 1960's, when Tverskaya Street was widened. To admire the fine detail, you can approach the arch through an underpass from either side of the avenue.

For information about the Italian restaurant **Gian Carlo** or the German **Triumf-Koenig Stube**, see Chapter 12, *Where to Eat.*

14. CULTURE

There are some 400 state-supported repertory theaters in Russia, according to the Ministry of Culture. These include more than 20 opera and ballet companies, usually combined, and 19 theaters for musical comedy. Russia boasts 80 large symphony orchestras. There are more than 200 major art museums.

Who would have thought that following half a century of brutal repression it would have come to this? After writers, composers, painters and poets had died for their art - not for lack of food, but rather for lack of artistic freedom - a long-sought opportunity finally arrived when they could express what they felt. But now the realities of Russia's economy seem just as restrictive as the Communists were before. There are signs of rebirth here and there, but the immediate image of the country's cultural life is one of poverty and creative paralysis.

What was once a comfortable life - at least for those artists willing to toe the Communist line - has now been deflated by reduced state subsidies and the ravages of inflation into a financial existence that is for some almost as terrifying as the knock on the door before dawn. Unknown artists and the largest cultural institutions in Russia have to compete for apathetic consumers who can barely afford their daily bread. Some artists must wonder which is worse: a totalitarian regime that bestowed on them dachas in the same breath as censors, or democracy with an uncertain future and excesses disguised as freedom of expression.

The lack of money and capitulation to the excesses of the West are noticeable everywhere, from museums that had their subsidies cut to films that mesmerize Muscovites with the worst examples of artistic freedom. Because of a lack of money, the central building at the Tretyakov Museum in Moscow was closed for ten years before reopening in 1995. The Bolshoy Theater needs a temporary home for its ballet and opera company during the reconstruction of its theater. Reconstruction started in 1996 and will probably shut it down for years at a cost of millions of dollars.

Many artists and observers believe that the level of Russian culture fell with the fall of the Soviet Union. And even those artistic groups that have remained at their former lofty heights are now so obsessed with earning hard currency in the West that a Londoner or a New Yorker must surely wonder whether there are any performers left in Moscow or St. Petersburg. It is not uncommon for a large Western city to play host to a Russian artist almost every other week.

The Russian Ministry of Culture, which in the former Soviet Union received between three and four percent of the national budget, now gets less than one percent. Municipalities, like Moscow, are supposed to make up the difference, but are unable to cope with inflation. Corporate sponsors have no real tax incentives to support the arts.

At the Bolshoy, some Russians can still qualify for discounted tickets to see a performance for which you may have to pay $50 a seat. But even at rock-bottom ruble prices, many Russians cannot afford to pay for a ticket, so they are drifting to television, which is practically free entertainment.

For tickets to many of Moscow's cultural events, or the circus, talk with the concierge at your hotel or buy them from **EPS Theater Box Office**, *Metropol Hotel, 1/4 Teatralny proyezd, Metro Teatralnaya, Tel. 927-6982 or 6983, Fax 250-9741.* Their hours are Monday through Friday, from 11am to 7pm; Saturdays and Sundays, from 10am to 3pm. They take orders for same-day performances until about 2pm. You will pay a healthy service charge, but will get good seats and can ask all your questions in English. While the prices for Bolshoy tickets range up to $100, most other events cost much less. You should be able to get good theater seats for under $25.

Getting them directly at the box office may be the next best thing, but always have someone call on your behalf to make sure tickets are still available and you are not wasting an hour of your time getting to the theater. The kiosk ticket sellers are a passable alternative, although you will probably pay as much as you would to the EPS but get lesser seats.

You can also get tickets for some cultural events at the main **Intourist** office, *13 Ulitsa Mokhovaya, Metro Okhotny Ryad, Tel. 203-6962*, near the Natsional Hotel, but call ahead for details.

CLASSICAL MUSIC

Evening theater and concert performances usually begin between 6:30 and 8pm. It is customary to check your coat and anything larger than a woman's purse, including your umbrella. There is no charge for this service, but try not to resist it because this rule goes back many years and applies to everyone. Wear jeans if you feel you absolutely must, and

Muscovites will understand if men skip the tie, but do not show up in shorts for a performance at the Tchaikovsky Concert Hall or the Bolshoy. Programs are sold in the lobby by the attendants who check your ticket. Concerts usually have one intermission, but plays and operettas may have two or even three. They each last up to 15 minutes and most theaters and concert halls have foyers large enough for you to stretch your numb feet and get a refreshment. You will usually hear three warning bells before a performance starts or resumes.

Russians are punctual to cultural events and the curtain goes up on time. You will not likely be admitted until the first act is over if you show up late. If someone else has taken your seat, do not fuss. It is a common practice that theatergoers appropriate better seats if they are still empty after a performance has begun.

Just a handful of Moscow theaters have anything approaching air-conditioning during the summer. Theaters are much more concerned about shielding you from numbing cold in the winter than cooling during a week or two in summer. A heat wave may last for a few days only, but if you are an unlucky patron sitting through such a time at the Lenkom Theater, let's say, you may never forget the stifling heat in the auditorium.

If at home you rush out before a play or concert is over, know that this is not what Russians do. Concert-goers at the Moscow Conservatory may applaud enthusiastically for five minutes after a performance has concluded, waiting to hear an encore. As impersonal as Muscovites may appear to you on the street, you will be amazed at the flowers and emotions they shower on their favorite artists.

These are the two most important concert halls in Moscow:

MOSCOW CONSERVATORY, *11 & 13 Ulitsa Bolshaya Nikitskaya, Metro Pushkinskaya or Arbatskaya. Tel. 229-8183 or 0042 or 7412. Performances usually begin at 7pm.*

Centrally located inside the Boulevard Ring Road, northwest of the Kremlin, and two blocks southwest of Tverskaya Street.

The Moscow Conservatory (also referred to as the Tchaikovsky Conservatory) was founded in 1866 by musician **Nikolay Rubinstein**, the year when **Peter Ilytich Tchaikovsky** wrote his *First Symphony*. In addition to Tchaikovsky, who taught here for twelve years, countless other Russian composers and performers were trained and also taught at the Conservatory, including Sergey Prokofiev and modernist Alfred Schnittke. Mstislav Rostropovich, who was exiled in 1974 for sheltering writer Aleksandr Solzhenitsyn, but had his citizenship restored by Gorbachev during the time of glasnost, taught here for 26 years.

The Conservatory's **Grand Hall** (Bolshoy zal), *13 Bolshaya Nikitskaya*, is an 18th century palace of Princess Yekaterina Dashkova. It was designed

FIRST PRIZE GOES TO AN AMERCIAN

*In 1958, a completely unknown Texas pianist, **Van Cliburn**, won the first Tchaikovsky International Piano Competition at the Conservatory against all odds for his performance of Tchaikovsky's First Piano Concerto in B Flat Minor and Rachmaninov's Third Piano Concerto in D Minor. Soviet pianist Lev Vlasenko shared second prize with a Chinese pianist. Composer Dmitry Shostakovich was chairman of its organizing committee.*

All this took place during the Cold War and set the precedent that talent would be recognized regardless of nationality. The Soviet Minister of Culture had to go directly to Premier Nikita Khrushchev, who had assumed office only a few weeks earlier, to get instructions as to what to do. Khrushchev supposedly asked him:

"Is he really the best?"

"Yes, he is the best," replied the minister.

"In that case, give him the first prize," said Khrushchev, who personally met the pianist and embraced him. And the rest is history.

Van Cliburn received a prize of 25,000 rubles, which in 1958 was officially valued as $6,230, a nice sum. He was also honored with a ticker tape parade in New York City.

Second-placed Vlasenko recalls that the whole of Moscow followed the competition; even taxi drivers asked him about the tall, blond American. Overnight, he became an idol for half the young women in the Soviet Union.

Van Cliburn now lives in Fort Worth, Texas, where he manages a piano competition under his own name every four years. He celebrated his 60th birthday with a performance in Los Angeles with the Moscow Philharmonic, the same orchestra he performed with when he won the 1958 Tchaikovsky Competition.

by Matvey Kazakov and purchased by Rubinstein in 1859. The first concert, dedicated to Tchaikovsky, who died five years earlier, was held in 1898. The 1750-seat hall has natural light streaming through glass panels in the ceiling. Also part of the Conservatory is the 500-seat **Chamber Hall** (Maly zal). The Conservatory's **Rachmaninov Hall**, *11 Bolshaya Nikitskaya Street, Tel. 229-0294*, is a former boyar mansion.

Tchaikovsky's portrait hangs above the Grand Hall's stage; the walls above the balcony are lined with oval portraits of other classical composers. In 1940, the portraits of George Frederick Handel, Franz Joseph Haydn, Felix Mendelssohn and Christoph Willibald Gluck were replaced by Modest Petrovich Mussorgsky, Nicholas Andreievich Rimsky-Korsakov, Frederic Chopin and Dargomyzhsky. Symphonic concerts, solo recitals and opera performances are given here. The Conservatory is also the largest music school in Russia.

The Tchaikovsky International Piano Competition is held here, as well as in Klin, 50 miles northwest of the capital, where the great Russian composer lived from 1885 until his death in 1893. In that year, after his return from England and after the first performance of his *Pathetique Symphony*, he is believed to have died of cholera.

There is a **statue** of Tchaikovsky, seated and with his arms raised as if writing music, outside the main entrance to the Conservatory. It was designed by **Vera Mukhina** (1889-1953), who also created the enormous monument *Worker and Collective Farm Woman* in front of the Russian Exhibition Center. Born in Latvia, Mukhina was two years old when her mother died and four years old when she lost her father. She came to Moscow at 11 and a year later began studying sculpture. Following a disfiguring toboggan accident, her relatives in 1912 granted her wish to study in Paris. She died in Moscow at 64.

Tchaikovsky was born in 1840, the same year that the Italian violin virtuoso Nicolò Paganini died. His father was an inspector of government mines. He studied law in St. Petersburg and worked as a clerk for the Ministry of Justice. He became a professor at the Moscow Conservatory in 1866, but on receiving an annuity from a wealthy widow, Nadezhda von Meck, whom he never met, Tchaikovsky was able to devote himself to composing entirely. He married in 1877, but frustrated by his homosexual preferences left his bride after a month. He toured London in 1888 and the US in 1891. Tchaikovsky wrote his first composition, *Symphony in G Minor*, when he was 26 years old and concluded his career with his *Third Piano Concerto* at the age of 53. He also produced 11 operas.

TCHAIKOVSKY CONCERT HALL, *4/31 Triumfalnaya ploshchad, Metro Mayakovskaya. Tel. 299-3957 or 3681. Performances usually begin at 7pm.*

Located northwest of the Kremlin, just inside the Garden Ring Road, and facing the statue of poet Vladimir Mayakovsky on Triumfalnaya Square.

Triumfalnaya Square was originally named after the triumphal arches that were built here in the 18th century to welcome tsars. Before the Revolution, this was the site of the Zon Comedy Theater. This gargantuan building with its ten-columned portico atop the Mayakovskaya metro station was originally built as a theater for the legendary avant-garde theatrical director Vsevolod Meyerhold (1874-1940) and was to contain two circular stages.

In 1938, when the bloody climate of political repression began frothing at the mouth and the director became increasingly isolated, the theater was converted into a concert hall and Meyerhold was hauled off to Siberia and died two years later. (For more about Meyerhold, please see **Mayakovsky Theater**.)

This large circular auditorium in the shape of half an amphitheater can seat 1,650. There is a huge pipe organ, with 7,800 pipes weighing 20 tons, which was made in the former Czechoslovakia and installed in 1959.

The State Symphony Orchestra regularly performs at the Tchaikovsky Concert Hall and many musical and other cultural events are held here.

Other Centrally Located Concert Halls

Kolonny Zal, *1 Ulitsa Bolshaya Dmitrovka, Tel. 292-4864*, is located inside the Boulevard Ring Road, across the street from Hotel Moskva and Teatralnaya metro station.

Prechistenka Concert Hall, *32 Ulitsa Prechistenka, Tel. 201-4986*, is located two blocks inside the Garden Ring Road, metro Park Kultury or Kropotkinskaya.

Rossiya Concert Hall, *Tel. 298-1124*, is centrally located inside the huge Rossiya Hotel, next to Red Square and St. Basil's Cathedral, metro Kitay-gorod.

State Kremlin Palace, *Tel. 917-2336*, is centrally located inside the Kremlin, with entrance at Trinity Gate, metro Aleksandrovsky sad.

THEATER

Until Russia's independence, theater, like most other arts had generous support, if not the intellectual freedom, of the omnipotent state. Actors were trained in specialized schools and practically guaranteed lifetime employment in one professional company or another.

Theater is popular with all classes of Russian society because most are exposed to theatrical arts from an early age and continue identifying with it through adulthood. There are four premier children's theaters in Moscow alone and many other subsidiary groups that cater to the young. There are also several puppet theaters in the capital and they often perform to full houses, almost as often for adults as for children.

LOOK FOR THE ASTERISK

While a basic knowledge of Russian will help you to appreciate the brilliance of the Russian theater, there are several stages in Moscow where you can have good time even if you do not understand the language. We have placed an asterisk on these theaters. For children's theaters, please see Chapter 9, Child's Play.

Ballet was introduced to the Russian imperial court in the 18th century during the reign of Empress Anna (1730-40). Russian ballet reached its absolute perfection under the direction of **Sergey Diaghilev** at the beginning of this century. Neither the 1917 October Revolution nor World War II could stop its complete world dominance. Only in the 1990's has lack of money and competition with other forms of popular entertainment created doubts as to what the future might bring.

The ballet season in Moscow does not include the summer months, from June through August, when the actors and dancers perform abroad or at special events throughout the country.

There never seems to be a consensus on the exact number of theaters, but there are more than one hundred opera and ballet, drama and comedy, musical comedy and variety, and marionette theaters in Moscow. Until now, most theatrical companies have been permanent and their repertoire consisted of seven to 15 productions. Russian classical playwright Aleksandr Ostrovsky, dead for 110 years, is the most popular author in Moscow, with at least half a dozen of his plays being performed every season. He is usually followed by Dostoyevsky or Gogol.

The show may change nightly at some theaters because actors can play several roles. It is unthinkable in Moscow to run the same show for years in one theater, as was done with Agatha Christie's *Mousetrap* in London or is the case with a number of Broadway musicals in New York.

THEATERS INSIDE THE BOULEVARD RING ROAD

BOLSHOY OPERA & BALLET THEATER*, *1 Teatralnaya ploshchad at Ulitsa Petrovka, Metro Teatralnaya. Tel. 292-9986 for information, 292-6690 for repertoire, 292-0050 or 3491 for tickets. Performances usually begin at 7pm.*

Centrally located north of the Kremlin, across the square from the Metropol and Moskva Hotels, and the Maly Theater.

The area where the Bolshoy Theater and the Metropol Hotel stand was known as Theater Square until 1919, when it was renamed Sverdlov Square, after the Russian revolutionary and politician. In 1991 it again became Teatralnaya ploshchad.

The Bolshoy is Moscow's oldest opera and ballet house and has enjoyed more than 220 seasons. It was founded in 1776 and has been at this location since 1780. After burning down in 1805, it was rebuilt in 1824. Thirty years later, after it burned down again, the Imperial Theatrical Society bought its site and commissioned the present building, which includes the colonnade of an earlier structure.

The statue of Phoebus in the Sun Chariot above the Ionic portico was sculpted by **Pyotr Klodt**. A fountain in front of the Bolshoy overlooks the Square. The theater's interior consists of five tiers of gilded boxes and about 2,200 seats. Its chandelier is composed of 13,000 pieces of cut glass. The ceiling has a huge painting, *Apollo and Muses*, that was completed in 1856 by Titov.

"Bolshoy," which translates into "grand" employs several hundred singers, dancers, and musicians, as well as another 1,900 behind-the-stage workers who are responsible for everything from costumes to special effects and cleaning. It nurtures new ballet dancers through its own ballet school. Many Bolshoy performers still earn wages comparable to factory workers, although the lucky ones who travel abroad make much more.

The Opera's repertoire over the years included Tchaikovsky's *The Maid of Orleans*, *Yevgeny Onegin* and *The Queen of Spades*, Borodin's *Prince Igor*, Glinka's *Life for the Tsar* and *Ruslan and Ludmila*, Musorgsky's *Boris Godunov* and Rimsky-Korsakov's *Mlada* and *Sadko*, Rachmaninov's one-act operas based on works by Pushkin, *Aleko* and *The Covetous Night*, as well as Puccini's *Madame Butterfly* and *Tosca*, Rossini's *The Barber of Seville*, and Verdi's *Il Trovatore*.

Beginning in 1778, the Bolshoy also gained a reputation for its ballet performances. Its repertoire now spans *Giselle*, *Swan Lake*, *Ivan the Terrible*, *Romeo and Juliet*, *Sleeping Beauty*, *Spartacus*, *Anna Karenina*, *The Nutcracker* and *La Bayadere* and *Le Corsaire*. In the opinion of those who would know, the quality of performances, whether in opera or ballet, has suffered measurably over the last few years. The Bolshoy still has one of the better orchestras.

Until the autumn of 1994, the Bolshoy operated under a system of lifelong tenure, whereby artistic directors reigned over their fiefdoms with an iron hand. They single-handedly decided which ballets the company performed and who traveled abroad. That year, President Yeltsin decreed that all Bolshoy staff members will henceforth be hired only on a contractual basis, as in most Western groupss.

Since 1996, the Bolshoy has been under a multi-million-dollar reconstruction effort and it is anybody's guess how long it will take. The theater is situated above the River Neglinka, which was forced underground after Napoleon's invasion of Moscow.

You can buy tickets at the Bolshoy box office, at the Intourist office three blocks southwest and next to the Natsional Hotel, or through the **EPS Theater Box Office**, which is located inside the Metropol Hotel. You can also buy tickets at theater kiosks in central Moscow or through your hotel. Expect to pay from $25 to $100 for a good ticket.

We advise against buying the $5-10 tickets from the scalpers around the Bolshoy. You will invariably end up in the second row of one of the high-tier boxes, where you will see practically nothing, unless you stand up and crane your neck during the entire performance.

The Bolshoy Theater's **Beethoven Hall**, which has existed in its current form since 1895, is one of the most elegant and acoustically desirable facilities in Moscow. It is the venue for daytime chamber orchestras and vocal concerts.

The **Museum of the Bolshoy Theater**, *8/2 Okhotny Ryad, Metro Okhotny Ryad, Tel. 292-0025*, was founded in 1920. It contains more than 11,000 sketches of decorations and costumes created for Bolshoy performances. The pictorial, graphic and sculpture sections number some 500 items. There are more than 600 other items, including theatrical costumes by such legends as Shalyapin.

THE BAT CABARET✱ (Letuchaya Mysh), *GITIS Theater, 10 Bolshoy Gnezdnikovsky pereulok, Metro Pushkinskaya or Tverskaya. Tel. 229-7087.*

Centrally located northwest of the Kremlin, inside the Boulevard Ring Road, in a narrow lane next to the original Russkoye Bistro, a Russian fast food restaurant.

The original Bat Cabaret was founded in 1908 by a Moscow Arts Theater actor who was responsible for preparing the theater's annual New Year's program of party sketches. Its mixture of satire, parody, and music and dance numbers proved wildly popular so the cabaret performed regularly on the small stage of what is now the GITIS Theater until 1913. In 1920, the company emigrated to Paris. Until the Great Depression it toured often and performed to great acclaim on Broadway.

The Bat Cabaret was resurrected in the early 1980s in Brezhnev Russia, where cabaret was not appreciated by the authorities. In May 1989, the GITIS theater gave permission for the use of its stage for ten performances to test the waters. Two months later, in the traditionally dead August season, the company rented the 1,000-seat Yermolova Theater on Tverskaya and sold out.

GELIKON OPERA (Helicon Opera), *19 Ulitsa Bolshaya Nikitskaya, Metro Arbatskaya. Tel. 290-0971 or 1323.*

Centrally located northwest of the Kremlin, one block east of the Boulevard Ring Road, at the Mayakovsky Theater address.

Gelikon Theater, now renamed Gelikon Opera, was established in 1990 when it began its repertoire with single-act operas by Stravinsky, Debussy, Hindemith and Prokofiev.

It has staged Bizet's *Carmen*, Tchaikovsky's *The Queen of Spades* and Verdi's *The Masked Ball* and *La Traviata*.

MALY THEATER, *1/6 Teatralnaya ploshchad, Metro Teatralnaya. Tel. 923-2621. Performances usually begin at 7pm.*

Centrally located northeast of the Kremlin, across the street from the Bolshoy Theater on one side and the Metropol Hotel on the other. One of Maly's two locations, the other is at 69 Bolshaya Ordynka Street, south of the Kremlin and just inside the Garden Ring Road.

Like its neighbor, the Bolshoy, Maly (which means "little," or the opposite of "bolshoy") was also designed by architect **Osip Bove**. It is located above the now-subterranean Neglinka River, with the Bolshoy Theater on the other shore. Inaugurated in 1824, Maly was Moscow's first dramatic theater and one of the best in Russia. It was administered by the emperor's court and controlled by an official committee.

Always closely connected with the development of progressive social thinking, it has often been said that "in Moscow one went to college, but studied in the Maly Theater." Maly played an important role in Russian theater by staging classical plays by Russian writers, such as Aleksandr Ostrovsky, whose statue you can see in front of the theater. Muscovites have nicknamed it Ostrovsky House because it produced 47 of the playwright's 48 works.

Chekhov's *The Cherry Orchard*, Ostrovsky's *Balzaminov's Marriage* and *Rags to Riches* were staged here. *The Victors' Feast*, Aleksandr Solzhenitsyn's play in verse about an intelligence unit at the end of World War II, was staged for the first time at the end of 1994.

MAYAKOVSKY THEATER, *19 Ulitsa Bolshaya Nikitskaya, Metro Arbatskaya. Tel. 290-4658 or 2725.*

Centrally located northwest of the Kremlin, one block east of Boulevard Ring Road, at the same address as Gelikon Opera.

This theater is named after **Vladimir Mayakovsky**, a poet who vigorously supported the Bolsheviks. You can see his statue in front of the **Tchaikovsky Concert Hall** on Triumfalnaya Square. The theater is a child of the October Revolution, the first such theater to be created by the Soviets and it caused a stir among the older theaters, which were producing classics.

But it flopped: its inexperienced actors performed on the back of tramways and at railway stations to Red Army men going to the front. The group was replenished with more qualified performers and given its own building. In 1926, the renowned theatrical director **Vsevolod Meyerhold** came on board, but even he could not get rid of the revolutionary deadwood. When in the 1930's Meyerhold staged the classic *Romeo and Juliet* it was so popular that it stayed in the repertory for decades. This was followed by productions of *Hamlet* and, during the height of Stalinism, of *Medea*. The theater, which has 1,060 seats, was named after Mayakovsky in 1954.

After *Pravda's* denunciation of Shostakovich's opera *Ledi Makbet* in 1936, Meyerhold was the only Soviet artist who publicly protested the denunciation, declaring that it was destroying Russian art and culture. He was immediately arrested and never seen again. American journalist David Remnick quotes a Russian researcher who said that while imprisoned Meyerhold had to drink his own urine and his interrogators broke his left arm and forced him to sign his "confession" with his right one. His wife Zinaida Raikh was just as brutally murdered a few weeks later. An employee of the NKVD (later KGB) climbed through her balcony window and stabbed her with a knife eight times.

MOSCOW ART THEATER (Chekhov), *3 Kamergersky pereulok, Metro Teatralnaya. Tel. 229-8760 or 5370.*

Centrally located north of the Kremlin, one block west of the Moscow Operetta Theater, and half a block east of Tverskaya Street.

This theater is better known by its initials, MKhAT, which stands for Moscow Art Academic Theater. The theater is sometimes called the House of Chekhov because it gained its prestige through the plays of Anton Chekhov. After a successful run of Chekhov's *The Seagull*, the bird became the theater's emblem. You will know you are near the theater by a large portrait of Chekhov painted on a wall across the street.

The Moscow Art Theater was founded in 1898, after stage directors **Konstantin Stanislavsky** and **Vladimir Nemirovich-Danchenko** conceived it over a 2pm lunch (in a private room in Moscow's oldest restaurant, Slavyansky Bazar) that continued at Stanislavsky's villa until 8am the following morning in June 1897. For almost 18 hours the two men quizzed each other, hardly believing the unanimity of their views about theater. They agreed that Nemirovich-Danchenko would have veto over literary matters and Stanislavsky over artistic ones. It was in this theater that Stanislavsky developed his "Stanislavsky Method," based on the traditions of Russian theater.

The Moscow Art Theater is a direct descendant of Savva Mamontov's dramatic circle and its offshoot, the **Private Opera**, which still stands at 6 Bolshaya Dmitrovka Street, although it is known today as the **Moscow Operetta Theater. Savva Mamontov** (1841-1918) was one of the wealthiest men of his time until his arrest in 1899, when he was accused of illegal dealings. Imprisoned for a year, but then exonerated, he lost his fortune and died in a Moscow suburb during the bitterly cold winter of 1918. For more about his patronage of the arts, see **Abramtsevo Estate** in Chapter 18, *Excursions & Day Trips*.

After MKhAT toured America in 1923, they staged Bulgakov's *Days of the Turbines* that the novelist himself dramatized, but it was banned by the Communist Party. Bulgakov appealed directly to Stalin and to everyone's astonishment the dictator himself showed up for a performance; later it was banned again as were all Bulgakov's plays.

Its repertoire today includes Chekhov's *The Seagull* and *Uncle Vanya*, Lermontov's *Mascarade*, Bulgakov's *A Cabal of Hypocrites*, and Pushkin's *Boris Godunov*.

This is also the home of **Woodstock-MkHAT**, a sober night club, which is open from noon to 5am.

MOSCOW ART THEATER (Gorky), *22 Tverskoy bulvar, Metro Pushkinskaya. Tel. 203-8791 or 7399.*

Located northwest of the Kremlin, on the Boulevard Ring, in this instance Tverskoy, which is the oldest Moscow boulevard that was written about by Tolstoy and Chekhov. Some consider this building a disgrace to Moscow architecture.

This theater, also known as Gorky MKhAT, has 1,360 seats, and is an extension of the MKhAT, above. It opened in 1973 and in the late 1980's MKhAT was divided into two: Chekhov and Gorky.

The theater stages Chekhov's *The Seagull*, Aleksandr Ostrovsky's *Enough Stupidity for a Wise Man*, Leo Tolstoy's *The Living Corpse*, and Ivan Turgenev's *Fathers and Sons*. It also stages *The White Guard*, an adaptation of Bulgakov's novel about the Civil War. When written, the play was rejected by the censor who, in turn, was overruled by Stalin; the carnivorous oppressor saw it 17 times.

If you happen to come by this theater, you will see a statue of the dissolute poet **Sergey Yesenin** (1895-1925) on Tverskoy Boulevard, almost in front of Gorky MKhAT. It was unveiled in 1995 to mark the 100th anniversary of his birth. Moscow's mayor and Nobel Prize winner Aleksandr Solzhenitsyn were on hand to praise the beloved poet and alcoholic scoundrel, who, in his own words "swore obscenely and created scandal" as a "naughty Muscovite playboy." He married his second wife, the American dancer Isadora Duncan, in 1924, beat her often, then left her. A complex figure given to flights of genius, Yesenin hanged himself at the age of 30, having penned his famous last lines in blood: "In this life there's nothing new in dying." Isadora was killed in an automobile accident two years later.

MOSCOW OPERETTA THEATER, *6 Ulitsa Bolshaya Dmitrovka, Metro Teatralnaya. Tel. 292-6377 or 0405.*

Centrally located north of the Kremlin, one block west of the Bolshoy Theater, and one block east of the Moscow Art Theater (Chekhov).

Built by the wealthy arts patron **Savva Mamontov** (1841-1918) in 1885, this theater was known before the Revolution as the avant-garde Private Opera. Mamontov was accused of illegal dealings and arrested in 1899. He served a one-year sentence and was later exonerated (see **Abramtsevo Estate** Chapter 18, *Excursions & Day Trips*).

CONTEMPORARY THEATER

Konstantin Stanislavsky (1863-1938), a stage director, actor and teacher, was one of the most important theorists on contemporary theater. Son of a wealthy merchant, tall, loose-limbed and energetic, he was the director of a manufacturing and trading company until 1917. He organized an amateur company in Moscow that performed plays with Stanislavsky often as the lead actor. He rejected the style of histrionic acting and declamatory speech then prevalent in Russian theater and sought a more realistic acting style, as well as sets and costumes.

Stanislavsky's greatest triumphs were his productions of Chekhov plays. The actors were trained in a new way of acting that brought out the inner psychological state of the characters. Stanislavsky rejected all elements of falsehood and strove for an illusion of reality. From 1912, he led the Moscow Art Theater's First Studio which aimed to train younger actors in the "Stanislavsky method." After suffering a heart attack on stage in 1928 while performing in Chekhov's Three Sisters, he had to abandon acting and concentrated on his pedagogical work. His influence in the West has been enormous, especially in the US.

*A member of the gentry, **Vladimir Nemirovich-Danchenko (1858-1943)** was one of Russia's leading stage directors. He had been educated at Moscow University and was the owner, through his wife, of a modest estate in the south of Russia. Dapper and rather stockily built, he wrote novels, but had become famous as the author of two successful plays produced in 1888 and 1890. The following year, he began to teach dramatic art at the Moscow Philharmonic Society drama school, where he used the opportunity to develop in practice his ideas on increased naturalism. After the Revolution, he also organized the Music Studio which in 1926 became the Nemirovich-Danchenko Music Theater, producing light operas.*

In the second half of the 19th century, all great Russian operas were first performed here. Classical composer Sergey Rachmaninov conducted at the Operetta Theater and operatic basso Fyodor Shalyapin sang there. Its reputation now lags that of the Bolshoy; mostly light classics are performed in this 1,850-seat theater. The Moscow Operetta was once a branch of the Bolshoy Theater and has had its current name since 1927.

Carrying on a tradition from the Private Opera, where tickets were always less expensive than at the Bolshoy, Moscow Operetta's admissions are still priced lower than most other established theaters in the city. Many performances are quickly sold out.

Among the productions staged here are Lehar's *The Merry Widow,* Kasagrande's *Pinocchio's Adventures,* and the operettas of Jacques Offenbach.

PUSHKIN THEATER, *23 Tverskoy bulvar, Metro Tverskaya or Pushkinskaya. Tel. 203-4221 or 8582.*

Located northwest of the Kremlin, on the Boulevard Ring Road, in this instance Tverskoy bulvar, and almost across the street from the Moscow Art Theater (Gorky).

Situated in a mansion that later became a theater in 1914, the Pushkin Theater was created in 1950 in lieu of the Chamber Theater of Moscow. It is named after the most famous Russian poet, born in Moscow, who in 1817 entered government service, but was exiled to southern Russia in 1820 for his liberal views. Legend has it that it was at 23 Tverskoy Boulevard that Pushkin met his beautiful 16-year-old future wife, Nataliya Goncharova, where she supposedly took dance classes. The poet perished tragically in a duel at age 37.

Pushkin's repertoire includes performances from August Strindberg's cycle of Shakespearean historical plays, *House of Fun* by Arkady Averchenko who is often called the Russian Mark Twain, and a stage version of F. Scott Fitzgerald's novel *Great Gatsby.*

Additional Sights Near the Pushkin Theater

Next door, at 25 Tverskoy is the **Yakovlev Mansion,** the birthplace of thinker and writer Aleksandr Gertsen (or spelled Hertzen), whose statue you can see in the courtyard; it is now the Gorky Literary Institute. For more about Gertsen, please see **Gertsen Museum** in Chapter 13, *Seeing the Sights.*

An outbuilding, located between the theater and Yakovlev Mansion, was once the residence to the great Russian poet **Osip Madelshtam** (1891-1938), who had perished in labor camps for an unflattering poem about Stalin.

STANISLAVSKY & NEMIROVICH-DANCHENKO MUSICAL THEATER*, *17 Ulitsa Bolshaya Dmitrovka, Metro Chekhovskaya or Teatralnaya. Tel. 299-8388.*

Located northwest of the Kremlin, southeast of Pushkin Square, and one block east of Tverskaya Street.

This theater was founded in 1941 with the intention to merge the Stanislavsky Opera and the Nemirovich-Danchenko Musical Theater. The quality of its ballets and operas sometimes rivaled those produced by the Bolshoy. This is another theater you might enjoy, regardless of how little Russian you understand.

Among the operas and ballets staged here are Tchaikovsky's ballet *Swan Lake,* Rimsky-Korsakov's opera *May Night,* and Aram Khachaturyan's ballet *Suite from Gayane*. Its repertoire also includes *The Snow Maiden*, a Tchaikovsky opera of Aleksandr Ostrovsky's fairy tale; Tchaikovsky opera *The Queen of Spades*, based on a Pushkin's tale of greed; and Rossini's *The Barber of Seville*.

In 1934, when the great Russian composer Dmitry Shostakovich was 27 years old, his opera *Lady Macbeth of Mtsensk* premiered at this theater and ran more than a hundred times to great critical success, much to the consternation of some Party members.

YERMOLOVA THEATER, *5 Ulitsa Tverskaya, Metro Okhotny Ryad. Tel. 202-3926 or 203-9063.*

Centrally located north of the Kremlin, between the Intourist Hotel and the Central Telegraph Office.

This theater was named after the Russian actress **Maria Yermolova** who died in 1928. Yermolova was a great actress of the Maly Theater for more than 50 years and as popular in Russia as Sarah Bernhardt was in the West.

The Yermolova theater was created in 1937 with the merger of two drama studios. When the Soviets took over, Yermolova was the first person to be awarded the title of People's Artist. The revolutionary theatrical director **Vsevolod Meyerhold** (1874-1940) worked here until 1938, when he was arrested and brutally murdered two years later.

During the war, this theater was evacuated to Eastern Russia and by 1945 it earned the reputation for its sharp social satire and irony. During the Khrushchev period, it was one of the first theaters that dared to stage plays that attacked Stalinism.

Its current repertoire includes a play woven from the short stories of the emigrant writer Ivan Bunin and another based on a Dostoyevsky's short story about a young woman who is driven to suicide to escape her loveless marriage.

For more about **Yermolova Theater Salon**, see Chapter 13, *Seeing the Sights.*

THEATERS BETWEEN THE BOULEVARD & GARDEN RING ROADS

ERMITAZH (Hermitage), *3 Ulitsa Karetny Ryad, Metro Chekhovskaya or Pushkinskaya. Tel. 209-2076 or 6681.*

Located north of the Kremlin, half a block south of the Garden Ring Road, in the once-beautiful Ermitazh Gardens that are now hardly recognizable, and where the Sfera Drama Theater is also located.

To help defray some of the costs of this theater, a night club was opened on its premises under the same name; see Chapter 15, *Nightlife & Entertainment* for more details.

Ermitazh has staged *Pugachev*, a dance interpretation of Sergey Yesenin's poem about the 1773 Cossack rebellion led by Yemelyan Pugachev, Shakespeare's *Othello*, and the works of Nikolay Gogol.

Across the street at 4 Karetny Ryad, the great theatrical director Konstantin Stanislavsky lived until 1918 .

ESTRADY THEATER* (Variety Theater), *20/2 Bersenevskaya nab., Metro Borovitskaya or Polyanka. Tel. 230-0444 or 1327.*

Located south of the Kremlin and across the Moskva River from the Cathedral of Christ the Savior, and one long block southwest of the British Embassy. It may take you 20 minutes to walk to Estrady from either metro station.

Estrady, another Moscow theater that Westerners might enjoy for its musicals and similar entertainment, was established in 1961. It does not have a regular theatrical company, but presents musical variety, rock opera, singers and comedians. Well-known Russian and international artists can be heard and seen here.

Additional Sights Near the Estrady Theater
The huge gray apartment complex next door, with more plaques than you will find on any Moscow building and wedged between Bersenevskaya Embankment and Serafomovicha Street as you cross the Maly Kamenny Bridge, is the well known **House on the Embankment**, which was popularized in a novel by Yuri Trifonov. Built in 1931 for high-level Bolsheviks, such as Lazar Kaganovich, it is to this day remembered for late-night visits by the secret police who carted away those who fell out of Stalin's favor.

LENKOM THEATER*, *6 Ulitsa Malaya Dmitrovka, Metro Chekhovskaya or Pushkinskaya. Tel. 299-0708.*

Located northwest of the Kremlin, northeast of Pushkin Square, in a 1909 building with a marble-clad interior that once housed the Merchant's Club.

Lenkom saw the light of day in 1927 when it was first named the Theater of Young Workers. It was renamed as the Theater of Lenin's Komsomol, thus Lenkom. From 1938 until 1951 it was guided by Ivan Bersenev.

This very popular theater now produces rock operas and Broadway-style musicals as well as regular theater performances. It is another theater whose shows you may enjoy even with just a smattering of Russian. Plan ahead because tickets are sometimes hard to get.

Lenkom's repertoire includes the perennially popular Chekhov and Ostrovsky classics, and Beaumarche's *Wedding of Figaro.*

Located in the basement of this theater is Tram restaurant, run by actors. It resembles the auditorium of a theater with descending rows of tables and shows old Soviet films.

THEATER NA MALOY BRONNOY, *2/4 Ulitsa Malaya Bronnaya at Tverskoy bulvar, Metro Pushkinskaya or Arbatskaya. Tel. 290-4093 or 0482.*

Located northwest of the Kremlin, one block west of the Boulevard Ring Road, almost across the street from the Chinese restaurant Panda.

This building was originally home to the famous State Yiddish Theater, which was liquidated under Stalin. Several of its directors and actors perished. It was here that Marc Chagall painted his famous Yiddish Theater frescoes, which were rediscovered on his visit to Russia in 1976.

This theater was organized in 1922 by graduates of the Maly Theater school. In 1946 it became the Moscow Dramatic Theater and staged a slew of foreign productions, including the works of Arthur Miller.

Staged now are Gogol's *The Marriage*, Aleksandr Ostrovsky's *Wolves and Sheep* and his satire *The Forest*, Turgenev's *A Month in the Country*, and Moliere's *A Husband Deceived.*

MOSSOVIET THEATER, *16 Ulitsa Bolshaya Sadovaya at Triumfalnaya ploshchad, Metro Mayakovskaya. Tel. 299-2035.*

Located northwest of the Kremlin, on the Garden Ring Road, behind Tchaikovsky Concert Hall and Satira Theater, in the Aquarium Gardens, next to Starlite Diner restaurant.

Before the 1917 Revolution there was a casino in this building and Mikhail Bulgakov was one of the regulars. This theater was established in 1923 and its first productions were performed in workers' clubs. It was led for 40 years by Yuri Zavadsky, a pupil of Vakhtangov and Stanislavsky.

Mossoviet's repertoire before perestroika included Andrew Lloyd Webber's *Jesus Christ Superstar.* This rock version of Jesus's life, which provoked outrage in the West, is still staged at this theater. Also produced are Edward Albee's dramatization of Nabokov's *Lolita*, as well as Bulgakov's *White Guard*, Gustave Flaubert's *Madame Bovary*, and Arthur Miller's *The Price.*

SATIRA THEATER, *2 Triumfalnaya ploshchad, Metro Mayakovskaya. Tel. 299-6305.*

Located northwest of the Kremlin, on the Garden Ring Road, next to Tchaikovsky Concert Hall and the Mossoviet Theater, and across the street from the Pekin Hotel.

The Theater of Satire began its activity in 1925 in a cabaret hall. Its repertory in the early years was a review of political and domestic themes, and later it began staging comedies. They were mostly flops.

The crisis deepened in the late 1920's with the Communist belief that the one thing Soviet society did not need was satire. But Satira survived on nonpolitical plays. After the death of Stalin, this theater began to flower on satires about the Soviet bureaucracy.

During the Khrushchev period, its satiric bite really began to sting. Of particular note is poet Tvardovsky's anti-Stalinist satire, *Tyorkin in the Other World*, in which the hero, killed in battle, goes to the other world only to find the same Stalinist bureaucracy. He cannot get into Hell until he proves he is dead.

Over the last couple of years, Satira, which has 1,200 seats to fill, staged Bulgakov's *Flight*, Gogol's *The Inspector-General*, Mayakovsky's *The Bed Bug* and Aleksandr Ostrovsky's *Crazy Money*.

SFERA THEATER STUDIO, *3 Karetny Ryad, Metro Pushkinskaya or Chekhovskaya. Tel. 209-9285.*

Located northwest of the Kremlin and Pushkin Square and inside the small Ermitazh Gardens. The Ermitazh Theater and night club are also located here.

This theater, which emphasized musical dramas, was established in 1984.

Sfera's repertoire includes Boris Pasternak's *Dr. Zhivago*, Vladimir Nabokov's *Lolita*, as well as Mikhail Bulgakov's play *Fateful Eggs*.

SOVREMENNIK THEATER (Contemporary Theater), *19a Chistoprudny bulvar, Metro Chistiye prudy. Tel. 921-6473.*

Located northeast of the Kremlin, just outside the Boulevard Ring Road, and three very long blocks southeast of the Chistiye prudy metro station, in a former cinema with a portico flanked by bas-reliefs of Greek gods.

This group was founded in 1956 by graduates of the Moscow Art Theater School and was led by actor **Oleg Efremov** until 1971. The Sovremennik, which was created as a vehicle of opposition to the Soviet State, at one time claimed Oleg Tabakov, who later established his own theater, as one of its own. It produced mostly contemporary Soviet authors writing about the younger generation. The *New York Times* calls the theater company "one of the most audacious and outspoken of Russia's artistic collectives."

In the early 1960's, the theater produced the politically risky Solzhenitsyn play *The Love-Girl and the Innocent*, based on his first year in the Gulag prison camp. As it reached a dress rehearsal, the Communist Party banned it, as it did all of Solzhenitsyn's work and eventually the author himself. In the 1970's, Sovremennik produced *Macbeth*, a play that had long been banned by the tsars and Stalin. The bloodiness of tyranny must have been too much for the Communist censors, for they banned it even before its premiere.

During its 1992 and 1996 American tours, the Sovremennik company performed Yevgenia Ginzburg's adaptation of her nightmarish novel of Stalin's terror, *Into the Whirlwind*, to great acclaim. Ginzburg's son, Vasily Aksyonov, is a respected novelist who lives in Washington.

Its repertoire also includes *Three Sisters*, one of Chekhov's best known plays, *The Karamazov and Hell*, based on Dostoyevsky's classic, and Gogol's *The Inspector General*.

STANISLAVSKY DRAMA THEATER, *23 Ulitsa Tverskaya at Mamonovsky pereulok, Metro Tverskaya. Tel. 299-7224.*

Located northwest of the Kremlin, two blocks northwest of Pushkin Square, and next door to the Museum of the Revolution. Behind Stanislavsky Theater is the Young Spectators' Theater.

Named after the Moscow-born actor, producer and teacher, **Konstantin Stanislavsky**, whose influence on theater remains undiminished with his "Stanislavsky Method."

This theater was created in 1948 with the participation of many leading actors of the Moscow Art Theater who worked with Stanislavsky between 1935 and 1938, and in 1943 it became part of the Drama and Opera Theater. In its earlier years, it produced mostly classics, such as Chekhov's *Three Sisters*.

Its repertoire now includes Mikhail Bulgakov's *The Heart of a Dog*, and an adaptation of Gabriel Garcia Marquez's short novel *No One Writes to the Colonel*. The theater seats 590.

For more about the **Stanislavsky Club**, formerly the theater's ground-floor buffet, please see Chapter 15, *Nightlife & Entertainment*.

The **Stanislavsky Museum**, *6 Leontiyevsky Lane*, is located about half a dozen blocks south of here, and a block north of Stanislavskogo restaurant, *2 Leontiyevsky*.

OLEG TABAKOV STUDIO THEATER, *1a Ulitsa Chaplygina at Bolshoy Kharitonyevsky pereulok, Metro Chistiye prudy. Tel. 921-2480 or 6504.*

Located northeast of the Kremlin, three blocks northeast of the Boulevard Ring Road, and two blocks north of Sovremennik Theater.

Named after **Oleg Tabakov**, its founder and director, the theater follows the traditions of the great Stanislavsky's old Moscow Art Theater (MKhAT). Tabakov acted in the MKhAT (Chekhov) Theater, as well as in film. His studio is a relatively young company. Tabakov's actors are fortunate to receive not only an irregular monthly salary from the state, but also financial support from their corporate sponsor, Inkombank, one of Russia's largest banks.

In the past, his company toured Japan to a great critical acclaim. Tabakov has also produced plays in theaters in the US, Great Britain, Germany and Finland. He was the first president of the Russian-American Performing Arts Center. This non-commercial organization, financed by the Ford Foundation, promotes contacts between the theaters of the two countries.

On Tabakov's 60th birthday, his wife bore him another child, and the weekly *Moscow News* observed: "His unique creative energy has made him one of the most brilliant artists without whom it is no longer possible to imagine the history of Soviet theater and cinematography, just like without Tabakov's pupils there would have been no current stage and screen hits."

U NIKITSKIH VOROT STUDIO THEATER, *23/9 Ulitsa Bolshaya Nikitskaya, Metro Pushkinskaya or Arbatskaya. Tel. 202-8219 or 4465.*

Centrally located northwest of the Kremlin, at the Boulevard Ring Road, near the site of the medieval Nikitskiye vorota, or St. Nicholas Gate.

Begun in 1981, this theater stages quality plays on a small stage and is guided by the respected director **Mark Rozhovsky**.

U Nikitskih Vorot's repertoire includes Nabokov's *The Dashing Fellow*, Chekhov's *Uncle Vanya*, Tolstoy-based *Triangle: Anna-Karenin-Vronsky*, a *Mein Kampf* farce, and a somewhat disappointing four-hour production of Shakespeare's *Romeo and Juliet*.

VAKHTANGOV THEATER, *26 Ulitsa Stary Arbat, Metro Smolenskaya or Arbatskaya. Tel. 241-0728.*

Located west of the Kremlin, four blocks east of the Garden Ring Road, and almost in the middle of Old Arbat Street.

This theater was named after Stanislavsky's pupil **Yevgeny Vakhtangov** (1883-1922), a master of the grotesque, in 1926. It was inaugurated in 1914 as the third Moscow Art Theater studio for training under Vakhtangov's direction.

During the Stalinist era, the Vakhtangov Theater created a storm of controversy because of its attempt to give Hamlet a Marxist interpretation, but the ever vigilant Communist Party condemned it for not being socialist realism. Stalin could not stand Hamlet. In 1941, the theater troupe was evacuated to Eastern Russia for 22 months and upon returning to Moscow found its 19th century building destroyed. The current theater was built in 1947.

Always pushing the limits, the Vakhtangov again stirred public opinion in 1974 with the play *Woman Behind the Green Door*. In the play, screams come from behind a door from a woman who is being methodically beaten to death by her husband, questioning the ethics of non-interference. Its current repertoire includes *Three Ages of Casanova*, written by poet Marina Tsvetayeva, Neil Simon's *The Sunshine Boys*, and Gozzi's *Princes Turandot*, the first and best known production that Vakhtangov staged before his death to inaugurate the theater.

THEATERS OUTSIDE THE GARDEN RING ROAD

GOGOL DRAMA THEATER, *8a Ulitsa Kazakova, Metro Kurskaya. Tel. 262-8348 or 9214.*

Located northeast of the Kremlin, two blocks east of the Garden Ring Road, and north of Kursky Railway Station.

The Gogol Drama Theater is named after Nikolay Gogol, the dramatist and novelist who became a legend through two masterpieces, the satire *Inspector-General* and the novel *Dead Souls*. Begun in 1926, the Gogol was a touring theater of the railway workers union and was named after the great writer in 1959.

It staged Boris Pasternak's translation of *Romeo and Juliet* in 1970 and was subsequently accused of distorting Shakespeare. The Gogol's repertoire includes the well-known Renaissance play *Decameron*.

MIMIKY I ZHESTA* (Pantomime Theater), *39/41 Izmaylovsky bulvar, Metro Pervomayskaya. Tel. 163-8141.*

Located northeast of the Kremlin, northeast of the Izmaylovo Estate, four long blocks north of Izmaylovsky Park, and one block north of the Pervomayskaya metro station.

This is still another theater where knowledge of Russian will be helpful, but you may enjoy its productions even if English is all you speak. The Moscow Theater of Mimicry & Gesture was established by two professors of the Yevgeny Vakhtangov theater school in 1962. Its actors, who are deaf, give theatrical performances in many countries. Theater workers in Sweden, Poland, Japan and Australia have studied their experiences to see how to duplicate their success in their own countries.

Its repertoire includes Shakespeare's *Romeo and Juliet*, Pushkin's *Boris Godunov*, Kipling's *Maugli*, and *Siberian Yankees*, a musical about the Russian emigre life in New York by a former Operetta choreographer who emigrated to America and is back in Moscow.

POKROVSKY MUSICAL THEATER, *71 Leningradsky prospekt, Metro Sokol. Tel. 198-7240.*

Located northwest of the Kremlin and southeast of the southern metro station Sokol; the theater is situated on the same block as the metro.

This theater house, established in 1972, has staged Gogol's play *The Marriage*, with Modest Mussorgsky's experimental music; Gogol's play *The Gamblers* with Prokofiev's music; *The Anti-Formalistic Farce*, a parodic work by Shostakovich; and Vainberg's opera based on Dostoyevsky's novel *The Idiot*.

RUSSIAN ARMY THEATER, 2 *Suvorovskaya ploshchad, Metro Novoslobodskaya. Tel. 281-5120 or 5719.*

Located north of the Kremlin, west of Frunze Army Park, and just east of the Dostoyevsky Museum. Situated northwest of the square named after field marshal Aleksandr Suvorov (1729-1800), a military genius whose only defeat was his marriage to a bride 20 years his junior and his discovery of her adultery.

The theater was designed in 1934 by the Armenian architect **Karo Alabyan**, a Communist Party member since age 20, but an architectural student from his 25th year, when the Armenian Communist Party sent him on a scholarship to Moscow. It is built - as you might expect for a site erected during the Stalinist era - in the shape of a large five-point star that can be recognized as such only from the air. The theater is owned by the Russian Defense Ministry, which may explain why its Great Hall has a stage large enough to enact battle scenes with armored cars and other real props.

The Russian Army Theater was organized in 1929 by the political arm of the Red Army to present in artistic form the tasks of the defense of the former Soviet Union. A child of the first Five-Year Plan, it grew with the Red Army itself and met with many initial creative difficulties. Its productions, of course, touted the glory of the Army.

But after its initial awkwardness, it began producing classics, such as Shakespeare's *Taming of the Shrew* and *Midsummer Night's Dream* and steadily gained in popularity. Its repertoire also includes Dostoyevsky's *The Idiot*, Shakespeare's *Much Ado About Nothing*, and, of all things, *The Wizard of Oz*.

SATIRIKON THEATER*, 9 *Ulitsa Sheremetyevskaya, Metro Rizhskaya. Tel. 289-7844.*

Located north of the Kremlin, north of Frunze Central Army Park, and northwest of the Rizhskaya metro station. This theater is probably too far to walk to for most, and definitely in the evening.

Satirikon was established in 1939 and has for many years been associated with the director **Konstantin Raikin** whose productions tend toward the musical and the dance show.

With Raikin in the title role as Cyrano, Satirikon stages *Cyrano de Bergerac*. Also shown are Shakespeare's *Romeo and Juliet*, *The Thief of Bagdad* from the Arabian fairy tale *A Thousand and One Nights*, Jean Genet's *The Housemaids*, and Franz Kafka's *The Metamorphosis*.

TAGANKA DRAMA & COMEDY THEATER, 76 *Zemlyanoy val at Taganskaya ploshchad, Metro Taganskaya. Tel. 915-1015.*

Located on the square of the same name southeast of the Kremlin and on the Garden Ring Road.

This theater was originally founded in 1946. The legendary director

Yuri Lyubimov took it over in 1964. For many years, through the sixties and seventies, this was Moscow's experimental theater, featuring plays by contemporary Russian writers, as well as those written in the West. As a result, the theater was often the center of theatrical controversy. It grew famous from the start as the conscience of the Russian intelligentsia.

Productions of contemporary classics, such as Bulgakov's novel *Master and Margarita*, adapted for the stage, were so popular it was impossible to obtain tickets. Yevtushenko wrote a poem for Taganka criticizing the US for the assassination of John F. Kennedy. In the 1970's, Taganka staged a controversial production of *Hamlet* in modern clothes, with Hamlet playing a guitar and singing a poem from Pasternak's banned novel, *Dr. Zhivago* (which Taganka premiered in 1993, accompanied by the music of Alfred Schnittke). In 1993, the theater became embroiled in a controversy when Lyubimov temporarily closed the playhouse in a dispute to privatize the theater, a step that he favored. A former Soviet culture minister opposed the privatization for its loss of jobs and Lyubimov lost the court case over the issue.

Lyubimov was deprived of his Soviet citizenship in 1983 while staging Dostoyevsky's *Crime and Punishment* in London. He directed performances in London, and other European capitals, as well as in Washington, D.C., and returned home five years later.

Among productions staged now are Dostoyevsky's *Crime and Punishment*, and *Boris Godunov*, a story about the life of the Russian tsar. *Boris Godunov*, as produced by Lyubimov, was rejected by the censors as recently as 1982. In 1996, Lyubimov staged Euripides's tragedy *Medea*, featuring a searing performance by Lyubov Selyutina in the title role.

Taganka was also the home of the Moscow-born poet, actor, singer and composer **Vladimir Vysotsky** (1938-1980), whose rebellious writings and premature death transformed him into a legend. He played the leading role in Lyubimov's extraordinary production of Hamlet. Vysotsky achieved near-legendary fame during his brief career at Taganka and in 26 films, but his fame as an actor paled before his celebrity as an officially forbidden bard who sang of the travails of his people.

When Vysotsky died during the 1980 Olympic Games, more than one hundred thousand admirers took part in the three-day mourning ceremonies. For more about the **Vysotsky Museum**, a block from here, see Chapter 13, *Seeing the Sights*.

CINEMA

Russians are five times more likely to go to the cinema than the British or French, but only see about half as many movies in theaters as do Americans.

Gone with the Wind, one of the better American films shown in Russia after 1991, was so popular that one large cinema on Novy Arbat showed it for an entire year.

Russian cinema has such a great tradition that what you find in an average Moscow movie house these days seems almost criminal. Do not expect to be able to see many great Russian films because the city has been flooded with American action junk and French erotica, often translated by one voice-over for all the protagonists.

But Muscovites seem hungry for the cultural kitsch they could not see for decades and you may be the only bored spectator inside the jammed cinemas. On the other hand, if you get homesick for a little English-language junk, you will have plenty of opportunities to indulge yourself with superfluous cultural calories.

A ten-day international film festival is held in Moscow every two years.

When viewing Soviet films made from the 1920's to 1940's, remember that no film could be released without the Stalin's personal approval and most of the time without his seeing it.

Moscow cinemas are usually open from 10am until midnight. Ticket holders are only admitted in the intervals between programs. The program often consists of a newsreel and a full-length feature. Non-stop showing of a film is unheard of in Moscow and your ticket entitles you to one showing only. After that, the auditorium is cleared before the next show; something akin to visiting the Armory, where admission is limited to four times a day and you can remain inside for less than two hours. More than one film may be shown at a cinema during one day. Smoking is not permitted in auditoriums. Seats are often numbered and reserved.

Among the 100-plus Moscow cinemas still operating, we recommend the following, located inside the Garden Ring Road. The first two theaters show first-run movies and are centrally located. The next four show English-language films with and without subtitles.

• **Oktyabr**, *42 Novy Arbat, Metro Arbatskaya, Tel. 291-2263*
• **Rossiya**, *2 Pushkin Square, Metro Pushkinskaya, Tel. 229-2111 or 7300*
• **Americom House of Cinema**, *Hotel Radisson Slavyanskaya, 2 Berezhkovskaya nab., Metro Kievskaya, Tel. 941-8890*
• **The Dome**, *Moscow Renaissance Hotel, 18/1 Olimpiysky prospekt, Metro Prospekt Mira, Tel. 931-9000*
• **Litva**, *29/8 Lomonosovsky prospekt, Metro Universitet, Tel. 147-2282*
• **Tsentralny detsky**, *25 Bakhrushina, Metro Paveletskaya, Tel. 233-3350*
• **Barrikady**, *21 Barrikadnaya, Metro Barrikadnaya, Tel. 254-2973*
• **Khudozhestvenny**, *14 Arbatskaya ploshchad, Metro Arbatskaya, Tel. 291-5598*
• **Kiev**, *30/32 Kutuzovsky prospekt, Metro Kievskaya, Tel. 249-1624*
• **Mir**, *11 Tsvetnoy bulvar, Metro Tsvetnoy bulvar, Tel. 924-9647*

• **Moskva**, *3 Triumfalnaya ploshchad, Metro Mayakovskaya, Tel. 251-5860 or 7222*

• **Zaryadye**, *1 Moskvoretskaya nab., Metro Kitay-gorod, Tel. 298-5686*

ART GALLERIES & EXHIBITION HALLS

Many successful private galleries have been opened with the help of well-placed former or current government officials, who sometimes bought up the available collections of artworks that may now be sold off through one of their friends or relatives. Other galleries have been set up by Russian artists with recognizable names in the West or by Russians who have formed partnerships with the Westerners.

One estimate has is that there are almost 150 state and private art galleries and exhibition halls in Moscow. New galleries keep popping up with some regularity, although they sometimes are no more than a few walls in an artist's apartment and known mostly to other artists. Some seem to close as soon as they open their doors. Several well-known galleries have sunk into oblivion over the last few years, only to resurface in a completely new configuration.

One such example is the **Aydan Gallery**, once a stylish gallery opened by the artist Aydan Salakhova, a young painter of Azeri origin. The prices at Aydan started at about $4,000 in its heyday. Today, Aydan still has her gallery, but showings are by appointment only. This is what Salakhova says about the state of art in Russia: "There are very few artists of the young generation who are really working hard now. There are very many galleries, but very few good artists. Even talented and famous artists aren't creating anything new at the moment; it's a real crisis of ideas."

In spite of the many new galleries, some artists still prefer to show their work in the state-run exhibition halls. The 23-room **Central House of Artists**, *10 Krimsky val, metro Oktyabrskaya or Park Kultury*, seems particularly popular. An artist can lease space there and also sell his or her artwork. Artists and art lovers alike feel this is because Central House's staff knows how to hold exhibitions properly. Another reason is that when several exhibitions are held at the same time, visitors attracted by one artist may go and see the remaining ones as well.

Useful information about Moscow art galleries is excruciatingly difficult to come by. The only known professional periodical to the city's museums, galleries and exhibition halls is the booklet, *Moscow Gallery Guide*, published monthly in Russian and English by Oleg Loginov. Mr. Loginov owns a private art gallery, **Moscow Collection Art Gallery** and the **Art-Tour Agency**, which assists Western art collectors with their purchases of artworks in Russia. The following list of galleries was prepared with his assistance.

GALLERIES & EXHIBITION HALLS
INSIDE THE BOULEVARD RING ROAD

ESTATE GALLERY, *5 Starosadsky pereulok, near Ulitsa Pokrovka, Metro Kitay-gorod. Tel. 928-7618. Open daily from noon to 6pm, closed Sundays and Mondays.*

Located east of the Kremlin and two blocks west of the Boulevard Ring Road.

This gallery was originally named Moscow Union of Artists, or Mosart, and was part of the Moscow branch of the Painters' Union of Russia, which has been in existence since 1932.

Established in 1991, the gallery's permanent display shows paintings and graphics from the late 19th and early 20th centuries, bronzes, and tapestry by Russian artists.

MALY MANEZH, *3/3 Georgiyevsky pereulok, Metro Teatralnaya or Okhotny Ryad. Tel. 292-0621. Open daily from 11am to 7pm, closed Mondays. Small admission fee.*

Centrally located north of the Kremlin, between Tverskaya and Bolshaya Dmitrovka Streets, behind the **Kolonny zal** (Hall of Columns or House of Unions) building on Okhotny Ryad Street. Georgiyevsky Lane is easy to miss: when heading north, watch for the first courtyard on your right at the foot of Tverskaya Street.

Maly Manezh was named after his big brother, Manezh Exhibition Hall (see below), which stands at the southwestern end of Manezhnaya Square. Situated in a renovated historical building and inaugurated in the summer of 1996, this is the newest state-owned gallery in Moscow and possibly the most pleasant one. Intimate and well lit with the help of roof skylights, it is just large enough to do justice to any individually featured artist.

MANEZH EXHIBITION HALL, *1 Manezhnaya ploshchad, Metro Okhotny Ryad. Tel. 202-9304. Open daily from 11am to 8pm, closed Tuesdays. Small admission fee.*

Centrally located northwest of the Kremlin, near the main Intourist office, and the Natsional and Moskva Hotels. Because of the billion-dollar construction on the square, Manezh Hall has been open only sporadically.

One of Moscow's most remarkable buildings, Manezh was erected as a monument to Russia's victory over Napoleon in 1812. Its opening in 1817 was marked by a parade of Russian troops engaged in those battles. The construction was supervised by the military engineer A. Betancourt, who succeeded in covering a 558-foot by 148-foot space with a roof that

ERNST NEIZVESTNY

After the artists hung their works, the Manezh building was cordoned off by security men and the gallery was searched. Soon about seventy government officials entered. Khrushchev had barely reached the top of the stairs when he began to yell: "This is dog shit! Filth! Disgrace! Who is responsible for this?"

Somebody in the entourage pointed at Ernst Neizvestny. Khrushchev then yelled at Neizvestny and Neizvestny yelled back: "You're the Premier, but not here. Here we shall discuss this as equals."

To those present this reply seemed more dangerous than Khrushchev's anger. Neizvestny turned and began to walk away. For a moment nobody moved and he knew that he was risking his life but continued walking. The onlookers were silent. Soon Khrushchev followed him and the two men began arguing again. Neizvestny was accused of being a homosexual, to which he replied: "Nikita Sergeyevich, this is awkward, but if you could find a girl, I will prove you wrong." Khrushchev laughed.

Gradually the conversation between them became more relaxed. Khrushchev asked Neizvestny what thought of the art produced under Stalin.

"I think it was rotten and the same kind of artists are still deceiving you," answered the artist, to which Khrushchev replied: "Stalin's methods were wrong, but the art itself was not."

For almost an hour, everyone had to remain standing, yet no one dared to interrupt Khrushchev until Neizvestny held out his hand and suggested that they stop arguing.

Leaving, Khrushchev turned around and said: "You're the kind of man I like. But there's an angel and a devil in you. If the angel wins, we will get along, if it's the devil, we will destroy you."

Neizvestny left, still expecting to be arrested before he reached Tverskaya Street, but was not. Today he is an American citizen and lives in New York.

had no intermediate supports. The designer of Manezh was the Italian architect Osip Bove.

Although intended primarily for equestrian exercises, the Manezh often served as a concert and exhibition hall. In 1867, the French composer Hector Berlioz performed here, conducting an orchestra and choir of 700. Since 1957, the Manezh has often been utilized as the Central Exhibition Hall for large presentations, such as that of Leningrad-born exponent of Soviet kitsch, the wealthy Ilya Glazunov, or the 700 religious and nature-inspired oils by Sergey Andriyaka.

But the event at the Manezh whose consequences reverberated around the world was an exhibition of experimental, unofficial art in

1962, which included the works of Ernst Neizvestny, born in 1926, who among other distinct sculptures created the gravestone for the deceased Nikita Khrushchev.

ROSIZO EXHIBITION HALL, *28/2 Ulitsa Petrovka at Petrovsky bulvar, Metro Pushkinskaya, then trolleybus #15 or #31. Tel. 928-1445, Fax 921-9291. Open daily from noon to 7pm, closed Sundays and Mondays.*

Centrally located north of the Kremlin, just south of the Boulevard Ring Road, and next to the Museum of Literature.

This is the state gallery of the Ministry of Culture that opened in 1992. It sold its artworks - which also include finely crafted folk toys, Gzhel porcelain, pottery by graduates of the prestigious Abramtsevo Art School, and tapestries made in Sergiyev Posad - to other Russian museums.

This is one of the few serious exhibition halls where you can buy handmade silver jewelry that starts at about $1,000. One of the most noteworthy artists to be regularly displayed at Rosizo is Aleksandr Ivanov, a glass and crystal designer from St. Petersburg who emigrated to the US. His avant-garde glass vases, bottles and figurines are in collections and museums across Europe and America. Ivanov is one of the few remaining glassmakers in Russia, where glassblowing is a dying art. There are no glass factories and glass masters left around Moscow.

GALLERIES & EXHIBITION HALLS
BETWEEN THE BOULEVARD & GARDEN RING ROADS

A-3 GALLERY, *39 Starokonyushenny pereulok, Metro Smolenskaya or Arbatskaya. Tel. and Fax 291-8484. Open daily from 11am to 7pm, Sundays from 11am to 6pm; closed Mondays and Tuesdays.*

Located west of the Kremlin, one block north of the Canadian Embassy, and half a block south of Stary Arbat Street.

Municipal, non-commercial projects of conceptual, avant-garde art are exhibited here, often in cooperation with the Goethe Institute in Moscow.

CENTRAL HOUSE OF ARTISTS (Tsentralny Dom Khudozhnika), *10 Krimsky val, Metro Oktyabrskaya or Park Kultury. Tel. 238-1245 or 4986. Open daily from 11am to 7pm, closed Mondays. Small admission fee.*

Located southwest of the Kremlin, northeast of Gorky Park and adjacent to the Moskva River.

The Central House is a steel and glass Soviet architectural monstrosity that has 23 exhibition halls where five thousand works of art can be shown at a time. There are several exhibitions on at any one time and they change about twice monthly. Most of the works on display are for sale. The House displays works from Russian provincial museums, as well as artists from throughout the Commonwealth of Independent States. You will also find exhibits from the West, such as a 1994 retrospective of the Spanish surrealist Salvador Dali that included 900 original graphics, lithographs and sculptures.

Also located here is the **Tretyakov Gallery Affiliate**, which exhibits the Soviet and post-Soviet art that was thrown out of Tretyakov Gallery.

And while there, be sure to see several of the statues that were attacked by mobs after the 1991 coup d'etat and brought here to await their disposition. The Moscow government gave the museum 50 acres of land behind the Central House to create the Mouseion, a fine arts park. For the time being, the grounds are home to more than a hundred Soviet political statues and monuments, the only such open-air museum in Russia.

The monument to "Iron Feliks" Dzerzhinsky, the founder of the Soviet secret police, which for many years stood on Lubyanka Square in front of the KGB headquarters, and those of his cronies Kalinin (after whom Novy Arbat Street was named) and Sverdlov (the square in front of the Bolshoy Theater held his name for many years) were the first three to be brought here after the 1991 coup d'etat attempt.

At that time, the Moscow Soviet passed a resolution to clear Moscow of at least 200 monuments which seemed inappropriate in the newly democratic Russia, but these efforts soon died down and now the idea is to preserve these artifacts for posterity.

CONTEMPORARY ART CENTER, *2/6 Ulitsa Bolshaya Yakimanka at Yakimanskaya nab., Metro Oktyabrskaya or Polyanka. Tel. 238-4422. Open daily from 10am to 6pm, closed Sundays and Mondays.*

Located south of the Kremlin, two blocks north of the President Hotel, in the historic Zamoskvorechye district, which was first mentioned in 1365 but is believed to go even farther back into history.

The Contemporary Art Center, established in 1991, is one of several apartment-sized galleries clustered in buildings that at one time were planned as an art community behind the **Central House of Artists**. It is often referred to as the Zone, a place for experimental artists.

DAR GALLERY OF NAIVE ART, *7/7 Ulitsa Malaya Polyanka, Bldg. 5, Metro Polyanka. Tel. 238-6554. Open daily from 2pm to 5pm, closed Mondays and Tuesdays.*

Located south of the Kremlin, one long block south of Polyanka metro station, in the historic Zamoskvorechye district, which in the 14th century was inhabited by craftsmen, followed by **streltsy** (musketeers), and then merchants in the 16th century.

Dar Gallery is a non-commercial art gallery created by art historians to support naive art, primitivism and traditional trends in folk art. It focuses on the work of self-educated artists.

DOM NASHCHOKINA GALLERY, *12 Vorotnikovsky pereulok, 2nd Floor, Metro Mayakovskaya. Tel. 299-4774 or 1178. Open daily from 10am to 6pm, closed Saturdays and Sundays.*

Located northwest of the Kremlin, just inside the Garden Ring Road, and on the premises of a film script publisher.

This gallery exhibits quality artworks by well-known contemporary artists and sells them at high prices. Sculptor Ernst Neizvestny, who was a thorn in the paw of the former Soviet Union for many years, is just one of the artists exhibiting here.

FOTOTSENTR, *8 Gogolevsky bulvar, Metro Kropotkinskaya or Arbatskaya. Tel. 290-4188. Open daily from noon to 7pm, closed Mondays.*

Located southwest of the Kremlin, on the Boulevard Ring Road, and a block north of the western metro station Kropotkinskaya. Reporter restaurant is next door in the same building.

This looks more like a second-hand poster shop, and they indeed carry more posters than you could ever want. Fototsentr is also one of the few Moscow places where a good selection of artistic photographs can be found. Regular photographic exhibitions are held here, from Japanese prints to photos showing the longtime **Taganka Theater** director Yuri Lyubimov at work. Old books and ceramics round out the selection.

Among the exhibits regularly recycled at Fototsentr are *The History of Erotic Art from Antiquity Until the Modern Age*, and *The History of Erotic Photography Over the Past 150 Years*.

Additional Sights Near the Fototsentr

Nearby, at 6 Gogolevsky bulvar, lived the wealthy art patron Sergey Tretyakov, who in 1850 funded the gallery named after him. Moscow actress Olga Knipper-Chekhova, the playwright's wife, lived on the other side of the boulevard. She died in 1959 at the age of 90.

GUELMAN GALLERY, *7/7 Ulitsa Malaya Polyanka, Bldg. 5, Metro Polyanka. Tel. 238-6654 or 8492. Open daily from noon to 7pm, closed Sundays.*

Located south of the Kremlin, one long block south of Polyanka metro station, in the historic Zamoskvorechye district.

Established by Marat Guelman, a native of Moldova, this gallery claims to be the first private art gallery in Moscow. His salon was once hailed by the business daily *Kommersant* as the leader of art galleries in Moscow. Guelman exhibits primarily contemporary Russian and international art. Thirty-six years old in 1997, he is inventive and a shrewd businessman. An engineer by profession, Guelman also speaks good English. In 1994, he brought the works of Western avant-garde artists

American Andy Warhol and German Josef Beuys to Moscow, for the first time.

THE MOSCOW COLLECTION ART GALLERY, *10 Shchetininsky pereulok, Metro Polyanka or Dobryninskaya. Tel. 238-3968, Fax 945-0768, Internet http://air.iki.rssi.ru/art in russia. Open daily from noon to 6pm, Saturdays and Sundays from 11am to 4pm; closed Tuesdays and Wednesdays. Shown by appointment only.*

Located south of the Kremlin and southeast of Tretyakov Gallery, between First Kazachy pereulok and Pogorelsky pereulok, in Zamoskvorechye, one of the oldest Moscow districts.

The Moscow Collection Art Gallery was initiated with an exhibition of 600 artworks at the Tretyakov Gallery by art collector Oleg Loginov in 1989, who specializes in Russian art of the 1920's.

His gallery exhibits works by the painter Nadezhda Udaltsova (1885-1961) and her husband Aleksandr Drevin (1889-1938). You can also see and buy the artworks of Sergey Chekhonin (1878-1936) who studied under the famed Ilya Repin. Also shown are works by the contemporary painter Vladimir Nemukhin, who was born in Moscow in 1925; his work can be seen at the Metropolitan Museum of Art and Museum of Modern Art, both in New York City. Also on display are works by Eduard Shteinberg, who was born in Moscow in 1937, and whose art can be seen at the Pushkin Museum of Fine Arts and the Tretyakov Gallery.

Mr. Loginov speaks fluent French and enough English to help you with your selection. Most of your purchases at his gallery include all the documentation required by the Ministry of Culture to take art out of Russia. He also provides consultations to Western buyers, who want to purchase Russian art, but do not speak the Russian language and are not familiar with the market. In Moscow and St. Petersburg, he offers tours through his **Art-Tour Agency**, through which you can visit private galleries and the studios of well-known artists. If you only want a customized guided tour of Moscow or St. Petersburg museums and galleries, the Art-Tour Agency will provide it at a fee in English.

This gallery occupies part of the basement of the **Tropinin Museum**, *Tel. 231-1799*, which is open daily from noon to 7pm, Saturdays 10am to 5pm, and is closed Tuesdays and Wednesdays. It is named after Vasily Tropinin (1776-1857), a serf portrait painter, who studied at the Academie, but was recalled by his owner to work on his estate as a gardener and valet. Tropinin is also exhibited at the Tretyakov Gallery. This museum was founded in 1969 and displays portraits from the mid-18th century to the first half of the 19th century.

MOSCOW FINE ART, *38 Ulitsa Stary Arbat at Spasopeskovsky pereulok, 4th Floor, Metro Smolenskaya or Arbatskaya. Tel. 241-1267. Open daily from 10am to 6pm, closed Saturdays and Sundays.*

Located west of the Kremlin, two blocks east of the Garden Ring Road, and two blocks west of Vakhtangov Theater.

The Moscow Fine Art Gallery was established in 1992. It features the works of Georgy Litichevsky, born in 1956 in the Ukraine. He graduated from Moscow State University, began exhibiting in 1986 and has since exhibited in Amsterdam, Rome, London, Munich and Madrid. His work can also be seen at Moscow's **Tsaritsino Museum**.

GALERIE LES OREADES, *Central House of Artists, Hall 5a, 10 Krimsky val, Metro Oktyabrskaya or Park Kultury. Tel. 238-0217, Fax 238-6066. Open daily from 11am to 7pm, closed Mondays.*

Located southwest of the Kremlin, across the Garden Ring Road from Gorky Park, and adjacent to the Moskva River.

The French-owned Les Oreades opened its Moscow gallery in 1989 and originally had a gallery on Tverskaya Street. It displays about a dozen carefully chosen paintings by about half a dozen artists. Les Oreades features 19th century and modern paintings, as well as 20th century Russian artists.

Other Les Oreades Galleries, which specialize in the 19th century and contemporary French and foreign painters, are based in Paris, as well as in Toulouse and Luchon.

SLAVYANSKY DOM, *3 Goncharnaya nab., Bldg 5, Metro Taganskaya. Tel. 915-6821. Open daily from 10am to 6pm, closed Sundays.*

Located southeast of the Kremlin, southwest of Taganka Square, adjacent to the Moskva River.

This is a porcelain and ceramics gallery of objects made to order at the former Imperial China Factory, such as old-style Moscow pottery, clay toys, and original works by contemporary masters of porcelain and ceramics.

YAKUT GALLERY, *5 Ulitsa Dolgorukovskaya, Metro Mayakovskaya. Tel. 973-3452, Fax 261-4154. Open daily from noon to 7 pm, closed Saturdays, Sundays and Mondays.*

Located northeast of the Kremlin, on the Garden Ring Road and less than a block southwest of the Glinka Museum of Musical Culture. Yakut is situated in a basement on the western corner of a building facing the Garden Ring Road.

The gallery was established in 1993 and is co-owned by a bank. Its director, Aleksandr Yakut, is the former director of the once highly successful Aydan Gallery. Among the artists on exhibit here is Moscow painter Semyom Faibisovich, born in 1949. Alyona Kirtsova, another Yakut artist, was born in 1954. She studied at the private studio of Vassily Sitnikov, a striking figure of the 1960's and 1970's, who had left for the US.

Vassily Sitnikov emigrated to the US in 1975 and died in the East Village in New York City in 1986. He was born in 1915 in a village on the river Don and moved to Moscow as a child. A bearded bohemian, Sitnikov lived in a small communal apartment he shared with several other families, close to the KGB headquarters at Lubyanka prison. Eccentric and unpredictable, he always seemed to be in conflict with the Soviet authorities. He had once been imprisoned in a mental institution to "shape up ideologically." Many of his works are in Norton Dodge's collection of nonconformist Soviet art at the Jane Voorhees Zimmerli Art Museum at Rutgers University in New Jersey.

GALLERIES & EXHIBITION HALLS OUTSIDE THE GARDEN RING ROAD

AYDAN GALLERY, *23/7 Ulitsa Novopeshchanaya at Peshchanaya ploshchad, Entrance 8, Top Floor, Metro Sokol or Oktyabrskoye pole. Tel. 943-5348. Open daily from noon to 6pm, closed Saturdays and Sundays. Shown by appointment only.*

Aydan Salakhova, who in 1989 established **First Gallery** to sell Soviet art for hard currency, is described by art critic Andrew Solomon as "dark and beautiful and mysterious, catlike, with enormous eyes, dramatically short black hair, and a quiet self-assurance that allows her to skate through the most difficult situations. She does not use her last name, partly because she has decided that to have only one name, in the mode of Halston, carries a certain chic; and partly because it is an oft-repeated 'fact' that she has severed all ties with her father and hates him.

"You never know whose side Aydan is on. She negotiates and arranges, and in the end things always seem to happen as she wants them to happen. Only in her twenties, she is the best that perestroika has to offer, a businesswoman, an artist, a socialite, replete with ambition you have no doubt she will fulfill."

KOVCHEG (Ark), *12 Ulitsa Nemchinova, Metro Timiryazevskaya. Tel. 977-0044. Open daily from 11am to 6pm, closed Mondays and Tuesdays.*

Located northwest of the Kremlin, east of Timiryazeva Academy Park, and about half a dozen long blocks northwest of the Timiryazevskaya metro station.

Although it is located far from central Moscow, Kovcheg is worthy of your visit if you are serious about art. Its director, Yuri Petukhov, an artist himself, puts on excellent exhibits, mostly from private collections.

L-GALLERY, *26 Ulitsa Oktyabrskaya at Ulitsa Trifonovskaya, Metro Novoslobodskaya or Mendeleyevskaya. Tel. and Fax 289-2491. Open daily from 11am to 7pm, closed Saturdays and Sundays.*

Located three long blocks north of the Frunze Army Park and slightly farther north from the Russian Army Theater and Dostoyevsky Museum.

L-Gallery's featured contemporary Russian conceptual artists are post-modernists: Yuri Albert; Ivan Chuykov (born 1935), whose work is on display at Centre George Pompidou in Paris; Igor Makarevich, who was born in Tblisi, Georgia, in 1943; Vladimir Zakharov, who was born in Tajikistan in 1959 and now works in Moscow and Cologne; husband-wife team of Konstantin Zvezdochetov, born in Moscow in 1958, and his wife Larissa Resun-Zvezdochetova, born the same year in Odessa, Ukraine.

MALAYA GRUZINSKAYA 28, *28 Ulitsa Malaya Gruzinskaya at Ulitsa Klimashkina, Metro Ulitsa 1905 goda or Barrikadnaya. Tel. 253-3688 or 7505. Open daily from noon to 8pm, closed Mondays.*

Located northwest of the Kremlin, about five blocks northeast of the Ulitsa 1905 goda metro station, and two blocks northwest of the Moscow Zoo.

Malaya Gruzinskaya 28, named after its street address, was established in 1975 by the painters who then were not members of the Communist-controlled Painters' Union. Some of its painters also established M'ARS Gallery, below.

International art critic Andrew Solomon, writing about the Soviet artists in time of glasnost says, "Malaya Gruzinskaya was tolerated by the KGB because it brought underground activity to the surface of society; it showed predominantly badly executed amateur still lifes, work that was neither official nor part of the unofficial movement. Still, as an unofficial but public space it attracted obsessive interest: every day lines wound around the block to see the exhibitions there."

M'ARS GALLERY, *32 Ulitsa Malaya Filyovskaya, near Ulitsa Polosukhina, Metro Pionerskaya or Kuntsevskaya. Tel. 146-2029 or 6335, Fax 146-8426. Open daily from noon to 8pm, closed Mondays.*

Located southwest of the Kremlin, northwest of Victory Park, and three blocks northwest of the Pionerskaya metro station.

M'ARS Gallery, established in 1988, is believed to be Moscow's oldest and one of its largest private galleries. It was started by seven Moscow artists from Malaya Gruzinskaya 28 gallery, above, who founded it with their own money. In their charter, the artists state as their chief goal the creation of a museum of modern art in Moscow. M'ARS features mostly contemporary Russian and international art, as well as artworks from the republics of the former Soviet Union. The gallery is sponsored by corporate clients.

Konstantin Khudyakov, one of the founders, said: "Surrounded as we are by economic and cultural decline, we want to salvage the honor of Russian art and to prevent it from being sold off on the cheap. We're interested only in those artists, who, in our opinion, are able to influence the nation's artistic taste."

Consensus has it that M'ARS tends to be erratic in the quality of its displays, but has a large stock of unframed canvases in the back room.

RED ART GALLERY, *10 Leningradsky prospekt, 8th Floor, Metro Belorusskaya. Tel. 214-3249. Open daily from 1pm to 8pm, closed Mondays.*

Located northwest of the Kremlin and a couple of blocks north of the Belorusskaya Railway Station.

Red Art Gallery was established in 1992 and until 1994 shared its former Tverskaya Street location with Les Oreades Gallery (described above).

Several Russian artists are on permanent exhibit here, among them the Moscow painter Dmitry Plavinsky, born in 1937. A non-conformist who had many a scrape with the former Soviet authorities, Plavinsky now lives in New York. Other Red Art artists include Aleksandr Kharitonov, born in Moscow in 1931, and Anatoly Zverev, born in 1931, who has exhibited throughout Europe. Also shown here is the work of famed artist Ernst Neizvestny, who locked horns with Nikita Khrushchev and ended up sculpting the stone on Khrushchev's grave.

15. NIGHTLIFE & ENTERTAINMENT

During the 1960s, an American journalist griped in print that "the visitor in Moscow can be kept busy every night for several months attending different performances of excellent opera, ballet and theater, but if he seeks the night life of Paris or New York he will be disappointed. Night clubs - there aren't any."

Even when a Russian travel guide, *Three Days in Moscow*, published its second revised edition in 1989, it stated flatly: "There are no night clubs in Moscow."

But that was in 1989, which seems like an ice age ago in fast-moving contemporary Moscow. Even in 1992, the opportunities for partying into the night could be counted on the fingers of two hands. As you can see below, things have changed drastically and we list only a sampling of such establishments. One estimate has it there are well over 600 clubs, pubs and bars in Moscow today.

A word of advice: do not plunge into the Moscow night alone - the larger your party the better. But do not get carried away by fear either. If you exercise the same caution you would in New York City, London or Los Angeles, you will do fine and make a few new acquaintances in the bargain.

The line between Moscow restaurants, casinos, clubs, pubs, and bars is often quite blurry. We segregate the restaurants in a separate section, but since all of the rest usually constitute nighttime entertainment we have bunched them together, first according to one of the three major geographical areas, and within those alphabetically.

Moscow casinos, to the amazement of many, have multiplied like an epidemic. You cannot pick up an English-language publication in Moscow these days without seeing advertisements with glamorous females beckoning you inside to try your luck. There seems to be one on every corner of central Moscow. Altogether, Moscow had 580 gambling facilities at the end of 1996, including 450 slot machine salons, a dozen bookmaking offices, and two bingo clubs.

The city mayor, who previously had tried to outlaw street kiosks and foreign-language - actually English - signs from the capital, claims there are more than 70 casinos in Moscow and that some are not even registered. The government wants to scale their numbers to just five in the city center and three in each of the eight prefectures on the outskirts to cut down on organized crime. But new casinos keep opening up and will probably do so for awhile, for it seems that Russians, unable to gamble openly for seven decades, are transfixed by the possibilities, no matter what the odds.

Like the restaurants, all nighttime establishments are divided into one of these three geographical areas: **Inside the Boulevard Ring Road**, or what Westerners might call the downtown area; **Between the Boulevard & Garden Ring Roads**, a donut-shaped band around central city and; **Outside the Garden Ring Road**, which encompasses the Moscow suburbs.

Because of the rapidly changing admissions to Moscow nightclubs, we do not specify the entrance fees or cover charges, except in extreme cases. Unlike restaurants, the nightclubs are listed alphabetically inside each of the above three geographical areas, not according to their prices.

BARS, CLUBS & CASINOS
INSIDE THE BOULEVARD RING ROAD

ALEKSANDR'S NO. 1 CLUB, *1 Ulitsa Bolshaya Dmitrovka, Entrance 6, Metro Teatralnaya or Okhotny Ryad. Tel. 292-0272 or 7123, Fax 292-0272 or 214-4303. Open daily from 8pm to 8am. Cover charge for men only. Major credit cards accepted. Jacket and tie are required for men.*

Centrally located north of the Kremlin, two blocks southeast of the Bolshoy Theater and three blocks east of the Metropol Hotel, on the street that until 1993 bore the name of the Russian national poet Pushkin. The club is situated in the historic Kolonny zal block.

Aleksandr's opened in 1992 and is considered one of the ten best nightclubs in Moscow, perhaps in the entire country. It has a casino, disco, bar and restaurant serving European-Russian cuisine at breakfast, lunch and dinner.

You will enjoy a small European style casino, with slots, blackjack, poker, and American roulette. If you plan to stay in Moscow for a while, you can save money on the cover and other fees by buying Aleksandr's Gold Card.

There is free champagne and an erotic cabaret, featured Fridays and Saturdays from midnight to 3am, other days from midnight to 12:30am only.

There are restaurants galore around here if you want to eat elsewhere before going in. In the Hotel Moskva alone there are two eateries: El Rincon Espanol on the southwest side, which closes at 11:30pm, and Paradise on the northwest, which closes at 1am. Azteca in the Intourist Hotel shuts down at 5am. See Chapter 12, *Where to Eat*, for details.

ARBAT BLUES CLUB, *11 Filippovsky pereulok, Building 2, Metro Arbatskaya or Kropotkinskaya. Tel. 291-1546. Open Fridays and Saturdays, from 8:30pm to 5:30am. Cover charge. Reservations after 7pm are advisable if you want a table. Cash only.*

Centrally located southwest of the Kremlin, south of Stary Arbat Street, and one block west of the Boulevard Ring Road, in this instance Gogolevsky Boulevard. Situated at the theater studio Na Starom Arbate on a twisting side street "built before mankind reached the level of consciousness needed for effective city planning."

Inaugurated in 1993, Arbat Blues Club is the oldest blues club in Moscow and caters predominantly to Western clientele in the heart of Moscow's tourist zone. Foreign journalists and professional musicians are the regulars. You will not find many Russians here. You can hear live blues and rock every weekend and there are always festivals, contests and jam sessions going on. The lounge room is casual and comfortable, the dance floor flooded in a 1960s lighting effects.

Drinks, such as beer, vodka, soft drinks, and coffee, or snacks, like pizza, sandwiches, salads or ice cream are as simple as the club, if a bit higher in price than you would expect. If you crave something more substantial, the touristy restaurant Praga (see Chapter 12, *Where to Eat*, for details) is nearby where the New and Old Arbat Streets merge, as well as more than half a dozen similar eating joints on both Arbats.

ARMADILLO TEX-MEX BAR, *1 Khrustalny pereulok at Ulitsa Varvarka, Metro Kitay-gorod or Ploshchad Revolutsiyi. Tel. and Fax 298-3982. Open daily from 5pm to 6am, Saturdays and Sundays from noon to 6am. Major credit cards accepted.*

Centrally located east of the Kremlin, roughly between the Rossiya Hotel and GUM department store on Red Square.

Armadillo claims to be Moscow's only true Tex-Mex bar, serving chili, burritos, guacamole, tequila, margaritas and Mexican beer. It's a classic all right.

There is live country & western and rock music and dancing nightly. Lack of a sufficient dance floor is a shortcoming. It has good atmosphere, but the prices keep rising. There are five pool tables and four dart boards.

"When full, it jumps," comments the alternative English-language weekly *Living Here*, "especially when people get stuck into their tequillas. Great billiards."

GABRIELLA CASINO, *on the ground floor of the Intourist Hotel, 3/5 Ulitsa Tverskaya, Metro Teatralnaya. Tel. 956-8448 or 8451 or 8321. Open 24 hours, 7 days a week. Cover charge returned in casino chips. Major credit cards accepted. Formal attire not required.*

Centrally located north of the Kremlin, three blocks southwest of the Bolshoy Theater, and two blocks southeast of the Central Telegraph Office.

This small casino has several blackjack tables, American roulette, poker, 5- and 7-card stud, and Texas Hold'em games.

If you get hungry, there are several restaurants nearby, including the Chinese restaurant Lili Wong on the southern side, which closes at midnight, and the 24-hour Patio Pizza in front of the hotel; see Chapter 12, *Where to Eat*, for details.

HUNGRY DUCK, *9/6 Ulitsa Pushechnaya at Ulitsa Rozhdestvenka, Metro Kuznetsky Most of Lubyanka. Tel. 923-6158. Open daily from noon until the last drunk is thrown out. Live entertainment of the unusual kind. Cash only.*

Centrally located northeast of the Kremlin, northwest of Lubyanka Square, north of Detsky Mir children's store, and next to the Kuznetsky Most metro station.

Wish you could have lived during the times of the Wild West? Wish no more, just come to Hungry Duck, one of the wildest bars since Dodge City started listening to classical music. This is a good place for men with a fourth-grade education who want to get drunk and create a ruckus. The bar is cited by Russians as a place where you can hear obnoxiously loud, educated Western women carry on. The food is good so you can drink even more.

KARO/UTOPIYA, *2 Pushkinskaya ploshchad, Metro Pushkinskaya or Chekhovskaya. Tel. 229-0003. Open daily from 9pm to 5am at Karo and 10pm to 5am at Utopiya. Substantial cover charge at Utopiya. Major credit cards accepted.*

Located north of the Kremlin, on the Boulevard Ring Road, across Pushkin Square from McDonald's fast food restaurant, and occupying a large part of the Rossiya Cinema building.

Karo is an upstairs casino with four American-style roulette tables, as well as five blackjack and three poker tables. "In the VIP bar," says the *Moscow Times*, "girls take off what precious little they have on and for a little extra will do a personal show on your table. It's best to hang back a little at this point, as the tables are on the wobbly side." Karo also features a European restaurant. There is a cabaret after midnight, Thursday through Sunday, and music entertainment all night.

Utopiya is a giant ground-floor discotheque and bar featuring dance music from the 1970's through the 1990's. Like most Moscow clubs, the guards behave as though the Soviet Union still rules. Now and then you can hear a known entertainer, such as Latoya Jackson. "Bar is a budget version of Stanislavsky/Zhar-Ptitsa scene," declares *Living Here*, the English-language alternative weekly, which also labels the club as "Vulgar, painful techno and Russky Pop." The *Moscow Times* reviewer sees it a bit differently: "You'd be hard pressed to find a better sound system in Moscow. The music is techno at its most up-to-date. The best night for dancing is Monday, student night, when you won't trip over Gucci bags on the dance floor."

In addition to McDonald's fast food restaurant a block away, there is also Pirata (Pirate) seafood restaurant on the ground floor and in the back of Utopiya; the waiters, of course, are dressed as buccaneers. One popular specialty is strawberries, which are flown in fresh daily. For more about Strastnoy 7, a restaurant one block north of here, at 7 Strastnoy bulvar, please see Chapter 12, *Where to Eat*.

KLUB MOSKOVSKY, *6 Ulitsa Tverskaya, near Kamergersky pereulok, Metro Okhotny Ryad. Tel. 292-1282, Fax 292-3688. Open daily from noon to 6am, disco opens at 10pm. Substantial cover charge from Friday through Sunday; no cover for unaccompanied women. Major credit cards accepted.*

Centrally located north of the Kremlin, south of Yuri Dolgoruky's statue on Tverskaya Square, and north across Tverskaya Street from the Central Telegraph Office.

There is a dance floor and bar on the first floor; casino with American roulette, blackjack and poker on the second floor, next to the restaurant. One cannot help but be suspicious of any nightclub with television sets; Moskovsky has a video wall showing mostly Eurosport. While berouged females are not quite as obvious as at **Night Flight**, you would have to be blind to miss them.

If the club's restaurant is not to your liking, you can walk over to the Italian-cuisine Artistiko, *6 Kamergersky pereulok*, which is open until midnight, or to the Georgian Aragvi in the opposite direction, which is open until 11pm. Both are described in Chapter 12, *Where to Eat*.

MAGNIFIQUE!, *5/9 Petrovsky pereulok at Ulitsa Petrovka, Metro Chekhovskaya or Pushkinskaya. Tel. 921-0993. Open daily from noon to 6am. Admission charge on concert nights. Cash only.*

Located north of the Kremlin, two long blocks east of Tverskaya Street, and one block south of the Boulevard Ring Road.

A good place to go to on weekends when bands are playing, perhaps as good as Krizis-Zhanra (see listing), although it has more dancing and seating space. Musicians range from rock to jazz to folk and the club boasts a somewhat young and artistic crowd. Food is no more than okay and is expensive.

Magnifique! is much less than magnificent on weeknights when no live acts are scheduled; as a matter of fact it is as dead as a grave.

If you get hungry, there is Moscow Bombay Express, *3 Glinishchevsky Lane*, a moderately-priced Indian restaurant open until 11:30pm, one block southwest of here. Pizza Hut on Tverskaya Street is just as close, but shuts down by 10pm. See Chapter 12, *Where to Eat*, for more on both.

MANHATTAN EXPRESS, *inside Hotel Rossiya, 6 Ulitsa Varvarka, Metro Kitay-gorod or Ploshchad Revolutsiyi. Tel. 298-5355 or 1372. Open daily from 7pm to 5am, restaurant from 8pm to 2am. Cover charge after 9pm. Major credit cards accepted.*

Centrally located on the northwest corner of Rossiya Hotel, facing the Kremlin and St. Basil's Cathedral.

This is a two-million-dollar New York-style dance and supper club which opened in 1993. Like so many joints of this sort, it has surly security people at the door and is expensive. Manhattan Express tries to be both, a bohemian hangout and large fancy nightclub; it does not succeed in either attempt. Live entertainment nightly, dancing starts at 10pm.

It has an expensive American-style restaurant in the back, serving large portions of such traditional meals as grilled steak with mushrooms and veal Madeira, seafood kebab and sirloin with mustard sauce. Your meal will cost at least $30.

Foreigners are admitted free with one guest before 1am every Thursday, but only if they show their passports. Half price for hotel guests.

CLUB MIRAMAR, *30/2 Ulitsa Myasnitskaya at Turgenevskaya ploshchad, Metro Chistiye prudy or Turgenevskaya. Tel. 924-1986, Fax 921-0471. Open 24 hours a day, 7 days a week; for hours of specific establishments, please see below. Live entertainment. Major credit cards accepted.*

Located northeast of the Kremlin on Garden Ring Road, and across the street from the Chistiye prudy metro station.

Club Miramar, once a modest Cuban cafe, has become a veritable United Nations of food, drink and entertainment. It consists of the following five establishments:

El Cocodrilo restaurant, open from 4pm to 6am, which serves decent Latin American cuisine with lots of seafood dishes. Appetizers include quesadilla especial (with ham, chorizo, sweet peppers and cheese) and tortilla guajira (banana omelette with four eggs). Jaiba rellena (stuffed crab) and pollo en salsa (chicken in Cuban sauce) are but two hot entrees, both priced under $20. But if you really want to eat and are able to reserve ahead, you can have a baked suckling pig for $80.

The Italian-Cuban cuisine restaurant **Montekatini**, open from 9am until midnight, is inexpensive with food that tastes accordingly. Cream of mushroom soup, cucumber and tomato salad, pasta with Italian sauce, and pizza are just a few of the offerings. Do not expect gourmet Italian delicacies from a Cuban chef.

Tequilla Smash Bar, open from 4pm to 6am, is perfect for frustrated Westerners who have been beating the pavement all day on some failed bureaucratic mission that Russia is so famous for. Here you will find a special wall against which you can smash empty bottles. And if you are really enraged over the delay in your visa, you can smash an unopened bottle. But if you truly want to be heard, write something profound, like "Life stinks," on this special wall to impress other Westerners, one of whom might add "for Jerks" to your missive.

O.K., next you can shoot a game of American pool at one of the three tables at **Johnnie's Pool Bar** (open 4pm to 6am) downstairs, but don't forget to get your tokens first. Drinks of almost any description can be had, depending on your mood. A tournament is held here every Sunday, starting at 2pm.

But if even chalking the cue is too much work for you, relax with a cocktail in the peaceful **Taverna Miramar** upstairs, which is open from noon until 6am.

NA NEGLINNOY, *8 Ulitsa Neglinnaya at Ulitsa Pushechnaya, Metro Kuznetsky Most. Tel. 924-5655 or 921-3541. Open daily from noon to 4am, lunch and dinner served from noon to midnight. A cover charge, mostly returned in casino chips. Major credit cards accepted.*

Centrally located north of the Kremlin, one block east of the Bolshoy Theater, and across Neglinnaya Street from the somewhat frowsy state-owned Central Department Store, commonly known under the acronym TsUM.

This casino, restaurant and bar, open in 1994 in a restored building, is named after the Neglinka River, which in centuries past has given the city a lot of headaches with unexpected flooding, but has now been forced underground and tamed. The food is cheap because you are expected to gamble, where the casino will recoup all such expenses.

The club has six roulette tables and a stud poker table.

The House food specialty is beef fillet with hot dressing. The most expensive item on the menu is under $15. Cold **zakuski** (appetizers) include tsar hors d'oeuvre with salmon, crabs, sturgeon and trout, and crabs dressed with mayonnaise. **Moskovian**-style sturgeon baked with crabs, Austrian-style trout, and sturgeon grilled on the sword with Oriental dressing are just three among the fish entrees. Meat courses include lamb shashlik (kebab) Georgian style, Aragvi River beef shashlik marinated in cognac, and Odessa-style veal.

THE NEWS PUB, *18 Ulitsa Petrovka at Stoleshnikov pereulok, Metro Kuznetsky Most. Tel. 921-1585 or 1238. Open daily from noon to 2am. Cover charge. Live entertainment. Cash only.*

Located north of the Kremlin, two blocks east of the Prince Dolgoruky statue and Aragvi restaurant on Tverskaya Square, and less than a block north of the Petrovsky Passazh Western-style shopping mall. Russkiye Uzory souvenir shop is next door.

Long ago, in 1992, this was one of the best pubs in Moscow. This is a place that seats more than a hundred, where not only can you meet journalists from all over the world, but it's also a sanctuary where you can relax over a drink and talk things over or read complementary newspapers and magazines as varied as *The Guardian, National Geographic, Le Monde* and *The Wall Street Journal.*

Since Russian management took over, this pub has lost its appeal. As in the good old days, however, you will still bump into curvaceous platinum-haired ladies that seem a lot more interested in dollars than dailies. Consider instead the wild Hungry Duck, *9 Ulitsa Pushechnaya,* two blocks southeast of here.

NIGHT FLIGHT, *17 Ulitsa Tverskaya, Metro Tverskaya or Pushkinskaya. Tel. 229-4165. Open daily, restaurant from noon to 4am, club from 9pm to 5am. Cover charge. Major credit cards accepted. Jacket and tie suggested for men.*

Centrally located north of the Kremlin, southeast of Pushkin Square in the Moscow's theater district.

This somewhat expensive restaurant and bar was opened in 1991 by Swedes. No-nonsense former KGB guards stand at the door to keep things in check. The dress code is somewhat arbitrary, but do not wear jeans or tennis shoes because you will be turned away for sure. Men must be 30 and women at least 21 years old to be admitted.

Night Flight sports red velvet interior in the 1920s Paris bordello style. The DJ plays mostly top 40 hits. The hostesses and other women outnumber the patrons at times.

If you are male and your hormones are acting up, you can meet a fille de joie here who will gladly join you at your pad – for $200 a night. Fifty-plus-year-old men often prowl this joint for under-20-year-old girls.

"Not for the politically correct or the religious," says the English-language alternative weekly *Living Here,* "Dead DJ. Whores are cheaper elsewhere."

OLD SQUARE PIANO BAR, *8 Bolshoy Cherkassky pereulok, Metro Kitay-gorod or Lubyanka. Tel. 298-4688 or 4738, Fax 298-4738. Open 24 hours. Live entertainment. Major credit cards accepted.*

Centrally located northeast of the Kremlin, two blocks south of Lubyanka Square, and two blocks west of the northern Kitay-gorod metro station.

Bills itself as an authentic American restaurant and piano bar, where you can relax over a decent meal and drink, while enjoying live music.

ROSIE O'GRADY'S BAR, *9/12 Ulitsa Znamenka at Maly Znamensky pereulok, Metro Borovitskaya or Arbatskaya. Tel. and Fax 203-9087. Open daily, from noon to 1am, on weekends until 1:30am. Major credit cards accepted. Live jazz Tuesday nights from 8pm to 10pm.*

Located west of the Kremlin, three blocks east of the Boulevard Ring Road, and one block southwest of the Russian State Library.

O'Grady's features Guinness, Harp and Killian's beer on tap, wine, spirits, sandwiches and a few hot meals, like Irish stew.

O'Grady's, a Russian-Irish joint venture, was constructed in Ireland, then shipped and assembled in Moscow as one of the first "Irish" bars in Moscow. When it opened in the early 1990's, this bar developed such strong customer loyalty that it was a favorite place for Moscow expatriates. Today there is very little of the Irish left at Rosie's except for the beer, and the prices are high.

SAVOY CASINO CLUB, *inside Hotel Savoy, 3 Ulitsa Rozhdestvenka, Metro Lubyanka. Tel. 929-8630. Open daily from 8pm to 4am. Major credit cards accepted. Jacket and tie are mandatory for men; no blue jeans.*

Centrally located northeast of the Kremlin, a block west of Lubyanka Square, and two blocks west of the Bolshoy Theater.

Savoy opened in 1989 and was the first casino in the former Soviet Union. Today it is the highest-rated casino in Russia by the International Casino Guide. It also has the best reputation because it can accommodate even the most demanding gamblers, which are usually international businessmen and tourists.

Savoy is a European style casino with ten thousand square feet of space. It has four blackjack tables and an American-style roulette table. A passport is required to enter and the minimum gaming age is 20 years.

There is a nightly show from Thursday through Sunday. It has a bar.

BARS, CLUBS & CASINOS BETWEEN THE BOULEVARD & GARDEN RING ROADS

B.B. KING BLUES CLUB, *4/2 Ulitsa Sadovaya-Samotechnaya at Likhov pereulok, Metro Tsvetnoy bulvar. Tel. 299-8206. Open daily from noon to 2am, Saturdays from noon to 5am. Lunch served from noon to 2:30pm, a la carte until 11pm. No cover charge after midnight. Major credit cards accepted.*

Located north of the Kremlin on Garden Ring Road, across the Ring Road from Obraztsov's famed Puppet Theater and next door to the Georgian restaurant Kolkhida.

One of the friendlier bars and restaurants in town, the African barmen really make a difference in perennially surly Moscow. Clean facilities, a balanced mix of expatriates and Russians, affordable food and drink prices make this an enjoyable evening out.

BEDNIYE LYUDI (Poor Folks), *11/6 Ulitsa Bolshaya Ordynka, Metro Tretyakovskaya. Tel. 231-3342. Open 24 hours. $100 membership card required for admission. Membership card not required for concerts, but there is entrance fee. Cash only.*

Located southeast of the Kremlin, one block north of Tretyakovskaya metro station, and tucked inconspicuously under a block of flats.

An unpretentious 24-hour candle-lit cellar bar with fake medieval tables and chairs. There are jazz and blues singers and alternative bands featured every night. It has a reasonably-priced bar. If you liked **Krizis Zhanra** (see listing), a club northwest of here and across the Moskva River, near Prechistenka Street, you will very likely enjoy Bedniye Lyudi. There is talk about eliminating the $100 membership card.

BULGAKOV, *10 Ulitsa Bolshaya Sadovaya, Metro Mayakovskaya. Tel. 209-9914 or 9723. Open daily from 7pm to 7am. Cover charge. Cash only.*

Located northwest of the Kremlin on Garden Ring Road, and southwest of the Aquarium Gardens.

Inaugurated in 1996, the basement-located Bulgakov is supposedly named after the great Russian satirist Mikhail Bulgakov, who had lived in a nearby flat for almost five years. (See Bulgakov Flat in Chapter 13, *Seeing the Sights*.) You will have to pass through a metal detector, an increasingly common practice in Moscow establishments.

If you get hungry, the American Starlite Diner (see Chapter 12, *Where to Eat*) inside the Aquarium Gardens, just a short distance from here might be a godsend since it is open all night and serves a terrific breakfast.

ERMITAZH (Hermitage), *3 Ulitsa Karetny Ryad, Metro Pushkinskaya or Chekhovskaya. Tel. 299-1160, Fax 299-7519. Open daily Thursday through Sunday from 10pm to 6am. Live entertainment after midnight. Cover charge. Major credit cards accepted. Reservations are suggested.*

Located north of the Kremlin and half a block south of the Garden Ring Road in the middle of Ermitazh Gardens.

The predecessor of today's Ermitazh, having the same name, was believed to be the best restaurant in Moscow until 1915. Writers Dostoyevsky and Turgenev often ate at the old Ermitazh; composer Peter Tchaikovsky held the party for his disastrously short and unconsumated marriage on its premises.

Today, Ermitazh is an informal disco club and food bar that seats 40. Opened in 1993, this club has established itself as a Moscow cult institution. Crowded, funky and crazy, Ermitazh is pulsating with a crowd of hip teenagers and artistic types.

There is dancing and a strip show after 9pm. Ermitazh is a favorite spot in Moscow for expatriates seeking dates. Ermitazh has a problem with toilets and air-conditioning. Russia's first international tattoo convention was held here.

KANADSKY BAR (Moosehead Candian Bar), *54 Ulitsa Bolshaya Polyanka, Metro Dobryninskaya or Polyanka. Tel. 230-7333. Open daily from noon to 5am, Saturdays and Sundays from 10am to 5am. Live entertainment Friday and Saturday nights. Major credit cards accepted.*

Located across Moskva River south of the Kremlin, in the historic Zamoskvorechye neighborhood, and one block north of the Garden Ring Road.

This may be called the Canadian Bar, but you won't find many Canadians inside. They are outnumbered by young Russian executives. "As expat bars go," noted the *Moscow News* restaurant critic, "it is delightfully free of prostitutes, making it an acceptable place to take your girlfriend." Moscow's alternative English-language weekly *Living Here* calls it "stuffy, predictable, ex-patty."

A 14-ounce T-bone steak with fries or rice is the most expensive item on the menu, at about $20. Buffalo wings are also popular. Several varieties of draft and bottled beer are available. Happy Hour is Monday and Tuesday, from 6pm to 8pm, when there are also food specials.

KRIZIS-ZHANRA, *22/4 Prechistensky pereulok, Metro Kropotkinskaya. Tel. 243-8605. Open daily Tuesday through Sunday, from noon to 1am. Free admission before 8pm, when the live entertainment begins. Cash only.*

Located southwest of the Kremlin, three blocks northeast of the Garden Ring Road - in this instance Smolensky Boulevard - and a block west of historic Prechistenka Street. Entrance is from the courtyard.

A pleasant cellar cafe with a young and hip crowd, although the place is small and you may have difficulty moving around after the band starts playing. There is a reasonable selection of drinks and limited food fare. The surly doormen may not be able to spoil your evening because this place has a nice European atmosphere.

METELITSA/CHERRY CASINO, *inside Metelitsa Entertainment Center, 21 Ulitsa Novy Arbat, Metro Smolenskaya or Arbatskaya. Tel. 291-1170 or 1130 or 1305. Open daily from 1pm to 8am. Before 8pm the $50 cover charge is refunded in gambling chips. Major credit cards accepted. Tie and jacket are mandatory for men.*

Located west of the Kremlin, two blocks southeast of the American Embassy, just steps east of the Garden Ring Boulevard, and next door to the questionable Arbat restaurant.

Metelitsa is one of the largest entertainment complexes in Moscow, consisting of **Cherry Casino**, **Black Jack**, a Swedish-cuisine restaurant, the **Snowstorm** night club, and three bars. You can even buy flowers and souvenirs. Before entering you will have to pass through a metal detector and, if you are a man, you will probably be frisked by armed guards.

The casino is on the first floor, featuring several American roulette wheels, craps, poker, and ten blackjack tables, where $10 is the minimum bet. Drinks are complimentary in the casino.

From about 1pm to 8pm, you can watch live horse and hound races in England and South Africa on a giant TV screen and place your bets.

On the second floor is the disco Snowstorm, open from 9pm to 5am, with dancing to 50,000 watts of sound. There is live entertainment every night at 1am and 2am; it includes such sought-after entertainers as Aleksandr Abdulov, the Russian TV and film actor. The restaurant on the second floor is open from 8pm to 8am, serving such gourmet delicacies as roast rack of lamb, coq au vin, and fillet of Salmon Veronique (with grape and white wine sauce), but be prepared to spend $100 per person. You will be served a breakfast buffet at 6am.

A courtesy bus is available to and from all major hotels.

011 CLUB, *19/2 Ulitsa Sadovaya-Kudrinskaya, Metro Mayakovskaya. Tel. 245-3272. Open Thursday through Sunday, from 9pm to 4am. Cover charge. Cash only.*

Located northwest of the Kremlin on Garden Ring Road, and two blocks northwest of Patriarshy Ponds of Bulgakov fame.

A mainstream, unpretentious, no-nonsense dance club located in a brick cellar. The clientele are mostly Russian and foreign students and the music is tunes from the Eurocharts and Russian pop.

If you get hungry, the American Starlite Diner is across Garden Ring Road and one very long block northeast of the club. It is open 24 hours and you will appreciate their breakfast at 4am.

SALLY O'BRIEN'S, *1/3 Ulitsa Bolshaya Polyanka at Kadashevskaya nab., Metro Polyanka or Tretyakovskaya. Tel. and Fax 230-0059. Open daily from noon to midnight. Major credit cards accepted.*

Located south of the Kremlin, at the foot of Polyanka Street, just across the Maly Kamenny Bridge over the canal. Tretyakov Gallery is within walking distance, southeast of here.

In 1991, this pub would have been a sensation beyond compare, today it seems like just another Western-style bar. Sally has lots of beers and Irish music to keep you entertained during your stay in Moscow. Try her chicken nuggets and chips. We never did find out whether that good-looking Irish lass behind the bar is Sally.

SHAMROCK BAR, *On the second floor of the Arbat Irish House, 13 Ulitsa Novy Arbat, Metro Arbatskaya. Tel. 291-7681. Open daily from 11am to midnight. Major credit cards accepted.*

Located west of the Kremlin, two blocks west of the Arbatskaya metro station, in the Arbat Irish House department store.

Until 1994, this was arguably one of the three most popular Western bars in Moscow and a place no English-speaking foreigner could ignore. Since the Russian partners have taken over, this is just another bar that you can safely ignore, except for its historical value. You may want to drop by just long enough to pick up the free English-language tabloid at the adjacent supermarket, and perhaps sit down for a beer and a quick snack.

STANISLAVSKY CLUB, *23 Ulitsa Tverskaya at Mamonovsky pereulok, Metro Tverskaya or Pushkinskaya. Tel. 564-8004 or 299-7686. Open daily from 6pm to 6am. Admission free until 10pm and 9pm on weekends, after that a hefty cover charge, half for women. Live entertainment starts at midnight. Cash only.*

Located northwest of the Kremlin, two blocks northwest of Pushkin Square, next to the Museum of the Revolution, and in the building that also houses the Stanislavsky Drama Theater.

Once just a lowly ground-floor theater buffet, Stanislavsky is now an elite club and French restaurant with a stylish interior that includes plenty of mirrors and lacquered wood. The clientele is more cultured than in many other similarly expensive spots, and Stanislavsky is expensive. The food is decent; this is supposedly one of a handful Moscow restaurants where you can choose a live crab to be cooked especially for you. The cabaret show and live bands are average.

ZHAR-PTITSA (Firebird), *1 Kudrinskaya ploshchad, Metro Barrikadnaya. Tel. 255-4228/4774. Open daily, restaurant from 6:30pm to 6am, discotheque from 9pm to 6am. Cover charge. Major credit cards accepted.*

Located northwest of the Kremlin on Garden Ring Road, two blocks south of the Planetarium, and one block north of the American Embassy.

One of the "new criminal rich" clubs, which, according to the Moscow press, also include Cherry Casino on Novy Arbat Street and Karusel on First Tverskaya-Yamskaya Street. If you want to meet a menacing Russian Godfather, this would be the place to go to.

There is a casino with two roulette tables and three blackjack and two poker tables. You can enjoy two cabaret shows early in the morning; a topless show is held on Saturdays.

BARS, CLUBS & CASINOS OUTSIDE THE GARDEN RING ROAD

ALEKSANDR BLOK CASINO, *aboard the M.S. Aleksandr Blok, 12 Krasnopresnenskaya nab., Metro Ulitsa 1905 goda. Tel. 255-9284 or 9281 or 9323. Open daily from 8pm to 5am. Major credit cards accepted.*

Located west of the Kremlin, east of Krasnaya Presnya Park, and in front of the Mezhdunarodnaya Hotel.

Named after the Russian poet Aleksandr Blok (1880-1921) who at first welcomed both the 1905 and 1917 Revolutions, but became disillusioned and suffered greatly in the times which followed the 1917 uprising. This floating ship casino is mostly for foreign-passport holders. It has three casino areas; games include blackjack, American roulette, and poker, where bets can go up to $500.

A courtesy casino limousine is available. Formal attire not required.

This floating ship also includes the Greek Restaurant, see Chapter 12, *Where to Eat*, and the Inflotel, see Chapter 11, *Where to Stay*.

GOLDEN PALACE, *15 Third Ulitsa Yamskogo pola, Metro Belorusskaya. Tel. 212-3909 or 3941. Open 24 hours. A sizeable admission fee. Major credit cards accepted.*

Located northwest of the Kremlin, southeast of the Aerostar Hotel, northeast of the Hippodrome racetrack, and one block east of Leningradsky Avenue. It's relatively easy to find, just look for the large neon sign.

This is one of the gaudiest casinos in all of Moscow. There are gun-toting guards falling over each other even before you get inside. There's an unusual cloakroom and a few other hokey surprises, but only worth seeing if you are a country lad. In that case you might also be impressed by a rotating BMW car on the lower level dance floor. If you are male, come with your own body guards because prostitutes here aim to get you by hook or by crook, no pun intended. The Vietnamese food is passable.

HIPPOPOTAM, *5/1 Ulitsa Mantulinskaya, Bldg. 6, Metro Ulitsa 1905 goda. Tel. 256-2346 or 2126 or 2487. Open daily from 10pm to 5am, closed Mondays and Tuesdays. Cover charge. Major credit cards accepted.*

Located west of the Kremlin, one block west of the Mezhdunarodnaya Hotel, near the entrance to Krasnaya Presnya Park, and directly below the Santa Fe restaurant (see Chapter 12, *Where to Eat*). The Hippopotam is far from the nearest metro station and unsafe at night so take a taxi.

This club, managed by Brits, has more theme nights than there are days in a week: Latin music, house music, funk, soul, jazz and blues. It's also a nightclub where you won't bump into quite as many prostitutes as in most other Moscow spots, primarily because it's popular with students.

"It's safe, it's sexy and it swims," pronounces the Moscow English-language alternative weekly *Living Here*, then adds, "Waitresses don't smile and drinks are pricey."

JAZZ ART CLUB, *inside the Vernisazh Theater, 5 Ulitsa Begovaya at Ulitsa Polikarpova, Metro Begovaya. Tel. 946-0165. Open Fridays from 7:30pm to 2am; also the first and third Sunday each month, from 5pm to midnight. Admission fee, students half-price. Cash only.*

Located northwest of the Kremlin, four long blocks northeast of the Begovaya metro station, and two blocks west of the Hippodrome racetrack.

This is an informal and clean jazz club with comfortable sofas and inexpensive drinks. There is live jazz on Fridays and experimental music on Sundays.

JOHN BULL PUB, *4 Kutuzovsky prospekt at Ukrainsky bulvar, Metro Kievskaya. Tel. and Fax 243-5688. Open daily from noon to 1am, Thursday through Saturday until 3am. Live entertainment. Major credit cards accepted.*

Located west of the Kremlin, southwest of the American Embassy and the Russian White House, and across Ukrainsky Boulevard from the Ukraina Hotel. Kentucky Fried Chicken and Pizza Hut are southwest and across the street at 17 Kutuzov Avenue.

Patterned carpet, varnished bar and tables, and polished brass all make for a pub that would thrive in the West. You can even speak English and make yourself understood. Only after you collapse into one of those thick green chesterfield sofas, after hours of shopping and sightseeing, will you realize what a godsend this pub is, whether to help you reduce the swelling in your aching joints or to finish last week's newspaper that you've been carrying around for days. There is a downstairs with a bar and a more quiet upstairs.

The menu includes caviar, salads and soups, and several meat and seafood dishes. Between noon and 3pm all hot meals are discounted. There is, of course, a variety of ales and lagers to wash down your provisions, as well as bottled and canned varieties, some of which are not even on the menu. Sunday mornings you can enjoy a full English breakfast.

Another equally pleasant and clean two-level John Bull Pub opened in the summer of 1996 on the Garden Ring Road at Novinsky Boulevard and Karmanitsky pereulok near the middle (one of three) Smolenskaya metro station entrance, and is northwest of McDonald's restaurant on Arbat Street. Other John Bull Pubs are planned for.

MOSCOW CASINO, *inside Hotel Leningradskaya, 21/40 Ulitsa Kalanchevskaya, Metro Komsomolskaya. Tel. and Fax 975-1967. Open daily from 2pm to 5am. American Express credit card accepted. Formal attire not required.*

Located inside Stalin's sky-rise northeast of the Kremlin, just east of the Kazansky and southeast of the Leningradsky and Yaroslavsky railway stations, and southeast of the International Post Office.

This was one of the first casinos in Moscow. American roulette, blackjack, slot machines, and poker are available.

Hotel Leningradskaya also has a popular bar, **Jacko's**, next door to the casino, which opens at 6pm. While run by an expatriate Scot, who drew disproportionately large crowds of foreigners, Jacko's was a cozy and friendly spot with live music and a famous pick-up spot for men. Since the Scot left, Jacko's just wasn't the same and has lost a lot of its patrons.

NE BEY KOPYTOM (No Horse Kicks), *at the Palace Night Club, 1 Ploshchad Izmaylovskaya at Ulitsa Pervomayskaya, Metro Izmaylovskaya. Tel. 165-6929 or 0283. Open Saturdays and Sundays, from 7pm to 6am. Live entertainment until 10pm only. Cover charge. Cash only.* Located northeast of the Kremlin, east of Izmaylovo Estate, and three blocks northwest of the Izmaylovskaya metro station.

This club is situated on two levels in an 18th century mansion and has a large dance floor and a good stage for bands. An unpretentious student hangout that opened in the spring of 1996, prices are quite reasonable compared with most spots in central Moscow. If you tire of all those pretentious downtown clubs, this one might turn out to be a welcome alternative.

PILOT/SOKHO, *6 Ulitsa Trekhgorny val, Metro Ulitsa 1905 goda or Krasnopresnenskaya. Pilot Tel. 252-2764, Sokho Tel. 205-6209. Open, Pilot Thursday through Sunday from 11pm to 6am; Sokho always. Both have a cover charge. Cash only.*

Located northwest of the Kremlin, southwest of the Moscow Zoo, and a couple of long blocks northeast of the World Trade Center and the Mezh Hotel.

Pilot is upstairs, cavernous, accessible and aeronautically designed, with a twin-engine plane suspended from the roof.

Sokho is downstairs, exclusive and futuristic, with mostly biznismeny clientele.

Both clubs are large, technically advanced, but lack warmth. Pilot has live bands regularly; Sokho has many celebrities, a pool table and good Irish beer.

If you get hungry there are several options: either you can go two very long blocks southwest to Santa Fe (there is another club beneath it, the Hippopotam) or three blocks northeast to the Pakistani restaurant Ravi, *7 Stoliarny Lane*, which closes at 11pm.

CASINO ROYALE, *at the Hippodrome Racecourse, 22 Ulitsa Begovaya, Bldg. 1, Metro Begovaya. Tel. 945-1410 or 4842, Fax 945-1854. Open daily from 8pm to 5am. Cover charge. Major credit cards accepted. Jacket and tie mandatory for men; no blue jeans. Minimum gaming age is 18 years.*

Located northwest of the Kremlin, west of Belorussky Railway Station, on the western side of the racetrack, in a former royal palace.

This is the largest and perhaps the most popular casino in Moscow. Royale is a conservative deluxe European style casino with 5,000 square feet on each of its two levels and Eastern European **biznismeny** are its chief clients. There are 16 blackjack and five roulette tables, punto banco, poker and 22 slot machines available.

From Thursday through Sunday there is no cover charge for members, who also get a 50 percent reduction on tickets for various entertainment events, which include concerts and cabaret shows. You can dance the night away in a fashionable discotheque. Complimentary transportation to and from major hotels is provided.

The elegant Fyodoroff restaurant, open from 7pm to 1am, gaming tables and slot machines are on the ground floor. Floor-to-ceiling glass on two sides of the restaurant allows diners to watch the casino action and horse racing. A majestic winding staircase leads to the second floor with additional tables and private gambling rooms. There are full service bars on both levels.

RUSSKAYA TROYKA, *inside Orlyonok Hotel, 15 Ulitsa Kosygina, Metro Leninsky prospekt. Tel. 938-1959 or 939-8679. Restaurant open daily, nightclub Thursday through Sunday from 9pm to 5am. Cover charge. Major credit cards accepted. Jacket and tie are suggested for men.*

Located southwest of the Kremlin, southeast of the Luzhniki Sports Complex across the Moskva River, three very long blocks southwest from Gagarin Square, and in the grim Soviet-era Orlyonok Hotel at the foot of Sparrow Hills.

Opened in 1993, it promotes itself as an up-scale striptease club, but it has a somewhat crude bare skin show that starts at 9pm. On Fridays, there are also variety and circus acts. If you want to just dance, there is a charge after 1:30am.

There are women lounging everywhere in their perennial search of a rich score. Secured parking and taxi service are available.

SHANS (Chance), *at Dom Kultury Serp i Molot (Hammer & Sickle House of Culture), 11/15 Ulitsa Volochayevskaya at Gzhelsky pereulok, Metro Ploshchad Ilyicha or Rimskaya. Tel. 956-7102. Open daily from 11pm to 6am. Live entertainment. Cover charge is almost double for men than for women, and is high for both sexes after midnight. Cash only. Casual dress.*

Located southeast of the Kremlin, two blocks northwest of the northern Ploshchad Ilyicha metro station, and immediately east of the Spasso-Andronikov Monastery. As you exit this metro station, walk away from the Lenin statue standing on the square until you reach Sergiya Radonezhskogo Street, then continue west toward the monastery. The second street on your right will be Khlebnikov Lane, with the restaurant Las Palmas on the corner. Turn right and continue in the northeasterly direction, past Cafe Agdam, and across Volochayevskaya Street.

This is considered the most liberal homosexual club in Moscow and definitely not for the squeamish. Entertainment includes scantily clad men dancing and naked men swimming to Tchaikovsky music in an aquarium. There is a large dance floor with a bar downstairs and a smaller one, also with a bar, upstairs; drinks are reasonably priced. Women make up almost 25 percent of the crowd and a few straight couples come for the show.

TRI OBEZYANY (Three Monkeys), *4 Trubnaya ploshchad, Metro Tsvetnoy bulvar. Tel. 208-4637. open daily from 6pm to 9am.* This is another gay club with a drag cabaret and with entrance by membership or invitation only. Also located here is the **Dyke** lesbian club, *Tel. 163-8002,* which is open from 6pm to 11pm. Both the Cuban Las Palmas and the Georgian Cafe Agdam are nearby and open until midnight should you wish to eat before clubbing. For details, see Chapter 12, *Where to Eat.*

TAGANKA BLUES, *15 Ulitsa Verkhnyaya Radishchevskaya, Metro Taganskaya. Tel. 915-1004 or 1056. Open daily from 8pm to midnight. Live entertainment. Cash only.*

Located southeast of the Kremlin, just inside the Garden Ring Road, two blocks northwest of the northern Taganskaya metro station, and one block west of Taganka Theater.

This club has a restaurant and bar that seats about 75. The entertainment is better than the food and many men seem to agree that the belly dancers on the stage are the best. Cossack and Russian singers prey on your sentiments with folk melodies.

The Italian restaurant Kaprichio, *8/40 Goncharny proyezd,* is about four blocks south of here and open until midnight, if Taganka's food does not please you.

SHELTER'S DISCO CLUB, *14 Ulitsa Presnensky val, Metro Ulitsa 1905 goda. Tel. 253-6653 or 6203. Open 24 hours. Live entertainment. Substantial cover charge in the evening. Cash only.*

Located northwest of the Kremlin, west of the Moscow Zoo, and two blocks from either metro station exit.

If you pine for rock & roll music, this is the place to go. The younger American set will appreciate the large variety of pinball and video machines, not to mention eight kinds of beer.

A block south of here, at 6 Presnensky val Street, is the Belgian pub **Sixteen Tons**, which from the outside and inside looks thoroughly English. Belgian drafts and bottled beers can be had, in addition to some basic pub meals.

If you continue southwest on Presnensky val, it becomes Trekhgorny val Street and four long blocks later you will find yourself in front of the Pilot/Sokho night clubs at 6 Trekhgorny val. Now you are within three blocks of the Golden Ostap restaurant and casino, as well as Santa Fe restaurant and the Hippopotam nightclub underneath it.

TITANIK, *inside the Young Pioneers' Stadium, 31 Leningradsky prospekt at Ulitsa Begovaya, Metro Dinamo. Tel. 213-4581. Open Thursday through Sunday, from 10pm to 6am. Cover charge. Cash only.*

Located northwest of the Kremlin, south of Dinamo Stadium, and north of the Hippodrome racetrack.

This is a trendy, boisterous, sprawling disco with three decks and a balcony overlooking a dance floor in the style of the ill-fated liner. It's so big you can get a thousand people inside. The Titanik is a bit expensive and the music is loud.

Two monstrously long blocks northwest from here lies the Hotel Aerostar, with the very expensive continental restaurant, Borodino, and a more bearable Cafe Taiga, should you get hungry; but eat first because they both close at 11pm.

ZOLOTOY OSTAP (Golden Ostap), *3 Shmitovsky proyezd at Second Zvenigorodskaya ulitsa, Metro Ulitsa 1905 goda. Tel. 259-4795 or 256-0939. The casino is open daily from 8pm to 4am, restaurant from 1pm to 4am; only restaurant patrons may gamble. Live entertainment. Major credit cards accepted. Jacket and tie are suggested for men. Reservations may be needed in the evening.*

Located west of the Kremlin, north of the World Trade Center and the Mezh Hotel, and four very long blocks southwest of the Ulitsa 1905 goda metro station. It's too far to walk to from the metro; take a taxi or a bus on Presnensky val Street nearby, across the street from Sixteen Tons restaurant and pub.

Zolotoy Ostap has a small casino with one blackjack and one American roulette table. First evening floor show starts at 9pm. For more about its restaurant, see Chapter 12, *Where to Eat.*

16. SPORTS & RECREATION

Muscovites, like so many other Europeans, are passionate about soccer, ice hockey, basketball, volley ball, and track and field. Soviets often tried to display their superiority through sporting events, so there are plenty of facilities all over the city. In this chapter you'll find a number of fitness centers where you can work out, swim, and play tennis and basketball. Under sport complexes, you'll see a number of places where you can attend professional soccer and hockey games, and tennis and vollyball tournaments, among other sports. I also include suggestions for two popular recreational activities, chess and public baths.

BASKETBALL

There is a regular pickup game, open only to expatriates, from 6pm to 8pm every Sunday at the **US Embassy's indoor court**. Enter the embassy compound through the south gate on Bolshoy Devyatinsky pereulok, but bring your passport. It costs about $5 to play. The gym sells cards for $25 that entitle you to five games or you can pay $50 for ten games. For more information, call the gym, *Tel. 252-2451*.

CHESS

The **Central Chess Club**, *14 Gogolevsky bulvar, Metro Kropotkinskaya or Arbatskaya, Tel. 291-0641*, is, judging by its modest facilities overlooking the park on the boulevard, also a social club for chess players.

FISHING & HUNTING

If you wish to go **fishing** or **hunting**, go to the Intourist office on Ulitsa Mokhovaya, next to the Hotel Natsional, to find out how to obtain a license.

FITNESS CENTERS

Jogging hit the spotlight in 1990 when actress Jane Fonda led several hundred joggers from Moscow's Red Square to the Moskva River to get her foot into the Russian market and sell more of her fitness tapes. Since then, some two dozen fitness centers have sprouted up in Moscow.

World Class Gym, *14 Ulitsa Zhitnaya, Bldg. 2, Metro Oktyabrskaya, Tel. 239-1994 or 238-5676*, located south of Kremlin and on the Garden Ring Road near the French Embassy, is a 1993 addition to the Moscow exercise scene. Spacious and clean, it has everything you expect from such facilities in the West.

Built by the Swedes and equipped with the latest top-of-the-line computerized equipment from that Nordic land, it offers weight rooms, tennis and squash courts, an aerobics room with certified instructors and a swimming pool. A trainer is available to answer your questions. Men's and women's locker rooms provide clean Western-standard showers and toilets, as well as secure lockers for valuables. Towels are also provided. A small bar offers drinks and sandwiches.

The owners want to keep the World Class Gym an exclusive club for foreign businessmen. A one-time visit will cost you $20-30, depending on what facilities you use. A full-year single membership is $2,500, or $1,800 for six months. Corporate membership is available. The use of the swimming pool only for one year is $1,200. The Gym is open daily from 7am to 10pm, Saturdays and Sundays from 9am to 9pm.

Nosorog (Rhino) **Fitness & Health Club**, *16 Maly Kazenny pereulok, Metro Kurskaya, Tel. 913-6473*, opened in 1995. Located northeast of the Kremlin and between the Boulevard and Garden Ring Roads, it boasts a step-aerobic studio as well as a spa with sauna and whirlpool. Professional massages are available. There is a CNN Bar with a large screen TV and valet parking.

Excell Health Club, *1 Ulitsa Zaporozhskaya, Metro Molodyozhnaya in the suburb of Kuntsevo, Tel. 448-0135 or 444-9464*, is situated east of the Kremlin, outside the Garden Ring, and near Iskra Stadium, close to the Moscow Circular Road, which delineates the boundaries of the city.

Swimming pool, sauna, workout room, solarium, massage, and table tennis are available Monday through Saturday, from 11am to 11pm. The club is closed Sundays.

Spartak Palace of Sports, *23a Maly Oleny pereulok (for membership), and 1a Shiryayevo pole (for the sports complex), both metro Sokolniki, Tel. 268-0888 or 8013, Membership, Tel. 268-1947*, is located northeast of the Kremlin and outside the Garden Ring Road. While the tennis courts are said to be almost always booked, you can go for a workout at any time. It is open Monday through Friday, from 7am to 11pm, and fees are payable in rubles only.

The **Chaika Sports Complex**, *3/5 Prechistenskaya nab., Metro Park Kultury, Tel. 246-1344*, is located southwest of the Kremlin and just inside the Garden Ring Road.

Chaika has one of the best swimming pools in Moscow, a gym, covered tennis courts, athletic facilities and sauna, but admission is difficult because a membership card is required, except Sundays. It is almost always full. Try a Sunday afternoon session, from 4pm to 8pm, when you can have access to the swimming pools, the sauna and the workout room for about $10. For more on swimming, see the Swimming section below.

Laetitia-Fizkultura, *Metallurg Hotel, 12 Oktyabrsky pereulok, Metro Rizhskaya or Mendeleyevskaya, Tel. 971-2108*, is northwest of the Kremlin and outside the Garden Ring Road. It has workouts and an American-style gym, solarium and massage services. Each visit costs about $10, while the massage and solarium are extra. Memberships are available. You can pay in rubles or with a currency credit card. Hours are from 10am to 8pm every day, except Saturday and Sunday.

Russian-style aerobics is available at the **Dinamo Stadium**, *36 Leningradsky prospekt, Entrance 14, 2nd Floor, Metro Dynamo, Tel. 212-8342*. Sunday classes meet at 1pm; Monday and Thursday sessions are at 7:45pm. The cost is a few dollars per month. To mark your spot at Dinamo aerobics, you are supposed to throw down a marker to be entitled to stand where you do. Otherwise, another person might throw down something like a glove or her keys and tell you to move. Women aged 18 to 50 exercise here.

The **International Women's Club**, *Tel. 479-5478 or 284-6396*, and its Isadora Duncan Center offer aerobics and dance classes.

GOLF

A 9-hole Swedish-built **Moscow Golf Club**, also known as **Tumba Golf Club**, *Tel. 147-8330 or 5480, Metro Universitet*, is situated in Sparrow Hills and has been open to the public since Communism went into oblivion.

The membership is $20,000 a year. Members can invite one guest to all club functions. The club also has a sauna, a conference room for 50 and a sporting goods shop on the premises. Golfing equipment can be rented. For more about the Chinese restaurant, Chopsticks, at the club, see Chapter 12, *Where to Eat*.

HORSE RACING

While casino gambling is a relative newcomer in Moscow entertainment, horse racing and betting have gone hand in hand even during the height of Communist folly.

Harness and thoroughbred horse racing with small-stake betting takes place each Sunday and Wednesday at the 1.1-mile **Hippodrome Racecourse**, *22 Ulitsa Begovaya, Metro Begovaya, Tel. 945-4516 or 0437*. It is situated northwest of the Kremlin, outside the Garden Ring Road, and west of the Belorussky Railway Station.

The Hippodrome has been run for many years by the Ministry of Agriculture under the guise of improving horse breeding. The 7,000-square-yard Hippodrome was reconstructed in 1993 to bring it up to international standards with seating for 8,000 spectators. Tickets are available all over the city, including at sidewalk stands, and prizes include cars, TV sets and cash. Bets range upward from a few cents and there is, at least theoretically, no maximum bet. The overwhelmingly male crowd can be rowdy. The Hippodrome is open in the winter for troika racing on Saturdays and Sundays, starting at 1pm.

If you wish to take riding lessons, call *Tel. 945-3224 or 5872.*

PUBLIC BATHS

Some 50 **banyi**, or public baths, remain in Moscow, down from 120 in 1946. Their numbers started dropping precipitously by the early 1960's, when bathrooms became widely available in new apartment buildings. If you should decide to try a public bath, we suggest you do so with Russian friends who know their way around. Do not go to a steam bath after a full meal, if you are hungry, if you have been drinking or if you are tired.

Public baths have separate sections for men and women. After you pay a small fee, you go to a communal room to change. You can clean yourself in a shower or at a bench with buckets of water. It is recommended that you keep your hair dry and not soap your body until the very end. Wear a cap moistened with cold water.

You can then proceed to a steam room, but gradual exposure to heat is the essence of the steam bath. How long should you stay? Some people say until the third drop of sweat streams down your nose. You should not sweat your brains out. It is recommended that you stay in the steam room from eight to twelve minutes in three steps of about three to four minutes each.

After coming out of the steam room, you should not lie down at once to rest, but walk around for a couple of minutes. Then take a one-minute warm shower. Jumping in a pool of cold water is a stereotype and is not recommended. Natural juices, tea and mineral water are suggested to quench your thirst, not alcohol and nothing ice cold. If you want a massage, you should make prior arrangements.

The following public baths have communal and private facilities for men and women:

Sandunovsky Baths, *14 Ulitsa Neglinnaya, Metro Kuznetsky Most, Tel. 928-4203, are centrally located north of the Kremlin and inside the Boulevard*

Ring. Open 8am to 10pm, but the cashier closes at 8pm. Closed Tuesdays. The entrance fee is $15.

Built in 1808 and showing their age, they are named after the Imperial Theater actor Sila Sandunov, son of a Georgian aristocrat. Fyodor Shalyapin, the famed operatic basso, came here every Wednesday and sang during a cold shower, much to the delight of his all-male admirers. The facility has a good hot room, large and hot enough so that you will need a sheet. There is a small snack area and a large rest room with two billiard tables and a set of weights.

A two-hour session, complete with exercise room, costs about $20 for a private suite with carpeting, refrigerator and samovar; it also includes linens. The plain **banya**, or bath, downstairs is about $5; the main difference between the $20 and $5 banya is the size of the swimming pool. Private bathing facilities for up to six persons can be reserved for about $75. A full-body massage is available at an additional cost.

Krasnopresnensky Baths, *7 Stolyarny pereulok, Metro Ulitsa 1905 goda, Tel. 253-8690, are located northwest of the Kremlin and outside the Garden Ring Road, west of the Moscow Zoo. Open 8am to 10pm, but the cashier closes at 8pm. Closed Mondays.*

These baths have an excellent plunge pool and a good dry sauna for those not accustomed to the heat of the banya. A two-hour session, complete with dry sauna, steam sauna and plunge pool in the soberly decorated facility (which has seen better days) is about $10. A full-body massage is available at an additional cost. Private bathing facilities for up to six persons can be reserved.

SPORTS COMPLEXES

Luzhniki Sports Complex

The **Luzhniki Sports Complex**, *24 Luzhnetskaya nab., Metro Sportivnaya, Tel. 201-0155 or 0995,* is a 445-acre sports facility located southwest of the Kremlin and outside the Garden Ring, practically enveloped by the snaking Moskva River. The Novodevichy Convent is just northeast of Luzhniki.

The all-purpose **Central Stadium**, formerly called the Central Lenin Stadium, seats more than 100,000 spectators, was privatized in 1992 and is the largest in the capital. Built three years after Stalin's death on a useless swamp along the banks of the Moskva River and directly opposite Moscow State University, it is undergoing a $100 million renovation to bring it up to European standards. A retractable dome will be added by the year 2000.

Thousands of laborers from the Komsomol youth movement, which often picked the Soviet Union's potato crops, came from all over the country to work night and day so that by the summer of 1956 the stadium could host the All-Soviet Summer Games. In 1982, the stadium was also the site of one of the worst sports-related tragedies in Europe; upon conclusion of a soccer match between Russian and Dutch teams a collision among the fans resulted in 360 deaths.

The **Grand Sports Arena**, *Tel. 246-6916 or 201-0928*, built in 1956, is used for track and field events and soccer matches. There are also 14 training gyms and swimming pools for men and women. For information about its physical fitness center call *Tel. 201-1655 or 1164 or 0321*. You will also find several cafes in this facility.

The **Small Sports Arena**, *Tel. 201-1413*, which seats 14,000, is used for volleyball and tennis competitions. Hockey matches and figure skating contests, as well as basketball, boxing, gymnastics and weight-lifting events are also held here.

There are two swimming pools for competition and one for warming up and training. The **Druzhba** (Friendship) building is used for training and various sports events.

The Luzhniki complex also has ten training soccer fields, 33 outdoor tennis courts, 22 gyms and sports grounds for children.

Krylatskoye Olympic Sports Center

The **Krylatskoye Olympic Sports Center**, *10 Ulitsa Krylatskaya, Metro Krylatskaya, Tel. 141-4440*, is a 300-acre complex that includes an archery range, as well as martial arts, fencing and gymnastic facilities scattered between the Moscow Circular Road and Ulitsa Nizhniye Mnevniki, west of the Kremlin. Krylatskoye is an ancient village which once belonged to the Romanov noblemen.

The complex also includes the following: the **Alpine Skiing Center**, *Tel. 140-4308*, a children's alpine ski school that is open daily from 10am to 6pm; **Bicycle Track**, *Tel. 148-2181*, open daily from 10am to 10pm, as well as a similar indoor facility; and **Grebnoy Kanal**, *Tel. 140-8658*, a rowing basin with two courses and grandstands for 3,000 people.

The **Dinamo Sports Complex**, *36 Leningradsky prospekt, Metro Dinamo, Tel. 212-7092*, is situated northwest of the Kremlin, north of the Hippo-drome racetrack, and outside the Garden Ring Road. The complex, which was built in 1928, takes up 100 acres. It is home to several major sports clubs, including the Dinamo Stadium and the Dinamo Fitness Center.

The **Dinamo Stadium**, *Tel. 212-2252*, named after a local club, can hold 60,000 soccer fans. It has been filled to near capacity whenever Michael Jackson gives a concert here. Soccer matches and track and field competitions are held at the Dinamo and the Central (see Luzhniki Sports Complex) stadiums, and hockey games are played at the Lenin and

Sokolniki Sports Palace. There is also the **Small Arena** with a gymnastics hall and ice rink.

Dinamo Fitness Center, *Tel. 212-1582*, includes physical fitness and cardiovascular exercise classes and limited equipment. It is open daily from 9am to noon and 3pm to 8pm.

If in the evening you should see an inordinate number of Mercedes-Benz and Volvo sedans around the Dinamo soccer stadium, you are probably close to **Grand Dinamo**, an exclusive private social club, where membership costs upwards of $3,000.

Olypmic Sport Complex, *16 Olimpiysky prospekt, Metro Prospekt Mira, Tel. 288-2018*, is north of the Kremlin and outside the Garden Ring Road, next to Moscow's only functioning mosque. It was built for the 1980 Moscow Olympic Games and has an array of sports facilities, such as the **Olympic Stadium** that seats 45,000. It can also be adjusted to make it suitable for circus and theatrical performances or New Year's parties. As you will recall, the US and several other countries did not participate in the 1980 Olympics because of the Soviet invasion of Afghanistan.

There are tennis courts, workout classes and saunas. You can take tennis lessons here. Also on the premises are basketball and volleyball courts. Hours are from 9am to 10pm daily.

The Olympic swimming pool, located in a smaller building next to the stadium, is open from 7am to 5pm. For more on that, see the Swimming section in this chapter.

SWIMMING

Basin Moskva, since 1960 a large open-air swimming pool on Kropotkinskaya nab. a block or so south of the Pushkin Museum, has been replaced by the **Cathedral of Christ the Savior**.

Chaika Health Club, *1/3 Turchaninov pereulok, Metro Park Kultury, Tel. 246-1344* is probably the best open-air swimming venue in the city. Monthly club membership is about $30. This is a favorite place for women who sunbathe topless and are not embarrassed by a male presence. You must have a medical certificate to be admitted, but if you do not, the club's doctor will examine you for a small fee.

Olympic Nautical Sports Center, *30 Ulitsa Ibragimova, northeast of the metro station Semenovskaya, Tel. 369-0649 or 4803*, is located northeast of the Kremlin, outside the Garden Ring Road, and near the Neptune Hotel.

There are eight swimming pools in this huge complex and open to everyone for about $5 per visit, although some pools are reserved for children and for swimming lessons. There are workout rooms, aerobics, a sauna, massage services, tennis, judo, karate and kung-fu. It is open daily from 7am to 10pm.

Olympic Sports Complex, *16 Olimpiysky prospekt, Metro Prospekt Mira, Tel. 288-3777 or 2018*, is located north of the Kremlin and outside the Garden Ring Road. It was built for the 1980 Moscow Olympic Games and has an array of sports facilities, including a swimming pool and sauna.

The swimming pool is open from 7am to 5pm, but first you must get a health certificate from the clinic inside the complex, which is usually just a formality for Westerners. The Olympic pool, like much of functioning Russia, is run by women of uncertain humor and iron authority. You will need a towel and soap. Your shoes better be clean or you might be scolded about carrying them into the changing room without putting them into a plastic bag first. The pool is heavily chlorinated. The shower room is not particularly pleasant, but it does have hot water. There are no drinking fountains, but a nearby kiosk sells juice, swimsuits and goggles.

Luzhniki Sports Complex, *Tel. 201-1164 or 0321 for the swimming pool, Tel. 246-4515 for the gym and health club*, is open to the public. See the description of the facility under Sports Complex in this chapter.

Among the luxury hotels, the following swimming facilities are available:

Baltschug Kempinsky Hotel, *Tel. 230-6500*, is located south and across the Moskva River from Red Square. It has a health club for its guests.

Kosmos Hotel, *150 Prospekt Mira, metro VDNkH, Tel. 217-0785*, is situated northeast of the Kremlin and outside the Garden Ring Road. It has an indoor swimming pool, *Tel. 217-1183*, a sauna, and a bowling alley, all of which are payable in rubles.

Metropol Hotel, *1 Teatralny Square, Metro Teatralnaya, Tel. 927-6000*, has a swimming pool, workout area and sauna.

Mezhdunarodnaya Hotel, *12 Krasnopresnenskaya nab., Metro Ulitsa 1905 goda, Tel. 253-1391*, is located near the World Trade Center. It has a bowling alley, gym, swimming pool and sauna.

Renaissance Moscow Hotel, *18/1 Olimpiysky prospekt, Metro Prospekt Mira, Tel. 931-9000*, is situated north of the Kremlin and outside the Garden Ring. It has a swimming pool and workout facilities.

Palace Hotel, *19 Ulitsa First Tverskaya-Yamskaya, Metro Mayakovskaya, Tel. 956-3152*, is located northwest of the Kremlin and outside the Garden Ring Road. It has a health club with jacuzzi, saunas, massage services, solarium, workout classes and aerobics, daily from 7am to 10pm. The fee is $30 for each visit or a one-month membership for $150, payable in rubles or with the credit card.

Radisson Slavyanskaya Hotel, *2 Berezhkovskaya nab., near Kievsky Railway Station and metro, Tel. 941-8027*, is west of the Kremlin and outside the Garden Ring Road. It has a health center, which includes a junior Olympic swimming pool, men's and women's saunas, and Nautilus exercise equipment. These facilities are available through the Gold and Silver Club.

Silver Club membership costs about $800 for six months and allows access from 8am to 4pm on weekdays and 7am to noon on weekends. The Gold Club costs $1,400 for six months and offers expanded hours. They are payable in rubles or with a credit card. There is a waiting list for both.

17. SHOPPING

Shopping in Moscow is unlike shopping anywhere else. Muscovites suggest that you always bring more cash than you think you will need and buy immediately whatever you like because it probably will not be there tomorrow.

Few things will irritate you more or help you better understand the Russian economic mess than Moscow's state-run stores and their sales personnel. First you stand in line to pick out your item. Then you have to line up again at the cashier to pay for it. And then you have to bring your receipt back to the counter to collect your merchandise. Two or three, or more people, are doing what in the West is almost always done by one person, except in the most exclusive establishments.

You will be startled, we promise you, when you hear the sales clerks actually yelling at customers in the state-owned stores. But Russians will tell you with a straight face that the trick is to keep your sense of humor and always have the right amount of money.

Even if you stare at a saleswoman - and they are overwhelmingly women - right in the eye to get her attention, she will not budge. She may be talking to a friend, or even reading a book, and at times you feel she is doing you a favor serving you at all. Your only recourse is to plead, **"Dyevushka!"** (Miss!) and hope she takes pity on you. You'll ask yourself more than once how in the world did the Communist-driven economy survive for seven decades? Would you like a hint? Terror and brute force.

On the other hand, it gives us pleasure to tell you that in today's Moscow you do not have to worry that a salesperson will try to sell you something that you are not interested in having or cannot afford. You will never receive telephone calls in the dead of night from pesky entrepreneurs trying to sell you solar-driven vacuum cleaners or soliciting for a charity for blue-eyed Albanians at Harvard. It is not uncommon for a saleswoman to tell you that a less expensive item is just as good or even better than what you are thinking of buying. Nobody, of course, knows how long this will last.

There were relatively few private name stores until hard-currency stores appeared in Moscow. For decades most shops had simple generic names like Fruits and Vegetables, Food Shop, Books, Cheese, Ice Cream, or Tea and Coffee and most of the state-run shops still have them.

Unlike at home where your purchases are likely to end-up in an expensive four-color paper or plastic shopping bag (making you wonder how much of the price goes for packaging), in Moscow's state stores you will seldom get a bag of any kind. You are expected to bring your own, whether for groceries or bread. Larger Western stores do provide free shopping bags, and you'll see some Muscovites toting around these bags until the print has completely rubbed off.

Whether you want Marlboro cigarettes, Tobler chocolate, Chanel perfume, Agfa film, wigs or light bulbs, you will find them all, and more, everywhere, from kiosks to one of the metro corridors. On some sidewalks, you will pass a gauntlet of sellers, from students to pensioners, trying to earn a few extra rubles by offering everything from socks to week-old puppies. The moment a policeman appears, these sellers dissolve into the crowds, only to reappear moments later.

There are several well-known Moscow streets, such as Stary Arbat and Novy Arbat Streets, where shopping and walking will be fun and they are discussed in this chapter.

WHERE TO SHOP

DEPARTMENT STORES

There are two large clusters of stores that will probably meet most of your needs. Both have a large variety of products and many Western companies selling them. One is the GUM department store –really more like a huge mall – and the other is Petrovsky Passazh Mall.

GUM STATE UNIVERSAL STORE, *3 Red Square, Metro Ploshchad Revolutsiyi. Tel. 926-3470 or 3471 or 5763 or 5692. Open daily from 8am to 8pm; no lunch break, closed Sundays. Major credit cards accepted in some of GUM's international shops.*

The site where GUM now stands has been the center of Moscow trade since time immemorial. Hundreds of small shops cluttered the Kitay-gorod (an area twice the size of the Kremlin) as well as Nikolskaya and Ilyinskaya Streets before the Revolution and earlier. Many of these shops were in a deplorable state of disrepair. In one store the floorboards were so rotten that a noblewoman who was trying on a dress on the second floor fell through to the ground floor and broke a leg. Concerned about safety, the Moscow governor issued an order that the shops be replaced by the Upper Trading Rows, or today's GUM.

When completed at the turn of the century, GUM was the largest store in Europe, and like the department stores of Paris and Stockholm it had three parallel and three perpendicular rows; an arcade with 240 small shops. An artesian well situated under the building provided up to 50,000 buckets of water needed for heating, the water system and fire hydrants. After the 1917 Revolution, GUM was converted into government offices, but upon Stalin's death in 1953 the building was renovated and reopened as a shopping mall and a "showcase of socialist trade."

More than a quarter-million shoppers throng its narrow passageways every day. It is Moscow's equivalent of Macy's in New York or Galerie Lafayette in Paris. Stretching across the entire northeast side of Red Square opposite the Kremlin Wall, GUM sells practically everything or houses stores that make such claims. Over each entrance to the building you can still see empty cases which used to hold magnificent icons.

GUM is a national monument so it cannot be privatized. But GUM Trading House has a 49-year lease on the property and also owns several other stores in Moscow. A joint-stock company, it was privatized through vouchers that were made available to Russian citizens. By the time it celebrated its 100th anniversary, the mall was crying for improvements and the smell would turn off some Western shoppers, but by 1995 it was in a renaissance of sorts and was being renovated everywhere. If you come on a rainy day, you may still have to dodge dripping water from its rounded glass roof, but you will enjoy its atmosphere, bridges and ornamental stucco design.

There are several souvenir shops on the ground floor, although we recommend the Old Arbat Street over GUM if you are looking for something like a Zhostovo tray, Palekh lacquer box, Khokhloma wood objects, or a matryoshka of any size and description.

The first rows on the first and second floor carry the most prestige and by the time you reach the third row, the stores become sloppy, disorganized and sorely lacking in service.

First Row, First Floor, From Ulitsa Nikolskaya toward Ilyinka:

Christian Dior: Large variety of makeup, accessories for men and women, purses, watches; **Clinique**: The complete skin care line, including makeup, moisturizers and creams; **Estee Lauder**: Good selection of women's cosmetics, perfumes and accessories; **Benetton**: Selection of men's, women's everyday clothes, pants, jackets, sweaters, suits; **Karstadt**: Mid-priced German department store selling men's and women's clothing, shoes; **Karstadt Optics**: Western-style optometrist with a variety of frames and accessories; **Benetton 12 Kids**: Sports clothing and toys for boys and girls to age 12, up to $100 apiece; **GUM Service**: Freshly cut flowers and flower arrangements for every occasion; **Galerie Lafayette**: French department store selling a variety of merchandise; **Statfall**: Writing instruments and stationery, briefcases and children's school supplies; **GUMIR**: Makeup, appliances, electronics, clothes, footwear, toys, food and snack bar; **JVC**: JVC electric appliances, Braun kitchenware, Bauknecht large appliances and cameras; **SoapBerry**: 200 biodegradable skin, hair and bath products for the environmentally conscious; **Wellfarm**: Siemens appliances, Playmobil toys, Henkel detergents, Black & Decker tools; and **Arrow Shirts**: Men's suits, jackets, slacks, sweaters, shirts, ties, socks and more.

First Row, Second Floor. All Stores Overlook Red Square:

Claude Litz: Individually designed furs, from $500 to $20,000, Canadian sable coats; **Escada**: Two salons, one selling women's clothes at outrageous prices, the other at moderate prices; **Karstadt Kids**: Clothes and toys for boys and girls to 12 years, Nintendo Game Boy; **Samsonite**: Belgian firm catering to male and female travelers with luggage and accessories; **Santens**: Quality men's and women's terry cloth bathrobes and towels, starting as low as $5; **Botany 500**: American men's clothing and accessories store, where suits go for $300-1,000; **GUM Business Center**: Relax in the bar, meet your date, call your boss, send a fax; **Steilmann Berlin**: Women's dresses, skirts, jackets, raincoats and various accessories; **Salamander**: Men's and women's shoes, boots, women's bags, wallets and other accessories. The Vetoshny proyezd side of the second floor consists mostly of Russian shops.

Second Row, First Floor, From Ulitsa Nikolskaya toward Ilyinka:

Lego: Legendary Scandinavian building blocks and other toys for your favorite tyke; **L'Oreal**: Perfumes, cosmetics, makeup and hair products for women from the French firm; **Russian Souvenirs**: Two shops face each other, selling the usual tourist fare; **Tefal**: Kitchen appliances, pots and pans, irons and hair dryers, variety of other items; **Yves Rocher**: Cosmetics, perfumes, soaps, makeup, jewelry, accessories, even men's ties; **Lakme**: Still more cosmetics, toiletries, perfumes, bags and accessories for women.

On the Second Row, Second Floor almost all stores are Russian, selling a variety of goods. You will also find here electric samovars, but if you are serious about buying one see the section on **Souvenirs & Antiques on Old Arbat Street**, below.

On the Third Row, First Floor there is a variety of businesses, such as a bank, food store, shops selling photographic supplies, electronics, kitchen ware, and garden supplies.

If you have time to browse, walk up and down Ilyinka and Nikolskaya Streets, which border GUM. You will find some surprisingly interesting stores that could have been inside GUM, but for the high cost of leases.

GUM Restaurants: The Chinese restaurant **Golden Dragon** is located on the second floor, on the Ilyinka Street side. Nearby is the **Copacabana** bar, serving quick sandwiches, desserts and beverages. The large **Rostik's** restaurant, located on the second floor of the third row, is a carbon copy of Kentucky Fried Chicken, with a few Russian touches. The opportunity to be able to sit down and rest will sometimes be more appreciated than the average food being served, but there are no rest rooms available at Rostik's. There are also a couple of stand-up **bars** on the ground floor, where you can grab a quick bite to eat before your next shopping expedition.

PETROVSKY PASSAZH BOUTIQUES, *10 Ulitsa Petrovka at Ulitsa Kuznetsky Most, Metro Kuznetsky Most or Teatralnaya. Tel. 923-6066 or 928-5047. Open Monday through Saturday from 8am to 8pm. Major credit cards accepted at some shops.*

Located north of the Kremlin and the Bolshoy Theater, and northwest of the Metropol Hotel. Petrovka Street, which runs in a northwesterly direction (and parallel with Tverskaya, see below) from Teatralnaya Square in front of the Bolshoy and Metropol to the Boulevard Ring Road, is about half a dozen blocks from Kuznetsky Street.

Petrovka Street is an old aristocratic street, which by the turn of the century was settled by merchants. It is well-known for its twin-arcaded Petrovsky Passazh shopping mall, which, after GUM on Red Square, has the second largest concentration of chic Western boutiques.

This shopping mall is a glassed-in two-story gallery of shops where prices are based on the exchange rate for the US dollar. On the ground floor you will find an **Avon Cosmetics** boutique, a bank, a flower shop, **Nina Ricci** clothing, a business center where you can make photocopies, an electronics store selling cameras, TV's and telephones, a food shop, an appliance store, flower and souvenir stores, a tiny print shop where you can have your business cards done, **L'Oreal** cosmetics store, a leather wear store, a casual men's and women's clothing store, an optical shop, a formal men's clothing store, a **Kodak** express photo counter where you can buy film and other supplies, and a stand-up snack bar.

On the second floor, there is a women's clothing store, **Olbi-Diplomat** electronics, **Pioneer** electronics, **Panasonic** electronics, and **Sony** electronics stores, a drug store, a **Samsonite** luggage store, followed by a **Parker Pen** stationery store, a compact disks counter, a leather goods store with jackets for men and women, a shoe store for men and women, a clothing shop for boys and girls, and a women's intimate apparel shop.

Next door to Petrovsky Passazh is **Russkiye Uzory** (Russian Ornaments), *Tel. 923-1883*, a crafts shop selling a fair selection of souvenirs, including samovars.

CENTRAL DEPARTMENT STORE (TsUM), *2 Ulitsa Petrovka, Metro Teatralnaya. Tel. 292-1157. Open daily Monday through Saturday, from 8am to 9pm. Cash only.* Centrally located north of the Kremlin and across the street from the Bolshoy Theater.

This large multi-level state-owned general department store has a little of everything and a lot of nothing. Back at home you would consider it a cheap discount store by its looks, but its prices are higher than that. This place is barely worth your time. A hundred years ago, one of the most exclusive department stores in Moscow stood at this site.

FARMERS MARKETS

The pickings at Moscow's farmers markets have improved considerably since individual farmers do what many collective farms were unable to do for decades, provide fresh, wholesome produce at competitive prices.

Whether to pick up fresh fruit and vegetables or just to observe the Soviet melting pot at work, you should visit one of the **rynky**, or farmer's markets. You can also buy fresh meat, but be prepared for what you would consider at home to be unacceptable hygienic practices. Honey, milk and flowers are also sold at the rynky. Fruit sellers are mostly from the southern republics. Prices are much higher than in the state stores, but lower than in the Western-style supermarkets, but the fruit and vegetables are of good quality.

Moscow's farmers markets are no different than a souk in Casablanca or feira in northeastern Brazil. To get the best possible price say as little as you can, but let your expression tell the seller that you are not impressed by the merchandise. The more you want something, the more disinterested you should act. Some hagglers will actually disparage the goods. The worst sin you can commit is showing foreign currency; if you do you will never get the price down.

Check out **Tsentralny rynok**, *15 Tsvetnoy bulvar, Metro Tsvetnoy bulv*ar, which is located northeast of the Kremlin, between the Garden and Boulevard Ring Roads. It's open from 7am until 6pm on weekdays and until 4pm on Sundays. It has the highest prices and the best selection. Opened in the mid-1950s, it is located in an area once known as Okhotny Ryad, or Hunters' Row. It is Moscow's largest market and you'll find it all here, but the prices are high. The mafia is alleged to be pervasive here.

Try **Novocheryomushkinsky rynok**, *1/64 Lomonosovsky prospekt, between Leninsky prospekt and Ulitsa Vavilova,* located southwest of the Kremlin and outside the Garden Ring Road. Take the metro to the Universitet station, then continue for three stops on a tram. Open daily from 7am to 6pm. You can observe Russian, Georgian, Armenian and Uzbeki farmers bringing in their best produce and selling it at their highest prices.

Danilovsky rynok, *74 Ulitsa Mytnaya, near Danilovskaya ploshchad and across the street from the Tulskaya metro station.* Located south of the Kremlin and outside the Garden Ring Road. Open daily from 7am to 7pm, Sundays 7am to 5pm. The prices are about average, but the selection is better than that. There is also a flea market at Danilovsky.

Leningradsky rynok, *11 Ulitsa Chasovaya, near Ambulatorny pereulok, Metro Aeroport or Sokol.* Located northwest of the Kremlin and outside the Garden Ring Road. Open daily from 7am to 7pm, Sundays from 7am to 5pm. It has among the lowest prices, but the selection is average. It's one of the newer markets.

Preobrazhensky rynok, *Preobrazhensky val.* Located northwest of Preobrazhenskoye Cemetery, southeast of the Preobrazhenskaya metro station, northeast of the Kremlin, and outside the Garden Ring Road. Open daily from 7am to 6pm, Sundays from 7am to 4pm. An excellent market with a good selection, but the prices are high. Charming and surrounded by 18th century churches.

Rizhsky rynok, *Prospekt Mira, near the Rizhskaya metro station.* Located northeast of the Kremlin and outside the Garden Ring Road. Open daily, from 7am to 7pm, Sundays from 8am to 8pm. The selection is fair, but prices are low. The surrounding area, with its grim poverty, will stick in your memory.

Tishinsky rynok, *Tishinskaya ploshchad, north of the Zoo, Metro Belorusskaya or Mayakovskaya,* was reconstructed in 1996. Located northwest of the Kremlin and outside the Garden Ring Road. Open daily from 6am until dusk, Sundays 8am until dusk. Selection and prices are average. This is the oldest among these markets. The new Tishinsky rynok was built in the form of a triangle, with 160,000 square feet of space. There is an underground parking garage.

KUZNETSKY MOST STREET

Kuznetsky Most (or Blacksmith's Bridge) is only four blocks long, bounded on the west by Bolshaya Dmitrovka Street and on the east by Bolshaya Lubyanka Street. All four blocks are roughly north of the Kremlin as well as the Bolshoy Theater and Metropol Hotel.

In the 15th century, Kuznetsky Most was the neighborhood for Moscow's blacksmiths, who lived along the banks of the Neglinka River (which has since been diverted underground). By the 19th century, it became one of the most fashionable shopping and browsing streets and remained so until the Communists impoverished it.

Today, the cobbled Kuznetsky Most, which for decades has had the largest concentration of booksellers and airline offices, is slowly regaining its prestige. The descendants of the august Faberge firm, which in the 19th century maintained a Moscow workshop, now have a modest jewelry store at 22 Kuznetsky Most. In one of the few authentic remaining buildings on Kuznetsky Most, across the street from today's Faberge store, is the former residence of the Suzdal archbishops. Two other fashionable retailers on Kuznetsky Most include:

CLAUDE LITZ SALON, *14 Ulitsa Kuznetsky Most, Metro Kuznetsky Most. Tel. 921-8171. Open daily Monday through Friday, from 10am to 7pm, Saturdays from 11am to 6pm. Major credit cards accepted.*

Exclusive fur coats, overcoats, sheepskin coats and accessories for men and women by this Parisian fashion designer are sold here. For the Claude Litz boutique on Red Square, please see GUM Department store.

GIANNI VERSACE, *19 Ulitsa Kuznetsky Most, Metro Kuznetsky Most. Tel. 921-5979 or 3289. Open daily Tuesday through Saturday, from noon to 8pm, Sundays noon to 6pm. Major credit cards accepted.*

Designers clothes and accessories for men and women, and perfumes and carpets are on sale here. In an ironic twist of fate, Versace is located in the very building where, in the 1850's, only Russian products were sold by Slavophiles.

NEW ARBAT STREET
Ulitsa Novy Arbat

During the first three or four years of Russian independence, Novy Arbat Street was a shopping promenade with more than a hundred kiosks lining both sidewalks, one next to the other, selling everything your imagination could conjure, from Lolita cigarettes to footwear.

What was, during the Soviet times, known as Prospekt Kalinina (named after the chairman of presidium of the Supreme Soviet, Mikhail Kalinin) runs east to west from the Praga Restaurant, and past the Arbat Irish House luxury shop on one side and Melodiya record store on the other side of the avenue, all the way to the Moskva River and the edge of the Russian White House and the mayor's office across Konyushkovskaya Street.

Novy Arbat, in comparison with Stary Arbat, is almost anticlimactic. Until the spring of 1962, this part of Moscow was just as interesting as Stary Arbat. The construction of this absurd new avenue cut through the neighborhood to enable the rulers of the Soviet Union to bring the celebrants of the Communist May Day celebrations directly to Red Square without having to navigate the ancient lanes of old Moscow. It took less than two years to destroy one of the most unique sections of Moscow.

Kiosks in central Moscow, which by 1994 numbered more than 16,000, rapidly began disappearing from streets like Novy Arbat, with most of them being removed on orders from the city to improve its image.

The north side of Novy Arbat sports a variety of stores and five open-book-like high-rises, each containing 280 apartments that were constructed between 1964 and 1968, after Nikita Khrushchev was toppled from power. One of the largest cinemas in Russia, the **Oktyabr Cinema**, seating 2,400 moviegoers, is located on Novy Arbat. The American classic *Gone with the Wind* played here to a packed house for a year. The south side of the street is crowded with stores, as well. There are also four large administrative blocks where a number of ministries have their offices.

The following stores on Novy Arbat may be of interest to you:

DOM KNIGI (House of Books), *8 Ulitsa Novy Arbat, Metro Arbatskaya. Tel. 290-4507 or 3580. Open Monday through Saturday, from 11am to 7:30pm. Cash only.*

Dom Knigi is the largest bookstore in Moscow. It occupies a two-story building almost across the street from the Arbat Irish House store. The largest unfortunately does not translate into the best. We believe that no one at Dom Knigi knows exactly what titles they have and where they are located. Although each section is labeled according to a specific subject, you'll find books on the same subject in more than one section.

The service is appalling; you can be standing at a counter right next to a saleswoman until doomsday and she will not care. The English-language book section, or what you can see of it across the counter on the ground floor, is still meager. Dom Knigi also sells antiques and souvenirs on the ground floor.

MELODIYA (Melody), *22 Ulitsa Novy Arbat, Metro Smolenskaya or Arbatskaya. Tel. 291-1421. Open Monday through Saturday, from 9am to 8pm, closed Sundays. Cash only.*

When it comes to CD's and cassette tapes of classical, pop or Russian folk music, you are advised to head for the state-owned Melodiya. It's on the same side of Novy Arbat Street as Dom Knigi (above), and just two blocks east of the Garden Ring Road. The selection of Russian classical music is marvelous and the prices are reasonable.

ARBAT IRISH HOUSE, *13 Ulitsa Novy Arbat, second floor, Metro Arbatskaya. Tel. 291-7641 or 7185. Open Monday through Saturday from 10am to 9pm; Sundays from 10am to 8pm. No lunch breaks. Major credit cards accepted.*

Irish House, which is hardly Irish anymore, consists of a clean, well-stocked Western-style supermarket with a good selection of meats and a baby section; a small department store of boutiques selling electronics, appliances, china, glassware, clothes, music and video tapes; as well as the **Shamrock Bar** (see Chapter 15, *Nightlife & Entertainment*).

In 1991, this was the first major Western shopping complex and until 1994 accessible only to those with credit cards and dollars. It was an oasis without which most foreigners swore they could not survive. In 1995, management of the Arbat House, which was among the first large Western joint ventures in Russia, was taken over by its Russian owners, which included the Moscow city government. The store's expatriate employees were unceremoniously sent home. The Arbat House has never been the same and is now just another supermarket, department store, and bar. The Shamrock Bar will still do when you need a rest room, although it is not as clean as it once was.

NOVOARBATSKY GASTRONOM, *13 Ulitsa Novy Arbat, ground floor, Metro Arbatskaya (same address as Arbat Irish House, above). Open Monday through Saturday from 9am to 9pm. Cash only.*

This large, clean, sometimes crowded, completely renovated delicatessen offers perhaps the best variety of raw, processed and ready-to-eat meats and other foods of all state-owned food establishments. The service is brisk and business-like. There is a busy bakery on one side and a pharmacy on the other, and even a counter where duplicate keys are made.

BRITISH HOME STORE, *15 Ulitsa Novy Arbat, Metro Arbatskaya. Tel. 202-3575. Open daily from 10am to 9pm, Sundays from 10am to 8pm. Major credit cards accepted.*

When it opened in the summer of 1996, the two-level British Home Store, or BHS as it is known in Europe, was probably the most Western department store in the capital. Airy and well-lit, clean and tastefully arranged, it even has fitting rooms with mirrors. A wide escalator takes you silently to the second floor and the only Soviet habit you cannot escape even at BHS are the surly guards at the entrance who insist that you open your shopping bags and show all your receipts.

Those of you who may have wandered all over Moscow to find some silly little item that should not take but a few minutes but didn't, will survey with satisfaction Western-type of racks with clothing and price tags attached, as well as shelves of shoes in most of the usual sizes, even if everything is more expensive than at home. There is everything from lingerie to umbrellas and leather bags. Sections include merchandise for men, women, teenagers, toddlers and tots, not to mention home and hearth. You will even see signs directing you to the Customer Service Desk and Gift Wrapping.

Interesting Sights on Novy Arbat

The only truly historic structure on Novy Arbat, near the intersection of Povarskaya Street, that has miraculously survived to this day is the **Church of St. Simon the Stylite**, which was built in 1676-79. Count

Nikolay Sheremetyev, one of the wealthiest Russian aristocrats, married his serf, Praskovia Kovalyova-Zhemchugova, who was a popular actress and a singer at **Ostankino Palace**, in this church (for more about this startling union that infuriated the nobles, please refer to Chapter 13, *Seeing the Sights*). Speculation has it that Praskovia's humble origins led the Soviets to spare the church, although they closed it in 1940 when its frescoes were destroyed.

Poet Vladimir Mayakovsky and Nobel Prize winning novelist and poet Boris Pasternak, born three years apart, went to a gymnasium-type secondary school nearby: the school was torn down in 1957.

One block north of Dom Knigi, on Malaya Molchanovka Street, is the wooden **Lermontov Home-Museum**; two blocks west of Lermontov's house stands the **Tsvetayeva Museum**, whose occupant was one of the most tragic figures in Russian literature; and at the foot of Arbat and just half a block north on Nikitsky bulvar you will find the **Gogol Memorial Rooms**, where the great satirist died in a religious fervor bordering on insanity. Details on all three museums can be found in Chapter 13, *Seeing the Sights*.

There are several restaurants located on this somewhat artificial street, among them **Arbat** and **Tropicana**, **Sports Bar** and **Palmas** in the Valdai Center, as well as nightspots, such as **Metelitsa/Cherry Casino** and the Arbat Irish House's **Shamrock Bar**. You'll also find the **Arbat Irish House** supermarket and **Novoarbatsky Gastronom** delicatessen.

OLD ARBAT STREET
Ulitsa Stary Arbat

This road runs at a 45-degree angle from New Arbat (Novy Arbat), and in a southwesterly direction from Praga Cafe past the 1,000-seat Vakhtangov Theater, the Pushkin Museum, and McDonald's restaurant to Smolenskaya Square, which is next to the gigantic Ministry of Foreign Affairs. The 500 year old street is about one kilometer long and traces its origins to the road that led to the ancient city of Smolensk.

This area was first mentioned in the 15th century. Paved with brick, Stary Arbat was Moscow's first pedestrian road. In 1812, when Napoleon occupied the city, most of Stary Arbat Street was burned to the ground. Because of that, its appearance was altered completely and new mansions, some of which you can still see, were built in the Empire style. Nine Arbat Street, where the Ukrainian Culture Center stands today, was a bohemian restaurant called Arbatsky Cellar where poets Pasternak, Yesenin and Mayakovsky read their verse in the early 1920s.

If you would like to capture a bit of the flavor of the Bolshevik Arbat before coming to Moscow, read Anatoly Rybakov's semi-fictional novel

Children of the Arbat. The author, incidentally, spent his childhood at 51 Arbat Street, which is the house next to the Pushkin Museum. Many of the once opulent homes, including the Pushkin Museum, were turned into **komunalky**, or communal apartments, and a few choice ones were taken over by Communist Party functionaries. The streetlights that run the length of Arbat were built in the early 1980's.

Like most counterpart streets and promenades the world over, a sort of Greenwich Village in New York, Arbat crawls with musicians, singers, artists, photographers, entrepreneurs, beggars, and acts of every conceivable shade. Some are so young they have not yet seen the inside of a school, but all are intent on separating you from a few hundred rubles so they can buy their next meal or drink.

Most of Stary Arbat is becoming as commercialized as any comparable historical street elsewhere, so unless you are willing to spend more rubles than you would elsewhere, we suggest you think twice before spending them on this street. Stary Arbat has many antique stores and bookstores. There are few places to sit down, without having to pay for a drink or a bite to eat, where you can admire the beautiful **Moskvichky** who are showing off their outrageous fashion styles.

The restaurants **Praga**, **Italia**, **Arbatskiye Vorota**, **Arbatsky Dvorik**, **Russky Traktir**, **McDonald's**, **John Bull Pub** and **Arbat Blues Club**, are a sampling of eateries on and immediately off Stary Arbat Street that are reviewed in Chapter 12, *Where to Eat* and Chapter 15, *Nightlife & Entertainment*. The food in all Arbat restaurants is average and somewhat expensive for what you get, the service is disinterested, and very few establishments accept credit cards. If you want something quick, stop for hot pita-like beef or chicken sandwiches at **Cafe Antalya**, *42 Arbat*, located near the Georgian Cultural Center. This was once one of the residences of Yekaterina Ushakova, another beautiful woman that Pushkin seduced and dropped after meeting his wife, Nataliya Goncharova. Unable to resist her poet, Ushakova did not marry until she was 44, after Pushkin died in a duel over his wife in 1837.

When walking down Arbat, stop at the **Peace Wall** (Stena mira), across the street from 23 Arbat and near Serebryany Lane. It consists of scores of tiles painted by Soviet schoolchildren as an answer to former President Ronald Reagan's Star Wars.

And then, wander over to the rock musician **Viktor Tsoy's Memorial Wall** at Arbat and Krivoarbatsky Lane, across the street from the Vakhtangov Theater. It is scribbled with messages from his fans. This will give you a sense of what has become of some Moscow teenagers under the influence of the West. Fans are particularly active here every August 15, marking the day in 1990 when the 28-year-old leader of the rock group Kino was killed in a car accident outside Riga, Latvia. From that day, a legend began which continues with the Tsoy Wall and his final resting place at the Bogoslovskoye cemetery. On the anniversary of his death, you can see hundreds of teenagers, all dressed in black.

While at Krivoarbatsky Lane, keep walking (you'll be parallel with Arbat Street) until you reach house number 10, the neglected 1927 cylindrical residence of **Konstantin Melnikov** (1890-1974). He was Russia's leading modernist architect, who, in 1936, was accused of 'formalism' and barred from his profession until his death at the age of 84. This is believed to be the only private residence built after the Bolshevik Revolution. Covered in scaffolding, the house has fallen into disrepair. It was declared a historic monument in 1987, and remains an international architectural embarrassment. Eleven of Melnikov's buildings have survived in Moscow.

Two blocks north of here, just beyond Arbat, is Spasopeskovsky Square. Here you'll find a statue of Pushkin and **Spaso House**, which was built in 1914 for a banker who was later murdered by a Red Army guard. Since 1933, it has been the residence of American ambassadors to Russia. Across the square is the **Church of the Savior on the Sands**, which was rebuilt in 1711. A disastrous fire that destroyed much of Moscow is said to have begun from a candle in this church in 1493.

Classical composer **Aleksandr Skryabin** lived in a hauntingly gloomy second-floor apartment on the same block, northeast of here off Arbat Street on Bolshoy Nikolopeskovsky Lane, for three years. For more about it, turn to Chapter 13, *Seeing the Sights*.

What to Buy on Old Arbat Street

Every country is known for an item or two that are forever more touted to foreigners. In Russia it is the **matryoshka**, a wooden nesting doll, painted in bright colors and lacquered. Legend has it that a matryoshka-like figurine from the Japanese island of Honshu was given to the family of the industrialist Savva Mamontov (see Abramtsevo in Chapter 18, *Excursions & Day Trips*) at the end of the 19th century. This figurine gave his craftsmen the idea for a Russian girl in folk attire. It soon became a much sought after Russian souvenir, but it was originally made only in Mamontov's Abramtsevo workshop.

The **matryoshky** were first mass-produced in **Sergiyev Posad** (see Chapter 18, *Excursions & Day Trips*), the Russian spiritual capital northeast of Moscow, where they were manufactured under a controlled design. Its **Toy Museum** has an excellent selection on exhibit. Other villages renowned for their matryoshky are Maidan, Polkhov, Semyonov, Tver and Vyatka. After the 1900 Paris Exposition, the new toy became popular all over Europe. Matryoshky range in scale from three to 40 pieces that fit inside one another, with the smallest sometimes the size of a thimble.

Matryoshky are usually turned out on a lathe. They are painted by hand with oil, gouache or aniline paint and then coated with a lacquer finish. The face and body are painted brightly but not extravagantly, and on the front there is usually a bouquet of flowers. Since perestroika, many matryoshky now depict political figures, such as Gorbachev and Yeltsin. The prices range widely, depending on the number of pieces, their size and particularly the quality of craftsmanship. You can be sure that anything under $20 is of inferior quality because it takes a month or longer to paint a well-done matryoshka. Prices for the best dolls go as high as $3,000. There are more than a thousand painters of matryoshky, but fewer than 50 are worth collecting.

Additional Russian handicrafts include wood carvings, ivory figurines, painted wooden articles, ceramics, stamped leather, enamelled and filigree metalwork, as well as rugs and embroidery.

One of the most appealing Russian crafts is wood objects uniquely painted by the artisans of **Khokhloma**, a village on the Volga River. Brilliantly colored Khokhloma artworks have been associated with this village for more than 300 years. The process of creating a Khokhloma object is time consuming: first logs are stripped of bark and the wood is seasoned for two years. With the help of wood-turning lathes that were already in use during the reign of Peter the Great, bowls, cups, vases and other objects take shape.

All carving is done by hand. These objects are then brought to the kiln room for drying. A thin layer of brown clay "primer" is applied, and they are kiln-dried again. Three coats of oil are then applied to each piece, which is left to dry until the oil becomes slightly sticky. After being tinned with powder aluminum, they are dried again, leaving them silver-colored. After that, it takes days, even weeks, for each piece to be individually painted. When the last coat is dry, several more coats of lacquer are applied and each piece is baked. Every item is a unique and different work of art. Bowls, plates and cups are lead-free, resistant to extreme temperatures and safe for serving food, although most of these objects are so appealing that few foreigners use them for anything but to display.

Thirty-seven miles southeast of Moscow lies the region of **Gzhel**, where the making of porcelain folk art began in the 14th century. The soil in Gzhel was too poor to farm successfully, but was abundant with red clay. In the 18th century, Gzhel began producing pottery. As pottery houses began to mass produce everything from inkwells to pitchers, handicrafts lost their prestige. This almost led to the end of Gzhel, but it was saved from extinction by the Bolsheviks who subsidized the native folk art. Ceramic tea and coffee services, samovars, dishes, vases and figurines are made of Gzhel porcelain and painted with a distinct blue glaze on a white background. Flowers, fairy-tale animals and abstract designs make Gzhel porcelain original and attractive. The best Gzhel ceramics can be seen at the **Kuskovo Estate Museum** in Chapter 18, *Excursions & Day Trips* and at the **Decorative & Folk Art Museum** detailed in Chapter 13, *Seeing the Sights*.

Nestled in the woods on a hill not far from the town of Sergiyev Posad, 46 miles northeast of Moscow, lies the village of **Bogorodskoye**, whose tradition of carved wooden toys goes back to the 17th century. With a knife and a set of chisels, Bogorodskoye artists carve toys from soft woods, such as linden and alder. Using no sketches, drawings or models, they carve quickly and exactly, avoiding superfluous details and striving for simplicity. A specialty of the Bogorodskoye masters are toys with moving parts, with the most popular being the bear whose paws move by means of a simple mechanism.

Russian lace in the form of tablecloths, bedspreads and napkins are lovely. Since ancient times, red, white and gold threads have decorated these linens, as well as Russian clothing and headdresses. Northern Russian embroidery with red thread on a white background is the classic form. Its densely woven pattern of colorful crossed stitches is unique in that it cannot be reproduced on a sewing machine; it is done by hand only. You should also be on the lookout for bright red or deep blue cotton shawls made in **Pavlovsky Posad**. These head scarves were worn before the Revolution by nearly every Russian woman. In a time-consuming process that continues to this day, special blocks of wood are used to apply patterns to the scarves.

You should also look for **shkatulky**, lacquered papier-mache objects that mostly come in the form of miniature boxes. A roll of cardboard is turned around a wooden shape of a box, then soaked in special oil, lacquered and pressed and finally dried over time. For more about these boxes, please see the descriptions of the villages of **Fedoskino** and **Palekh** in Chapter 18, *Excursions & Day Trips*. Other excursions in the same chapter detail trips to **Dulyovo**, known for its porcelain, and **Zhostovo**, which excels in the production of metal trays.

TVERSKAYA STREET
Ulitsa Tverskaya

Tverskaya Street is the Fifth Avenue of Moscow. It was named Ulitsa Gorkogo after the writer Maksim Gorky (1932 to 1990). Tverskaya runs in a northwesterly direction from Manezhnaya Square and the Natsional Hotel (north of the Kremlin), along the Intourist Hotel, **Yermolova Theater**, **Central Telegraph Office**, Prince Yuri Dolgoruky equestrian statue, and Pushkin Square, all the way to the **Tchaikovsky Concert Hall** and **Satira Theater** on Triumfalnaya Square. From Triumfalnaya Square to the 100-year-old **Belorussky Railway Station** its name changes to First Tverskaya-Yamskaya Street. From the Belorussky station, Tverskaya becomes Leningradsky prospekt, which leads directly to Sheremetyevo 2 International Airport.

Starting at Manezhnaya Square, Tverskaya's even numbered building will be on your right. It is a splendid idea to walk the whole length of this street at least once, but it will take you well over one hour, maybe two. You can always change your mind and ride the the metro from any of these stations that span Tverskaya: Okhotny Ryad-Tverskaya/Pushkinskaya-Mayakovskaya-Belorusskaya. The ride will take only ten minutes or so.

Tverskaya Street is so name because it connected Moscow with the ancient Russian town of Tver, 160 miles northeast of Moscow. Tverskaya gained in importance after the construction of St. Petersburg since it was the initial part of the direct route, via Tver, to the new capital. By the 16th century, Tverskaya was a well-known trade route. Even after Peter the Great transferred the capital from Moscow to St. Petersburg, the new tsars entered Moscow along Tverskaya Street.

Originally a tiny, uneven, winding road, Tverskaya's width was tripled in the mid-1930s when some houses were torn down and others were moved back. The construction of the many large buildings that you see today, with shops on the ground floor, began soon afterwards. The Intourist Hotel, unfortunately, is an eyesore in comparison with the surrounding buildings. Before the Revolution, the street was well-known for its fashionable stores, luxurious hotels, and aristocratic mansions. The first electric lamps and the first trams in Moscow were installed on Tverskaya. Muscovites love to tell the story about the red granite lining in some of the buildings on Tverskaya, although few seem to know the truth behind it. They say the granite was brought to Moscow by the Germans to build a colossal monument in honor of their victory over Russia in World War II. Parts of Moscow, according to this scenario, were to be turned into a lake.

Today, Ulitsa Tverskaya, still a bit ragged from years of Communist depravation, again boasts some of the most expensive real estate and the most exclusive stores in the capital. There are many shops along the street, together with sights that you will find detailed elsewhere, as noted. We highlight the Moskva Bookstore, Troyka Gallery, the Souvenir Shop, and Yeliseyevsky Gastronom.

MOSKVA BOOKSTORE, *8 Ulitsa Tverskaya, Metro Tverskaya or Pushkinskaya. Tel. 229-6483. Open daily from 10am to 7pm, closed Sundays. Cash only.*

Located northwest of the Kremlin, inside the Boulevard Ring Road, and in the first building north of Prince Dolgoruky's statue on Tverskaya Square.

If you are looking for a book, map of Moscow, souvenir, antique and more, this is a good place to try to find it. Books in Russian only are sold, but the selection is larger than it might seem as you enter. The southern part of Moskva also sells antiques and silver objects, including icons, some of which you cannot take out of the country. In the northern part of the store, you can have your business cards printed, as well as your film developed.

TROYKA GALLERY, *16 Ulitsa Tverskaya at Pushkin Square, Metro Tverskaya, Pushkinskaya or Chekhovskaya. Tel. 250-1412. Open daily from 11am to 7pm, closed Sundays. Cash only.*

Located northwest of the Kremlin, on the Garden Ring Road, and east across Pushkin Square from McDonald's fast food restaurant.

A good place in central Moscow to educate yourself about lacquered boxes and other souvenirs, perhaps to even buy one. Prices start at about $25 and go into the thousands. Troyka exhibits and sells lacquered boxes from throughout Russia. With direct links to the factories and artists in Fedoskino, Palekh, Mstyora and Kholuy, the gallery maintains a representative selection of works from Russia's leading schools of lacquered miniatures. All boxes purchased here come with an official certificate of authenticity and permission is not required to take them out of the country.

In Chapter 18, *Excursions & Day Trips*, you can find out more about **Fedoskino** and **Palekh**, where you will be able to buy their boxes at lower prices, but will need the time to travel there.

SOUVENIR SHOP, *10 Ulitsa Tverskaya, Metro Tverskaya or Pushkinskaya. Tel. 292-2264 or 371-7703. Open daily from 11am to 7pm, Saturdays 11am to 5pm, closed Sundays. Cash only.*

Located northwest of the Kremlin, in the Tsentralnaya hotel and restaurant building, with entrance between the Pizza Hut and Filippov Bakery. Take the elevator to the fourth floor, then walk the stairs up to office 447.

The shop sells crafts from Fedoskino, Kholuy, Mstyora and Palekh, as well as painted eggs. If you should take a guided tour to **Fedoskino** (see Chapter 18, *Excursions & Day Trips*), there is a good chance that the manager of this shop will accompany your group and answer your questions.

The bread shop situated here is the once-famous Filippov Bakery, particularly beloved for its pastries and meat pies. If all this talk about food makes you hungry there is help just one block northwest of here at Yeliseyevsky, or Gastronom #1, as it was known during Soviet times.

YELISEYEVSKY (Gastronom #1), *14 Ulitsa Tverskaya, Metro Tverskaya or Pushkinskaya. Tel. 209-0760. Open daily Monday through Saturday, from 9am to 9pm, Sundays from 8am to 7pm. Cash only.*

Located northwest of the Kremlin, inside the Boulevard Ring Road, and half a block south of Pushkin Square. Next door is the Wax Museum; on the floor above it the Bolshevik-inspired Nikolay Ostrovsky Museum. Before the 1917 Revolution, this was the biggest specialty food store in Moscow. When it opened in 1901, Yeliseyevsky was the most opulent food emporium ever built in Moscow and known for such idiosyncratic foodstuffs as sausages carved in the shape of the Kremlin. Thousands thronged its large hall when it opened and they still do today, although the place looks worn down. Even during Soviet times, this was the one store where Muscovites could hope to find some sort of sausage or vodka.

The founder, Pyotr Yeliseyev, was a serf who bought his freedom from his owner and came to Moscow with a basket of goods on his shoulders. He saved enough to open a shop in St. Petersburg in 1813. Business was so good that by 1845 his son Grigory needed his own fleet to transport wines sold in his stores. In 1892, the firm received a gold medal in Paris for nothing more than its excellence in storing French wines.

The building has had many owners and the Yeliseyevsky store even sheltered Princess Volkonskaya, who organized literary soirees here. In 1897, Grigory Yeliseyev was among the founders of the first Russian car factory and in St. Petersburg he built a huge refuge for the disabled. He was awarded a hereditary noble rank in 1910. He offered his eldest son one million rubles and unlimited credit to open a chain of stores in the US, but none of his five sons wanted to follow in their father's footsteps. Immensely wealthy, Yeliseyev unexpectedly fell in love with the wife of a leading jeweler and his sons publicly renounced their inheritance. Two weeks after his wife committed suicide, he married this woman, ran away and settled down in Paris, where he died in 1942.

The busts of Grigory's five sons, as well as the ornate woodwork and magnificent chandeliers in the store will still catch your attention. Now that imports are flowing in, you can again find many delicacies. Also available are fresh fruit, vegetables, canned goods, cakes and meats. Rare is the moment when you will walk in and not have to stand in lines to select merchandise, to pay for it and, again, to pick it up.

A Western development company plans to incorporate Yeliseyevsky into a shopping and office complex and move the gastronom's current entrance to its original position on the corner of Tverskaya Street and Kozitsky Lane, named after a rich Siberian gold magnate Kozitskaya for whom the Yeliseyevsky building was erected at the end of the 18th century. During its projected closing in 1997-98, Yeliseyevsky is to set up a temporary shop in the basement of a building across Kozitsky Lane. The **Nikolay Ostrovsky Museum** (see the entry in Chapter 13, *Seeing the Sights*) is to be relocated to the center's fifth floor.

The selection of food in early 1990s Moscow was so poor you could not ignore this shop, but today, if the lines get on your nerves, there are other delicatessens all over the town. The nearest one is the Armenian delicatessen practically across the street, on the corner of Tverskaya Street and Tverskoy Boulevard. This shop, by the way, was once the famed confectionery shop Armenia, built in 1900.

If you wish to sit down and have a real meal there is no dearth of places to eat on and around Tverskaya and First Tverskaya-Yamskaya Street. The following restaurants inside the Boulevard Ring Road, listed here in a descending order based on their cost, are reviewed in Chapter 12, *Where to Eat*: **Maxim's de Paris** at the Natsional Hotel, **U Dyady Guilyaya**, **Azteca**, **Skazka**, **Lili Wong** and **Patio Pizza** at the Intourist Hotel, **El Rincon Espanol** and **Paradise** at the Moskva Hotel, **Pizza Hut**, **Artistiko**, **Aragvi**, **La Cantina**, **Moscow Bombay Express**, **Tsentralny**, **Kombi's**, **McDonald's**, and **Russkoye Bistro**.

Eateries on Tverskaya between the Boulevard and Garden Ring Roads include **Ampir**, **Pekin**, **American Bar & Grill**, **Starlite Diner**, **Tandoor**, and **Baku/Livan-Nassr**. Restaurants located on Tverskaya's extension (First Tverskaya-Yamskaya Street), outside the Garden Ring Road, include **Yakor**, **Vienna**, and **Lomonosov** at Palas Hotel, **Aleksandrovsky**, and **Karusel**. These restaurants are also reviewed in Chapter 12, *Where to Eat*.

Gabriella Casino, **Klub Moskovsky**, **Night Flight**, **Stanislavsky Club**, and **Karusel** are the nightclubs on these streets; for more information see Chapter 15, *Nightlife & Entertainment*. Hotels on and off Tverskaya include **Moskva**, **Natsional**, **Intourist**, **Minsk**, **Tverskaya** and **Palace**.

WHERE TO FIND CERTAIN ITEMS

ANTIQUES

The antiques market is a fairly recent phenomenon in Moscow. Until now, the few articles available were mostly sold in state commission stores for a flat fee.

Perhaps the only Russian antique shops worth visiting are those in Moscow and St. Petersburg and, again, unless you know what you are doing, you may be hauling junk home. The one-kilometer-long Stary Arbat probably has the largest concentration of antique stores in Moscow (list of stores follows). Prices at state-owned salons are a bit lower compared with those in private shops. And make sure you can take the antique out of the country before you purchase it.

The following are among the best known auction houses:
ALFA-ART, *Central Artist's House, 10 Krymsky val, Metro Oktyabrskaya or Park Kultury. Tel. 230-0091. Open daily from 11am to 8pm, closed Mondays. Major credit cards accepted.*
Located southwest of the Kremlin, inside the Garden Ring Road, and northeast of Gorky Park.
Alfa-Art is the largest and most prestigious of all the antique firms in Moscow. It is the only dealer in Moscow that holds regular auctions and publishes an illustrated catalogue. The semi-private Alfa-Art was founded by Alfa Bank in 1991. The auction house has had a spat with the former Ministry of Culture, which attempted to ban an auction because the Ministry felt that the trade in antiques was slipping out of its control.
Alfa specializes in 18th to 20th century Russian and Western art. Due to its reputation, practically everything that Alfa puts on the auction block is quickly sold. Alfa is also quite successful in their auctions of Russian paintings; prices of some domestic works are actually higher at Alfa than in the West.
GELOS ANTIQUITY GALLERIES, *2/6 First Botkinsky proyezd, Metro Dinamo. Tel. 946-0977 or 945-4410. Open daily from 10am to 7pm, closed Sundays. Major credit cards accepted.*
Located northwest of the Kremlin and outside the Garden Ring Road, one block northeast from the Botkin Hospital and one block southwest of the Hippodrome racetrack.
You will find some fine antiques in this two-story shop. Check out their displays of paintings, applied art, silver table accessories, vases, Gardner porcelain and porcelain from the Emperor's Porcelain Factory. Faberge, Khlebnikov, and Ovchinnikov silver objects, gold jewelry, and bronzes of the 17th to 20th centuries are also for sale. There is a restoration workshop on the premises.
The store also has on exhibit a collection of ceramic figurines by Gardner, a well-known pre-Revolutionary porcelain maker who had a factory in Moscow, but the collection is not for sale. And while there, look at an unusual album on the history and architecture of the Cathedral of Christ the Savior, which is also not for sale.
Stary Arbat is well known for its many antique and souvenir stores, all of them accessible through Arbatskaya or Smolenskaya metro stations. Antique and souvenir stores on this street are listed in the ascending order of their addresses:
RUSSKAYA IKONA (Russian Icon), *6/2 Old Arbat Street, Bldg. 1-2, with entrance on Arbatsky pereulok, Tel. 202-0571.* Located in the same store as Zolotoy Larets (below), it sells icons and sculptures from the 16th to 19th centuries. The stores are open daily from 10am to 7pm and closed on Sundays.

ZOLOTOY LARETS (Golden Casket), *6/2 Old Arbat Street, Bldg. 1-2, with entrance on Arbatsky pereulok, Tel. 203-7666 or 6926.* Located in the same building as Russkaya Ikona (above) this store also sells icons and sculptures from the 16th to 19th centuries. The stores are open daily from 10am to 7pm and closed on Sundays.

ALEKSANDR CO., *9 Ulitsa Stary Arbat, Tel. 291-7034.* It sells antique furniture, porcelain and paintings and is open daily from 10am to 8pm.

ARBATSKAYA NAHODKA (Arbat Treasure), *11 Old Arbat Street.* You will find glass objects, bronze, porcelain and paintings by Russian artists. Vases and lamps of Emil Gallet are sold here. It is open daily from 10am to 6pm, but closed Sundays.

KUPINA, *18 Old Arbat Street, Tel. 202-4100 or 4462.* This is an interesting antique store that sells a variety of antiques, priced up to $20,000. You will also find gold and diamond jewelry, bronze, porcelain, furniture, rugs, tapestries, Palekh boxes, and old books. Kupina usually has a reasonable selection of Tula samovars made in the 18th and 19th centuries; some are restored and for display only because of the oxidation in the metal. Their prices range $50-1,500. Kupina is open Monday through Saturday, from 10am to 8pm.

Two other Kupina shops are located at 4 Stary Arbat, where books and antiques are available, and at 21 Stary Arbat, which is called **Zvezda** (Star), *Tel. 291-7143*, where you can buy books, antiques and cameras.

PODARKY (Gifts), *23 Ulitsa Stary Arbat, Tel. 203-1111.* Podarky shares its space with Suveniry (below). It sells a large variety of souvenirs. Decorated electric samovars with matching teapots and trays are also for sale. Both are open daily from 10am to 6pm, but closed Sundays

SUVENIRY (Souvenirs) *23 Ulitsa Stary Arbat, Tel. 291-7158.* Located at the same address as Podarky (above), it sells a large variety of souvenirs. Decorated electric samovars with matching teapots and trays are also for sale. Both are open daily from 10am to 6pm, but closed Sundays.

ARBATSKAYA LAVITSA (Arbat Shop), *27 Old Arbat Street, Tel. 241-6135.* Arbatskaya Lavitsa shares this location with Skazki Starogo Arbata (below). You will find shawls, Khokhloma wooden objects, matryoshka dolls and Russian wooden toys. They are open daily from 10am to 8pm.

SKAZKI STAROGO ARBATA (Old Arbat Fairy Tales), *27 Old Arbat Street, Tel. 241-6135.* As with Arbatskaya Lavitsa (above), which shares the same space, you will find shawls, Khokhloma wooden objects, matryoshka dolls and Russian wooden toys. They are open daily from 10am to 8pm.

RARITET (Rarity), *31 Ulitsa Stary Arbat, Tel. 241-2381.* This is perhaps Moscow's oldest antique shop. It claims that the American pop singer Michael Jackson is but only one famous visitor to their premises. The store's collection of bracelets and rings, adorned with diamonds, sapphires and rubies, goes as high as $20,000.

GUSTAV FABERGE

Silver objects are perhaps Russia's most popular antique and Faberge the most sought after item by Westerners. While other Russian silver producers, such as the Grachev Brothers, Khlebnikov and Sarkizov did fine work, few items attain the perfection of Faberge.

Gustav Faberge, who was of French and German heritage, was born in Estonia in 1814. He opened a small workshop in St. Petersburg which his son Peter Karl expanded into a thriving business that at its prime employed more than 500 craftsmen. His name became synonymous with the best in silver and jewelry works. By 1880's, the House of Faberge had won the title Supplier to the Imperial Court, and in 1885 it produced its first Imperial Easter Egg, which contained a tiny golden hen. The firm opened a branch in Moscow in 1897 and in London in 1903. Over the years, Faberge sold more than 150,000 objects worldwide. In 1918, Karl Faberge was forced to flee to Switzerland, where he died two years later.

*Of the 56 Imperial Easter Eggs made by Faberge for Aleksandr III and his son Nicholas between 1885 and 1917, only ten remain in the Kremlin's Armory collection, although not all are shown. The Forbes Collection in New York contains 12, more than anyone else, at **Forbes Galleries**, 62 Fifth Avenue, New York City, Tel. 212/206-5548, open Tuesday through Saturday, from 10am to 4pm. The **New Orleans Museum of Art**, Tel. 504/488-2631, has three Imperial Easter Eggs. Two were acquired by Queen Mary in 1929 and 1934.*

A large portion of Faberge works are already in Russian and Western museums and good articles are difficult to find. Expect to pay a minimum of $500 for anything genuine by this firm. There are many fake Faberge objects everywhere; do not rely on hallmarks or signatures alone, ask for an authentication certificate.

VYSHIVKA (Needlework), *31 Ulitsa Stary Arbat*. Located at the same address as Raritet (above), handmade textiles are sold exclusively at Vyshivka. Both are open daily from 10am to 6pm, but closed Sundays.

BUKINIST, *36 Old Arbat Street*. Bukinist translates as second-hand bookstore. Founded in 1937, the Bukinist moved to its present location in 1960. Aside from old books and maps, it also stocks silverware, jewelry, medals, and statuettes. Japanese and Russian engravings are also for sale. It is open daily from 10am to 7pm, with lunch break from 2-3pm, but closed Sundays.

ARBATSKY DVOR (Arbat Courtyard), *43 Stary Arbat, Building 4*. This antique shop is hidden in the courtyard off 43 Stary Arbat. You will find some gold and silver jewelry, as well as 19th century chinaware. Since it is owned by the Society of Book and Art Lovers, one of its rooms is devoted to antique books, old postcards, engravings and lithographs. It is open daily from 10am to 6pm, but closed Sundays.

On weekends, you may also want to check out the huge outdoor market at Izmaylovsky Park, Metro Izmaylovo, located northeast of the Kremlin and outside the Garden Ring Road, where everything from unadulterated kitsch to $1,000 antiques and artworks are for sale.

BOOKS

If you care about such things, it may sadden you, as you walk along Moscow's sidewalks and browse the rickety stalls along the way, to see that Agatha Christie and James Bond are overtaking the great Russian literary tradition. The very men and women who so many times risked their lives for a few pages of Bulgakov or Solzhenitsyn in **samizdat**, or Nabokov and Pasternak, often reading deep into the night to be able to pass the pages on to the next person in the morning, are now reading mindless trash. Seldom will you find anything more than Solzhenitsyn's trilogy on the street and, one suspects, even those sell mostly for their shock value. Tarzan and television are rapidly and inalterably supplanting Turgenev and Tolstoy.

There is still a shortage of books in parts of the Commonwealth of Independent States, where some 280 million people read the same language. More than one-half of Russians specified reading as their chief leisure activity in a poll, and ranked it just behind such necessities as food, clothing and footwear.

Books are reasonably priced in Russia, including art books, but take nothing for granted and check them page by page before buying anything. On your return home, you may find that a few pages are glued together or there is some other printing blemish that should have been spotted during the quality control check.

From a Western point of view, most Moscow bookstores are completely inadequate, compared with their counterparts in the US. Here is a list of the major English-language bookstores:

SHAKESPEARE & CO., *5/7 First Novokuznetsky pereulok, Metro Paveletskaya or Novokuznetskaya. Tel. 231-9360. Open Monday through Saturday from 11am to 7pm. Cash only.*

Located southeast of the Kremlin and inside the Garden Ring Road. Exiting from the Paveletskaya metro station, turn right and go north on Novokuznetskaya Street until the second cross-street on your left, which is First Novokuznetsky pereulok. Turn left and keep walking in a semi-circle until you reach the building with **Ad Marginem Press**, *Tel. 231-9360*, a store that sells philosophy books. Shakespeare & Co. is tucked away in the basement of an apartment building, across the street from a small Russian Orthodox church with a wooden belfry.

Shakespeare & Co. has our vote for the best and friendliest English-language bookstore in Moscow. Once you have been to Shakespeare & Co., few other bookstores in the capital will give you as much satisfaction. After a two-year struggle with red tape and construction hassles, the store opened in 1996.

Mary Duncan, a former professor at San Diego State University, is the co-owner of the bookery along with publisher Aleksandr Ivanov, who owns Ad Marginem Press. You can sit down and chat with the owners or browse among the hundreds of books of literature, culture and the arts, most selling at list prices or below, something that you will not find in other English-language bookstores. About one-third of the books are used and brought in by customers who want to exchange them for something else. The store is also a miniature cultural center with lectures, book readings and evenings with writers, such as the former US federal prosecutor William Pease, who turned writer and lives in Moscow.

ZWEMMER'S BOOKSHOP, *18 Ulitsa Kuznetsky Most near Ulitsa Rozhdestvenka, Metro Kuznetsky Most. Tel. 928-2021 or 2921. Open Monday through Friday from 10am to 7pm, Saturdays from 11am to 6pm, closed Sundays. Major credit cards accepted.*

Centrally located north of the Kremlin, inside the Boulevard Ring Road, and a couple of blocks northeast of the Bolshoy Theater.

Moscow's foreign community had high hopes for this store, originally a British bookseller, which opened the capital's first truly Western English-language bookshop in 1994. But even while run by the British, Zwemmer's sales personnel were somewhat surly. After the store was taken over by Russians, it became a veritable icebox of hostility. Sales-clerks behave as though they are doing you a favor just by answering your questions and the quality of service has dropped noticeably.

Some 9,000 titles are available in the one-room store, with a good selection of coffee-table art and travel volumes, fiction, reference books, children's books and paperbacks. Prices are sky-high, you could pay almost double what some books would cost you in the US.

Zwemmer's companion store, whose service and civility are just as low and the prices just as high, is **RUBICON**, *1 Kaluzhskaya ploshchad, Tel. 230-0483*, located just west of the Oktyabrskaya metro station, in a building that also houses a Russian children's library. Rubicon's ground floor houses books in Russian, while the second floor is stocked with an average selection of English-language fiction and non-fiction books.

BIBLIO-GLOBUS, *6 Ulitsa Myasnitskaya, Metro Lubyanka. Tel. 925-8232. Open daily from 10am to 7pm, closed Sundays; Lunch break from 2-3pm. Cash only.*

Centrally located across Lubyanka Square, east of Detsky Mir children's store and next to the Mayakovsky Museum.

Like at Rubicon, its Russian-language books are sold on the ground floor, and foreign books, including those in English, are on the second floor, along with office supplies. They have a good selection of artbooks. There is a souvenir section in the room on your right from the entrance. Also located in the store is a DHL courier window, a travel agency, a photocopier and a place where you can get passport photos in ten minutes.

INOSTRANNAYA KNIGA, *16 Ulitsa Malaya Nikitskaya, Metro Barrikadnaya. Open Monday through Saturday, from 10am to 7pm; Lunch break 2-3pm.*

Located northwest of the Kremlin, between the Boulevard and Garden Ring Roads, and about half a block west of the Big Ascension Church.

This is an interesting used-books and antiques store, where you never know what you'll find in which language.

For information about **Dom Knigi**, Moscow's largest bookstore, see details under the description of Novy Arbat Street; for information on **Moskva Bookstore**, look under Tverskaya Street. Details about the excellent **Progress Bookstore**, on Garden Ring Road near the Park Kultury metro station, can be found under **Progress Supermarket** in the section on food in this chapter.

There is at least one library in Moscow that you might consider visiting:

FOREIGN LITERATURE LIBRARY, *1 Ulitsa Nikoloyamskaya at Bernikovskaya nab., Metro Taganskaya. Tel. 915-3636 or 3621, Fax 915-3637. Open Monday through Friday from 9am to 8pm, Saturdays 10am to 6pm.*

Founded in 1922, this library has more than four million books and publications in almost 100 languages.

In 1993, the **American Center**, *Tel. 956-3260*, joined the British Resource Center on the third floor of this library. They both provide research facilities, books and periodicals in English. Visitors can sit in the library lounge and browse through some 5,000 English-language books on law, business and economics, as well as up to 100 periodicals, including the Sunday edition of the New York Times. However, you will need a proof of permanent residence to check any of the materials out. There is no charge for these services. The American Center is open Monday through Friday, from 10am to 8:30pm, Saturdays from 10am to 5:30pm.

Next to the American Center is the **British Resource Center**. A BBC viewing room is available on the fourth floor. The Resource Center is open Monday through Friday, from 10am to 8pm, Saturdays from 10am to 6pm.

CLOTHING & FOOTWEAR

A first-time visitor to Moscow generally leaves with the impression that Russian sales staff in many Western-style stores, just like in most state-owned shops, are there to guard the store against badly dressed intruders instead of coming forward to serve you with a smile. If you are a Westerner, you will probably just ignore them, but woe be to the Russian who does not quite look the part to be left alone to browse in such a shop. You can almost feel the icicles in the air.

Western-style stores still have far superior service and their personnel speak at least some English. Some of these shops are overcrowded and most are overpriced. A few popular ones only let in a limited number of customers at regular intervals to better control and follow them through the store. None will accept travelers checks and increasingly more and more will take a credit card.

As a rule, the prices in Western-style stores are much higher than what you would pay at home. Some clothing, footwear and accessories can cost twice as much as in the West, sometimes even more. You will search in vain for those smashing bargains you love so much at home. A sale in Moscow is not that dissimilar from a sale in some other European countries: picked-over junk that few Westerners will even want to look at.

WOMEN'S CLOTHING & SHOE SIZES

Clothes

American	6	8	10	12
British	8	10	12	14
Russian	34	36	38	40

Shoes

American	6	7	8	9
British	4.5	5.5	6.5	7.5
Russian	37	38	39	40

It is safe to generalize that, except for Russian designer clothes, most Russian-made men's and women's clothing sold in state stores is unattractive, ill-fitting, of inferior quality and relatively expensive. The choice of sizes, colors and styles is practically nonexistent even today.

Avoid, if you can, finding yourself in situations where you have to buy clothes in Russia because you, women in particular, will be hard pressed to find anything that will give you pleasure wearing. If you take the trouble of searching through the Western clothing and footwear stores listed below, you will find a more satisfying selection, but the sizes, colors and styles will still be lacking, compared with what you can find at home.

The following list consists of stores inside the Garden Ring metro circle, although there are many more stores in the suburbs. Major credit cards are accepted unless otherwise noted.

BENETTON, *13/36 Ulitsa Stary Arbat, Metro Arbatskaya. Tel. 291-7083. Open daily from Monday through Saturday, from 10am to 7pm.*

Cotton or lamb wool shirts, skirts and pants. (Also at GUM on Red Square.)

CARLO PAZOLINI, *1/2 Novinsky bulvar, Metro Smolenskaya. Tel. 241-8775/4674. Open daily Monday through Saturday, from 10am to 8pm.*

Men's and women's Italian fashions, from Armani to Valentino. (Also has stores at 22, 37a and 57 Leninsky prospekt.)

CROCUS, *20/5 Ulitsa Bolshaya Dmitrovka, Metro Kuznetsky Most. Tel. 229-7019. Open daily Monday through Saturday, from 10am to 8pm.*

Men's and women's shoes and accessories. (Other stores are located at 5a Tsvetnoy bulvar, 8 Ulitsa Malaya Dmitrovka, and 9 Stoleshnikov pereulok, Bldg 1.)

DOM MODY SLAVY ZAITSEVA (Zaitsev Showroom), *21 Prospekt Mira, Metro Prospekt Mira. Tel. 971-4114 or 1122. Open daily Monday through Saturday, from 10am to 6pm; Lunch break from 2-3pm.*

Located northeast of the Kremlin and two very long blocks north of the Garden Ring Road.

Slava Zaitsev, born in 1938 in Ivanovo, has been in the fashion business for 30 years and is the best known Russian fashion designer. His showroom features men's and women's clothes and winter coats. His shows have been held worldwide and his Moscow Fashion House is an institution of high quality design and construction.

Since 1970, he has created costumes for most of the major Moscow theaters, whether for Mozart's opera *The Marriage of Figaro* or Chekhov's play *The Three Sisters*. Discussing men's and women's fashions, he said this in an interview with the *Moscow News*:

"I permitted myself to elevate man, together with woman, to the pedestal and tried, using the art of clothing, to help them draw closer to each other, to reestablish harmony. But women always come first. Always.

"'Fashion is a noun of feminine gender in Russian. My interest in men's clothing has been provoked by a desire to see a woman being surrounded with men worthy of her attention, and dressed the way she would like them to be.

"So that with their clothing they should not obscure her world of dreams and wishes, but tone up and stimulate her. However hard we may try to pass this over in silence, clothing always, for all its functionalism and utilitarianism, carries a sexual charge."

GAP, *15 Komsomolsky prospekt, Metro Park Kultury. Tel. 246-2142. Open daily Monday through Friday, from 10am to 8pm.*
Jeans and other Gap clothing.

GREKOFF FASHION GALLERY, *1 Ulitsa Malaya Kaluzhskaya at Ulitsa Akademika Petrovskogo, Metro Shabolovskaya. Tel. 955-3311 or 3014. Open daily Monday through Friday from 10am to 8pm, Saturdays from noon to 6pm.*
Located southwest of the Kremlin, outside the Garden Ring Road, and one block east of Leninsky prospekt.

Aside from Slava Zaitsev and Valentin Yudashkin, the 35-year-old **Aleksey Grekoff** is one of Russia's top three high-quality, ready-to-wear clothes designers.

In 1988, as a student at the Moscow Textile Academy, Grekoff came up with some print designs for fabrics that were later manufactured at the Ivanovo factory outside Moscow. The fabrics were such a hit that the designer barely managed to get enough material to sew a skirt for his future wife. In 1990, he graduated from the Textile Academy, won the Nina Ricci design competition and began his dizzying ascent. Grekoff is especially popular among Russia's new rich.

KALINKA-STOCKMANN BOUTIQUE, *73/8 Leninsky prospekt, Metro Universitet. Tel. 134-3546. Open daily Monday through Saturday, from 10am to 9pm.*
Clothing and footwear for men, women and children by the Finnish company that also owns a supermarket. (Also at 2 Ulitsa Dolgorukovskaya, Metro Novoslobodskaya.)

LEVI STRAUSS ORIGINAL JEANS, *9 Stoleshnikov pereulok, Metro Teatralnaya or Kuznetsky Most. Tel. 924-4821. Open daily Monday through Saturday, from 10am to 8pm; Sundays from 11am to 5pm. Cash only.*
Men's and women's jeans, shirts, sweaters and belts. (Also at GUM on Red Square, 3 Ulitsa Sadovaya-Spasskaya, Metro Sukharevskaya.)

NIKE, *1 Ulitsa Sadovo-Kudrinskaya, Metro Barrikadnaya. Tel. 255-4491. Open daily Monday through Saturday, from 10am to 8pm; Sundays from 11am to 3pm.*
Men's and women's brand-name American footwear and apparel. (Also at 30 Ulitsa Bolshaya Polyanka, Metro Polyanka.)

OVEN, *99 Prospekt Mira, Metro Alekseyevskaya. Tel. 287-0610. Open daily Monday through Saturday, from 10am to 6pm.*
The most expensive men's and women's American and European jeans store in Moscow, with Versace jeans costing up to $300 a pair.

REEBOK USA, *28/35 Novinsky bulvar, Metro Barrikadnaya. Tel. 291-7873. Open daily Monday through Saturday, from 10am to 8pm.*
Women's, men's and children's brand-name American footwear and apparel.

RIFLE JEANS, *10/8 Ulitsa Kuznetsky Most, Metro Kuznetsky Most. Tel. 928-5525 or 923-2458. Open daily Monday through Saturday, from 10am to 7pm; Lunch break 2-3pm.*
Italian men's and women's clothing and accessories.

SADKO FASHION, *9 Kutuzovsky prospekt, Metro Kievskaya. Tel. 245-5103. Open daily Monday through Friday, from 10am to 8pm, Saturdays from 10am to 6pm; Lunch break 2-3pm.*
One of Moscow's first Western clothing stores.

SANDRA STAR, *27 Ulitsa Tverskaya, Metro Pushkinskaya. Tel. 299-5595. Open daily Monday through Saturday, from 10am to 8pm.*
Top-of-the-line women's clothing and accessories: blazers go up to $1,000, pullovers $550, Italian shoes $350, slacks, skirts and blouses $600, evening wear to $2,000.

TEXAS, *12 Ulitsa Bolshaya Serpuhovskaya, Metro Serpuhovskaya. Tel. 236-8116. Open daily Monday through Saturday, from 10am to 6pm.*
Lee and Wrangler jeans, skirts and jackets. (Also at 11 Ulitsa Bolshaya Cherkizovskaya, Metro Preobrazhenskaya ploshchad.)

VALENTIN YUDASHKIN SHOWROOM, *19 Kutuzovsky prospekt, Metro Kievskaya. Tel. 240-1189. Open Monday through Friday, from 10am to 7pm. Major credit cards accepted.*
Located west of the Kremlin, outside the Garden Ring Road, and two long blocks southwest of the Ukraina Hotel.
Together with Slava Zaitsev and Aleksey Grekoff, Valentin Yudashkin is one of the top three Russian fashion designers. In this showroom you can buy his exclusive formal or casual clothes, mostly hand-made.

Winter Boots

If you're in Moscow during the winter and you need winter boots, try:
EVROPA, *13 Ulitsa First Tverskaya-Yamskaya, Metro Mayakovskaya or Belorusskaya. Tel. 250-3323. Open daily Monday through Saturday.*
Large selection of high quality boots for men and women.

GIORGIO, *Proyezd Sopunova, next to the GUM stores on Red Square, Metro Ploshchad Revolutsiyi. Open daily Monday through Saturday.*
An upscale Italian men's and women's store, where style take precedence over rugged durability.

CARLO PAZOLINI, *6 Ulitsa Pyatnitskaya, Metro Novokuznetskaya. Tel. 231-5826. Open daily Monday through Saturday.*
A glamorous Moscow boot shop, where a pair of boots can cost hundreds of dollars.

ECCO, *Valdai Center at 28 Novy Arbat, Metro Arbatskaya. Tel. 291-2014 or Salon Nataly, at 17 Ulitsa Pyatnitskaya, Metro Novokuznetskaya. Tel. 231-1210. Both open daily Monday through Saturday.*
Danish-made Ecco boots for men and women are the rage in Moscow.

NORRIS INTERNATIONAL, *33a Leningradsky prospekt, Metro Dinamo. Open daily Monday through Saturday.*
Quality German-made boots for men and women.
LE MENAGE, *1 Khrustalny pereulok, Metro Kitay-gorod or Ploshchad Revolutsiyi. Tel. 298-5856.*
A favorite among Moscow's fashionable set, Le Menage sells boots for men and women.

FOOD

Even today, food is not nearly as accessible in Moscow as it is in the West. Although you will unlikely undertake an expedition like your weekly supermarket trip at home, you may well need a thing or two, particularly a non-food item.

Listed below are half a dozen major food and specialized stores, predominantly in central Moscow, where you should be able to find food, clothing and other items without the benefit of a car or taxi. You can manage nicely with the help of the metro, provided you are amenable to a little walking. A couple of stores outside the Garden Ring metro circle have been included because of their reputation or the selection of merchandise they carry.

With the possible exception of Progress Supermarket, do not expect the kind of selection you are accustomed to at home; you will learn to be grateful that certain items are available at all if you are in Russia long enough. Read all labels carefully until you familiarize yourself with brands that are thrown together from manufacturers all over Europe, indeed the world. All stores accept major credit cards, unless stated otherwise.

All bags and packages, regardless of size, have to be checked in before you will be allowed inside any of these stores. Be prepared to be followed around by the stores' security personnel from one aisle to the next.

Two stores previously mentioned in this chapter that you should keep in mind are the **Arbat Irish House**, under the section on Novy Arbat Street, and **Yeliseyevsky**, under Tverskaya Street.

CAESAR PARK, *20 Nakhimovsky prospekt, Bldg. 1, Metro Profsoyuznaya. Tel. 120-4122, Fax 120-7297. Open daily from 10am to midnight.*
Located southwest of the Kremlin, outside the Garden Ring Road, and half a block northwest of the Profsoyuznaya metro station.

This is one of the best supermarkets in southern Moscow. It has a good selection of meats, cheeses, juices, snack foods, cookies, wine and other alcoholic beverages. The fruit and vegetable selection is average. Prices are high, especially for various salads and ready-to-eat cold pastas prepared on the premises. There is a small bar with a few tables.

COLOGNIA-INTERCAR, *5/1 Ulitsa Bolshaya Sadovaya, Metro Mayakovskaya. Tel. 209-6561 or 251-6903, Fax 250-9741. Open daily Monday through Friday from 10am to 8pm, Saturdays and Sundays from 11am to 7pm.* Located northwest of the Kremlin on Garden Ring Road, in the Pekin Hotel building, with the entrance on Bolshaya Sadovaya Street. Garden Ring Irish Supermarket is situated at the other end of the same block.

Colognia-Intercar has a good meat and cheese department, home-made breads, Italian pasta and yogurt. It also has a well organized, courteous staff.

GARDEN RING IRISH SUPERMARKET, *1 Ulitsa Bolshaya Sadovaya, Metro Mayakovskaya. Tel. 209-1517, Fax 956-6394. Open daily from 9am to 9pm.*

Located northwest of the Kremlin on Garden Ring Road, and southwest of the Pekin Hotel. Colognia-Intercar supermarket is situated northeast of here, in the Pekin Hotel building, although its entrance is on Bolshaya Sadovaya Street.

You'll find a good meat selection, and a variety of groceries, produce and bread. It is clean and friendly.

KALINKA-STOCKMANN, *2 Ulitsa Zatsepsky val, Metro Paveletskaya. Tel. 231-1924, Fax 233-2602. Open 7 days a week from 10am to 9pm.*

Located southeast of the Kremlin on Garden Ring Road, and across the street from the Paveletsky Railway Station.

A civilized Finnish supermarket, the oldest Western-style food store, and in some ways still one of the best. This store is well-stocked with dairy products, meats and cheeses, breads, snack foods, fruit and produce. Also has a good selection of European and American news, fashion and entertainment magazines, all marked up. The professional service comes with a smile.

PROGRESS SUPERMARKET, *17 Zubovsky bulvar, Metro Park Kultury. Tel. 246-9976 or 9078, Fax 246-5551. Open daily from 10am to 8:30pm, Sundays from 11am to 8pm.*

Located southwest of the Kremlin on Garden Ring Road, two blocks west of the Moskva River, and half a block west of the Park Kultury metro station.

One of the largest, and by far the best supermarket in Moscow, with a decidedly French flavor. The large second floor is brimming with French, Canadian and American foods and household goods. There is an excellent selection of meats, cheeses, juices, snacks, canned goods, and other items you might not find in many other places; towelettes and Kleenex paper tissues being just two. A smaller third-floor has limited men's and women's clothing and footwear, and a children's shop. Prices are just as high as at other Western-style stores.

On the ground floor, there is a good **bookshop**, with books in Russian, English, French and German, dictionaries, art books, and maps of Moscow. French and other European home appliances, and school and office supplies are also sold on the ground floor. It has a film developing kiosk and a foreign exchange booth. This is the only Moscow store we could find that will exchange American Express traveler's checks, but only at a hefty fee.

SADKO, *16 Ulitsa Bolshaya Dorogomilovskaya, Metro Kievskaya. Tel. 243-6659 or 1016. Open daily from 10am to 8pm, Sundays from 10am to 6pm; Lunch break 3-4pm.*

Located west of the Kremlin, outside the Garden Ring Road, one block south of Kutuzov Avenue, and near the Pizza Hut.

Good selection of groceries, oriental foods, wines and liquors.

SADKO ARCADE, *1 First Krasnogvardeysky proyezd, Metro Ulitsa 1905 goda. Tel. 259-5656. Open daily from 9am to 9pm.*

Located west of the Kremlin, outside the Garden Ring Road, west of the World Trade Center, and inside Ekspotsentr exhibition park.

You'll find a good selection of American meats, fresh-baked breads, and plenty of frozen foods.

ICONS

Icons are holy images that began as mosaics in the 10th century. Icons are also oil paintings, generally on wood, that depict religious scenes. Sometimes painted by teams of painters, with each artist creating a part of the body, icons were considered the bible for the illiterate and were at first painted by monks. A painting does not have to show Christ to be an icon; just about any Christian theme will do, from St. George slaying the dragon to portraits of Kiril and Mephody, the brothers who invented the Cyrillic alphabet. Some icons are adorned with silver or gold leaf, the engraving of which can be as artistic as the painting itself.

Before the 1917 Revolution, there were about 80 million families in Russia and all of them had at least one icon in their home, and usually they had from two to six. A simple calculation will tell you that Moscow and, indeed, the whole country is saturated with icons. Add to that the cheap imitations for sale at Izmaylovo outdoor market and the number can get mind-numbing. The quality varies greatly; there are some fine icons by well-known artists and tons of the flea-market variety that sell for $20.

The price range for icons is very wide. You will pay a few dollars for an unskilled rendition of the Madonna and Child on chipped, cracking wood, or you can spend $25,000 for one that you would not be allowed to take out of the country. The store where you shop for your icon will tell you whether the one you like can be exported or not and they will likely provide whatever paperwork you need to take it abroad.

Requirements for Export of Russian Art: The rules on taking art and antiques out of Russia are a mess and very confusing, and even the customs officials no longer seem to know which law applies when. The customs forms at the airport say that you cannot take out of the country "antiques and objects of art (paintings, drawings, icons, sculptures, etc.)." An antique, according to Russia's customs department, is anything that was created before 1945.

If you pay more than $500 for any art object, the dealer should take care of all these formalities for you, or take your business elsewhere. Trying to do it by yourself would be a needless waste of your time. Allow at least two days for the processing of paperwork.

MUSIC - CD's & TAPES

When it comes to **CDs** and **cassette tapes** of classical, pop or Russian folk music, we advised you to head for the state-owned **Melodiya** store on Novy Arbat, described in the section on New Arbat Street in this chapter.

Other places, where you can sometimes find a good selection of Russian classical music, is the area near the cloak room in the basement of the **Pushkin Museum of Fine Arts**, on Ulitsa Volkhonka, southeast of the Kremlin. **Danilovsky Monastery**, metro Tulskaya, south of the Kremlin and outside the Garden Ring Road, is a place to look for CDs of Russian folk and religious music.

Also check the **kiosks** on the north side of Novy Arbat. They specialize in predominantly pop and rock music. The cluster of kiosks at many centrally-located metro stations, such as Arbatskaya, also have a good selection of popular music.

You will be surprised at the vitality and originality of Russian pop music, which is almost unknown in the West. If you want to sample Russian pop music, turn to Channel 3 on your television. This is the nation's first commercial channel and is known as "2 X 2" (until 6pm).

TOILETRIES & COSMETICS

If you are particular about the brand of your toiletries, we suggest you bring everything with you from home. Never expect to find shampoo, soap, moisturizer or a sewing kit in your hotel room, except in the most luxurious Moscow hotels. Make sure you bring enough of your own.

Women should carry a good supply of feminine hygiene supplies and your own contraceptives. Tampons appear to be more of a luxury than a necessity in Russia, although they are easier to find these days. Contraceptives may be harder to find.

A roll or two of toilet paper, depending on how particular you are about such things and how long you will stay, would not be a bad idea either.

Here is a short list of stores where you will find cosmetics and toiletries from the West. We include easily accessible stores only. All are located inside the Garden Ring metro circle and you can reach them without a car or taxi. If you do not feel like searching out any one of these individual stores, then we recommend you head for GUM department store on Red Square or Petrovsky Passazh shopping mall on Ulitsa Petrovka and Kuznetsky Most, north of the Bolshoy Theater. Both have clusters of stores that will likely satisfy your needs and are described in this chapter. Credit cards are accepted unless otherwise noted.

CHRISTIAN DIOR, see GUM on Red Square.

ESTEE LAUDER, *at Parfyumeriya, 6 Ulitsa Tverskaya, Metro Okhotny Ryad. Tel. 292-6421 or 2967. Open daily Monday through Saturday, from 10am to 7pm; Lunch break 2-3pm. Cosmetics, perfumes and lotions.* (Also at GUM on Red Square.)

L'OREAL PARIS, see GUM on Red Square.

YVES ROCHER, *4 Ulitsa Tverskaya, Metro Okhotny Ryad. Tel. 923-5885 or 0606. Open daily Monday through Friday, from 9:30am to 7pm, lunch break 2-3pm; Saturdays from 9:30am to 4:30pm, lunch break 2-2:30pm.*

French perfumes, cosmetics and toiletries are sold. The Yves Rocher beauty salon at the same address (almost across the street from the Intourist Hotel or the Central Telegraph Office), does permanents, cutting, dyeing and styling, as well as facial massages, manicures and pedicures. Appointments are sometimes required several days in advance.

JACQUES DESSANGE, *7 Ulitsa First Tverskaya-Yamskaya, Metro Mayakovskaya. Tel. 200-5744. Open daily Monday through Saturday, from 10am to 7pm.*

For the ultimate in self-indulgence, but at a price, consider Jacques Dessange hair and beauty salon. One of 500 Dessange salons worldwide, the one in Moscow boasts 50 hairdressers and cosmetologists, all trained in Paris. The salon is also a full-fledged beauty institute that includes the latest technology from France. In the boutique downstairs, you can buy a plethora of Dessange products.

18. EXCURSIONS & DAY TRIPS

These are sights you can comfortably visit in one day by yourself, through Patriarshy Dom, or through Intourist, often with time left over for a leisurely lunch in the countryside. The only excursion that may not fit into a one-day format is a visit to Tolstoy's estate in Yasnaya Polyana, 120 miles south of Moscow.

We suggest that you take these excursions on a comfortable bus arranged for you through Patriarshy Dom, although you can rent a car and drive yourself, something we never recommend. When you see a red diagonal stripe across the name of a town's sign, it means you are leaving it. Before you decide to drive, ask yourself a few questions (what would you do if you have a flat tire in the fields of Borodino; where would you go if you run out of gas on the way to Yasnaya Polyana?)

ABRAMTSEVO ESTATE & MUSEUM

Located in the town of Abramtsevo. Tel. 253-2470. Open Wednesday through Sunday, from 11am to 5pm. Closed during the months of April and October, also Mondays and Tuesdays, and the last Thursday of each month. Admission fee.

The Abramtsevo Estate is located about 45 miles northeast of Moscow. You can start out north on Prospekt Mira, which becomes Yaroslavskoye shosse on road M8 to Sergiyev Posad (formerly Zagorsk). When you near the villages of Leshkovo or Vozdvizhenskoye, look for the signs for the turn off to Abramtsevo. Watch for signs to Abramtsevo and Khotkovo as you pass the 61st kilometer post.

You can also take an 80-minute train ride to Abramtsevo from Moscow's Yaroslavsky Railway Station, metro Komsomolskaya. Look for any train going to Sergiyev Posad, although Abramtsevo is situated less than four miles south of Sergiyev Posad. The estate is more than a mile from the railway station.

The Abramtsevo estate was once a thriving artists' colony. The village dates back to the 17th century, when it was called Obramkovo. The main estate house was built in 1771 and in 1843 became the home of writer and government censor **Sergey Aksakov** (1791-1859) who acquired it because of its proximity to the religious center of Sergiyev Posad. His oldest son Konstantin became the principal theorist of the Slavophile movement in their intellectual battles with Westernizers, like the revolutionary writer Aleksandr Gertsen. The younger Aksakov left Moscow University on foot every Friday afternoon and arrived at Abramtsevo the following morning, walking the entire 70-plus kilometers.

Writers Nikolay Gogol and Ivan Turgenev spent time at Abramtsevo and both read their prose on the estate. Gogol, who lived upstairs in a garret of the main building, would sometimes pace back and forth for hours every day, while writing the second volume of *Dead Souls*, which he later destroyed at his Moscow home (for more information see **Gogol Memorial Rooms** in Chapter 13, *Seeing the Sights*).

The estate was bought in 1870 by the railway baron and art connoisseur **Savva Mamontov** (1841-1918), who transformed it into an artists colony of Russian painters, writers and playwrights. Painter such as Mikhail Nesterov, Vasily Polenov, Ilya Repin, brothers Vasnetsov, and Mikhail Vrubel lived here permanently, all of whom's work you can see on display at the Tretyakov Gallery. Echoes of this artistic tradition continued even after the 1917 Revolution with painter Robert Falk (1886-1958), who continued working here.

Classical composers Sergey Rachmaninov and Nikolay Rimsky-Korsakov often came to the estate. Operatic basso singer Fyodor Shalyapin made his debut here in one of the operas that was staged in a large music room and the famous theatrical actress Mariya Yermolova was also a regular at Abramtsevo. They all admired the richness of their Russian cultural heritage and the underlying national traditions. About 90 percent of Russian artistic life was said to be centered on this estate at the time.

The buildings, which overlook the Vorya River, are well restored and there are several parks where you can walk to your heart's content. Most rooms of the main house, which was expanded in 1880, are preserved as they were originally built, although the second floor is closed to visitors. There is authentic furniture and many artworks are on display. Photographs, but particularly paintings created by Polenov, Repin, Serov and Vasnetsov during that period, are on display.

You can catch up with a copy of Valentin Serov's well-known work, *The Girl with Peaches*, in the very dining room where it was painted; the girl was Mamontov's daughter Vera, who died of cholera at age 24 and is buried on the estate, together with her parents. The original can be seen at the Tretyakov Gallery. In one of the rooms, you can see a ceramic tiled stove with a lion's head decorated by Vrubel (1856-1910), the half-mad genius who anticipated the cubists. His wife had him committed to a mental hospital, while she lived comfortably on his art. Another of Vrubel's creations is a ceramic park bench behind the main building.

Mamontov's wife, Yelizaveta Mamontova, ran the estate and made it possible for all those idiosyncratic geniuses to thrive, as is the case with many Russian women in Russia's past and present. She also founded a school for the children of Abramtsevo's peasants. Unfortunately, all five of her own children died before the age of 25.

Her husband, who among other icons of cultural life, founded in 1885 his Private Opera, which still stands at 6 Bolshaya Dmitrovka Street and is known today as the **Moscow Operetta Theater** (see Chapter 14, *Culture*). Rachmaninov and Shalyapin began their careers at this theater. Mamontov lost his fortune on the stock exchange, was accused of illegal dealings and arrested in 1899. He served one year and was later exonerated. He spent the next 14 years on this estate and died in 1918.

In 1882, a 12th century-style Orthodox church named **Not Made by Human Hand** (in its English translation) was built in the woods at the back of the estate. Many of the above artists contributed; Repin, Nesterov and Apollinary Vasnetsov the wooden iconostasis (a screen that separates the sanctuary from the nave), Vasnetsov's brother Viktor the mosaic floor, and Vrubel the tiled stove. Mamontov built a ceramics factory here in the 1890s. The ceramics studio near the main building is a log cabin in the tradition of the Russian **izba**, or peasant hut, displaying Vrubel's ceramics. The **Hut on Chicken Legs**, which Viktor Vasnetsov built for the estate's kids, is based on the fairy tale of the witch Baba Yaga, who for generations has been scaring Russia's children.

In the village of Lesnoy, about 24 miles out of Moscow (by the 41st kilometer post), just off the Yaroslavskoye Highway, is the restaurant **Russkaya Skazka** (Russian Fairy Tale), which is inside a traditional wooden building. It is perhaps the only decent eatery in the area.

ARKHANGELSKOYE ESTATE & MUSEUM

Located in the town of Arkhangelskoye. Tel. 561-9456. Open Wednesday through Sunday, from 11am to 6pm; closed Mondays and Tuesdays and last Friday of each month. Admission fee.

This estate, located on the banks of Moskva River, is about 16 miles west of Moscow. First head northwest on Leningradsky Avenue, then continue along the Volokolamskoye Highway M9 after the Sokol metro station and turn left onto the Ilyinskoye Highway a few miles after the Moscow Circular Road. You can also take the metro as far as the

Tushinskaya station, then continue for another thirty minutes by bus #549, which stops opposite the back gates.

This estate has been under reconstruction for years and it is not known when it will reopen; check with Patriarshy Dom or Intourist. But even if the museum is closed, you might still enjoy the park and the outer buildings, which date from the 18th and 19th centuries. Named after the 17th century **Church of the Archangel Michael**, the estate took 40 years to complete and ended up as one of the finest aristocratic estates in the region; some called it Moscow's Versailles.

In the late 17th century, the land belonged to Prince Cherkassky and was bought in 1731 by Golitsyn. His grandson, Prince Nikolay Golitsyn (1751-1809) remodeled the estate into a large palace ensemble, but died while it was still under construction. In 1810, Arkhangelskoye was purchased by the art patron and collector **Prince Nikolay Yusupov** (1751-1831), who was also one of the wealthiest property owners in Russia, with more than 20,000 serfs. In the spring of 1812, Yusupov's art collection of more than 500 paintings by European masters was brought to Arkhangelskoye, together with a collection of sculpture, antique furniture, tapestries, and china with Yusupovs's portrait on them, and can still be seen today.

That same year, the estate was first ravaged by the French during the Napoleonic invasion, then by a peasant revolt and in 1820 by fire. It was rebuilt in 1825 and Yusupov turned the palace into a museum that rivaled many European state art collections. The poet Pushkin visited Yusupov's library on the second floor several times and was impressed by its more than 16,000 volumes. The palace, which is surrounded by an ornamental garden and a park and literally strewn with classical statues, became a state museum in 1918.

Behind the palace, Yusupov built a temple dedicated to Catherine the Great, who is sculpted as a goddess of justice. Pushkin is also immortalized with a bust erected on a lane named after him in 1899, the centenary of his birth. The church, some distance from the palace and overlooking the Moskva River, has stood here since 1667. The wooden serf theater, built in 1818 by a serf architect, could seat 400 and was one of the best theaters at the time.

The Yusupov mausoleum, completed the year before the Bolsheviks climbed to power, never served its intended purpose. That year, Feliks Yusupov (1887-1967) and his fellow conspirators poisoned, shot and drowned Rasputin, one of the most influential and perhaps the most unsavory character at the court of Tsar Nicholas II. On April 11, 1919, Yusupov and his wife just barely escaped the Bolsheviks by sailing to Constantinople, then settled down in Paris, where they lived on the proceeds from hundreds of precious stones they brought from Russia; in

1922, a black pearl necklace alone netted them $400,000. They received another $400,000 for two Rembrandt canvases and spent it all.

The Yusupovs sailed to New York to sue over the terms of the Rembrandt sale in 1923 and had more jewels confiscated by American customs officials who thought the stones were part of the Russian crown jewels. After six months in New York, the couple sank so low they subsisted on nightclub leftovers from an acquaintance. Yusupov lost the court case and the two Rembrandts ended up at the National Gallery of Art in Washington, D.C. In 1927, he wrote his controversial book about his involvement in the murder of Rasputin and later that year fled to Spain fearing arrest over a bank fraud. The following year, his many homosexual affairs finally caught up with him and compromised him even further in his circles. He died in his bed in 1967 and his wife died three years later of a heart attack.

Since 1934, when a military sanatorium opened on the estate grounds, Arkhangelskoye has been part of the Defense Ministry. The museum's restoration has not been high on the Ministry's list of priorities.

There are two restaurants nearby, **Arkhangelskoye** across the street from the estate and **Russkaya Izba** next to the bridge in nearby Ilyinskoye village. Arkhangelskoye is open from 11am to 11pm; it is located in a birch grove and is particularly appealing in the summer. Russkaya Izba is open from noon to midnight; it overlooks the Moskva River and is built in the style of old Russian peasant homes with carved wooden beams.

BORODINO BATTLEFIELD & MUSEUM

Located in the town of Borodino. Open from 10am to 6pm, Tuesday through Sunday; closed Monday and last Friday of each month. Admission fee.

The village of Borodino lies 75 miles southwest of Moscow on the Moscow-Minsk Highway. A train ride from the Belorussky Railway Station takes about two and a half hours, a Patriarshy Dom bus excursion about two hours.

If driving, start out in southwesterly direction on Kutuzov Avenue, past Kutuzov's equestrian statue on one side and Victory Park on the other, then continue on Mozhayskoye Highway M1 to the 96th or 108th kilometer post, where you can turn off to Borodino. We recommend that you do not drive by yourself, but instead take a guided tour. The terrain is so large and there are so many detours that you have to know where you are going to see at least the major sights in a one-day excursion.

This village will forever be immortalized as the site of the **Battle of Borodino**. On August 26, 1812 (September 7 by today's calendar), 120,000 Russian troops, including 10,000 badly trained militia from Moscow and 600 cannons, commanded by field marshall **Mikhail Kutuzov** (1745-1813) fought an indecisive battle against Napoleonic forces. These forces consisted of 130,000 men and 587 cannons, who had earlier that year invaded Russia as a contingent of 450,000 men that crossed the Neman River on June 25, 1812.

Napoleon had made up his mind to attack Russia a year earlier. Although warned about the climate and the obstinacy of the Russians, he dismissed such warnings with: "Bah! I will finish Alexander and his fortifications of sand. He's feeble." But Napoleon did not expect that his war machine would begin breaking down just days after crossing into Russia. Pillaging, sickness and desertions soon became commonplace. By the time he had reached Vilno, 20,000 horses had died and the equivalent of supplies for two large battles were lost. When Napoleon occupied Smolensk at the end of August, Moscow was only two hundred miles away.

The entire Borodino battlefield area, now a national park, measures 42 square miles. It is estimated that "an experienced soldier had to go through 14 steps and took one minute to load and shoot his musket. During the 15-hour battle, starting at six o'clock in the morning and ending in a pouring rain, more than 80,000 soldiers were killed. The Russian positions had been captured, but the Russian army had not been broken and only 750 prisoners were taken. The French casualties, 30,000 men and 42 generals, were astonishing. Kutuzov lost more than 50,000 men. Napoleon, who until now chased the retreating Russians, was on his way to Moscow, but still unaware that Borodino was the beginning of the end for him.

When Tsar Aleksandr I appointed Prince Kutuzov as commander of Russian forces, it was against Kutuzov's will, for he was already 67 years old, blind in one eye, suffering from rheumatism and barely able to sit on a horse. Kutuzov had already fought Napoleon at Austerlitz in 1805 and was defeated. Now he fought an indecisive battle at Borodino. Contrary to the romantic legends of the times, Kutuzov spent most of the Borodino battles sitting down, following the action through his field glasses, and issuing orders a couple of miles away. Napoleon, too, could see very little of the actual battles. But no opponent could have been more dangerous to Napoleon and Kutuzov never underestimated his old adversary. After the Russians retreated, Kutuzov held council with his generals at what is today known as **Kutuzov Hut**, on the avenue named after him, and made the difficult decision of abandoning Moscow. He believed it was the only way to preserve his army and win the war.

The city, which then had about a million inhabitants, was deserted; almost 900,000 Muscovites followed the Russian army in their retreat. The next day, September 2, Napoleon stood on Poklonnaya gora (Hill of Greeting), catching his first glimpse of Moscow. After waiting in vain for six hours to get a formal surrender notice from the deputation of nobles, as was the custom at the time, he rode into the silent, empty city. That night great fires broke out in many places and with the help of strong winds raged for five days, consuming everything in sight. They forever destroyed Napoleon's dream of ruling Russia. He could not comprehend that the tsar would not and could not negotiate a surrender because he would be deposed or assassinated if he did. More than three-quarters of Moscow's buildings, many made of wood and covered with plaster, were destroyed.

The weather in October 1812 was unusually mild in the Moscow region, November was slightly colder than usual, but by December an unbelievably brutal cold set in. Napoleon, defeated as much by the elements as by invisible Russians, left Moscow with almost 100,000 men, but was slowed down by the sick and wounded, as well as hundreds of cannons. He was so uncharacteristically desperate that he ordered his men to blow up the Kremlin, but it never took place. His army was decimated by hunger, his cavalry was on foot because the cold killed all the horses, and by the time he reached Viazma, Kutuzov's 50,000-strong army, Cossacks and partisans, all accustomed to the frigid weather, attacked his rear guard. Only the emperor had all the comforts and food he desired to the end, including fresh linen and his favorite beef and mutton, with rice and beans.

By the time Napoleon's armies had regrouped behind the Neman River, he had, according to the most optimistic estimates, less than 40,000 troops left. Kutuzov pursued him across Russia and into Poland and Prussia, where the field marshall died in 1813. In March of 1814, the victorious Tsar Aleksandr I himself rode into Paris.

Lev Tolstoy visited Borodino in the 1860's and spent two weeks here, riding and walking in the area to commit it to memory while he worked on his epic novel *War and Peace.*

In the autumn of 1941, in this same field, Soviet forces held off the Nazis advancing on to Moscow for six days.

Twenty-seven years later, the main monument of Borodino, a structure more than 85 feet high, was erected on Krasny kholm (Red Hill). By 1912, to mark the 100th anniversary of the battle, 34 monuments were erected on the battlefield. Today, more than 300 monuments and historic objects are scattered throughout the fields of Borodino, most of them along the road from Borodino to Gorky. On October 18, 1975, a memorial to the French who had died at Borodino was unveiled by French president Valery Giscard d'Estaing.

The **Borodino Military History Museum**, opened just south of the village in 1912, displays documents and exhibits relating to this monumental battle. You will see displayed original weapons, uniforms and personal effects, such as Kutuzov's snuffbox and Napoleon's cot. There is an interesting diorama exhibit. The only sour note on this excursion are the smelly and primitive toilets behind the museum, which would not be a credit to even ancient Mesopotamia.

You will need a comfortable pair of shoes to walk the extensive battlefield grounds. There are no restaurants in the area, but if you take the Patriarshy Dom tour you will likely get a sack lunch to tie you over until you return to Moscow.

Every year, usually during the first Sunday in September, hundreds of members of the Russian Military Historical Club reenact the Borodino battle amid the blaring bugles and booming cannons. A memorial service usually starts at about 9am and the actual battle soon after noon. Each participant must make from scratch his uniform and weapons, using only authentic methods, to be able to participate. Some spend years just getting their uniforms ready, investing virtually all their spare time and money to get ready for this once-a-year event. Government assistance is limited to supplying tents, food and water for the weekend. Call Patriarshy Dom or Intourist for more details.

For details about the **Battle of Borodino Panorama Museum** and Kutuzov Hut on Kutuzov Avenue, see Chapter 13, *Seeing the Sights*.

Aside from Borodino, two other battlefields have a special meaning for Russians:

Kulikovo: More than six centuries ago, in 1380, on a large battlefield between the Don River and its small tributary, the Nepriadva, in the Tula region south of Moscow, the 100,000 troops of Grand Prince Dmitry of Moscow defeated the larger forces, almost four times larger, of the Golden Horde led by Khan Mamai. This victory marked the beginning of the liberation of Old Russia from Tartar oppression. The Battle of Kulikovo did not stop the bondage, but it did raise Russia's self-awareness.

Poltava: Three hundred years later, in 1709, another great battle crucial to Russia was fought near Poltava in the Ukraine. During the **Northern War** between Sweden and Russia, which lasted from 1700 to 1721, a Swedish force of 35,000 invaded the northern Ukraine and advanced toward Poltava, which was then the center of a series of defense installations protecting the southern approaches to Moscow. The Swedes laid siege to the fortress of Poltava, which only had 6,500 soldiers and civilians to defend it, for three months. A larger force led by emperor Peter the Great began approaching Poltava. On July 8, 1709, the major battle of the Northern War was fought. The Russians defeated the army of King Charles XII and established the position of Russia in Europe.

DULYOVO PORCELAIN WORKS

Located in the town of Dulyovo. Parts of factory are open sporadically.

There is a large porcelain museum on the premises, exhibiting hundreds of objects, none of which is for sale. Check with Patriarshy Dom, the only Moscow tour operator conducting irregular excursions to Dulyovo in the summer. They can also arrange for a privately guided shopping trip to Dulyovo.

Dulyovo, a town of about 7,000 is located some 75 miles east of Moscow and probably does not have another sight worthy of your time, aside from the porcelain works. A bus excursion which takes about two hours and 15 minutes each way, starts out at Taganka Square and Ryazansky Avenue and continues along Oktyabrsky Avenue to R105. A commuter train from Moscow's **Kursky Railway Station** goes east to Orekhovo-Zuyevo, then south to Likino-Dulyovo.

The Dulyovo Porcelain Works was founded in 1832, just twenty years after Napoleon's invasion of Russia. According to sympathetic Russian sources, Dulyovo was once one of the largest factories of china in Russia, employing more than 3,000 poeple and producing 75 million items annually. This craft started in Gzhel, a village some 16 miles away, because wood was more readily available for the baking process.

Today, Dulyovo is but a shadow of the once proud artisan community that employed nearly the entire town. There is the unmistakable smell of the former Soviet Union around the aged, dilapidated, rusty factory whose ineffective management may yet force it into insolvency. Instead of promoting its products at home and abroad, Dulyovo is in such a financial vise that it apparently cannot afford to open an independent store in Moscow and does not have a salesman competent enough to sell its wares to foreign enterprises. Because of falling demand, the factory operates well below its capacity. Depending on when you visit, you will see but small clusters of mostly female workers in just a few sections of the factory, completely unprotected against dust so thick you could cut it with your pocket knife. The management claims that demand for the time-consuming hand-painted and primitively baked Dulyovo porcelain has dropped sharply in the West, where there is greater demand for plain white porcelain.

Adjacent to the factory is the **Kuznetsov Workshop**, an attempt to resurrect the old style of artistic porcelain modeled after what Kuznetsov produced for the imperial household. Its whiteness and thinness are its standard trademarks of quality.

If you survive the courtyards and byways piled with water, trash and construction materials, you can admire the work of the few remaining Kuznetsov artisans and place your customized order right then and there. It takes up to two weeks to fulfill your request and your china can be delivered to a prearranged address in Moscow. Although considerably more expensive than the run of the mill porcelain sets sold in the official factory store, Kuznetsov pieces will likely turn out to be a bargain compared with what you would pay in New York or Toronto. In a wonderfully Soviet style, however, it may take you longer to pay for your order in Dulyovo's antiquated office than it will to collect your wares.

FEDOSKINO LACQUERED BOXES

Located in the town of Fedoskino.
Whether taking a Patriarshy Dom excursion that starts at the south gate of the American Embassy compound or driving yourself, you will go out on Dmitrovskoye Highway and continue on A-104 for about one hour, passing through thick woods on a scenic road to Fedoskino.

Fedoskino, a village of one thousand, lies about 18 miles north of Moscow and is believed to be the oldest school of lacquer painting still in existence in Russia. By the 18th century, Fedoskino painters excelled in icon painting.

Lacquer arts originated in China before the birth of Christ. In the 18th century, lacquer workshops opened in France. A Russian merchant brought the art of this craft from Germany to Fedoskino. There were originally two villages here, Danilovo and Fedoskino, separated by a river, and the boxes were made in Fedoskino and painted in Danilovo. **Pyotr Lukutin** opened the original workshop and was followed by his son who is responsible for the development of this craft.

In 1828, the reputation of the factory declined under Lukutin's grandson, who ran the operations from Moscow. By 1904, the factory was almost bankrupt and in 1910 a number of Lukutin's artists started another cooperative which operated until the 1960's. Before the 1917 Revolution, Fedoskino artisans painted icons, but turned to these lacquer boxes because the Bolsheviks would not tolerate the religious tone of their work. In 1943, the Communists reconstructed the Fedoskino factory, which had long before become a state-run facility.

The process is the same today as it was 200 years ago, when Fedoskino craftsmen started producing lacquered boxes, called **shkatulky**. First a roll of pressed paper is turned around a wooden shape of the box, which is cut, glued and pressed. It is then dipped in linseed oil and dried for 24 hours. The carpenter shapes the box as if it were made of wood and, if needed, adds hinges. After it has been polished, the box goes to the painter who first colors the large surfaces, then covers them with oil lacquer and lets the box dry for up to six hours. Following this, additional details are added, such as eyes, lacquers it, dries and polishes the box again. After the artist adds ornaments, the box goes to the polishing workshop where it is covered with additional layers of lacquer and polished several more times. From the time a box is painted the first time, it takes about ten days to finish the job. The boxes are usually black on the outside and red inside. Two or three shkatulky are painted at the same time with brushes so fine they have to be custom made at the factory.

Quality Fedoskino boxes usually cost from $200 to $5,000 and most are exported for hard currency. The Fedoskino cooperative has a shop in Chicago. If you take this tour, be careful before spending hundreds of dollars; an investment-grade lacquer miniature is difficult for an inexperienced eye to appraise.

Although almost 300 Fedoskino artists work at the factory or in their homes, fewer than a dozen, called People's Artists, have free hands to create what they please; the rest have to churn out work copied from the People's Artists. While other villages producing lacquered miniatures often rely on fairy tales to express themselves artistically, Fedoskino's miniatures are painted more realisticly, based on old masters, and on Renaissance and Dutch painters. Since 1931, there has been a school in Fedoskino that teachs students how to paint lacquer boxes, but the students better be patient because it takes five years or longer to learn the craft. It is those students, not the masters, that you will be able to observe for a few minutes before you are guided to the ground-floor shop, where you will likely succumb to a purchase. Only rubles are accepted.

Upon your return, you might also stop at an artisan cooperative initiated in 1986 in the town of Dolgoprudny, just outside of greater Moscow, where you will be given one more chance to leave behind some cash, in rubles or dollars. It is located on Parkovaya Street.

The best of Fedoskino lacquered art can be seen in the museum right inside the Fedoskino factory, as well as in Moscow's **Decorative & Folk Museum** (turn to Chapter 13, *Seeing the Sights* for details).

ISTRA & THE NEW JERUSALEM MONASTERY

Located in the town of Istra. Open Wednesday through Sunday, from 10am to 5pm; closed Mondays and Tuesdays, last Friday of each month.

The town of Istra is located 35 miles northwest of Moscow on the banks of the Istra River. To get there by car, start out along the Volokolamskoye Highway and continue through Dedovsk and Snegiry, or take the hourly train from the **Rizhsky Railway Station** to the New Jerusalem stop; after that the monastery can be reached by bus. The journey takes an hour and a half.

Istra became prominent in the 17th century when the **New Jerusalem Monastery** was erected about a mile from the village. The **Resurrection Cathedral** in the center of the monastery grounds, built in 1685, is a replica of the Christian church in Jerusalem. Patriarch Nikon is buried in the cathedral. Unfortunately, the cathedral's tent-shaped roof collapsed under its own weight in 1723 and had to be rebuilt all over again; three years later the cathedral was damaged by fire. After many years as a museum, the monastery is a practicing Orthodox church again.

In World War II, retreating Germans bombed it heavily. Restoration has been going on since 1958 and has not yet been completed. Armor, Russian paintings and porcelain, books and music scores are on exhibit on two floors at the **Baroque Nativity Church.** The **Museum of Wooden Architecture** is outside the monastery's north wall in the park along the river, where you can have a picnic. A church from 1647, peasant cottages, granaries and a windmill have been brought from all over the country for permanent display.

THE KLIN TCHAIKOVSKY HOME

48 Ulitsa Tchaikovskogo, Klin. Tel. 539-8196. Open from 10am to 6pm, Friday through Tuesday; closed last Monday of each month. Admission fee.
Klin is an ancient Russian town about 50 miles northwest of Moscow. Patriarshy Dom arranges tours to the composer's home almost every month and throws a sack lunch into the bargain. The bus ride takes about an hour and a half each way. You can also travel to Klin by train from Leningradsky Railway Station, a journey that takes a little over an hour; once there a local bus can bring you into the town. If you prefer to drive on your own, which we never recommend, start out in a northwesterly direction on Leningradskoye Highway M10 and continue through Zelenograd and Solnechnogorsk.

Klin was founded on the banks of the Sestra River in 1318 and was given to his son by Ivan the Terrible in 1572. It later became the property of the Romanovs. The city, which now has a population of more than 100,000, was home to the great Russian composer **Pyotr Tchaikovsky** (1840-1893) from 1885 until his death. "I have become so attached to Klin," he once wrote, "that I cannot imagine myself living anywhere else." Belonging to a local lawyer, this was the last of the four houses in Klin that the composer lived in. He loved the two-story cottage on the outskirts of town because it was situated in a quiet wooded area that gave him the privacy to compose undisturbed and, although suffering periods of intense guilt about it, also afforded him a sexual lifestyle that most citizens of Klin did not approve of.

The house has been a museum since his brother, Modest Tchaikovsky, bought it. Modest lived in the added wing of the house as a caretaker of the museum until he died in 1916. It is believed that Modest burned up to one-third of his brother's correspondence after Tchaikovsky's death for fear that he would be compromised.

The composer wrote the *Fifth* and *Sixth Symphonies* and the *Third Piano Concerto*, as well as *Sleeping Beauty* and *Nutcracker Suite* ballets here.

The house is furnished and decorated as it was when the composer lived here. His black Becker grand piano, a present from the manufacturer, still stands in the center of the large second-floor living room, although Tchaikovsky is said never to have played it. It was seldom used even by his visitors, however, while the composer was out walking, the children from the family that lived downstairs would pound it out of tune.

Tchaikovsky's quarters were also on the second floor. His cane, boots and steamer trunks are still in the hallway. A small bed, writing desk and a bookcase, including Dostoyevsky in French, stand in the bedroom where he composed, and is separated from his living room by a curtain. You can also see the gown that he received, together with an honorary doctorate, from the University of Cambridge, which he visited in the year of his death. There is a music library, including the complete works of Mozart whose music Tchaikovsky loved. Many original manuscripts are kept in the house, but out of reach of visitors. The composer loved being photographed and this house is said to contain more photos than the home of any other well-known Russian artist.

Germans occupied Klin in 1941 and destroyed much of his house, but the house was restored and reopened four years later on the 105th anniversary of the composer's birth.

Twice a year, on the anniversaries of his birth and death, visiting composers and musicians from various countries come to play in Klin and pay tribute to the great master in the museum's 400-seat concert hall, which was built within walking distance of the house in 1963.

Fort Worth, Texas, pianist **Van Cliburn**, who won the first Tchaikovsky International Piano Competition in Moscow, visited Klin in 1958 and was granted the honor of playing Tchaikovsky's piano. Since then a tradition has taken place that every four years on May 7, the composer's birthday, the winner of this competition performs on the master's piano.

There is a large park around Tchaikovsky's house, where trees have been planted by visitors from abroad, including an oak planted by the American conductor Leopold Stokowski.

KOLOMENSKOYE ESTATE & MUSEUM

39 Prospekt Andropova, Metro Kolomenskaya, then a leisurely 15-minute walk. Tel. 115-2309 or 2768, Fax 112-0414. Open Thursdays, Saturdays and Sundays, from 11am to 5pm; Wednesdays and Fridays, from noon to 8pm; closed Mondays and Tuesdays. Admission fee.

Constructed atop a steep bank of the Moskva River, this estate lies about six miles southeast of the Kremlin. Rest rooms are available at the Church of Our Lady of Kazan.

The history of this estate goes back to the 6th century B.C. Kolomenskoye was mentioned in the will of Moscow Prince Ivan Kalita in 1336. The village also witnessed the triumphant return of Dmitry Donskoy's troops after they defeated the Tartars at Kulikovo in 1380. Peter the Great's troops also stopped here after their victory at Poltava in 1709. For more information on both of these events, please see the entry immediately following the **Borodino Battlefield** description in this chapter. Kolomenskoye served for many years as a fortress defending the roads to Moscow. Legend has it that it was founded by the refugees from **Kolomna** (see the end of this section) who fled from the Tatar Khan Baty in the early 13th century. Later the estate became the country residence of Russian princes and czars, including Ivan Grozny (Ivan the Terrible), who was truly cruel, and Pyotr Veliky (Peter the Great), who was 6 feet and 4 inches tall. Receptions for foreign ambassadors were also held here.

The earliest architectural monument on the estate is the **Church of the Ascension**, built in 1532 by Grand Prince Vassily III to commemorate the birth of his son, the future tsar Ivan the Terrible. More than 200 feet tall, it was one of the tallest Russian buildings in the 16th century and one of the first stone churches in the Russian tent-roof style. The church also served as a watchtower. The French classical composer Hector Berlioz (1803-1869), who visited Russia in 1847, was deeply affected by its beauty and wrote: "Here before my gaze stood beauty of perfection and I gasped in awe."

Across the ravine on the hill in the nearby village of Dyakovo, one of the most ancient settlements around Moscow, there is yhe 16th century **Church of St. John the Baptist**, which is believed to be the direct forerunner of St. Basil's Cathedral in Red Square.

In 1640, the first tsar of the Romanov dynasty, Mikhail Fyodorovich, ordered the construction of a luxurious wooden palace at Kolomenskoye. Although having 250 rooms and 3,000 windows, it was built in a year entirely without saws or nails. The murals painted by Simon Ushakov took more than a decade. Thirty years later, a covered gallery connected the palace with the newly-built **Church of Our Lady of Kazan**, a striking blue-domed structure which is the first sight that you will see upon entering through the northern **Savior Gate**, where orchards once stood. After additions were made by Tsar Aleksey, the palace became known as the "eighth wonder of the world." In 1768, the somewhat neglected palace was torn down by Catherine the Great, who ordered the construction of a new palace near the Ascension Church. The Napoleonic invaders devastated Catherine's palace in 1812. The 1673 stone-made **Palace Gate**, which greeted visitors to the estate from the Moskva River, however, has survived to this day and houses a museum.

The museum is comprised of old armaments, period furnishings and decorations, historical documents and paintings. You will also see an interesting medieval collection of bells and clock mechanisms. And there are icons, wood carvings and early printed books to see.

In 1930, an open air museum of Russian wooden architecture was opened in the area of the former servants' quarters. Seventeenth and 18th century wooden structures were brought to the Kolomenskoye park from all over the country, including a 1702 six-room wooden cottage of Peter the Great which was brought from the Arkhangelsk region in 1934. The estate, which was declared a state preserve in 1974, is surrounded by a park with oak trees up to 600 years old. Russian film director Sergey Eisenstein shot some of the footage for his classic *Ivan the Terrible* at Kolomenskoye.

The estate is a favorite summer spot for the Muscovites who want to escape the heat and smog. Musical concerts are held in the **Pavilion**, which was built in 1825. An annual festival of Russian sacred music takes place in the Church of the Ascension. Around the last Sunday in May, you can also see an annual celebration of Peter the Great's birthday, which includes a parade.

In 1994, the two-headed eagle, the symbol of imperial Russia, once again crowned the gates of Kolomenskoye park. It was the first reinstallation of a tsarist crest on a building anywhere in Russia since the 1917 Revolution. Originally made in Germany, the eagle was removed after the Bolshevik takeover and broken into pieces. The pieces were kept, however, and later reassembled.

If you wish to visit the town of **Kolomna**, you can take a local train from the **Kazansky Railway Station**, which takes about two and a half hours. The last stop on the local tram in Kolomna is also the location of a museum. Kolomna was founded in 1177 and at one time had the protection of Prince Dmitry Donskoy (1350-1389), who married a Suzdal princess here. In the 16th century, Vassily III built a 90-feet high stone kremlin, or defensive wall.

KUSKOVO ESTATE & MUSEUM

2 Ulitsa Yunosty, Metro Ryazansky prospekt, then by bus #133 or #208 for six more stops. Tel. 370-0150 or 0160. From April 1 through October 1, it is open daily from 10am to 5pm; closed Mondays and Tuesdays, and last Wednesday of the month. Admission fee.

Kuskovo estate lies within Moscow city limits and is located about ten miles east of the Kremlin, just inside the Moscow Circular Road. Take a guided tour or call before going by yourself because estate may be closed due to humidity and other conditions.

The land that makes up the Kuskovo estate had been owned by the Sheremetyevs since the 16th century. Most villages around Kuskovo were also the property of the family, which also owned several other residences. Sheremetyevo International Airport is named after the clan because it was constructed on what was family property for almost 300 years. In 1775, Count Pyotr Sheremetyev, who was from one of the oldest Russian noble families who owned 200,000 serfs, built a summer palace here to escape the noise and heat of the capital, which in 1760 already numbered 150,000 inhabitants, as well as to entertain. The Sheremetyevs never lived here. The wooden mansion on a white stone foundation is covered with plaster, was designed by serf architects, and has a columned portico with a ramp by which coaches brought invited guests right to the entrance. Its interior is decorated with antique furniture, Flemish tapestries, and parquet floors, and houses one of the largest collections of 18th century Russian art. Also on display are paintings by French, Italian and Flemish artists. Starting with the entrance hall, there are 19 rooms, including, card, billiard, portrait and music rooms, some of which are closed to visitors. The palace's main reception and ballroom is the **Hall of Mirrors**, with gilded walls, rock crystal chandeliers and a ceiling painting. When balls were held here, the orchestra would be seated outside on the balcony, while hundreds of candles were lit inside.

From the ballroom in the back of the palace and overlooking the gardens, you can see the **Orangery** whose wings served as a winter garden where oranges and pineapples were grown even in the dead of the frigid Russian winters. Since 1932, it has housed the **State Museum of Ceramics**, the only exhibit of its kind in Russia, even if it feels a bit out of place here. It contains a collection of 27,000 pieces of Russian, French, German, English and Chinese porcelain, glass and ceramics, although just a small part of it is actually displayed. Part of this trove belonged to the family of Ivan Morozov, a Moscow merchant whose valuable art collection of Impressionists had been expropriated by the Bolsheviks. With large glass surfaces on one side, this part of the Orangery gets very hot in the summer.

By the time the palace was finished, the compound also included such necessary additions as the kitchen and coach facilities, the Hermitage, as well as Dutch, Italian and Swiss Houses. A grotto near the entrance was decorated with sea shells and pebbles brought from the Mediterranean. The **Church of the Holy Trinity & The Bell Tower** were among the last structures to be built in 1792.

Kuskovo gardens were immaculate and how could they not be, they were maintained by 300 gardeners. It's a far cry from what you will see today, with scraggly linden trees, bushes and patches of grass here and there, making you wonder where your $6 admission fee goes. Fifty-four statues are displayed throughout the estate, most of them from 18th century Italian masters, including one of Minerva to celebrate the visit of Catherine the Great in 1775. The marble statues on the estate are covered in wooden boxes during the winters to shelter them from the extreme cold.

In the 1760s and 80s, the estate owners entertained as many as 30,000 guests in a single day and it was the Moscow aristocracy's favorite playground for more than a hundred years. The festivities would include sumptuous balls, fireworks, folk dances, theater performances, rowing on the lake, choir singing, horn orchestras and merry-go-rounds. The receptions rivaled those at the royal court. The estate today is said to be only one-tenth the size of the original property.

At his other estate in **Ostankino**, Pyotr's son, Count Nikolay Sheremetyev, built one of the best theaters in Russia to accommodate his attraction for a slave girl he later married. His theatrical company numbered 230 serfs and had a repertoire the size of the Moscow and St. Petersburg theaters. (For more details, see the entry in Chapter 13, *Seeing the Sights*.) Kuskovo had an open-air theater (built in 1763) where his serf, Parasha Kovalyova-Zhemchugova, entertained her lord. She died of tuberculosis at age 34 and was followed by the heartstricken Sheremetyev six years later. Their son Dmitry died at Kuskovo. After the Revolution, several prominent Sheremetyevs were executed and some escaped and now live in Europe and the US. Four Sheremetyev female descendants are believed to still live in Moscow.

The palace, which overlooks an artificial pond built during the famine of 1770, has been a museum since 1918. The pond was used to stage war games and still sports a small island where noble ladies were invited to trade gossip and powder their noses. Regretfully, the pond is littered with Coca-Cola cans and other garbage, crying out against the obviously inadequate maintenance.

In the summer, chamber music concerts are held at the Kuskovo palace's 250-seat mirrored hall, usually on Tuesday, Wednesday, Thursday and Sunday evenings at 7pm.

THE MELIKHOVO ESTATE OF CHEKHOV

Located in the town of Melikhovo, about 37 miles south of Moscow.

Chekhov bought this estate in 1892 and lived in it until 1899. You may want to consider stopping in Melikhovo on your way to Tolstoy's House in Yasnaya Polyana. You can take a train from the Kursky Railway Station to Chekhov and then continue by local bus to Melikhovo. If driving, you start out on Varshavskoye Highway until the Circular Road and continue on Simferopolskoye Highway M2 through Podolsk, then go east from Chekhov.

During his seven years at Melikhovo, the author wrote his plays *The Seagull* and *Uncle Vanya*. While here, Chekhov was also instrumental in building three local schools.

The son of a shopkeeper and the grandson of a serf, he studied medicine at Moscow University and received his doctorate in 1884. He began writing as a student and just a few years after qualifying as a doctor was able to earn living as a writer. He seldom practiced, except during the cholera epidemic of 1892-93. His great play *The Seagull* was a flop on publication in 1896. Stage director Vladimir Nemirovich-Danchenko persuaded him to let the **Moscow Art Theater** revive it two years later. Produced by the great Konstantin Stanislavsky, *The Seagull* was such a success that Chekhov wrote his next three masterpieces, *Uncle Vanya* in 1900, *The Three Sisters* a year later, and *The Cherry Orchard* in 1904, for the same house. In 1900, he was elected a fellow of the Moscow Academy of Science, but resigned when his fellow-member, Maksim Gorky, was dismissed by the tsar. At age 40 he married an actress, Olga Knipper, who long after her husband's death interpreted the female parts from his plays.

For more about the **Chekhov Museum** in Moscow, please refer to Chapter 13, *Seeing the Sights*.

Tchaikovsky also lived for a time in Melikhovo.

PALEKH LACQUERED BOXES

Located in the town of Palekh.

Palekh is a town of about 6,000 in the Ivanovo region. It is 40 miles southeast of the city of Ivanovo, a textile center with predominantly female workers that have a reputation as being among the most aggressive pursuers of men in Russia. Situated along the banks of the Paleshka River, Palekh is one of the oldest villages in the area.

Palekh, together with Kholuy and Mstyora, might be part of your itinerary if you visit the so-called Golden Ring cities. These cities are a ring of ancient towns northeast of Moscow that were built between the 11th and 17th centuries and are considered the centers of Russian culture. Starting with Sergiyev Posad and continuing clockwise, they also include Pereslavl Zalessky, Rostov, Yaroslavl, Kostroma, Ivanovo, Suzdal and Vladimir. We suggest a guided excursion with Patriarshy Dom because hotel space is limited and often reserved in advance.

There is one bus daily to Palekh from Moscow. You can also take a train to Ivanovo from Moscow's **Yaroslavsky Railway Station**; it takes about six hours. Take road M7 if driving, and continue on to Nizhny Novgorod for another 37 miles. To get to Kholuy from Ivanovo, take the two-hour bus or drive to Yuzha. To get to Mstyora, take the train from Vladimir, then the local bus.

Palekh, Kholuy and Mstyora, all located in the Ivanovo region about 200 miles northeast of Moscow, were once renowned as centers of icon painting of the Vladimir-Suzdal school. Palekh icons and frescoes in particular were considered to be among the best until the beginning of the 19th century, when icon painting became so common it was considered just a craft with little artistic significance. When they could no longer carry on their traditional craft of painting icons after the Communists took over, they transferred their skills to Russian lacquered art, or miniature painting on papier-mache boxes. In this process, a roll of cardboard is turned around a wooden shape of a box, is then pressed, soaked in linseed oil, painted and lacquered several times, and dried over time. For more details on how to make a **shkatulka**, please see Fedoskino in this chapter.

Other centers of exceptional artisanship include Fedoskino and **Khokhloma** (see Souvenirs & Antiques on Old Arbat Street in Chapter 17, *Shopping*). Palekh and Fedoskino are probably the most highly valued by collectors.

Palekh lacquer miniatures, produced by about 100 artists, are noted for their range of colors, especially the details in gold, and recognizable by the predominance of black paint. There are boxes of every conceivable shape, cigarette cases, powder boxes and brooches. Expect to pay at least $25 for even a decent fake Palekh lacquer box of any size on Arbat Street or at the Izmaylovo open market. A real Palekh box will costs you from $200 to $4,000, or more, and is crafted to last for centuries. Not many of them are found in Moscow because most are exported. The most highly sought are those painted by about two dozen top artists of the Tovarishchestvo cooperative in Palekh, which was founded in 1924.

The town is also well-known for its embroidery. If you go to Palekh, visit its **Museum of Applied Art** and the **House of Ivan Golikov** (1886-1937), the founder of Palekh's lacquered miniature art. Also worthy of your attention are the **New Palekh Museum** and the **Artists' Workshop**. These villages were closed to foreigners until 1991.

Kholuy, within one hour's drive and located on the banks of the Teza River, produces more realistic miniatures without Palekh's overwhelming black backgrounds.

Fedoskino, north of Moscow, is perhaps the oldest school of lacquer painting still in existence in Russia. You will also come across the bright red and black wooden articles made by craftsmen from the village of Khokhloma that have a 300-year tradition. They include wooden cups, spoons, goblets and trays painted in a traditional style.

PEREDELKINO WRITERS COLONY

Located in the town of Peredelkino. Pasternak's House is open daily from 10am to 4pm; closed Mondays, Tuesdays and Wednesdays. Admission fee.

Peredelkino is the village home to a writers' colony that was established in 1936 in Moscow's southwest suburbs during the Stalinist era. It is located about 15 miles from the city.

Patriarshy Dom has regular monthly excursions to Peredelkino during the summer. You can also take a 30-minute **elektrichka**, a suburban train, from Moscow's Kievsky Railway Station, next to the

Slavyanskaya Hotel, then continue by local bus #47. If you prefer to walk, it will take about 20 minutes from the Peredelkino railway station to Pasternak's house. By car, start out on Kutuzovsky prospekt, continue on the Minsk Highway M1, until you turn left at the 21 kilometer marker.

Boris Pasternak (1890-1960) is the author of *Dr. Zhivago,* a love story about a doctor and poet whose life is disrupted by the Civil War. Many Americans know the story from the movie starring Omar Sharif and Julie Christie. When the author submitted the manuscript to a Moscow literary journal it was rejected. Published in Italy in 1957, it was awarded the Nobel Prize for Literature the following year, although Pasternak was compelled to decline it. The epic tale quickly became an international best-seller translated into 18 languages. Pasternak was expelled from the Union of Soviet Writers and *Dr. Zhivago* was not published in his homeland until 1987.

A world-class poet, Pasternak was also an elegant translator of Shakespeare and Goethe, which is how he earned a living when his poetry was not appreciated. He lived in Peredelkino from 1939 until his death of lung cancer at age 70, spending his final years tending to his garden. Although disgraced by the Soviets, thousands came to Pasternak's funeral in 1960.

In 1990, after a hard-fought campaign by his supporters, his house was turned into the Pasternak Museum. Chances are, unless you come with a guided tour, you won't have a clue as to where the large brown wooden house with a glassed-in oblong porch on Pavlenko Street is located. A simple way to ask is: **Izvinite, gdye dom Pasternaka?** (Where is Pasternak's house?) The house was built by his father, the eminent painter Leonid Pasternak. Although it is somewhat bare, the furniture and photos on the walls are authentic, his boots and coat are still near a bookshelf with novels by Virginia Woolf, as though Pasternak will be back any minute. Also upstairs, in his study, you can see the writing armoire where the author wrote standing up.

Novelist Aleksey Tolstoy, poet Yevgeny Yevtushenko, cellist and conductor Mstislav Rostropovich and his wife, opera singer Galina Vishnevskaya, all have lived here, amid luxuries that most Russians could only dream about. The well-known poet Andrey Voznesensky is said to still reside here. It was in Peredelkino that Rostropovich and his wife gave refuge to Aleksandr Solzhenitsyn, another Nobel Prize winner for literature. A few writers still remain to this day, but Peredelkino has now become a favorite place for the rich New Russians to escape Moscow's pollution and keep out of the limelight.

Before glasnost and perestroika, it was dangerous to be seen here, but now the worst that could happen to you is that you will be spoken to in Russian and you might not understand it. So go ahead and make the pilgrimage to the Pasternak's grave in the village cemetery opposite the well-preserved 15th century **Church of the Transfiguration**. Pasternak wanted to be buried near the three pine trees next to his grave and his wish was granted, although only two of the trees have survived. Expect lots of company if you come on May 30, the anniversary of the poet's death.

You can have lunch or dinner at the former Young Communist resthouse, now the Italian Villa Peredelkino, *Tel. 435-1211 or 8345.* Located near the railway's arrival platform, it is open from noon to midnight, and accepts credit cards. This pricey eatery, whose food is mostly imported from Italy, will give you a peek at how the privileged lived in the past and how some still do today.

SERGIYEV POSAD

*The **Monastery**, Krasnogorskaya Ploshchad, Tel. 973-0823, is open daily from 10am to 5pm, closed Mondays, but check with Patriarshy Dom, Intourist or call Tel. (8-254) 45-356 or 45-350 from Moscow for more details. The **Museums** are open daily from 10am to 6pm; closed Mondays. The **Toy Museum** is open daily Wednesday through Sunday, from 10am to 5pm; also closed last Monday of the month. Admission fees are much higher for foreigners than for Russians. There is a $5 charge to take still photos on the grounds and $11 for video cameras, but not inside the churches. The toilets are near the main entrance to the monastery.*

Sergiyev Posad, a city of just over 120,000, is located 45 miles northeast of central Moscow, on the Yaroslavskoye Highway M8; you can start out on Prospekt Mira. You can also get here on a train from the Yaroslavsky Railway Station, which runs about every 45 minutes. Travel time is one hour and a half, then a 15 minute walk two blocks west from the station and north to the monastery.

To spare yourself the aggravation, we strongly recommend that you visit Sergiyev Posad with a guided tour company, such as Patriarshy Dom or Intourist. The monastery today has become, much like the Kremlin, a tourist circus and a comedy of errors. No one seems to know what the rules concerning tourists are and when they apply.

You will show respect for Russian customs by being properly dressed: shorts and sandals are not appropriate for either men or women under any circumstance. Women must wear a dress or skirt, not jeans or pants, and should also bring along a head scarf to cover their hair, while men must always remove their head covering and no one may smoke on the grounds. If you should detect a slight backlash against Western tourists, particularly loud Americans, it will not surprise you after you see visitors dressed in a most disrespectful way. Thongs and cutoffs may be fine in Miami, but in Sergiyev Posad they only accentuate a visitor's ignorance and disrespect for a thousand years of tradition.

Sergiyev Posad is the most popular among the eight Golden Ring towns, all of them located northeast of Moscow, and the only one you can comfortably see in a day. In 1987, British Prime Minister Margaret Thatcher made a much publicized visit to Sergiyev Posad, just as President Ronald Reagan did the following year when he visited the Danilovsky Monastery during the 1988 Moscow summit meeting. But the American pop singer Michael Jackson was discouraged from coming here by the Orthodox Church during his 1993 Russian tour because of now well known sex-related accusations.

The **Holy Trinity Monastery of St. Sergius** is one of Russia's most important spiritual and historical landmarks. Tens of thousands made a pilgrimage here every year before the Revolution and they continue to do so again now that the Bolsheviks are gone. Until a few years ago it was also the headquarters of the Russian Orthodox Church. Although the headquarters has since been moved to Moscow's Danilovsky Monastery, St. Sergius still represents the essence of Russian Orthodoxy and houses its seminary. The monastery was originally encircled by wooden ramparts, which in the late 1540's gave way to a high brick wall that measures almost a mile in circumference.

To get to what was until 1991 crudely called Zagorsk, after Communist Party Secretary Vladimir Zagorsky who was blown up by a bomb in 1919, you will drive through some dreary Moscow suburbs until you reach the countryside. While Sergiyev Posad will remind you of the former Soviet Union even before you get to the monastery, the sight of the blue domes and gold stars on the Assumption Cathedral up on the hill ahead of you will quickly erase these stilted impressions. You are about to enter a most magnificent collection of Orthodox churches, even if you have to pass through a gauntlet of beggars, souvenir peddlers and annoying tourists of every nationality. You enter through the single-dome **Red Gate Tower** that dates from 1600 and beyond it through the frescoed arch under the **Church of John the Baptist**, which was completed 99 years later, and today serves as a confessional for Orthodox pilgrims.

St. Sergius is one of only four Russian monasteries to hold the title of **lavra**, which is reserved for the monasteries of the highest rank. This status, granted in 1744, lies with **St. Sergius of Radonezh** (1314-1392), the patron saint of Russia and founder of the Holy Trinity Lavra here. He was born into the family of a pious Rostov nobleman. Since his childhood he was deeply devotional. He lived with his parents in the small hamlet of Radonezh (about 200 people) where you can see a monument in his honor on your way to **Abramtsevo** (see entry in this chapter). In 1337, Sergius and his brother Stepan built a small church in the midst of a dense forest where they lived in seclusion for long periods of time, as was customary in the Russian Orthodox community until recently. Seventeen years later Patriarch Philotheos of Constantinople sent a pectoral cross to Sergius as encouragement to continue his work in the monastery. As the centuries passed, his disciples founded more than 50 monasteries.

It was Sergius who blessed Prince Dmitry Donskoy and his 100,000 troops, spurring them on to defend the honor of Russia in the battle at Kulikovo in 1380, where Tartars suffered the first major defeat in more than a century. In 1408, the monastery was again devastated by the Tartars; it remained an important fortress defending Moscow from foreign invaders until the end of the 17th century. In the Time of Troubles, 1608-10, a mere 1,500 defenders of the monastery withstood a 16-month siege by an army of 30,000 well-armed Polish troops.

What you see comprises numerous churches and chapels, architectural monuments and towers. Once inside any one of the churches, you will notice that there are no pews, no music and very few statues, but it's filled with icons. The churches are full of praying elderly Russian women, called **babushki**, scarved and oblivious to the rest of the world. You will be impressed by the services in the **Cathedral of the Assumption**, the largest of the ensemble, which was modeled after the Assumption Cathedral in the Kremlin. It is located one-third of the way through the monastery grounds, on your right. Begun in 1585 and completed 26 years later, it was built to commemorate Ivan the Terrible's victory over the Tartars in Kazan. A century later its murals were painted by Yaroslavl craftsmen and the tsar's icon painter Simon Ushakov took part in the design of the iconostasis (a screen that separates the sanctuary from the nave).

It was Ivan the Terrible who granted St. Sergius monastery large parcels of land and Moscow nobility who donated large sums of money. These donations made it the largest landowner in Russia for centuries. They also made it possible for the lavra to own 106,000 serfs peasants. St. Sergius traded in grain, honey, wax and salt and sent its own merchant ships to Norway. It was the second most important cultural center after Kiev. The monastery had 20,000 fighting men ready to defend it at all times.

Catherine the Great thought most monasteries entirely too powerful and wealthy and just a couple of years upon ascending the throne in 1762, she confiscated many of their landholdings and soon afterwards deprived the church of its right to own serfs. Outside, on the northwest corner of the Assumption Cathedral is the tomb of Boris Godunov, the sole tsar not buried in the Kremlin or St. Petersburg's Peter and Paul Cathedral. West of the cathedral you will spot a small octagonal chapel built over a spring that monks discovered in 1644. Pilgrims from everywhere can be seen filling jars and bottles with the supposedly holy water, believing it has healing properties.

Heading southwest of here, you will pass by the **Church of the Descent of the Holy Spirit**, built in 1477 by architects from Pskov; the top of its dome was once a watchtower. The nearby **Holy Trinity Cathedral**, built by St. Sergius' successor, Patriarch Nikon, in 1427, was built over the grave of St. Sergius, whose remains are buried in a silver sarcophagus that was a gift from Ivan the Terrible. The cathedral replaced a wooden monastery that was burned down by the Tartars. The **Chapel of St. Nikon** nearby dates from 1548.

If you are allowed to enter the Holy Trinity, you might be able to observe part of the memorial service to St. Sergius that goes on all day. Access to this church has been restricted and foreigners may be barred from entering it because they interfere with the services. Most of its 42 priceless icons were painted by Russia's foremost iconist, monk Andrey Rublev, a St. Sergius pupil, in the 1420's. Rublev's spectacular **Trinity** icon, which you can see on display at the **Tretyakov Gallery** (see Chapter 13, *Seeing the Sights*), was originally painted for this church, but was later replaced by a copy. Patriarch Nikon was buried in a church near the cathedral in 1548.

The northern one-third of the monastery, with the **Tsar's Palace** and **Theological Academy** seminary, and another small part of the monastery in the south are closed to tourists. The monastery's **Bell Tower**, which once had 40 bells, soars 289 feet high and is perhaps the tallest in Russia; it is located north of Trinity Cathedral. Just northwest from the tower stands the **Church of Our Lady of Smolensk**, dating from 1748. The long building on your left, as you walk toward Trinity Cathedral, was once the refectory, used to feed thousands of pilgrims who came here on feast days.

If you have time, take your kids to the **Toy Museum**, the large red brick building on Krasnoy Armiyi Avenue, which was founded in Moscow in 1918 and transferred to Sergiyev Posad in 1931. It is open Tuesday through Sunday, from 10am to 5pm. They can see more than 30,000 toys from the Bronze Age and from all over the country. Sergiyev Posad woodworks go back to the 14th century and **matryoshka** wooden dolls have a 100-year-long tradition here. Your kids can buy a toy at the souvenir shop, while you pick up a tiny reproduction of Rublev's icon. The **Zolotoye Koltso** (Golden Ring) restaurant is nearby and has passable rest rooms, but you will have to pay to use them. **Russky Dvorik** is a small restaurant located across the street from the monastery entrance.

On your way to and from Sergiyev Posad, you could also stop at Russkaya Skazka, a quaint state-run restaurant. Skazka, which is located in Lesnoy village, at the 41st kilometer (21st mile) post, or about halfway toward Sergiyev Posad, is open daily from noon to 11 pm. While at the restaurant, take advantage of their toilets because the ones in Sergiyev Posad are primitive.

TSARITSINO RUINS & MUSEUM

1 Ulitsa Dolskaya. Tel. 321-0743. Museum open April through October, Wednesday through Friday, from 11am to 5pm, Saturdays and Sundays from 10am to 6pm; closed Mondays and Tuesdays.

Tsaritsino is about nine miles southeast of Red Square, beyond Kolomenskoye and west of the Kashirskoye Highway. It's bound on its south side by the Moscow Circular Road which delineates the capital's boundary. By metro, you can go to Tsaritsino or Orekhovo stations, then walk to the estate entrance. We suggest a guided tour with Patriarshy Dom.

At the beginning of the 18th century this village was given to the satiric poet Prince Antiokh Kantemir by Peter the Great. But Catherine the Great bought it back in 1775 because she wanted to have another residence in the vicinity of Moscow. Originally named Black Mud, the village became Tsaritsino (Tsarina's Village) upon her purchase.

Trained in philosophy and literature, the tsarina was more than a mere ruler. She corresponded with the great writers and philosophers of her time and wrote tragedies and comedies as well as philosophical studies.

A thousand-acre park was selected on a southern Moscow hill and the construction of two palaces, an opera house and other buildings began soon after her purchase. Two small rivers were dammed, leading to the formation of picturesque ponds at the foot of the hill. Construction was almost completed when Catherine visited her new residence, but did not like it. Exasperated by the purely Russian style of the buildings, she fired the architect Vasily Bazhenov, who had worked on the property for ten years, and hired the famous Matvey Kazakov. He tore down practically everything, except the entrance gate and the opera house, and reconstructed it to his own taste, but the new design failed to please Catherine's court and in 1787 construction was discontinued altogether for lack of funding.

Tsaritsino castle is probably the most unusual of all Moscow's architectural relics. Its uniqueness lies in its unfinished construction. You can still see the skeletons of the original buildings, which have been under restoration for several years. The park at Tsaritsino has been immortalized by writer Ivan Turgenev in his novel *On the Eve*. There is a small museum at Tsaritsino with a collection of icons, glass and china.

Down the hill near the water is a restored summer house where a traditional Russian restaurant, Usadba, is located. It's open daily from noon to 11 pm. Behind the restaurant are the horse riding stables, where, from 9am to 9pm, you can hire a horse on an hourly basis.

YASNAYA POLYANA TOLSTOY'S ESTATE

Located in the hamlet of Yasnaya Polyana near Tula. Open Wednesday through Sunday from 10am to 5pm; closed Mondays and Tuesdays, last Wednesday of the month and on very humid days. Admission fee.
The sole claim to fame this town has is the almost lifelong residence of novelist **Lev Tolstoy**. This town, near Tula and about 120 miles south of Moscow, is where he spent more than half a century. A small cafe is located opposite the main gate. The public rest rooms are primitive.

Tula, an industrial city of about 550,000, is polluted and of interest to those who like antique guns and samovars of yesteryear. Tula's **Weapon's Museum** is located in the former Epiphany Cathedral. The **Samovar Museum**, which is located just outside the kremlin entrance, exhibits more samovars than you may care to see. Gun-making began here in 1712 when Peter the Great founded an arms factory; a samovar industry flourished in the late 18th and early 19th centuries and has since become extinct.

Unless *War and Peace* and *Anna Karenina*, both of which were written here, have a special meaning for you, this place may be too far. Driving time is almost three hours each way; it will take you a full day to visit and you won't know for sure whether the museum will be open until you get there. We suggest that you take a Patriarshy Dom guided tour. If you drive, take the Varshavskoye Highway out of Moscow and follow the signs on the M2 Highway to Tula, then continue another eight or nine miles south to Yasnaya Polyana, which translates as Bright Glade. The estate, which was created by Tolstoy's relatives, lies about a mile from the main road.

Tolstoy was born here in 1828. He was educated privately and led a gay life until 1851 when he joined an artillery regiment and began his literary career. It is said that he walked more than once from Yasnaya Polyana to Moscow - and it took a week. After marrying in 1862, he settled on his estate and began working on *War and Peace*. His wife dutifully transcribed her husband's daily scribbles in what have since become great Russian classics.

In *What is Art?* he argued that only simple works constitute great art. Everything sophisticated and detailed, such as his own novels, he condemned as worthless. He turned over his fortune to his wife, who gave him 13 children, and tried to live simply as a peasant. Marital arguments, which consisted mostly of lifelong, extreme jealousy on the part of both Tolstoys, finally compelled him to leave the house on the night of October 28, 1910 at the age of 82. He came down with pneumonia and died at the railway station in the village of Astapovo. His unmarked grave is a little distance away from the museum, in the park and surrounded by nine oaks. His wife Sofiya died in 1919.

Tolstoy's house on the one-million-acre estate became a museum two years later. It is a rich find of authentic memorabilia and attests to visitors like classical writers Anton Chekhov and Ivan Turgenev. Portraits of the writer by painters Ilya Repin and Ivan Kramskoy are on display. You can also see a phonograph that was presented to Tolstoy by Edison and a portrait of the real Anna Karenina. The desk at which Tolstoy's wife transcribed *War and Peace* has also been preserved and is shown in her bedroom. Tolstoy's library contained 22,000 books in 35 languages and some insist that he spoke several himself. The **Literature Museum** nearby was once Tolstoy's school for peasant children. The original Volkonsky Mansion is closed to visitors.

To ease the strain on the buildings, the museum has had to limit the number of visitors to 300,000 a year. In 1993, President Yeltsin declared it a national treasure entitled to special protection by the government. Tolstoy's descendants have been bickering with the local bureaucracy for years as to who should look after the estate.

In Tolstoy's time, there was a tall elm tree near this house. Every morning, people would gather on a bench under that tree seeking Tolstoy's advice. The elm became known as the "poor people's tree." It died after more than 200 years, but in 1971, a young elm was planted in its place.

ZHOSTOVO TRAYS

Located in the village of Zhostovo, some 18 miles north of Moscow.

Zhostovo has a population of about a thousand and a reputation for producing the best hand-painted metal serving trays in Russia. Patriarshy Dom organizes 75-minute shopping excursions to Zhostovo, which takes more than half a day. Should you be adventurous enough to drive by yourself, start out on the Dmitrovskoye Highway and continue on A104, as though going to Fedoskino, or by turning east on the Moscow Circular Road and continuing north through the villages of Borodino (not of Napoleonic fame) and Belyaninovo. But regardless of which way you go, you will be surprised at the numbers of luxurious **dachas** (summer homes) strewn everywhere on your way. These dachas belong to the rich New Russians.

The artisanship of hand painting metal trays has been in existence since lacquer arts reached Europe in the late 17th century. In this area, it is believed to have started around 1825 when the Vishnyakov family started producing snuffboxes in the nearby village of Ostashkovo. Zhostovo artisans began producing metal trays in 1840 and now numerous individuals paint the pre-cut mass-produced trays at a cavernous five-story Soviet-style factory or in their homes.

As you will notice in the factory museum, fantasy flowers are the usual feature on Zhostovo trays, which traditionally are painted on a black background. Usually two artisans work on each tray, one prepares the tray for the artist, the other paints it by hand. The least expensive Zhostovo trays, or the countless knock-offs that litter Moscow and the countryside, only have two layers of lacquer topping the design. The best trays have up to seven layers and can cost up to $1,000 each, depending on the complexity of the design and the size.

While the Zhostovo factory has hundreds of trays in many sizes and price ranges in its store and warehouse, for the best bargains ask the Patriarshy Dom guide to take you to a family of artisans who work from their homes. The **Antipovs** are one such family that use their tiny living room as a miniature gallery to display the range of their artisanship. Trays with traditional Russian scenes, instead of the usual flowers, are fairly rare and more difficult to find, but artisan-entrepreneurs like the Antipovs always keep a few such pieces in their stock. There is a bit of room for negotiation and you can buy good quality trays from $25 to $200 each, depending on their size. You can pay with rubles or dollars.

19. ST. PETERSBURG

St. Petersburg was built on the marshy grounds of the Neva River in the Gulf of Finland by Peter the Great in 1703. Peter believed that only rapid westernization would pull his backward nation to the forefront of Europe, and he spared no expense or human life to attain his goal. Tens of thousands of serfs perished while building the city, which remained Russia's capital until the Bolshevik arrival in 1918.

During World War I, St. Petersburg was renamed Petrograd and in 1924, the year of Lenin's death, Leningrad. In September 1941, Germans surrounded the city and, during a blockade that lasted 872 days, caused the death of more than 660,000 Leningraders, mostly due to starvation. The city of five million was renamed St. Petersburg by a referendum in 1991.

ARRIVALS & DEPARTURES

By Air

To fly to St. Petersburg you can buy tickets at Intourist, Intourservice, Intourtrans or a Western-style travel agency. See Chapter 7, *Getting Around Moscow* for addresses and telephone numbers. Car rental companies are listed in the same chapter, although we never recommend that you drive. You can also buy tickets from Aeroflot or, preferably Transaero, which has more civilized service (see Chapter 6, *Arrivals & Departures* for more details).

Pulkovo Airport, Domestic Flights Information, *Tel. (812) 104-3611* and International Flights Information, *Tel. (812) 104-3444*, is located about 17 miles south of central St. Petersburg. A taxi downtown will cost you at least $30. For an idea of what to expect from taxis see Chapter 6, *Arrivals & Departures.*

Airlines: Aeroflot international flights, *Tel. (812) 104-3444;* **Air France**, *Tel. (812) 325-8252*, Pulkovo, *Tel. (812) 104-3433;* **British Airways**, Nevsky Palace Hotel, *Tel. (812) 325-6222*, Pulkovo, *Tel. (812) 104-3749;* **Delta Airlines**, *Tel. (812) 311-5819*, Pulkovo, *Tel. (812) 104-3438;*

Finnair, *Tel. (812) 315-9736;* **Lufthansa**, *Tel. (812) 314-4979,* Pulkovo, *Tel. (812) 104-3432;* **SAS**, Nevsky Palace Hotel, *Tel. (812) 314-5086,* Pulkovo, *Tel. (812) 104-3443.*

By Train

The much less expensive alternative is to take an overnight train from the Leningradsky Railway Station in Moscow. Please see **Railway Stations** in the section on trains in Chapter 6, *Arrivals & Departures* for details on how and where to purchase railway tickets in Moscow. In St. Petersburg, tickets can be bought at the Intourist counter inside the Moscow Railway Station, at any travel agency or, if you are willing to pay extra, at most luxury hotels.

There are more than a dozen trains departing daily in both directions between Moscow and St. Petersburg. Most travelers take the overnight sleeper train to save a night's accommodations. Express trains usually leave either city before midnight and arrive at their destinations between 6am and 8am. The cost is about $35 for first class.

WHERE TO STAY

St. Petersburg has several Western-style hotels that will satisfy even the most demanding tourists and business travelers. Most of them have at least one restaurant, a cafe, and sometimes a combination of a bar, pub and nightclub. Always reserve your St. Petersburg lodgings before you leave Moscow.

Taking a taxi outside a luxury hotel is usually not a good idea because you will be considered fair game for high fares. To hire a **taxi** day or night, call *Tel. (812) 312-0022.*

Expensive

ASTORIA HOTEL, *39 Ulitsa Bolshaya Morskaya, Metro Nevsky prospekt or Gostiny Dvor. Tel. (812) 210-5757, Fax 210-5059, Telex 121213 ASTOR SU. Major credit cards accepted.*

Centrally located, clean, and modern, this six-story two-block luxury hotel was built in 1913 and accommodates about 330 guests. It overlooks St. Isaac's Cathedral. The complex also includes the former Angleterre Hotel, where poet Yesenin committed suicide in 1925. Singles start at $175 and doubles at $225 a night.

Restaurants include the **Winter Garden**, *Tel. 210-5906*, with live entertainment, and the **Angleterre** and the **Astoria**, both of which have good reputations. Intourist, which provides city tours, car rentals, and tickets to various events, has a desk at the hotel. A bank and fitness center are also on the premises.

GRAND HOTEL EUROPE, *1/7 Ulitsa Mikhaylovskaya, Metro Nevsky prospekt or Gostiny Dvor. Tel. (812) 329-6000, Fax 329-6001, Telex 64121073. Major credit cards accepted.*

The Grand Hotel Europe is centrally located, clean, wheelchair-accessible, and overlooks Nevsky prospekt and the Russian Museum. This former Evropeyskaya Hotel has a business center, and an American Express office, *Tel. 329-6060*, which is open weekdays from 9am to 5pm and will cash your personal checks or give you an advance on your Amexco credit card. There are 300 suites and rooms starting at $300 and going all the way to $1,000 for the top suites.

Evropeysky, which dates from 1905, is perhaps the most formal and expensive restaurant in St. Petersburg. Other well-regarded Grand eateries include The Brasserie, Sadko's and the Atrium Cafe. Bars, shops and a health club are also on the premises.

HOTEL MERCURY, *39 Ulitsa Tavricheskaya, Metro Chernyshevskaya. Tel. and Fax (812) 325-6444, Fax 276-1977, International Tel. and Fax (7 502) (201) 222-3388. Major credit cards accepted.*

This small but rather expensive hotel is located near Tavrichesky Park and Smolny Cathedral. It caters mostly to foreign business travelers. A restaurant and bar are on the premises.

NEVSKY PALACE HOTEL, *57 Nevsky prospekt, Metro Mayakovskaya. Tel. (812) 275-2001 or 2004, Fax 310-7323 Telex 121279 HERMS SU. Major credit cards accepted.*

The Nevsky Palace Hotel is centrally located, wheelchair-accessible, and restored. Formerly the Baltiskaya Hotel, which dates from 1861, it has 287 suites and rooms and is managed by the Austrian company Marco Polo Hotels. Its restaurants are among the best in the city and comparably priced. Singles start at $300 and doubles at $350 a night, with the presidential suite going for $1,200.

A DHL express mail office, *Tel. (812) 325-6100*, open Monday through Friday, is located here, in addition to British Airways, SAS, and Swissair airline offices.

Moderate

HOTEL HELEN (Sovyetskaya), *43/1 Lermontovsky prospekt, Metro Baltiyskaya, then trolleybus #3 or #8, or tram #29 to get to Nevsky prospekt. Tel. (812) 329-0181 or 0182 or 0186, Fax 329-0188, Telex 121705 XOTS SU. Major credit cards accepted.*

This Russian-Finnish venture overlooking the Fontanka Canal is only a couple of miles southwest of the Hermitage. Singles start at about $75. Hotel Helen has three restaurants and a bar as well as three cafes on the premises.

WHERE TO EAT

In addition to the restaurants mentioned in Where to Stay in St. Petersburg, some of which are among the best in the city and also serve breakfast, there are several additional restaurants included in the description of Nevsky Avenue in Seeing the Sights. The following restaurants are also worthy of note:

AUSTERIA (Old Russian cuisine), *at the Peter and Paul Fortress, Metro Gorkovskaya. Tel. (812) 232-7580 or 238-4262. Open daily from noon to midnight. Cash only.*

A friendly and pleasant eatery.

DADDY'S STEAK ROOM (Steaks), *73 Moskovsky prospekt, next to Frunzenskaya metro station. Tel. (812) 252-7744, Fax 298-9552. Open daily from noon to 11pm. Major credit cards accepted.*

Daddy's boasts of having "The Best Steaks in St. Petersburg," but there are a few such establishments in the city. They also serve pizza.

DOM ARKHITEKTORA (Russian cuisine), *52 Ulitsa Bolshaya Morskaya. Tel. (812) 311-4557. Open daily from noon to 11pm. Major credit cards accepted. Reservations suggested.*

An elegant, expensive restaurant that once served the Union of Architects exclusively.

OKEAN (Seafood), *31b Primorsky prospekt. Tel. (812) 239-6305. Open daily from noon to midnight. Cash only.*

A boat restaurant with traditional Russian cuisine and live entertainment.

1001 NIGHTS (Uzbeki cuisine), *21/6 Ulitsa Millionnaya, several blocks northwest of metro station Nevsky prospekt, but near the Hermitage. Entrance on Zaporozhsky pereulok. Tel. (812) 312-2265. Open daily from noon to midnight. Live entertainment. Cash only.*

Reasonably priced, good Uzbeki food served in a relaxed atmosphere. Belly dancing in the evening.

SCHWABSKY DOMIK (German cuisine), *28/19 Krasnogvardeysky prospekt, Metro Novocherkasskaya. Tel. (812) 528-2211. Open daily from 11am to midnight. Major credit cards accepted.*

Simple, pleasant, friendly and full of German expatriates. Live entertainment.

ST. PETERSBURG (Russian & European cuisine), *5 Nab. Kanala Yekaterininsky, still widely known as Nab. Kanala Griboyedova. Tel. (812) 314-4947. Open daily from noon to 1:30am. Major credit cards accepted.*

An expensive, tourist trap opposite the Church of the Resurrection of Christ. The live entertainment starts at 9pm.

SEEING THE SIGHTS

As in Moscow, you can stay in St. Petersburg for months and only see half of its riches. Below are two large clusters of major sights that you can explore at your leisure. To get the flavor of Moscow, you would walk the length of Tverskaya Street or Stary Arbat; to sample St. Petersburg, walk down Nevsky Avenue, a long and straight shopping and sightseeing avenue.

The second cluster covers such indispensable sights as Palace Square and the Hermitage Museum, Senate Square and the Admiralty, as well as sights on nearby Isaac's Square.

Although St. Petersburg covers an area of 150 square miles, most of the sights of interest to Westerners are located downtown. You are advised to seem them on foot because the metro and bus lines are not the most convenient means for getting around. Almost everything said about the Moscow metro applies to St. Petersburg's as well.

Mosquitos are a nuisance in St. Petersburg so bring a repellent if you plan to spend a lot of time outdoors.

Nevsky Avenue
Nevsky prospekt

We suggest you start your walk at the **Admiralty**, the neo-classical building you will recognize by its gilded spire, or the triple arch of the **General Staff Building**. The nearest metro station is Nevsky prospekt. Buses #7 and #44 and trolleybuses #1, #7, #10 and #22 run along Nevsky Avenue between the Admiralty and the Moscow Railway Station. Your walking tour could easily take a couple of hours on this three-mile road, but you can always take public transportation back to the city center.

Nevsky prospekt is St. Petersburg's favorite street, the center of business as well as social and cultural activities. There are theaters, concert halls, cinemas, galleries, hotels, restaurants, pubs, shops, and quiet public gardens for you to enjoy. Nevsky Avenue is adjoined by squares and crossed by the Moika and Fontanka Rivers, and the Griboyedov Canal.

The initial road was cut through swamps in 1710 to connect the Admiralty with **Aleksandr Nevsky Monastery** at the other end of this avenue. Paved with logs, it soon became the main street of the new capital and it was named Nevsky prospekt in 1730. Many nobles built their mansions along the avenue. In 1863, a horse-drawn railway was laid here and twenty years later electric street lamps were installed.

The gray granite house at 7/9 Nevsky Avenue and Malaya Morskaya Street, at the outset of the avenue, was built in 1912 for the St. Petersburg Bank of Trade and now houses **Aeroflot** Russian airlines.

The great Russian writer **Nikolay Gogol** lived nearby at 17 Malaya Morskaya and the house at number 13 was the last residence of the composer **Pyotr Tchaikovsky**. A couple of blocks down the next side street to your right, at 24 Ulitsa Bolshaya Morskaya, is the **Hotel Astoria**, which once housed the famous Faberge workshop.

But back to Nevsky prospekt: house number 8 was built in the second half of the 18th century and has served as an art salon for many years; there are several such salons on this avenue. Number 14 is one of almost 600 secondary schools in St. Petersburg. House number 15 was built for the St. Petersburg police chief in 1760; later writers Denis Fonvizin and Aleksandr Griboyedov visited here. After the 1917 Revolution, it was known as the House of Arts, where poet Osip Mandelshtam and satirist Mikhail Zoshchenko lived; it is now the **Barrikady Cinema**. **Cafe Druzhba**, *Tel. (812) 315-9536*, is also located in this building. At house number 16 is the **Iskusstvo** bookstore, and on the first street to your left, *3/5 Bolshaya Morskaya Street*, is the **Central Telephone and Telegraph**, where you can place calls overseas.

The house at 17 Nevsky Avenue, overlooking the Moika embankment, is known as the **Stroganov Palace**, which is now part of the Hermitage. It was built in 1754 for Count Aleksandr Stroganov, president of the Academy of Arts, by the well-known baroque architect Bartolomeo Rastrelli. Also at this address, is a rather formal Russian and Italian restaurant **Stroganov**, *Tel. (812) 312-1859*, open daily from noon to 11pm.

On the opposite corner, at number 18, where the Moika crosses Nevsky prospekt, you will find the vastly overrated bohemian **Literary Cafe**, *Tel. (812) 312-6057*, which is open daily from noon to 11pm. It was here, on January 27, 1837, that poet Aleksandr Pushkin met his dueling second for his last meal before the fateful encounter that cut short his prodigal literary life. The cafe was opened in his honor and is usually mobbed by tourists, although there is little to recommend it for but the classical music you can hear inside. **Pushkin's House**, *12 Moika Embankment, Tel. (812) 312-1962*, is now a museum, open Wednesday through Monday, from 11am to 5pm. This was the poet's last residence and the place where he was brought to die after his duel with Baron Georges d'Anthes for the honor of his wife in January 1837.

At 22 Nevsky prospekt you will find **Apteka No. 6**, *Tel. (812) 311-2077*, one of the few centrally-located pharmacies that are open 24 hours a day; the **Bristol Cafe**, *Tel. (812) 311-7490*, is at the same address. The **House of Books**, *28 Nevsky prospekt, Tel. (812) 219-6402 or 9422*, is St. Petersburg's largest bookstore, open Monday–Saturday from 11am to 7pm, an imposing building with large windows built at the beginning of this century for the American Singer Sewing Machine Company. Today it houses several publishers. Set behind it is **St. Peter's Lutheran Church**.

Across the street is **Kazan Cathedral** (open Thursday through Tuesday, from 11am to 5pm), constructed in Russian classical style in 1811 on the plans of Count Stroganov's serf, who was eventually granted his freedom. The 70-meter-high cruciform structure is modeled on St. Peter's Cathedral in Rome. In 1813, field marshall **Mikhail Kutuzov**, the commander of the Russian forces during the 1812 Napoleonic invasion of Russia, was laid to rest here. In 1837, monuments to Kutuzov and another hero of the 1812 war were erected on the Nevsky prospekt side of the cathedral.

During the Soviet era, the cathedral housed the Museum of Atheism, which is now the **Museum of Religion**, *Tel. (812) 311-0495*. Where Nevsky Avenue is crossed by the Yekaterininsky Kanal, still widely known as Griboyedov Kanal, you can see the **Kazansky Bridge**, which was built in 1766 by Kutuzov's father.

House number 30 was once St. Petersburg's major music center where such illustrious composers as Hector Berlioz, Richard Wagner and Franz Liszt performed. It is now the location of the **Glinka Philharmonic Hall**, *Tel. (812) 311-8333*, which was incorporated into the Nevsky prospekt metro below it. On the side, you will see the large **Church of the Resurrection**, built in 1907 on the spot where Tsar Aleksandr II was assassinated in 1881. Designed in a Russian style, it resembles St. Basil's Cathedral in Moscow.

Following Nevsky prospekt metro and set back from the avenue is the 18th century **Roman Catholic Church of St. Catherine**. On your right, at number 33 is the building of the former **City Duma**, with a pentagonal tower, which is the highest structure on Nevsky prospekt. In years past, concerts and literary parties were held in the duma hall, attended by such luminaries as novelist Fyodor Dostoyevsky and poet Aleksandr Blok.

From here Mikhaylovskaya Street leads you to **Arts Square**, laid out by architect Carlo Rossi, where you will find the well-known **Russian Museum**, *Tel. (812) 219-1615*, open Wednesday through Monday, from 10am to 6pm. This building, erected in 1825, was once the palace of Grand Prince Mikhail Pavlovich, the younger brother of Emperor Aleksandr I. It was bought by the state at the close of the last century and turned into a museum of exclusively Russian art.

The museum opened in 1898 with 500 paintings and 100 sculptures; today there are more than a quarter million artworks on exhibit here, including some 6,000 icons in some 100 rooms. You can admire the work of iconist Andrey Rublev and paintings by such masters as Ilya Repin, Ivan Kramskoy and Isaak Levitan, as well as works of the Russian avant-garde represented by Kandinsky and Malevich. Folk art, lacework, embroidery, painted chests and lacquered miniatures are also on display.

The **Ethnographic Museum**, *Tel. (812) 219-1174*, is open Tuesday through Sunday, from 10am to 6pm, and displays thousands of objects and photographs in the same building as the Russian Museum. In 1883, the Mikhaylovsky Theater opened in Arts Square and was renamed the **Maly Theater** in 1918. Composer Dmitry Shostakovich worked here until the Stalinist regime destroyed him. The former Noblemen's Assembly, built in 1839, is now the **Shostakovich Philharmonic Hall**. And, finally, a larger-than-life **statue of Pushkin**, erected in 1957, greets you in the middle of the square.

Still farther north of here is the **Field of Mars**, a huge square that for more than 200 years served as military parade grounds. It now honors those killed in the Civil War and the 1917 Revolution. East of Mars Field is the **Summer Garden**, which was laid out in 1704. In the 18th century this was Russia's first sculpture garden, with more than 250 statues and busts. Each spring, more than 2,000 trees come into leaf in the garden, which is open from 8am to 10pm in the summer and closed in April. On the northeastern edge of the Summer Garden and on the bank of the Fontanka River, you can see Peter the Great's **Summer Palace**, built in 1714 by Domenico Trezzini. South of here is the **Engineering Castle**, built for the mad Tsar Paul I, who had moved in out of fear for his life even before the red building adjacent to the Moika and Fontanka Rivers was finished. Sadly, he was strangled 42 days later by close associates who staged a coup.

Where the widest part of Nevsky prospekt begins is also where the city's two oldest shopping galleries, the **Gostiny Dvor** and the **Passazh**, are located. Gostiny Dvor (Merchant Arcade), *35 Nevsky prospekt, Tel. (812) 312-4165*, is open from 9am to 9pm; and the Passazh (Arcade), *48 Nevsky prospekt, Tel. (812) 254-4359*, is open from 10am to 9pm. They face each other at the Gostiny Dvor metro station. The block-long Gostiny Dvor building, where more than 100,000 shoppers thronged daily even before it was closed for restoration, was erected in 1785. If you are looking for souvenirs or antiques, it is a good bet that you will find them on Nevsky Avenue because there are several such shops that cater to visitors.

While here, you can buy tickets to cultural events, including the famed Kirov Ballet, at the **Central Theatrical & Concert Ticket Office**, *42 Nevsky prospekt, Tel. (812) 311-0593*, opposite Gostiny Dvor. Also near Gostiny Dvor, at 34 Nevsky prospekt is **Nike**, the sneaker and accessories store, open from 11am to 8pm. **Levi's** jean store is at 102 Nevsky Avenue. And if you are looking for a pub, there is a German-style bar, **Dr. Oetker**, *40 Nevsky prospekt, Tel. (812) 312-2457*, which is open from noon to midnight.

Russia's second largest library, after the Russian State Library in Moscow, the **Saltykov-Shchedrin Library**, is located where Sadovaya

Street crosses Nevsky prospekt. Built in 1801, it displays the statue of Pallas Athena, the goddess of wisdom, on its top. The library is part of **Aleksandrinskaya Square**, where a monument to Catherine the Great is prominently displayed in front of the **Pushkin Drama Theater**. Here Gogol's play *Inspector-General* premiered. Before he was brutally murdered by the Soviets, Vsevolod Meyerhold directed several productions here.

If your joints are swelling from walking, you can go to 46 Nevsky prospekt and sit down at the German fast-food cafe **Grillmaster**, *Tel. (812) 110-4555*, which is open from 9am to 6pm, but has no rest rooms. North of it, at 13 Ulitsa Italianskaya, parallel with Nevsky prospekt, is the **Musical Comedy Theater**, *Tel. (812) 277-4177 or 4760*, and not far from it is the **Komissarzhevskaya Drama Theater**, *Tel. (812) 311-0849*, which is located at 19 Italianskaya Street. At house number 52, you will find the **Puppet Theater**, *Tel. (812) 311-1900*, one of three such theaters in the city, and at 56 Nevsky is the **Akimov Comedy Theater**, *Tel. (812) 312-4555*. You will find four different locations for **Yeliseyevsky** food store on Nevsky Avenue, at 44, 54, 56 and 78; for more about the history of this famous store, please see Chapter 17, *Shopping*.

After the **Lancome** cosmetics store, *64 Nevsky Avenue, Tel. (812) 312-3495*, you will soon approach the **Anichkov Bridge** that crosses the Fontanka River and named after the man who built the first wooden bridge here in the early 18th century. The bridge is interesting for the four rearing horses decorating its corners. In the 18th century, the Fontanka marked St. Petersburg's boundaries. On this end of the bridge is **Anichkov Palace**, which Elizabeth, the daughter of Peter the Great, presented to Count Aleksey Razumovsky, her favorite. Tsar Nicholas I gave balls in this palace, and where Pushkin's wife Nataliya often dazzled everyone with her beauty, including the tsar.

You can stop here and return to the city center or push on. There is another pharmacy here before you cross the bridge. On the other side, you will pass three more cinemas, then two Finnish restaurants, **Afrodita** and **Art**, *84 Nevsky, Tel. (812) 275-7620* (same phone), which are open daily from noon to midnight. Almost across the avenue is the luxury **Nevsky Palace Hotel**, *57 Nevsky prospekt* (see Where to Stay for more information). Next to it is **Yves Rocher**, *Tel. (812) 113-1496*, a cosmetics shop at house number 61.

Nevsky Restaurant, *71 Nevsky Avenue, Tel. (812) 311-3093*, open from noon to midnight, is located near the Mayakovskaya metro station. After several more establishments, such as **John Bull Pub**, *Tel. (812) 164-9877*, and **Baskin-Robbins**, *Tel. 164-6456*, the ice cream shop, you will reach Ploshchad Vosstaniya and the **Moskovsky Railway Station**, *Tel. 168-0111*. This station receives trains from Moscow and is the largest of five in St.

Petersburg. It was built in 1851 simultaneously with the **Leningradsky Railway Station** in Moscow. The first trains between the two cities took almost 22 hours each way, now the ride can take as little as five hours. While in the area, you can visit the **Dostoyevsky Museum**, *5/2 Kuznechny pereulok, Tel. (812) 164-6950*, which is open Tuesday through Sunday, from 10:30am to 5:30pm. Just make a detour from the railway station down Ligovsky prospekt to reach the apartment where the great writer lived from 1878 to 1881 and wrote *The Brothers Karamazov*. Also nearby is the **Museum of the Arctic and Antarctic**, *24a Ulitsa Marata, Tel. (812) 311-2549*.

Southeast of the railway station lies the **Aleksandr Nevsky Monastery**, *Tel. (812) 274-4464*, open daily from 8am to 2pm, which was founded by Peter the Great in 1710 to commemorate a military commander of Old Rus, i.e. the old Russian, pre-communist state. It is one of only a handful of monasteries that was granted the title of **lavra**, or the highest religious status in the Russian Orthodox Church. Its **Cathedral of Trinity** was one of only about a dozen churches that functioned in the Soviet era and services are still held daily. The lavra's oldest building is the **Church of the Annunciation**, which is also the resting place of Russia's great general Aleksandr Suvorov, whose statue you will find in front of the **Russian Army Theater** in Moscow. Its necropolis also holds the remains of Dostoyevsky and Tchaikovsky. In the square north of the monastery is the **Hotel Moskva**, *Tel. (812) 274-3001 or 2051*, and the Aleksandr Nevsky metro station right underneath it.

Also located here is the **Aleksandr Nevsky Bridge**, almost one kilometer long and the longest of all the Neva River bridges. There are some 330 bridges spanning rivers in St. Petersburg.

And, finally, if you are looking for one more opportunity to eat around 142 Nevsky prospekt, you will find **Le Cafe**, *Tel. (812) 271-2811*, a German bakery, restaurant and cafe at the upper end of this avenue (accepts major credit cards).

Palace Square, Hermitage Museum, & Senate Square

The starting point for this walking tour is the **Admiralty** and the nearest metro station is Nevsky prospekt. This trip takes about two hours.

The history of **Palace Square** goes back to 1704, when Peter the Great laid the foundation of the **Admiralty Yard**, a shipyard and fortress on the left bank of the Neva River. By then, the **Peter and Paul Fortress** had already been built on the opposite bank to guard the entrance to the river. After the Admiralty was constructed, the island was named Admiralty Island. Military engineering of the time did not allow for the construction of any buildings adjacent to the Admiralty so two squares, Palace Square and Senate Square, were formed in front of this fortification.

In 1838, the **Admiralty** was reconstructed and its wooden tower replaced with a stone one. The Admiralty was reconstructed several more times and the building was handed to the Russian navy in the 1840s. The dome and the spire of the previous tower were preserved. There are 28 statues on top of the upper columns of the tower. The Admiralty spire with the caravelle on top of it is the symbol of St. Petersburg. In front of Admiralty, statues of composer Mikhail Glinka, poet Mikhail Lermontov, and satirist Nikolay Gogol are on display.

Palace Square, created by architect Carlo Rossi, is the focal point of St. Petersburg. It was formed after the construction of the **Winter Palace** (now the **Hermitage Museum**), the residence of Russian tsars. Two long buildings, with a total length of 1,739 feet and connected by an arch, form a horseshoe around the square in front of the Winter Palace. This ensemble is called the **General Staff Building**, which traditionally served as Russia's military headquarters. The **Triumphal Arch** connecting the two parts of the General Staff Building carries the **Chariot of Victory** drawn by six horses.

In the center of the square is the 230-ton **Aleksandr Column**, which was erected in 1834. Both the 155-foot-high column and the arch commemorate the Russian's victory over Napoleon. The angel on top of the column symbolizes peace in Europe after the Napoleonic invaders were defeated. Palace Square bore witness to many historical events, including **Bloody Sunday** in January 1905, when tsarist soldiers massacred unarmed demonstrators. Twelve years later, the Bolshevists also attacked the Winter Palace from this square.

Collections in the **Hermitage Museum**, *Tel. (812) 110-9625 or 9604*, open Tuesday through Sunday from 10:30am to 6pm, closed Mondays, consist of some 2.7 million artworks exhibited in 400 of the Palace's 1,057 rooms. This museum is one of the largest and best art museums in the world and also one of the most congested during the tourist season. Its origins go back to 1764, when a Berlin merchant brought a collection of 226 paintings to St. Petersburg to pay off his debts. Only two years later the first Rembrandt was acquired and still later other collections from auctions in France, England and Germany were added. Today, the museum occupies several buildings on the banks of the Neva River. After the Revolution, many priceless collections were plundered by the Bolsheviks from nobles like the Sheremetyevs and the Yusupovs and incorporated into the museum.

You can visit the Hermitage through a half-day Intourist tour or on your own with the help of an English-language plan of the museum. The main entrance is on the north side, overlooking the Neva River. Admission for Westerners is about $9, as opposed to about 25 cents for Russians. Tickets are sold until one hour before closing. Be prepared for an onslaught of tourists if you come during the summer. According to its director, the museum route is 12 miles long and it would take you ten years just to glance at each object stored in the Hermitage. Less than one-quarter of all available artworks are shown at any one time. If you only have an hour or two to spare, he recommends that you hurry to the immortal *Madonna Lita* by Leonardo da Vinci and Raphael's *Madonna and Child* nearby, both on the second floor of the **Large Hermitage**, one of the three interlinked Hermitage buildings. The Hermitage's Room 254 is filled with some two dozen canvases by Rembrandt; only Holland has more of his works. Do not miss the extraordinary collection of French Impressionist paintings in the Winter Palace's south wing.

Southwest of the Admiralty is **Senate Square**, which, together with the **Synod**, was built in 1834. The square originally served as parade grounds. In the garden between the Senate and the Admiralty is the statue *Bronze Horseman*, made famous by Aleksandr Pushkin's poem of the same name. It is a monument to Peter the Great and was erected in 1782 by Catherine the Great. It was sculpted from a granite block that weighed 1,600 tons and took 400 men four months to roll it from the Gulf of Finland.

During Soviet times, Senate Square was called **Decembrist Square** to honor the liberal guard officers who on December 14, 1825 staged an unsuccessful overthrow of Tsar Nicholas I by refusing to swear allegiance to the newly-crowned emperor. The five leaders of the Decembrists, as the participants are now remembered, were hanged in the nearby Peter and Paul Fortress, and several hundred others were exiled to Siberia. Pushkin, although a sympathizer of the Decembrist movement, escaped with a warning from the tsar.

Incidently, the **Peter and Paul Fortress** on Hare Island, just across the Neva, is open Thursday through Tuesday, from 11am to 5pm, but closed Wednesdays. Inside its cathedral lie the remains of most of Russia's tsars, from Peter the Great on. Many a prisoner languished in its infamous prison, from Dostoyevsky to Lenin's brother. The **Cabin of Peter the Great** (open Wednesday through Monday, from 11am to 6pm), from which Peter supervised the fortress' construction, is just northeast of here and not far from the **Cruiser Aurora**, which is docked opposite the **St. Petersburg Hotel**. The cruiser has been converted into a museum and you can visit it Monday-Tuesday and Thursday-Friday from 11am to 5pm; Saturdays and Sundays, from 1:30pm to 5pm.

Aurora fired a blank round in the direction of the Winter Palace as a signal for the Bolshevists to storm the palace in 1917. If you visit the cabin or the cruiser, you might also consider the **Russian Political History Museum**, *4 Kuybysheva Street, Tel. (812) 233-7052*, which is open Friday through Wednesday, from 10am to 5:30pm. This is the former mansion of the ballerina Mathilde Kseshinskaya, who was a mistress to Nicholas II.

Adjacent to the southwestern corner of Senate Square is **St. Isaac's Square** with the magnificent gold-domed **St. Isaac's Cathedral**, *Tel. (812) 315-9732*, open Thursday through Tuesday from 11am to 6pm. Begun in 1818, it took 40 years and more than 400,000 workers to complete. The cathedral's vaults, walls and pylons are decorated with some 150 murals depicting biblical subjects. There are 62 mosaic panels in the cathedral.

The structure was named after St. Isaac of Dalmatia whose day, according to the church calendar, is May 30, when Peter the Great was born. Three hundred and thirty-five feet high, it is believed to be one of the tallest domed buildings in the world. The cathedral can accommodate 14,000 worshipers. Climb the 262 steps to the colonnade and enjoy the city's panorama.

The eight-column portico building next to the cathedral is the **Prince Lobanov-Rostovsky House**, also mentioned in Pushkin's poem *The Bronze Horseman*. In the middle of St. Isaac's Square is a monument to Tsar Nicholas I. Across the square from the cathedral, on the bank of the Moika River, stands **Mariinsky Palace**, which was built in 1844 for Nicholas's daughter Mariya. Also looking onto this square is the **Hotel Astoria**, built in 1912. On the opposite end of the hotel you will see the building that houses the **Vavilov Institute**, which is known for its collection of more than 160,000 plant seeds.

Next to it is the **Intourist** office and another building away you will find the **Museum of Musical Instruments**, *5 Isaakiyevskaya Square, Tel. (812) 314-5345*, displaying 19th and 20th century instruments. It's open Wednesday through Sunday from noon to 5:30pm.

St. Petersburg's ballet and opera companies were organized in 1738 and have been housed in the Mariinsky Theater since it was built in 1860. The **Mariinsky Theater of Opera and Ballet**, *1 Teatralnaya ploshchad, Tel. (812) 114-5264*, is the home of the famed Kirov Opera and Kirov Ballet and is several blocks southwest of St. Isaac's Square.

NIGHLIFE & ENTERTAINMENT

As in Moscow, the nightclub scene in St. Petersburg is constantly changing and with the exception of a few clubs, come and go all the time.

COURIER, *58 Ulitsa Bolshaya Morskaya. Tel. (812) 311-4678. Open Wednesday through Friday and Sunday, from 7pm to 10:30pm, Saturdays from 7pm to 5am. Cover charge. Cash only.*

An interesting disco next to the Okoshky Art Cafe.

DOMENICO'S, *70 Nevsky prospekt, between the Fontanka River and Rubinshteyna Street, Metro Gostiny Dvor or Mayakouskaya. Tel. (812) 272-5717, Fax 273-3973. Open daily from noon to 5am. Cover charge. Cash only.*

Open since 1994, this restaurant and disco nightclub is popular with Westerners and Russians.

JOY, *1/27 Ulitsa Lomonosova at Nab. Kanala Yekaterininsky, still widely known as Nab. Kanala Griboyedova, Metro Nevsky prospekt. Tel. (812) 311-3540. Open daily from 2pm to 6am. Cover charge. Cash only.*

This restaurant, bar and discotheque is popular with those who have money to throw away.

THE TUNNEL, *Lubyansky pereulok at Ulitsa Zverinskaya, Metro Gorkovskaya. Tel. (812) 233-2562. Open Thursday through Saturday from 2pm to 6am. Cover charge. Cash only.*

The Tunnel is a popular nightclub located in a bomb shelter.

PRACTICAL INFORMATION

American Consulate, *15 Ulitsa Furshtadtskaya, Metro Chernyshevskaya. Tel. (812) 275-1701 or 274-8235. Open Monday through Friday, from 9am to 5pm.*

Canadian Consulate, *32 Malodetskoselsky prospekt, Metro Tekhnologichesky Institut. Tel. (812) 325-8448.*

American Medical Center, *77 Nab. Reki Fontanki. Tel. (812) 325-6101, Fax 325-6120.* This is the place to contact for medical emergencies while in St. Petersburg.

Central Post Office, *9 Ulitsa Pochtamtskaya, a couple of blocks southwest of St. Isaac's Cathedral. Tel. (812) 312-8302 or 8305. Open daily from 9am to 8pm.*

Central Telephone and Telegraph, *3/5 Ulitsa Bolshaya Morskaya, not far from Nevsky Avenue. Tel. (812) 312-2085 or 326-0332.*

Peter TIPS, *86 Nevsky prospekt, in the House of Actors. Tel. (812) 279-0037.* This is a German-owned travel company that provides free practical information, handles visas, provides tickets at a fee, and offers reasonably priced tours in and around St. Petersburg.

INDEX

THINGS CHANGE!

Phone numbers, prices, addresses, quality of food, etc, all change. If you come across any new information, we'd appreciate hearing from you. No item is too small! Drop us an e-mail note at: Jopenroad@aol.com, or write us at:

Moscow Guide
Open Road Publishing, P.O. Box 20226
Columbus Circle Station, New York, NY 10023